Koren Talmud Bavli
THE NOÉ EDITION

MOED KATAN

Steinsaltz Center

KOREN

תלמוד בבלי

KOREN TALMUD BAVLI

THE NOÉ EDITION

מועד קטן

MOED KATAN

Daf 13b through Daf 29a

COMMENTARY BY

Rabbi Adin Even-Israel Steinsaltz

EDITOR-IN-CHIEF

Rabbi Dr Tzvi Hersh Weinreb

SENIOR CONTENT EDITOR

Rabbi Dr Shalom Z Berger

EXECUTIVE EDITOR

Rabbi Joshua Schreier

•

STEINSALTZ CENTER

KOREN PUBLISHERS JERUSALEM

MATANEL
FOUNDATION
GRANTED TO GIVE

Supported by the Matanel Foundation

Koren Talmud Bavli, The Noe Edition
Vol. 12b: Tractate Moed Katan, Daf 13b through Daf 29a
Paperback, ISBN, 978-965-7765-61-6

First Hebrew/English paperback edition, 2021

Koren Publishers Jerusalem Ltd.
PO Box 4044, Jerusalem 91040, ISRAEL
PO Box 8531, New Milford, CT 06776, USA
www.korenpub.com

Steinsaltz Center

Steinsaltz Center is the parent organization of institutions established by Rabbi Adin Even-Israel Steinsaltz

PO Box 45187, Jerusalem 91450 ISRAEL
Telephone: +972 2 646 0900, Fax +972 2 624 9454
www.steinsaltz-center.org

הִנֵּה יָמִים בָּאִים, נְאֻם אֲדֹנָי יֱהֹוִה, וְהִשְׁלַחְתִּי רָעָב בָּאָרֶץ,
לֹא־רָעָב לַלֶּחֶם וְלֹא־צָמָא לַמַּיִם, כִּי אִם־לִשְׁמֹעַ אֵת דִּבְרֵי יהוה.

Behold, days are coming – says the Lord God – I will send a hunger to the land, not a hunger for bread nor a thirst for water, but to hear the words of the Lord. (AMOS 8:11)

The Noé edition of the Koren Talmud Bavli
with the commentary of Rabbi Adin Even-Israel Steinsaltz
is dedicated to all those who open its covers
to quench their thirst for Jewish Knowledge,
in our generation of Torah renaissance.

This beautiful edition is for the young, the aged,
the novice and the savant alike,
as it unites the depth of Torah knowledge
with the best of academic scholarship.

Within its exquisite and vibrant pages,
words become worlds.

It will claim its place in the library of classics,
in the bookcases of the Beit Midrash,
the classrooms of our schools,
and in the offices of professionals and business people
who carve out precious time to grapple with its timeless wisdom.

For the Student and the Scholar

DEDICATED BY LEO AND SUE NOÉ

Steinsaltz Center

Executive Director, Steinsaltz Center
Rabbi Meni Even-Israel

Managing Editor
Rabbi Jason Rappoport

Senior Content Editor
Rabbi Dr. Shalom Z. Berger

Editors
Rabbi Joshua Amaru, *Coordinating Editor*
Rabbi Yehoshua Duker
Rabbi Yonatan Shai Freedman
Raz Hartman
Gila Hock
Rabbi Adin Krohn
Catriel Lev
Rabbi Jason Lieb
Adina Luber
Rabbi Avishai Magence, *Content Curator*
Sarit Nagus
Rabbi David Sedley
Shira Shmidman
Rabbi Michael Siev
Avi Steinhart
Rabbi David Strauss
Amiel Vick

Copy Editors
Aliza Israel, *Coordinator*
Bracha Hermon
Ita Olesker
Debbie Ismailoff
Shira Finson
Ilana Sobel
Deena Nataf
Eliana Kurlantzick Yorav
Nava Wieder

Language Consultants
Dr. Stephanie E. Binder, *Greek & Latin*
Rabbi Yaakov Hoffman, *Arabic*
Dr. Shai Secunda, *Persian*
Shira Shmidman, *Aramaic*

KOREN

Design & Typesetting
Raphaël Freeman, *Design & Typography*
Dena Landowne Bailey, *Typesetting*
Rina Ben Gal, *Typesetting*
Tani Bayer, *Jacket Design*

Images
Eliahu Misgav, *Illustration & Image Acquisition*

Introduction by the Publisher

The Talmud has sustained and inspired Jews for thousands of years. Throughout Jewish history, an elite cadre of scholars has absorbed its learning and passed it on to succeeding generations. The Talmud has been the fundamental text of our people.

Beginning in the 1960s, Rabbi Adin Even-Israel Steinsaltz שליט״א created a revolution in the history of Talmud study. His translation of the Talmud, first into modern Hebrew and then into other languages, as well the practical learning aids he added to the text, have enabled millions of people around the world to access and master the complexity and context of the world of Talmud.

It is thus a privilege to present the *Koren Talmud Bavli*, an English translation of the talmudic text with the brilliant elucidation of Rabbi Steinsaltz. The depth and breadth of his knowledge are unique in our time. His rootedness in the tradition and his reach into the world beyond it are inspirational.

Working with Rabbi Steinsaltz on this remarkable project has been not only an honor, but a great pleasure. Never shy to express an opinion, with wisdom and humor, Rabbi Steinsaltz sparkles in conversation, demonstrating his knowledge (both sacred and worldly), sharing his wide-ranging interests, and, above all, radiating his passion. I am grateful for the unique opportunity to work closely with him, and I wish him many more years of writing and teaching.

Our intentions in publishing this new edition of the Talmud are threefold. First, we seek to fully clarify the talmudic page to the reader – textually, intellectually, and graphically. Second, we seek to utilize today's most sophisticated technologies, both in print and electronic formats, to provide the reader with a comprehensive set of study tools. And third, we seek to help readers advance in their process of Talmud study.

To achieve these goals, the *Koren Talmud Bavli* is unique in a number of ways:

- The classic *tzurat hadaf* of Vilna, used by scholars since the 1800s, has been reset for great clarity, and opens from the Hebrew "front" of the book. Full *nikkud* has been added to both the talmudic text and Rashi's commentary, allowing for a more fluent reading with the correct pronunciation; the commentaries of *Tosafot* have been punctuated. Upon the advice of many English-speaking teachers of Talmud, we have separated these core pages from the translation, thereby enabling the advanced student to approach the text without the distraction of the translation. This also reduces the number of volumes in the set. At the bottom of each *daf*, there is a reference to the corresponding English pages. In addition, the Vilna edition was read against other manuscripts and older print editions, so that texts which had been removed by non-Jewish censors have been restored to their rightful place.
- The English translation, which starts on the English "front" of the book, reproduces the *menukad* Talmud text alongside the English translation (in bold) and commentary and explanation (in a lighter font). The Hebrew and Aramaic text is presented in logical paragraphs. This allows for a fluent reading of the text for the non-Hebrew or non-Aramaic reader. It also allows for the Hebrew reader to refer easily to the text alongside. Where the original text features dialogue or poetry, the English text is laid out in a manner appropriate to the genre. Each page refers to the relevant *daf*.

- Critical contextual tools surround the text and translation: personality notes, providing short biographies of the Sages; language notes, explaining foreign terms borrowed from Greek, Latin, Persian, or Arabic; and background notes, giving information essential to the understanding of the text, including history, geography, botany, archaeology, zoology, astronomy, and aspects of daily life in the talmudic era.
- Halakhic summaries provide references to the authoritative legal decisions made over the centuries by the rabbis. They explain the reasons behind each halakhic decision as well as the ruling's close connection to the Talmud and its various interpreters.
- Photographs, drawings, and other illustrations have been added throughout the text – in full color in the Standard and Electronic editions, and in black and white in the Daf Yomi edition – to visually elucidate the text.

This is not an exhaustive list of features of this edition, it merely presents an overview for the English-speaking reader who may not be familiar with the "total approach" to Talmud pioneered by Rabbi Steinsaltz.

Several professionals have helped bring this vast collaborative project to fruition. My many colleagues are noted on the Acknowledgments page, and the leadership of this project has been exceptional.

RABBI MENACHEM EVEN-ISRAEL, DIRECTOR OF THE STEINSALTZ CENTER, was the driving force behind this enterprise. With enthusiasm and energy, he formed the happy alliance with Koren and established close relationships among all involved in the work.

RABBI DR. TZVI HERSH WEINREB שליט״א, EDITOR-IN-CHIEF, brought to this project his profound knowledge of Torah, intellectual literacy of Talmud, and erudition of Western literature. It is to him that the text owes its very high standard, both in form and content, and the logical manner in which the beauty of the Talmud is presented.

RABBI JOSHUA SCHREIER, EXECUTIVE EDITOR, assembled an outstanding group of scholars, translators, editors, and proofreaders, whose standards and discipline enabled this project to proceed in a timely and highly professional manner.

RABBI MEIR HANEGBI, EDITOR OF THE HEBREW EDITION OF THE STEINSALTZ TALMUD, lent his invaluable assistance throughout the work process, supervising the reproduction of the Vilna pages.

RAPHAËL FREEMAN, EXECUTIVE EDITOR OF KOREN, created this Talmud's unique typographic design which, true to the Koren approach, is both elegant and user friendly.

It has been an enriching experience for all of us at Koren Publishers Jerusalem to work with the Steinsaltz Center to develop and produce the *Koren Talmud Bavli*. We pray that this publication will be a source of great learning and, ultimately, greater *avodat Hashem* for all Jews.

Matthew Miller, Publisher
Koren Publishers Jerusalem
Jerusalem 5772

Contents

For the vocalized Vilna Shas layout, please open as a Hebrew book.

Introduction to **Perek III**

And the children of Israel wept for Moses in the plains of Moab thirty days; so the days of weeping in the mourning for Moses were ended.

(Deuteronomy 34:8)

And Joab sent to Tekoa, and fetched from there a wise woman, and said to her: "I pray you, feign yourself to be a mourner, and put on mourning apparel, I pray you, and do not anoint yourself with oil, but be as a woman that had a long time mourned for the dead."

(II Samuel 14:2)

Also the word of the Lord came to me, saying: "Son of man, behold, I take away from you the desire of your eyes with a stroke; yet neither will you make lamentation nor weep, nor shall your tears run down. Sigh in silence; make no mourning for the dead, bind your headwear upon yourself, and put your shoes on your feet, and do not cover your upper lip, and eat not the bread of men."

(Ezekiel 24:15–17)

Then Job arose, and rent his mantle, and shaved his head, and fell down upon the ground, and worshipped.

(Job 1:20)

And that whoever does not come within three days, according to the counsel of the princes and the elders, all his substance should be forfeited, and himself separated from the congregation of the captivity.

(Ezra 10:8)

The *mishnayot* in this chapter deal primarily with the *halakhot* of the intermediate days of the Festival. Specifically, they discuss the prohibitions of laundering, haircutting, and writing during these days. Also discussed are the various circumstances when the Sages permitted these activities for particular reasons. The Gemara brings in other topics, particularly regarding the *halakhot* of mourning and of ostracism. These *halakhot* are included here because there is a certain similarity between the seven days of rejoicing of a Festival and the seven days of mourning. Furthermore, the Gemara discusses how to behave when both a Festival and a mourning period occur at the same time.

Many of the *halakhot* of mourning, as well as those of ostracism and excommunication, are mentioned in various places in the Bible. However, they are not written as a complete, systematic description of the *halakha*. Therefore, when it comes to matters of practical *halakha* there are many unresolved issues. For example, there is a custom of tearing garments when one is in mourning, but the Bible gives no details of when, for whom, or how to tear. Concepts such as comforting mourners and overturning the beds are alluded to in the Bible, but again no halakhic details are provided, such as when or how these activities are to be performed. Even the number of days of mourning isn't fixed. The Gemara explains which of the activities mentioned in the Bible are *halakha* and obligatory on all mourners, and which are only customs of suffering that certain people took upon themselves.

There are many other, related issues and practical questions. For example, when precisely does mourning begin? What is the *halakha* in a case when someone heard of a relative's death some time later? Also, how must one act when the days of mourning occur on Shabbat or Festivals?

The *halakhot* of ostracism and excommunication are likewise only alluded to in the Bible, yet the Torah does not explicate many of their numerous practical aspects therein. For example, when and for what violations are people ostracized? For how long is someone ostracized? How should one who has been ostracized or excommunicated behave, and how should others act toward him?

These questions and others are the main topics discussed in this chapter.

Perek **III**
Daf **13** Amud **b**

מתני׳ וְאֵלּוּ מְגַלְּחִין בַּמּוֹעֵד: הַבָּא מִמְּדִינַת הַיָּם, וּמִבֵּית הַשִּׁבְיָה, וְהַיּוֹצֵא מִבֵּית הָאֲסוּרִין, וְהַמְנוּדֶּה שֶׁהִתִּירוּ לוֹ חֲכָמִים, וְכֵן מִי שֶׁנִּשְׁאַל לְחָכָם וְהוּתַּר, וְהַנָּזִיר וְהַמְּצוֹרָע מִטּוּמְאָתוֹ לְטׇהֳרָתוֹ.

MISHNA And these may shave and cut their hair[N] **on** the intermediate days of **a Festival: One who comes from a country overseas;**[N] **and** one who is released **from a house of captivity; and one who comes out of prison** on the intermediate days of a Festival; **and one who had been ostracized** and therefore prohibited from cutting his hair, **and the Sages released him** from his decree of ostracism on the intermediate days of the Festival; **and similarly, one who** had vowed not to cut his hair and then **requested of a Sage** to dissolve his vow **and was released** from it on the intermediate days of the Festival; **and the nazirite** whose term of naziriteship ended on the intermediate days of a Festival; **and the leper**[N] who needs to purify himself on the intermediate days and must shave his entire body in order to leave **his** state of ritual **impurity**[N] and regain **his** ritual **purity.** Since these people were not able to cut their hair on the eve of the Festival, they are permitted to do so on the intermediate days of the Festival.[H]

וְאֵלּוּ מְכַבְּסִין בַּמּוֹעֵד: הַבָּא מִמְּדִינַת הַיָּם וּמִבֵּית הַשִּׁבְיָה, וְהַיּוֹצֵא מִבֵּית הָאֲסוּרִין,

And these may launder their clothes **on** the intermediate days of **a Festival: One who comes from a country overseas; and one who** is released **from a house of captivity; and one who comes out of prison** on the intermediate days of a Festival;

HALAKHA

Those who are permitted to shave and cut their hair on the intermediate days of the Festival – הַמּוּתָּרִין בְּתִגְלַחַת בַּמּוֹעֵד: Both one who came out of captivity or was freed from jail during a Festival and one who had been ostracized and was released from his decree of ostracism during a Festival are permitted to shave on the Festival (*Shulḥan Arukh Oraḥ Ḥayyim* 531:4).

NOTES

And these may shave and cut their hair – וְאֵלּוּ מְגַלְּחִין: The Ritva and *Tosafot* ask why the mishna begins with the conjunctive: And, although there is no apparent connection to the previous chapters of mishna. *Tosafot* explain the connection: The previous two chapters listed exceptional cases, where certain activities are permitted during the intermediate days of a Festival. Similarly, this mishna continues with exceptions to the prohibitions against cutting hair and laundering during the intermediate days of a Festival. The Ritva explains that this mishna continues to discuss the subject matter of the previous chapters, which is activities that are permitted during the intermediate days of a Festival because they could not have been performed earlier.

One who comes from a country overseas – הַבָּא מִמְּדִינַת הַיָּם: Some explain that this is not necessarily referring to another country but to any distant place (*Talmid Rabbeinu Yehiel of Paris*). The Ritva holds that anyone coming from outside the city is included in this category with regard to the intermediate days of the Festival.

The nazirite and the leper, etc. – הַנָּזִיר וְהַמְּצוֹרָע וכו׳: There is a dispute as to whether a priest may rule on a case of leprosy during the intermediate days of a Festival. The commentaries point out that according to Rabbi Meir, who holds that the priest may rule on the status of a leper, the priest may instruct the leper to shave the hair around the site of the leprosy, and the leper may shave during the intermediate days of the Festival. This case is different than the case of the leper listed in the mishna. The mishna is referring to shaving once he has completed the purification process, whereas this case is referring to shaving that is part of the process of ascertaining whether or not one is impure. This case is not included in the mishna because it is not shaving for aesthetic purposes but for a halakhic purpose (Ran, citing Rashi; see Ritva and *Melekhet HaShulhan*).

And the leper his impurity – וְהַמְּצוֹרָע מִטּוּמְאָתוֹ: The Rambam and other early authorities had a version of the text that did not specify the leper, but read: And the one ascending from his state of ritual impurity. The Rambam writes that all who purify themselves are permitted to shave on the Festival. In the *Mishne LeMelekh* it is explained that it is not appropriate for an impure person to beautify himself with a haircut. Therefore, when he purifies himself it is considered as if he did not have time to cut his hair on the eve of the Festival (see *Dikdukei Soferim*).

Perek **III**
Daf **14** Amud **a**

וּמְנוּדֶּה שֶׁהִתִּירוּ לוֹ חֲכָמִים, וְכֵן מִי שֶׁנִּשְׁאַל לְחָכָם וְהוּתַּר.

and one who had been ostracized and the Sages released him from his decree of ostracism; **and similarly, one who** had vowed not to launder his clothes and he **requested from a Sage**[N] to dissolve his vow **and was released** from it on the intermediate days of a Festival.

NOTES

One who requested from a Sage – מִי שֶׁנִּשְׁאַל לְחָכָם: Some explain that this means that one was prohibited by his oath from washing clothes, and he changed his mind on the Festival (manuscript of Rashi; Rabbeinu Yehonatan of Lunel). Others explain that in such a case it is not permitted, and the only cases in which it is permitted are when the oath was for a specific duration that expired during the Festival, or if one did not find a Sage to permit him to do so until the Festival (Rosh and *Tosafot*, citing the Jerusalem Talmud).

מִטְפְּחוֹת הַיָּדַיִם, וּמִטְפְּחוֹת הַסַּפָּרִים, וּמִטְפְּחוֹת הַסְּפָג, הַזָּבִין וְהַזָּבוֹת וְהַנִּדּוֹת וְהַיּוֹלְדוֹת, וְכׇל הָעוֹלִין מִטּוּמְאָה לְטׇהֳרָה – הֲרֵי אֵלּוּ מוּתָּרִין. וּשְׁאָר כׇּל אָדָם אֲסוּרִין.

Hand towels;[H] **and barbers' towels,**[N] which are used to cover a person having a haircut; **and body-drying towels,** all of which get quickly soiled, may be laundered on the intermediate days of a Festival. ***Zavim,*** men suffering from an impure venereal emission; ***zavot,***[H] women who experience a flow of menstrual-type blood on three consecutive days during a time of the month when they do not expect to experience menstrual bleeding; **menstruating women; women who have** just **given birth; and all others who leave** a state of **ritual impurity for** a state of **ritual purity** on the intermediate days of the Festival, **these** people **are** all **permitted** to launder their clothes in order to purify themselves. **But all other people are prohibited** from laundering during the intermediate days of the Festival.

גמ׳ וּשְׁאָר כׇּל אָדָם מַאי טַעְמָא אֲסוּרִין?

GEMARA The Gemara asks: **What is the reason** that **all other people are prohibited** from performing these actions during the intermediate days? Why are these actions not included in the category of actions that are permitted in deference to the Festival?

כִּדְתְנַן: אַנְשֵׁי מִשְׁמָר וְאַנְשֵׁי מַעֲמָד אֲסוּרִין לְסַפֵּר וּלְכַבֵּס, וּבַחֲמִישִׁי מוּתָּרִין, מִפְּנֵי כְּבוֹד הַשַּׁבָּת.

The Gemara answers: **As we learned** in a mishna (*Taanit* 15b): Both **the members of the priestly watch**[B] whose week it is to serve in the Temple **and the members of the non-priestly watch**[HB] who accompanied the members of the watch to Jerusalem **are prohibited from cutting** their **hair**[N] **or laundering** their clothes during that week. **But on the Thursday** of that week **they are permitted**[N] to do so **in deference to Shabbat.**

וְאָמַר רַבָּה בַּר בַּר חָנָה אָמַר רַבִּי אֶלְעָזָר: מַאי טַעְמָא? כְּדֵי שֶׁלֹּא יִכָּנְסוּ לְמִשְׁמַרְתָּן כְּשֶׁהֵן מְנוּוָּלִין. הָכָא נַמִי: כְּדֵי שֶׁלֹּא יִכָּנְסוּ לָרֶגֶל כְּשֶׁהֵן מְנוּוָּלִין.

And Rabba bar bar Ḥana said in the name of Rabbi Elazar: What is the reason that the members of the priestly and non-priestly watch are prohibited from cutting their hair and laundering their clothes? It is **in order that they not enter their watch when they are untidy.** If it were permitted for them to cut their hair and launder their clothes during the week of their watch, they would leave their haircuts and laundry until the middle of that week and begin their service in a disorderly state. **Here, too,** ordinary people are prohibited from cutting their hair or laundering their clothes on the intermediate days of a Festival, **in order that they** complete all necessary preparations beforehand and **not enter the Festival when they are untidy.**

NOTES

Barbers' [*sapparim*] towels – מִטְפְּחוֹת הַסַּפָּרִים: Some say that these were the towels used during the haircut for those who were permitted to have their hair cut during the Festival (Rabbi Ovadya MiBartenura). Some explain that these are the cloth covers of *sefarim*, holy books (Meiri). Others, based on a slightly different version of the text, explain that it means cloths of the *soferim*, scribes, which they place over their manuscripts to protect them from ink blots and dirt (see Meiri and Rabbeinu Yehonatan of Lunel).

The prohibition against cutting hair on the intermediate days of a Festival – אִיסּוּר תִּסְפּוֹרֶת בַּמּוֹעֵד: According to most commentaries and halakhic authorities, cutting hair is a prohibited labor (see *Tosafot*). However, there are cases of leniency for the sake of beautifying oneself, since doing so is not an exertion (*Talmid Rabbeinu Yeḥiel of Paris*). Others hold that it is considered like other necessary activities that are permitted from the outset on the intermediate days of a Festival (Ritva).

But on the Thursday they are permitted – וּבַחֲמִישִׁי מוּתָּרִין: The early and later authorities discuss the following question: Why are members of the non-priestly watch permitted to cut their hair on Thursday in deference to Shabbat, whereas cutting hair on the Thursday of the intermediate days of a Festival is prohibited? Some write that because cutting hair throughout the Festival is a prohibited labor, if others see a person cutting his hair on a Thursday they will think it is permitted during all the intermediate days and will come to be lenient on those days as well (Rid).

Haircutting and shaving is prohibited during the intermediate days and during the watch, so that people will cut their hair and shave before the Festival or watch begins. Some explain that since the priestly watch always begins on Sunday, Thursday is always at the end of the shift, and permitting haircutting or shaving on that day does not discourage people from doing so before the watch begins. However, a Festival can begin on any day of the week. Sometimes Thursday is near the beginning of the Festival, so there is concern that people will not make themselves look nice before the Festival, but wait until the Thursday to do so.

Another reason is that for the members of the watch, the prohibition against shaving was a rabbinic decree, but on the intermediate days of the Festival there is a Torah prohibition against performing labor (Meiri). The later authorities reached the same conclusion (see *Tal Ḥayyim*).

With regard to the general mitzva to cut one's hair on a Thursday when it is not a Festival, to show deference to Shabbat, some write that it is also permitted to cut one's hair on Friday (Commentary on *Moed Katan*; Ritva). Others write that it is permitted only on Thursday, but not on Friday, so as not to add extra tasks on Friday (manuscript of Rashi; see Meiri).

HALAKHA

Washing hand towels, etc. – כִּבּוּס מִטְפְּחוֹת הַיָּדַיִם וכו׳: On the intermediate days of a Festival it is permitted to wash hand towels, barbers' towels, and body towels, even in public, but this is not the accepted custom (Rema). Baby clothes, such as diapers, may be washed, even several at once, based on the ruling in the Jerusalem Talmud (*Shulḥan Arukh, Oraḥ Ḥayyim* 534:1).

Zavim and *zavot*, etc. – הַזָּבִין וְהַזָּבוֹת וכו׳: *Zavim, zavot,* menstruating women, women who have given birth, and all who are purifying themselves from their ritual impurity during the Festival are permitted to wash their clothes on the intermediate days of the Festival (Rambam *Sefer Zemanim, Hilkhot Yom Tov* 7:21).

The members of the priestly watch and the members of the non-priestly watch – אַנְשֵׁי מִשְׁמָר וְאַנְשֵׁי מַעֲמָד: The members of the priestly watch and the members of the non-priestly watch are prohibited from cutting their hair and laundering their clothes during the whole week of their watch. However, on Thursday they are permitted to do so in deference to Shabbat (Rambam *Sefer Avoda, Hilkhot Kelei HaMikdash* 6:11 and *Hilkhot Biat HaMikdash* 1:12).

BACKGROUND

Priestly watch – מִשְׁמָר: The priests who served in the Temple were divided into twenty-four groups, called watches. Each watch served for one week at a time. In this manner, each watch performed the Temple service for approximately two weeks every year. During the pilgrimage Festivals, the members of all the watches went to the Temple and performed the Temple service together. Each watch received the priestly gifts that were contributed to the Temple during their week of Temple service. The watches were divided into extended patrilineal families. The priests were originally divided into watches in the time of King David. However, during the Second Temple period, many of the Jews who had been exiled to Babylonia after the destruction of the First Temple remained in Babylonia. Therefore, those priestly families who returned to Eretz Yisrael had to be divided again into twenty-four watches.

Non-priestly watch – מַעֲמָד: Each priestly watch was responsible for sacrificing the offerings for their week. Corresponding to each of these watches was a group of non-priests who constituted a non-priestly watch. The Jewish men of Eretz Yisrael were divided into twenty-four non-priestly watches, and each time a priestly watch went to Jerusalem to sacrifice offerings, part of the corresponding non-priestly watch went there as well. The remainder of the non-priestly watch stayed at home. During that week, those at home would fast each day, from Monday to Thursday, read certain portions from the Torah, and say special prayers.

בָּעֵי רַבִּי זֵירָא: אָבְדָה לוֹ אֲבֵידָה עֶרֶב הָרֶגֶל, כֵּיוָן דַּאֲנִיס – מוּתָּר, אוֹ דִּלְמָא: כֵּיוָן דְּלָא מוֹכְחָא מִילְּתָא – לָא?

Rabbi Zeira asks: If one lost an item on the eve of a Festival and he was busy searching for it and had no time to cut his hair or launder his clothes before the Festival commenced, can one say that **since** he was **a victim of circumstances beyond his control,** which prevented from taking care of these matters prior to the Festival, **he is permitted** to cut his hair and launder his clothes on the intermediate days of the Festival? **Or perhaps since it is not** clearly **evident** to others that he failed to cut his hair or launder his clothes due to unavoidable circumstances, he is **not** permitted to perform these actions during the Festival week.

אָמַר אַבַּיֵי, יֹאמְרוּ: כׇּל הַסְּרִיקִין אֲסוּרִין סְרִיקֵי בַּיְיתוֹס מוּתָּרִין?!

Abaye said, in answer to this question, that there is a principle of the Sages that applies here. They prohibited the baking of decorated Syrian cakes for Passover, lest people tarry in their preparation of these elaborate cakes and the cakes become leavened. When Baitos ben Zunen,[P] wished to prepare the cakes in a way that would not lead to a violation of any prohibition, the Sages nevertheless prohibited it. They explained that were they to permit him to do so, others **would say: All the** decorated **Syrian cakes are forbidden,** but **the Syrian cakes of Baitos**[L] **are permitted?** This teaches that the Sages do not permit exceptions when the reason for leniency is not clearly evident, like in the case of one who was busy looking for a lost item.

וּלְטַעְמִיךְ, הָא דְּאָמַר רַבִּי אַסִּי אָמַר רַבִּי יוֹחָנָן: כׇּל מִי שֶׁאֵין לוֹ אֶלָּא חָלוּק אֶחָד – מוּתָּר לְכַבְּסוֹ בְּחוּלּוֹ שֶׁל מוֹעֵד, הָתָם נַמִי: יֹאמְרוּ כׇּל הַסְּרִיקִין אֲסוּרִין סְרִיקֵי בַּיְיתוֹס מוּתָּרִין!

Rabbi Zeira retorted: **And according to your reasoning,**[N] **that which Rabbi Asi said** that **Rabbi Yoḥanan said: Anyone who has only one shirt is permitted to launder it on the intermediate days of a Festival, there too,** one should apply the principle that others **will say: All the** decorated **Syrian cakes are forbidden** but **the Syrian cakes of Baitos are permitted.** There, too, it is not clearly evident that the reason for leniency is that one has only one shirt.

הָא אִתְּמַר עֲלַהּ, אָמַר מָר בַּר רַב אַשִׁי: אֵיזוֹרוֹ מוֹכִיחַ עָלָיו.

The Gemara rejects this argument: **Wasn't it** already **said about this** that **Mar, son of Rav Ashi, said: His belt is proof for him,**[N] as when he launders his only shirt he will have to wear his outer garment tied with his belt so that his body is not exposed, and everyone will understand that he has no other shirt to wear.

רַב אַשִׁי מַתְנֵי: בָּעֵי רַבִּי זֵירָא אוּמָּן שֶׁאָבְדָה לוֹ אֲבֵידָה עֶרֶב הָרֶגֶל מַהוּ? כֵּיוָן דְּאוּמָּן הוּא – מוֹכְחָא מִילְּתָא, אוֹ דִּלְמָא: כֵּיוָן דְּלָא מוֹכְחָא מִילְּתָא כִּי הָנָךְ – לָא? תֵּיקוּ.

Rav Ashi taught a different version of this passage, as follows: **Rabbi Zeira asks:** With regard to **a craftsman who lost an item**[N] **on the eve of a Festival** and was busy searching for it, **what is** the *halakha*? Is it permitted for him to launder his clothes and cut his hair on the intermediate days of the Festival because he had been unable to do so before the Festival? The Gemara explains the two sides of the question: Can one say that **since he is a craftsman, it is** clearly **evident** why he did not launder his clothes and cut his hair before the Festival, as many people would have come to his place of work and seen that he was busy looking for his lost article? **Or perhaps since** the special circumstances **are not** as clearly **evident as in those** cases in the mishna, it is **not** permitted for him to cut his hair or launder his clothes during the intermediate days of the Festival. The dilemma **shall stand** unresolved.

PERSONALITIES

Baitos ben Zunen – בַּיְיתוֹס בֶּן זוּנֵן: Baitos was a wealthy man who lived in Lod during the time of Rabban Gamliel of Yavne. From many sources in the Talmud, it appears that he was a major importer and exporter, and he owned a great deal of land. He was apparently closely associated with the house of the *Nasi*, and he would insist that all of his actions be in accordance with the *halakha* and the opinion of Sages. Therefore, proofs for the proper *halakha* are derived from his actions. His father may have been the Zunen who was appointed by Rabban Gamliel. It is also possible that the Zunen mentioned as an important man during the days of Rabbi Yehuda HaNasi was the son of Baitos.

LANGUAGE

Baitos – בַּיְיתוֹס: From the Greek βοηθός, *Boethos*, meaning helper or assistant, like the name Ezra in Hebrew.

NOTES

And according to your reasoning, etc. – וּלְטַעְמִיךְ וכו׳: According to Rabbi Zeira's opinion, since the essence of the prohibition against cutting hair is a rabbinic decree, there is no need to add another stricture lest others misunderstand the reason behind the leniency. But according to Abaye's opinion, that even exceptional cases are included within the original decree against haircuts, why does the same principle not apply to laundering as well, such that it is prohibited even when one has only one piece of clothing (Ritva)?

His belt is proof for him – אֵיזוֹרוֹ מוֹכִיחַ עָלָיו: There are many explanations suggested for this expression. According to Rashi, one who has no clothing wraps himself in a coat and ties it with a belt (see Rabbeinu Gershom *Meor HaGola* and *Arukh*, citing Rabbis of Mainz). Rabbeinu Ḥananel explains that when others see a person who is wearing only an outer garment, they understand that he has no clothing. Some explain that the custom was to transfer the belt from one piece of clothing to another, and consequently, clothing was laundered without a belt. If others would see a person washing a piece of clothing with a belt or sending it to the launderer, they would know that he has no other clothing (manuscript of Rashi; Rashi on *Ḥullin* 108a; *Tosefot HaRosh*). Some explain that one who has no clothing wraps his waist with a cloth in order to cover himself, and all know that he has no other item of clothing (Rabbeinu Shlomo ben HaYatom). Others explain that one who has no clothing and wears a shirt alone does not tie it with a belt, so that his outer coat, which is made of wool, not scratch him (*Talmid Rabbeinu Yeḥiel of Paris*). Still others write the converse, that one who has no clothing ties his coat tightly in order to be warmed by the coat (Meiri).

A craftsman who lost an item – אוּמָּן שֶׁאָבְדָה לוֹ אֲבֵידָה: Some explain that this is referring to any craftsman whose services are needed on the eve of the Festival. People know that he is not at home because he is searching for his lost object or because he is concerned due to his loss (Rashi). Some say that this is referring specifically to a barber (Commentary on *Moed Katan*; Rabbeinu Shlomo ben HaYatom). Some add to this explanation that since a barber could cut his own hair and did not, it is clear that it was because he was concerned with something else and had no time to do so (Ran).

״מִמְּדִינַת הַיָּם״. מַתְנִיתִין דְּלָא כְּרַבִּי יְהוּדָה, דְּתַנְיָא, רַבִּי יְהוּדָה אוֹמֵר: הַבָּא מִמְּדִינַת הַיָּם – לֹא יְגַלֵּחַ, מִפְּנֵי שֶׁיָּצָא שֶׁלֹּא בִּרְשׁוּת.

§ The mishna taught: One who comes **from a country overseas**[N] on the intermediate days of a Festival is permitted to cut his hair.[H] The Gemara comments: **The mishna is not in accordance with** the opinion of **Rabbi Yehuda, as it is taught** in a *baraita* that **Rabbi Yehuda says: One who comes from a country overseas** on the intermediate days of a Festival **must not shave** or cut his hair, **due to** the fact that **he left** his home **without permission.**

אָמַר רָבָא: לָשׁוּט – דִּבְרֵי הַכֹּל אָסוּר; לִמְזוֹנוֹת – דִּבְרֵי הַכֹּל מוּתָּר; לֹא נֶחְלְקוּ אֶלָּא לְהַרְוִיחָא. מָר מְדַמֵּי לֵיהּ כְּלָשׁוּט, וּמָר מְדַמֵּי לֵיהּ כִּלְמְזוֹנוֹת.

The Gemara continues to explain the definition and parameters of leaving without permission. **Rava said:** If one left Eretz Yisrael **to travel, all agree** that **it is prohibited** for him to shave during the intermediate days of the Festival because he left on his own initiative, and this is not considered an unavoidable circumstance. If he left **for** basic **sustenance,** i.e., due to financial difficulty, **all agree** that **it is permitted** for him to shave upon his return because he is regarded as having left due to circumstances beyond his control. **They disagree only** with regard to the case where he left **to** earn greater **profit,** i.e., he had enough to live on in Eretz Yisrael, but he left in order to increase his income. **One Sage,** Rabbi Yehuda, **compares him** to one who left **to travel, and the other Sage,** the Rabbis of the mishna, **compare him** to one who left **for** basic **sustenance.**

מֵיתִיבִי, אָמַר רַבִּי: נִרְאִין דִּבְרֵי רַבִּי יְהוּדָה כְּשֶׁיָּצָא שֶׁלֹּא בִּרְשׁוּת, וְדִבְרֵי חֲכָמִים כְּשֶׁיָּצָא בִּרְשׁוּת. מַאי שֶׁלֹּא בִּרְשׁוּת? אִילֵימָא לָשׁוּט – וְהָאָמְרַתְּ דִּבְרֵי הַכֹּל אָסוּר. וְאֶלָּא לִמְזוֹנוֹת – וְהָאָמְרַתְּ דִּבְרֵי הַכֹּל מוּתָּר! אֶלָּא פְּשִׁיטָא – לְהַרְוִיחָא.

The Gemara **raises an objection** from the following *baraita*: **Rabbi** Yehuda HaNasi **said:** The **statement of Rabbi Yehuda seems** more reasonable in a case **when he left without permission, and the statement of the Rabbis** seems more reasonable **when one left with permission.** The Gemara clarifies: **What is** meant by **without permission? If we say** that it means that he left **to travel, didn't you say** that in this case **all agree** that **it is prohibited** for him to cut his hair upon his return? **Rather,** say that it means that he left **for** basic **sustenance. But didn't you say** that **all agree** that **it is permitted** for him to cut his hair in such a case? **Rather,** it is **obvious** that it means that he left in search of greater **profit.**

אֵימָא סֵיפָא: נִרְאִין דִּבְרֵי חֲכָמִים כְּשֶׁיָּצָא בִּרְשׁוּת. מַאי בִּרְשׁוּת? אִילֵימָא לִמְזוֹנוֹת – הָא אָמְרַתְּ דִּבְרֵי הַכֹּל מוּתָּר. וְאֶלָּא לְהַרְוִיחָא – וְהָא אָמְרַתְּ נִרְאִין דִּבְרֵי רַבִּי יְהוּדָה בְּהָא!

Say the latter clause of the *baraita* as follows: **The statement of the Rabbis seems** more reasonable in a case **when one left with permission.** The Gemara clarifies: **What is** meant by **with permission? If we say** that he left **for** basic **sustenance, didn't you say** that **all agree** that **it is permitted** for him to cut his hair upon his return? **Rather,** say that it means that he left **for** greater **profit. But didn't you say** in the first clause that **the statement of Rabbi Yehuda seems** more reasonable **in this** case? Therefore, according to Rava's distinctions, there is an internal contradiction within the *baraita.*

הָכִי קָאָמַר: נִרְאִין דִּבְרֵי רַבִּי יְהוּדָה לְרַבָּנַן כְּשֶׁיָּצָא שֶׁלֹּא בִּרְשׁוּת, וּמַאי נִיהוּ – לָשׁוּט, שֶׁאֲפִילּוּ חֲכָמִים לֹא נֶחְלְקוּ עָלָיו אֶלָּא לְהַרְוִיחָא, אֲבָל לָשׁוּט – מוֹדוּ לֵיהּ. וְנִרְאִין דִּבְרֵי רַבָּנַן לְרַבִּי יְהוּדָה כְּשֶׁיָּצָא בִּרְשׁוּת, וּמַאי נִיהוּ – לִמְזוֹנוֹת, שֶׁאֲפִילּוּ רַבִּי יְהוּדָה לֹא נֶחֱלַק עֲלֵיהֶם אֶלָּא לְהַרְוִיחָא, אֲבָל לִמְזוֹנוֹת – מוֹדֶה לְהוּ.

The Gemara resolves the difficulty: **This is what** Rabbi Yehuda HaNasi **is saying: The statement of Rabbi Yehuda seems** more reasonable **to the Rabbis** in the case **where one left without permission. And what is** meant by without permission? It means a case where one left **to travel, as even the Rabbis disagree with** Rabbi Yehuda **only** when one left **for** greater **profit, but** when one left **to travel they agree with** Rabbi Yehuda that it is prohibited for one to shave and cut his hair. **And the statement of the Rabbis seems** more convincing **to Rabbi Yehuda** in the case **where one left with permission. And what is** meant by with permission? It is a case where one left **for** basic **sustenance, as even Rabbi Yehuda disagrees with** the Rabbis **only** when one left **for** greater **profit, but** when he left **for** basic **sustenance** Rabbi Yehuda **concedes to them** that it is permitted for him to shave and cut his hair. Therefore, Rabbi Yehuda HaNasi's intent was not to decide between the opinions of the Rabbis and Rabbi Yehuda but to clarify their dispute.

אָמַר שְׁמוּאֵל: קָטָן הַנּוֹלָד בַּמּוֹעֵד – מוּתָּר לְגַלֵּחַ בַּמּוֹעֵד, שֶׁאֵין לְךָ בֵּית הָאֲסוּרִין גָּדוֹל מִזֶּה. בַּמּוֹעֵד – אִין, מֵעִיקָּרָא – לָא.

§ **Shmuel said:** If **a baby was born on a Festival** and he has long hair that is bothering him, **it is permitted to cut** his hair **on the** intermediate days of the **Festival, as there is no greater prison than this,** the womb of his mother, due to which his hair could not have been cut prior to the Festival. A precise reading of Shmuel's statement indicates that if the child was born **on the Festival, yes,** his hair may be cut. However, if he was born **before** the Festival, but for some reason his hair was not cut, **no,** it is not permitted to cut it on the intermediate days of the Festival because there was time to do so before the Festival.

NOTES

One who comes from a country overseas – מִמְּדִינַת הַיָּם: Some explain that the difference between leaving for sustenance and leaving for travel applies specifically to one who leaves Eretz Yisrael, since leaving Eretz Yisrael was permitted only under duress. Since one left, despite the fact that his leaving was not entirely necessary, the Sages did not permit him to cut his hair on the intermediate days of the Festival (Ra'avad; Rabbi Yitzḥak ibn Giat; *Sefer Hashlama*; Ritva; Meiri). Others hold that it is referring to anyone leaving his home to travel.

Talmid Rabbeinu Yeḥiel of Paris explains that one who leaves for his sustenance is considered to be leaving under duress and is therefore like the others who are permitted to cut their hair during the intermediate days of the Festival. However, one who leaves for pleasure could have made sure to cut his hair on the eve of the Festival. The only disagreement pertains to the case of one who goes out to earn greater profit; the disagreement is with regard to whether this is comparable to the other cases in the mishna or not.

Some learn from the discussion in Jerusalem Talmud on this issue that Rabbi Yehuda's statement applies to leaving from any place, whereas leaving from Eretz Yisrael is always considered to be leaving without permission (Vilna Gaon).

HALAKHA

One who comes from a country overseas – מִמְּדִינַת הַיָּם: If one comes to Eretz Yisrael from overseas on the intermediate days of the Festival or on the eve of the Festival and did not have time to cut his hair beforehand, it is permitted for him to shave and cut his hair during the intermediate days, provided that he is not simply returning from a leisure travel in the Diaspora. This ruling is in accordance with the opinion of the Rabbis, following the conclusion of the Gemara (*Shulḥan Arukh, Oraḥ Ḥayyim* 531:4).

מְתִיב רַב פִּנְחָס: כׇּל אֵלּוּ שֶׁאָמְרוּ מוּתָּר לְגַלֵּחַ בַּמּוֹעֵד – מוּתָּר לְגַלֵּחַ בִּימֵי אֶבְלוֹ. הָא אָסוּר לְגַלֵּחַ בַּמּוֹעֵד – אָסוּר לְגַלֵּחַ בִּימֵי אֶבְלוֹ.

Rav Pineḥas raised an objection from that which is taught in a *baraita*: **All of those** about **whom** the Sages **said: It is permitted to shave** and cut his hair **on** the intermediate days of the **Festival, it is** also **permitted to shave** and cut his hair **during the days of his mourning. But** from this it follows that **one who is prohibited from shaving** and cutting his hair **on** the intermediate days of **a Festival is** also **prohibited from shaving** and cutting his hair **during the days of his mourning.**

Perek **III**
Daf **14** Amud **b**

וְאִי אָמְרַתְּ קָטָן אִית בֵּיהּ פְּלוּגְתָּא – נִמְצֵאת אֲבֵילוּת נוֹהֶגֶת בְּקָטָן.

And if you say that with regard to **a baby there is a distinction** between being born before the Festival and being born on it, and in some cases it is prohibited to cut the hair of a baby, then **you find that mourning** is **practiced** even **with a minor.**

וְהָתַנְיָא: מְקָרְעִין לְקָטָן מִפְּנֵי עָגְמַת נֶפֶשׁ!

Isn't it taught in a *baraita*: **One rends** the clothes of **a minor**[H] whose relative has passed away, **due to** the desire to bring about feelings of **grief** among those who see him? However, there is no inherent requirement for the minor to observe any of the *halakhot* of mourning.

אָמַר רַב אַשִׁי, מִי קָתָנֵי: הָא אֲסוּרִין?! דִּלְמָא: יֵשׁ מֵהֶן אָסוּר, וְיֵשׁ מֵהֶן מוּתָּר.

Rav Ashi said: Is it taught explicitly in the first *baraita* cited by Rav Pineḥas that if it is prohibited for one to have a haircut during the Festival, **it is** likewise **prohibited** to have a haircut during the week of mourning? That was merely an inference. **Perhaps there are** those **among them,** i.e., those listed in the mishna, for whom it is **prohibited,** while **there are** others **among them** for whom it is **permitted,** and the *halakhot* of mourning do not apply to a baby.

אַמֵימָר, וְאִי תֵּימָא רַב שֵׁישָׁא בְּרֵיהּ דְּרַב אִידִי, מַתְנֵי הָכִי: אָמַר שְׁמוּאֵל: קָטָן מוּתָּר לְגַלְּחוֹ בַּמּוֹעֵד, לָא שְׁנָא נוֹלַד בַּמּוֹעֵד וְלָא שְׁנָא נוֹלַד מֵעִיקָּרָא.

Ameimar, and some say it was **Rav Sheisha, son of Rav Idi, taught** that statement **in this manner. Shmuel said:** With regard to **a baby, it is permitted to cut his** hair[H] **during the Festival.** It **is no different** whether **he was born during the Festival, and it is no different** whether **he was born beforehand.**

אָמַר רַב פִּנְחָס, אַף אֲנַן נַמִי תָּנֵינָא: כׇּל אֵלּוּ שֶׁאָמְרוּ מוּתָּר לְגַלֵּחַ בַּמּוֹעֵד – מוּתָּר לְגַלֵּחַ בִּימֵי אֶבְלוֹ. הָא אֲסוּרִין לְגַלֵּחַ בַּמּוֹעֵד – אֲסוּרִין לְגַלֵּחַ בִּימֵי אֶבְלוֹ.

Rav Pineḥas said: We, too, learn in the *baraita* a support for this statement: **All of those** about **whom** the Sages **said: It is permitted to shave** and cut his hair **on** the intermediate days of the **Festival, it is** also **permitted to shave** and cut his hair **during the days of his mourning. But** from this it follows that **one who is prohibited from shaving** and cutting his hair **on** the intermediate days of **a Festival is** also **prohibited from shaving** and cutting his hair **during the days of his mourning.**

אִי אָמְרַתְּ קָטָן אָסוּר – נִמְצֵאת אֲבֵילוּת נוֹהֶגֶת בְּקָטָן. וְתַנְיָא: מְקָרְעִין לְקָטָן מִפְּנֵי עָגְמַת נֶפֶשׁ.

If you say that with regard to **a baby it is prohibited** to cut his hair, then **you find that mourning** is **practiced** even **with a minor. And it was taught** in a *baraita*: **One rends** the clothes of **a minor** whose relative has passed away **due to** the desire to bring about feelings of **grief** among those who see him. However, there is no inherent requirement for the minor to observe any of the *halakhot* of mourning.

אָמַר רַב אַשִׁי, מִי קָתָנֵי: הָא אֲסוּרִין? דִּלְמָא: יֵשׁ מֵהֶן אָסוּר וְיֵשׁ מֵהֶן מוּתָּר.

Rav Ashi said: Is it taught explicitly in the first *baraita* cited by Rav Pineḥas that if it is prohibited for one to shave during the Festival, it is likewise **prohibited** to shave during the week of mourning? That was merely an inference. **Perhaps there are** those **among them** for whom it is **prohibited,** while **there are** others **among them** for whom it is **permitted.** If so, there is no clear support from this *baraita* for Shmuel's statement.

אָבֵל אֵינוֹ נוֹהֵג אֲבֵילוּתוֹ בָּרֶגֶל, שֶׁנֶּאֱמַר: ״וְשָׂמַחְתָּ בְּחַגֶּךָ״.

§ **A mourner does not practice** the *halakhot* of **his mourning on a Festival, as it is stated: "And you shall rejoice in your Festival"** (Deuteronomy 16:14).

HALAKHA

One rends the clothes of a minor – מְקָרְעִין לְקָטָן: If a minor has a close relative who dies, he rends his garment in order to arouse feelings of grief in those around him (*Shulḥan Arukh, Yoreh De'a* 340:27).

Cutting the hair of a baby – גִּילּוּחַ שַׂעֲרוֹת קָטָן: During the intermediate days of the Festival, it is permitted for one to cut a baby's hair if it is bothering him, regardless of whether he was born before or during the Festival. This is permitted even in public (Rema; *Shulḥan Arukh, Oraḥ Ḥayyim* 531:6).

אִי אֲבֵילוּת דְּמֵעִיקָּרָא הוּא – אָתֵי עֲשֵׂה דְּרַבִּים, וְדָחֵי עֲשֵׂה דְּיָחִיד. וְאִי אֲבֵילוּת דְּהַשְׁתָּא הוּא – לָא אָתֵי עֲשֵׂה דְּיָחִיד וְדָחֵי עֲשֵׂה דְּרַבִּים.

The Gemara explains: **If it is a mourning** period that had already begun **at the outset** of the Festival, **the positive mitzva of** rejoicing on the Festival, which is incumbent upon **the community, comes and overrides the positive mitzva of** the **individual,**[N] i.e., the mourning. **And if the mourning** period began only **now,** i.e., the deceased died during the Festival, **the positive mitzva of the individual does not come and override the positive mitzva of the community.**

מְנוּדֶּה, מַהוּ שֶׁיִּנְהוֹג נִידּוּיוֹ בָּרֶגֶל? אָמַר רַב יוֹסֵף, תָּא שְׁמַע: דָּנִין דִּינֵי נְפָשׁוֹת, וְדִינֵי מַכּוֹת, וְדִינֵי מָמוֹנוֹת. וְאִי לָא צָיֵית דִּינָא – מְשַׁמְּתִינַן לֵיהּ.

The Gemara asks: With regard to **one who was ostracized, what** is the *halakha*? Must he **observe the practices of ostracism,** or are they overridden by the mitzva to rejoice **on the Festival? Rav Yosef said: Come** and **hear** an answer from that which is taught: During the Festival **the court judges** cases of **capital law,** cases of **lashes,** and cases of **monetary law.**[H] It is known that **if one does not listen to** and follow **the judgment,** among the possibilities of enforcement is that **we ostracize him**[N] until he accepts the verdict.

וְאִי סָלְקָא דַּעְתָּךְ אֵינוֹ נוֹהֵג נִידּוּיוֹ בָּרֶגֶל – מְשׁוּמָּת וְאָתֵי מֵעִיקָּרָא – אָתֵי רֶגֶל דָּחֵי לֵיהּ, הַשְׁתָּא מְשַׁמְּתִינַן לֵיהּ אֲנַן?!

And if it enters your mind that one does not observe the practices of ostracism during the Festival, the following *a fortiori* argument can be made: If, for **one who has already been ostracized at the outset** of the Festival, **the Festival comes and overrides his** observance of that status, is it reasonable that **now we,** the court, should **ostracize he** who does not listen to the judgment of the court during the Festival itself? Rather, it must be that one does observe the practices of ostracism, even during the Festival.

אֲמַר לֵיהּ אַבַּיֵי: וְדִלְמָא לְעַיּוּנֵי בְּדִינֵיהּ. דְּאִי לָא תֵּימָא הָכִי דִּינֵי נְפָשׁוֹת דְּקָתָנֵי, הָכָא נַמִי דְּקָטְלִין לֵיהּ?

Abaye said to him: There is no proof from here, **as perhaps** when the *baraita* states that the court judges cases, what it meant is that it **deliberates in judgment** on the Festival, but it does not actually reach a verdict. Therefore, the court never ostracizes someone during the Festival. Accordingly, there is no *a fortiori* argument proving that one observes the practices of ostracism during the Festival. **Because if you do not say so,** that the *baraita* is referring to deliberation, then in the cases of **capital law that are taught, here too, would we put someone to death** on the Festival?

וְהָא קָא מִימַּנְעִי מִשִּׂמְחַת יוֹם טוֹב. דְּתַנְיָא, רַבִּי עֲקִיבָא אוֹמֵר: מִנַּיִן לְסַנְהֶדְרִין (שֶׁרָאוּ בְּאֶחָד) שֶׁהָרְגוּ אֶת הַנֶּפֶשׁ שֶׁאֵין טוֹעֲמִין כׇּל אוֹתוֹ הַיּוֹם? תַּלְמוּד לוֹמַר: ״לֹא תֹאכְלוּ עַל הַדָּם״.

But if so, the judges **would be prevented from rejoicing on the Festival, as it is taught** in a *baraita* that **Rabbi Akiva says: From where** is it derived with regard **to the Sanhedrin who put someone to death that they may not taste** any food or drink **for the entire rest of the day?**[H] **The verse states: "You shall not eat with the blood"** (Leviticus 19:26). It is not appropriate to eat during the same day that they caused bloodshed.

אֶלָּא – לְעַיּוּנֵי בְּדִינֵיהּ; הָכָא נַמִי – לְעַיּוּנֵי בְּדִינֵיהּ. אֲמַר לֵיהּ: אִם כֵּן נִמְצֵאתָ מְעַנֶּה אֶת דִּינוֹ!

Rather, the statement of the *baraita*, that the court judges cases of capital law, must be referring **to deliberating in judgment** and not actually reaching a verdict. **Here too,** in cases of monetary law and of lashes, it is referring **to deliberating in judgment,** without the possibility of ostracizing anyone during the Festival. Rav Yosef said **to him: If so,** if only deliberations are conducted during the Festival, **you find a perversion of justice** by delaying **his** verdict.

אָתוּ מִצַּפְרָא וּמְעַיְּינִי בְּדִינֵיהּ, וְעָיְילִי וְאָכְלִי וְשָׁתוּ כּוּלֵּי יוֹמָא, וַהֲדַר אָתוּ בִּשְׁקִיעַת הַחַמָּה וְגָמְרִינַן לְדִינֵיהּ, וְקָטְלוּ לֵיהּ.

Rather, the judges **come in the morning** as usual **and deliberate in judgment.** They then **enter** their homes **and eat and drink all day,** i.e., as much as they desire, in order to rejoice fully on the Festival. **Then they come** back to the courthouse close to **sunset and complete his judgment,** i.e., they dispense the verdict, and if necessary, **they kill him.**[H] In this manner, they are not prevented from enjoying the Festival properly.

אָמַר אַבַּיֵי, תָּא שְׁמַע: וּמְנוּדֶּה שֶׁהִתִּירוּ לוֹ חֲכָמִים.

Abaye said: Come and **hear** another support from a *baraita*: **And** it is the case with regard to **one who is ostracized, that the Sages permitted him** to get a haircut during the intermediate days of the Festival. This indicates that one who is ostracized need not observe the practices of ostracism during the Festival.

NOTES

Overrides the positive mitzva of the individual – דָּחֵי עֲשֵׂה דְּיָחִיד: The language of the Gemara here implies that mourning is a positive mitzva by Torah law, and many halakhic authorities rule in this manner (see Rambam). They bring support from verse: "And if I had eaten the sin-offering today" (Leviticus 10:19), which is written in reference to Aaron the priest after the death of two of his sons (Rambam). Another verse states: "Make for yourself mourning, as for an only son" (Jeremiah 6:26), which implies that the mourning rituals were well established before the time of Jeremiah (Rabbeinu Gershom *Meor HaGola*; Rashi; Rid). There are also other verses that refer to mourning practices (see Ezekiel 24:17, 31:15).

However, other authorities hold that only the first day of mourning is by Torah law, and there is also a dispute with regard to the following evening (Rif on tractate *Berakhot*). The statement here that mourning is a positive mitzva of the individual is only according to the opinion of certain *tanna'im*. Rabbeinu Shlomo ben HaYatom writes that the term used by the Gemara here is referring only to the first day of the mourning period. Others write that while most of the *halakhot* of mourning are by rabbinic law, the Gemara here is referring specifically to the prohibition against haircutting, which is derived from the Torah itself in reference to Aaron and his sons (Ra'avad; *Sefer Hashlama*).

Some authorities hold that all the *halakhot* of mourning are by rabbinic law, and when the Gemara uses the term positive mitzva it means by rabbinic law. It uses shorthand rather than explaining at length that a positive mitzva incumbent upon the community by Torah law overrides a positive mitzva of an individual by rabbinic law (Rosh). Another possibility is that the positive mitzva of the community to rejoice on a Festival is also referring to a rabbinic mitzva (see *Tosafot*; *Ba'al Halakhot Gedolot*).

If one does not listen to the judgment we ostracize him – אִי לָא צָיֵית דִּינָא מְשַׁמְּתִינַן לֵיהּ: *Tosafot* question this, as normally the court would seize property as collateral and ostracize only as a last resort. However, it could be argued that ostracism is a more universal judgment, since if one does not own property, he can still be forced to listen to the court by being ostracized (*Ramat Shmuel*).

HALAKHA

Judgment during the Festival – דִּין בְּמוֹעֵד: A court may judge cases of capital or monetary law on the intermediate days of a Festival, and it may ostracize one who refuses to listen to its judgment (*Shulḥan Arukh, Oraḥ Ḥayyim* 545:10).

The fast of the Sanhedrin – צוֹם הַסַּנְהֶדְרִין: If the Sanhedrin condemns someone to death, the judges may not eat the entire day. This is derived from the verse: "You shall not eat with the blood" (Rambam *Sefer Shofetim, Hilkhot Sanhedrin* 13:4).

One who is liable to be put to death during the Festival – חַיָּיב מִיתָה בְּמוֹעֵד: If one is liable to be put to death by the court during the Festival, the court deliberates for the entire day, allowing the judges to eat and drink during that time. They then convict him just before sunset and put him to death (Rambam *Sefer Shofetim, Hilkhot Sanhedrin* 13:5).

אָמַר רָבָא: מִי קָתָנֵי שֶׁהִתִּירוּהוּ חֲכָמִים? שֶׁהִתִּירוּ לוֹ חֲכָמִים קָתָנֵי, דַּאֲזַל וּפַיְּיסֵיהּ לְבַעַל דִּינֵיהּ, וְאָתֵי קַמֵּי דְּרַבָּנַן, וְשָׁרוּ לֵיהּ.

Rava said: Is it taught in the *baraita*: **That they permitted it,** which would indicate that **the Sages** permitted all those who were ostracized to cut their hair on the intermediate days of the Festival? Rather, **it is taught: They permitted him.** This indicates that it is referring to an individual case, **where one went and appeased his** opposing **litigant and the Sages came and released him** from his decree of ostracism.

מְצוֹרָע מַהוּ שֶׁיִּנְהַג צָרַעְתּוֹ בָּרֶגֶל? אָמַר אַבַּיֵּי, תָּא שְׁמַע: וְהַנָּזִיר וְהַמְּצוֹרָע מִטּוּמְאָתוֹ לְטׇהֳרָתוֹ. הָא בִּימֵי טוּמְאָתוֹ – נָהֵיג.

§ The Gemara asks a similar question: With regard to **a leper,**[B] **what is the** *halakha*? Must he **observe the practices of his leper status,** or are they overridden by the mitzva to rejoice **during the Festival?**[NH] **Abaye said: Come** and **hear** a proof from a *baraita*: **And** both **the nazirite and the leper** who transfers **from his** state of **ritual impurity to his** new state of **purity** may shave on the intermediate days of the Festival. **This** implies that if **during the days of his impurity** he must **observe** all of the ordinary practices, even during the Festival.

לָא מִיבַּעְיָא קָאָמַר; לָא מִיבַּעְיָא בִּימֵי טוּמְאָתוֹ דְּלָא נָהֵיג, אֲבָל לְטׇהֳרָתוֹ – נִיגְזוֹר שֶׁמָּא יַשְׁהֶה קׇרְבְּנוֹתָיו. קָמַשְׁמַע לַן.

The Gemara rejects this proof: The *baraita* **is speaking** employing the didactic style of: **Needless to say. Needless to say, during the days of his impurity** on the Festival, **he does not observe** the practices of ostracism. **However,** with regard to one who regains **his** state of **purity** during the intermediate days of the Festival, one might think that **we should issue a decree** that he not be permitted to shave, **lest he delay** sacrificing **his offerings** until the last day of the Festival, when it is prohibited to sacrifice offerings of an individual. Perhaps prohibiting him from shaving will prevent this possibility. Therefore, because one might have thought that shaving should be prohibited, the *baraita* **teaches us** that it is, in fact, permitted for him to shave during the intermediate days of the Festival.

אָמַר רָבָא, תָּא שְׁמַע: ״וְהַצָּרוּעַ״ – לְרַבּוֹת כֹּהֵן גָּדוֹל. וְהָא כֹּהֵן גָּדוֹל, דְּכׇל הַשָּׁנָה כְּרֶגֶל לְכוּלֵּי עָלְמָא דָּמֵי, דִּתְנַן: כֹּהֵן גָּדוֹל מַקְרִיב אוֹנֵן וְאֵינוֹ אוֹכֵל. שְׁמַע מִינָּהּ: נוֹהֵג צָרַעְתּוֹ בָּרֶגֶל. שְׁמַע מִינָּהּ.

Rava said: Come and **hear** another source. The verse states: "**And the leper**[N] in whom the plague is, his clothes shall be rent" (Leviticus 13:45). The extra emphasis of the phrase: "And the leper" comes **to include the High Priest,** teaching that all the *halakhot* of the leper apply to him. **And** the status of **the High Priest** during **the entire year is like** that of **everyone on a Festival, as we learned** in a mishna (*Horayot* 12b): The **High Priest sacrifices** animals when he has the status of **an acute mourner,**[H] i.e., before the burial of a close relative who died, **but he may not eat** of the offering. **Learn from it** that a leper **practices the customs of his leprosy during the Festival.** The Gemara concludes: Indeed, **learn from it** that this is so.

אָבֵל אָסוּר בְּתִסְפּוֹרֶת, מִדְּקָאָמַר לְהוּ רַחֲמָנָא לִבְנֵי אַהֲרֹן ״רָאשֵׁיכֶם אַל תִּפְרָעוּ״ – מִכְּלָל דְּכוּלֵּי עָלְמָא אָסוּר.

§ The source for the *halakha* that **it is prohibited for a mourner** to receive **a haircut**[H] is derived **from** the fact that **the Merciful One states to the sons of Aaron: "Let not the hair of your heads go loose"** (Leviticus 10:6). It was prohibited for them to let their hair grow long during their period of mourning over the death of their brothers, Nadav and Avihu. **By inference,** it is teaching **that for everyone** else, i.e., non-priests, **it is prohibited** to cut their hair during the period of mourning.

NOTES

A leper during the Festival – מְצוֹרָע בָּרֶגֶל: Some explain that the question is whether or not all the *halakhot* of the leper should be observed on the Festival (Rashi; Rabbeinu Gershom *Meor HaGola*). However, the Rid finds this explanation difficult and explains that the only question is with regard to the rabbinic prohibitions pertaining to the leper, such as washing clothes or greeting people. However, those activities that are prohibited by Torah law, such as cutting one's hair or entering the camp, certainly remain in effect (see *Talmid Rabbeinu Yeḥiel of Paris*).

And the leper – וְהַצָּרוּעַ: Some explain that this derivation is based on the apparently superfluous letters *vav* and *heh* at the beginning of the word (Rabbeinu Shlomo ben HaYatom). Others suggest that the entire word seems to be extraneous (*Talmid Rabbeinu Yeḥiel of Paris*). Still others hold that it is not this word that is unnecessary, but the following phrase: "In whom the plague is" (see *Korban Aharon*).

HALAKHA

A leper on Shabbat and during the Festival – מְצֹרָע בְּשַׁבָּת וְיוֹם טוֹב: Even on Shabbat and Festivals, a leper observes all of his normal practices, including those that are similar to mourning (Rambam *Sefer Tahara, Hilkhot Tumat Tzara'at* 10:6).

The High Priest sacrifices as an acute mourner – כֹּהֵן גָּדוֹל מַקְרִיב אוֹנֵן: The High Priest may perform the service in the Temple, even when he is an acute mourner. However, he may not eat from consecrated meat (Rambam *Sefer Avoda, Hilkhot Biat HaMikdash* 2:6, 8).

A mourner with regard to receiving a haircut – אָבֵל בְּתִסְפּוֹרֶת: It is prohibited for a mourner to have a haircut or to shave (*Shulḥan Arukh, Yoreh De'a* 390:1).

BACKGROUND

Leprosy [*tzara'at*] – צָרַעַת: Traditionally rendered as leprosy, the term *tzara'at* used in the Torah is not necessarily identical with leprosy as defined by modern medicine. The Torah term refers to symptoms that cause severe ritual impurity. The *halakhot* governing these symptoms are detailed at length in Leviticus, chapters 13–15, and in the Mishna in tractate *Nega'im*. There can be leprosy of the skin, hair, articles of clothing, or houses.

When a symptom appears, it is examined by a priest. Only a priest is authorized to determine whether to quarantine the affected person for a certain period or to declare immediately that the symptom is, or is not, leprosy.

Leprosy is one of the primary sources of ritual impurity, and any item touched by a leper also becomes impure. While the Jews were in the desert, one afflicted with leprosy was sent out of the Israelite camp, and when the Jewish people lived in Eretz Yisrael, a leper was sent out of any walled city. The leper was obligated to live alone until his affliction was cured.

A garment affected by leprosy is burned, and a contaminated house is entirely destroyed and its rubble disposed of in a ritually impure place. A cured leper must undergo special purification rites outside the city and a purification ceremony in the Temple itself. He is obligated to bring special offerings as part of his purification.

מנודין ומצורעין מה הן בתספורת? תא שמע: מנודין ומצורעין אסורין לספר ולכבס.

The Gemara asks: **What** is the *halakha* governing **those who are ostracized and lepers,**[N] with regard to **a haircut?** The Gemara answers: **Come** and **hear that which** was taught in a *baraita*: **Those who are ostracized**[H] **and lepers**[H] **are prohibited from cutting** their hair **and laundering** their clothes.

מנודה שמת – בית דין סוקלין את ארונו. רבי יהודה אומר: לא שיעמידו עליו גל אבנים כגלו של עכן, אלא: בית דין שולחין ומניחין אבן גדולה על ארונו. ללמדך שכל המתנדה ומת בנידויו בית דין סוקלין את ארונו.

It was further taught there: If **one who is ostracized dies, the court** places **stones on his coffin. Rabbi Yehuda says:** This does **not** mean **that they pile up a heap of stones over him like the heap** of stones that was placed over the grave **of Achan**[N] (see Joshua 7:26). **Rather, the court sends** its agents, **who place a large stone**[N] **on his coffin** as a symbolic gesture. This comes **to teach you** that **anyone who is ostracized and dies while in his** period of **ostracism,** without seeking to be released from it, **the court** places **stones on his coffin.**[H]

אבל חייב בעטיפת הראש. מדקאמר ליה רחמנא ליחזקאל: "ולא תעטה על שפם" – מכלל דכולי עלמא מיחייבי.

§ The Gemara continues: **A mourner is obligated to wrap** his **head** as a sign of mourning, covering his head and face.[H] This is derived from the fact **that the Merciful One says to Ezekiel,** while he is in mourning: **"And cover not your upper lip"** (Ezekiel 24:17). God commands Ezekiel not to display outward signs of mourning, which proves **by inference that everyone** else **is obligated** to wrap their heads in this manner.

מנודה מהו בעטיפת הראש? אמר רב יוסף, תא שמע: והן מתעטפין ויושבין כמנודין וכאבלים עד שירחמו עליהם מן השמים. אמר ליה אביי: דלמא מנודה לשמים שאני דחמיר.

The Gemara asks: **What is** the *halakha* governing **a person who is ostracized,** with regard to **wrapping of the head?**[NH] **Rav Yosef said: Come** and **hear** that which was taught in a *baraita* about those who were fasting for rain and whose prayers were not answered: **And they wrap themselves and sit as those who are ostracized and as mourners, until they are shown mercy from Heaven.** This implies that those who are ostracized must wrap their heads like mourners. **Abaye said to him: Perhaps one who is ostracized by Heaven is different, as that is more serious** than being ostracized by an earthly court.

מצורע מהו בעטיפת הראש? תא שמע: "ועל שפם יעטה" – מכלל שחייב בעטיפת הראש. שמע מינה.

The Gemara continues and asks: **What is** the *halakha* in the case **of a leper** with regard to **wrapping of the head?**[H] **Come and hear** a proof based upon the verse: **"And he shall cover his upper lip"** (Leviticus 13:45), from which it may be learned **by inference that he is obligated to wrap** his **head.** The Gemara concludes: Indeed, **learn from here** that this is the case.

NOTES

Those who are ostracized and lepers – מנודין ומצורעין: The early authorities ask: Isn't it implicit in the mishna that one who is ostracized or a leper may not cut his hair? Why is it necessary to seek evidence from another source (see Rid; *Talmid Rabbeinu Yeḥiel of Paris*)? Similarly, the answers to some of the questions of the Gemara appear to be stated explicitly in the verse, e.g., the question concerning the wrapping of a leper's head.

Some suggest that perhaps the Gemara here holds in accordance with the opinion of Rabbi Akiva, that the verse there is referring to a different issue. The Ritva writes that perhaps these questions are asked because this is the style of the Gemara. In the manuscript of Rashi, this idea is taken further. It is suggested there that these questions are not actually necessary and are only mentioned to increase Torah learning. Therefore, when asking these questions, the Gemara uses a set formula to ask questions: A question is asked based on a *halakha* that applies to a mourner, and the Gemara asks if it applies to a person who was ostracized or to a leper. In order to maintain this formula, the Gemara also asks questions for which there are straightforward answers (see *Tal Ḥayyim*).

Like the heap of Achan – כגלו של עכן: Achan was notorious for having taken from the spoils of Jericho, which had been set aside for God. His theft led to casualties in the subsequent war against the city of Ai. Once his trespass was discovered, Achan was put to death and a pile of stones was heaped upon his grave (see Joshua 7:26).

Who place a large stone – ומניחין אבן גדולה: Rashi explains that placing the stone is meant to serve only as a reminder of the decree of ostracism (manuscript of Rashi). It is intended to publicize the matter (*Talmid Rabbeinu Yeḥiel of Paris*). According to Rabbi Shlomo ben HaYatom, this also warns others about the severity of the deceased's sin. He further explains that it is sufficient to place only one stone on the grave because when a court rules that one is to be stoned, a single large stone is first placed on his chest, and if he dies he is not stoned further. Therefore, the placement of one stone is defined as stoning by *halakha*. Based on this, the halakhic authorities understand that all those mourning customs that show respect for the deceased are not practiced in the case of one who was ostracized, and only those customs that are meant to honor the living mourners apply in such a case (see Rif).

A person who is ostracized wrapping his head – מנודה בעטיפה: Some say that an ostracized person is required to wrap his head. Abaye is merely rejecting the proof, but not the *halakha*, which is in accordance with the opinion of Rav Yosef (Rav Hai Gaon).

HALAKHA

One who has been ostracized with regard to cutting hair and laundering clothes – מנודה בתספורת וכביסה: One who has been ostracized may not cut his hair or launder his clothes (*Shulḥan Arukh, Yoreh De'a* 334:2).

A leper with regard to cutting hair and laundering clothes – מצורע בתספורת וכביסה: A leper may not cut his hair or launder his clothes as long as he is quarantined (Rambam *Sefer Tahara, Hilkhot Tumat Tzara'at* 10:6).

One who is ostracized and dies – המתנדה ומת: If one who was ostracized died without having his decree of ostracism removed, then the court appoints emissaries to place a stone on his coffin. The relatives of such a person do not rend their clothes, remove their shoes, or deliver eulogies for the deceased.

This applies to those who were ostracized for committing sins; however, one who was ostracized as a penalty for not meeting his financial obligations is treated with the honor due to any other person who passed away. The reason for this is because one becomes exempt from such a penalty once he passes away (*Shulḥan Arukh, Yoreh De'a* 334:3).

A mourner wrapping his head – אבל בעטיפה: A mourner is required to wrap his head in such a way that the end of a scarf or shawl covers his mouth and nose. According to the Rema, it is not customary to carry out this practice today because shawls are not ordinarily worn, and one should not be stringent (*Shulḥan Arukh, Yoreh De'a* 386:1).

A person who is ostracized wrapping his head – מנודה בעטיפה: One who has been ostracized is not required to wrap his head. This is because the issue is left unresolved by the Gemara, and the *halakha* generally follows the lenient opinion in unresolved issues concerning rabbinic mitzvot (*Shakh*; *Shulḥan Arukh, Yoreh De'a* 334:1).

A leper wrapping his head – מצורע בעטיפה: A leper is required to wrap his head and cover his upper lip (Rambam *Sefer Tahara, Hilkhot Tumat Tzara'at* 10:6).

אָבֵל אָסוּר לְהָנִיחַ תְּפִילִּין. מִדְּקָאָמַר לֵיהּ רַחֲמָנָא לִיחֶזְקֵאל: ״פְּאֵרְךָ חֲבוֹשׁ עָלֶיךָ״ – מִכְּלָל דְּכוּלֵּי עָלְמָא אָסוּר.

§ The Gemara moves on to another *halakha*: **A mourner is prohibited from donning phylacteries.**[H] This is derived from the fact **that the Merciful One says to Ezekiel,** while he is in mourning: **"Bind your headwear [*pe'er*] upon yourself"** (Ezekiel 24:17).[N] The word *pe'er* alludes to phylacteries. Ezekiel was unique in that he was commanded to put on phylacteries while in mourning, which proves **by inference that everyone** else **is prohibited** from doing so.

מְנוּדֶּה מַהוּ בִּתְפִילִּין? תֵּיקוּ. מְצוֹרָע מַהוּ בִּתְפִילִּין? תָּא שְׁמַע: ״וְהַצָּרוּעַ״ – לְרַבּוֹת כֹּהֵן גָּדוֹל; ״בְּגָדָיו יִהְיוּ פְרוּמִים״ – שֶׁיְּהוּ מְקוֹרָעִים; ״וְרֹאשׁוֹ יִהְיֶה פָרוּעַ״ – אֵין פְּרִיעָה אֶלָּא גִּידּוּל שֵׂעָר, דִּבְרֵי רַבִּי אֱלִיעֶזֶר.

The Gemara asks: **What is the** *halakha* governing **one who is ostracized,** with regard to phylacteries? The dilemma **shall stand** unresolved. The Gemara proceeds to its next question: **What is** the *halakha* in the case of **a leper** with regard to phylacteries? The Gemara suggests: **Come** and **hear** a proof from the following *baraita*: The verse states: **"And the leper"** (Leviticus 13:45); as explained earlier, this comes **to include the High Priest** in all the *halakhot* of the leper. The verse states there: **"His garments shall be *perumim*,"** meaning **that they shall be rent.** The verse continues: **"And his head shall be *parua*,"** and this ***peria*** means **only growing the hair long;** this is **the statement of Rabbi Eliezer.**

רַבִּי עֲקִיבָא אוֹמֵר: נֶאֶמְרָה הֲוָיָה בְּרֹאשׁ וְנֶאֶמְרָה הֲוָיָה בְּבֶגֶד. מַה הֲוָיָה הָאֲמוּרָה בְּבֶגֶד – דָּבָר שֶׁחוּץ מִגּוּפוֹ, אַף הֲוָיָה בְּרֹאשׁ – דָּבָר שֶׁחוּץ מִגּוּפוֹ. מַאי לָאו אַתְּפִילִּין?

Rabbi Akiva says: The meaning of these terms is derived through a verbal analogy. The verse **states** a form of the verb **being, with regard to** one's **head** in the verse: "His head shall be," teaching that a leper must perform a certain action with his head. **And the verse states** a form of the verb **being with regard to** a leper's **garment,** in the verse: "His garment shall be." **Just as** the term **being stated with regard to** his **garment** is referring to **an object external to his body, so too,** the term **being** used **with regard to** his **head** is referring to **an object external to his body.** The Gemara derives from this: **What, is it not** referring to **phylacteries,** and the verse teaches that it is prohibited for a leper to wear phylacteries?

אָמַר רַב פַּפָּא: לָא, אַכּוּמְתָא וְסוּדָרָא.

Rav Pappa said: No, there is no proof from here, as the verse may be referring **to a cap [*kumta*]**[L] **or a scarf [*sudara*],**[L] which people wear on their heads. It is possible to explain that according to Rabbi Akiva, it is prohibited for a leper to wear such headwear because it is excessive adornment.[H]

אָבֵל אָסוּר בִּשְׁאִילַת שָׁלוֹם, דְּקָאָמַר לֵיהּ רַחֲמָנָא לִיחֶזְקֵאל: ״הֵאָנֵק דּוֹם״.

§ The Gemara continues: **A mourner is prohibited from greeting** others or be greeted.[H] This is derived from the fact **that the Merciful One says to Ezekiel: "Sigh in silence"** (Ezekiel 24:17),[N] implying that aside from what was absolutely essential, he was prohibited from speaking.

HALAKHA

A mourner and phylacteries – אָבֵל וּתְפִילִּין: On the first day of mourning, a mourner is prohibited from donning phylacteries, even if the deceased was buried the night before. From the second day of mourning onward, one should don phylacteries. However, different customs exist with regard to whether or not this may be done only in private (*Mishna Berura*; *Shulḥan Arukh, Oraḥ Ḥayyim* 38:5 and *Yoreh De'a* 388:1).

A leper growing his hair and rending his garments – מְצוֹרָע בִּפְרִיעָה וּבִפְרִימָה: Every leper must let his hair grow long and rend his garments, even if he is the High Priest (Rambam *Sefer Tahara, Hilkhot Tumat Tzara'at* 10:6).

A mourner with regard to greeting others – אָבֵל בִּשְׁאִילַת שָׁלוֹם: A mourner may not greet others or be greeted (*Shulḥan Arukh, Yoreh De'a* 385:1).

LANGUAGE

Cap [*kumta*] – כּוּמְתָא: The *ge'onim* explain that this word refers to a soft hat or a beret. It is related to the Arabic كمة, *kumma*, which has the same meaning.

Scarf [*sudara*] – סוּדָרָא: From the Latin sudarium, meaning scarf or towel. Here and in other cases, this word refers to a scarf wrapped around the head, which was worn by married rabbis. Similarly, it is customary in several communities for the rabbi to wrap a special scarf around his turban.

NOTES

Bind your headwear [*pe'er*] upon yourself – פְּאֵרְךָ חֲבוֹשׁ עָלֶיךָ: In tractate *Berakhot* this conclusion is reached in a different manner. It is stated there that phylacteries are referred to as *pe'er*, literally meaning splendor, and it is not appropriate for a mourner to be crowned with such splendor. Additionally, when a mourner wears phylacteries it is disrespectful toward the mitzva of phylacteries, as the mourner is in a lowly state, and it is inappropriate that words describing God's glory rest upon him. In *Tosefot HaRosh* it is noted that these two explanations complement each other. While the *halakha* is derived from the Gemara here, the reasoning behind it is explained in tractate *Berakhot*.

Sigh in silence – הֵאָנֵק דּוֹם: *Tosafot* allude to the difficulty with this proof. The Gemara has already shown that Ezekiel's mourning was an exceptional case, and ordinary mourners should do the opposite of everything he was instructed to do. If so, how is it possible to prove that a mitzva of silence stated with regard to Ezekiel also applies to other mourners?

The early authorities who address this issue answer it in several different ways. Some say that the instruction: "Sigh in silence," applies to Ezekiel and other mourners as well. Immediately afterward he was instructed: "Make no mourning for the dead" (Ezekiel 24:17), with regard to the further instructions, which were unique to him (Ra'avad; *Talmid Rabbeinu Yeḥiel of Paris*). The reason for this is because mourning is not immediately evident through a mourner's silence (*Talmid Rabbeinu Yeḥiel of Paris*).

Others suggest that God instructed Ezekiel to deviate from the common practice in this case as well. Therefore, the verse should be understood as: Sighing in silence and mourning for the dead, do not do. If this is the case, then this proof is similar to those cited for the other practices mentioned here (Rabbi Shlomo ben HaYatom; *Nimmukei Yosef*, citing Rabbi Meir HaLevi).

Tosefot HaRosh gives a simple explanation: Certainly the Merciful One was not stricter with Ezekiel than with other mourners, and therefore any stringency that applied to him certainly also applies to other mourners as well. A similar explanation appears in several places in *Tosafot*. Others explain that all these proofs are meant only as support or allusions and should not be read too carefully. Instead, the Sages relied upon traditions or made decrees on their own (*Sefer HaMe'orot*).

מְנוּדֶּה מַהוּ בִּשְׁאִילַת שָׁלוֹם? אָמַר רַב יוֹסֵף: תָּא שְׁמַע: וּבִשְׁאִילַת שָׁלוֹם שֶׁבֵּין אָדָם לַחֲבֵרוֹ, כִּבְנֵי אָדָם הַנְּזוּפִין לַמָּקוֹם. אֲמַר לֵיהּ אַבַּיֵי: דִּלְמָא מְנוּדֶּה לַשָּׁמַיִם שָׁאנֵי, דַּחֲמִיר.

The Gemara asks: **What is the** *halakha* governing **one who is ostracized** with regard to **greeting** others? **Rav Yosef said: Come** and **hear** a proof from a *baraita* dealing with those who were fasting for rain and whose prayers were not answered. These people were prohibited **from greeting one another, as people who are reprimanded by the Omnipresent.**[H] This indicates that those who are ostracized must not greet each other, just as mourners may not greet each other. **Abaye said to him: Perhaps one who is ostracized by Heaven is different, as that is more serious** than being ostracized by an earthly court.

מְצוֹרָע מַהוּ בִּשְׁאִילַת שָׁלוֹם? תָּא שְׁמַע: ״וְעַל שָׂפָם יַעְטֶה״ – שֶׁיְּהוּ שִׂפְתוֹתָיו מְדוּבָּקוֹת זוֹ בָּזוֹ, שֶׁיְּהֵא כִּמְנוּדֶּה וּכְאָבֵל, וְאָסוּר בִּשְׁאִילַת שָׁלוֹם. שְׁמַע מִינָּהּ.

The Gemara continues and asks: **What is** the *halakha* concerning **a leper** with regard to **greeting** others? The Gemara suggests: **Come** and **hear** a proof from the following *baraita*: The verse states: **"And he shall cover his upper lip"** (Leviticus 13:45). This means that **his lips should be stuck together, that he should be like one who is ostracized and like a mourner, and he is prohibited from greeting** others or being greeted. The Gemara concludes: Indeed, **learn from this** that this is so.

וְנִיפְשׁוֹט מִינָּהּ לִמְנוּדֶּה! אָמַר רַב אַחָא בַּר פִּנְחָס מִשְּׁמֵיהּ דְּרַב יוֹסֵף: מִי קָתָנֵי שֶׁאָסוּר? שֶׁיְּהֵא כִּמְנוּדֶּה וּכְאָבֵל [קָתָנֵי] – בְּמִילֵּי אַחֲרָנְיָיתָא, וְאָסוּר נַמִי בִּשְׁאִילַת שָׁלוֹם.

The Gemara asks: If this is the case, then **we should** also **resolve** the question asked above **with regard to one who is ostracized** and say that such a person is prohibited from offering greetings. **Rav Aḥa bar Pineḥas said in the name of Rav Yosef: Does it** explicitly **teach** that a leper **is prohibited** from greeting others, like one who is ostracized? **It teaches** only **that he should be** treated **like one who is ostracized and like a mourner,** i.e., he should be like them **with regard to other things, and** that **he is also prohibited from greeting** others. This being the case, no proof can be derived from here with regard to whether or not one who is ostracized may offer greetings.

אָבֵל אָסוּר בְּדִבְרֵי תוֹרָה, מִדְּקָאָמַר רַחֲמָנָא לִיחֶזְקֵאל ״דֹּם״.

§ The Gemara moves on to a new topic: **A mourner is prohibited** from studying **words of Torah.**[H] This prohibition is derived **from** the fact **that the Merciful One says to Ezekiel:** "Sigh in **silence**" (Ezekiel 24:17). Ezekiel was commanded to be silent and not discuss even Torah matters.

מְנוּדֶּה מַהוּ בְּדִבְרֵי תוֹרָה? אָמַר רַב יוֹסֵף, תָּא שְׁמַע: מְנוּדֶּה – שׁוֹנֶה וְשׁוֹנִין לוֹ, נִשְׂכָּר וְנִשְׂכָּרִין לוֹ.

The Gemara asks: **What is** the *halakha* concerning **one who is ostracized** with regard to speaking **words of Torah? Rav Yosef said: Come** and **hear that which** was taught in the following *baraita*: **One who is ostracized may teach** Torah to others, **and** others **may teach him** Torah. Similarly, **he may be hired** for work by others, **and** others **may be hired by him.**[H]

מוּחֲרָם – לֹא שׁוֹנֶה וְלֹא שׁוֹנִין לוֹ, לֹא נִשְׂכָּר וְלֹא נִשְׂכָּרִין לוֹ. אֲבָל שׁוֹנֶה הוּא לְעַצְמוֹ שֶׁלֹּא יַפְסִיק אֶת לִמּוּדוֹ. וְעוֹשֶׂה לוֹ חֲנוּת קְטַנָּה בִּשְׁבִיל פַּרְנָסָתוֹ.

One who has been excommunicated,[NH] which is a more severe form of ostracism, **may not teach** Torah to others **and** others **may not teach him. He may not be hired** by others, **and** others **may not be hired by him. However, he may study by himself,** so **that he will not interrupt his study** entirely and forget everything he knows. **And he may build a small store for his livelihood,** so that he can earn enough money to cover his most basic needs, but not more.

וְאָמַר רַב: זַבּוּנֵי מַיָּא בְּפַקְתָּא דַּעֲרָבוֹת. שְׁמַע מִינָּהּ.

And Rav said: What is the small store referred to here? This is referring to **selling water in the valley of Aravot,**[NB] where no water was to be found. One selling water there could earn a small income. The Gemara concludes: Indeed, **learn from this** *baraita* that one who is ostracized is permitted to study Torah.

מְצוֹרָע מַהוּ בְּדִבְרֵי תוֹרָה? תָּא שְׁמַע: ״וְהוֹדַעְתָּם לְבָנֶיךָ וְלִבְנֵי בָנֶיךָ יוֹם אֲשֶׁר עָמַדְתָּ לִפְנֵי ה׳ אֱלֹהֶיךָ בְּחוֹרֵב״, מַה לְהַלָּן בְּאֵימָה וּבְיִרְאָה וּבִרְתֵת וּבְזִיעַ.

The Gemara asks: **What is** the *halakha* with regard to **a leper** speaking **words of Torah?**[H] The Gemara answers: **Come** and **hear** that which is taught in a *baraita*: It is written: **"And you shall impart them to your children and your children's children; the day that you stood before the Lord your God in Horeb"** (Deuteronomy 4:9–10). **Just as there,** the revelation at Sinai was **in reverence, fear, and trembling,** so too, here, in every generation, Torah must be studied in a similar fashion.

HALAKHA

Mourning practices during a time of drought – אֲבֵלוּת בַּעֲצִירַת גְּשָׁמִים: If there is a drought and the thirteen fasts have been carried out without rain falling, then people should begin to greet each other with less emotion, and Torah scholars should not greet each other at all (*Shulḥan Arukh, Oraḥ Ḥayyim* 575:7).

A mourner with regard to Torah study – אָבֵל בְּדִבְרֵי תוֹרָה: A mourner is prohibited from studying Torah for all seven days of mourning. This includes the Bible, Talmud, and *halakha*. He may read the prophecies that speak about catastrophes in the books of Jeremiah and Job. Similarly, he may study this third chapter of *Moed Katan* and the *halakhot* of mourning (*Pitḥei Teshuva*; *Arukh HaShulḥan*; *Shulḥan Arukh, Yoreh De'a* 384:1).

One who has been ostracized with regard to earning a livelihood and studying Torah – מְנוּדֶּה בְּפַרְנָסָה וְתוֹרָה: One who has been ostracized may study, teach, or be taught Torah. In addition, he may earn a livelihood by hiring other people to work for him or by hiring himself out to others (*Shulḥan Arukh, Yoreh De'a* 334:2).

One who has been excommunicated – מוּחֲרָם: One who has been excommunicated may not teach or be taught Torah. However, he may study Torah on his own, so that he will not forget what he has learned. He may not be hired for work, and he may not hire other people to work for him. However, he may establish a small store in order to earn a minimal income (*Shulḥan Arukh, Yoreh De'a* 334:2).

A leper with regard to Torah study – מְצוֹרָע בְּדִבְרֵי תוֹרָה: Like others who are impure, a leper may study Torah (Rambam *Sefer Tahara, Hilkhot Tumat Tzara'at* 10:6).

NOTES

Ostracized and excommunicated – מְנוּדֶּה וּמוּחֲרָם: Most authorities explain that these terms refer to two different levels within the same concept. One is ostracized as a warning, and if he fails to listen and have his decree of ostracism reversed then he will be excommunicated afterward. According to the Ra'avad, between excommunication and ostracism there is an intermediate level of banishment: *Shamta*.

Selling water in the valley of Aravot – זַבּוּנֵי מַיָּא בְּפַקְתָּא דַּעֲרָבוֹת: Some say that this is meant to serve merely as a suggestion. Since one who is excommunicated cannot hire other people or be hired, and he may earn a livelihood only by selling his property, he is permitted to earn this small amount of income (Rabbeinu Yehonatan of Lunel). Some say that this statement teaches something novel: He is permitted to sell water in a place where it is needed. Similarly, he may earn his livelihood by providing any goods or services that are necessities (Ritva). Others suggest that he may be involved only in businesses that involve minimal interaction with other people (see *Beit Yosef*). Others say that he is permitted to work only in a place where few people are present (Rabbi Shlomo ben HaYatom).

BACKGROUND

Valley [*pakta*] of Aravot – פַּקְתָּא דַּעֲרָבוֹת: The word *pakta* is another form of the word *bakta*, meaning valley or plain. From other sources, it is known that people worked and lived in such places, although they did not have sources of water. One could earn money by selling water in such places; however, one was able to earn only a small profit by doing so.

מִכָּאן אָמְרוּ: הַזָּבִין וְהַמְּצוֹרָעִין וּבוֹעֲלֵי נִדּוֹת מוּתָּרִין לִקְרוֹת בַּתּוֹרָה וּבַנְּבִיאִים וּבַכְּתוּבִים, וְלִשְׁנוֹת בַּמִּדְרָשׁ וּבַתַּלְמוּד, בַּהֲלָכוֹת וּבָאַגָּדוֹת, וּבַעֲלֵי קְרָיִין אֲסוּרִין. שְׁמַע מִינָּהּ.

From here the Sages stated: *Zavim*, lepers, and those who had intercourse with menstruating women despite their severe ritual impurity are permitted to read the Torah, Prophets, and Writings, and to study midrash, Talmud, *halakhot*, and *aggada*. But those who experienced a seminal emission are prohibited[N] from doing so.[H] The reason for this distinction is that the cases of severe impurity are caused by ailment or other circumstances beyond one's control; as a result, they do not necessarily preclude a sense of reverence and awe as one studies Torah. However, a seminal emission usually occurs due to frivolity and a lack of reverence and awe, and it is therefore inappropriate for one who experiences a seminal emission to engage in matters of Torah. The Gemara concludes: Indeed, **learn from this** that a leper is permitted to study words of Torah.

אָבֵל אָסוּר בְּתִכְבּוֹסֶת, דִּכְתִיב: ״וַיִּשְׁלַח יוֹאָב תְּקוֹעָה וַיִּקַּח מִשָּׁם אִשָּׁה חֲכָמָה וַיֹּאמֶר אֵלֶיהָ הִתְאַבְּלִי נָא וְלִבְשִׁי נָא בִגְדֵי אֵבֶל וְאַל תָּסוּכִי שֶׁמֶן וְהָיִית כְּאִשָּׁה זֶה יָמִים רַבִּים מִתְאַבֶּלֶת עַל מֵת״.

§ The Gemara proceeds to discuss another issue: **A mourner is prohibited from laundering his clothes,**[NH] **as it is written: "And Joab sent to Tekoa, and fetched from there a wise woman, and said to her, I pray you, feign yourself to be a mourner, and put on now mourning apparel, and do not anoint yourself with oil, but be as a woman that had a long time mourned for the dead"** (II Samuel 14:2).

מְנוּדִּין וּמְצוֹרָעִין מַהֵן בְּתִכְבּוֹסֶת? תָּא שְׁמַע: מְנוּדִּין וּמְצוֹרָעִין אֲסוּרִין לְסַפֵּר וּלְכַבֵּס. שְׁמַע מִינָּהּ.

The Gemara asks: **What** is the *halakha* concerning **laundering** with regard to **those who are ostracized or lepers? Come** and **hear** that which is taught in a *baraita*: **Those who are ostracized or lepers are prohibited from cutting** their hair **or laundering** their clothes. The Gemara concludes: Indeed, **learn from** here that they are prohibited from laundering their clothes.

אָבֵל חַיָּיב בִּקְרִיעָה. דְּקָאָמַר לְהוּ רַחֲמָנָא לִבְנֵי אַהֲרֹן: ״לֹא תִפְרוֹמוּ״ – מִכְּלָל דְּכוּלֵּי עָלְמָא מִיחַיְּיבִי.

The Gemara continues: **A mourner is obligated to rend** his clothes.[H] This is derived from the fact **that the Merciful One says to the sons of Aaron: "Neither rend** your clothes" (Leviticus 10:6), which proves **by inference that everyone** else, all other mourners, **are obligated** to rend their clothes.

מְנוּדֶּה מַהוּ בִּקְרִיעָה? תֵּיקוּ.

The Gemara asks: **What is the** *halakha* of **rending** clothes with regard to **one who is ostracized?**[H] No answer is found, and the question **shall stand** unresolved.

מְצוֹרָע מַהוּ בִּקְרִיעָה? תָּא שְׁמַע: ״בְּגָדָיו יִהְיוּ פְרוּמִים״ – שֶׁיְּהוּ מְקוֹרָעִין. שְׁמַע מִינָּהּ.

The Gemara continues: **What is** the *halakha* concerning **a leper** with regard to **rending? Come** and **hear that which** is taught in the following *baraita*: The verse states: **"His garments shall be rent"** (Leviticus 13:45), meaning **that they shall be torn.** The Gemara concludes: Indeed, **learn from here** that this is the case.

אָבֵל חַיָּיב בִּכְפִיַּית הַמִּטָּה, דְּתָנֵי בַּר קַפָּרָא:

§ The Gemara moves to a different issue: **A mourner is obligated to overturn** his **bed,**[H] so that he sleeps on the underside of it, **as bar Kappara taught** a *baraita* that states:

NOTES

But those who experienced a seminal emission are prohibited – וּבַעֲלֵי קְרָיִין אֲסוּרִין: *Talmid Rabbeinu Yeḥiel of Paris* explains that when the Torah was given the men were instructed to separate themselves from the women. Therefore, one suffering from this type of impurity is prohibited from learning Torah. However, there was no mention of other types of impurity at the time that the Torah was given.

A mourner is prohibited from laundering his clothes – אָבֵל אָסוּר בְּתִכְבּוֹסֶת: Most commentaries explain that the proof from this verse is that the woman was instructed to wear mourner's clothes, meaning clothes that were dirty and black (Rashi; *Talmid Rabbeinu Yeḥiel of Paris*; Rabbi Shlomo ben HaYatom).

HALAKHA

One who experienced a seminal emission with regard to Torah study – בַּעַל קֶרִי בְּדִבְרֵי תוֹרָה: Ezra the Scribe decreed that one who experiences a seminal emission is prohibited from studying Torah until he has immersed. In the era of the *amora'im*, this decree was nullified, and today it is permitted for such a person to study Torah without immersing. However, it is still the custom of the pious to be strict and immerse before studying Torah (*Shulḥan Arukh, Oraḥ Ḥayyim* 88:1).

A mourner with regard to laundering clothes – אָבֵל בְּתִכְבּוֹסֶת: A mourner may not launder his clothes for all seven days of mourning (*Shulḥan Arukh, Yoreh De'a* 389:1).

A mourner with regard to rending clothes – אָבֵל בִּקְרִיעָה: Upon hearing that one of his close family members has passed away, one is required to rend his clothes (*Shulḥan Arukh, Yoreh De'a* 340:1).

One who is ostracized with regard to rending clothes – מְנוּדֶּה בִּקְרִיעָה: One who has been ostracized is not required to rend his clothes because the issue is left unresolved by the Gemara, and the ruling is generally lenient in cases of doubtful issues of *halakha* concerning rabbinic decrees (*Shakh*; *Shulḥan Arukh, Yoreh De'a* 334:1).

Overturning the bed – כְּפִיַּית הַמִּטָּה: A mourner is required to overturn his bed. However, for many generations this has no longer been the custom. The reason is either because the gentiles will view this as a practice of witchcraft or because this act is not noticeable with contemporary beds (*Tur*, citing Rosh). Some say that a mourner is required to sleep on the ground (*Shakh*), but others disagree (*Panim Meirot*). The custom today is not to be stringent with regard to this *halakha* (*Arukh HaShulḥan*; *Shulḥan Arukh, Yoreh De'a* 387:1–2).

דְּמוּת דְּיוֹקְנִי נָתַתִּי בָּהֶן, וּבַעֲוֹנוֹתֵיהֶם הֲפַכְתִּיהָ – כְּפוּ מִטּוֹתֵיהֶן עָלֶיהָ. מְנוּדֶּה וּמְצוֹרָע מַה הֵן בִּכְפִיַּית הַמִּטָּה? תֵּיקוּ.

God stated: **I have placed the likeness of My image** [***deyokan***][L] **within** humans, as they were created in My image, **and owing to their sins I have overturned it,** as when this person died the Divine image in him was removed. Therefore, you must also **overturn your beds on account of this.** The Gemara asks: **What is the** *halakha* governing **one who was ostracized or a leper,** with regard to **overturning the bed?**[NH] The Gemara has no answer, and the question **shall stand** unresolved.

אָבֵל אָסוּר בַּעֲשִׂיַּית מְלָאכָה, דִּכְתִיב: ״וְהָפַכְתִּי חַגֵּיכֶם לְאֵבֶל״. מַה חַג אָסוּר בִּמְלָאכָה – אַף אָבֵל אָסוּר בִּמְלָאכָה.

§ The Gemara proceeds to the next topic: **A mourner is prohibited from performing work, as it is written: "And I will turn your Festivals into mourning"** (Amos 8:10). The Gemara infers: **Just as a Festival** is a time when it is **prohibited to work, so too, a mourner is prohibited from performing work.**[H]

מְנוּדֶּה מַהוּ בַּעֲשִׂיַּית מְלָאכָה? אָמַר רַב יוֹסֵף, תָּא שְׁמַע: כְּשֶׁאָמְרוּ אָסוּר בַּעֲשִׂיַּית מְלָאכָה – לֹא אָמְרוּ אֶלָּא בַּיּוֹם, אֲבָל בַּלַּיְלָה מוּתָּר. וְכֵן אַתָּה מוֹצֵא בִּמְנוּדֶּה וּבְאָבֵל. מַאי לָאו – אַכּוּלְּהוּ? לָא, אַשְּׁאָרָא.

The Gemara asks: **What is the** *halakha* concerning **one who was ostracized** with regard to **the performance of work? Rav Yosef said: Come** and **hear** that which is taught in the following *baraita*: **When** the Sages **said that the performance of work is prohibited** on a communal fast due to lack of rain, **they meant only** that work is prohibited **during the day** of the fast, **but during the night** of the fast **it is permitted.**[H] **And you find a similar** *halakha* **with regard to a person** who was **ostracized and** with regard to **a mourner. What, is it not with regard to all** of the prohibitions stated that the *baraita* says that they apply to one who was ostracized as well, including the prohibition to engage in work? The Gemara rejects this argument: **No,** this **is referring to the rest** of the prohibitions, but not to work.

תָּא שְׁמַע: מְנוּדֶּה שׁוֹנֶה וְשׁוֹנִין לוֹ, נִשְׂכָּר וְנִשְׂכָּרִין לוֹ. שְׁמַע מִינָּהּ. מְצוֹרָע מַהוּ בַּעֲשִׂיַּית מְלָאכָה? תֵּיקוּ.

The Gemara offers a different proof: **Come** and **hear that** which was taught in the following *baraita*: **One who is ostracized may teach Torah** to others, **and** others **may teach him** Torah. Similarly, **he may be hired** for work by others, **and** others **may be hired by him.** The Gemara concludes: **Learn from here** that it is permitted for one who is ostracized to engage in work. The Gemara asks: **What is** the *halakha* concerning **a leper,** with regard to **the performance of work?** An answer is not found, and the question **shall stand** unresolved.

אָבֵל אָסוּר בִּרְחִיצָה, דִּכְתִיב: ״וְאַל תָּסוּכִי שֶׁמֶן״, וּרְחִיצָה בִּכְלָל סִיכָה.

§ The Gemara discusses a different prohibition: **A mourner is prohibited from bathing, as it is written: "And do not anoint yourself with oil,** but be as a woman that had for a long time mourned for the dead" (II Samuel 14:2). **And bathing is included in** the category of **anointing,**[N] as both activities have a similar goal, i.e., cleanliness.

מְנוּדֶּה מַהוּ בִּרְחִיצָה? אָמַר רַב יוֹסֵף, תָּא שְׁמַע: כְּשֶׁאָמְרוּ אָסוּר בִּרְחִיצָה – לֹא אָמְרוּ אֶלָּא כָּל גּוּפוֹ, אֲבָל פָּנָיו יָדָיו וְרַגְלָיו – מוּתָּר. וְכֵן אַתָּה מוֹצֵא בִּמְנוּדֶּה וּבְאָבֵל. מַאי לָאו אַכּוּלְּהוּ? לָא, אַשְּׁאָרָא. מְצוֹרָע מַהוּ בִּרְחִיצָה? תֵּיקוּ.

The Gemara asks: **What is** the *halakha* concerning **one who is ostracized** with regard to **bathing? Rav Yosef said: Come** and **hear that** which was taught in the following *baraita*: **When** the Sages **said that bathing is prohibited** on a communal fast, **they meant only** that a person may not wash **his entire body, but** washing **his face, his hands, and his feet is permitted. And you find a similar** *halakha* **with regard to a person who was ostracized and** with regard to **a mourner. What, is it not with regard to all** the prohibitions stated in the *baraita*, including the prohibition against bathing, that they apply also to one who is ostracized? The Gemara rejects this argument: **No,** this **is referring to the rest** of the prohibitions, but not to bathing. The Gemara asks: **What is** the *halakha* concerning **a leper** with regard to **bathing?** An answer is not found, and the question **shall stand** unresolved.

LANGUAGE

Image [*deyokan*] – **דְּיוֹקָן:** This word has a Greek root, and some claim that it is related to the Greek **δείκανον**, *deikanon*, meaning a drawn or woven image. However, the *ge'onim* understand it to mean *dio-iconin*, from the Greek **εἰκών**, *eikon*, meaning image or form. Together with the prefix this word is said to mean double image or copy.

NOTES

One who was ostracized or a leper with regard to overturning the bed – **מְנוּדֶּה וּמְצוֹרָע...בִּכְפִיַּית הַמִּטָּה:** The Ritva asks: The explanation offered for this custom in the case of a mourner does not apply to these other two groups. Therefore, why would they be required to overturn their beds? He explains that since their world has turned upside down, and they are distanced from other people, it is appropriate for them to overturn their beds.

Bathing is included in anointing – **רְחִיצָה בִּכְלָל סִיכָה:** This verse does not mention bathing, which makes the proof somewhat problematic. The Ritva explains that there is never a case in which anointing is prohibited and bathing is permitted. Furthermore, it is clear that the verse compares the two of them. The Rambam explains, as does the Meiri in greater detail, that the common practice was to bathe and afterward to anoint oneself with oil. Since the verse states that the woman from Tekoa was instructed not to anoint herself, she must have been prohibited from bathing as well.

HALAKHA

A leper with regard to overturning the bed – **מְצוֹרָע בִּכְפִיַּית הַמִּטָּה:** A leper is not required to overturn his bed. The ruling is lenient with regard to this *halakha* because the question is one of rabbinic law that is left unresolved (Rambam *Sefer Tahara, Hilkhot Tumat Tzara'at* 10:6).

Working while mourning – **מְלָאכָה בַּאֲבֵילוּת:** A mourner is prohibited from working for all seven days of the mourning period (*Shulḥan Arukh, Yoreh De'a* 380:1).

The final fast days for lack of rain – **מִנְהָג בְּתַעֲנִיּוֹת אַחֲרוֹנוֹת שֶׁל גְּשָׁמִים:** During the final stage of fast days for a drought, it is prohibited to perform work during the day, but working at night is permitted. In addition, one may not wash his entire body with hot water; however, he may wash his hands, face, and feet. It is likewise prohibited to walk with shoes in the city (*Shulḥan Arukh, Oraḥ Ḥayyim* 575:3).

אָבֵל אָסוּר בִּנְעִילַת הַסַּנְדָּל, מִדְּקָאָמַר לֵיהּ רַחֲמָנָא לִיחֶזְקֵאל: ״וּנְעָלֶיךָ תָּשִׂים בְּרַגְלֶיךָ״ – מִכְּלָל דְּכוּלֵּי עָלְמָא אָסוּר.

§ The Gemara moves to the next topic: **A mourner is prohibited from wearing shoes.**[H] **Since the Merciful One says to** Ezekiel with regard to how his mourning rites should differ from the accepted custom: **"And put your shoes upon your feet"** (Ezekiel 24:17), which shows **by inference that everyone** else, i.e., all other mourners, **is prohibited** from wearing shoes.

מְנוּדֶּה מַהוּ בִּנְעִילַת הַסַּנְדָּל? אָמַר רַב יוֹסֵף, תָּא שְׁמַע: כְּשֶׁאָמְרוּ אָסוּר בִּנְעִילַת הַסַּנְדָּל – לֹא אָמְרוּ אֶלָּא בָּעִיר, אֲבָל בַּדֶּרֶךְ – מוּתָּר. הָא כֵּיצַד? יָצָא לַדֶּרֶךְ – נוֹעֵל; נִכְנָס לָעִיר – חוֹלֵץ. וְכֵן אַתָּה מוֹצֵא בִּמְנוּדֶּה וּבְאָבֵל. מַאי לָאו אַכּוּלְּהוּ? לָא, אַשְּׁאָרָא.

The Gemara asks: **What is the** *halakha* concerning **one who is ostracized** with regard to **wearing shoes?**[H] **Rav Yosef said: Come** and **hear that which** is taught in the following *baraita*: **When the** Sages **said** that **wearing shoes is prohibited** on a communal fast, **they meant only** that one may not wear shoes when he is walking about **in the city, but** if he set out to travel **on the road,** wearing shoes **is permitted. How so?** When **he sets out on the road, he may put on** his shoes. But as soon as **he enters the city** once again, **he must take off** his shoes and continue barefoot. **And you find a similar** *halakha* **with regard to a person** who was **ostracized and** with regard to **a mourner. What, is it not with regard to all** of the prohibitions stated in the *baraita*, including the prohibition against wearing shoes, that they apply also to one who was ostracized? The Gemara rejects this argument: **No, this is referring to the rest** of the prohibitions, but not to wearing shoes.

מְצוֹרָע מַהוּ בִּנְעִילַת הַסַּנְדָּל? תֵּיקוּ.

The Gemara asks: **What is the** *halakha* concerning **a leper** with regard to **wearing shoes?**[H] No answer is found, and the question **shall stand** unresolved.

אָבֵל אָסוּר בְּתַשְׁמִישׁ הַמִּטָּה, דִּכְתִיב: ״וַיְנַחֵם דָּוִד אֵת בַּת שֶׁבַע אִשְׁתּוֹ וַיָּבֹא אֵלֶיהָ״ – מִכְּלָל דְּמֵעִיקָּרָא אָסוּר.

§ The Gemara considers another issue: **A mourner is prohibited from engaging in sexual relations,**[H] **as it is written: "And David comforted Bath-Sheba his wife, and went into her,** and lay with her" (II Samuel 12:24), after their son had died. This proves **by inference that initially,** during the period of mourning, sexual relations **were forbidden.**

מְנוּדֶּה מַהוּ בְּתַשְׁמִישׁ הַמִּטָּה? אָמַר רַב יוֹסֵף, תָּא שְׁמַע: כׇּל אוֹתָן שָׁנִים שֶׁהָיוּ יִשְׂרָאֵל בַּמִּדְבָּר מְנוּדִּין הָיוּ, וְשִׁימְּשׁוּ מִטּוֹתֵיהֶן. אֲמַר לֵיהּ אַבַּיֵּי: וְדִלְמָא מְנוּדֶּה לַשָּׁמַיִם שָׁאנֵי, דְּקִיל.

The Gemara asks: **What is the** *halakha* concerning **one who is ostracized** with regard to **sexual relations? Rav Yosef said: Come** and **hear that which** is taught in a *baraita*: **All those years that the Jewish people were in the wilderness they were ostracized,**[N] **and yet they engaged in sexual relations,** as there were children born to them during that period. It follows that it is permitted for one who is ostracized to engage in sexual relations. **Abaye said to him: Perhaps one who is ostracized by Heaven is different, as that is less serious**[N] than being ostracized by an earthly court.

קִיל?! וְהָא אָמְרַתְּ חָמִיר! סַפּוּקֵי מְסַפְּקָא לֵיהּ, זִיל הָכָא – קָמַדְחֵי לֵיהּ, וְזִיל הָכָא – קָמַדְחֵי לֵיהּ.

The Gemara asks in astonishment: Is it **less serious? But didn't you,** Abaye, **say** elsewhere that a decree of ostracism imposed by Heaven is **more serious** than one issued by an earthly court? For this reason, Abaye rejected several proofs of Rav Yosef from the previously cited *baraita*. The Gemara answers: Abaye **is uncertain** whether a decree of ostracism imposed by Heaven is more or less serious than one imposed by an earthly court. Therefore, when **he goes in this** direction **he rejects** the argument, **and** when **he goes in that** direction **he rejects** the argument. Abaye asserts that since the issue is in doubt, no proof can be derived from ostracism issued by Heaven.

HALAKHA

A mourner with regard to wearing shoes – **אָבֵל בִּנְעִילַת הַסַּנְדָּל**: A mourner may not wear shoes for all seven days of the mourning period (*Shulḥan Arukh, Yoreh De'a* 380:1).

One who is ostracized with regard to wearing shoes – **מְנוּדֶּה בִּנְעִילַת הַסַּנְדָּל**: One who has been ostracized may not wear shoes, like a mourner, because many sources imply that one who has been ostracized is required to remove his shoes. The *Beit Yosef* explains the opinion of the Rivash, who cites the Rashba, and maintains that it is permitted for such a person to wear shoes. The common practice follows this opinion (*Shakh*; *Shulḥan Arukh, Yoreh De'a* 334:2).

A leper with regard to bathing and wearing shoes – **מְצוֹרָע בִּרְחִיצָה וּבִנְעִילַת הַסַּנְדָּל**: A leper is permitted to bathe and to wear shoes. The ruling is lenient with regard to these *halakhot* and other similar cases because the issue is left unresolved, and the law itself is rabbinic (Rambam *Sefer Tahara, Hilkhot Tumat Tzara'at* 10:6).

A mourner with regard to sexual relations – **אָבֵל בְּתַשְׁמִישׁ**: A mourner may not engage in sexual relations for all seven days of the mourning period (*Shulḥan Arukh, Yoreh De'a* 380:1).

NOTES

In the wilderness they were ostracized – **בַּמִּדְבָּר מְנוּדִּין הָיוּ**: The early authorities find evidence of this ostracism in that which is stated after the sin of the spies: "For every day a year, you shall bear your sins…and you shall know My displeasure" (Numbers 14:34; manuscript of Rashi). Others derive evidence of ostracism from the fact that God did not speak to Moses throughout the years following the sin of the spies until that generation had died out (Rabbi Shlomo ben HaYatom).

One who is ostracized by Heaven…that is less serious – **מְנוּדֶּה לַשָּׁמַיִם...דְּקִיל**: A simple explanation for this opinion is that people are generally less afraid of God than they are of other people (Commentary on *Moed Katan*). The Ra'avad explains that being ostracized by Heaven is dependent upon God, Who does not want to prevent one from observing mitzvot such as sacrificing offerings or having children. Instead He only prohibited one from activities that relate to other people. However, a court that has imposed ostracism does not make this distinction and prohibits such a person from both types of activities (*Tosefot HaRosh*).

מְצוֹרָע מַהוּ בְּתַשְׁמִישׁ הַמִּטָּה? תָּא שְׁמַע, דְּתַנְיָא: ״וְיָשַׁב מִחוּץ לְאָהֳלוֹ״ – שֶׁיְּהֵא כִּמְנוּדֶּה וּכְאָבֵל, וְאָסוּר בְּתַשְׁמִישׁ הַמִּטָּה. וְאֵין אָהֳלוֹ אֶלָּא אִשְׁתּוֹ, שֶׁנֶּאֱמַר: ״לֵךְ אֱמוֹר לָהֶם שׁוּבוּ לָכֶם לְאָהֳלֵיכֶם״. שְׁמַע מִינָּהּ.

The Gemara continues: **What is** the *halakha* concerning **a leper** with regard to **sexual relations?**[H] **Come and hear** a proof, **as it is taught** in a *baraita*: The verse concerning a leper states: **"But he shall remain outside his tent** seven days" (Leviticus 14:8), from which it is derived **that** a leper **should be like one who is ostracized and like a mourner, and he is prohibited** from engaging **in sexual relations.** How is this derived? The **only** meaning of the term **"his tent"** is **his wife, as is stated** after the giving of the Torah: **"Go say to them, return again to your tents"** (Deuteronomy 5:27). This statement rendered it permitted for the men to once again engage in sexual relations with their wives after they had previously been prohibited to do so in anticipation of the giving of the Torah, as expressed in the verse: "Come not near a woman" (Exodus 19:15). The Gemara concludes: Indeed, **learn from this** that it is prohibited for a leper to engage in sexual relations.

וְנִיפְשׁוֹט נַמִי לִמְנוּדֶּה! אָמַר רַב הוּנָא בְּרֵיהּ דְּרַב פִּנְחָס מִשְּׁמֵיהּ דְּרַב יוֹסֵף: מִי קָתָנֵי ״שֶׁאָסוּר״? שֶׁיְּהֵא כִּמְנוּדֶּה וּכְאָבֵל – בְּמִילֵּי אַחֲרָנְיָיתָא, וְאָסוּר נַמִי בְּתַשְׁמִישׁ הַמִּטָּה.

The Gemara asks: If this is the case, then **can we** also **resolve** the question raised above with regard to **one who is ostracized,** by saying that it is prohibited for such a person to engage in sexual relations? **Rav Huna, son of Rav Pineḥas, said in the name of Rav Yosef: Is it taught** that a leper **is prohibited** from engaging in sexual relations like one who is ostracized? **It states** only that **he should be** treated **like one who is ostracized and like a mourner,** i.e., he should be like them **with regard to other things, and in addition he is prohibited** from engaging in **sexual relations.** Therefore, no proof can be derived from here with regard to one who is ostracized that he, too, is prohibited from engaging in sexual relations.

אָבֵל אֵינוֹ מְשַׁלֵּחַ קָרְבְּנוֹתָיו, דְּתַנְיָא, רַבִּי שִׁמְעוֹן אוֹמֵר: ״שְׁלָמִים״ – בִּזְמַן שֶׁהוּא שָׁלֵם, וְלֹא בִּזְמַן שֶׁהוּא אוֹנֵן.

§ The Gemara continues: **A mourner may not send his offerings** to the Temple,[H] **as it is taught** in a *baraita*: **Rabbi Shimon says: A peace-offering [*shelamim*]**[B] is given this name also to teach us that one may sacrifice it only **at a time when he is whole [*shalem*]**[N] and his mind is settled,[N] **but not at a time when he is an acute mourner,**[N] i.e., on the first day of his bereavement, when he is distressed.

מְנוּדֶּה מַהוּ שֶׁיְּשַׁלַּח קָרְבְּנוֹתָיו? אָמַר רַב יוֹסֵף, תָּא שְׁמַע: כׇּל אוֹתָן שָׁנִים שֶׁהָיוּ יִשְׂרָאֵל בַּמִּדְבָּר מְנוּדִּין הָיוּ, וְשִׁלְּחוּ קָרְבְּנוֹתֵיהֶן. אֲמַר לֵיהּ אַבָּיֵי: וְדִלְמָא מְנוּדֶּה לַשָּׁמַיִם שָׁאנֵי, דְּקִיל.

The Gemara asks: **What is** the *halakha* concerning **one who is ostracized** with regard to **sending his offerings** to the Temple? **Rav Yosef said: Come** and **hear** a proof from that which is taught in a *baraita*: **All those years that the Jewish people were in the wilderness they were ostracized, and yet they sent their offerings.**[N] **Abaye said to him: Perhaps one who is ostracized by Heaven is different, as that is less serious** than being ostracized by an earthly court.

קִיל?! וְהָאָמְרַתְּ חֲמִיר! סַפּוּקֵי מְסַפְּקָא לֵיהּ, וּמַדְחֵי לֵיהּ.

The Gemara asks in astonishment: Is it **less serious? But certainly you,** Abaye, **said** elsewhere that being ostracized by Heaven is **more serious** than being ostracized by an earthly court. The Gemara offers a resolution: Abaye **is uncertain** whether being ostracized by Heaven is more or less serious than being ostracized by an earthly court, and therefore **he rejects** Rav Yosef's arguments in both directions.

HALAKHA

A leper with regard to sexual relations – מְצוֹרָע בְּתַשְׁמִישׁ: A quarantined leper may engage in sexual relations (Rambam *Sefer Tahara, Hilkhot Tumat Tzara'at* 10:6).

Sending offerings – שִׁילּוּחַ קָרְבָּנוֹת: A mourner may not send offerings for all seven days of the mourning period. Similarly, a leper may not send offerings because as long as he is unfit to enter the camp, he is also unfit to sacrifice an offering. This is the case even if he sends it with a messenger. It is unclear whether or not one who has been ostracized may send an offering; therefore, if an offering is sacrificed on his behalf it is accepted (Rambam *Sefer Avoda, Hilkhot Biat HaMikdash* 2:11).

BACKGROUND

Peace-offering – שְׁלָמִים: Male and female cattle or sheep may be sacrificed as peace offerings (see Leviticus, chapter 3). They are offerings of lesser holiness and may be slaughtered anywhere within the Temple courtyard. Their blood is sprinkled on the two opposite corners of the altar in such a manner that it will drip down on each of the altar's four sides. Part of each peace-offering is burned on the altar, and the breast and the right hind leg are given to the priests. The rest is eaten by one bringing the offering, with his family. They may eat of the offering anywhere in the city, on the day the animal is sacrificed and during the following night and day. With the exception of the Festival peace-offering and a few other cases, the peace-offerings were voluntary gifts. The word offering used without qualification usually means a peace-offering.

NOTES

A peace-offering [*shelamim*] at a time when he is whole [*shalem*] – שְׁלָמִים בִּזְמַן שֶׁהוּא שָׁלֵם: Some say that the word *shelamim*, which is written in Hebrew in the plural, indicates that both the animal being sacrificed and the one sacrificing it must be whole [*shalem*]. In a *baraita* it is taught that this principle applies to other offerings as well, not only to peace-offerings.

At a time when he is whole and his mind is settled – בִּזְמַן שֶׁהוּא שָׁלֵם: According to Rashi, this statement indicates that his mind is whole and he is settled. Similarly, in the manuscript of Rashi it is written that this expression means he must be joyous. Others explain that such a person must not be lacking anything, and when one member of his immediate family is lacking he can no longer be considered whole (*Talmid Rabbeinu Yeḥiel of Paris*; Commentary on *Moed Katan*).

When he is an acute mourner – שֶׁהוּא אוֹנֵן: Some of the early authorities write that the prohibition against sending an offering refers specifically to an acute mourner, whose pain is very intense (Rid; Ra'avad on *Sifra*). However, the majority of the commentaries disagree, and they show from the *Tosefta* that a mourner is prohibited from sending an offering for the entire seven-day period of mourning.

They were ostracized and they sent their offerings – מְנוּדִּין הָיוּ וְשִׁלְּחוּ קָרְבְּנוֹתֵיהֶם: *Tosafot* note that the Torah does not explicitly mention that the people sacrificed offerings during the forty years in the wilderness. Some explain that it can be assumed that they sacrificed the daily offering and the additional offerings (*Talmid Rabbeinu Yeḥiel of Paris*). Others write that because they did not eat non-consecrated meat in the desert, according to the opinion of Rabbi Yishmael, whenever the Torah mentions that they ate meat it must be referring to eating meat from peace-offerings (Rabbi Shlomo ben HaYatom; see *Turei Aven*).

מצורע מהו שישלח קרבנותיו? תא שמע, דתניא: "ואחרי טהרתו" – אחר פרישתו מן המת; "שבעת ימים יספרו לו" – אלו שבעת ימי ספירו; "וביום באו אל הקודש אל החצר הפנימית לשרת בקודש יקריב חטאתו" –

The Gemara asks: **What is** the *halakha* with regard to **a leper sending his offerings**[N] to the Temple? The Gemara answers: **Come and hear** a proof, **as it is taught** in a *baraita* with regard to a priest who became ritually impure: "And after he is purified, they shall count for him seven days" (Ezekiel 44:26). The verse should be understood as follows: **"And after he is purified"; after he has separated from** his **deceased** relative.[N] **"They shall count for him seven days"; these are the seven days of his counting**[N] before he may purify himself. **"And on the day that he goes into the Sanctuary, into the inner court, to minister in the Sanctuary, he shall sacrifice his sin**-offering, says the Lord God" (Ezekiel 44:27);

NOTES

What is the *halakha* with regard to a leper sending his offerings – מצורע מהו שישלח קרבנותיו: The doubt in this case is not due to impurity, as other impure people are permitted to send offerings. Here, the question is whether a leper falls into the same category as a mourner, who is not considered to be whole (Rid).

After he has separated from his deceased relative – אחר פרישתו מן המת: The reason that the Gemara does not explain this phrase according to the simple meaning of the words, i.e., that it is referring to counting after the purification of the one who became ritually impure, is because after he has become pure there is no clear reason for him to continue counting (Ra'avad) In the commentary on *Moed Katan*, it is written that this verse is referring to the High Priest. Immediately after he has left the deceased he may return to sacrificing offerings, because he is permitted to do so while he is a mourner, unlike other priests (Rid).

These are the seven days of his counting – אלו שבעת ימי ספירו: In the manuscript of Rashi, it is explained that since the verse is referring to these days as counting, it must be referring to the purification of a leper, whose purification process involves counting. *Talmid Rabbeinu Yeḥiel of Paris* explains slightly differently, noting that since the verse lists the days of one's counting, it must be referring to a purification process that involves counting after the impurity has passed, i.e., the purification of a leper.

Perek **III**
Daf **16** Amud **a**

זו עשירית האיפה שלו, דברי רבי יהודה.

this is the meal-offering of **a tenth of an ephah** of flour, which every priest would bring on the day he began serving in the Temple. But as long as he is ritually impure, whether because he had come into contact with a corpse or due to leprosy, he may not send his offerings to the Temple; this is **the statement of Rabbi Yehuda.**

רבי שמעון אומר: "בבאו יקריב" – בזמן שראוי לביאה ראוי להקרבה; בזמן שאינו ראוי לביאה – אינו ראוי להקרבה.

Rabbi Shimon says: The verse states: "And on the day that **he goes into** the Sanctuary, into the inner court, to minister in the Sanctuary **he shall sacrifice** his sin offering." This teaches that **when he is fit to enter**[N] the Sanctuary, **he is fit to sacrifice** an offering. But **when he is not fit to go into** the Sanctuary, i.e., when he is ritually impure, **he is not fit to sacrifice** an offering. This implies that a leper may not send his offerings to the Temple to be sacrificed on the altar, as he himself is not fit to enter the Temple.

אמר רבא: מנלן דמשדרין שליחא דבי דינא, ומזמנינן ליה לדינא? דכתיב: "וישלח משה לקרא לדתן ולאבירם בני אליאב". ומנלן דמזמנינן לדינא? דכתיב: "ויאמר משה אל קרח אתה וכל עדתך".

§ Having discussed some of the restrictions applying to a person who was ostracized, the Gemara explains some of the basic principles relating to ostracism: **Rava said: From where do we** derive **that a court agent is sent**[N] **to summon** the defendant **to** appear before the **court** before he is ostracized? **As it is written: "And Moses sent to call Dathan and Abiram, the sons of Eliab"** (Numbers 16:12). **And from where do we** derive **that we summon** the defendant, that he himself must appear before the **court?**[H] **As it is written: "And Moses said to Korah: Be you and all your congregation** before the Lord, you and they, and Aaron, tomorrow" (Numbers 16:16).

NOTES

When he is fit to enter – בזמן שראוי לביאה: Everyone agrees that this principle does not apply in all cases, since impure people may send their animals as offerings. Rather, this statement applies to those whose level of impurity is as severe as that of a leper, including, according to the Rambam, one who is impure due to contact with a corpse. This verse implies that due to the serious nature of their impurity they may not sacrifice offerings (Ritva).

From where do we derive that a court agent is sent, etc. – מנלן דמשדרין שליחא וכו׳: According to the version of the text used by some of the early authorities, it was Korah himself who was sent by the court to summon the rest of his congregation (see Ran).

HALAKHA

Summoning to court – הזמנה לדין: The court sends messengers that summon one to court on a specific day. If he does not come the first time, he is summoned a second time. If he does not come the second time, he should be summoned a third time. If he does not come at any time during that day, he is ostracized on the next day (*Shulḥan Arukh*, *Ḥoshen Mishpat* 11:1).

לְקַמֵּי גַּבְרָא רַבָּה – דִּכְתִיב: ״לִפְנֵי ה׳״. אַתְּ וּפְלָנְיָא – דִּכְתִיב: ״אַתָּה וָהֵם וְאַהֲרֹן״. דְּקָבְעִינַן זִימְנָא – דִּכְתִיב: ״מָחָר״. זִימְנָא בָּתַר זִימְנָא – דִּכְתִיב: ״קָרְאוּ שָׁם פַּרְעֹה מֶלֶךְ מִצְרַיִם שָׁאוֹן הֶעֱבִיר הַמּוֹעֵד״.

From where is it derived that the defendant must be told that he is being summoned to appear **before a great man? As it is written:** "And Moses said to Korah: Be you and all your congregation **before the Lord**" (Numbers 16:16). From where is it derived that the summons must mention the names of both parties: **You and so-and-so,** the plaintiff? **As it is written: "You, and they, and Aaron"** (Numbers 16:16). From where is it derived **that we set a date** for the court proceedings? **As it is written: "Tomorrow"** (Numbers 16:16). From where is it derived that a second **date** must be set **after** the first **date,** if the defendant did not heed the first summons? **As it is written: "They did cry there, Pharaoh,**[N] **king of Egypt is but a noise; he has passed the time appointed…** Surely as Tabor is among the mountains, and as Carmel by the sea, so shall he come" (Jeremiah 46:17). Although a time had been appointed and it had passed, it was not canceled entirely but pushed off to a later date.

וּמְנָלַן דְּאִי מִתְפַּקַּר בִּשְׁלִיחָא דְּבֵי דִּינָא, וְאָתֵי וְאָמַר, לָא מִיתְחֲזֵי כְּלִישָּׁנָא בִּישָׁא – דִּכְתִיב: ״הַעֵינֵי הָאֲנָשִׁים הָהֵם תְּנַקֵּר״.

And from where do we derive **that if** the summoned person **behaves disrespectfully toward the agent of the court, and** the agent **comes** back **and reports** his conduct, that **this is not considered slander?**[H] **As it is written: "Will you put out the eyes of these men?"** (Numbers 16:14). Dathan and Abiram spoke these words to the messenger that Moses had sent to them, and the messenger reported them back to Moses.

וּמְנָלַן דִּמְשַׁמְּתִינַן? דִּכְתִיב: ״אוֹרוּ מֵרוֹז״. דְּהָכִי סְבָרָא דְּגַבְרָא רַבָּה, דִּכְתִיב: ״אָמַר מַלְאַךְ ה׳״. וּמְנָלַן דְּמַחְרְמִינַן? דִּכְתִיב: ״אוֹרוּ אָרוֹר״.

From where **do we** derive **that we ostracize** one who does not obey a court summons? **As it is written: "Curse Meroz"** (Judges 5:23), who was ostracized for not coming to battle after having been summoned. From where is it derived that the ostracized person must be told **that it** was **the decision of a great man** to ostracized him? **As it is written:** "Curse Meroz, **said the messenger of the Lord**" (Judges 5:23).[N] **And from where do we** derive **that,** if he fails to mend his ways, **we excommunicate** such a person more harshly, putting him under the most severe form of excommunication? **As it is written:** "Curse Meroz… **curse bitterly** its inhabitants" (Judges 5:23), implying that one curse is followed by another, i.e., lesser ostracism is followed by harsh excommunication.

דְּאָכֵיל וְשָׁתֵי בַּהֲדֵיהּ וְקָאֵי בְּאַרְבַּע אַמּוֹת דִּידֵיהּ – דִּכְתִיב: ״יוֹשְׁבֶיהָ״. וּמְנָלַן דְּפָרְטִינַן חֶטְאֵיהּ בְּצִיבּוּרָא? דִּכְתִיב: ״כִּי לֹא בָאוּ לְעֶזְרַת ה׳״.

From where is it derived **that** the curse applies to anyone who **eats or drinks with, or stands within, four cubits of** the ostracized person?[H] **As it is written:** "Curse bitterly **its inhabitants**" (Judges 5:23), in reference to all those sitting together with Meroz. **And from where do we** derive **that we detail his sin in public?**[H] **As it is written:** "Curse bitterly its inhabitants, **because they did not come to the help of the Lord**" (Judges 5:23).

וְאָמַר עוּלָּא: בְּאַרְבַּע מְאָה שִׁיפּוּרֵי שַׁמְתֵּיהּ בָּרָק לְמֵרוֹז. אִיכָּא דְּאָמְרִי: גַּבְרָא רַבָּה הֲוָה. וְאִיכָּא דְּאָמְרִי: כּוֹכְבָא הֲוָה, שֶׁנֶּאֱמַר: ״מִן שָׁמַיִם נִלְחָמוּ הַכּוֹכָבִים״.

And Ulla said: Barak ostracized Meroz with the blowing **of four hundred** ***shofarot*** due to his failure to come. As for the identification of Meroz, **some say** that **he was a great man** and that he was ostracized because he did not join in the war effort. **And others say** that the reference is to **a star** and not a human being, and that it did not aid the Jewish people in their battle, **as it is stated: "The stars fought from heaven;** in their courses they fought against Sisera," (Judges 5:20). This star, which did not help the Jewish people, was cursed.

וּמְנָלַן דְּמַפְקְרִינַן נִכְסֵיהּ? דִּכְתִיב: ״וְכֹל אֲשֶׁר לֹא יָבוֹא לִשְׁלֹשֶׁת הַיָּמִים בַּעֲצַת הַשָּׂרִים וְהַזְּקֵנִים יָחֳרַם כָּל רְכוּשׁוֹ וְהוּא יִבָּדֵל מִקְּהַל הַגּוֹלָה״.

And from where do we derive **that** the court **may declare the property of** one who does not obey its orders **as ownerless?**[H] **As it is written: "And that whoever would not come within three days, according to the counsel of the princes and the Elders, all his substance shall be forfeited** [*yaḥoram*] **and himself separated from the congregation of the exiles"** (Ezra 10:8). "Shall be forfeited" is referring to excommunication.

וּמְנָלַן דְּנָצֵינַן וְלָיְיטִינַן וּמָחֵינַן וְתָלְשִׁינַן שֵׂיעָר וּמַשְׁבְּעִינַן? דִּכְתִיב: ״וָאָרִיב עִמָּם וָאֲקַלְלֵם וָאַכֶּה מֵהֶם אֲנָשִׁים וָאֶמְרְטֵם וָאַשְׁבִּיעֵם״.

And from where do we derive **that we may contend with** such a person, **and curse**[H] him, **and beat** him, **and pull out** his **hair, and make** him **take an oath** in order to prevent him from sinning? **As it is written: "And I contended with them, and cursed them, and beat some of them, and pulled out their hair, and made them take oath** by God" (Nehemiah 13:25).

NOTES

They did cry there, Pharaoh, etc. – קָרְאוּ שָׁם פַּרְעֹה וכו׳: In the manuscript of Rashi, it is explained that Jeremiah set a time for the downfall of Pharaoh, and although it did not occur at that time, it was to occur at another time. The Ritva writes that although God set a time for the downfall of Pharaoh at the hands of Nebuchadnezzar, Nebuchadnezzar arrived late. Despite this, God did not punish Nebuchadnezzar because he did eventually arrive. If so, certainly a Jew who is threatened with ostracism should be given a second chance even if he misses the first opportunity. Some explain that Pharaoh made noise in joy because he thought that the time for the war had passed, and he was informed that there would be another time for war later (Rabbeinu Yehonatan of Lunel; Ran).

Said the messenger of the Lord – אָמַר מַלְאַךְ ה׳: Most of the commentaries explain that it was Barak who served as God's messenger. However, some say that Barak was a messenger for the decree of the Lord's angel (Ran).

HALAKHA

One who shows disrespect toward the court's messenger – הַמְבַזֶּה שְׁלִיחַ בֵּית דִּין: The testimony of a court's messenger carries the weight of two witnesses, if he testifies that he was treated disrespectfully. He may tell the court what occurred, and it is not considered to be slanderous speech (Rema). The one who acted disrespectfully toward the court's messenger is ostracized (*Shulḥan Arukh*, *Ḥoshen Mishpat* 11:1 and *Yoreh De'a* 334:43).

Who eats or drinks with him, etc. – דְּאָכֵיל וְשָׁתֵי בַּהֲדֵיהּ וכו׳: When the courts see that a person is transgressing a serious prohibition and they wish to separate him from it, they may excommunicate not only the one committing the sin but even those who are eating, drinking, and standing within four cubits of him (*Shulḥan Arukh*, *Yoreh De'a* 334:9).

We detail his sin in public – פָּרְטִינַן חֶטְאֵיהּ בְּצִיבּוּרָא: A court, if it deems it appropriate, is permitted to ostracize a person who is not strictly liable for ostracism, in order to serve as a warning to others. His sin should be made public, and it should be made known that he was ostracized or excommunicated by the court (Rambam *Sefer Shofetim*, *Hilkhot Sanhedrin* 24:7).

The court may declare his property ownerless – מַפְקְרִינַן נִכְסֵיהּ: A court is permitted to declare a person's property ownerless or destroy it in order to prevent sins that are widespread at that time (*Shulḥan Arukh*, *Ḥoshen Mishpat* 2:1, and in the comment of Rema).

We may contend with and curse – נָצֵינַן וְלָיְיטִינַן: A judge is permitted to purposely antagonize the defendant when appropriate, curse, strike, pull out hair, and force a person to take an oath. Similarly, he is permitted to seize the guilty party, imprison him, and punish him with any type of punishment (Rambam *Sefer Shofetim*, *Hilkhot Sanhedrin* 24:8–9).

וּמְנָלַן דְּכָפְתִינַן וְאָסְרִינַן וְעָבְדִינַן הַרְדָּפָה? דִּכְתִיב: ״הֵן לְמוֹת הֵן לִשְׁרוֹשִׁי הֵן לַעֲנָשׁ נִכְסִין וְלֶאֱסוּרִין״. מַאי לִשְׁרוֹשִׁי? אָמַר אַדָּא מָרִי אָמַר נְחֶמְיָה בַּר בָּרוּךְ אָמַר רַב חִיָּיא בַּר אָבִין אָמַר רַב יְהוּדָה: הַרְדָּפָה. מַאי הַרְדָּפָה? אָמַר רַב יְהוּדָה בְּרֵיהּ דְּרַב שְׁמוּאֵל בַּר שֵׁילָת מִשְּׁמֵיהּ דְּרַב: מְנַדִּין לְאַלְתַּר, וְשׁוֹנִין לְאַחַר שְׁלֹשִׁים, וּמַחֲרִימִין לְאַחַר שִׁשִּׁים.

And from where do we derive **that we may shackle** his hands and feet, **chain him, and apply pressure?**[N] **As it is written: "Whether it be for death, or for banishment** [*lishroshi*], **or for confiscation of goods, or for imprisonment"** (Ezra 7:26). The Gemara asks: **What** is the meaning of the word "*lishroshi*," translated here as banishment? **Adda Mari said** that **Neḥemya bar Baruch said** that **Rav Ḥiyya bar Avin said** that **Rav Yehuda said:** This is **pressure.** Since this expression is also unclear, the Gemara asks: **What is pressure? Rav Yehuda, son of Rav Shmuel bar Sheilat, said in the name of Rav** that this term refers to the following series of actions: **They ostracize** him **immediately,** and then once **again after thirty** days, and if he still does not repent, **they excommunicate him after sixty** days.

אֲמַר לֵיהּ רַב הוּנָא בַּר חִינָּנָא, הָכִי אָמַר רַב חִסְדָּא: מַתְרִין בֵּיהּ שֵׁנִי וַחֲמִישִׁי וְשֵׁנִי. הָנֵי מִילֵּי – לְמָמוֹנָא. אֲבָל לְאַפְקִירוּתָא – לְאַלְתַּר.

Rav Huna bar Ḥinnana said to him: Rav Ḥisda said as follows: Before excommunicating a person, the court **warns him** three times, on **Monday, Thursday, and** the following **Monday.** The Gemara notes: **This applies** in a case where one ignores **a monetary judgment** that was issued against him. He is warned three times that he must repay his debt.[H] **But** in a case where one **behaves disrespectfully** toward a Torah scholar, he is **immediately** ostracized.[H]

הַהוּא טַבָּחָא דְּאִיתְפַּקַר בְּרַב טוֹבִי בַּר מַתָּנָה, אִימְנוּ עֲלֵיהּ אַבַּיֵי וְרָבָא וְשַׁמְתוּהוּ. לַסּוֹף אֲזַל פַּיְּיסֵיהּ לְבַעַל דִּינֵיהּ. אֲמַר אַבַּיֵי: הֵיכִי לִיעֲבִיד? לִישְׁרֵי לֵיהּ – לָא חָל שַׁמְתָּא עֲלֵיהּ תְּלָתִין יוֹמִין. לָא לִישְׁרֵי לֵיהּ – קָא בָּעוּ רַבָּנַן לְמֵיעַל!

§ The Gemara relates that **a certain butcher behaved disrespectfully toward Rav Tuvi bar Mattana. Abaye and Rava were appointed** to the case **and ostracized him. In the end** the butcher **went and appeased his disputant,** Rav Tuvi. **Abaye said: What should we do** in this case? Shall **he be released** from his decree of ostracism? **His** decree of **ostracism has not** yet **been in effect for** the usual **thirty days.** On the other hand, **shall he not be released** from ostracism? But **the Sages wish to enter**[N] his shop and purchase meat, and they are presently unable to do so. What, then, is the most appropriate course of action?

אֲמַר לֵיהּ לְרַב אִידִי בַּר אָבִין: מִידִי שְׁמִיעַ לָךְ בְּהָא? אֲמַר לֵיהּ: הָכִי אָמַר רַב תַּחְלִיפָא בַּר אֲבִימִי אָמַר שְׁמוּאֵל: טוּט אָסַר, וְטוּט שָׁרֵי. אֲמַר לֵיהּ: הָנֵי מִילֵּי – לְמָמוֹנָא, אֲבָל לְאַפְקִירוּתָא – עַד דְּחָיְילָא שַׁמְתָּא עֲלֵיהּ תְּלָתִין יוֹמִין.

He said to Rav Idi bar Avin: Have **you heard anything with regard to such** a case? Rav Idi bar Avin **said to** Abaye: **Rav Taḥlifa bar Avimi said** that **Shmuel said as follows:** A *shofar* **blast**[N] at the time of the ostracism **makes** it **binding, and** a *shofar* **blast releases** it.[H] In other words, the *shofar* should be sounded now, as it had been sounded when the decree of ostracism was pronounced, and it should be canceled, although thirty days have not passed. Abaye **said to him: This applies** in a case where one ignores **a monetary judgment** that was issued against him; **but** in a case where one **behaves disrespectfully,** there must be no release **until the** decree of **ostracism has been in effect for thirty days.**[N]

אַלְמָא קָסָבַר אַבַּיֵי: הָנֵי בֵּי תְּלָתָא דְּשַׁמִּיתוּ – לָא אָתוּ תְּלָתָא אַחֲרִינֵי וְשָׁרוּ לֵיהּ.

The Gemara comments: **Apparently, Abaye maintains** that if **three** people **ostracized** one, **three others may not come and release him.** This is derived from the fact that Abaye was concerned about releasing the butcher from ostracism and did not delegate the task to someone else.

NOTES

Pressure [*hardafa*] – הַרְדָּפָה: The *ge'onim* have a different version of the text, according to which the word *hardafa* refers to a method of imprisonment similar to solitary confinement. Similarly, many of the early authorities understood this term to be a separate type of punishment, different from ostracism and excommunication, such as lashes (see Rabbeinu Gershom *Me'or HaGola*), or that the quality of life of one who was admonished would be lowered through other types of persecution (Rid; see Rambam).

The Sages wish to enter – בָּעוּ רַבָּנַן לְמֵיעַל: This is the text of the standard edition of the Talmud, and it is the text that Rashi follows (see Ritva). However, the manuscript of Rashi has a version that reads: To go, meaning that the Sages wished to return home and Abaye wished to keep them there until they nullified the decree of ostracism, in accordance with his opinion that three other people could nullify his decree of ostracism. This is the explanation of most commentaries, although many have a version that reads: That they wished to take leave of their teacher.

Blast [*tut*] – טוּט: The word used by the Gemara here is a form of onomatopoeia and is meant to mimic the sound of the *shofar* itself. Similar words can be found in every language (Rabbeinu Shlomo ben HaYatom). According to *Tosafot* on tractate *Menaḥot*, this word is related to the term *tat*, which the Talmud explains to mean two. Here, this expression is referring to the two people who enacted the decree of ostracism, and it teaches that these two are also able to nullify it. In the manuscript of Rashi, it is explained that the numerical value of the word *tut* is twenty-four, which alludes to the twenty-four actions for which one may be ostracized.

Ostracism for thirty days – נִידּוּי שְׁלֹשִׁים: In the Jerusalem Talmud an allusion to this time period is found in the verse: "But a whole month, until it comes out at your nostrils" (Numbers 11:20), referring to the punishment that God gave the Jewish people in the desert.

HALAKHA

Warning before ostracism – הַתְרָאָה לִפְנֵי נִידּוּי: When one is ostracized because he has not repaid loans, he is warned three times: On Monday, on Thursday, and on the following Monday, before he is ostracized. This ruling is in accordance with the opinion of Rav Ḥisda (*Shulḥan Arukh, Yoreh De'a* 334:1, and in the comment of the Rema).

Ostracism due to disrespect – נִידּוּי לְאַפְקִירוּתָא: When one is ostracized because he has shown disrespect, he is ostracized immediately. However, it is the accepted practice to first give him a warning (*Shakh*; *Shulḥan Arukh, Yoreh De'a* 334:1).

Nullifying ostracism – הַתָּרַת נִידּוּי: If one was told that he is ostracized for thirty days, his decree of ostracism may still be nullified immediately once he repays the money that he owes or once he makes amends with the one toward whom he acted disrespectfully. Some say that his decree of ostracism should be reversed after thirty days when he comes to the court after thirty days and asks for his decree of ostracism to be nullified, even if he has not repented. However, if he does not make such a request, he remains ostracized until his death. Some disagree and say that if one does not repent then he remains ostracized, and one who makes amends can have his decree of ostracism nullified only after thirty days (Rema). Others say that if he makes amends then his decree of ostracism may be nullified immediately (*Taz*; *Shulḥan Arukh, Yoreh De'a* 334:13).

דְּאִיבַּעְיָא לְהוּ: הָנֵי בֵּי תְּלָתָא דְּשַׁמִּיתוּ, מַהוּ לְמֵיתֵי תְּלָתָא אַחֲרִינֵי וְשָׁרוּ לֵיהּ? תָּא שְׁמַע: מְנוּדֶּה לָרַב – מְנוּדֶּה לַתַּלְמִיד; מְנוּדֶּה לַתַּלְמִיד – אֵינוֹ מְנוּדֶּה לָרַב.

As a dilemma was raised before the Sages: If **three** people **ostracized** someone, **what is** the *halakha* with regard to **three others coming and releasing him** from his decree of ostracism? The Gemara suggests: **Come** and **hear** a proof from that which is taught in a *baraita*: **One who was ostracized by the teacher** of Torah for having acted disrespectfully toward him **is** considered **ostracized with regard to the student,** and the latter must keep his distance from him. However, **one who was ostracized by the student is not** considered **ostracized with regard to the teacher.**[H]

מְנוּדֶּה לְעִירוֹ – מְנוּדֶּה לְעִיר אַחֶרֶת; מְנוּדֶּה לְעִיר אַחֶרֶת – אֵינוֹ מְנוּדֶּה לְעִירוֹ. מְנוּדֶּה לַנָּשִׂיא – מְנוּדֶּה לְכָל יִשְׂרָאֵל; מְנוּדֶּה לְכָל יִשְׂרָאֵל – אֵינוֹ מְנוּדֶּה לַנָּשִׂיא. רַבָּן שִׁמְעוֹן בֶּן גַּמְלִיאֵל אוֹמֵר: אֶחָד מִן הַתַּלְמִידִים שֶׁנִּידָּה וּמֵת – חֶלְקוֹ אֵינוֹ מוּפָר.

One who was ostracized by his own **city is** considered **ostracized with regard to another city.** However, **one who was ostracized by another city is not** considered **ostracized with regard to his** own **city.**[H] **One who was ostracized by the** *Nasi* of the Sanhedrin **is** considered **ostracized with regard to all the Jewish people;** but **one who was ostracized by all the Jewish people is not** considered **ostracized with regard to the** *Nasi* of the Sanhedrin.[H] **Rabban Shimon ben Gamliel says:** If **one of the students** sitting as a judge on the court **had ostracized** someone, **and he died** before releasing him from the decree of ostracism, **his portion** of the decree of ostracism **is not nullified.**

שְׁמַע מִינָּהּ תְּלָת. שְׁמַע מִינָּהּ: תַּלְמִיד שֶׁנִּידָּה לִכְבוֹדוֹ – נִידּוּיוֹ נִידּוּי. וּשְׁמַע מִינָּהּ: כָּל אֶחָד וְאֶחָד מֵיפֵר חֶלְקוֹ. וּשְׁמַע מִינָּהּ: הָנֵי בֵּי תְּלָתָא דְּשַׁמִּיתוּ – לָא אָתוּ תְּלָתָא אַחֲרִינֵי וְשָׁרוּ לֵיהּ.

The Gemara says: **Learn three** *halakhot* **from this** *baraita*. **Learn from this** that in the case of **a student who ostracizes** someone **due to** an insult to **his dignity**[H] and not because the ostracized person was guilty of some transgression, **his** decree of **ostracism is valid.** Were the case one where one was ostracized due to sin, everyone is required to respect the decree of ostracism, even the student's teacher. **And learn from this** that **each and every one** who participated in the decree of ostracism **nullifies his** own **portion**[H] of the decree of ostracism, as the *baraita* speaks of: His portion. **And learn from this** that if **three** people **ostracized** another person, **three other** people **may not come and nullify** the decree of ostracism. Were this not the case, it wouldn't matter if a certain person's portion was not nullified. His portion could be nullified by someone else.

אֲמַר אַמֵימָר: הִלְכְתָא, הָנֵי בֵּי תְּלָתָא דְּשַׁמִּיתוּ – אָתוּ בֵּי תְּלָתָא אַחֲרִינֵי וְשָׁרוּ לֵיהּ. אֲמַר לֵיהּ רַב אַשִׁי לְאַמֵימַר: וְהָא תַּנְיָא רַבָּן שִׁמְעוֹן בֶּן גַּמְלִיאֵל אוֹמֵר: אֶחָד מִן הַתַּלְמִידִים שֶׁנִּידָּה וּמֵת – חֶלְקוֹ אֵינוֹ מוּפָר. מַאי לָאו – אֵינוֹ מוּפָר כְּלָל? לֹא, עַד דְּאָתוּ בֵּי תְּלָתָא אַחֲרִינֵי וְשָׁרוּ לֵיהּ.

Ameimar[P] **said: The** *halakha* **is** that if **three** people **ostracize** another person, **three others may come and nullify** the decree of ostracism.[H] **Rav Ashi said to Ameimar: But isn't it taught in** a *baraita*: **Rabban Shimon ben Gamliel says:** If **one of the students had ostracized** another person, **and he died** before releasing him from the decree of ostracism, **his portion is not nullified? What, is it not that it is not nullified at all,** i.e., it cannot be nullified by another person? The Gemara rejects this argument: **No,** this means that the decree of ostracism remains in force **until three other people come and nullify** it.

HALAKHA

One who is ostracized by a teacher and a student – מְנוּדֶּה לָרַב וְלַתַּלְמִיד: One who has been ostracized by a teacher of Torah is also ostracized with respect to that teacher's students. However, other rabbis are not obligated to observe this ban (Rema).

If one is ostracized by a student, people who are not Torah scholars are bound by this ban, but this student's teacher and other Torah scholars are not (Rema). According to some authorities, scholars of lesser status than the student are bound by the ban (*Shakh*). In the presence of his teacher, a student may not ostracize another without permission (*Shulḥan Arukh, Yoreh De'a* 334:15).

One who is ostracized by his city and by another city – מְנוּדֶּה לְעִירוֹ וּלְעִיר אַחֶרֶת: One who has been ostracized by his city is ostracized by another city as well, even when it is bigger than his city (Rema). One who has been ostracized by another city is not ostracized by his city; however he is ostracized by other cities, since they are considered like the city from which he was originally ostracized.

This distinction applies only if one was ostracized because he acted disrespectfully. However, if one was ostracized because he did not listen to the ruling of the court or because he had sinned, then he is ostracized by his own city as well (*Shakh*). The people of his city are not required to treat him as though he were ostracized; however, he is required to observe the restrictions of ostracism on his own (*Pitḥei Teshuva*, citing *Levushei Serad*; *Shulḥan Arukh, Yoreh De'a* 334:20).

One who is ostracized by the ***Nasi*** **of the Sanhedrin and by all the Jewish people – מְנוּדֶּה לַנָּשִׂיא וּלְיִשְׂרָאֵל:** One who is ostracized by the *Nasi* of the Sanhedrin is ostracized by all Jewish people; however, one who is ostracized by the entire Jewish people is not ostracized by the *Nasi* of the Sanhedrin (*Shulḥan Arukh, Yoreh De'a* 334:21).

A student who ostracizes due to his dignity – תַּלְמִיד שֶׁנִּידָּה לִכְבוֹדוֹ: A Torah scholar is permitted to ostracize one who acts disrespectfully toward him, even if he did not explicitly show disrespect to him but intended to do so (Rema). If he showed disrespect in a manner that makes him worthy of being ostracized according to the *halakha*, then he is ostracized by everyone. However, if he showed disrespect in a different manner, he is ostracized only from people of smaller stature than that Sage (*Shulḥan Arukh, Yoreh De'a* 334:15).

Each and every one nullifies his portion – כָּל אֶחָד וְאֶחָד מֵיפֵר חֶלְקוֹ: One who has been ostracized by three people cannot have his decree of ostracism nullified by two of the three unless the third has given them permission. If many people were present when one was ostracized, all of them must participate in nullifying his decree of ostracism. All those who join in ostracizing a person must also join together in order to reverse his decree of ostracism. However, any of those involved in the ostracism may nullify his own portion by himself, and it is not necessary to gather them together, even if they were together when he was ostracized (*Shulḥan Arukh, Yoreh De'a* 334:26).

Another court may nullify ostracism – בֵּית דִּין אַחֵר הַמַּתִּיר נִידּוּי: If one was ostracized by a court of three people who have moved away, his decree of ostracism may be nullified by three other people, on condition that he has abandoned his sin. Rav Hai Gaon writes that those three must be of the same stature as the original three people, i.e., they must be as wise, as great, and of the same age (Rema). These requirements apply only if they perform the nullification within the initial period of ostracism (*Shakh*, citing Ra'avad; *Shulḥan Arukh, Yoreh De'a* 334:25).

PERSONALITIES

Ameimar – אֲמֵימָר: Ameimar was one of the great talmudic Sages of the fifth and sixth generation of Babylonian *amora'im*. Ameimar was born and raised in Neharde'a, where he studied and taught Torah, although it is likely that he studied with the Sages of Pumbedita as well. The teachings that he quotes are mainly from fifth-generation *amora'im* who were students of Abaye and Rava. It appears that he served as rabbi and religious judge in Neharde'a, where he established various rabbinic regulations. However, he also wielded influence in many other places, such as Meḥoza. The leaders of the following generation, e.g., Rav Ashi, were his students and came before him for judgment. He had at least one son, named Mar, who studied with Rav Ashi while Ameimar was still alive.

תנו רבנן: אין נידוי פחות משלשים יום, ואין נזיפה פחות משבעה ימים. ואף על פי שאין ראיה לדבר - זכר לדבר, שנאמר: "ואביה ירק ירק בפניה הלא תכלם שבעת ימים".

§ **The Sages taught** the following *baraita*: **Ostracism does not apply for less than** a period of **thirty days, and admonition,**[N] which is less severe than ostracism, **does not apply for less than** a period of **seven days.**[H] **And although there is no proof with regard to the matter,** i.e., the standard duration of admonition, there is **an allusion to the matter, as it is stated: "If her father had but spit in her face, should she not be ashamed for seven days?"** (Numbers 12:14). This implies that admonition lasts for seven days.

אמר רב חסדא: נידוי שלנו כנזיפה שלהן. ונזיפה דידהו שבעה, ותו לא? והא רבי שמעון בר רבי ובר קפרא הוו יתבי וקא גרסי, קשיא להו שמעתא. אמר ליה רבי שמעון לבר קפרא: דבר זה צריך רבי. אמר ליה בר קפרא לרבי שמעון: ומה רבי אומר בדבר זה?

Rav Ḥisda said: Our decree of **ostracism** in Babylonia has the power **of their admonition** in Eretz Yisrael. Since the authorities in Eretz Yisrael are ordained with the title Rabbi, their admonition carries more weight than a decree of ostracism issued in Babylonia. The Gemara asks: Is **their admonition** in Eretz Yisrael only **seven** days **and no more? But isn't** it related that **Rabbi Shimon, son of Rabbi** Yehuda HaNasi,[P] **and bar Kappara**[P] **were sitting and studying,** and they posed **a difficulty with** a certain ***halakha*****. Rabbi Shimon said to bar Kappara: This issue requires** my father, **Rabbi** Yehuda HaNasi, to explain it. **Bar Kappara said to Rabbi Shimon,** somewhat mockingly: **And what can** your father, **Rabbi** Yehuda HaNasi, **say**[N] **about this** issue? What can he add and teach us about it?

אזל אמר ליה לאבוה. איקפד. אתא בר קפרא לאיתחזויי ליה, אמר ליה: בר קפרא, איני מכירך מעולם. ידע דנקט מילתא בדעתיה, נהג נזיפותא בנפשיה תלתין יומין.

Rabbi Shimon **went and told his father,** Rabbi Yehuda HaNasi, what bar Kappara had said, and Rabbi Yehuda HaNasi **became angry** with him. When **bar Kappara came** at some later point **to visit,** Rabbi Yehuda HaNasi **said to him: Bar Kappara, I do not know you at all.** Bar Kappara **understood that** Rabbi Yehuda HaNasi **had taken** his **statement to heart,** i.e., was insulted. He subsequently **behaved** as if he had been **admonished,** as a self-imposed punishment, **for thirty days.**

שוב, פעם אחד גזר רבי שלא ישנו לתלמידים בשוק. מאי דרש? "חמוקי ירכיך כמו חלאים", מה ירך בסתר

Once again, on another occasion, Rabbi Yehuda HaNasi **decreed that students not be taught in the marketplace** but only in a study hall. **What** verse did he **expound** to serve as the basis for this decree? The verse states: **"Your rounded thighs are like jewels,** the work of the hands of an artist" (Song of Songs 7:2). **Just as a thigh is** ordinarily **hidden** and kept covered with clothes,

NOTES

Admonition – נזיפה: The punishment of admonition is not expressed through the way others act toward the admonished person. Rather, the onus is on this person to conduct himself as if he had been admonished, like one who has been publicly shamed and who is embarrassed to show his face in public (Ra'avad).

And what can Rabbi Yehuda HaNasi say – ומה רבי אומר: Most commentaries who explain this statement claim that Rabbi Shimon understood that bar Kappara wished to mock him and to state: This question is challenging, and will Rabbi Yehuda HaNasi have anything to say about it? Others suggest that he was upset because bar Kappara used the title Rabbi and not the greater honorific *Rabbeinu*, meaning: Our Rabbi (Ran).

HALAKHA

Ostracism and admonition – נידוי ונזיפה: Generally, ostracism lasts for thirty days, and admonition lasts for seven days. However, in Babylonia ostracism lasts for seven days and admonition lasts for only one day, in accordance with the opinion of Rav Ḥisda (*Shulḥan Arukh, Yoreh De'a* 334:1).

PERSONALITIES

Rabbi Shimon, son of Rabbi Yehuda HaNasi – רבי שמעון בר רבי: Rabbi Shimon was the youngest son of Rabbi Yehuda HaNasi and his close student. In addition, he was especially close to Rabbi Ḥiyya, who also his close friend and partner in the silk business. In many places, it is noted that he was very meticulous about his honor, which he saw as related to the honor of the office of *Nasi*. In particular, he was careful to ensure that nothing he did would imply offense to his great father. At least one of his sayings is found in the Mishna itself, although he was actually in the transitional generation between *tanna'im* and *amora'im*. His sayings are often introduced by the word *itmar*, meaning: It was said, a term used for *amora'im*.

Rabbi Yehuda HaNasi considered Rabbi Shimon to be a great scholar. Before Rabbi Yehuda HaNasi's death, he appointed Rabbi Shimon to be the *Ḥakham*, which was the third-highest position in the Sanhedrin after the *Nasi* and the Head of the Court, although he appointed Rabbi Shimon's older brother, Rabban Gamliel, to replace him as *Nasi*.

Bar Kappara – בר קפרא: Bar Kappara was one of the Sages of Eretz Yisrael during the transitional generation between *tanna'im* and *amora'im*. His first name is unknown, although some say his name was Shimon. It is unclear whether he was related to Elazar HaKafar, and if so, what their relationship was. Bar Kappara was one of the more important students of Rabbi Yehuda HaNasi and a colleague of Rabbi Ḥiyya. He assembled a unique collection of *baraitot* that are introduced in the Talmud with the words: Bar Kappara teaches. His halakhic statements are mentioned many times in the Talmud. His aggadic statements and expositions appear in both the Babylonian and Jerusalem Talmud.

Bar Kappara was well known for his sharp personality and intellect. He was considered to be well-versed in the Bible, so much so that even Rabbi Yehuda HaNasi asked him about the meaning of certain verses. Because he was prone to making harsh statements, it sometimes happened that certain members of Rabbi Yehuda HaNasi's family were insulted; however, Rabbi Yehuda HaNasi himself thought very highly of bar Kappara, praised him, and was the first to offer a eulogy for him. Almost all of the first generation of *amora'im* were his students, including his nephew, Rabbi Yehuda ben Padda.

He lived, at least toward the end of his life, in the Galilee and was buried in the city of Parod.

אַף דִּבְרֵי תוֹרָה בְּסֵתֶר.

so too, the words of Torah, which are "the work of the hands of an artist," i.e., God, must remain **hidden** in the study hall.

יָצָא רַבִּי חִיָּיא וְשָׁנָה לִשְׁנֵי בְּנֵי אֶחָיו בַּשּׁוּק, לְרַב וּלְרַבָּה בַּר בַּר חָנָה. שְׁמַע רַבִּי – אִיקְפַּד. אֲתָא רַבִּי חִיָּיא לְאִיתְחֲזוֹיֵי לֵיהּ. אֲמַר לֵיהּ: עִיָּיא, מִי קוֹרֵא לְךָ בַּחוּץ? יָדַע דִּנְקַט מִילְּתָא בְּדַעְתֵּיהּ, נְהַג נְזִיפוּתָא בְּנַפְשֵׁיהּ תְּלָתִין יוֹמִין.

Despite Rabbi Yehuda HaNasi's decree, **Rabbi Ḥiyya**[P] **went out and taught his two nephews, Rav and Rabba bar bar Ḥana, in the marketplace. Rabbi** Yehuda HaNasi **heard** what he had done and **became angry** with him. When **Rabbi Ḥiyya came** at some later date **to visit him,** Rabbi Yehuda HaNasi mockingly **said to him: Iyya, who is calling you outside?**[N] By asking this question Rabbi Yehuda HaNasi was intimating that Rabbi Ḥiyya should leave his house. Rabbi Ḥiyya **understood that** Rabbi Yehuda HaNasi **had taken the matter to heart** and was insulted, and so **he conducted** himself as if he had been **admonished,** as a self-imposed punishment, **for thirty days.**

בְּיוֹם תְּלָתִין שְׁלַח לֵיהּ: תָּא; הֲדַר שְׁלַח לֵיהּ דְּלָא לֵיתֵי.

On the thirtieth day, Rabbi Yehuda HaNasi **sent him** a message, saying: **Come** and visit me. However, **he later** reversed his opinion and **sent him** another message, telling him **not to come.**

מֵעִיקָּרָא מַאי סָבַר וּלְבַסּוֹף מַאי סָבַר? מֵעִיקָּרָא סָבַר: מִקְצָת הַיּוֹם כְּכוּלּוֹ; וּלְבַסּוֹף סָבַר: לָא אָמְרִינַן מִקְצָת הַיּוֹם כְּכוּלּוֹ.

The Gemara asks: **At the outset what did he hold, and ultimately what did he hold? Initially,** Rabbi Yehuda HaNasi **held that** the legal status of **part of the day is like** that of **an entire** day, and since the thirtieth day already begun, Rabbi Ḥiyya's time of admonition had ended. **But ultimately he held** that with regard to this issue **we do not say** that the legal status of **part of the day is like** that **of an entire** day.

לְסוֹף אֲתָא. אֲמַר לֵיהּ: אַמַּאי אָתֵית? אֲמַר לֵיהּ: דִּשְׁלַח לִי מָר דְּלֵיתֵי. וְהָא שְׁלַחִי לָךְ דְּלָא תֵּיתֵי? אֲמַר לֵיהּ: זֶה רָאִיתִי, וְזֶה – לֹא רָאִיתִי. קְרֵי עֲלֵיהּ: "בִּרְצוֹת ה׳ דַּרְכֵי אִישׁ גַּם אוֹיְבָיו יַשְׁלִים אִתּוֹ".

In the end Rabbi Ḥiyya **came** on that same day. Rabbi Yehuda HaNasi **asked him: Why have you come?** Rabbi Ḥiyya **responded: Because** you, **Master, sent** me a message that **I should come.** He said to him: **But I sent** you a second message **that you should not come. He responded: This** messenger that you sent, i.e., the first one, **I saw** him and I did as he said, **but that** messenger, i.e., the second one, **I did not see.** Rabbi Yehuda HaNasi **read** the verse **about** Rabbi Ḥiyya: **"When a man's ways please the Lord, He makes even his enemies to be at peace with him"** (Proverbs 16:7), as it was clear to him that Rabbi Ḥiyya had merited divine assistance.

מַאי טַעְמָא עֲבַד מָר הָכִי? אֲמַר לֵיהּ: דִּכְתִיב: "חָכְמוֹת בַּחוּץ תָּרֹנָּה". אֲמַר לֵיהּ: אִם קָרִיתָ – לֹא שָׁנִיתָ, וְאִם שָׁנִיתָ – לֹא שִׁילַּשְׁתָּ, וְאִם שִׁילַּשְׁתָּ, לֹא פֵּירְשׁוּ לָךְ.

§ Concerning the issue with which the entire incident had begun, Rabbi Yehuda HaNasi asked Rabbi Ḥiyya: **What is the reason that** you, **the Master, acted as** you did, ignoring my instructions not to teach Torah in the marketplace? Rabbi Ḥiyya **said to him: As it is written: "Wisdom cries aloud in the streets"** (Proverbs 1:20), which implies that Torah should be publicized in the streets. Rabbi Yehuda HaNasi **said to him: If you read** this verse once, **you** certainly **did not read it a second time**[N] in greater depth; **and if you read it a second time, you** certainly **did not read it a third time;** and **if you read** it **a third time,** then **it was not** adequately **explained to you,** as it is clear that you do not understand it properly.

"חָכְמוֹת בַּחוּץ תָּרֹנָּה" – כִּדְרָבָא. דְּאָמַר רָבָא: כָּל הָעוֹסֵק בַּתּוֹרָה מִבִּפְנִים – תּוֹרָתוֹ מַכְרֶזֶת עָלָיו מִבַּחוּץ.

The words: **"Wisdom cries aloud in the streets,"** should be understood **in accordance** with the opinion **of Rava. As Rava said:** With regard to **everyone who occupies himself with Torah** study **inside** the privacy of his home, **his Torah** knowledge **will proclaim his** greatness **outside,** as it will be revealed to the masses and they will see his greatness.

וְהָא כְּתִיב: "לֹא מֵרֹאשׁ בַּסֵּתֶר דִּבַּרְתִּי"! הַהוּא בְּיוֹמֵי דְּכַלָּה.

The Gemara asks: **But isn't it written: "From the beginning I have not spoken in secret"** (Isaiah 48:16), implying that the Torah should be taught and proclaimed in public? The Gemara answers: **That** verse is referring to **the days of the *kalla*,**[N] the gathering for Torah study held during Elul and Adar, when many people come to listen to Torah discourses. During this time, it is not only permitted but even recommended to teach Torah to the masses. In this way, the verse can be explained in accordance with the opinion of Rabbi Yehuda HaNasi.

PERSONALITIES

Rabbi Ḥiyya – רַבִּי חִיָּיא: Rabbi Ḥiyya, son of Abba, from the Babylonian city of Kafri, was one of the last of the *tanna'im*. He was a contemporary of Rabbi Yehuda HaNasi.

Rabbi Ḥiyya was born to an important family that traced its roots to King David and included many important Sages. Rabbi Ḥiyya was recognized as a leading Torah scholar even while living in Babylonia. As the Gemara attests, his efforts were credited by many with saving the Torah from oblivion. Upon moving to Eretz Yisrael, Rabbi Ḥiyya became a close friend and colleague of Rabbi Yehuda HaNasi. He also became a close friend of Rabbi Yehuda HaNasi's son, Rabbi Shimon, with whom he became partners in trade. A powerful force in his generation, he also worked closely with Rav, who was recognized as the leader of the Jewish people in Babylonia, but still learned from Rabbi Ḥiyya.

Rabbi Ḥiyya's greatest work was his *Tosefta*, a collection of oral traditions that were not included in the Mishna compiled by Rabbi Yehuda HaNasi. This collection, which was assembled with the assistance of Rabbi Ḥiyya's disciple-colleague, Rabbi Oshaya, was viewed as authoritative to the extent that the Talmud states that any *baraita* that was not found in his work should not be discussed in the study hall (*Hullin* 141a–b). Some hold that Rabbi Ḥiyya edited the *Tosefta* that exists today.

While it appears that Rabbi Ḥiyya was financially supported by others when he first came to Eretz Yisrael, ultimately he was a successful merchant who dealt in international business ventures, and in particular the silk trade. He had twin daughters, Pazi and Tavi, and twin sons, Yehuda and Ḥizkiya, who were leading Sages in the generation between the *tanna'im* and *amora'im*. His sons apparently took over his yeshiva in Tiberias after his passing.

NOTES

Iyya, who is calling you outside – עִיָּיא, מִי קוֹרֵא לְךָ בַּחוּץ: When Rabbi Yehuda HaNasi called Rabbi Ḥiyya by this name it was meant to show his displeasure. Rabbi Ḥiyya was unable to pronounce guttural consonants, and in his accent *ḥet* and *ayin* sounded the same. Therefore, calling him Iyya was a way of mocking his accent. In addition, Rabbi Yehuda asked: Who is calling you outside, in order to hint that he taught Torah outside (Maharsha). Others claim that he was suggesting that someone else had called him outside, as if to say: I, Rabbi Yehuda HaNasi, did not call you (Rabbi Shlomo ben HaYatom; see Rashi).

If you read, you did not read a second time – אִם קָרִיתָ לֹא שָׁנִיתָ: Some explain this expression as follows: If you have read this only one time without reviewing it, then you certainly have forgotten what you read. If you have read it a second and third time and have not forgotten it, then certainly it was not explained to you. Therefore, you do not properly understand what is written in this verse (Commentary on *Moed Katan*).

***Kalla* – כַּלָּה:** The *kalla* is a uniquely Babylonian Jewish tradition, though it may have its early roots in Eretz Yisrael. The *kalla* is essentially a gathering of all the Sages. It took place twice a year, in Adar and in Elul, and focused on a specific tractate, which the Sages would analyze and interpret. Thousands of people would attend the days of the *kalla* [*yarḥei kalla*], which also served as an extraordinary occasion of paying homage to the Torah.

ורבי חייא, האי "חמוקי ירכיך" מאי עביד לה? מוקי לה בצדקה ובגמילות חסדים.

The Gemara asks: **And what did Rabbi Ḥiyya do with this** verse: **"Your rounded thighs are like jewels"?** How did he understand it? This verse implies that the Torah must be kept hidden in the study hall and not publicized in the marketplace. The Gemara explains: **He interprets it** not as a reference to Torah, but as referring **to** acts of **charity and loving-kindness,** which should certainly be performed in private.

אלמא, נזיפה דידהו תלתין יומין! נזיפת נשיא שאני.

This incident demonstrates **that, apparently, admonition of those** who live in Eretz Yisrael lasts for **thirty days** and not for seven days. The Gemara answers that this is not a conclusive proof, since Rabbi Yehuda HaNasi was the *Nasi*. **The admonition of the *Nasi*** of the Sanhedrin **is different** i.e., more severe, than the admonition of anyone else.

ונזיפה דידן כמה הוי? חד יומא. כי הא דשמואל ומר עוקבא, כי הוו יתבי גרסי שמעתא – הוה יתיב מר עוקבא קמיה דשמואל ברחוק ארבע אמות, וכי הוו יתבי בדינא – הוה יתיב שמואל קמיה דמר עוקבא ברחוק ארבע אמות. והוו חייקי ליה דוכתא למר עוקבא בציפתא ויתיב עילויה, כי היכי דלישתמען מיליה.

The Gemara asks: **And how long is our admonition**[H] in Babylonia? The Gemara answers: It is only **one day, as in** the case involving **Shmuel and** the Exilarch **Mar Ukva.**[P] **When they would sit and study *halakha*, Mar Ukva would sit before Shmuel at a distance of four cubits** as a sign of respect. Mar Ukva would conduct himself as though Shmuel were his teacher because Shmuel was much greater than him in Torah matters. **And when they would sit** together **in judgment, Shmuel would sit before Mar Ukva at a distance of four cubits** because Mar Ukva was the Exilarch and the chief judge. **But they would lower a place for Mar Ukva in the matting** upon which he sat, **and he would sit on it so that he could hear** Shmuel's **words**[N] of Torah even when they were engaged in judgment.

כל יומא הוה מלוי ליה מר עוקבא לשמואל עד אושפיזיה. יומא חד איטריד בדיניה. הוה אזיל שמואל בתריה. כי מטא לביתיה אמר ליה: לא נגה לך? לישרי לי מר בתיגריה! ידע דנקט מילתא בדעתיה, נהג נזיפותא בנפשיה חד יומא.

Every day, Mar Ukva would accompany Shmuel to his lodgings, in the manner that a student would show honor toward his teacher. **One day,** Mar Ukva **was** so heavily **preoccupied with a case** that had been brought before him for judgment that he did not realize that **Shmuel was walking behind him** to show him respect due to his position as the Exilarch. **When** Mar Ukva **reached his home,** Shmuel **said to him: Is it not enough for you**[N] that I accompanied you until here? **Release me, Master, from my obligation,** so that I may return home. Mar Ukva **understood that** Shmuel **had taken the matter to heart** and was insulted. Therefore, **he conducted** himself as if he had been **admonished, for one day** as a self-imposed punishment.

ההיא איתתא דהוות יתבה בשבילא, הוות פשטה כרעה וקא מניפה חושלאי, והוה חליף ואזיל צורבא מרבנן, ולא איכנעה מקמיה. אמר: כמה חציפא ההיא איתתא! אתאי לקמיה דרב נחמן. אמר לה: מי שמעת שמתא מפומיה? אמרה ליה: לא. אמר לה: זילי, נהוגי נזיפותא חד יומא בנפשיך.

It was related that **a certain woman was sitting alongside a path** with **her leg extended** while **she was sifting barley. A Torah scholar passed** by her on this path, **but she did not yield to him** and move her leg to make room for him. **He said: How rude is that woman!** The woman **came before Rav Naḥman** to ask if this statement should be deemed as excommunication. **He said to her: Did you hear** the word **excommunication** explicitly issue **from his mouth? She said to him: No. He said to her:** If this is the case, then **go and observe an admonition for one day,** as it appears that the Torah scholar sought only to admonish you.

HALAKHA

Our admonition – נזיפה דידן: Admonition lasts for one day (*Shulḥan Arukh, Yoreh De'a* 334:1).

PERSONALITIES

Mar Ukva – מר עוקבא: Mar Ukva was the Exilarch during the time of Rav and Shmuel. Generally, the title *Mar* was added to the name of the Exilarch and those in his family. He was a direct descendant of the house of David and was appointed by the Persians as Exilarch. For these two reasons, Mar Ukva had authority to rule in monetary cases. In this regard, the great Sages of Babylonia deferred to the Exilarch, and Mar Ukva's court, which had a permanent location near the city of Sura, was considered to be the most respected court.

Mar Ukva was very knowledgeable in Torah, and based upon several sources it seems that he saw himself as the primary student of Shmuel. In fact, many of Shmuel's statements are transmitted through Mar Ukva. There was also a close friendship between them, and Shmuel served as Mar Ukva's doctor. Apparently, Mar Ukva outlived Shmuel.

In addition to his greatness in Torah, Mar Ukva was also very generous. Many stories are told about the charity that he gave, which was not only given in large sums but was also given secretly, so as not to embarrass the recipients. Similarly, due to his modest nature he did not use his position of power to fight those who tried to harm him. Several Sages from the following generation cite statements in his name.

NOTES

So that he could hear Shmuel's words – כי היכי דלישתמען מיליה: According to this version of the text, they would give Mar Ukva an elevated seat, on a cushion, so that his words could be heard and so people would humbly accept them (*Talmid Rabbeinu Yeḥiel of Paris*).

Some explain that this statement emphasizes that they would lower Mar Ukva's seat a bit so that his seat would not be much higher than Shmuel's, and that Shmuel was honored by being offered a position from which his words could be heard (manuscript of Rashi). The version of Rashi printed on the page seems to relate to a different version of the talmudic text. According to this version, Mar Ukva lowered his seat so that he would not be far from Shmuel, in order to hear what Shmuel said.

Is it not enough [*nega*] for you – לא נגה לך: Some explain that this expression is related to *noga*, light, and Shmuel implied: Have you not yet been enlightened as to how much you are troubling me (Rabbi Shlomo ben HaYatom)? Others claim that the word *nega* means evening, and he implied: Will it become dark while you are still dragging me behind you (manuscript of Rashi)?

זוּטְרָא בַּר טוֹבִיָּה הֲוָה קָפְסֵיק סִידְרָא קַמֵּיהּ דְּרַב יְהוּדָה. כִּי מְטָא לְהַאי פְּסוּקָא: "וְאֵלֶּה דִּבְרֵי דָוִד הָאַחֲרוֹנִים", אֲמַר לֵיהּ: אַחֲרוֹנִים – מִכְּלָל דְּאִיכָּא רִאשׁוֹנִים. רִאשׁוֹנִים מַאי נִינְהוּ?

§ **Zutra bar Toviyya** was once **reading the portion**[N] of the Bible **before Rav Yehuda. When he reached the verse: "Now these are the last words of David"** (II Samuel 23:1), Zutra bar Toviyya **said to** Rav Yehuda: If it is written that these are the **last** of David's words, **by inference there are first**[N] words as well. If this is the case, **what are these first** words of David? Prior to this, it mentions only David's song, but not his words.

שָׁתֵיק וְלָא אֲמַר לֵיהּ וְלָא מִידִּי. הֲדַר אֲמַר לֵיהּ: אַחֲרוֹנִים מִכְּלָל דְּאִיכָּא רִאשׁוֹנִים. רִאשׁוֹנִים מַאי הִיא? אֲמַר לֵיהּ: מַאי דַּעְתָּךְ? דְּלָא יָדַע פֵּירוּשָׁא דְּהַאי קְרָא – לָאו גַּבְרָא רַבָּה הוּא? יְדַע דִּנְקַט מִילְּתָא בְּדַעְתֵּיהּ, נְהַג נְזִיפוּתָא בְּנַפְשֵׁיהּ חַד יוֹמָא.

Rav Yehuda **remained silent and said nothing to him.** Zutra bar Toviyya thought that Rav Yehuda did not hear what he had said, so he **then said to him** a second time: If it is written that these are the **last** of David's words, **by inference there are first** words as well. If this is the case, **what are these first** words of David? **He said to him: What do you think?** Do you think that anyone **who does not know the meaning of this verse is not a great man?** Why are you stressing the fact that I do not know the answer to your question? Zutra bar Toviyya **understood that** Rav Yehuda **had taken the matter to heart** and was insulted. Therefore, **he conducted** himself as if had been **admonished for one day** as a self-imposed punishment.

וּדְאָתָן עֲלָהּ, מִיהָא אַחֲרוֹנִים – מִכְּלָל דְּאִיכָּא רִאשׁוֹנִים, רִאשׁוֹנִים מַאי הִיא? "וַיְדַבֵּר דָּוִד לַה' אֶת דִּבְרֵי הַשִּׁירָה הַזֹּאת בְּיוֹם הִצִּיל ה' אוֹתוֹ מִכַּף כָּל אוֹיְבָיו וּמִכַּף שָׁאוּל".

The Gemara asks: **But** now **that we have come** to discuss this issue, since the verse mentions David's **last** words, **by inference there are** also **first** words. **What** then **are these first** words of David? The Gemara answers: The first words are: **"And David spoke to the Lord the words of this song in the day that the Lord delivered him out of the hand of his enemies, and out of the hand of Saul"** (II Samuel 22:1), as that song is also referred to as words.

אָמַר לוֹ הַקָּדוֹשׁ בָּרוּךְ הוּא לְדָוִד: דָּוִד, שִׁירָה אַתָּה אוֹמֵר עַל מַפַּלְתּוֹ שֶׁל שָׁאוּל? אִלְמָלֵי אַתָּה שָׁאוּל וְהוּא דָּוִד – אִיבַּדְתִּי כַּמָּה דָּוִד מִפָּנָיו.

The Gemara elaborates: **The Holy One, Blessed be He, said to David: David, do you recite a song over the fall of Saul? Had you been Saul**[N] **and he were David,** then **I would have destroyed many Davids before him.** Although I decreed that Saul's kingdom would not continue, as an individual he was far greater and more important than you.

הַיְינוּ דִּכְתִיב: "שִׁגָּיוֹן לְדָוִד אֲשֶׁר שָׁר לַה' עַל דִּבְרֵי כוּשׁ בֶּן יְמִינִי". וְכִי כּוּשׁ שְׁמוֹ? וַהֲלֹא שָׁאוּל שְׁמוֹ! אֶלָּא: מַה כּוּשִׁי מְשׁוּנֶּה בְּעוֹרוֹ – אַף שָׁאוּל מְשׁוּנֶּה בְּמַעֲשָׂיו.

The response to this admonishment **is** found in the verse, **as it is written: "Shiggaion of David, which he sang to the Lord, concerning the words of Cush the Benjaminite"** (Psalms 7:1). **Is Cush his name? Saul is his name.**[N] **Rather,** this is a designation that indicates: **Just as a Cushite,** a native of the ancient kingdom of Cush in eastern Africa, **is distinguished by his** dark **skin, so too, Saul was distinguished by his actions,**[N] as he was absolutely righteous and performed many good deeds. Therefore, David uses the word *shiggaion* as an allusion to the error [*shegia*] that he had made when he sang a song of praise over Saul's downfall.

כַּיּוֹצֵא בַּדָּבָר אַתָּה אוֹמֵר: "עַל אוֹדוֹת הָאִשָּׁה הַכּוּשִׁית אֲשֶׁר לָקָח". וְכִי כּוּשִׁית שְׁמָהּ? וַהֲלֹא צִיפּוֹרָה שְׁמָהּ! אֶלָּא: מַה כּוּשִׁית מְשׁוּנָּה בְּעוֹרָהּ – אַף צִיפּוֹרָה מְשׁוּנָּה בְּמַעֲשֶׂיהָ. כַּיּוֹצֵא בַּדָּבָר אַתָּה אוֹמֵר: "וַיִּשְׁמַע עֶבֶד מֶלֶךְ הַכּוּשִׁי". וְכִי כּוּשִׁי שְׁמוֹ? וַהֲלֹא צִדְקִיָּה שְׁמוֹ! אֶלָּא: מַה כּוּשִׁי מְשׁוּנֶּה בְּעוֹרוֹ – אַף צִדְקִיָּה מְשׁוּנֶּה בְּמַעֲשָׂיו.

The Gemara notes: **Similarly, you can explain** the verse: "And Miriam and Aaron spoke against Moses **due to the Cushite woman whom he had married,** for he had taken a Cushite woman" (Numbers 12:1). **But is her name Cushite? Zipporah is her name. Rather, just as a Cushite is distinguished by his** dark skin, **so too, Zipporah was distinguished by her actions.** The Gemara continues: **Similarly, you can explain** the verse: **"Now when Ebed-Melech the Cushite heard"** (Jeremiah 38:7). **Is his name Cushite? Zedekiah is his name. Rather, just as a Cushite is distinguished by his** dark **skin, so too, Zedekiah was distinguished by his** righteous **actions.**[N]

כַּיּוֹצֵא בַּדָּבָר אַתָּה אוֹמֵר: "הֲלֹא כִבְנֵי כוּשִׁיִּים אַתֶּם לִי בֵּית יִשְׂרָאֵל". וְכִי כּוּשִׁיִּים שְׁמָן? וַהֲלֹא יִשְׂרָאֵל שְׁמָן! אֶלָּא: מַה כּוּשִׁי מְשׁוּנֶּה בְּעוֹרוֹ – אַף יִשְׂרָאֵל מְשׁוּנִּין בְּמַעֲשֵׂיהֶן מִכָּל הָאוּמּוֹת.

Similarly, you can explain the verse: **"Are you not as much Mine as the children of the Cushites, O children of Israel?"** (Amos 9:7). **Is their name Cushite? Israel is their name. Rather, just as a Cushite stands out** because of **his dark skin, so too, the Jewish people are distinguished by their actions,** and they are different **from all the other nations.**

NOTES

Reading the portion – קָפְסֵיק סִידְרָא: It was customary for the Sages of the Talmud to divide the Bible into portions, so that they would complete all of the Bible in one year. This practice is similar to the current division of the Torah into weekly portions. Perhaps the Sages' division is parallel to the divisions that are used today (see *Talmid Rabbeinu Yeḥiel of Paris*).

Last, by inference there are first – אַחֲרוֹנִים, מִכְּלָל דְּאִיכָּא רִאשׁוֹנִים: According to Rashi, Zutra bar Toviyya asked: How can the verse write "these are the last words of David" (II Samuel 23:1), when "words of David" is a unique expression found only here in the Bible? Where is it possible to find other words of David? Where is similar language used?

Other commentaries understand that Zutra bar Toviyya assumes that the verse in II Samuel, chapter 23, actually refers back to the previous chapter, as the word "these" in "these are the last words of David" can function as a concluding remark on II Samuel, chapter 22, which is a song that David sang after he was saved from Saul. If this is the case, Zutra bar Toviyya asked: Where else did David speak about Saul (Ra'avad; *Tosefot HaRosh*)?

Alternatively, there are those who maintain that "the words of David" indicates prophecy. If so, Zutra bar Toviyya asked: Where is there another case where David relayed words that God had spoken to him, but the text does not explicitly say so (Ritva)?

Had you been Saul – אִלְמָלֵי אַתָּה שָׁאוּל: Many explain that this expression means: Had it not been an issue of destiny, Saul would have prevailed, as he surpassed you, David, in righteousness (Rashi). Some say: If you were Saul, meaning: If you were humble like Saul, then this attribute alone would tip the scale in your favor (see Rabbeinu Gershom *Meor HaGola*). Others say that were it not for the heavenly decree that you, David, would rule, then you would not have been worthy of inheriting the kingship from Saul (Rabbi Shlomo ben HaYatom). Similarly, others explain that were it not stated from the outset that David become king after Saul, then he would not have ruled. It is stated elsewhere in the Talmud that because of his prestigious lineage, Saul's rule did not continue, unlike David, whose lineage was questionable (*Yoma* 22b; Ran; *Tosefot HaRosh*). Others suggest that the tribe of Benjamin, to which Saul belonged, was not chosen to rule forever. Instead, David's tribe, the tribe of Judah, was designated to have lasting monarchy (*Iyyun Ya'akov*).

Cush and Saul – כּוּשׁ וְשָׁאוּל: Some explain that the names Cush and Kish are actually the same name, and the verse in Psalms alludes to Saul, son of Kish (*Talmid Rabbeinu Yeḥiel of Paris*).

Saul was distinguished by his actions – שָׁאוּל מְשׁוּנֶּה בְּמַעֲשָׂיו: Some explain that the term distinguished is referring to Saul's righteousness and humility. Others state that it points to the fact that he was physically outstanding, as he was extremely tall.

Similarly, some say that the term distinguished, in the case of Zipporah, is referring to her good deeds and modesty, while others claim that it points to her unique beauty (manuscript of Rashi; *HaKotev*).

Zedekiah was distinguished by his actions – צִדְקִיָּה מְשׁוּנֶּה בְּמַעֲשָׂיו: According to this explanation, the verse is read as follows: The servant [*eved*] of the king [*melekh*] called Cushite. Zedekiah was called this because he was righteous in a generation of wicked people (*Talmid Rabbeinu Yeḥiel of Paris*).

אָמַר רַבִּי שְׁמוּאֵל בַּר נַחְמָנִי אָמַר רַבִּי יוֹנָתָן: מַאי דִּכְתִיב: ״נְאֻם דָּוִד בֶּן יִשַׁי וּנְאֻם הַגֶּבֶר הוּקַם עָל״? נְאֻם דָּוִד בֶּן יִשַׁי, שֶׁהֵקִים עוּלָּהּ שֶׁל תְּשׁוּבָה.

§ Having mentioned the last words of David, the Gemara continues to explain other expressions in that passage. **Rabbi Shmuel bar Naḥmani said in the name of Rabbi Yonatan: What is** the meaning of that **which is written: "The saying of David, son of Yishai, and the saying of the man who was raised up on high [*al*]"** (II Samuel 23:1)? It means as follows: **The saying of David, son of Yishai, who raised the yoke of [*ulla*] repentance,**[N] as through his actions he taught the power of repentance. The word *al*, on high, and the word *ulla* are comprised of the same consonants in Hebrew.

״אָמַר אֱלֹהֵי יִשְׂרָאֵל לִי דִּבֶּר צוּר יִשְׂרָאֵל מוֹשֵׁל בָּאָדָם צַדִּיק מוֹשֵׁל יִרְאַת אֱלֹהִים״. מַאי קָאָמַר? אָמַר רַבִּי אַבָּהוּ, הָכִי קָאָמַר, אָמַר אֱלֹהֵי יִשְׂרָאֵל: לִי דִּבֶּר צוּר יִשְׂרָאֵל, אֲנִי מוֹשֵׁל בָּאָדָם. מִי מוֹשֵׁל בִּי? צַדִּיק, שֶׁאֲנִי גּוֹזֵר גְּזֵרָה וּמְבַטְּלָהּ.

The passage continues: **"The God of Israel said, the Rock of Israel spoke to me, He that rules over men must be righteous, ruling in the fear of God"** (II Samuel 23:3). The Gemara asks: **What is** this verse **saying?** What does it mean? **Rabbi Abbahu said: This is what** the verse **is saying: The God of Israel said, the Rock of Israel spoke to me:** Although **I rule over man, who rules over Me?** It is **a righteous person.** How is it possible to say that a righteous person rules over God, as it were? **As I,** God, **issue a decree** and the righteous person **nullifies it.**

״אֵלֶּה שְׁמוֹת הַגִּבּוֹרִים אֲשֶׁר לְדָוִד יוֹשֵׁב בַּשֶּׁבֶת״ וגו׳. מַאי קָאָמַר? אָמַר רַבִּי אַבָּהוּ, הָכִי קָאָמַר, וְאֵלֶּה שְׁמוֹת גְּבוּרוֹתָיו שֶׁל דָּוִד:

Similarly, the verse states there: **"These are the names of David's warriors; Josheb-Basshebeth** a Tahchemonite, chief of the captains; the same was Adino the Eznite; he raised his spear against eight hundred, whom he slew at one time" (II Samuel 23:8). The Gemara asks: **What is** this verse **saying? Rabbi Abbahu said: This is what** the verse **is saying: These are the names of the mighty actions of David.**[N] These expressions should not be read as names of people but instead as descriptions of David's good deeds.

״יוֹשֵׁב בַּשֶּׁבֶת״ – בְּשָׁעָה שֶׁהָיָה יוֹשֵׁב בִּישִׁיבָה לֹא הָיָה יוֹשֵׁב עַל גַּבֵּי כָּרִים וּכְסָתוֹת, אֶלָּא עַל גַּבֵּי קַרְקַע. דְּכָל כַּמָּה דַּהֲוָה רַבֵּיהּ עִירָא הַיָּאִירִי קַיָּים – הֲוָה מַתְנֵי לְהוּ לְרַבָּנָן עַל גַּבֵּי כָּרִים וּכְסָתוֹת, כִּי נַח נַפְשֵׁיהּ – הֲוָה מַתְנֵי דָּוִד לְרַבָּנַן, וַהֲוָה יָתֵיב עַל גַּבֵּי קַרְקַע. אֲמַרוּ לֵיהּ: לֵיתֵיב מָר אַכָּרִים וּכְסָתוֹת! לָא קַבֵּיל עֲלֵיהּ.

Josheb-Basshebeth [*yoshev bashevet*] indicates that **when** David **would sit** [*yoshev*] **in the study hall, he would not sit upon pillows and cushions,** as an important person ordinarily would. **Rather,** he would sit **on the ground** like one of the students. **For as long as** David's **teacher, Ira the Jairite, was alive,** Ira **would teach the Sages** while sitting **on pillows and cushions. When Ira passed away, David would teach the Sages, and he** did this while **sitting on the ground. They said to him: Master,** you **should sit upon pillows and blankets. He did not accept** their suggestions, since in his humility he did not wish to appear as the teacher of the Jewish people.

״תַּחְכְּמוֹנִי״ – אָמַר רַב: אָמַר לוֹ הַקָּדוֹשׁ בָּרוּךְ הוּא, הוֹאִיל וְהִשְׁפַּלְתָּ עַצְמְךָ – תְּהֵא כָּמוֹנִי, שֶׁאֲנִי גּוֹזֵר גְּזֵרָה – וְאַתָּה מְבַטְּלָהּ.

In this verse, David is described as **"a Tahchemonite [*taḥkemoni*]." Rav said: The Holy One, Blessed be He, said to him: Since you have humbled yourself, be you** now **like Me [*tehe kamoni*].** How so? **As I issue a decree, and you,** owing to your righteousness, **may nullify it.**

״רֹאשׁ הַשָּׁלִישִׁים״ – תְּהֵא רֹאשׁ לִשְׁלֹשֶׁת אָבוֹת. ״הוּא עֲדִינוֹ הָעֶצְנִי״ – כְּשֶׁהָיָה יוֹשֵׁב וְעוֹסֵק בַּתּוֹרָה – הָיָה מְעַדֵּן עַצְמוֹ כְּתוֹלַעַת; וּבְשָׁעָה שֶׁיּוֹצֵא לַמִּלְחָמָה – הָיָה מַקְשֶׁה עַצְמוֹ כְּעֵץ.

David is also described here as **"chief of the captains** [*rosh hashalishim*]" because God said to him: **You will be the head [*rosh*] of the three [*sheloshet*] Patriarchs.**[N] **"The same was Adino the Eznite";** this alludes to the fact that **when** David **would sit and occupy himself with Torah, he would make himself soft [*me'aden*] as a worm,**[N] **and when he would go out to war, he would make himself hard** and strong **as a tree [*etz*].**

״עַל שְׁמוֹנֶה מֵאוֹת חָלָל בְּפַעַם אֶחָת״ – שֶׁהָיָה זוֹרֵק חֵץ וּמַפִּיל שְׁמוֹנֶה מֵאוֹת חָלָל בְּפַעַם אַחַת, וְהָיָה מִתְאַנֵּחַ עַל מָאתַיִם. דִּכְתִיב: ״אֵיכָה יִרְדֹּף אֶחָד אֶלֶף״.

The expression: **"Against eight hundred people, which he slew at one time,"** means **that he would throw an arrow** in the air **and** with it **kill eight hundred people at one time. And** David **would sigh over the two hundred** who were missing from fulfillment of the Torah's promise, **as it is written: "How should one man chase a thousand"** (Deuteronomy 32:30).[N]

יָצְתָה בַּת קוֹל וְאָמְרָה: ״רַק בִּדְבַר אוּרִיָּה הַחִתִּי״.

A Divine Voice issued forth and said by way of explanation as to why the promise was not entirely fulfilled: "Because David did that which was right in the eyes of the Lord, and turned not aside from anything that He commanded him all the days of his life, **save only the matter of Uriah the Hittite"** (I Kings 15:5). Had David not committed this sin, then all of the promises mentioned in the Torah would have been fulfilled in their entirety through him.

NOTES

Who raised the yoke [*ulla*] of repentance – שֶׁהֵקִים עוּלָּהּ שֶׁל תְּשׁוּבָה: Some explain that the word *ulla* is related to the word *ol*, yoke, and repentance rested upon David like a yoke rests upon an ox (*Talmid Rabbeinu Yeḥiel of Paris*). In the manuscript of Rashi, it is understood that, according to this expression, David showed the *to'elet*, great power and value, of repentance.

These are the names of the mighty actions of David – אֵלֶּה שְׁמוֹת גְּבוּרוֹתָיו שֶׁל דָּוִד: It is possible to explain the names listed in the verse as descriptions as David himself because they do not sound like names of people, e.g., Josheb-Basshebeth a Tahchemonite (Ran).

Head of the three Patriarchs – רֹאשׁ לִשְׁלֹשֶׁת אָבוֹת: Rashi and others explain that in the future David will be listed before the three Patriarchs. Rabbi Shlomo ben HaYatom explains this to mean that David will be equivalent to the three Patriarchs. Just as in the *Amida* prayer, the first blessing concludes with: Shield of Abraham, so the Gemara states that the blessing recited after the *haftara*, the portion read from the Prophets, concludes with: Shield of David (*Pesaḥim* 117b). Lastly, there are those who explain that according to this statement, he will be the leader over the descendants of the three Patriarchs (Ran).

He would make himself soft [*me'aden*] as a worm – הָיָה מְעַדֵּן עַצְמוֹ כְּתוֹלַעַת: Some explain that this means that he would bend himself like a worm. David would bend his hands and legs almost like a link in a chain, and this meaning is alluded to in the verse: "Can you bind the chains [*ma'adannot*] of Pleiades" (Job 38:31; manuscript of Rashi). Others explain that this is related to the phrase "polluted garment" [*begged idin*] (Isaiah 64:5), which refers to a decomposing garment that is filled with worms (Ran).

How should one man chase a thousand – אֵיכָה יִרְדֹּף אֶחָד אֶלֶף: Although this verse speaks about the defeat of the Jews at the hands of other nations, God's goodness, when the Jewish people defeat their enemies, will certainly be even greater than this. Therefore, this verse will be fulfilled to an even greater degree when Jews act properly (manuscript of Rashi; see Maharsha).

אמר רבי תנחום בריה דרבי חייא איש כפר עכו אמר רבי יעקב בר אחא אמר רבי שמלאי, ואמרי לה אמר רבי תנחום אמר רב הונא, ואמרי לה אמר רב הונא לחודיה:

The Gemara returns to the *halakhot* of ostracism and mentions that **Rabbi Tanḥum, son of Rabbi Ḥiyya, of the village of Akko, said** that **Rabbi Ya'akov bar Aḥa said** that **Rabbi Simlai said, and** some **say** that this tradition was transmitted in the following manner: **Rabbi Tanḥum said** that **Rav Huna said, and** others **say** that **Rav Huna himself** made this statement without the chain of transmission:

Perek **III**
Daf **17** Amud **a**

תלמיד שנידה לכבודו – נדויו נידוי. דתניא: מנודה לרב – מנודה לתלמיד; מנודה לתלמיד – אינו מנודה לרב. לרב הוא דאינו מנודה, הא לכולי עלמא – מנודה.

If **a student ostracized** someone else **due to** an insult to **his dignity,** and not because the ostracized person was guilty of some transgression, **his** decree of **ostracism is valid, as it is taught** in a *baraita*: **One who is ostracized by the teacher is** considered **ostracized with regard to the student.** However, **one who is ostracized by the student is not** considered **ostracized with regard to the teacher.** The Gemara attempts to draw an inference from a careful reading of this *baraita*: **He is not** considered **ostracized with regard to the teacher,** which implies **that he is** considered **ostracized with regard to everyone** else.

למאי? אי במילי דשמיא – "אין חכמה ואין תבונה ואין עצה לנגד ה'"! אלא לאו – לכבוד עצמו?

The Gemara clarifies the case: **For what** reason was he ostracized? **If** it was **for a matter relating to Heaven,**[H] i.e., because he sinned, then why, if he was ostracized by the student, should he not be considered ostracized with regard to the teacher? Doesn't the verse state: **"There is no wisdom or understanding or counsel against the Lord"** (Proverbs 21:30)? This means that when a sin is committed and God's name is desecrated, all other considerations are ignored, even the eminence and knowledge of the teacher, and therefore he too must treat the offender as ostracized. **Rather, is it not** that the Gemara is referring to a case where the student ostracized the other person due to an insult **to his own dignity?** Therefore, it is apparent that his decree of ostracism is valid and binding upon all, with the exception of his teacher.

אמר רב יוסף: צורבא מרבנן עביד דינא לנפשיה במילתא דפסיקא ליה.

Rav Yosef said: A Torah scholar may execute judgment for himself[N] **with regard to a matter about which he is certain,**[H] and he is not required to first go to court and have the case decided for him. The same applies when another person behaves in a disrespectful manner toward him; he is permitted to go ahead on his own and ostracize him.

HALAKHA

For a matter relating to Heaven – במילי דשמיא: If one is ostracized over one of the matters that are normally punishable by ostracism, as opposed to acting disrespectfully toward a Torah scholar, then the *Nasi* and all the Jewish people are required to respect the decree of ostracism until it is nullified. This is the *halakha* even if the one who declared the ostracism is the least important person (*Shulḥan Arukh, Yoreh De'a* 334:17).

Ruling for himself – עושה דין לעצמו: One may rule for himself when he is certain that the *halakha* is in accordance with his opinion; however, the details of when and how this may be done are very complex (*Shulḥan Arukh, Hoshen Mishpat* 4).

NOTES

A Torah scholar may execute judgment for himself – צורבא מרבנן עביד דינא לנפשיה: Some explain that according to this statement, a Torah scholar may ostracize someone who owes him money, if the loan has not been repaid and it is clear that the *halakha* is in accordance with the opinion of the Torah scholar (Rid; Ran). However, many authorities disagree and say that this behavior could lead to a desecration of God's name. Instead, they explain that the statement in the Gemara is referring to a Torah scholar who ostracizes someone over his honor. If one acts disrespectfully concerning a matter that is explicitly prohibited, then the Torah scholar may ostracize him (Rabbeinu Ḥananel). Others add that in that case, all people must ostracize him (Rosh). Some say that this statement is not referring to ostracism at all; it is actually referring to the more general concept that one is permitted to determine his own ruling with regard to money that has been stolen from him, and he is not required to wait for the court to rule on the issue. If so, the only novel element of this statement is that it teaches that even a Torah scholar is permitted to act in this manner, although it is preferable for a Torah scholar to act generously and to go above and beyond what is strictly permitted by the *halakha* (Ritva; Ran).

הַהוּא צוּרְבָּא מֵרַבָּנַן דַּהֲווֹ סָנוּ שׁוּמְעָנֵיהּ. אֲמַר רַב יְהוּדָה: הֵיכִי לִיעֲבִיד? לְשַׁמְתֵּיהּ – צְרִיכִי לֵיהּ רַבָּנַן. לָא לְשַׁמְתֵּיהּ – קָא מִיתְחִיל שְׁמָא דִשְׁמַיָּא.

There was a certain Torah scholar who gained a bad reputation[N] due to rumors about his conduct. **Rav Yehuda**[P] **said: What should be done? To excommunicate him** is not an option. **The Sages need him,**[N] as he is a great Torah authority. **Not to excommunicate him** is also not an option, as then **the name of Heaven would be desecrated.**[N]

אֲמַר לֵיהּ לְרַבָּה בַּר בַּר חָנָה: מִידֵי שָׁמִיעַ לָךְ בְּהָא. אֲמַר לֵיהּ: הָכִי אֲמַר רַבִּי יוֹחָנָן, מַאי דִּכְתִיב: ״כִּי שִׂפְתֵי כֹהֵן יִשְׁמְרוּ דַעַת וְתוֹרָה יְבַקְשׁוּ מִפִּיהוּ כִּי מַלְאַךְ ה׳ צְבָאוֹת הוּא״? אִם דּוֹמֶה הָרַב לְמַלְאַךְ ה׳ – יְבַקְשׁוּ תוֹרָה מִפִּיו; וְאִם לָאו – אַל יְבַקְשׁוּ תוֹרָה מִפִּיו.

Rav Yehuda **said to Rabba bar bar Ḥana:** Have **you heard anything with regard to this** issue? **He said to him: Rabbi Yoḥanan said as follows: What is** the meaning of that **which is written: "For the priest's lips should keep knowledge, and they should seek Torah at his mouth; for he is a messenger** [*malakh*] **of the Lord of hosts"** (Malachi 2:7)? This verse teaches: **If the teacher is similar to an angel** [*malakh*] **of the Lord,** then **seek Torah from his mouth,** but if he is **not** pure and upright, then **do not seek Torah from his mouth;** even if he is knowledgeable about Torah, do not learn from him.[H]

שַׁמְתֵּיהּ רַב יְהוּדָה. לַסּוֹף אִיחֲלַשׁ רַב יְהוּדָה. אָתוּ רַבָּנַן לְשַׁיּוּלֵי בֵּיהּ, וַאֲתָא אִיהוּ נַמִי בַּהֲדַיְיהוּ. כַּד חַזְיֵיהּ רַב יְהוּדָה חַיֵּיךְ,

Based on this statement, **Rav Yehuda ostracized** that Torah scholar. **In the end,** after some time had passed, **Rav Yehuda took ill** and was on the verge of death. **The Sages came to inquire about his well-being, and** the ostracized scholar came along **with them as well. When Rav Yehuda saw him,** that scholar, **he laughed.**

אֲמַר לֵיהּ: לָא מִסְתַּיֵּיךְ דְּשַׁמְתֵּיהּ לְהַהוּא גַּבְרָא אֶלָּא אַחוּכֵי נַמִי חַיֵּיךְ בִּי?! אֲמַר לֵיהּ: לָאו בְּדִידָךְ מְחַיַּיכְנָא. אֶלָּא דְּכִי אָזְלִינָא לְהַהוּא עָלְמָא בְּדִיחָא דַּעֲתַאי, דַּאֲפִילּוּ לְגַבְרָא כְּוָותָךְ לָא חֲנִיפִי לֵיהּ.

The ostracized scholar **said to him: Was it not enough that you excommunicated that man,** i.e., me, **but** now **you** even **laugh at me?** Rav Yehuda **said to him: I was not laughing at you; rather, I am happy as I go to that** other **world that I did not flatter even** a great **man like you,** but instead I treated you fairly in accordance with the *halakha*.

נַח נַפְשֵׁיהּ דְּרַב יְהוּדָה. אֲתָא לְבֵי מִדְרְשָׁא אֲמַר לְהוּ: שְׁרוּ לִי! אֲמַרוּ לֵיהּ רַבָּנַן: גַּבְרָא דַּחֲשִׁיב כְּרַב יְהוּדָה לֵיכָּא הָכָא דְּלִישְׁרִי לָךְ. אֶלָּא זִיל לְגַבֵּיהּ דְּרַבִּי יְהוּדָה נְשִׂיאָה דְּלִישְׁרִי לָךְ. אֲזַל לְקַמֵּיהּ. אֲמַר לֵיהּ לְרַבִּי אַמִי: פּוּק עַיֵּין בְּדִינֵיהּ. אִי מִיבָּעֵי לְמִישְׁרֵא לֵיהּ – שְׁרֵי לֵיהּ.

Rav Yehuda died. The ostracized scholar **came to the study hall and said** to the Sages: **Release me** from the decree of ostracism. **The Sages said to him: There is no man here as eminent as Rav Yehuda who can release you** from the ostracism. **Rather, go to Rabbi Yehuda Nesia** in Eretz Yisrael, as only **he can release you.** That scholar **came before** Rabbi Yehuda Nesia. Rabbi Yehuda Nesia **said to Rabbi Ami: Go and examine his case. If it is necessary to release him** from his decree of ostracism, **release him** on my behalf.

עַיֵּין רַבִּי אַמִי בְּדִינֵיהּ. סְבַר לְמִישְׁרֵא לֵיהּ. עָמַד רַבִּי שְׁמוּאֵל בַּר נַחְמָנִי עַל רַגְלָיו וְאָמַר: וּמָה שִׁפְחָה שֶׁל בֵּית רַבִּי לֹא נָהֲגוּ חֲכָמִים קַלּוּת רֹאשׁ בְּנִידּוּיָהּ שָׁלֹשׁ שָׁנִים – יְהוּדָה חֲבֵירֵינוּ עַל אַחַת כַּמָּה וְכַמָּה!

Rabbi Ami examined his case and **thought** at first **to release him** from his ostracism. But **Rabbi Shmuel bar Naḥmani**[P] **rose up on his feet and said: If the maidservant in the house of Rabbi** Yehuda HaNasi once ostracized another person,[N] and **the Sages did not relate frivolously to her** decree of **ostracism** and did not revoke it until **three years** had passed, **all the more so, with regard to** a decree of ostracism placed by **Yehuda our colleague,** we must take it seriously and not release this scholar.

NOTES

Gained a bad reputation – דַּהֲווֹ סָנוּ שׁוּמְעָנֵיהּ: Some say that this Torah scholar engaged in activities that were not appropriate for one of his stature, e.g., frivolous song or studying heretical works (Rabbeinu Ḥananel). Most commentaries explain that he was accused of adultery or some other type of sexual immorality (*Talmid Rabbeinu Yeḥiel of Paris*; Commentary on *Moed Katan*; see *Tosafot*). The Ritva explains that the Torah scholar did not violate any Torah prohibition but instead was lenient or ignored rabbinic prohibitions, such as the *halakhot* pertaining to seclusion with a woman or other similar *halakhot*.

To excommunicate him is not an option, the Sages need him – לְשַׁמְתֵּיהּ צְרִיכִי לֵיהּ רַבָּנַן: The question is raised: Why would ostracizing him be a problem; it was already stated that one who has been ostracized may study and teach Torah? The Ritva explains that it would not be appropriate for the students to sit four cubits away from him, as was the practice for one who had been ostracized. Some learn from here that there is a distinction between standard ostracism [*niddui*] and a more severe form of ostracism [*shamta*]. Although it is permitted for one who has been ostracized to teach Torah, it is prohibited for one severely ostracized to teach Torah, and that decree does not lapse after thirty days (Rabbeinu Yehonatan of Lunel).

The name of Heaven would be desecrated – מִיתְחִיל שְׁמָא דִשְׁמַיָּא: God's name could be desecrated either because failing to excommunicate could teach others to be lenient with regard to prohibitions, or because others will claim that Torah scholars do not judge fairly and do not render the appropriate punishment for other Sages who have violated transgressions (*Talmid Rabbeinu Yeḥiel of Paris*).

The ostracism of Rabbi Yehuda HaNasi's maidservant – נִדּוּיָהּ שֶׁל אַמְתָּא דְּרַבִּי: The early authorities ask: Why was this decree of ostracism, and that of the Torah scholar, nullified only after a period of time had passed? Some say that ostracism cannot be nullified unless the one who has been ostracized abandons the sin for which he was ostracized. In this case, since he did not, his decree of ostracism could not be nullified (Rabbeinu Yehonatan of Lunel). Others say that ostracism cannot be nullified unless those who nullify it are of equal or greater stature than the one who initially declared the ostracism. In this case, Rabbi Yehuda HaNasi's maidservant was wise and sin fearing, and therefore it took a long time to find someone who could nullify the decree of ostracism that she had declared (Rosh, citing Ra'avad).

HALAKHA

A Torah scholar who sins – תַּלְמִיד חָכָם שֶׁסָּרַח: When a Torah scholar sins, the court does not rush to ostracize him; rather, they distance themselves from him. However, if he is liable to receive lashes for his sin, he may be punished in private. If he has earned a bad reputation by involving himself in prohibited matters, and his fellow scholars are embarrassed due to his behavior, and the name of Heaven is desecrated, then he should be ostracized (*Shulḥan Arukh*, *Yoreh De'a* 334:42).

PERSONALITIES

Rav Yehuda – רַב יְהוּדָה: Rav Yehuda bar Yeḥezkel was one of the great Babylonian Sages of the second generation of *amora'im*. He studied under both Rav and Shmuel. Shmuel's love and respect for Rav Yehuda were such that he often spoke highly of him and even remarked in admiration: This cannot be an ordinary mortal. Following Shmuel's death, Rav Yehuda was appointed head of the Neharde'a academy in his stead. He moved the academy to his hometown of Pumbedita, where it remained for over seven hundred years, producing many prominent Sages.

Rav Yehuda's life was devoted entirely to Torah study, and he lived in poverty until he was instated as head of the academy. Most of scholars of the third generation of *amora'im* were Rav Yehuda's students, including his son, Rav Yitzhak. Even those who studied in the academy in Sura became his students after the death of Rav Huna, head of that academy.

Though Rav Yehuda believed that there are biblical verses prohibiting one from moving to Eretz Yisrael from Babylonia, he was well known for his love of Eretz Yisrael. The majority of his students moved there and became leading *amora'im* of Eretz Yisrael.

Rabbi Shmuel bar Naḥmani – רַבִּי שְׁמוּאֵל בַּר נַחְמָנִי: Rabbi Shmuel bar Naḥmani was an *amora* in Eretz Yisrael during the second to third generation of *amora'im* there. He was probably born in Eretz Yisrael, however he may have also spent some time in Babylonia. He was a main student of the *amora* Rabbi Yoḥanan, but he also studied under Rabbi Yehoshua ben Levi. He was considered to be one of the greatest scholars of *aggada* in the Talmud. He was one of the best known masters of *aggada* of his generation. His statements appear throughout the Jerusalem Talmud and other midrashic literature.

Rabbi Shmuel bar Naḥmani also made halakhic statements, which were transmitted by other Sages. It was primarily the students of Rabbi Yoḥanan who asked him different questions and transmitted Torah statements in his name. Additionally, Rabbi Shmuel bar Naḥmani had a unique status in that he was one of the few Sages who knew the secret of the movement of celestial bodies, necessary for calculating the New Moon. He was called: One of the great men of the generation. He also represented the Jewish people before the Roman Emperor Diocletian.

Rabbi Shmuel bar Naḥmani lived to a very old age, until the time when Rabbi Ami was the head of the study hall, when he no longer was able to go there regularly. However, it appears that he had his own personal study hall, in which the emphasis may have been more on the study of *aggada*.

BACKGROUND

A wasp came and stung him – אֲתָא זִיבּוּרָא וּטְרַקֵיהּ: A wasp sting is very painful, and in a sensitive area this pain is even greater. Approximately one percent of the population is allergic to these stings and the poison injected through the stinger. For such people, even one sting is dangerous and without quick treatment may lead to death.

Wasp stinger with dripping venom about to enter human skin

HALAKHA

One who strikes an adult son – הַמַּכֶּה בְּנוֹ הַגָּדוֹל: A father who strikes his grown child is ostracized for transgressing the prohibition: "You shall not place a stumbling block before the blind." According to some, one's child is an adult child from the age of twenty-two; others say from the age of twenty-four (*Shulḥan Arukh, Yoreh De'a* 334:43).

אֲמַר רַבִּי זֵירָא: מַאי דְּקַמָּן דַּאֲתָא הָאִידָּנָא הַאי סָבָא בְּבֵי מִדְרָשָׁא, דְּהָא כַּמָּה שָׁנֵי לָא אֲתָא. שְׁמַע מִינָּהּ לָא מִיבָּעֵי לְמִישְׁרָא לֵיהּ. לָא שְׁרָא לֵיהּ. נְפַק כִּי קָא בָּכֵי וְאָזֵיל.

Rabbi Zeira said: What caused **this Elder,** Rabbi Shmuel bar Naḥmani, **to come before us in the study hall** today **though for many years he did not come,** and now he comes precisely during this discussion. **Learn from this** that **it is not necessary to release him** from his decree of ostracism, as this combination of events is certainly not a coincidence. Rather, it should be viewed as an instructive sign from Heaven. Consequently, Rabbi Ami **did not release him** from the ostracism, and the ostracized scholar **left in tears.**

אֲתָא זִיבּוּרָא וּטְרַקֵיהּ אַאַמְּתֵיהּ, וּשְׁכֵיב. עַיְּילוּהוּ לִמְעָרְתָּא דַּחֲסִידֵי – וְלָא קִיבְּלוּהוּ. עַיְּילוּהוּ לִמְעָרְתָּא דְּדַיָּינֵי – וְקִיבְּלוּהוּ.

A wasp came and stung the ostracized scholar[B] **on his penis**[N] **and he died.** Because he was a great Torah scholar, **they took him into the caves in which the pious** are interred in order to bury him there, **but** the caves **did not accept him.** A snake stood at the entrance of the caves and did not let them pass. **They** then **took him into the caves of the judges, and they accepted him.**

מַאי טַעְמָא? דַּעֲבַד כְּרַבִּי אִילְעַאי. דְּתַנְיָא, רַבִּי אִילְעַאי אוֹמֵר: אִם רוֹאֶה אָדָם שֶׁיִּצְרוֹ מִתְגַּבֵּר עָלָיו – יֵלֵךְ לְמָקוֹם שֶׁאֵין מַכִּירִין אוֹתוֹ, וְיִלְבַּשׁ שְׁחוֹרִים וְיִתְעַטֵּף שְׁחוֹרִים, וְיַעֲשֶׂה מַה שֶּׁלִּבּוֹ חָפֵץ, וְאַל יְחַלֵּל שֵׁם שָׁמַיִם בְּפַרְהֶסְיָא.

The Gemara asks: **What is the reason** that he was accepted there? The Gemara answers: Even though he sinned, **he** still **acted in accordance with** the opinion of **Rabbi Ilai,**[N] **as it is taught** in a *baraita*: **Rabbi Ilai says: If a person sees that his** evil **inclination is gaining control over him** and he cannot overcome it, then **he should go to a place where he is not known. He should wear black, and he should wrap his** head **in black,** as if he were a mourner. Perhaps these changes will influence him, so that he not sin. Even if these actions do not help, **he should** at least **do as his heart desires** in private **and not desecrate the name of Heaven in public.**[N] Although this person had sinned, he did so in private and in a manner that did not publicly desecrate God's name, and therefore it was fitting that he be given an honorable burial.

שִׁפְחָה שֶׁל בֵּית רַבִּי מַאי הִיא? דְּאַמְתָא דְּבֵי רַבִּי חֲזִיתֵיהּ לְהַהוּא גַּבְרָא דַּהֲוָה מָחֵי לִבְנוֹ גָּדוֹל. אֲמַרָה: לֶיהֱוֵי הַהוּא גַּבְרָא בְּשַׁמְתָּא, דְּקָעָבַר מִשּׁוּם: ״וְלִפְנֵי עִוֵּר לֹא תִתֵּן מִכְשׁוֹל״. דְּתַנְיָא: ״וְלִפְנֵי עִוֵּר לֹא תִתֵּן מִכְשׁוֹל״ – בְּמַכֶּה לִבְנוֹ גָּדוֹל הַכָּתוּב מְדַבֵּר.

The Gemara asks: **What is** the story mentioned by Rabbi Shmuel bar Naḥmani involving **the maidservant in the house of Rabbi** Yehuda HaNasi? It was related **that the maidservant in Rabbi** Yehuda HaNasi's **house saw a certain man who was striking his adult son.**[H] **She said: Let that man be excommunicated, due to** the fact that **he has transgressed** the injunction: **"You shall not place a stumbling block before the blind"** (Leviticus 19:14), **as it is taught** in a *baraita* that the verse states: **"You shall not place a stumbling block before the blind,"** and **the verse speaks** here **of one who strikes his adult son,** as the son is likely to become angry and strike his father back, thereby transgressing the severe prohibition against hitting one's parent.

NOTES

Stung him on his penis [*ametei*] – וּטְרַקֵיהּ אַאַמְּתֵיהּ: Some explain that he was stung on his hand (Ritva), and others have a version of the talmudic text containing the word forehead [*aputei*] (Rabbi Shlomo ben HaYatom).

He acted in accordance with Rabbi Ilai – דַּעֲבַד כְּרַבִּי אִילְעַאי: There are various versions of this text, and consequently there are also many explanations of it. Some say that the question is why the unnamed ostracized scholar was not taken into the cave of the pious. The Gemara answers that this was because he did not act in accordance with Rabbi Ilai, but sinned in his home town. This is based on a version of the text that reads: Because he transgressed the opinion of Rabbi Ilai.

Others understand this Gemara in the opposite way. According to them, the Gemara asks why he was taken into the cave of judges. In response to this question, the Gemara answers that he acted in accordance with Rabbi Ilai. In fact, there are those who say that even if one acts in accordance with Rabbi Ilai but does not overcome his evil inclination, he is not considered to be pious (see *Talmid Rabbeinu Yeḥiel of Paris*; Rabbeinu Yehonatan of Lunel).

One whose evil inclination is gaining control over him – מִי שֶׁיִּצְרוֹ מִתְגַּבֵּר עָלָיו: Rabbeinu Ḥananel explains in the name of the *ge'onim* that this directive does not refer to one who intends to violate actual transgressions. Rather, it applies to someone who plans to enjoy pleasures or spend time in places that the Sages do not approve of. In that case, it is preferable that one who can no longer control himself go to a different place, where he is not known.

Many note, in the name of Rav Hai Gaon, that Rabbi Ilai does not claim that it is permitted for one to sin. Rather, he claims that if one goes to a different place and wears black, which is mourner's clothing, then he will be able to overcome his evil inclination. Similarly, others write that the hassle of traveling will reduce his inclination (Rabbeinu Yehonatan of Lunel). Alternatively, if he goes to a place where he is a stranger and is not respected, he will be humbled (*Talmid Rabbeinu Yeḥiel of Paris*; Rabbeinu Yehonatan of Lunel).

רֵישׁ לָקִישׁ הֲוָה מְנַטֵּר פַּרְדֵּיסָא. אֲתָא הַהוּא גַּבְרָא וְקָאָכֵיל תְּאֵינֵי. רְמָא בֵּיהּ קָלָא, וְלָא אַשְׁגַּח בֵּיהּ. אֲמַר: לֶיהֱוֵי הַהוּא גַּבְרָא בְּשַׁמְתָּא. אֲמַר לֵיהּ: אַדְּרַבָּה, לֶיהֱוֵי הַהוּא גַּבְרָא בְּשַׁמְתָּא! אִם מָמוֹן נִתְחַיַּיבְתִּי לְךָ – נִידּוּי מִי נִתְחַיַּיבְתִּי לְךָ?

Similarly, it was related that **Reish Lakish**[P] **was guarding an orchard** for payment when **a certain man came and ate** some **figs** that were growing there. Reish Lakish **raised his voice** and yelled at him, **but** this man **paid no attention to him** and kept eating. Reish Lakish **said: Let that man be** in a state of **excommunication.** The man eating the figs **said to him: On the contrary, let that man,** i.e., Reish Lakish, **be** in a state of **excommunication,** for even **if I have become liable to you for payment,** as I have eaten of the figs without permission, **have I become liable to you for excommuncation?**[N] With that statement, the man left.

אֲתָא לְבֵי מִדְרְשָׁא. אֲמַר לֵיהּ: שֶׁלּוֹ – נִידּוּי; שֶׁלְּךָ – אֵינוֹ נִידּוּי.

Reish Lakish **went to the study hall** to inquire about the *halakha* with regard to this man. The other Sages **said to him: His** decree of **ostracism is** valid, but **your** decree of **ostracism is not.**[H] In other words, that man was correct and Reish Lakish should not have ostracized him in response to his actions.

וּמַאי תַּקַּנְתֵּיהּ? זִיל לְגַבֵּיהּ דְּלִישְׁרֵי לָךְ. לָא יָדַעְנָא לֵיהּ. אֲמַרוּ לֵיהּ: זִיל לְגַבֵּי נְשִׂיאָה דְּלִישְׁרֵי לָךְ, דְּתַנְיָא: נִידּוּהוּ וְאֵינוֹ יוֹדֵעַ מִי נִידָּהוּ – יֵלֵךְ אֵצֶל נָשִׂיא, וְיַתִּיר לוֹ נִדּוּיוֹ.

Reish Lakish then asked: If so, **what is the remedy** for this decree of ostracism? The Sages answered him: **Go to him so that he may release you** from it. Reish Lakish replied: **I do not know him. They said to him:** Go then **to the** ***Nasi*****, so that he may release you** from the ban, **as it is taught** in a *baraita*: If one **was ostracized, but he does not know who ostracized him,**[H] **he should go to the** ***Nasi*****,** and the *Nasi* **may release** him from **his** decree of **ostracism.**

אָמַר רַב הוּנָא, בְּאוּשָׁא הִתְקִינוּ: אַב בֵּית דִּין שֶׁסָּרַח – אֵין מְנַדִּין אוֹתוֹ, אֶלָּא אוֹמֵר לוֹ: ״הִכָּבֵד וְשֵׁב בְּבֵיתֶךָ״. חָזַר וְסָרַח – מְנַדִּין אוֹתוֹ, מִפְּנֵי חִילּוּל הַשֵּׁם.

The Gemara continues: **Rav Huna said** that **in Usha it was enacted:** If **the president of the court sinned,**[H] **he is not ostracized.** Although this would be the appropriate punishment, he is not ostracized, so as not to cause a desecration of God's name. **Rather,** they **say to him** the words of the verse: **"Keep your honor and stay at home"** (II Kings 14:10).[N] That is to say, to preserve your dignity, it would be best if you were to stay at home, resign your position, and refrain from further public appearances. If **he sins again, he is ostracized, due to the desecration of God's name** that would ensue were people to think that he was spared his rightful punishment due to his high position.

וּפְלִיגָא דְּרֵישׁ לָקִישׁ. דְּאָמַר רֵישׁ לָקִישׁ: תַּלְמִיד חָכָם שֶׁסָּרַח – אֵין מְנַדִּין אוֹתוֹ בְּפַרְהֶסְיָא, שֶׁנֶּאֱמַר: ״וְכָשַׁלְתָּ הַיּוֹם וְכָשַׁל גַּם נָבִיא עִמְּךָ לָיְלָה״ – כַּסֵּהוּ כַּלַּיְלָה.

The Gemara comments: This opinion **disagrees with** that of **Reish Lakish,** for **Reish Lakish said: If a Torah scholar sins, he is not ostracized** at all **in public, as it is stated: "Therefore, shall you fall in the day, and the prophet also shall fall with you in the night"** (Hosea 4:5). This is explained to mean: If a prophet or any other important person sins, his offense **should be concealed like the night** and not punished in public.

מָר זוּטְרָא חֲסִידָא, כִּי מִיחַיַּיב צוּרְבָא מֵרַבָּנַן שַׁמְתָּא – בְּרֵישָׁא מְשַׁמֵּית נַפְשֵׁיהּ, וַהֲדַר מְשַׁמֵּית לְדִידֵיהּ. כִּי הֲוָה עָיֵיל בְּאוּשְׁפִּיזֵיהּ – שָׁרֵי לֵיהּ לְנַפְשֵׁיהּ וַהֲדַר שָׁרֵי לֵיהּ לְדִידֵיהּ.

With regard to this issue, it was related that **when a Torah scholar would become liable** to be punished with **excommunication before Mar Zutra the Pious,** Mar Zutra **would first excommunicate himself**[N] as a mark of respect for the Torah scholar, **and afterward he would ostracize** the Torah scholar. This self-imposed excommunication was meant only as a show of honor to the other Torah scholar, and therefore **when** Mar Zutra **would enter his house** of lodging, **he would release his** own excommunication, **and afterward he would release** the other's excommunication.

PERSONALITIES

Reish Lakish – רֵישׁ לָקִישׁ: Rabbi Shimon ben Lakish, typically referred to as Reish Lakish, was among the greatest *amora'im* in Eretz Yisrael. He was the friend and brother-in-law of Rabbi Yoḥanan.

Reish Lakish had an amazing life story. He studied Torah from a young age, but, perhaps due to dire financial straits, he sold himself to a Roman circus as a gladiator. There are many stories in the Talmud that attest to his great strength. Sometime later, after meeting Rabbi Yoḥanan, he resumed his Torah study, first as a student of Rabbi Yoḥanan, then as a friend and colleague. He married Rabbi Yoḥanan's sister.

The Talmud records many halakhic disagreements between Reish Lakish and Rabbi Yoḥanan with regard to central issues of *halakha*. Rabbi Yoḥanan treated him with great respect, often saying: My peer disagrees with me. Reish Lakish was known for his strict piety, to the extent that anyone who was seen conversing in public with Reish Lakish was said to be able to borrow money without guarantors, as Reish Lakish only associated with people beyond reproach. When he died, he was survived by his wife and son, who was a child prodigy.

NOTES

The ostracism that Reish Lakish declared – נִדּוּיוֹ שֶׁל רֵישׁ לָקִישׁ: Several questions are asked with regard to this incident. Apparently this person was a thief; why, then, was he not deserving of ostracism? Some say that the common practice in this place was to take fruit and pay afterward (see *Tosafot*). Others explain that Reish Lakish would have been permitted to ostracize the thief before he stole, but not after he had already stolen, when instead Reish Lakish could take him to court and sue for damages (Rosh).

With regard to the ostracism introduced by the phrase: On the contrary, there are those who claim that the ostracism has an impact only when directed toward an important person. Similarly, in the Jerusalem Talmud this story is told somewhat differently. According to that version, those stealing the figs were bandits, and it was Reish Lakish himself who was unsure if it was appropriate to ostracize them. These differences serve as the basis for the dispute between the Babylonian and Jerusalem Talmud with regard to this *halakha*.

Keep your honor and stay at home – הִכָּבֵד וְשֵׁב בְּבֵיתֶךָ: Some explain that the president of the court is essentially ostracized, however the court does not make explicit reference to it. Rather, they allude to it by encouraging him to remain at home and not leave (Rabbeinu Yehonatan of Lunel; Ran).

He would first excommunicate himself – בְּרֵישָׁא מְשַׁמֵּית נַפְשֵׁיהּ: Some write that this was the common practice when it was necessary to ostracize an important person. The one who would pronounce the ostracism would first ostracize himself, so that he would not cause additional embarrassment to the one being ostracized (Commentary on *Moed Katan*). Some say that the expression: When he would enter his house of lodging, is referring not to Mar Zutra, but to the one who had been ostracized, and his decree of ostracism would be nullified before he returned to his residence (*Talmid Rabbeinu Yeḥiel of Paris*).

HALAKHA

One who incorrectly ostracizes – הַמְנַדֶּה שֶׁלֹּא כַּדִּין: If one ostracizes another without a proper basis for doing so, and the second person says to him: On the contrary you are ostracized, then the first is ostracized. This is the *halakha* provided that the second person who declared the ostracism is an important person, even if he is not a Torah scholar (Rema). This is also the case if the first does not know who this second person is, and there is a chance that he is an important person. However, if the second person is not a Torah scholar or a Torah student, then he cannot say: On the contrary, etc. If the first person only stated that the act is punishable by ostracism, and the second person responded: On the contrary, etc., then the first person is not ostracized. The reason for this is because the first person did not explicitly ostracize the second (*Shulḥan Arukh, Yoreh De'a* 334:39, and in the comment of Rema).

If one was ostracized and does not know who ostracized him – נִידּוּהוּ וְאֵינוֹ יוֹדֵעַ מִי נִידָּהוּ: If one was ostracized but does not know who ostracized him, then he should go to the *Nasi* to have his decree of ostracism nullified (Rambam *Sefer HaMadda, Hilkhot Talmud Torah* 7:10).

If the president of the court sinned – אַב בֵּית דִּין שֶׁסָּרַח: If the head of a court or an eminent Torah scholar sins, he should not be publicly ostracized unless he committed major transgressions and is leading other members of the community astray, like Jeroboam ben Nebat. If he repents but commits other sins, then he should be punished with lashes in private (*Shulḥan Arukh, Yoreh De'a* 334:42).

אָמַר רַב גִּידֵּל אָמַר רַב: תַּלְמִיד חָכָם מְנַדֶּה לְעַצְמוֹ, וּמֵיפֵר לְעַצְמוֹ. אֲמַר רַב פַּפָּא: תֵּיתֵי לִי דְּלָא שַׁמִּיתִי צוּרְבָא מֵרַבָּנַן מֵעוֹלָם. אֶלָּא, כִּי קָא מִיחַיַּיב צוּרְבָא מֵרַבָּנַן שַׁמְתָּא הֵיכִי עָבֵיד? כִּי הָא, דִּבְמַעַרְבָא מִימְנוּ אַנְּגִידָא דְּצוּרְבָא מֵרַבָּנַן וְלָא מִימְנוּ אַשַּׁמְתָּא.

Rav Giddel said that **Rav said: A Torah scholar may ostracize himself,**[N] **and he may** similarly **release himself** from self-imposed ostracism.[H] **Rav Pappa said: I have good coming to me,** for I am praiseworthy, **as I have never ostracized a Torah scholar.** The Gemara asks about this: **If so, when a Torah scholar was liable to be ostracized, what would he do?** The Gemara answers: He did **as they do in the West,** Eretz Yisrael, where **they appoint** a court **to give a Torah scholar lashes, but they do not appoint** a court **to ostracize him.** That is to say, lashes were preferred over ostracism.

מַאי שַׁמְתָּא? אָמַר רַב: שָׁם מִיתָה. וּשְׁמוּאֵל אָמַר: שְׁמָמָה יִהְיֶה, וּמְהַנְיָא בֵּיהּ כִּי טִיחְיָא בְּתַנּוּרָא.

The Gemara proceeds with a discussion that explains the severity of the punishment of excommunication: **What** is the meaning of the word **excommunication** [*shamta*]?[L] **Rav said:** This word is a contraction of the expression **there is death** [*sham mita*], alluding to the deathly aspect of excommunication. **And Shmuel said:** *Shamta* means that **he will be a desolation** [*shemama yiheyeh*], **and it is effective upon him like fat** smeared **on an oven.** Just as some of the fat will always remain absorbed in the walls of the oven, so too some aspect of the curse contained in the excommunication will continue to adhere to him even after the excommunication has been nullified.

וּפְלִיגָא דְּרֵישׁ לָקִישׁ. דְּאָמַר רֵישׁ לָקִישׁ: כְּשֵׁם שֶׁנִּכְנֶסֶת בְּמָאתַיִם וְאַרְבָּעִים וּשְׁמוֹנָה אֵיבָרִים, כָּךְ כְּשֶׁהִיא יוֹצְאָה – יוֹצְאָה מִמָּאתַיִם וְאַרְבָּעִים וּשְׁמוֹנָה אֵיבָרִים.

The Gemara comments: **And** this opinion **disagrees with** the opinion of **Reish Lakish, for Reish Lakish said: Just as** ostracism **enters the two hundred and forty-eight organs** of one's body when it is first pronounced, **so too when it leaves, it leaves from** his **two hundred and forty-eight organs.**

כְּשֶׁהִיא נִכְנֶסֶת – דִּכְתִיב: ״וְהָיְתָה הָעִיר חֵרֶם״, ״חֵרֶם״ בְּגִימַטְרִיָּא מָאתַיִם וְאַרְבְּעִים וּשְׁמוֹנָה הָווּ. כְּשֶׁהִיא יוֹצְאָה – דִּכְתִיב: ״בְּרוֹגֶז רַחֵם תִּזְכּוֹר״ ״רַחֵם״ בְּגִימַטְרִיָּא הָכִי הָווּ.

The following allusion is offered in support of the opinion of Reish Lakish: **When it enters,** it enters all the organs, **as it is written: "And the city shall be a curse [*ḥerem*]"** (Joshua 6:17),[N] **and the numerical value [*gimatriyya*]**[L] of the word ***ḥerem*,** a concept similar to ostracism, **is two hundred and forty-eight.** Therefore, the verse alludes to the fact that a decree of ostracism penetrates one's two hundred and forty-eight organs. **When it leaves,** it leaves all the organs, **as it is written: "In wrath remember mercy [*raḥem*]"** (Habakkuk 3:2), **and the numerical value** of the word ***raḥem* is also** two hundred and forty-eight, thereby teaching that when the decree of ostracism is revoked, it disappears entirely.

אֲמַר רַב יוֹסֵף: שְׁדֵי שַׁמְתָּא אַגְּנוּבְתָּא דְּכַלְבָּא – וְאִיהִי דִּידָהּ עַבְדָה. דְּהַהוּא כַּלְבָּא דַּהֲוָה אָכִיל מְסָאנֵי דְּרַבָּנָן, וְלָא הָווּ קָא יָדְעִי מַנּוּ. וְשַׁמְתּוּ לֵיהּ. אִיתְלִי בֵּיהּ נוּרָא בִּגְנוּבְתֵּיהּ, וַאֲכַלְתֵּיהּ.

The Gemara continues discussing the power of a ban. **Rav Yosef said: Cast an excommunication on the tail of a dog and it,** the excommunication, **will do its work** and harm the dog. It was related that there was **a certain dog that would eat the shoes of the Sages, and they did not know who it was** causing this damage. They thought that it was a person, **and so they excommunicated** whoever was doing it. Soon thereafter, the dog's **tail caught fire and got burnt.** This shows that excommunication can have a harmful effect even on a dog.

הַהוּא אַלָּמָא דַּהֲוָה קָא מְצַעַר לֵיהּ לְהַהוּא צוּרְבָא מֵרַבָּנָן. אֲתָא לְקַמֵּיהּ דְּרַב יוֹסֵף. אֲמַר לֵיהּ: זִיל שַׁמְתֵּיהּ. אֲמַר לֵיהּ: מִסְתְּפִינָא מִינֵּיהּ.

It was further related that there was **a violent person who** caused **suffering to a certain Torah scholar.** This Torah scholar **came before Rav Yosef** to ask what he should do. Rav Yosef **said to him: Go and ostracize him.** This Torah scholar **said to him: I am afraid of him,** that he will harass me even more.

אֲמַר לֵיהּ: שְׁקִילִי פְּתִיחָא עֲלֵיהּ. כׇּל שֶׁכֵּן דְּמִסְתְּפִינָא מִינֵּיהּ. אֲמַר לֵיהּ: שְׁקַלֵיהּ אַחֲתֵיהּ בְּכַדָּא,

Rav Yosef **said to him: Take** out, i.e., publish **a written** ostracism **against him.**[B] The Torah scholar said to him: **All the more so I am fearful of him,** for if I publicize the matter he will certainly come after me. Rav Yosef **said to him** to do as follows: **Take the** written ostracism **and place it in a jug,**

NOTES

Ostracizes himself [*le'atzmo*] – מְנַדֶּה לְעַצְמוֹ: The word *le'atzmo* is explained in two ways. Some say it means that he ostracized himself. Others say that it means he may ostracize someone else for his own sake or due to his honor (Rashi manuscript).

And the city shall be a curse [*ḥerem*] – וְהָיְתָה הָעִיר חֵרֶם: The Maharsha comments that the word *ḥerem* is used many times earlier in the Bible, and therefore he asks why the Gemara specifically quotes the verse from the book of Joshua. He explains that the verse's indirect reference to the inhabitants with the word "city" indicates that there is something to be derived from it. He goes on to explain that the Gemara understands the word "city" here as an allusion to the body. Therefore, it is befitting to use this specific verse in a discussion with regard to *ḥerem* and the body. The *Iyyun Ya'akov* explains more simply that this is the first place where the enactment of such a *ḥerem* is found in the Bible.

HALAKHA

A Torah scholar may ostracize himself, and he may release himself – תַּלְמִיד חָכָם מְנַדֶּה לְעַצְמוֹ וּמֵיפֵר לְעַצְמוֹ: A Torah scholar can ostracize himself and release himself from ostracism, even if he was ostracized at the instruction of someone else, or was ostracized because he had sinned. Some say that if he was liable to be ostracized and is deserving of this punishment, he cannot release himself from ostracism (*Shulḥan Arukh, Yoreh De'a* 334:33).

LANGUAGE

Excommunication [*shamta*] – שַׁמְתָּא: This word is Aramaic and means to ostracize or to excommunicate. The explanations offered by the Sages for this word are not meant to teach about its etymology, but rather are meant to allude to the severity of ostracism.

Numerical value [*gimatriyya*] – גִּימַטְרִיָּא: From the Greek γεωμετρία, *geometria*, which means measurement or calculation in general, although it later came to refer to a specific type of calculation. In rabbinic literature, it also refers broadly to mathematical calculations, and specifically for tabulating the numerical value of the letters.

BACKGROUND

Document of ostracism – פְּתִיחָא: The *ge'onim*, who had a tradition with regard to this matter, understood that this is a document written for someone who refuses to appear in court or pay what he owes. It is given this name because it is the first document that the court writes for him. If, after some time, he still does not obey the court's orders, they then write a document of excommunication, which is more severe than the initial document of ostracism (see *Bava Kama* 112b).

וְאַחֲתֵיהּ בֵּי קִבְרֵי, וּקְרֵי בֵּיהּ אַלְפָּא שִׁפּוּרֵי בְּאַרְבָּעִין יוֹמִין. אֲזַיל עֲבֵיד הָכִי. פְּקַע כַּדָּא, וּמִית אַלָּמָא. מַאי שִׁפּוּרֵי? שֶׁנִּפְרָעִין מִמֶּנּוּ.

and set it down in a cemetery,[N] where nobody is found, **and sound a thousand,** i.e., many, ***shofar*** **blasts over the course of forty days.**[N] That man **went and did this. The jug burst and the violent man died.** The Gemara asks: **What** is the reason that ***shofarot*** are sounded when a decree of ostracism is pronounced? The *shofarot* allude to the fact **that they extract punishment** [*shenifra'in*] **from** the excommunicated person.

מַאי תַּבְרָא? אָמַר רַב יִצְחָק בְּרֵיהּ דְּרַב יְהוּדָה: תַּבְרֵי בָּתֵּי רָמֵי. דְּתַנְיָא, אָמַר רַבָּן שִׁמְעוֹן בֶּן גַּמְלִיאֵל: כָּל מָקוֹם שֶׁנָּתְנוּ חֲכָמִים עֵינֵיהֶם – אוֹ מִיתָה אוֹ עוֹנִי.

The Gemara asks further: **What** is the reason that **broken** blasts are sounded on the *shofar* when the excommunication is pronounced? **Rav Yitzḥak, son of Rav Yehuda, said: It breaks tall buildings,**[N] i.e., a decree of ostracism can harm and break even the high and mighty, **as it is taught** in a *baraita*: **Rabban Shimon ben Gamliel said: Wherever** it says that **the Sages set their eyes** in anger upon a particular person, it causes **either death or poverty.**

״וְהַנָּזִיר וְהַמְּצוֹרָע מִטּוּמְאָתוֹ לְטָהֳרָתוֹ״. בְּעָא מִינֵּיהּ רַבִּי יִרְמְיָה מֵרַבִּי זֵירָא: בְּשֶׁלֹּא הָיָה לָהֶם פְּנַאי, אוֹ דִּלְמָא אַף בְּשֶׁהָיָה לָהֶם פְּנַאי?

§ It is taught in the mishna: **And the nazirite** whose term of naziriteship ended on the intermediate days of a Festival, **and the leper** who needs to purify himself on the intermediate days and must shave his entire body in order to leave **his** state of ritual **impurity** and regain **his** ritual **purity,** these people are permitted to cut their hair on the intermediate days of the Festival because they were not able to do so on the eve of the Festival. **Rabbi Yirmeya raised a question before Rabbi Zeira:** Is this allowance limited to the case **where they did not have the time** to cut their hair before the Festival, as it was prohibited for them to do so beforehand? **Or perhaps** they may cut their hair **even** in a case **where they had the time** to do so beforehand.

אֲמַר לֵיהּ: תַּנֵּינָא, כָּל אֵלּוּ שֶׁאָמְרוּ מוּתָּרִין לְגַלֵּחַ בַּמּוֹעֵד – בְּשֶׁלֹּא הָיָה לָהֶם פְּנַאי, אֲבָל הָיָה לָהֶם פְּנַאי – אֲסוּרִים.

He said to him: We already **learned** this in a *baraita*: With regard to **all those** about whom **the** Sages **said** that they **are permitted to cut their hair on** the intermediate days of **a Festival,** they may do so only **if they did not have time** to cut their hair before the Festival. **But if they had time** before the Festival began, then **they are prohibited** from doing so.

נָזִיר וּמְצוֹרָע, אַף עַל פִּי שֶׁהָיָה לָהֶם פְּנַאי – מוּתָּרִים, שֶׁלֹּא יַשְׁהוּ קָרְבְּנוֹתֵיהֶן.

However, **a nazirite and a leper, even if they had the time** to do so before the Festival, **they are permitted** to cut their hair. Why are they granted this special allowance? So **that they will not delay** bringing **their offerings.**[N] Both a nazirite and a leper must cut their hair before sacrificing their offerings in completion of their purification process. Therefore, if they are not permitted to cut their hair, they will not be able to sacrifice their offerings at the proper time.[H]

תָּנָא: הַכֹּהֵן וְהָאָבֵל מוּתָּרִין בְּגִילּוּחַ. הַאי אָבֵל הֵיכִי דָּמֵי? אִילֵימָא שֶׁחָל שְׁמִינִי שֶׁלּוֹ בְּעֶרֶב הָרֶגֶל – אִיבְּעֵי לֵיהּ לְגַלּוּחֵי בְּעֶרֶב הָרֶגֶל. אֶלָּא שֶׁחָל שְׁמִינִי שֶׁלּוֹ לִהְיוֹת בְּשַׁבָּת עֶרֶב הָרֶגֶל,

In was **taught** in a *baraita*: **A priest and a mourner are permitted to cut their hair** during the intermediate days of a Festival. The Gemara asks: **What are the circumstances** when the **mourner** is permitted to do so? **If we say that the eighth** day of **his** mourning **occurred on the eve of the Festival,** then **he should have cut his hair on the eve of the Festival,** as the more stringent restrictions of his mourning no longer applied. **Rather,** it must be that we are dealing with a case **where the eighth** day of **his** mourning **occurred on a Shabbat**[N] **that was the eve of the Festival,** and so he could not have cut his hair on the Festival eve.

NOTES

Cemetery – **בֵּי קִבְרֵי**: The simple reason for this is because it is a place where people are not present. *Talmid Rabbeinu Yeḥiel of Paris* adds that by doing this, it is as though the dead were his community and they agreed to this decree of ostracism.

A thousand ***shofar*** **blasts over the course of forty days** – **אַלְפָּא שִׁפּוּרֵי בְּאַרְבָּעִין יוֹמִין**: Rabbi Shlomo ben HaYatom explains that this does not mean that he should sound the ram's horn exactly one thousand times, but rather that it should be blown numerous times. However, he writes that the number forty alludes to the forty days when a fetus is first formed so that this curse of death parallels the time when this person was first created. See also Maharsha who offers a similar explanation.

It breaks tall buildings [*tavrei batei ramei*] – **תַּבְרֵי בָּתֵּי רָמֵי**: In the manuscript of Rashi, it is noted that an alternative version of the Talmud text reads: That breaks, builds, and casts away [*tavrei, batei, verami*] (see Commentary on *Moed Katan*).

So that they will not delay bringing their offerings – **שֶׁלֹּא יַשְׁהוּ קָרְבְּנוֹתֵיהֶם**: Rabbi Shlomo ben HaYatom writes that one who is required to bring these offerings transgresses a positive mitzva every day that he delays doing so. *Talmid Rabbeinu Yeḥiel of Paris* explains that in this case the Sages did not prohibit haircutting during the intermediate days, as they did not want their decree to prevent one from bringing his offering in the proper time.

Tosafot ask: The nazirite's haircut is not a prerequisite for sacrificing his offering, so why is he permitted to cut his hair during the intermediate days? They answer that although he is not required to do so, it is a mitzva for him to cut his hair at that time. *Talmid Rabbeinu Yeḥiel of Paris* adds that normally one wants to perform all of the associated mitzvot at the same time, and if he is not permitted to cut his hair then he will similarly delay bringing his offering.

Where the eighth day…occurred on a Shabbat – **שֶׁחָל שְׁמִינִי...בְּשַׁבָּת**: *Tosafot* note that the mourning period begins only once the deceased has been buried. Since burials may not be performed on Shabbat, how is it possible for the eighth day of the mourning period to fall on Shabbat? This question is answered by the Jerusalem Talmud in several different ways: Either the deceased was killed and dragged away by a wild animal on Shabbat, in which case there is no burial and the mourning period begins immediately, or gentiles completed the burial after Shabbat had already begun. The Meiri adds that it is possible that the deceased drowned on a boat on Shabbat.

HALAKHA

Haircutting for a nazirite and leper during the intermediate days – **תִּגְלַחַת נָזִיר וּמְצוֹרָע בַּמּוֹעֵד**: When it is time for a nazirite or a leper to cut his hair, he is permitted to do so, even during the intermediate days of the Festival, so that he does not delay bringing his offerings. Even if his time to cut his hair occurred before the Festival, but he delayed for whatever reason, he may still cut his hair during the intermediate days to avoid further delay in bringing his offerings (Rambam *Sefer Zemanim*, *Hilkhot Yom Tov* 7:19).

אִיבָּעֵי לֵיהּ לְגַלּוּחֵי עֶרֶב שַׁבָּת, דְּאָמַר רַב חִסְדָּא אָמַר רָבִינָא בַּר שֵׁילָא: הֲלָכָה כְּאַבָּא שָׁאוּל. וּמוֹדִים חֲכָמִים לְאַבָּא שָׁאוּל בְּשֶׁחָל שְׁמִינִי שֶׁלּוֹ לִהְיוֹת בְּשַׁבָּת עֶרֶב הָרֶגֶל, שֶׁמּוּתָּר לְגַלֵּחַ בְּעֶרֶב שַׁבָּת!

But if this is the case, **he should have cut his hair on Friday, for Rav Ḥisda said that Ravina bar Sheila said: The *halakha* is in accordance with** the opinion of **Abba Shaul.** If the deceased was buried seven days before the Festival, then not only has the mourner completed the seven-day mourning period, but he is even regarded as having begun the thirty-day mourning period, and so the Festival cancels this thirty-day period of mourning. **And the Rabbis concede** to the opinion of **Abba Shaul when the eighth** day of **his** mourning **occurs on a Shabbat that is the eve of the Festival,** and they maintain **that he is permitted to cut his hair on Friday.** Since he is unavoidably prevented from cutting his hair on the eighth day, the Rabbis allowed him to cut it already on the seventh day.[H]

לָא צְרִיכָא, שֶׁחָל שְׁבִיעִי שֶׁלּוֹ לִהְיוֹת בְּשַׁבָּת עֶרֶב הָרֶגֶל.

The Gemara answers: **No,** the ruling of the *baraita* is **necessary** in the case **where the seventh** day of **his** mourning **occurs on a Shabbat that is the eve of the Festival.** In that case, he certainly cannot cut his hair on Friday because it is only the sixth day of his mourning, and so he is permitted to cut his hair on the intermediate days of the Festival.

תַּנָּא בָּרָא סָבַר לָהּ כְּאַבָּא שָׁאוּל, דְּאָמַר מִקְצָת הַיּוֹם כְּכוּלּוֹ, וְיוֹם שְׁבִיעִי עוֹלֶה לוֹ לְכָאן וּלְכָאן. וְכֵיוָן דְּשַׁבָּת הָוֵי – אָנוּס הוּא.

The Gemara comments: **The *tanna* of the *baraita*,** who permits a mourner to cut his hair during the intermediate days of the Festival, **holds in accordance with** the opinion of **Abba Shaul, who said:** The legal status of **part of the day is like** that of **an entire** day, **and** therefore **the seventh day counts as both** the final day of the seven-day mourning period and the first day of the thirty-day mourning period. From the perspective of the *halakhot* of mourning, one would be permitted to cut his hair; however **since** this day **is Shabbat, he is unavoidably prevented** from doing so, and therefore he is permitted to cut his hair during the intermediate days of the Festival.

תַּנָּא דִּידַן סָבַר לָהּ כְּרַבָּנַן, דְּאָמְרִי: לָא אָמְרִינַן מִקְצָת הַיּוֹם כְּכוּלּוֹ, וְאַכַּתִּי לָא שְׁלִים אֲבֵילוּת דְּשִׁבְעָה.

The *tanna* of **our** mishna, on the other hand, who does not mention that a mourner is permitted to cut his hair on the intermediate days of a Festival, **holds in accordance with** the opinion of the **Rabbis, who say: We do not say** that the legal status of **part of the day is like** that of **an entire** day for a mourner. Therefore, **he has not yet completed** his **seven**-day period of **mourning,** and consequently he will not be permitted to cut his hair even after the Festival, until the completion of the thirty-day mourning period.

הַאי כֹּהֵן הֵיכִי דָּמֵי? אִילֵימָא דִּשְׁלִים מִשְׁמַרְתּוֹ עֶרֶב הָרֶגֶל – אִיבָּעֵי לֵיהּ לְגַלּוּחֵי עֶרֶב הָרֶגֶל!

The Gemara continues and asks: The case of **this priest,** who is permitted to cut his hair during the intermediate days of a Festival, **what are the circumstances? If we say that he completed his watch on the eve of the Festival,** then **he should have cut his hair on the eve of the Festival.**

לָא צְרִיכָא, דִּשְׁלִים מִשְׁמַרְתּוֹ בָּרֶגֶל. תַּנָּא דִּידַן סָבַר: כֵּיוָן דִּתְנַן: בִּשְׁלֹשָׁה פְּרָקִים בַּשָּׁנָה הָיוּ כׇּל הַמִּשְׁמָרוֹת שָׁווֹת בְּאֵימוּרֵי הָרְגָלִים וּבְחִילּוּק לֶחֶם הַפָּנִים. כְּמַאן דְּלָא שְׁלִים מִשְׁמַרְתּוֹ בָּרֶגֶל דָּמֵי. וְתַנָּא בָּרָא סָבַר: אַף עַל גַּב דְּשַׁיָּיךְ בַּהֲנָךְ מִשְׁמָרוֹת – מִשְׁמַרְתֵּיהּ מִיהָא שְׁלִימָא לֵיהּ.

The Gemara answers: **No,** the ruling of the *baraita* is **necessary** in the case **where one completed his watch during the Festival** week itself.[H] **The *tanna*** of **our** mishna **holds that since we learned** in a mishna (*Sukka* 55b): **At the year,** i.e., the three pilgrimage Festivals, **all of the priestly watches share equally in the Festival offerings**[N] **and in the division of the shewbread**[B] among the priests on Shabbat that occurs on the Festival,[H] therefore, **he is** considered **like one whose watch was not completed during the Festival,** and he may not cut his hair until after the Festival. **And the *tanna* of the *baraita* holds that although** he **belongs** also **to those** other **watches** serving during the Festival, **nevertheless, his own watch was completed** before the Festival, and so he is permitted to cut his hair.[N]

HALAKHA

The time that a mourner may cut his hair – זְמַן גִּילּוּחַ לְאָבֵל: If one buried his deceased relative seven days before the Festival and mourned for seven days, the Festival cancels the thirty-day period of mourning known as *sheloshim*. This applies even if the seventh day occurs on the day before the Festival, due to the principle that part of a day has the halakhic status of an entire day, in accordance with the opinion of Abba Shaul. In addition, such mourners are permitted to cut their hair, launder their clothes, and bathe on the day before a Festival, close to nightfall. On the day before Passover, a mourner may perform these activities from midday onward so that he may bring the Paschal offering at the proper time. Others say that it is preferable for him to cut his hair before midday (Rema).

Similarly, if the eighth day of his mourning falls on Shabbat on the day before a Festival, then he may cut his hair, launder his clothes, and bathe on Friday, which is his seventh day of mourning. If he did not cut his hair in these cases, then he is prohibited from doing so during the intermediate days. However, he may do so after the conclusion of the Festival. If his seventh day of mourning falls on Shabbat on the day before a Festival, then he is permitted to cut his hair during the intermediate days, since he was unable to do so before the Festival (*Shulḥan Arukh, Yoreh De'a* 399:3).

A priest serving immediately prior to the Festival – כֹּהֵן הַמְשַׁמֵּשׁ סָמוּךְ לָרֶגֶל: The members of the priestly watch whose week of Temple service ends during the Festival may cut their hair during the intermediate days. However, if the watch completed its service on the day before a Festival, then the priests should cut their hair at that time, and they are prohibited from cutting their hair during the Festival (Rambam *Sefer Zemanim, Hilkhot Yom Tov* 7:19 and *Sefer Avoda, Hilkhot Biat HaMikdash* 1:13).

Watches during the Festivals – הַמִּשְׁמָרוֹת בָּרְגָלִים: During the three pilgrimage Festivals, all of the priestly watches have equal standing; they equally divide the shewbread and all of the offerings that were sacrificed during the Festival. Additionally, on *Shavuot* they share the two loaves (Rambam *Sefer Avoda, Hilkhot Kelei HaMikdash* 4:4–5).

BACKGROUND

The shewbread – לֶחֶם הַפָּנִים: The Torah describes the offering of the twelve loaves of shewbread that were placed on the sacred table in the Sanctuary each Shabbat (Leviticus 24:5–9). The bread of the previous week was divided among the priests and eaten by them. The shewbread was unleavened and placed on the table in two arrangements of six loaves each. Two bowls of frankincense were placed between them, or, according to other opinions, on top of them.

Priests with shewbread

NOTES

The Festival offerings [*imurei*] – אֵימוּרֵי הָרְגָלִים: In tractate *Sukka*, it is explained that the term used here for offerings refers specifically to those portions that were burnt on the altar. The priests have no benefit from those portions. Some explain that the word *imurei* here should be understood not as offerings, but as: What is said [*ne'emar*] to be done during the Festivals, or to the other offerings from which the priests would receive a portion (*Talmid Rabbeinu Yeḥiel of Paris*; Ritva).

A priest's haircut – תִּגְלַחַת הַכֹּהֵן: Rashi asks: Why does he not cut his hair on Thursday, just before the conclusion of his watch? In answer, he explains that the *baraita* refers to a case where the Festival itself occurs on Thursday. The Meiri offers a similar explanation. Rashi in the manuscript writes that initially the priest is permitted only to launder his clothes, but not to cut his hair on Thursday. The Ritva offers a similar explanation.

תָּנוּ רַבָּנַן: כׇּל אֵלּוּ שֶׁאָמְרוּ מוּתָּרִין לְגַלֵּחַ בַּמּוֹעֵד – מוּתָּרִין לְגַלֵּחַ בִּימֵי אֶבְלָן.

§ **The Sages taught** the following *baraita*: **All those about whom it was said** that they **are permitted to cut their hair on** the intermediate days of **a Festival**[H] because they were unable to do so beforehand, **they may** similarly **cut their hair during the period of their mourning** if they had been unable to do so beforehand.

וְהָתַנְיָא אֲסוּרִים! אָמַר רַב חִסְדָּא אָמַר רַב שֵׁילָא: כִּי תַּנְיָא הָכָא מוּתָּרִין – בְּשֶׁתְּכָפוּהוּ אֲבֵלָיו.

The Gemara asks: **But isn't it taught** in another *baraita*: **They are** nevertheless **prohibited** from cutting their hair during the period of their mourning? **Rav Ḥisda said** that **Rav Sheila said: When it is taught** in the *baraita* that **they are permitted** to cut their hair, it is referring to one **for whom** two periods of **mourning applied in succession.** In other words, this person was required to practice one period of mourning immediately following another period of mourning, and he is unable to endure the prescribed restrictions for such an extended period.

אִי בְּשֶׁתְּכָפוּהוּ אֲבֵלָיו מַאי אִירְיָא כׇּל אֵלּוּ שֶׁאָמְרוּ? אֲפִילּוּ כּוּלֵּי עָלְמָא נָמֵי! דְּתַנְיָא: תְּכָפוּהוּ אֲבֵלָיו זֶה אַחַר זֶה, הִכְבִּיד שְׂעָרוֹ – מֵיקֵל בְּתַעַר, וּמְכַבֵּס כְּסוּתוֹ בְּמַיִם!

The Gemara asks: **If** this is referring to a case **where his mourning applied in succession,** then **why specifically** does the *baraita* discuss **all those about whom it was said** that they may cut their hair? The allowance should apply **even to everyone,** not only to those who had been unavoidably prevented from cutting their hair in the preceding period, **as it is taught** in a *baraita*: If **one's mourning** periods **applied in succession, one after the other,** and **his hair** grew long and **became heavy, he may lighten** it by cutting his hair **with a razor,**[N] **and he may wash his garment in water,** so that he does not suffer for such a long time without cutting his hair or washing his clothes.

הָא אִתְּמַר עֲלָהּ, אָמַר רַב חִסְדָּא: בְּתַעַר וְלֹא בְּמִסְפָּרַיִם; בְּמַיִם וְלֹא בְּנֶתֶר וְלֹא בְּאָהָל. אָמַר רַב חִסְדָּא: זֹאת אוֹמֶרֶת: אָבֵל אָסוּר בְּתַכְבּוֹסֶת.

The Gemara answers: **But wasn't it said with regard to that** *baraita*: **Rav Ḥisda said:** When it states that one may cut his hair, it means that he may do so **with a razor, but not with scissors?** Similarly, when it states that one may wash his clothes, it means that he may launder them **with water, but not with** ***neter***[B] **or soap.**[B] Therefore, the *baraita* teaches that if one had been unavoidably prevented from performing these actions beforehand and then had to observe a double mourning period, he may cut his hair in an ordinary manner, without performing these actions in an altered way. **Rav Ḥisda said: That is to say** that, generally speaking, **a mourner is prohibited from laundering** his clothes.[NH]

תָּנוּ רַבָּנַן: כְּשֵׁם שֶׁאָמְרוּ אָסוּר לְגַלֵּחַ בַּמּוֹעֵד – כָּךְ אָסוּר לִיטּוֹל צִפּוֹרְנַיִם בַּמּוֹעֵד, דִּבְרֵי רַבִּי יְהוּדָה. וְרַבִּי יוֹסֵי מַתִּיר.

The Sages taught the following *baraita*: **Just as** the Sages **said** that **it is prohibited to cut one's hair during the** intermediate days of **a Festival, so too it is prohibited to cut one's nails during the** intermediate days of **a Festival;**[N] this is **the statement of Rabbi Yehuda, whereas Rabbi Yosei permits** cutting nails.

HALAKHA

Those who are permitted to cut their hair on the intermediate days of a Festival, etc. – **הַמּוּתָּרִים לְהִתְגַּלֵּחַ בַּמּוֹעֵד וכו׳**: If one from those categories of people whom the Sages permitted to cut their hair during the intermediate days becomes a mourner, it is prohibited for him to cut his hair during the mourning period. However, if he had two consecutive mourning periods, he may cut his hair in an ordinary manner during the second seven-day period. Anyone else who has two consecutive periods of mourning may cut his hair in an unusual manner, such as with a razor, as opposed to using scissors. This must be done in private (*Shulḥan Arukh*, *Yoreh De'a* 390:3, and in the comment of Rema).

A mourner is prohibited from laundering his clothes – **אָבֵל אָסוּר בְּתַכְבּוֹסֶת**: A mourner may not launder his clothes for the entire seven-day period of mourning, and he is similarly prohibited from wearing freshly laundered clothes. After these seven days, it is permitted. However, the common practice is to refrain from wearing freshly laundered clothes for the entire thirty-day period. In order to observe this custom, it is common practice to permit the mourner to wear clean clothes after they have first been worn by another person for a short time (Rema).

If a person in one of the categories of people who are permitted to launder their clothes during the intermediate days became a mourner, he is prohibited from laundering his clothes while in mourning. However, if he experiences two consecutive periods of mourning, then he may launder clothes in an ordinary manner in private.

Anyone who experiences two consecutive periods of mourning may launder clothes only in water, without soap or lye. If he must wash his clothes because they are dirty and he is not doing so for pleasure, then he is permitted to launder them properly (*Shulḥan Arukh*, *Yoreh De'a* 389:1; *Pitḥei Teshuva*, citing *Responsa Laḥmei Toda*).

NOTES

Lighten it with a razor – **מֵיקֵל בְּתַעַר**: According to some, this expression means that one is permitted only to neaten his hair by trimming several of the longer strands, but he may not have a proper haircut (*Talmid Rabbeinu Yeḥiel of Paris*). Others write that this means that he may cut the lower parts of his hair so that the haircut is not apparent to others (Rid). The Ran presents both opinions.

That is to say a mourner is prohibited from laundering his clothes – **זֹאת אוֹמֶרֶת אָבֵל אָסוּר בְּתַכְבּוֹסֶת**: The early authorities ask: Why did Rav Ḥisda need to make this statement when it was already taught that a mourner may not launder his clothes, based on the instructions given to the Tekoite woman (see *Tosafot*)? *Talmid Rabbeinu Yeḥiel of Paris* writes that the verse cannot serve as a proof but merely as an allusion to the *halakha*, making Rav Ḥisda's statement necessary. Others write that there the *baraita* taught only about laundering clothes in an ordinary manner. However, here Rav Ḥisda teaches that it is prohibited to launder clothes even in cold water (Ran; Ritva; see *Tosefot HaRosh*).

Cutting nails during the intermediate days – **נְטִילַת צִפּוֹרְנַיִם בַּמּוֹעֵד**: Some explain that according to Rabbi Yosei's opinion nothing is accomplished by cutting one's nails before a Festival because they grow so quickly. Even cutting them immediately before the Festival does not prevent the need to cut them during the intermediate days (Ran). Others suggest that long fingernails are especially repulsive, and the Sages were not strict with such a minor type of work (Ritva).

BACKGROUND

Neter – **נֶתֶר**: This is apparently sodium carbonate, Na_2CO_3, which is found in colorless clusters that crystallize from evaporating water. In nature, sodium carbonate is found in desert regions. However, in ancient times it was often produced from the ash of sea algae. Also called washing soda, this compound easily dissolves in water, and its solubility causes a strong basic reaction. Due to hydrolysis, which produces Na_2, it can dissolve many different types of fats, and therefore it was used as a cleaning agent, even during the biblical period. Some say that it refers to natron, a naturally occurring mixture of sodium carbonate decahydrate.

Soap [*ohal*] – **אָהָל**: Many plants with the name *ohal* are found in Eretz Yisrael. One of them, known as the common ice plant or *Mesembryanthemum crystallinum* L., is an annual plant that grows in the Sharon and Shephela regions of Eretz Yisrael, in rocks and walls that face the sea. The surface of these plants is covered in small translucent sacs that appear like ice crystals, which give it the name ice plant. This plant contains a noticeable amount of raw soda and was used for laundering clothes and bathing.

Common ice plant

וכשם שאמרו: אבל אסור לגלח בימי אבלו – כך אסור ליטול צפורנים בימי אבלו, דברי רבי יהודה. ורבי יוסי מתיר.

And just as the Sages said that a **mourner is prohibited from cutting his hair during the period of his mourning, so too he is prohibited from cutting his nails during the period of his mourning;** this is **the statement of Rabbi Yehuda, whereas Rabbi Yosei permits** a mourner to cut his nails.[N]

אמר עולא: הלכה כרבי יהודה באבל, והלכה כרבי יוסי במועד, שמואל אמר:

Ulla said: The *halakha* is in accordance with the opinion of **Rabbi Yehuda with regard to mourning, but the *halakha* is in accordance with** the opinion of **Rabbi Yosei with regard to the** intermediate days of the **Festival. Shmuel said:**

NOTES

Nail cutting for a mourner – נטילת צפורנים באבל: The Ran writes in the name of Rabbi Aaron HaLevi that it is possible to derive the prohibition against nail cutting during the mourning period from the biblical passage that describes the beautiful captive woman. She must mourn for her family for seven days, and it is written that she must "do her nails" (Deuteronomy 21:12). This is understood as meaning that she must let her nails grow during the period when she mourns her family.

Rabbi Yosei does not learn this derivation, either because the mitzva that the beautiful woman grow her nails is part of the requirement that she make herself unattractive, or because he maintains that "do her nails" does not mean grow her nails, but rather cut her nails (Ran; see Ritva).

Perek **III**
Daf **18** Amud **a**

הלכה כרבי יוסי במועד ובאבל. דאמר שמואל: הלכה כדברי המיקל באבל.

The *halakha* is in accordance with the opinion of **Rabbi Yosei with regard to** the intermediate days of **the Festival**[H] **and with regard to mourning, as Shmuel said** this general principle: **The *halakha* is in accordance with the statement of the** more **lenient** authority **in** matters relating to **mourning.**[H]

פנחס אחוה דמר שמואל, איתרע ביה מילתא. על שמואל למישאל טעמא מיניה. חזנהו לטופרי דהוו נפישן. אמר ליה: אמאי לא שקלת להו? אמר ליה: אי בדידיה הוה, מי מזלזלת ביה כולי האי?

It was related that **something** unpleasant **happened to Pineḥas, brother of Mar Shmuel,** that is to say, one of his close relatives died. **Shmuel entered to ask him the reason,** i.e., to console him. **He saw that** Pineḥas's **nails were long, and said to him: Why do you not cut them?** Pineḥas **replied: If it were your** relative who died,[N] and you were in mourning, **would you treat** the matter **so lightly** and cut your nails?

הואי "כשגגה שיצא מלפני השליט", ואיתרע ביה מילתא בשמואל. על פנחס אחוה למישאל טעמא מיניה, שקלינהו לטופריה חבטינהו לאפיה. אמר ליה: לית לך ברית כרותה לשפתים?

Pineḥas's words **were: "Like an error that proceeds from a ruler"** (Ecclesiastes 10:5).[N] As soon as he uttered them they came true, even though he did not intend them. Shortly after Pineḥas made his comment, **something** unpleasant **happened to Shmuel,** and one of his close relatives died. **Pineḥas, his brother, entered to ask him the reason,** i.e., to offer words of comfort. Shmuel **took his nails and cast them in** Pineḥas's face.[N] Shmuel then **said to him:** Do **you not** know the principle that **a covenant is made with the lips?** In other words, do you not know that what one says influences future events?

HALAKHA

Cutting nails during the intermediate days of a Festival – נטילת צפורנים במועד: It is permitted to cut both one's fingernails and toenails during the intermediate days of a Festival, even using a pair of scissors. This is because the *halakha* is in accordance with the opinion of Rabbi Yosei, as is stated by Shmuel.

The Rema writes that there are those who rule stringently and prohibit the use of scissors. The custom is not to cut one's nails using any implement, with the exception of a woman preparing for mandatory ritual immersion, who may cut her nails in an ordinary manner. However, even according to those who are strict, it is permitted to trim nails with one's teeth or hands. In exceptional circumstances, if one was preoccupied before the Festival, then he may cut his nails with scissors during the Festival, even according to those who are stringent (*Arukh HaShulḥan*). Practically speaking, Ashkenazic communities follow the Rema, and even many Sephardic communities do as well, and one should not act differently in a place where this is the custom (*Kaf HaḤayyim; Shulḥan Arukh, Oraḥ Ḥayyim* 532:1).

Cutting nails while in mourning – נטילת צפורנים באבל: The *halakha* follows the opinion of Rabbi Yosei, as ruled by Shmuel, that a mourner may cut his nails. However, the *halakha* also follows the opinion of Rav, and the nails should be cut with one's hands or teeth but not with a utensil.

Once the first seven days of mourning have passed, but before the thirty-day period of mourning is over, a woman who is preparing for her ritual immersion should ask a gentile woman to cut her nails for her. Some say that another Jewish woman may also cut them on her behalf (Rema). However, others disagree and say that it is prohibited for another Jewish woman to cut them for her (*Shakh*), but this is not the custom (*Arukh HaShulḥan; Shulḥan Arukh, Yoreh De'a* 390:7).

NOTES

If it were your relative who died – אי בדידיה הוה: This refers to a child, rather than any other relative, which explains why it was a close relative of Pineḥas, but not a close relative of Pineḥas's brother, Shmuel (Rashi manuscript).

Like an error that proceeds from a ruler – כשגגה שיצא מלפני השליט: In the manuscript of Rashi, it is explained: This is similar to a case where a ruler stated that a person deserves to be sentenced to death. Although the ruler did not actually intend for him to be killed, his servant carried out this order.

Took his nails and cast them in his face – שקלינהו לטופריה חבטינהו לאפיה: Shmuel was not concerned about throwing his fingernail clippings on the ground, although subsequently the Gemara explains that one who does so is wicked. Shmuel was not concerned, either because he collected them afterward (Rashi), or because he was in a place where women were not present (*Talmid Rabbeinu Yeḥiel of Paris*).

דְּאָמַר רַבִּי יוֹחָנָן: מִנַּיִן שֶׁבְּרִית כְּרוּתָה לַשְּׂפָתַיִם – שֶׁנֶּאֱמַר: ״וַיֹּאמֶר אַבְרָהָם אֶל נְעָרָיו שְׁבוּ לָכֶם פֹּה עִם הַחֲמוֹר וַאֲנִי וְהַנַּעַר נֵלְכָה עַד כֹּה וְנִשְׁתַּחֲוֶה וְנָשׁוּבָה אֲלֵיכֶם״, וְאִסְתַּיְּיעָא מִלְּתָא דַּהֲדוּר תַּרְוַויְיהוּ.

This is as **Rabbi Yoḥanan said: From where** is it derived **that a covenant is made with the lips,** and that one's speech has the power to change events? **For it is stated: "And Abraham said to his young men: Stay here with the donkey, and I and the lad will go onward; and we will worship, and we will come back to you"** (Genesis 22:5). Abraham said this even though he thought that he was going to sacrifice his son as an offering and that Isaac would not be returning, **yet this had an influence and they both came back.**

סְבוּר מִינֵּיהּ: דְּיָד – אִין, דְּרֶגֶל – לָא. אָמַר רַב עָנָן בַּר תַּחְלִיפָא: לְדִידִי מִפָּרְשָׁא לִי מִינֵּיהּ דִּשְׁמוּאֵל: לָא שְׁנָא דְּיָד, וְלָא שְׁנָא דְּרֶגֶל.

With regard to this *halakha* pertaining to a mourner cutting his nails: They initially **concluded from this:** With regard to the nails on his **hand, yes,** a mourner may cut them; but as for the nails on his **foot, no,** he may not cut them, because long toenails are less repulsive. **Rav Anan bar Taḥlifa said: It was explained to me by Shmuel** himself: **It is not different** if it is the nails on the **hand and it is not different** if it is the nails on the **foot,** as in both cases cutting the nails is permitted.

אָמַר רַב חִיָּיא בַּר אַשִׁי אָמַר רַב: וּבִגְנוּסְטְרָא אָסוּר. אָמַר רַב שֶׁמֶן בַּר אַבָּא: הֲוָה קָאֵימְנָא קַמֵּיהּ דְּרַבִּי יוֹחָנָן בֵּי מִדְרָשָׁא בְּחוּלּוֹ שֶׁל מוֹעֵד, וְשַׁקְלִינְהוּ לְטוּפְרֵיהּ בְּשִׁינֵּיהּ וְזַרְקִינְהוּ.

Rav Ḥiyya bar Ashi said that **Rav said: But with scissors** [*genustera*][L] specifically for nail cutting **it is prohibited,** i.e., the mourner should cut his nails in an alternate manner. **Rav Shemen bar Abba said:** I once **stood before Rabbi Yoḥanan in the study hall during the intermediate days of a Festival, and he cut his nails with his teeth and threw them** down.

שְׁמַע מִינָּהּ תְּלָת; שְׁמַע מִינָּהּ: מוּתָּר לִיטּוֹל צִפָּרְנַיִם בְּחוּלּוֹ שֶׁל מוֹעֵד. וּשְׁמַע מִינָּהּ: אֵין בָּהֶן מִשּׁוּם מִיאוּס. וּשְׁמַע מִינָּהּ: מוּתָּר לְזוֹרְקָן.

The Gemara comments: **Learn from this** incident of Rabbi Yoḥanan **three** *halakhot*:[N] **Learn from this that it is permitted to cut one's nails on the intermediate days of a Festival. And learn from this** that nails **have no** prohibition **due to** the fact that they are **repulsive,** i.e., there is no prohibition against biting them on that basis. Inasmuch as one is prohibited from placing something repulsive in his mouth, this incident teaches that nails do not fall into this category. **And** also **learn from this** that **it is permitted** to throw **nails** away.

אִינִי? וְהָתַנְיָא: שְׁלֹשָׁה דְּבָרִים נֶאֶמְרוּ בְּצִפָּרְנַיִם: הַקּוֹבְרָן – צַדִּיק; שׂוֹרְפָן – חָסִיד; זוֹרְקָן – רָשָׁע. טַעְמָא מַאי? שֶׁמָּא תַּעֲבוֹר עֲלֵיהֶן אִשָּׁה עוּבָּרָה וְתַפִּיל.

The Gemara asks: **Is that so? But isn't it taught** in a *baraita*: **Three things were said about nails: One who buries them** in the ground **is** deemed **righteous. One who burns them** is even better, as he **is** considered **pious.**[N] **One who** merely **throws them** away is regarded as **wicked.**[H] The Gemara explains: **What is the reason** that it is prohibited to throw away nail clippings? This is prohibited **lest a pregnant women pass over them**[N] **and miscarry,** for the Sages had a tradition that it is dangerous for a pregnant woman to walk over fingernails.

אִשָּׁה בֵּי מִדְרָשָׁא לָא שְׁכִיחָא. וְכִי תֵּימָא: זִימְנִין דְּמִיכַּנְשִׁי לְהוּ וְשָׁדֵי לְהוּ אַבָּרַאי, כֵּיוָן דְּאִשְׁתַּנֵּי – אִשְׁתַּנֵּי.

The Gemara answers: **A woman is not usually** found **in the study hall,** and therefore Rabbi Yoḥanan was not concerned about throwing his nail clippings there. **If you say** that **sometimes** the nails **are gathered** together when the floor is swept **and** then **thrown outside** where a pregnant woman may walk over them, this is not a problem. **Once** their place **has changed**[N] the nails themselves **change** and are no longer harmful.

אָמַר רַב יְהוּדָה אָמַר רַב: זוּג בָּא מֵחֲמָתָן לִפְנֵי רַבִּי, וּמָר זוּטְרָא מַתְנֵי: זוּג בָּא מֵחֲמָתָן לִפְנֵי רַבִּי, וּבִקְּשׁוּ מִמֶּנּוּ צִפָּרְנַיִם – וְהִתִּיר לָהֶם. וְאִם בִּקְּשׁוּ מִמֶּנּוּ שָׂפָה – הִתִּיר לָהֶם. וּשְׁמוּאֵל אָמַר: אַף בִּקְּשׁוּ מִמֶּנּוּ שָׂפָה וְהִתִּיר לָהֶם.

Rav Yehuda said that **Rav said: A pair** of Sages **from Ḥamatan came before Rabbi** Yehuda HaNasi. **And Mar Zutra taught**[N] it without the names of Rav Yehuda and Rav, simply as: **A pair** of Sages **from Ḥamatan came before Rabbi** Yehuda HaNasi. **And they asked him** whether or not a mourner is permitted to cut his **nails, and he permitted** it **to them. And had they asked him** whether or not a mourner may trim his **mustache, he would** also **have permitted** it **to them. And Shmuel said: They also asked him** about trimming **a mustache,**[N] and **he permitted** it **to them.**

HALAKHA

What is done with nail clippings – מַה עוֹשִׂים בְּצִפָּרְנַיִם: When one cuts his nails it is preferable that he does not throw away the clippings, but instead he should bury or burn them (*Shulḥan Arukh, Oraḥ Ḥayyim* 260:1; *Magen Avraham*).

LANGUAGE

Scissors [*genustera*] – גְּנוּסְטְרָא: The origin of this word is Greek. Some say it originates from the Greek κνηστήρ, *knestèr*, meaning a nail file, which was used for nail cutting. Others say, based on a version of the Talmud text that reads *negusterei*, that this may be from the Greek ὄνυξ, *onux*, meaning nail, and ῥίνη, *rhinè*, meaning clipper or cutter, which also refers to a utensil used for cutting nails.

NOTES

Learn from this incident three *halakhot* – שְׁמַע מִינָּהּ תְּלָת: Based on the fact that the Gemara specifically mentions three *halakhot* and not four, there are those who understand that Rabbi Yoḥanan's actions do not teach the prohibition against cutting fingernails on the intermediate days with scissors (Rif). Instead, he did not use scissors either because he did not have any available to him at that time or because one may not take metal tools into a study hall (Rabbi Shlomo ben HaYatom; see Ran). Some say that there is no evidence as to whether or not one may use scissors to cut nails on the intermediate days because this list of three only includes leniencies and not stringencies (Rid; see Ran).

One who burns them is pious – שׂוֹרְפָן חָסִיד: There are several reasons why such a person is called pious: Perhaps it is difficult to find an appropriate place to burn fingernails; burning fingernails smell unpleasant; or it may be particularly painful for one to burn something that was once part of his body (*Talmid Rabbeinu Yeḥiel of Paris*).

Lest a pregnant woman pass over them – שֶׁמָּא תַּעֲבוֹר עֲלֵיהֶן אִשָּׁה עוּבָּרָה: Some say that this means that the fingernails are repulsive and may thereby cause her to miscarry (*Talmid Rabbeinu Yeḥiel of Paris*). However, others explain that there is a spiritual reason that fingernails cause women to miscarry. For example, *Eliya Rabba* gives kabbalistic reasons for this.

Once their place has changed – כֵּיוָן דְּאִשְׁתַּנֵּי: Based on this expression, most explain that once nail clippings have been moved they no longer have the power to cause harm. Others suggest that once a certain amount of time has passed their power is negated (see *Talmid Rabbeinu Yeḥiel of Paris*).

Mar Zutra taught – וּמָר זוּטְרָא מַתְנֵי: According to the text of the Babylonian Talmud, there is no difference between the two versions of this statement, aside from the fact that Mar Zutra taught this statement as a *baraita* and not as a statement made by Rav. According to Rabbi Shlomo ben HaYatom, the text should read: A pair came from Ḥamatan before Rabbi Ḥiyya. In the Jerusalem Talmud, it is stated that two pairs of Sages came, each one from a different place, and each asked a different question.

They also asked him about a mustache – אַף בִּקְּשׁוּ מִמֶּנּוּ שָׂפָה: Rabbeinu Gershom *Me'or HaGola* and Rashi explain this question to be: In general, is trimming a mustache prohibited as a form of removing one's beard? However, most commentaries explain that the question is whether or not it is permitted to trim one's mustache during the intermediate days of a Festival (Rid; Rabbeinu Yehonatan of Lunel; *Talmid Rabbeinu Yeḥiel of Paris*). In the Jerusalem Talmud, there is a long dispute as to whether the question applies to the intermediate days of a Festival or to a mourning period. According to the Ra'avad, a mourner may not trim his mustache. In order to support his opinion, he cites Mephibosheth, who did not trim his mustache while he was mourning (II Samuel 19:25).

אָמַר אֲבִיטוּל סַפְרָא מִשְּׁמֵיהּ דְּרַב פַּפָּא: שָׂפָה מִזָּוִית לְזָוִית. אָמַר רַבִּי אַמִי: וּבְשָׂפָה הַמְעַכֶּבֶת. אָמַר רַב נַחְמָן בַּר יִצְחָק: לְדִידִי כְּשָׂפָה הַמְעַכֶּבֶת דָּמֵי לִי.

Avitul the scribe said in the name of Rav Pappa: A mustache may be trimmed **from** one **corner to** the other **corner**[N] of the mouth. **Rabbi Ami said:** One may trim only the portion of the **mustache that interferes** with normal eating, but one may not trim the mustache for beautification. **Rav Naḥman bar Yitzḥak said: For me,** my entire mustache **is** considered **like a mustache that interferes** with normal eating, as I am particularly sensitive, and so I may trim my entire mustache.[H]

וְאָמַר אֲבִיטוּל סַפְרָא מִשְּׁמֵיהּ דְּרַב פַּפָּא: פַּרְעֹה שֶׁהָיָה בִּימֵי מֹשֶׁה הוּא אַמָּה וּזְקָנוֹ אַמָּה, וּפַרְמַשְׁתָּקוֹ אַמָּה וָזֶרֶת, לְקַיֵּים מַה שֶּׁנֶּאֱמַר: ״וּשְׁפַל אֲנָשִׁים יְקִים עֲלַהּ״.

§ Having mentioned Avitul the scribe, the Gemara records other statements of his: **And Avitul the scribe said in the name of Rav Pappa: The Pharaoh who lived in the days of Moses**[N] **was a cubit** tall, his **beard was a cubit** long, **and his penis** [*parmashtako*][L] was **a cubit and a span,** i.e., a cubit and the distance between the thumb and the little finger, in length, **in order to fulfill what is stated: "And He sets up over it the lowest of men"** (Daniel 4:14), which teaches that Pharaoh was extremely short and lowly.

וְאָמַר אֲבִיטוּל סַפְרָא מִשְּׁמֵיהּ דְּרַב פַּפָּא: פַּרְעֹה שֶׁהָיָה בִּימֵי מֹשֶׁה אַמְגּוּשִׁי הָיָה, שֶׁנֶּאֱמַר: ״הִנֵּה יֹצֵא הַמַּיְמָה״ וגו׳.

Avitul the scribe also **said in the name of Rav Pappa:** The **Pharaoh who lived in the days of Moses was a sorcerer** [*amgushi*],[L] **as it is stated: "Behold, he goes out to the water"** (Exodus 7:15). Pharaoh would regularly go out to the water in order to engage in witchcraft.

״וְאֵלּוּ מְכַבְּסִין בַּמּוֹעֵד הַבָּא מִמְּדִינַת הַיָּם״. אָמַר רַב אַסִּי אָמַר רַבִּי יוֹחָנָן: מִי שֶׁאֵין לוֹ אֶלָּא חָלוּק אֶחָד – מוּתָּר לְכַבְּסוֹ בְּחוּלּוֹ שֶׁל מוֹעֵד.

§ The mishna taught: **And these** people **may launder** their clothes **on** the intermediate days of **a Festival: One who comes from a country overseas. Rav Asi said** that **Rabbi Yoḥanan said: Anyone who has only one shirt is permitted to launder it on the intermediate days of a Festival.**[H]

מֵתִיב רַבִּי יִרְמְיָה: אֵלּוּ מְכַבְּסִין בַּמּוֹעֵד, הַבָּא מִמְּדִינַת הַיָּם כו׳. הָנֵי – אִין, מִי שֶׁאֵין לוֹ אֶלָּא חָלוּק אֶחָד – לָא!

Rabbi Yirmeya raised an objection from what was taught in the mishna: **And these** people **may launder** their clothes **on the** intermediate days of a **Festival: One who comes from a country overseas,** and one who is released from a house of captivity, and one who comes out of prison, and one who had been ostracized and the Rabbis released him from his decree of ostracism, **etc.** It may be inferred: **Those** who are mentioned in the mishna, **yes,** they may launder their clothes during the intermediate days of the Festival, but **one who has only one shirt** may **not** launder it.

אֲמַר לֵיהּ רַבִּי יַעֲקֹב לְרַבִּי יִרְמְיָה: אַסְבְּרָה לָךְ. מַתְנִיתִין – אַף עַל גַּב דְּאִית לֵיהּ תְּרֵי וּמְטַנְּפִי.

Rabbi Ya'akov said to Rabbi Yirmeya: I will explain it to you. The mishna is referring to those cases where one is permitted to launder his clothes even if **he has two** changes of garments **and** they are **dirty.** Rabbi Yoḥanan speaks about one who has only one garment, and he rules that he may launder it in all circumstances.

שְׁלַח רַב יִצְחָק בַּר יַעֲקֹב בַּר גִּיּוֹרֵי מִשְּׁמֵיהּ דְּרַבִּי יוֹחָנָן: כְּלֵי פִשְׁתָּן מוּתָּר לְכַבְּסָן בְּחוּלּוֹ שֶׁל מוֹעֵד. מֵתִיב רָבָא: מִטְפְּחוֹת הַיָּדַיִם, מִטְפְּחוֹת

Rav Yitzḥak bar Ya'akov bar Giyorei sent a message **in the name of Rabbi Yoḥanan:** With regard to **linen garments,**[N] **it is permitted to launder them during the intermediate days of the Festival** because they are easily soiled.[H] **Rava raised an objection** from what is taught in the mishna: **Hand towels, the towels**

NOTES

A mustache may be trimmed from one corner to the other corner – שָׂפָה מִזָּוִית לְזָוִית: Many of the early authorities have a version of the text that includes the expression: But any part of the *hanaḥa* is prohibited. However, it is not in the standard text because in the manuscript of Rashi it is written that he did not find a way to explain the term *hanaḥa*. Neither the Rif nor the Rambam had these words in their talmudic text.

Many early authorities understand that *hanaḥa* refers to the sides of the mouth, and it means that one is permitted to cut only the mustache itself, but hair on the sides of the mouth must be left untrimmed, along with the rest of the beard, unless it interferes with eating (Rabbeinu Ḥananel).

Others explain that the terms mustache here refers to the hair immediately above the mouth, and the word *hanaḥa* refers to the hair above that (Meiri). Alternatively, there are those who claim the word *hanaḥa* refers to the hair near the lower lip, which is below [*naḥa*] the mouth (see Ritva).

Pharaoh who lived in the days of Moses – פַּרְעֹה שֶׁהָיָה בִּימֵי מֹשֶׁה: Rabbi Shlomo ben HaYatom has a different version of the Talmud text. It adds that Pharaoh's name was Girsi. The verse: "He sets up over it the lowest of men," is actually referring to Nebuchadnezzar, who was only one cubit tall. However, the Gemara understands that Pharaoh was also this height (*Talmid Rabbeinu Yeḥiel of Paris*).

Linen garments – כְּלֵי פִּשְׁתָּן: Some say that the reason for this allowance is that they become dirty quickly and can be laundered without much effort (Rashi manuscript).

LANGUAGE

His penis [*parmashtako*] – פַּרְמַשְׁתָּקוֹ: This word appears to be Persian. However, its actual source is unclear. Although there are similar words in Persian and Sanskrit, none of them have the meaning that Rashi and others ascribe to it.

It is possible that the depiction of Pharaoh here is based on other similar ancient Egyptian statues and objects that show dwarflike figures containing all the elements of the description here.

Sorcerer [*amgushi*] – אַמְגּוּשִׁי: The origin of the word is magus, a term used for Zoroastrian priests in Iranian languages. It was then adopted by Greek and Aramaic.

HALAKHA

Cutting one's mustache – נְטִילַת שָׂפָם: One may trim the mustache hairs above his upper lip during the intermediate days of the Festival, even in public (*Shulḥan Arukh, Oraḥ Ḥayyim* 531:8, and in the comment of Rema).

One who has one shirt – מִי שֶׁיֵּשׁ לוֹ חָלוּק אֶחָד: One who has only one garment may launder it in an ordinary manner during the intermediate days of a Festival, and he may even use different types of soap and launder it in public. However, he may launder only one garment at a time. One may wash other items, such as children's clothes or diapers, if they are soiled, in larger quantities (*Shulḥan Arukh, Oraḥ Ḥayyim* 534:1).

Laundering linen garments – כִּיבּוּס כְּלֵי פִּשְׁתָּן: In accordance with Rabbi Yoḥanan's opinion, one may launder linen garments during the intermediate days of the Festival. However, the common practice is to refrain from doing so. This type of laundering falls into the category of activities that are customarily avoided, although they are technically permitted. Therefore, one may not openly state that such an activity is permitted. Some say that one may give such garments to a gentile to be laundered during the intermediate days (*Ḥayyei Adam*, citing *Eliya Rabba* and *Perisha*; *Shulḥan Arukh, Oraḥ Ḥayyim* 534:2).

הַסַּפָּרִים. הָנֵי – אִין, כְּלֵי פִשְׁתָּן – לָא!

of barbers that are used to cover a person having a haircut, and body-drying towels may all be laundered on the intermediate days of a Festival. This statement implies that **these** garments, **yes,** they may be laundered, but other types of **linen garments, no,** they may not be laundered.

אֲמַר לֵיהּ אַבָּיֵי: מַתְנִיתִין אֲפִילּוּ דִּשְׁאָר מִינֵי. אֲמַר בַּר הֶדְיָא: לְדִידִי חֲזֵי לִי יַמָּה שֶׁל טְבֶרְיָה, דְּמַפְּקִי לַהּ מְשִׁיכְלֵי דְּמָנֵי כִּיתָּנָא בְּחוּלָּא דְמוֹעֲדָא.

Abaye said to him: This is not a contradiction: **The mishna** is referring to garments made **even of other types** of materials; linen garments, however, may be laundered even when they serve other purposes. **Bar Hedya said: I myself saw the Sea of Tiberias,**[B] the Sea of Galilee, **to which basins full of linen garments were brought out** to be laundered **during the intermediate days of a Festival.**

מַתְקִיף לַהּ אַבָּיֵי: מַאן לֵימָא לַן דְּבִרְצוֹן חֲכָמִים עָבְדִי? דִּלְמָא שֶׁלֹּא בִּרְצוֹן חֲכָמִים עָבְדִי.

Abaye strongly objects to this: This report cannot be adduced as proof for the *halakha*, for **who says to us** that **they did** this **in accordance with the will of the Sages? Perhaps they did** it **without the will of the Sages.**

מתני׳ וְאֵלּוּ כּוֹתְבִין בַּמּוֹעֵד: קִדּוּשֵׁי נָשִׁים, וְגִיטִּין, וְשׁוֹבְרִין, דְּיָיתֵיקִי, מַתָּנָה, וּפְרוֹזְבּוֹלִין, אִיגְּרוֹת שׁוּם, וְאִיגְּרוֹת מָזוֹן,

MISHNA And these are the documents that **may be written on** the intermediate days of a **Festival:**[NH] Documents of **betrothal of wives,**[N] through which bridegrooms betroth their brides; **bills of divorce;**[N] **receipts** for the repayment of debts; **wills** [*deyateiki*];[L] deeds of **gift;** ***perozbolin***,[L] documents through which lenders authorize the courts to collect their loans on their behalf, thereby preventing the Sabbatical year from canceling their debts; **letters of valuation,** which were drawn up by the court when they valued property and transferred it to the lender; and **letters of sustenance,**[N] which were drawn up when one accepted upon himself to maintain another, e.g., his step-daughter.

NOTES

These may be written during the intermediate days of a Festival – וְאֵלּוּ כּוֹתְבִין בַּמּוֹעֵד: The early authorities disagree as to why writing these documents during the intermediate days is permitted. Some say that each document is, to some degree, something that would cause a loss, as in each case delaying the writing of the document may cause financial loss or some other type of harm.

Although this reason may not apply in some particular cases, the *halakha* nevertheless applies in every case without distinction. The commentaries explain in detail what the loss is in each case (Rashi manuscript; Rabbeinu Yehonatan of Lunel; *Talmid Rabbeinu Yehiel of Paris*; Meiri). Some say that the writing of the prohibited labor is only writing business documents, and none of these documents is directly related to business. For this reason they may be written during the intermediate days of a Festival (Rid; Ran). However, the Rambam explains that most of these documents may be written because the public requires them (see Ra'avad).

Documents of betrothal of wives – קִידּוּשֵׁי נָשִׁים: Although it is explained in the Talmud that this refers to financial documents, the conclusion indicates that it also applies to actual documents of betrothal (Rashi manuscript; Rabbeinu Yehonatan of Lunel).

Bills of divorce – גִּיטִּין: Rashi in the manuscript explains that this is referring to a case where one is setting out on a journey during the intermediate days and does not wish to leave his wife bound in the event that he does not return. Alternatively, it is referring to one who is on his deathbed and wants to prevent his wife from having to marry in a levirate marriage. Rabbi Shlomo ben HaYatom explains that by giving his wife a bill of divorce, a husband ends the fighting within his home, and therefore writing such a document is considered to be for the sake of the joy of the Festival. In the Jerusalem Talmud, it is asked why writing a divorce document is permitted. Since it causes pain, it should not be an appropriate activity for a time of joy. It is explained there that once one has made up his mind to divorce his wife, it is no longer considered to be painful for him to give her the document of divorce.

Letters of sustenance – אִגְּרוֹת מָזוֹן: Some explain that such a document guaranteed that a widow would receive money for her basic needs from the property of her deceased husband (Jerusalem Talmud; Rabbeinu Yehonatan of Lunel).

LANGUAGE

Wills [*deyateiki*] – דְּיָיתֵיקִי: From the Greek διαθήκη, *diatèkè*, meaning a will. The Sages expound upon it as though it were Aramaic: *Da tehei lemeikam* meaning: This will stand.

Perozbul **– פְּרוֹזְבּוּל:** Through this document one transfers all outstanding loans owed to him to the court, so that the court will collect them. This was instituted by Hillel to circumvent the cancellation of loans in the Sabbatical Year and to thereby prevent lenders from refusing to grant loans.

The origin of the word is Greek, although it is unclear exactly which word it was taken from. Some say that it was related to the word προβολή, *probolè*, meaning the presentation of a message to the court or to a public gathering. It can also refer to a loan. Some say that it is related to the Greek προσβολή, *prosbolè*, which means application or the conclusion of a sale. However, the issue has not been conclusively resolved and there are also other opinions with regard to the word's origins.

BACKGROUND

Sea of Tiberias – יַמָּה שֶׁל טְבֶרְיָה:

Aerial view of the Sea of Tiberias, also known as the Sea of Galilee

HALAKHA

Writing during the intermediate days of a Festival – כְּתִיבָה בְּחוֹל הַמּוֹעֵד: During the intermediate days of the Festival it is permitted to write documents of betrothal; documents of stipulation; bills of divorce; receipts for repayment of debt; wills; gift documents; *perozbolin*; letters of valuation; letters of sustenance, and some say this includes a document in which a man writes that he will support his step-daughter (Rema); documents of *halitza*; documents of refusal; documents of arbitration; and decrees of the court.

Some say that it is permitted to write a marriage document, and some say that it is prohibited (Rema). Some permit one to write down novel ideas he has about Torah, lest he forget them. Some permit the writing of greeting letters, based on the Jerusalem Talmud, and others prohibit it. In many places it is customary to be stringent (Rema).

Some authorities say that writing is permitted, as long as it is not in the script used for writing Torah scrolls, because ordinary script is not considered to be the work of an expert. Those who write in an ordinary manner during the intermediate days of the Festival do so based on this opinion. Some require that each letter be written in an unusual manner (*Taz*; *Shulhan Arukh*, *Orah Hayyim* 545:5).

שְׁטָרֵי חֲלִיצָה, וּמֵיאוּנִים, וְשִׁטְרֵי בֵּירוּרִין, גְּזֵרוֹת בֵּית דִּין, וְאִיגְּרוֹת שֶׁל רָשׁוּת.

The list continues: **Documents of the ritual through which the brother-in-law frees the *yevama* of her levirate bonds [*ḥalitza*]**, thereby freeing her from the obligation to marry one of her deceased husband's brothers; documents in which the court records the **refusal** of a girl upon reaching majority to remain married to the man to whom her mother or brothers married her as a minor after the death of her father; **documents of arbitration,**[N] in which the court summarizes a conflict that had been resolved through arbitration; **court rulings; and** the official **correspondence of the** ruling **authorities.**[N]

גמ׳ אָמַר שְׁמוּאֵל: מוּתָּר לְאָרֵס אִשָּׁה בְּחוּלּוֹ שֶׁל מוֹעֵד, שֶׁמָּא יְקַדְּמֶנּוּ אַחֵר. לֵימָא מְסַיַּיע לֵיהּ: וְאֵלּוּ כּוֹתְבִין בַּמּוֹעֵד: קִדּוּשֵׁי נָשִׁים.

GEMARA **Shmuel said: It is permitted to betroth** a woman **on the intermediate days of a Festival, lest another** come and betroth her **first.** The Gemara asks: **Let us say that** the mishna **supports** Shmuel, who said: **And these** are the documents that **may be drawn up on the** intermediate days of a **Festival: Documents of betrothal.**

מַאי לָאו שִׁטְרֵי קִדּוּשִׁין מַמָּשׁ? לָא, שִׁטְרֵי פְּסִיקָתָא, וְכִדְרַב גִּידֵּל אָמַר רַב.

What, is the mishna **not** referring to **actual documents of betrothal,** through which one would actually betroth a woman? The Gemara rejects this: **No,** the mishna is referring to **documents of stipulation** recording the amounts that the parents agree to pay as the dowry of their respective son or daughter, **in accordance with** what **Rav Giddel said** that **Rav said.**

דְּאָמַר רַב גִּידֵּל אָמַר רַב: ״כַּמָּה אַתָּה נוֹתֵן לִבְנְךָ״ – כָּךְ וְכָךְ; ״כַּמָּה אַתָּה נוֹתֵן לְבִתְּךָ״ – כָּךְ וְכָךְ. עָמְדוּ וְקִדְּשׁוּ – קָנוּ. הֵן הֵן הַדְּבָרִים הַנִּקְנִין בַּאֲמִירָה.

For Rav Giddel said that **Rav said:** When two families negotiate the terms of marriage for their respective children, and one side says to the other: **How much do you give**[H] **to your son** as a dowry? And the second side says: I give **such and such** amount; **how much do you give to your daughter?** And the first side responds: **Such and such** amount, then, once the bride and groom **arose and** pronounced **the betrothal** formula, then all of these obligations are **acquired** and therefore binding. **These are** among **the things that are acquired through words** alone. In other words, there is no need to perform an additional act of acquisition in order to confirm the agreement, and the mishna is referring to a document recording such an agreement. Although such a document may be drawn up even on the intermediate days of a Festival, this does not mean that one may actually betroth a woman during this period.

לֵימָא מְסַיַּיע לֵיהּ: אֵין נוֹשְׂאִין נָשִׁים בַּמּוֹעֵד, לֹא בְּתוּלוֹת וְלֹא אַלְמָנוֹת, וְלֹא מְיַבְּמִין, מִפְּנֵי שֶׁשִּׂמְחָה הִיא לוֹ. הָא לְאָרֵס – שָׁרֵי!

The Gemara asks: **Let us say** that the following mishna **supports** Shmuel: **One may not marry a woman on the** intermediate days of a **Festival, neither a virgin nor a widow; nor may one** then **perform levirate marriage** with his sister-in-law, if his brother died childless, **because that** would be **a joyous** occasion **for him.** This statement implies that it is only marrying that is prohibited, **but betrothing is permitted.**

לָא מִיבַּעְיָא קָאָמַר; לָא מִיבַּעְיָא לְאָרֵס – דְּלָא קָעָבֵיד מִצְוָה, אֶלָּא אֲפִילּוּ לִישָּׂא נַמִי, דְּקָא עָבֵיד מִצְוָה – אָסוּר.

The Gemara rejects this argument: This is not the correct way to understand the mishna, as **it is speaking in the style of: Needless to say.** It is **needless to say** that **betrothal** is not permitted, because the groom **does not perform a mitzva**[N] through betrothal. **Rather,** the same is true **even of marriage, through which one performs a mitzva,** as marriage is preparation for fulfilling the mitzva of procreation. It is still **not permitted.**

תָּא שְׁמַע, דְּתָנָא דְּבֵי שְׁמוּאֵל: מְאָרְסִין אֲבָל לֹא כּוֹנְסִין, וְאֵין עוֹשִׂין סְעוּדַּת אֵירוּסִין, וְלֹא מְיַבְּמִין, מִפְּנֵי שֶׁשִּׂמְחָה הִיא לוֹ. שְׁמַע מִינָּהּ.

The Gemara offers another support for Shmuel: **Come** and **hear that** which a Sage **of the school of Shmuel taught** in the following *baraita*: **One may betroth** a woman on the intermediate days of a Festival,[H] **but he may not marry** her, **nor may he make a betrothal feast, nor may he perform levirate marriage, because that** would be **a joyous** occasion **for him,** and one may not mix the joy of a wedding with the joy of the Festival. The Gemara concludes: **Learn from this** a support for Shmuel's opinion.

NOTES

Documents of arbitration – שִׁטְרֵי בֵּירוּרִין: Rashi, the Rid, and Ran explain that this means arbitration to resolve a dispute. In the Jerusalem Talmud it is explained that this document gives power of attorney to investigators to look into a dispute (a similar explanation appears in the Rashi manuscript, and in Rambam's Commentary on the Mishna). Others explain that these documents contained each side's claims before the court (Riaz).

Official correspondence of the authorities [*rashut*] – אִיגְּרוֹת שֶׁל רָשׁוּת: The early authorities disagree about the way this word should be vocalized and consequently also about its meaning. According to those who read the word *rashut*, these were official documents sent to the ruling government (Rashi) or they contained calculations that were delivered to the government (Meiri). The *ge'onim* explain that it refers to a document in which the *Nasi* or the Exilarch appoints a judge for a certain community (see Rabbeinu Yehonatan of Lunel). However, others read this word *reshut*, based on the Jerusalem Talmud, where it is stated that this expression refers to letters of greetings. Some explain that it is permitted to write such letters because doing so does not require a great deal of precision, and is therefore considered a layman's activity (Rambam).

Some explain that the *halakha* permitting letters of greeting specifically refers to a case in which one will not find a messenger with whom he can send the letter after the Festival, and therefore he will incur some degree of loss by not mailing such a letter at this time (*Tosefot HaRosh*). Others suggest that this type of correspondence will increase the joy of the Festival (Ritva).

Betrothal, because he does not perform a mitzva – לְאָרֵס, דְּלָא קָעָבֵיד מִצְוָה: The later authorities mention that the Rambam, apparently, disagrees with this Gemara. He maintains that there is a mitzva to betroth a woman. Rabbi Shlomo ben HaYatom explains that there is no apparent contradiction, as this opinion in the Gemara holds that betrothal does not complete the mitzva, as marriage does.

HALAKHA

How much do you give – כַּמָּה אַתָּה נוֹתֵן: When there is an arrangement between a man and a woman that they will marry, the man asks his future wife: How much money will you give to me as a dowry? She answers that it will be a particular amount of money. He makes a similar statement to her. After the betrothal declaration has been made, this money is transferred through their statement, provided that the property belonged to them when they committed to it, and they do not need to perform any other method of transfer. There is no distinction between a first and second marriage (*Shulḥan Arukh, Even HaEzer* 51:1, and in the comment of Rema).

Betrothal during the intermediate days of a Festival – אֵירוּסִין בַּמּוֹעֵד: One may not marry or perform levirate marriage during the intermediate days of a Festival. However, one may betroth a woman, though without a betrothal feast, during the intermediate days (*Shulḥan Arukh, Oraḥ Ḥayyim* 546:1).

וּמִי אָמַר שְׁמוּאֵל שֶׁמָּא יְקַדְּמֶנּוּ אַחֵר? וְהָאָמַר רַב יְהוּדָה אָמַר שְׁמוּאֵל: בְּכׇל יוֹם וָיוֹם בַּת קוֹל יוֹצֵאת וְאוֹמֶרֶת: בַּת פְּלוֹנִי לִפְלוֹנִי, שְׂדֵה פְּלוֹנִי לִפְלוֹנִי!

The Gemara raises a question about the ruling itself: **And did Shmuel** actually **say** that we are concerned that **perhaps another** man will come and betroth the woman **first? But didn't Rav Yehuda say that Shmuel said: Every day a Divine Voice issues forth and says: The daughter of so-and-so is** destined to be the wife of **so-and-so; the field of so-and-so** will belong **to so-and-so?**[N] If this is the case, why should one be concerned lest another betroth her first? It is predestined that he will marry his designated mate.

אֶלָּא: שֶׁמָּא יְקַדְּמֶנּוּ אַחֵר בְּרַחֲמִים.

Rather, Shmuel's statement should be understood as follows: **Perhaps another** man will come and betroth her **first by means of** praying for divine **mercy.** In other words, Shmuel is concerned that the rival may beseech God to cancel the decree of the Divine Voice, and therefore the first man needs to hurry and betroth the woman before the other one has a chance to pray that he should take her from him.

כִּי הָא דְּרָבָא שַׁמְעֵיהּ לְהַהוּא גַּבְרָא דְּבָעֵי רַחֲמֵי וַאֲמַר: תִּזְדַּמֵּן לִי פְּלָנִיתָא. אֲמַר לֵיהּ: לָא תִּיבְּעֵי רַחֲמֵי הָכִי. אִי חַזְיָא לָךְ – לָא אָזְלָא מִינָּךְ; וְאִי לָא – כָּפְרַתְּ בַּה׳. בָּתַר הָכִי שַׁמְעֵיהּ דְּקָאָמַר: אוֹ אִיהוּ לֵימוּת מִקַּמָּהּ, אוֹ אִיהִי תָּמוּת מִקַּמֵּיהּ. אֲמַר לֵיהּ: לָאו אָמֵינָא לָךְ לָא תִּיבְּעֵי עֲלַהּ דְּמִילְּתָא?

This is **like this** incident, in **which Rava heard a certain man asking for mercy,** i.e., praying, **who said: Grant me so-and-so** as a wife. Rava **said to him: Do not** pray and **ask for mercy** in **this** way. **If** she **is fit for you,** and it has been decreed that she will be your wife, **she will not go away from you. And if** she is **not** destined to be your wife, **you will** come to **deny the Lord**[N] when you see that your prayer is not answered. **After** the man married this woman, Rava **heard him say** in prayer: Please **either let him die before her or let her die before him.** He was speaking about himself and his wife because he had grown to hate her so much. Rava **said to him: Did I not say to you not to pray for this matter?**

הָכִי אֲמַר רַב מִשּׁוּם רַבִּי רְאוּבֵן בֶּן אִיצְטְרוֹבִּילִי: מִן הַתּוֹרָה וּמִן הַנְּבִיאִים וּמִן הַכְּתוּבִים מֵה׳ אִשָּׁה לְאִישׁ. מִן הַתּוֹרָה – דִּכְתִיב: ״וַיַּעַן לָבָן וּבְתוּאֵל וַיֹּאמְרוּ מֵה׳ יָצָא הַדָּבָר״. מִן הַנְּבִיאִים – דִּכְתִיב: ״וְאָבִיו וְאִמּוֹ לֹא יָדְעוּ כִּי מֵה׳ הִיא״. מִן הַכְּתוּבִים – דִּכְתִיב: ״בַּיִת וָהוֹן נַחֲלַת אָבוֹת וּמֵה׳ אִשָּׁה מַשְׂכָּלֶת״.

Rav said in the name of Rabbi Reuven ben Itzterobili[P] **as follows: From the Torah, and from the Prophets, and from the Writings;**[N] it implies that the decree that a specific **woman** is destined to be married **to** a specific **man is from God.** From where is this derived? It is **from the Torah, as it is written: "Then Laban and Bethuel answered and said: The thing comes from the Lord,** we cannot speak to you either bad or good" (Genesis 24:50). **From the Prophets, as it is written: "But his father and his mother knew not that it was of the Lord"** (Judges 14:4). **From the Writings, as it is written: "House and riches are the inheritance of fathers; but a prudent woman is from the Lord"** (Proverbs 19:14).

וְאָמַר רַב מִשּׁוּם רַבִּי רְאוּבֵן בֶּן אִיצְטְרוֹבִּילִי, וְאָמְרִי לָהּ בְּמַתְנִיתָא תָּנָא, אָמַר רַבִּי רְאוּבֵן בֶּן אִיצְטְרוֹבִּילִי: אֵין אָדָם נֶחְשָׁד בְּדָבָר אֶלָּא אִם כֵּן עֲשָׂאוֹ; וְאִם לֹא עָשָׂה כּוּלּוֹ – עָשָׂה מִקְצָתוֹ; וְאִם לֹא עָשָׂה מִקְצָתוֹ – הִרְהֵר בְּלִבּוֹ לַעֲשׂוֹתוֹ; וְאִם לֹא הִרְהֵר בְּלִבּוֹ לַעֲשׂוֹתוֹ – רָאָה אֲחֵרִים שֶׁעָשׂוּ, וְשָׂמַח.

§ Apropos a teaching of Rabbi Reuven ben Itzterobili, the Gemara states that **Rav said in the name of Rabbi Reuven ben Itzterobili, and some say** that it was **taught in a** ***baraita*** that **Rabbi Reuven ben Itzterobili said: A man is suspected of** having done **something** wrong **only if he** has indeed **done so. And if he did not do it wholly,** then probably **he did it partly. And if he did not do it** even **partly,** then probably **he thought in his heart to do it. And if he did not** even **think to himself to do it,** then certainly **he saw others doing it and was happy.** Suspicions do not arbitrarily arise about a person; therefore is certainly some basis for them.

מְתִיב רַבִּי יַעֲקֹב: ״וַיְחַפְּאוּ בְנֵי יִשְׂרָאֵל דְּבָרִים אֲשֶׁר לֹא כֵן עַל ה׳ אֱלֹהֵיהֶם״! הָתָם לְהַכְעִיס הוּא דַּעֲבוּד.

Rabbi Ya'akov raised an objection: Does the verse not say: **"And the children of Israel fabricated matters that were not right against the Lord their God"** (II Kings 17:9), which indicates that it is possible to make up stories about someone else even though they are entirely baseless. The Gemara answers: **There they did it in order to anger** God, but they did not actually think that what they were saying was true.

NOTES

The field of so-and-so to so-and-so – שְׂדֵה פְּלוֹנִי לִפְלוֹנִי: According to the Ran, this statement is also connected to marriage, as it refers to property transferred to the groom through the dowry.

You will come to deny the Lord – כָּפְרַתְּ בַּה׳: The commentary here follows Rashi's version of the text, according to which, in this case, unanswered prayers lead one to heresy, while answered prayers do not actually benefit him. The *Arukh* explains the passage in a similar manner. However, others have a version of the text which reads: You will come to deny her, meaning that such a person will renounce this woman in the end. In other words, he will regret having married this woman and he will become disgusted with her (*Talmid Rabbeinu Yeḥiel of Paris*; Ran).

From the Torah and from the Prophets and from the Writings – מִן הַתּוֹרָה וּמִן הַנְּבִיאִים וּמִן הַכְּתוּבִים: Some expound on this statement and note that these three verses refer to three different types of couples. The verse from the Torah describes the marriage of Isaac and Rebecca, which was a marriage between a righteous man and a righteous woman. The verse from the Prophets describes the marriage of Samson and his first wife, which was a marriage between a righteous man and a wicked woman. The verse from Writings speaks in general about a marriage between a wicked man and a righteous woman (Riaf; *Iyyun Ya'akov*).

PERSONALITIES

Rabbi Reuven ben Itzterobili – רַבִּי רְאוּבֵן בֶּן אִצְטְרוֹבִּילִי: Rabbi Reuven ben Itzterobili was a *tanna* in the generation of Rabbi Akiva. It is told that he was able to intervene with the powerful people in Rome and cancel any decree made against Israel. Several statements are mentioned in his name in the Talmud and midrashic literature. His two sons were also Torah scholars and became students of Rabbi Yehuda HaNasi. The name Itzterobili appears to be from the Greek στρόβιλος, *strobilus*, meaning round, spinning.

תָּא שְׁמַע: ״וַיְקַנְאוּ לְמֹשֶׁה בַּמַּחֲנֶה לְאַהֲרֹן קְדוֹשׁ ה׳״ – רַב שְׁמוּאֵל בַּר יִצְחָק אָמַר: מְלַמֵּד שֶׁכׇּל אֶחָד קִינֵּא לְאִשְׁתּוֹ מִמֹּשֶׁה! הָתָם מִשּׁוּם שִׂנְאָה הוּא דַּעֲבוּד.

Come and hear a challenge from a different source: The verse states: **"And they were jealous of Moses in the camp, of Aaron the Lord's holy one"** (Psalms 106:16). **Rav Shmuel bar Yitzḥak said:** This verse **teaches that every man warned his wife** against seclusion **with Moses**[N] because he was jealous. This implies that every man thought that his wife had secluded herself with Moses and sinned, although this was certainly not the case. This demonstrates that it is possible to suspect an absolutely innocent person. The Gemara answers: **There they did it out of hatred** for Moses. They did not actually suspect him of wrongdoing. Instead, their goal was to degrade him by leveling these false accusations against him.

תָּא שְׁמַע, אָמַר רַבִּי יוֹסֵי: יְהֵא חֶלְקִי עִם מִי שֶׁחוֹשְׁדִין אוֹתוֹ בְּדָבָר וְאֵין בּוֹ. וְאָמַר רַב פַּפָּא: לְדִידִי חָשְׁדוּן וְלָא הֲוָה בִּי!

The Gemara raises another challenge, based on yet another source: **Come and hear that which Rabbi Yosei said: May my portion** in the future world **be with one who is suspected** of a certain wrongdoing **but is innocent,** as the pain that such a person experiences atones for his sins. This statement also appears to imply that it is possible to suspect an absolutely innocent person. **And Rav Pappa said: They suspected me** of a certain wrongdoing **but I was not** guilty.

לָא קַשְׁיָא; הָא – בְּקָלָא דְּפָסֵיק; הָא – בְּקָלָא דְּלָא פָּסֵיק. וְקָלָא דְּלָא פָּסֵיק עַד כַּמָּה? אָמַר אַבַּיֵי: אָמְרָה לִי אֵם: דּוּמֵי דְּמָתָא יוֹמָא וּפַלְגָא.

The Gemara answers: **It is not difficult. This** is referring **to a rumor that stops,** and therefore it is possible that it is groundless, whereas **that** is referring **to a rumor that does not stop,** and in that case there must be a factual basis for the suspicion. The Gemara asks: To be considered **a rumor that does not stop, for how long** must it persist? **Abaye**[P] **said: My nurse told me: Local gossip lasts for a day and a half,** and then it is deemed to be a rumor that does not stop.

וְהָנֵי מִילֵּי – דְּלָא פָּסַק בֵּינֵי בֵּינֵי; אֲבָל פָּסַק בֵּינֵי בֵּינֵי – לֵית לָן בַּהּ. וְכִי פָּסַק בֵּינֵי בֵּינֵי – לָא אֲמָרַן אֶלָּא דְּלָא פָּסַק מֵחֲמַת יִרְאָה, אֲבָל פָּסַק מֵחֲמַת יִרְאָה – לָא.

The Gemara comments: **This applies only** if the rumor **did not stop in between,** during the day and a half, **but if it stopped in between then we have no** problem **with it,** and it is not a persistent rumor. **And if** the rumor **stopped in between, we said** that it is considered baseless **only** if it **stopped** of its own accord and **not out of fear,** i.e., because the suspect is violent and therefore people are afraid to speak badly about him. But if the rumor **stopped out of fear,** then this dispensation does **not** apply, and it is still assumed that there must be some basis to the rumor.

וְלָא אֲמָרַן אֶלָּא דְּלָא הֲדַר נָבַט, אֲבָל הֲדַר נָבַט – לָא. וְלָא אֲמָרַן אֶלָּא דְּלֵית לֵיהּ אוֹיְבִים, אֲבָל אִית לֵיהּ אוֹיְבִים – אוֹיְבִים הוּא דְּאַפְּקוּהָ לְקָלָא.

And we said that a rumor that stopped is assumed to be baseless **only if it did not arise again.**[N] **But if it arose again,** then this does **not** apply. **And we said** that a rumor that does not stop must be taken seriously **only if** the slandered person **has no enemies. But if he** has known **enemies,** then it can be assumed that **it was the enemies who disseminated the rumor.**

מתני׳ אֵין כּוֹתְבִין שִׁטְרֵי חוֹב בַּמּוֹעֵד. וְאִם אֵינוֹ מַאֲמִינוֹ, אוֹ שֶׁאֵין לוֹ מַה יֹּאכַל – הֲרֵי זֶה יִכְתּוֹב.

MISHNA One may not write bills of debt on the intermediate days of a **Festival. But if** the lender **does not trust** the borrower, and he is concerned that the borrower will later deny the loan, **or** if the scribe **has nothing to eat,** then **he may write** a bill of debt during the Festival week.

אֵין כּוֹתְבִין סְפָרִים, תְּפִילִּין וּמְזוּזוֹת בַּמּוֹעֵד, וְאֵין מַגִּיהִין אוֹת אַחַת אֲפִילּוּ בְּסֵפֶר עֶזְרָא. רַבִּי יְהוּדָה אוֹמֵר: כּוֹתֵב אָדָם תְּפִילִּין וּמְזוּזוֹת לְעַצְמוֹ,

One may not write Torah **scrolls,**[H] **phylacteries, or** ***mezuzot*** **on the** intermediate days of **a Festival, nor may one correct a single letter, even in the** Torah **scroll of Ezra,**[N] which was kept in the Temple and upon which all the Jewish communities relied. **Rabbi Yehuda says: One may write phylacteries and** ***mezuzot*** **for himself** on the intermediate days of a Festival if he needs them.

NOTES

Warned his wife against seclusion with Moses – קִינֵּא לְאִשְׁתּוֹ מִמֹּשֶׁה: This statement is based primarily on the similarity between the verse: "And they were jealous of Moses [*vaykanu leMoshe*]" (Psalms 106:16), and the verse that describes what happens when a man becomes suspicious about his wife: "And the spirit of jealousy come upon him, and he be jealous of his wife [*vekineh et ishto*]" (Numbers 5:14).

Many explanations are offered for this somewhat surprising statement. Some say that because Moses had a tent outside the camp, people were suspicious that the women who came there would be alone with him in a prohibited manner (Riaf). The author of the commentary *HaKotev* in the *Ein Ya'akov* explains that the Gemara is referring to the congregation of Korah, who warned their wives that Moses was power hungry.

Did not arise again – דְּלָא הֲדַר נָבַט: Rashi in the manuscript has a different version of the talmudic text. He explains that when people other than the rumor's subject actively deny and try to quiet it, it is considered a rumor that stops.

Even in the Torah scroll of Ezra [*sefer Ezra*] – אֲפִילּוּ בְּסֵפֶר עֶזְרָא: This is Rashi's version of the talmudic text, according to which this statement is referring to the Torah scroll written by Ezra. This scroll was central in that it was the Torah scroll that was used to correct every other Torah scroll (Meiri).

However, most authorities have a version of the Gemara that reads: The Torah scroll of the courtyard [*sefer azara*]. This term refers to the Torah scroll that was kept in the Temple courtyard. It was used by the High Priest when he read on Yom Kippur (Rabbeinu Yehonatan of Lunel; see Rashi manuscript). Others suggest that it was the king who read from this Torah scroll during the time of *hakhel* (Rabbi Shlomo ben HaYatom; Meiri).

PERSONALITIES

Abaye – אַבַּיֵי: Abaye was one of the most famous of the Babylonian *amora'im*. The disagreements between Abaye and his colleague Rava recorded in the Gemara are so essential that the Gemara itself is referred to as the discussions of Abaye and Rava. Among those hundreds of discussions, the ruling follows Abaye in only six cases.

Abaye was orphaned at the time of his birth and raised bsy his paternal uncle, Rabba. The nurse who raised him impressed upon him many life lessons, which he quotes in the Gemara in her name. There are a number of stories in the Gemara that illustrate his intelligence even as a child, including some in which Rabba tests him with questions.

Abaye was chosen to head the academy in Pumbedita. He celebrated the study of Torah and would announce a holiday for the scholars whenever one of them completed a tractate. Growing up in his uncle's home, he was aware of the difficulties of scholars who were without financial means. The Gemara in tractate *Berakhot* (35b) relates that he testified that many were successful following the path of Rabbi Yishmael, who instructed his students to plow, plant, and harvest in the appropriate time. Only very few were successful following the path of Rabbi Shimon bar Yoḥai, who taught that one should devote himself entirely to Torah and ignore worldly concerns.

HALAKHA

Writing a Torah scroll – כְּתִיבָה בְּסֵפֶר: It is prohibited to write or correct even one letter in a Torah scroll during the intermediate days of a Festival. Some say this is prohibited even if it is needed for communal use during the Festival. The accepted custom is to permit writing in ordinary handwriting and to prohibit only the special scribal writing used for Torah scrolls (*Shulḥan Arukh, Oraḥ Ḥayyim* 545:1, and in the comment of Rema).

וְטוֹוֶה עַל יְרֵיכוֹ תְּכֵלֶת לְצִיצִיתוֹ.

And one may spin sky-blue wool[B] **for his ritual fringes on his thigh,**[HB] but not in the ordinary manner with a spindle, as this procedure must be performed in an altered manner on the intermediate days of a Festival.

גמ׳ תָּנוּ רַבָּנַן: כּוֹתֵב אָדָם תְּפִילִּין וּמְזוּזוֹת לְעַצְמוֹ, וְטוֹוֶה עַל יְרֵיכוֹ תְּכֵלֶת לְצִיצִיתוֹ; וְלַאֲחֵרִים בְּטוֹבָה, דִּבְרֵי רַבִּי מֵאִיר. רַבִּי יְהוּדָה אוֹמֵר מַעֲרִים וּמוֹכֵר אֶת שֶׁלּוֹ, וְחוֹזֵר וְכוֹתֵב לְעַצְמוֹ. רַבִּי יוֹסֵי אוֹמֵר: כּוֹתֵב וּמוֹכֵר כְּדַרְכּוֹ כְּדֵי פַּרְנָסָתוֹ.

GEMARA **The Sages taught** the following *baraita*: **A person may write phylacteries**[N] **and** *mezuzot* **for himself**[N] **and spin sky-blue** wool **for his fringes on his thigh. And for others** he may do these things **as a favor,** but not for payment. This is **the statement of Rabbi Meir. Rabbi Yehuda says:** If he initially made them for himself, **he may employ artifice, sell his own and** then **go back and write** new ones **for himself. Rabbi Yosei says: He may write and sell** them **in his** usual **manner,** in the amount that is **enough** to provide **for his livelihood.**[N]

BACKGROUND

Sky-blue wool – תְּכֵלֶת: This was made with a special dye produced from a species of snail. In talmudic times, this dye was already quite rare, and the means of preparing it, including the species of snail used, were eventually forgotten. In recent generations, efforts have been made to identify the snail and to resume use of the dye. A common identification today is the *Murex trunculus*. Others have suggested the common cuttlefish, *Sepia officinalis*, or the raft snail, *Janthina janthina*.

The Torah requires wool that is dyed sky-blue for two purposes: It is used for ritual fringes; some of the four threads of each fringe must be dyed with this special blue dye, and they are wound around the other threads. However, the mitzva to wear fringes is not contingent on one of the threads being dyed, and today all ritual fringes are made without the dyed thread. In addition, in the priestly vestments, wool dyed this color is used in all or part of the sash, the entire cloak, the *ephod*, and the breastplate.

Murex

Common cuttlefish

Raft snail

Methods of spinning – דַּרְכֵי טְוִיָּה: Spinning fibers of linen, cannabis, cotton, or wool in order to form strings was done with special utensils and complex spindles. Instead of a spindle, which is turned in order to wind the strings, it is also possible to use a stone. Without a spindle or stone, it is possible to spin in a simpler way, without the use of any external utensil, by winding strings around one's thigh.

Woman spinning wool with a spindle

HALAKHA

Making phylacteries and ritual fringes during a Festival – עֲשִׂיַּית תְּפִילִּין וְצִיצִית בְּמוֹעֵד: One may write phylacteries and *mezuzot* for himself and spin strings on his thigh for ritual fringes. If his income is minimal or if he needs to make more money in order to cover the expenses of the Festival then he may write these items and sell enough of them to others so that he can earn a living. If he writes phylacteries in order to wear them during the intermediate days of the Festival then it is permitted for him to write them in any case (Rema), because the *halakha* is in accordance with the opinion of Rabbi Yehuda and Rabbi Yosei (*Shulḥan Arukh*, *Oraḥ Ḥayyim* 545:3).

NOTES

A person may write phylacteries – כּוֹתֵב אָדָם תְּפִילִּין: Nevertheless, one may not write a Torah scroll. This is because the mitzvot of fringes and phylacteries are completed when work on them is finished. However, the mitzva pertaining to a Torah scroll is not completed when it is written, as Torah scrolls are written in order to fulfill the mitzva of teaching Torah (*Commentary on Rif*).

Write phylacteries…for himself – כּוֹתֵב...תְּפִילִּין...לְעַצְמוֹ: Many of the early authorities discuss a question not mentioned by the Gemara: Should one wear phylacteries during the intermediate days of a Festival? The dispute exists primarily between the early authorities, many of whom say that one may not wear phylacteries during the intermediate days because this period is considered to be like a Festival, during which wearing phylacteries is prohibited (Rif; Rambam; Rashba). The Meiri states that this was the common custom in Spain. Others say that one is required to wear phylacteries during the intermediate days (Rash; Ritva; *Sefer HaMeorot*). The Meiri writes that this is the accepted custom in all of France. Some say that since there is a doubt with regard to this issue, it is preferable to wear phylacteries without reciting a blessing (see Ran; Meiri). This dispute remains unresolved, and the standard Ashkenazic custom is to wear phylacteries and recite the blessings over them (Rema). However, the Sephardic and Hasidic customs, and the custom in Eretz Yisrael, is to not wear phylacteries during this period.

The simple explanation of the statements of the *tanna'im* in the *baraita* is in accordance with those who are of the opinion that phylacteries should be worn during the intermediate days of a Festival, and this also seems to be the opinion stated in the Jerusalem Talmud (see Meiri).

According to those who say that phylacteries should not be worn during the intermediate days of a Festival, this *baraita* is referring to one who is writing phylacteries for himself so that he will have them immediately after the Festival. Similarly, one who is selling phylacteries to others is doing this so that other people will have them when they are needed (Rif).

Some explain that the question of whether or not phylacteries are worn on the intermediate days is the basis of the dispute in the mishna. Rabbi Meir and Rabbi Yehuda claim that one is required to wear phylacteries during the intermediate days of a Festival because they say, in accordance with an opinion that is rejected, that one is required to wear phylacteries on Shabbat and on Festivals as well. However, Rabbi Yosei holds that one may not wear phylacteries during the intermediate days of a Festival (Rabbeinu Yehonatan of Lunel).

Enough to provide for his livelihood – כְּדֵי פַּרְנָסָתוֹ: The *Ba'al Halakhot Gedolot* explains that this expression refers to one who has nothing to eat. Many of the early authorities challenge this opinion, as if this were the case then certainly even Rabbi Meir would agree that it would be permitted. Consequently, they explain that the expression: Enough to provide for his livelihood, includes earning enough to cover expenses beyond one's most basic needs, such as the additional expenses of the Festival. With regard to the reason for this, some explain that once writing phylacteries is permitted, it is possible to expand this leniency and claim that one may write phylacteries in order to sell them (Rid).

אורי ליה רב לרב חננאל, ואמרי לה רבה בר בר חנה לרב חננאל: הלכה, כותב ומוכר כדרכו כדי פרנסתו.

Rav ruled for Rav Ḥananel, and some say it was **Rabba bar bar Ḥana** who ruled **for Rav Ḥananel: The *halakha* is** that **one may write and sell** them **in his** usual **manner,** in the amount that is **enough** to provide **for his livelihood.**

״וטווה על יריכו תכלת״. תנו רבנן: טווה אדם על יריכו תכלת לציציתו, אבל לא באבן, דברי רבי אליעזר. וחכמים אומרים: אף באבן. רבי יהודה אומר משמו: באבן, אבל לא בפלך. וחכמים אומרים: בין באבן בין בפלך.

§ The mishna taught: **And one may spin sky-blue** wool **for** his **ritual fringes on his thigh. The Sages taught** a *baraita*: **A person may spin sky-blue** wool **for his ritual fringes on his thigh, but not with a stone,** which can be used to form a small spindle and ease the spinning process; this is **the statement of Rabbi Eliezer. But the Rabbis say:** One may spin the sky-blue wool **even with a stone. Rabbi Yehuda said in** the name of Rabbi Eliezer: It is permitted **with a stone, but not with a spindle. And the Rabbis say:** One may spin this wool **with either a stone or a spindle.**

אמר רב יהודה אמר שמואל, וכן אמר רבי חייא בר אבא אמר רבי יוחנן: הלכה, בין באבן בין בפלך. והלכה: כותב כדרכו ומוכר כדי פרנסתו.

Rav Yehuda said that **Shmuel said, and similarly Rabbi Ḥiyya bar Abba said** that **Rabbi Yoḥanan said:** The *halakha* is that one may spin the sky-blue wool for fringes on the intermediate days of a Festival, **both with a stone and with a spindle,** owing to the importance of the mitzva of ritual fringes. **And** similarly **the *halakha* is: One may write** phylacteries and *mezuzot* on the intermediate days of a Festival **in his** usual **manner and sell enough** to provide **for his livelihood.**

מתני׳ הקובר את מתו שלשה ימים קודם לרגל – בטלה הימנו גזרת שבעה. שמונה – בטלו הימנו גזרת שלשים.

MISHNA **One who buries his deceased** relative **three days before a pilgrimage Festival**[N] has **the decree of** the **seven**-day period of mourning, i.e., the *halakhot* and prohibitions associated with that period, **nullified for him** by the Festival. He is not required to complete this seven-day mourning period after the Festival. If one buries his deceased relative **eight** days before a pilgrimage Festival, then **the decree of thirty** days **is nullified for him.** The restrictions that ordinarily apply during this thirty-day mourning period no longer apply after the Festival.[N]

מפני שאמרו: שבת עולה ואינה מפסקת, רגלים – מפסיקין ואינן עולין.

This is **because** the Sages **said**[N] a principle with regard to this issue: **Shabbat counts** as one of the days of mourning, although one may not mourn on it **and it does not interrupt**[H] the mourning period, which continues after Shabbat. The **pilgrimage Festivals,** on the other hand, **interrupt** the mourning period,[N] so that if one began mourning before such a Festival, then the mourning period is canceled by the Festival. **They do not,** however, **count.**[H] If one did not begin mourning before the Festival, or if his relative died during the Festival, then he is required to complete his mourning period afterward, as the days of the Festival do not count toward the requisite days of mourning.

רבי אליעזר אומר: משחרב בית המקדש עצרת כשבת.

Rabbi Eliezer says: From the time that the Temple was destroyed, *Shavuot* is like Shabbat, because nowadays the days following *Shavuot* are not treated like Festival days. When the Temple stood, many of the Festival's offerings that could not be sacrificed on *Shavuot* itself would be sacrificed during the six days following the Festival. Nowadays, however, when offerings are no longer sacrificed, *Shavuot* lasts for only one day in Eretz Yisrael, and therefore it is treated like Shabbat with regard to mourning: It counts as one of the days of mourning, but does not interrupt the period of mourning.

NOTES

Three days before a pilgrimage Festival – שלשה ימים קודם הרגל: The reason for this is because the first three days of mourning are considered to be the most stringent in several ways, as will be explained later. Consequently, they are treated as a separate entity, e.g., with regard to wearing phylacteries according to many authorities (Ritva; see *Sefat Emet*).

The decree of seven…the decree of thirty – גזרת שבעה...גזרת שלשים: They are referred to by the term decree because all the *halakhot* of mourning are based on rabbinic decree (Rabbi Shlomo ben HaYatom).

Because they said – מפני שאמרו: The Ritva questions this wording, which seems to introduce a new issue, but in fact only restates what is previously mentioned in the mishna. He explains that because all the *halakhot* of mourning are of rabbinic origin, it is the Sages who decide both what the *halakhot* of mourning are and how they are counted. Rabbi Shlomo ben HaYatom explains that the phrase: Because they said, introduces a quotation of a tradition that was transmitted by Moses from Sinai, and this quotation serves as the basis for the *halakha* in the mishna.

Shabbat and Festivals – שבת ויום טוב: Several explanations are offered for the difference between Shabbat and Festivals. Some say that the difference between them is that one may not perform a public display of mourning on Shabbat; however, mourning applies in private. For this reason, Shabbat counts as part of the mourning period. It has already been noted that this opinion fits with the opinion that there is no private mourning during a Festival (see Jerusalem Talmud, Rambam's Commentary on the Mishna; Rabbeinu Yehonatan of Lunel).

In the Jerusalem Talmud it is explained that Shabbat does not interrupt the mourning because if it did then there would never be a seven-day period of mourning. Some of the early authorities (*Ba'al Halakhot Gedolot*; *She'iltot*) make the following distinction: One is required to have enjoyment from Shabbat, and therefore one may not engage in public displays of mourning during it. Yet one may still be slightly sad during Shabbat. On the other hand, one is commanded to be joyous during the Festival, and therefore the *halakhot* of mourning are nullified altogether.

HALAKHA

Shabbat counts and it does not interrupt – שבת עולה ואינה מפסקת: Shabbat is counted as one of the days of mourning, although the restrictions of mourning do not apply during it. It does not interrupt the mourning period (*Shulḥan Arukh, Yoreh De'a* 400:1).

Festivals interrupt, they do not count – רגלים מפסיקין ואינן עולין: If one began mourning before a Festival, the Festival interrupts his mourning, and he does not continue mourning upon the conclusion of the Festival. However, if he did not begin observing mourning practices before the Festival, then the days of the Festival are not counted toward his mourning period, and he must observe the mourning in its entirety afterward. In the Diaspora, where two Festival days are observed, the last day of the Festival is counted as one of the seven days of mourning, so only six more days are observed after the Festival ends (*Shulḥan Arukh, Yoreh De'a* 399:2).

רַבָּן גַּמְלִיאֵל אוֹמֵר: רֹאשׁ הַשָּׁנָה וְיוֹם הַכִּפּוּרִים כִּרְגָלִים. וַחֲכָמִים אוֹמְרִים: לֹא כְּדִבְרֵי זֶה וְלֹא כְּדִבְרֵי זֶה, אֶלָּא: עֲצֶרֶת – כִּרְגָלִים, רֹאשׁ הַשָּׁנָה וְיוֹם הַכִּפּוּרִים – כְּשַׁבָּת.

Rabban Gamliel says: Even **Rosh HaShana and Yom Kippur** are considered **like the pilgrimage Festivals,** in that they interrupt the mourning period but are not counted toward the days of mourning.[H] **And the Rabbis say:** The *halakha* **is neither in accordance with the statement of** Rabbi Eliezer **nor in accordance with the statement of** Rabban Gamliel. **Rather,** with regard to mourning, ***Shavuot*** is treated **like the** other **pilgrimage Festivals,** whereas **Rosh HaShana and Yom Kippur** are treated **like Shabbat.**[N]

גמ׳ אָמַר רַב: גְּזֵרַת – בָּטְלוּ, יָמִים – לֹא בָּטְלוּ. וְכֵן אָמַר רַבִּי הוּנָא: גְּזֵרַת – בָּטְלוּ, יָמִים – לֹא בָּטְלוּ. וְרַב שֵׁשֶׁת אָמַר: אֲפִילּוּ יָמִים נַמִי בָּטְלוּ.

GEMARA With regard to the mishna's statement that the seven- and thirty-day periods of mourning are nullified, **Rav said:** The **decree,** meaning the main prohibitions of the period, **was nullified,** but **the days** of mourning themselves **were not** entirely **nullified.**[N] Instead, these periods of mourning remain to some degree. **And so said Rav Huna: The decree was nullified,** but **the days** of mourning themselves **were not nullified. And Rav Sheshet said: Even the days** of mourning **were also nullified.**

מַאי טַעְמָא יָמִים לֹא בָּטְלוּ? שֶׁאִם לֹא גִּילַּח עֶרֶב הָרֶגֶל – אָסוּר לְגַלֵּחַ אַחַר הָרֶגֶל.

The Gemara asks: **What is the reason that the days** themselves **were not nullified?** The Gemara explains: It is so **that if** one observed eight days of mourning before the Festival, so that the prohibition against hair cutting was nullified before the Festival, but for whatever reason **he did not cut his hair on the eve of the Festival, he is prohibited from cutting his hair after the Festival** until the end of the thirty-day period of mourning. In other words, the mourning period was not entirely nullified, and since he did not take advantage of the allowance to cut his hair before the Festival, he must observe the prohibitions applying during the thirty-day period of mourning after the Festival as well.

HALAKHA

Rosh HaShana and Yom Kippur with regard to mourning – רֹאשׁ הַשָּׁנָה וְיוֹם כִּפּוּר בַּאֲבֵילוּת: The *halakha* is in accordance with the opinion of Rabban Gamliel that Rosh HaShana and Yom Kippur have the same status as other Festivals with regard to mourning (*Shulhan Arukh, Yoreh De'a* 399:6).

NOTES

The opinions of the *tanna'im* in the mishna – שִׁיטוֹת הַתַּנָּאִים בַּמִּשְׁנָה: The Ramban explains that, according to Rabbi Eliezer, because Passover and *Sukkot* last for seven days, it interrupts the mourning and ends all of the mourning obligations. However, this does not apply to a Festival that lasts for only one day, and after the Temple was destroyed *Shavuot* was celebrated for only one day. It is therefore treated like Shabbat.

Alternatively, Rabban Gamliel says that the difference between Shabbat and Festivals with regard to mourning is related to the nature of the days and not to their length. Festivals, which are days of joy, cancel mourning entirely, and therefore all Festivals are included in this group, even *Shavuot*. The Rabbis essentially agree with Rabbi Eliezer; however, they say that since the additional six days were added to make up the offerings of *Shavuot*, it therefore falls into the same category as other Festivals, especially since it is listed together with them in the Bible. However, this is not the case with regard to Rosh HaShana and Yom Kippur.

The days were not nullified – יָמִים לֹא בָּטְלוּ: Some explain that, according to Rav, the harsh decrees of mourning are nullified. However, the days of mourning themselves are not nullified. Therefore, after the Festival one is required to make up the days on which he did not mourn by refraining from cutting his hair during that time (Rabbi Shlomo ben HaYatom).

וְהָתַנְיָא: הַקּוֹבֵר אֶת מֵתוֹ שְׁלֹשָׁה יָמִים קוֹדֶם לָרֶגֶל – בָּטְלָה הֵימֶנּוּ גְּזֵרַת שִׁבְעָה. שְׁמוֹנָה יָמִים קוֹדֶם לָרֶגֶל – בָּטְלָה הֵימֶנּוּ גְּזֵרַת שְׁלֹשִׁים. וּמְגַלֵּחַ עֶרֶב הָרֶגֶל. אִם לֹא גִּילַּח עֶרֶב הָרֶגֶל – אָסוּר לְגַלֵּחַ אַחַר הָרֶגֶל.

But isn't it taught[N] in a *baraita*: In the case of **one who buries his dead** relative **three days before a pilgrimage Festival, the decree** of the **seven**-day period of mourning is **nullified for him.** If one buries his dead relative **eight** days before a Festival, **the decree of thirty** days **is nullified for him,** and therefore he may **cut his hair on the eve of the Festival. If,** however, **he did not cut his hair on the eve of the Festival, he is prohibited from cutting his hair after the Festival**[N] until the end of the thirty-day period of mourning.

אַבָּא שָׁאוּל אוֹמֵר: מוּתָּר לְגַלֵּחַ אַחַר הָרֶגֶל. שֶׁכְּשֵׁם שֶׁמִּצְוַת שְׁלֹשָׁה מְבַטֶּלֶת גְּזֵרַת שִׁבְעָה – כָּךְ מִצְוַת שִׁבְעָה מְבַטֶּלֶת גְּזֵרַת שְׁלֹשִׁים.

Abba Shaul says: Even if he failed to cut his hair on the eve of the Festival, **he is permitted to cut his hair after the Festival, for just as** his observance of **the mitzva of three** days of mourning prior to the Festival **cancels the decree of** the **seven**-day period of mourning, and so if the deceased was buried three days before the Festival, the mourner is no longer required to continue this period of mourning after the Festival, **so too,** his observance of **the mitzva of seven** days of mourning before the Festival **cancels the decree** of the **thirty**-day period of mourning.

NOTES

But isn't it taught – וְהָתַנְיָא: Most of the commentaries explain that the expression: But isn't it taught, which normally introduces a challenge, introduces a support in this case. However, there is a dispute about the details of this support. Some say that it serves as proof for Rav Huna's opinion, based on the first *tanna*, who makes an explicit statement in accordance with his opinion (*Tosafot*, see *Yad David*). Some say the expression: But isn't it taught, means here: Like the dispute between *tanna'im*, and note that the dispute between Rav Huna and Rav Sheshet parallels an explicit tannaitic dispute (Rid; *Talmid Rabbeinu Yehiel of Paris*; Ritva). However, others claim that it is not possible to say that this dispute is like the dispute between *tanna'im* because the dispute between *amora'im* is about how to explain the mishna. It is not a dispute concerning the *halakha* itself (*Tal Hayyim*).

There is another opinion, according to which the expression: But isn't it taught, is meant to introduce a challenge by Rav to Rav Huna's opinion, based on Abba Shaul's statement, which is the accepted *halakha*. According to this explanation, it was not Abaye who said that the *halakha* is in accordance with the opinion of Abba Shaul with regard to the seventh day of mourning, but Rav. This also explains Rav's answer that the *halakha* is not in accordance with Abba Shaul with regard to every issue (Rabbeinu Hananel).

He is prohibited from cutting his hair after the Festival – אָסוּר לְגַלֵּחַ אַחַר הָרֶגֶל: Some say that this serves as a sort of punishment. Because this mourner did not mind entering into the Festival while he was disheveled, the Festival no longer cancels the restrictions that apply during his thirty-day period of mourning (*Talmid Rabbeinu Yehiel of Paris*).

שִׁבְעָה? וְהָאֲנַן שְׁמוֹנָה תְּנַן! קָסָבַר אַבָּא שָׁאוּל: מִקְצָת הַיּוֹם כְּכוּלּוֹ, וְיוֹם שְׁבִיעִי עוֹלֶה לוֹ לְכָאן וּלְכָאן. אָמַר רַב חִסְדָּא אָמַר רָבִינָא בַּר שֵׁילָא: הֲלָכָה כְּאַבָּא שָׁאוּל.

The Gemara asks: Why does Abba Shaul speak of the observance of **seven** days of mourning? **But didn't we learn** in the mishna that it requires **eight** days? The Gemara explains: **Abba Shaul maintains** that the legal status of **part of the day is like** that of **an entire day,** and therefore **the seventh day counts as both** the final day of the seven-day period of mourning and the first day of the thirty-day period of mourning. **Rav Ḥisda said** that **Ravina bar Sheila said: The *halakha* is in accordance with** the opinion of **Abba Shaul.**[H]

וּמוֹדִים חֲכָמִים לְאַבָּא שָׁאוּל כְּשֶׁחָל שְׁמִינִי שֶׁלּוֹ לִהְיוֹת בְּשַׁבָּת עֶרֶב הָרֶגֶל, שֶׁמּוּתָּר לְגַלֵּחַ בְּעֶרֶב שַׁבָּת.

And furthermore, even **the Rabbis concede to Abba Shaul that when one's eighth** day of mourning **occurs on a Shabbat,** which is also **the eve of a Festival, he is permitted to cut his hair on Friday,** which is the seventh day. Since he is unavoidably prevented from cutting his hair on the eighth day, as it is prohibited for him to cut his hair on Shabbat, he may do so already on Friday, although it is only his seventh day of mourning.

כְּמַאן אָזְלָא הָא דְּאָמַר רַב עַמְרָם אָמַר רַב: אָבֵל, כֵּיוָן שֶׁעָמְדוּ מְנַחֲמִין מֵאֶצְלוֹ – מוּתָּר בִּרְחִיצָה. כְּמַאן? כְּאַבָּא שָׁאוּל.

The Gemara asks: **In accordance with whose** opinion **is that which Rav Amram said** that **Rav said:** With regard to **a mourner, once the comforters have stood up** to leave **his** house on the seventh day of his mourning, **he is immediately permitted to bathe? In accordance with whose** opinion? **In accordance** with the opinion of **Abba Shaul.** He maintains that a part of the seventh day is treated as an entire day with regard to this issue.

אָמַר אַבָּיֵי: הֲלָכָה כְּאַבָּא שָׁאוּל בְּיוֹם שִׁבְעָה, וּמוֹדִים חֲכָמִים לְאַבָּא שָׁאוּל בְּיוֹם שְׁלֹשִׁים, דְּאָמְרִינַן: מִקְצָת הַיּוֹם כְּכוּלּוֹ.

Abaye said: The *halakha* is in accordance with the opinion of **Abba Shaul with regard to the seventh** day of mourning, **and the Rabbis concede to Abba Shaul with regard to the thirtieth day,**[N] for with regard to the thirtieth day **we** certainly **say** that the legal status of **part of the day is like** that of **an entire** day, and so a mourner may already cut his hair on the morning of the thirtieth day.

רָבָא אָמַר: הֲלָכָה כְּאַבָּא שָׁאוּל בְּיוֹם שְׁלֹשִׁים, וְאֵין הֲלָכָה כְּאַבָּא שָׁאוּל בְּיוֹם שִׁבְעָה. וּנְהַרְדָּעֵי אָמְרִי: הֲלָכָה כְּאַבָּא שָׁאוּל בָּזוֹ וּבָזוֹ. דְּאָמַר שְׁמוּאֵל: הֲלָכָה כְּדִבְרֵי הַמֵּיקֵל בְּאֵבֶל.

Rava said: The *halakha* is in accordance with the opinion of **Abba Shaul with regard to the thirtieth day** of mourning, **but the *halakha* is not in accordance with Abba Shaul with regard to the seventh** day. **And the** Sages of **Neharde'a say: The *halakha* is in accordance with** the opinion of **Abba Shaul with regard to both** the seventh day and the thirtieth day, for **Shmuel said: The *halakha* follows the statement of the** more **lenient** authority **in** matters relating to **mourning.**

שְׁלֹשִׁים יוֹם מְנָלַן? יָלֵיף ״פֶּרַע״ ״פֶּרַע״ מִנָּזִיר. כְּתִיב הָכָא: ״רָאשֵׁיכֶם אַל תִּפְרָעוּ״, וּכְתִיב הָתָם: ״גַּדֵּל פֶּרַע שְׂעַר רֹאשׁוֹ״, מָה לְהַלָּן שְׁלֹשִׁים – אַף כָּאן שְׁלֹשִׁים.

§ The Gemara asks now about the thirty-day mourning period: **From where do we** derive the **thirty-day** period of mourning?[N] The Gemara answers: **It is learned** by way of a verbal analogy **between** one instance of the word ***pera*** and a different instance of the word ***pera*** stated with regard to **a nazirite. Here,** in the instructions given to Aaron not to mourn the deaths of his sons, **it is written: "Let the hair of your heads not grow loose [*tifra'u*]"** (Leviticus 10:6), which indicates that ordinary mourners are required to grow their hair long. **And there,** with regard to a nazirite, **it is written: "He shall let the hair of his head grow long [*pera*]"** (Numbers 6:5). **Just as there,** in the case of the nazirite, he must grow his hair for **thirty** days, **so too, here** a mourner must grow his hair for **thirty** days.

וְהָתָם מְנָלַן? אָמַר רַב מַתָּנָה: סְתָם נְזִירוּת שְׁלֹשִׁים יוֹם. מַאי טַעְמָא? אָמַר קְרָא: ״קָדוֹשׁ יִהְיֶה״. יִהְיֶה בְּגִימַטְרִיָּא תְּלָתִין הָווּ.

The Gemara asks: **And there,** with regard to a nazirite, **from where do we** derive that he must grow his hair for thirty days? Nowhere is this explicitly stated with regard to a nazirite. The Gemara answers: **Rav Mattana said: An unspecified naziriteship,**[H] when one takes a vow of naziriteship without specifying for how long, extends for **thirty days. What is the reason** for this? **The verse states: "He shall be sacred,** and he shall let the hair of his head grow" (Numbers 6:5), and **"He shall be [*yihye*],"** which is written *yod, heh, yod, heh,* **has a numerical value [*gimatriyya*] of thirty,** as *yod* has a numerical value of ten and *heh* has a numerical value of five. This implies that an unspecified naziriteship extends for thirty days, and by way of the verbal analogy, this is applied to mourning as well.

HALAKHA

The *halakha* is in accordance with the opinion of Abba Shaul – הֲלָכָה כְּאַבָּא שָׁאוּל: The *halakha* is in accordance with the opinion of Abba Shaul with regard to the seven- and thirty-day mourning periods, and it is in accordance with the Sages of Neharde'a, based on the principle that the *halakha* follows the lenient opinion with regard to mourning. Therefore, once those who have come to console the mourner stand to leave on the seventh day, the prohibitions of the seven-day mourning period cease to apply. Similarly, the legal status of part of the day is like that of an entire day with regard to the thirty-day period of mourning, and the restrictions of mourning cease at sunrise of the thirtieth day. The Rema writes, based on the Rosh, that in places where the consolers do not come on the seventh day, the restrictions of the seven-day period end one hour after the time of prayer (*Shulḥan Arukh, Yoreh De'a* 395:1).

Unspecified naziriteship – סְתָם נְזִירוּת: If one took an oath to become a nazirite without specifying for how long it would be in effect, he is required to act as a nazirite for thirty days (Rambam *Sefer Hafla'a, Hilkhot Nezirut* 3:1).

NOTES

The Rabbis concede…with regard to the thirtieth day – וּמוֹדִים חֲכָמִים...בְּיוֹם שְׁלֹשִׁים: The reason for this is because the thirty-day period of mourning is considered to be a less serious type of mourning, and therefore the Rabbis are not stringent with regard to this issue. Instead ,they agree that one may rely upon the principle that a portion of the day is considered to be like the entire day (Rabbeinu Yehonatan of Lunel; *Talmid Rabbeinu Yeḥiel of Paris*).

From where do we derive the thirty-day period of mourning – שְׁלֹשִׁים יוֹם מְנָלַן: As is explained in a later passage (20a), the seven-day period of mourning is derived from the Bible (Rashi manuscript). In addition, this derivation from a nazirite serves as the basis for the dispute between the Rabbis and Abba Shaul. In the case of a nazirite, the unique restrictions apply to him for thirty days, and he is permitted to cut his hair on the thirtieth day itself. However, the *tanna'im* disagree as to why the *halakhot* of a nazirite should be compared to the *halakhot* of a mourner (*Tosefot HaRosh*; see *Tosafot*).

אָמַר רַב הוּנָא בְּרֵיהּ דְּרַב יְהוֹשֻׁעַ: הַכֹּל מוֹדִין כְּשֶׁחָל שְׁלִישִׁי שֶׁלּוֹ לִהְיוֹת עֶרֶב הָרֶגֶל שֶׁאָסוּר בִּרְחִיצָה עַד הָעֶרֶב.

Rav Huna, son of Rav Yehoshua, said: Everyone, including Abba Shaul, who says that part of a day is treated like a full day, **agrees** that **when his third** day of mourning **occurs**[N] **on the eve of the Festival,**[H] the mourner **is prohibited from bathing** his body **until the evening.** In this case, the principle that the legal status of part of the day is like that of an entire day does not apply. Rather, one must observe three full days of mourning. He must therefore wait until the evening and wash himself with cold water, or wait until the intermediate days of the Festival and bathe in hot water.

אֲמַר רַב נְחֶמְיָה בְּרֵיהּ דְּרַב יְהוֹשֻׁעַ: אַשְׁכַּחְתִּינְהוּ לְרַב פַּפִּי וּלְרַב פַּפָּא דְּיָתְבִי וְקָאָמְרִי: הֲלָכָה כְּרַב הוּנָא בְּרֵיהּ דְּרַב יְהוֹשֻׁעַ. אִיכָּא דְּאָמְרִי, אֲמַר רַב נְחֶמְיָה בְּרֵיהּ דְּרַב יוֹסֵף: אַשְׁכַּחְתִּינְהוּ לְרַב פַּפִּי וּלְרַב פַּפָּא וּלְרַב הוּנָא בְּרֵיהּ דְּרַב יְהוֹשֻׁעַ דְּיָתְבִי וְקָאָמְרִי: הַכֹּל מוֹדִים שֶׁאִם חָל שְׁלִישִׁי שֶׁלּוֹ לִהְיוֹת עֶרֶב הָרֶגֶל – שֶׁאָסוּר בִּרְחִיצָה עַד הָעֶרֶב.

Rav Neḥemya, son of Rav Yehoshua, said: I once **found Rav Pappi**[P] **and Rav Pappa sitting** together **and saying: The** ***halakha*** **is in accordance** with the opinion **of Rav Huna, son of Rav Yehoshua. There are** those who **say** a different version of this tradition: **Rav Neḥemya, son of Rav Yosef, said:** I once **found Rav Pappi, Rav Pappa, and Rav Huna, son of Yehoshua, sitting** together **and saying: Everyone concedes** that **when the third** day of mourning **occurs on the eve of a Festival,** the mourner **is prohibited from bathing** his body **until the evening.**[N]

בְּעָא מִינֵּיהּ אַבַּיֵי מֵרָבָא: קְבָרוֹ בָּרֶגֶל, רֶגֶל עוֹלֶה לוֹ לְמִנְיַן שְׁלֹשִׁים, אוֹ אֵין רֶגֶל עוֹלֶה לוֹ לְמִנְיַן שְׁלֹשִׁים? לְמִנְיַן שִׁבְעָה לָא קָמִיבַּעְיָא לִי – דְּלָא נָהֲגָא מִצְוַת שִׁבְעָה בָּרֶגֶל. כִּי קָא מִיבַּעְיָא לִי – לְמִנְיַן שְׁלֹשִׁים, דְּקָא נָהֲגָא מִצְוַת שְׁלֹשִׁים בָּרֶגֶל. מַאי?

Abaye inquired of Rava: If **one buried** his dead relative **on the Festival** itself, **does the Festival count toward his thirty**-day period of mourning, **or does the Festival not count toward his thirty**-day period of mourning? Abaye elaborated on his question: **I do not ask** whether or not the Festival counts toward his **seven**-day period of mourning because **the obligation** to observe **seven** days of mourning **does not apply** at all **during the Festival,** and therefore he must certainly observe the seven-day mourning period, beginning from after the Festival. **What I am asking is** with regard to the **thirty**-day period of mourning, because certain aspects of the **mitzva of** the **thirty**-day mourning period **do** in fact **apply during the Festival,**[N] e.g., the prohibitions to launder clothes and cut hair. **What,** then, is the *halakha*: Do the days of the Festival count toward the thirty days or not?

אֲמַר לֵיהּ: אֵינוֹ עוֹלֶה. אֵיתִיבֵיהּ: הַקּוֹבֵר אֶת מֵתוֹ שְׁנֵי יָמִים קוֹדֶם הָרֶגֶל – מוֹנֶה חֲמִשָּׁה יָמִים אַחַר הָרֶגֶל, וּמְלַאכְתּוֹ נַעֲשֵׂית עַל יְדֵי אֲחֵרִים, וַעֲבָדָיו וְשִׁפְחוֹתָיו עוֹשִׂים בְּצִינְעָא בְּתוֹךְ בֵּיתוֹ, וְאֵין רַבִּים מִתְעַסְּקִין עִמּוֹ,

Rava **said to him:** The Festival **does not count** toward the thirty days. Abaye **raised an objection to** Rava's opinion from the following *baraita*: If **one buries his dead** relative **two days before a Festival, he must count five days** of mourning **after the Festival, and** during this period **his work is performed** for him **by others.**[N] **And his menservants and maidservants do** this work **in private inside his house, and the public need not occupy themselves with him** by coming to console him,

HALAKHA

The third day occurs on the eve of the Festival – חָל שְׁלִישִׁי בְּעֶרֶב הָרֶגֶל: If a Festival interrupts one's seven-day mourning period, he may launder his clothes on the day preceding the Festival, though he may not wear laundered clothes until the Festival begins at night. However, he is prohibited from bathing until nightfall. Some permit him to bathe after the afternoon prayer, immediately before it becomes dark. The Rema writes that this is prohibited because the custom not to bathe during the thirty-day period applies, as the Festival does not cancel the thirty-day period of mourning. The same is true with regard to laundering in places where it is customary for a mourner to refrain from laundering his clothes for thirty days. However, it is the common practice to be lenient (*Magen Avraham*; Rema; *Shakh*; *Taz* on *Shulḥan Arukh, Yoreh De'a* 399:5; *Shulḥan Arukh, Oraḥ Ḥayyim* 548:10).

PERSONALITIES

Rav Pappi – רַב פַּפִּי: Rav Pappi was one of the fourth generation of *amora'im* in Babylonia and a primary student of Rava. There are cases of Rav Pappi discussing halakhic issues with his colleagues, mainly with other students of Rava, such as Rav Huna, son of Rabbi Yehoshua, and Rav Pappa. It appears that Rav Pappi was connected to the house of the Exilarch, that there were warm relations between them, and that eventually he joined the Exilarch's court.

Several members of the next generation of Sages and even his younger colleagues transmitted statements in his name, and the *amora* Rav Ashi is listed as one of his students.

NOTES

When his third day of mourning occurs – כְּשֶׁחָל יוֹם שְׁלִישִׁי שֶׁלּוֹ: There are those who explain that this statement specifically refers to the third day (see *Or Zarua* and Ra'avya). However, most of the commentaries explain that the prohibition against bathing on the eve of the Festival before nightfall does not specifically apply to the third day. Rather, this *halakha* applies to any day during the seven-day period of mourning, with the exception of the seventh day. This day is mentioned only because the wording of the mishna is preserved (*Ba'al Halakhot Gedolot*).

He is prohibited from bathing until the evening – אָסוּר בִּרְחִיצָה עַד הָעֶרֶב: The halakhic authorities explain that bathing is specifically prohibited until the evening. However, this is not the case with regard to laundering and cutting hair, which are permitted on account of the principle that the legal status of part of the day is like that of an entire day. The reason for this distinction is because the latter group of activities may not be performed during the Festival itself, whereas bathing may be performed in a certain way during the Festival (Ra'avad; Rosh).

Certain aspects of the mitzva of the thirty-day mourning period do apply during the Festival – דְּקָא נָהֲגָא מִצְוַת שְׁלֹשִׁים בָּרֶגֶל: Some explain that this does not mean that the thirty-day period of mourning actually applies during the Festival. However, since it is prohibited to launder clothes and cut one's hair during the intermediate days of the Festival, it is as though the restrictions of the thirty-day period of mourning extended into the Festival itself (Rashi; Rabbeinu Ḥananel; Rid).

However, there are others who hold that the thirty-day period of mourning actually applies during the Festival, and therefore a mourner may not wear ironed clothes during the Festival. Similarly, he must avoid joyous social gatherings. According to this opinion, because laundering and hair cutting are similarly prohibited during the Festival, observing these restrictions does not appear to be a public display of mourning (Ramban; Ran).

His work is performed by others – מְלַאכְתּוֹ נַעֲשֵׂית עַל יְדֵי אֲחֵרִים: *Tosafot* question the reasoning behind this leniency. The Ramban explains that because one is not permitted to perform work during the Festival, the Sages were not stringent and did not prohibit him from having his work performed by others after the Festival.

שֶׁכְּבָר נִתְעַסְּקוּ בּוֹ בָּרֶגֶל. כְּלָלוֹ שֶׁל דָּבָר: כָּל שֶׁהוּא מִשּׁוּם אֵבֶל – רֶגֶל מַפְסִיקוֹ; וְכָל שֶׁהוּא מִשּׁוּם עִסְקֵי רַבִּים – אֵין רֶגֶל מַפְסִיקוֹ.

for they already occupied themselves with him when they came to console him **during the Festival. The** general **principle with regard to the matter** is as follows: **Any** activity **that** is prohibited to the mourner **because it is** an expression of **mourning is interrupted by the Festival**[N] and remains prohibited afterward. **And anything that involves the public's occupation** with the mourner,[N] e.g., coming to the mourner to offer him comfort and condolence, **is not interrupted by the Festival,** for people console the mourner during the Festival as well.

קְבָרוֹ שְׁלֹשָׁה יָמִים בְּסוֹף הָרֶגֶל – מוֹנֶה שִׁבְעָה אַחַר הָרֶגֶל. אַרְבָּעָה יָמִים הָרִאשׁוֹנִים – רַבִּים מִתְעַסְּקִין בּוֹ. שְׁלֹשָׁה יָמִים הָאַחֲרוֹנִים – אֵין רַבִּים מִתְעַסְּקִין בּוֹ, שֶׁכְּבָר נִתְעַסְּקוּ בָּרֶגֶל, וְרֶגֶל עוֹלֶה לוֹ.

If **he** buries his relative **three days** before **the end of the Festival,** the mourner **must count seven** days of mourning **after the Festival** because his mourning never began. On the **first four days** of his mourning, **the public must occupy themselves with him** and come to console him. On **the three last days,** however, **the public need not occupy themselves with him, as they already occupied themselves with him during the Festival.** That is to say, they certainly came to console him during the Festival, although the period of mourning did not actually begin until afterward. **And the Festival counts for him** toward the thirty-day mourning period.

מַאי לָאו אַסֵּיפָא? לָא, אָרֵישָׁא.

With regard to the statement of the *baraita* that the Festival counts toward the thirty-day period of mourning: **What, is it not** referring to **the latter clause**[N] of that *baraita,* which speaks about a case where the burial was performed during the Festival itself? If this is the case, then a refutation of Rava's opinion is stated explicitly, that the Festival counts toward the thirty-day mourning period, even if the deceased was buried on the Festival itself. Rava rejects this argument: **No,** it is referring to **the first clause,** which discusses a case where the burial was performed before the Festival, and since rites of mourning were observed already before the Festival, the Festival is counted toward the thirty-day period of mourning. Therefore, it is not a refutation of Rava's *halakha.*

אֵיתִיבֵיהּ: רֶגֶל עוֹלֶה לוֹ לְמִנְיַן שְׁלֹשִׁים. כֵּיצַד? קְבָרוֹ בִּתְחִילַּת הָרֶגֶל – מוֹנֶה שִׁבְעָה אַחַר הָרֶגֶל, וּמְלַאכְתּוֹ נַעֲשֵׂית עַל יְדֵי אֲחֵרִים, וַעֲבָדָיו וְשִׁפְחוֹתָיו עוֹשִׂין בְּצִנְעָא בְּתוֹךְ בֵּיתוֹ, וְאֵין רַבִּים מִתְעַסְּקִין בּוֹ, שֶׁכְּבָר נִתְעַסְּקוּ בּוֹ בָּרֶגֶל, וְרֶגֶל עוֹלֶה לוֹ! תְּיוּבְתָּא.

Abaye **raised an objection to** Rava's opinion from another *baraita,* in which it was taught: **A pilgrimage Festival counts toward the thirty**-day period of mourning. **How so?** If one **buried** his dead relative **at the beginning of a pilgrimage Festival,**[N] **he must count seven** days of mourning **after the Festival, and** during this period **his work is performed by others. And his menservants and maidservants perform** this work **in private inside his house, and the public need not occupy themselves with him** and come to console him, **for they already occupied themselves with him during the Festival. And the Festival counts for him.** Here it is explicitly stated that the Festival counts toward the thirty-day period of mourning, even when the deceased was buried during the Festival itself. The Gemara concludes: This is indeed **a conclusive refutation** of Rava's opinion.

כִּי אֲתָא רָבִין אָמַר רַבִּי יוֹחָנָן: אֲפִילּוּ קְבָרוֹ בָּרֶגֶל. וְכֵן אוֹרֵי לֵיהּ רַבִּי אֶלְעָזָר לְרַבִּי פְּדָת בְּרֵיהּ: אֲפִילּוּ קְבָרוֹ בָּרֶגֶל.

When Ravin came from Eretz Yisrael to Babylonia, **he said** that **Rabbi Yoḥanan said: Even if one buried** his dead relative **during the Festival,** the Festival counts toward his thirty-day period of mourning. **And, similarly, Rabbi Elazar ruled for Rabbi Pedat, his son: Even if one buried** his dead relative **during the Festival** it counts towards his thirty days.[H]

תָּנוּ רַבָּנַן, קִיֵּים כְּפִיַּית הַמִּטָּה שְׁלֹשָׁה יָמִים קוֹדֶם הָרֶגֶל – אֵינוֹ צָרִיךְ לִכְפּוֹתָהּ אַחַר הָרֶגֶל, דִּבְרֵי רַבִּי אֱלִיעֶזֶר. וַחֲכָמִים אוֹמְרִים: אֲפִילּוּ יוֹם אֶחָד, אֲפִילּוּ שָׁעָה אַחַת.

§ **The Sages taught** the following *baraita*: **If one fulfilled the** obligation of **overturning the bed**[N] **for three days before the pilgrimage Festival, he is** no longer **required to overturn it after the Festival;** this is **the statement of Rabbi Eliezer. But the Rabbis say: Even** if one overturned his bed for only **one day,** or **even** for only **one hour,** he is not required to overturn it after the Festival.

NOTES

It…is interrupted by the Festival – רֶגֶל מַפְסִיקוֹ: Some note that the expression: Is interrupted by the Festival, does not mean the same thing here as it does in most other places. Usually the phrase means that the Festival nullifies the rest of the mourning period. However, in this case the term means that the mourning is put on hold and is continued after the conclusion of the Festival (Rashi manuscript).

Public's occupation with the mourner – עִסְקֵי רַבִּים: According to all opinions, this expression refers to people coming to console the mourner. With regard to the meal eaten after the burial, some say that it is eaten even during the intermediate days (Ritva; see *Tosafot*). However, according to the Jerusalem Talmud, this meal may not be eaten during the intermediate days of the Festival, or on Hanukah or Purim.

What, is it not referring to the latter clause – מַאי לָאו אַסֵּיפָא: In other words, does it not refer to all of the *halakhot* stated in this *baraita,* including those mentioned it the latter clause? (Ritva).

He buried his relative at the beginning of a pilgrimage Festival – קְבָרוֹ בִּתְחִילַּת הָרֶגֶל: The Gemara is referring only to the beginning of the Festival in order to present the most extreme case. Although an entire seven-day Festival passed since one relative died, he is still required to observe seven days of mourning (*Talmid Rabbeinu Yeḥiel of Paris*).

He fulfilled the overturning of the bed – קִיֵּים כְּפִיַּית הַמִּטָּה: From the wording of this *baraita,* the Ra'avad learns that the matter is not connected to one's status as a mourner, but rather to his observance of even some of the *halakhot* of mourning, for the Gemara mentions only overturning the bed but not the relative's burial. This is also the opinion of most authorities. However, the Meiri states that the wording used is not conclusive. In his opinion, the Festival nullifies the mourning of one who has buried his relative, even if he had not yet observed the mourning customs.

HALAKHA

Someone whose relative died during the Festival – מִי שֶׁמֵּת לוֹ מֵת בָּרֶגֶל: One whose close relative dies during the intermediate days of a Festival observes the *halakhot* of acute mourning before the burial, and afterward he privately observes the customs of mourning. In such a case, the Festival counts toward the thirty-day mourning period. The public comes to console him during the Festival, and he may perform any work if refraining from it would cause him to incur a loss, as is the case for anyone else during the intermediate days. Any work that does not fall into this category may be performed by his servants and maidservants in private (Rema). Once seven days have passed from the time of the burial, even though he has not completed his seven-day mourning period, his work may be performed by others in their houses. Consolation by others is only for the remainder of the seven days minus the days that he was mourning during the Festival. He practices the seven-day mourning period in an ordinary manner after the Festival. In the Diaspora, he includes the last day of the Festival as one of his seven days, although in practice he does not mourn on it, and therefore he observes only six days of mourning (*Shulḥan Arukh, Yoreh De'a* 399:2).

אָמַר רַבִּי אֶלְעָזָר בְּרַבִּי שִׁמְעוֹן: הֵן הֵן דִּבְרֵי בֵּית שַׁמַּאי, הֵן הֵן דִּבְרֵי בֵּית הִלֵּל. שֶׁבֵּית שַׁמַּאי אוֹמְרִים: שְׁלֹשָׁה יָמִים, וּבֵית הִלֵּל אוֹמְרִים: אֲפִילּוּ יוֹם אֶחָד.

Rabbi Elazar, son of Rabbi Shimon, said: This is the statement of Beit Shammai, and that is the statement of Beit Hillel. In other words, Rabbi Eliezer and the Rabbis disagreed about a matter that was the subject of an earlier dispute between Beit Shammai and Beit Hillel, **for Beit Shammai say: Three days, and Beit Hillel say: Even one day.**

אָמַר רַב הוּנָא אָמַר רַבִּי חִיָּיא בַּר אַבָּא אָמַר רַבִּי יוֹחָנָן, וְאָמְרִי לָהּ אָמַר לֵיהּ רַבִּי יוֹחָנָן לְרַבִּי חִיָּיא בַּר אַבָּא וּלְרַב הוּנָא: אֲפִילּוּ יוֹם אֶחָד, אֲפִילּוּ שָׁעָה אַחַת. רָבָא אָמַר: הֲלָכָה כְּתַנָּא דִּידַן, דְּאָמַר שְׁלֹשָׁה.

Rav Huna said that **Rabbi Ḥiyya bar Abba said** that **Rabbi Yoḥanan said, and some say** a different version of this line of transmission: **Rabbi Yoḥanan said to Rabbi Ḥiyya bar Abba and to Rav Huna: Even one day, even one hour.** The Gemara cites **Rava,** who **said: The** ***halakha*** **is in accordance with** the opinion of **the** ***tanna*** **of our** mishna, who **said three** days. Based on this, we rule that the mourning rites are not canceled after the Festival unless they were observed for at least three days before the Festival.[H]

רָבִינָא אִיקְּלַע לְסוּרָא דִּפְרָת. אֲמַר לֵיהּ רַב חֲבִיבָא לְרָבִינָא: הִלְכְתָא מַאי? אֲמַר לֵיהּ אֲפִילּוּ יוֹם אֶחָד, וַאֲפִילּוּ שָׁעָה אַחַת.

Ravina happened to come to the city of **Sura on the** banks of the **Euphrates** River. **Rav Ḥaviva said to Ravina: What is the** ***halakha*** with regard to this issue? **He said to him: Even one day, and even one hour.**

יְתֵיב רַבִּי חִיָּיא בַּר אַבָּא וְרַבִּי אַמִי וְרַבִּי יִצְחָק נַפָּחָא אַקִּילְעָא דְּרַבִּי יִצְחָק בֶּן אֶלְעָזָר. נְפַק מִילְּתָא מִבֵּינַיְיהוּ: מִנַּיִן לַאֲבֵילוּת שִׁבְעָה? דִּכְתִיב: ״וְהָפַכְתִּי חַגֵּיכֶם לְאֵבֶל״ מַה חַג שִׁבְעָה – אַף אֲבֵילוּת שִׁבְעָה.

§ It was related that **Rabbi Ḥiyya bar Abba, Rabbi Ami, and Rabbi Yitzḥak Nappaḥa were** once **sitting in the pavilion of Rabbi Yitzḥak ben Elazar** and were conversing. **A matter emerged from among them: From where** is it derived that the rites of **mourning** are observed for **seven** days?[N] **As it is written: "And I will turn your Festivals into mourning"** (Amos 8:10).[N] **Just as a Festival** lasts for **seven** days, **so too mourning** lasts for **seven** days.

וְאֵימָא עֲצֶרֶת, דְּחַד יוֹמָא! הַהוּא מִיבָּעֵי לֵיהּ לְכִדְרֵישׁ לָקִישׁ, דְּאָמַר רֵישׁ לָקִישׁ מִשּׁוּם רַבִּי יְהוּדָה נְשִׂיאָה: מִנַּיִן לִשְׁמוּעָה רְחוֹקָה שֶׁאֵינָהּ נוֹהֶגֶת אֶלָּא יוֹם אֶחָד? דִּכְתִיב: ״וְהָפַכְתִּי חַגֵּיכֶם לְאֵבֶל״, וְאַשְׁכַּחַן עֲצֶרֶת דְּאִיקְּרִי חַד יוֹמָא חַג.

The Gemara asks: **And say** that perhaps mourning is like ***Shavuot***, **which is only one day.** The Gemara rejects this argument: **That** derivation, from the one day of *Shavuot*, **is required for** what was stated by **Reish Lakish, as Reish Lakish said in the name of Rabbi Yehuda Nesia: From where** is it derived **that** mourning in the case of **distant tidings,** i.e., when one hears that one of his relatives died a long time ago, **applies for only one day? As it is written: "And I will turn your Festivals into mourning," and we find** with regard to ***Shavuot*** **that one day is** also **called a Festival.**

תָּנוּ רַבָּנַן: שְׁמוּעָה קְרוֹבָה נוֹהֶגֶת שִׁבְעָה וּשְׁלֹשִׁים; שְׁמוּעָה רְחוֹקָה אֵינָהּ נוֹהֶגֶת אֶלָּא יוֹם אֶחָד. אֵיזוֹ הִיא קְרוֹבָה וְאֵיזוֹ הִיא רְחוֹקָה? קְרוֹבָה – בְּתוֹךְ שְׁלֹשִׁים; רְחוֹקָה – לְאַחַר שְׁלֹשִׁים, דִּבְרֵי רַבִּי עֲקִיבָא. וַחֲכָמִים אוֹמְרִים: אַחַת שְׁמוּעָה קְרוֹבָה וְאַחַת שְׁמוּעָה רְחוֹקָה – נוֹהֶגֶת שִׁבְעָה וּשְׁלֹשִׁים.

The Sages taught the following *baraita*: In the case of **recent tidings** of a relative's death, mourning **applies for seven- and thirty-**day periods. In the case of **distant tidings, it applies only for one day. What are** considered **recent tidings and what are** considered **distant tidings? Recent** tidings are news that arrives **within thirty** days of the person's death. **Distant** tidings are news that arrives **after thirty** days; this is **the statement of Rabbi Akiva. And the Rabbis say: Both** in the case of **recent tidings** and in the case of **distant tidings,** mourning **applies for seven- and thirty-**day periods.[H]

HALAKHA

One who buries his dead before a Festival – הַקּוֹבֵר מֵתוֹ לִפְנֵי לָרֶגֶל: When one buries a close relative before a Festival and begins observing mourning practices, even in private, and even for a short period of time, the remainder of his seven days of mourning are nullified by the Festival. In such a case, the days of the Festival also count toward the thirty-day period of mourning.

However, if one did not observe any mourning practices beforehand, whether intentionally or accidentally, the Festival does not nullify the mourning. Therefore, one must observe the mourning customs in private during the Festival, and comforters come to visit and console him in his home. Then he observes the seven-day period of mourning after the Festival. During those days, his work is performed by others, since he refrained from working during the Festival and was consoled. However, the Festival counts toward the thirty-day mourning period, because he observed the customs of this thirty-day period during the intermediate days of the Festival (*Shulḥan Arukh*, *Yoreh De'a* 399:1).

Recent and distant tidings – שְׁמוּעָה קְרוֹבָה וּשְׁמוּעָה רְחוֹקָה: If one receives news that his relative has passed away within thirty days of the death, then he acts as if the day he heard this news were the day of the burial, even if this news arrives on the thirtieth day. Therefore, the mourner rends his clothes and observes the seven- and thirty-day periods of mourning.

If one heard about the death after the thirtieth day, then he is required to observe mourning only for one hour, whether he heard this news during the day or at night, because of the principle that the legal status of part of a day is like that of a whole day.

For one's father or mother, mourning practices are observed even after the thirtieth day, and one may not cut his hair until others rebuke him for looking disheveled. If one receives news about his father's or mother's death more than twelve months after it occurred, then he practices only one day of mourning (*Shulḥan Arukh*, *Yoreh De'a* 402:1).

NOTES

From where is it derived that the rites of mourning are observed for seven days – מִנַּיִן לַאֲבֵילוּת שִׁבְעָה: The Jerusalem Talmud offers different sources for the seven-day mourning period, and the clearest of them is based on the verse that states that Joseph "made seven days of mourning for his father" (Genesis 50:10). However, this proof is rejected by the Jerusalem Talmud because *halakha* cannot be derived from events that occurred before the giving of the Torah. Furthermore, *Tosafot* point out that Joseph's mourning occurred before the burial, and therefore is not a valid source for current practice. Another source is from that which is stated before the flood: "And it came to pass after the seven days, that the waters of the flood were upon the earth" (Genesis 7:10). This is understood as a reference to either God's or Methuselah's time of mourning for the world that would be destroyed. Similarly a proof is derived from a verse describing Miriam, who was afflicted with leprosy and confined for seven days. The verse says there: "Let her not, I pray, be as one dead" (Numbers 12:12), and therefore her case is compared to that of the dead. The Jerusalem Talmud there mentions the details of each of these proof texts and the difficulties with learning from each one.

And I will turn your Festivals into mourning – וְהָפַכְתִּי חַגֵּיכֶם לְאֵבֶל: The Ritva writes that Reish Lakish bases his exposition on the word "Festivals," in plural. He maintains that this word must be referring to two Festivals: A seven-day Festival in the case of recent tidings and a one-day Festival in the case of distant tidings. In the Jerusalem Talmud, it is asked: Why can't this verse be used to conclude that there is an eight-day mourning period from the festival of *Sukkot*, which is eight days long? The answer given there is that the Eighth Day of Assembly is a separate Festival, and therefore none of the Festivals are longer than seven days.

BACKGROUND

Bei Ḥozai – בֵּי חוֹזָאֵי: This is the Aramaic name for the portion of the Persian kingdom near Shatt al Arab, the river formed by the confluence of the Euphrates and the Tigris. Bei Ḥozai is known today as Khuzestan, which is derived from the original name Ḥozai. This area was distant from the centers of Jewish life in Babylonia, and it took several months to make the trip. However, due to the strong business relations between Bei Ḥozai, Babylonia, and Eretz Yisrael, there was constant contact between these places.

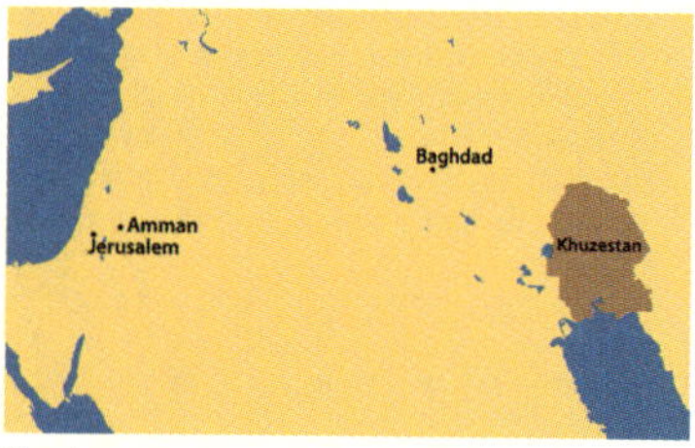

Khuzestan

Ginzak – גִּינְזַק: The Sages identify Ginzak as the biblical Gozan (see I Chronicles 5:26). However, the location of the city is unknown. Some explain that this is the ancient city Ganzak, which stood somewhere south of Lake Urmia. Others hold that it is south of the Caspian Sea, while still others maintain that it is in the vicinity of Nahrawan. It seems that this Jewish center was separate from the primary centers of Jewish life in Babylonia, though it was important enough that several Jewish leaders visited there.

אָמַר רַבָּה בַּר בַּר חָנָה אָמַר רַבִּי יוֹחָנָן: כָּל מָקוֹם שֶׁאַתָּה מוֹצֵא יָחִיד מֵקֵל וְרַבִּים מַחֲמִירִין – הֲלָכָה כְּרַבִּים, חוּץ מִזּוֹ, שֶׁאַף עַל פִּי שֶׁרַבִּי עֲקִיבָא מֵקֵל וַחֲכָמִים מַחֲמִירִין – הֲלָכָה כְּרַבִּי עֲקִיבָא. דְּאָמַר שְׁמוּאֵל: הֲלָכָה כְּדִבְרֵי הַמֵּקֵל בְּאֵבֶל.

Rabba bar bar Ḥana said that Rabbi Yoḥanan said: Wherever you find an individual being lenient and the majority being stringent, the *halakha* is in accordance with the majority, except for this case, **for even though Rabbi Akiva is lenient and the Rabbis are stringent, the *halakha* is in accordance with** the opinion of **Rabbi Akiva.** This is in keeping with the principle **stated by Shmuel: The *halakha* follows the statement of the** more **lenient** authority **in** matters relating to **mourning.**

רַב חֲנִינָא אֲתְיָא לֵיהּ שְׁמוּעָה דַּאֲבוּהּ מִבֵּי חוֹזָאֵי. אֲתָא לְקַמֵּיהּ דְּרַב חִסְדָּא. אֲמַר לֵיהּ: שְׁמוּעָה רְחוֹקָה אֵינָהּ נוֹהֶגֶת אֶלָּא יוֹם אֶחָד. רַב נָתָן בַּר אַמִּי אֲתָא לֵיהּ שְׁמוּעָה דְּאִימֵּיהּ מִבֵּי חוֹזָאֵי. אֲתָא לְקַמֵּיהּ דְּרָבָא. אֲמַר לֵיהּ: הֲרֵי אָמְרוּ: שְׁמוּעָה רְחוֹקָה אֵינָהּ נוֹהֶגֶת אֶלָּא יוֹם אֶחָד בִּלְבָד.

It was related that **Rav Ḥanina received** distant **tidings of his father's death from Bei Ḥozai.**[B] **He came before Rav Ḥisda** to ask what he should do. Rav Ḥisda **said to him:** In the case of **distant tidings,** mourning **applies for only one day.** It was similarly related that **Rav Natan bar Ami received a report about his mother's** death **from Bei Ḥozai. He came before Rava,** and Rava **said to him: They said** that in the case of **distant tidings,** mourning **applies for only one day.**

אֵיתִיבֵיהּ: בַּמֶּה דְּבָרִים אֲמוּרִים – בַּחֲמִשָּׁה מֵתֵי מִצְוָה, אֲבָל עַל אָבִיו וְעַל אִמּוֹ – שִׁבְעָה וּשְׁלֹשִׁים!

Rav Natan **raised an objection to** Rava's opinion based on what was taught in a *baraita*: **In what** case **is this statement** that mourning applies for only one day **said?** In the case of **the** other **five close relatives,** over whose **death** it is **a mitzva** to mourn, i.e., son, daughter, brother, sister, and spouse. **But for one's father or mother,** one is required to mourn for **seven and thirty** days, even when the report of the parent's death is received some time after the event.

אֲמַר לֵיהּ: יְחִידָאָה הִיא, וְלָא סְבִירָא לָן כְּוָותֵיהּ. דְּתַנְיָא: מַעֲשֶׂה וּמֵת אָבִיו שֶׁל רַבִּי צָדוֹק בְּגִינְזַק, וְהוֹדִיעוּהוּ לְאַחַר שָׁלֹשׁ שָׁנִים, וּבָא וְשָׁאַל אֶת אֱלִישָׁע בֶּן אֲבוּיָה וּזְקֵנִים שֶׁעִמּוֹ, וְאָמְרוּ: נְהוֹג שִׁבְעָה וּשְׁלֹשִׁים. וּכְשֶׁמֵּת בְּנוֹ שֶׁל רַבִּי אֲחִיָּה בַּגּוֹלָה יָשַׁב עָלָיו שִׁבְעָה וּשְׁלֹשִׁים.

Rava **said to him: This is an individual** opinion,[N] **and we do not hold in accordance with his** opinion, **as it is taught** in a *baraita*: There was **an incident and the father of Rabbi Tzadok died in** the city of **Ginzak,**[B] **and they informed him** of his father's passing only **after three years. He came and asked Elisha ben Avuya and the Elders with him** what he should do. **And** Elisha ben Avuya **said** to him: **Observe** the rites of mourning for **seven and thirty** days. **And when the son of Rabbi Aḥiyya died in the Diaspora,** and Rabbi Aḥiyya was informed about his passing a long time afterward, he **sat** in mourning for **seven and thirty** days. Therefore, it is clear that this opinion was held only by a few individual Sages, but it was not generally accepted.

אִינִי? וְהָא רַב, בַּר אֲחוּהּ דְּרַבִּי חִיָּיא, דְּהוּא בַּר אַחְתֵּיהּ דְּרַבִּי חִיָּיא. כִּי סְלֵיק לְהָתָם, אֲמַר לֵיהּ: אַבָּא קַיָּים?

The Gemara asks: **Is that so,** that this is Rabbi Aḥiyya's opinion? **But Rav was the son of Rabbi Ḥiyya's brother and** also **the son of Rabbi Ḥiyya's sister,** for Rav's father, Aivu, was Rabbi Ḥiyya's paternal half brother, and Rav's mother was Rabbi Ḥiyya's maternal half sister. **When** Rav **went there,** Eretz Yisrael, his uncle Rabbi Ḥiyya **said to him: Is** your **father,** Aivu, still **alive?**

NOTES

This is an individual opinion – יְחִידָאָה הִיא: In other words, this is the opinion only of Elisha ben Avuya, as will be explained shortly. However, as noted by *Tosafot*, it seems that there are other Sages who also hold that one is required to observe seven- and thirty-day periods of mourning in the case of distant tidings. Therefore, this statement is referring only to the opinion in the *baraita* that accepts the distinction between recent and distant tidings. Elisha ben Avuya essentially agrees with Rabbi Akiva's opinion. However, he also presents a third opinion, according to which Rabbi Akiva's opinion distinguishes between mourning a parent and mourning another relative, and in this respect his is an individual opinion (see Ritva; see *Sefat Emet*, and *Tal Ḥayyim*).

One can ask why this opinion is called individual when it was held by other Sages as well as Elisha ben Avuya. The answer is that, notwithstanding their numbers, they are referred to as an individual in opposition to the majority, which does not accept their opinion (*Tosefot HaRosh*; see Ya'avetz). This supports the Rambam's opinion, according to which even when an individual opinion is mentioned in the Mishna, it does not mean that it was held by only one Sage. Rather, the individual Sage represented the most important member from among the group of minority Sages who agree with him.

אֲמַר לֵיהּ: אִימָּא קַיֶּימֶת? אֲמַר לֵיהּ: אִימָּא קַיֶּימֶת? אֲמַר לֵיהּ: אַבָּא קַיָּים?! אֲמַר לֵיהּ לְשַׁמָּעֵיהּ: חֲלוֹץ לִי מִנְעָלַי, וְהוֹלֵךְ אַחֲרַי כֵּלַי לְבֵית הַמֶּרְחָץ.

Not wishing to deliver unfortunate news, Rav **said to him: Is my mother** still **alive?**[N] In other words, why do you not ask me about my mother, who is your sister, whether she is still among the living? Rabbi Ḥiyya **said to him: Is** your **mother** still **alive?** Rav **said to him: Is my father** still **alive?** Rabbi Ḥiyya understood from Rav's failure to provide him with straight answers that both his brother and his sister had passed away.[P] Rabbi Ḥiyya immediately **said to his servant: Remove my shoes** as a sign of mourning, and afterward **carry my clothes behind me,** as I am going **to the bathhouse.**

שְׁמַע מִינַּהּ תְּלָת: שְׁמַע מִינָּהּ: אָבֵל אָסוּר בִּנְעִילַת הַסַּנְדָּל; וּשְׁמַע מִינָּהּ: שְׁמוּעָה רְחוֹקָה אֵינָהּ נוֹהֶגֶת אֶלָּא יוֹם אֶחָד; וּשְׁמַע מִינָּהּ: מִקְצָת הַיּוֹם כְּכוּלּוֹ.

The Gemara comments: **Learn three** *halakhot* **from this**[N] incident with Rabbi Ḥiyya. **Learn from this** that **a mourner is prohibited from wearing shoes,**[N] and therefore Rabbi Ḥiyya removed his shoes upon hearing of the deaths of his brother and sister. **And learn from this** that in the case of **distant tidings** of a relative's death, the mourning rites **apply for only one day** and no more. **And learn from this** that the legal status of **part of the day is like** that **of an entire** day, as immediately following the removal of his shoes, Rabbi Ḥiyya went to the bathhouse.

רַבִּי חִיָּיא – לְחוּד, רַבִּי אֲחִיָּיה – לְחוּד.

In any case, Rabbi Ḥiyya observed only one day of mourning after receiving a belated report of his siblings' passing, in contrast to Rabbi Aḥiyya, who observed seven and thirty days. The Gemara's question assumes that Rabbi Ḥiyya and Rabbi Aḥiyya are the same person. The Gemara answers: This is not difficult, for **Rabbi Ḥiyya is a discrete** person **and Rabbi Aḥiyya is a discrete** person; despite the similarity between their names, these are two different people.[L]

אָמַר רַבִּי יוֹסֵי בַּר אָבִין: שָׁמַע שְׁמוּעָה קְרוֹבָה בָּרֶגֶל, וּלְמוֹצָאֵי הָרֶגֶל נַעֲשֵׂית רְחוֹקָה – עוֹלֶה לוֹ, וְאֵינוֹ נוֹהֵג אֶלָּא יוֹם אֶחָד. תָּנֵי רַבִּי אַדָּא דְּמִן קֵסָרִי קַמֵּיהּ דְּרַבִּי יוֹחָנָן: שָׁמַע שְׁמוּעָה קְרוֹבָה בְּשַׁבָּת, וּלְמוֹצָאֵי שַׁבָּת נַעֲשֵׂית רְחוֹקָה – אֵינוֹ נוֹהֵג אֶלָּא יוֹם אֶחָד.

§ **Rabbi Yosei bar Avin said: If one received recent tidings** of a relative's death **during a Festival,** when it is prohibited to mourn, **and after the Festival they became distant** tidings, as after the Festival thirty days had already elapsed since the relative's passing, the Festival **counts for him** toward the number of days that make it a belated report. **And,** consequently, after the Festival **he observes only one day** of mourning.[H] Similarly, **Rabbi Adda of Caesarea taught** a *baraita* **before Rabbi Yoḥanan: If one received recent tidings** of a relative's passing **on Shabbat, and at the conclusion of Shabbat it became distant tidings, he observes only one day** of mourning.

NOTES

He said to him, Is mother alive – אֲמַר לֵיהּ, אִימָּא קַיֶּימֶת: There are many different versions of this story, and there are different explanations of each version. Rabbeinu Ḥananel and other early authorities had a version that read: Is Father alive? He said to him: Abba is alive. He said to him: Is Mother alive? He said to him: Imma is alive.

According to this version of the story, Rabbi Ḥiyya asked about the well-being of his own father and mother, i.e., Rabbi Abba bar Aḥa and his wife, who were Rav's grandfather and grandmother. Rav responded that Rav's father, Aivu, and his mother, who were the brother and sister of Rabbi Ḥiyya, were alive, and based on this Rabbi Ḥiyya understood that his own father and mother had died. Rabbeinu Ḥananel derives from here the *halakha* in a case of distant tidings with regard to one's parents.

However, there is another version of the story that is more similar to the one in the Gemara, and most commentaries base their explanations on it. According to this version, Rabbi Ḥiyya asked about Rav's father, Aivu, and his mother. Rav answered with two other questions: Is mother alive, and is father alive? Based on this, Rabbi Ḥiyya understood that his brother and sister had died (Rashi; Rabbeinu Yehonatan of Lunel; Ran).

Some explain, based on this version, that Rav's words constituted a statement rather than a question: My mother is alive, and: My father is alive, and Rabbi Ḥiyya understood, based on the fact that Rav did not answer him directly, that they were no longer alive. Rashi, who offers this explanation, questions it, as it is inconceivable that Rav would tell a lie. Rabbi Shlomo ben HaYatom explains that Rav was speaking through euphemism, as it is stated elsewhere that the righteous are considered alive even after their death. For this reason, he stated that they were alive.

Learn three ***halakhot*** **from this** – שְׁמַע מִינַּהּ תְּלָת: There are two other *halakhot* that can be learned from this story: One can fulfill his obligation to mourn over several deceased relatives at one time (Rabbi Yitzḥak ibn Giat), and one may rely on the testimony of an individual relative with regard to mourning (Ramban). The Ritva writes that these *halakhot* are not mentioned in the Talmud because they were considered to be obvious.

A mourner is prohibited from wearing shoes – אָבֵל אָסוּר בִּנְעִילַת הַסַּנְדָּל: This *halakha*, as it applies to a mourner, is certainly not novel, and therefore some explain that this statement indicates that one who is mourning over distant tidings is prohibited from wearing shoes. According to the Ramban, it means that one can fulfill his obligation to mourn with even a small act, e.g., removing his shoes.

PERSONALITIES

Rabbi Ḥiyya and Rav – רַבִּי חִיָּיא וְרַב: This diagram shows the relationship between Rabbi Ḥiyya and Rav. Rabbi Abba married his first wife and had a son named Ḥana, the father of Rabba bar Ḥana. He also had three other sons, Sheila, Marta, and Aivu. Aivu was Rav's father. Afterward, Rabbi Abba married his second wife, who brought with her a daughter called Ima, from a previous marriage. Rabbi Abba and the second wife had a son named Ḥiyya. Later, Aivu, Rabbi Ḥiyya's half brother, married his stepsister, the daughter of Rabbi Ḥiyya's mother, and their son was named Rav. Therefore, Rav was the son of Rabbi Ḥiyya's brother as well as the son of his sister.

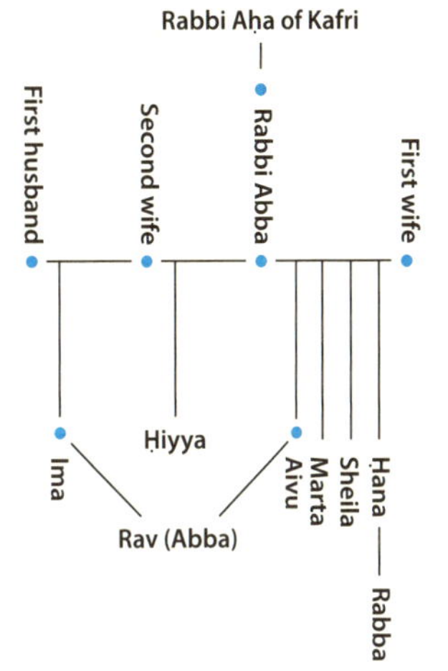

Family tree of Rabbi Ḥiyya and Rav

HALAKHA

Distant tidings on Shabbat and Festivals – שְׁמוּעָה רְחוֹקָה בְּשַׁבָּת וּמוֹעֵד: If one hears on Shabbat or a Festival that a close relative has passed away, and by the end of that day the news will become a distant tiding, then news of the passing is already considered to be a distant tiding when it is received. Consequently, the mourner observes mourning practices in private on Shabbat or the Festival itself. On the following day, he observes only a single day of public mourning (*Shulḥan Arukh, Yoreh De'a* 402:5).

LANGUAGE

Ḥiyya, Aḥiyya – חִיָּיא, אֲחִיָּיה: The name Ḥiyya, like the names of many other *tanna'im* and *amora'im*, is Aramaic. However, there were many common Hebrew names that had an Aramaic version or a shortened form, while the person's actual Hebrew name was rarely used. The name Yosei, which is referred to in the Jerusalem Talmud as Yosa either with an *alef* or a *heh* at the end, is a shortened form of the Hebrew name Yosef. In addition, some say that the name Ezra is actually an Aramaic nickname for the Hebrew name Azariya. The same applies for many different names. Consequently, the Gemara thought that the name Ḥiyya was an Aramaic version of the name Aḥiyya, which is both phonetically similar and has a similar meaning to the name Ḥiyya.

HALAKHA

Rending garments over distant tidings – **קְרִיעָה עַל שְׁמוּעָה רְחוֹקָה**: One is not required to rend his clothes upon hearing distant tidings for other relatives. However, one is always required to rend his clothes upon hearing about the death of a parent or a great person with whom he discussed *halakha* (*Shakh*). This ruling is in accordance with the opinions of Rabbi Mani and Rabbi Zeira (*Shulḥan Arukh, Yoreh De'a* 402:4).

One did not have his own garment – **מִי שֶׁאֵין לוֹ חָלוּק**: One who does not have a garment when he hears that his close relative has died may rend his clothes later if he happens to acquire a garment during the seven-day period of mourning. However, after hearing about the death of one of his parents, he is required to rend his garment at any time afterward, in accordance with the opinion of Rabbi Zeira (*Shulḥan Arukh, Yoreh De'a* 340:18).

קוֹרֵעַ אוֹ אֵינוֹ קוֹרֵעַ? רַבִּי מָנִי אָמַר: אֵינוֹ קוֹרֵעַ. רַבִּי חֲנִינָא אָמַר: קוֹרֵעַ. אָמַר לֵיהּ רַבִּי מָנִי לְרַבִּי חֲנִינָא: בִּשְׁלָמָא לְדִידִי, דְּאָמֵינָא אֵינוֹ קוֹרֵעַ, הַיְינוּ דְּלָא אִיכָּא אֲבֵילוּת שִׁבְעָה. אֶלָּא לְדִידָךְ דְּאָמְרַתְּ קוֹרֵעַ, קְרִיעָה בְּלָא שִׁבְעָה מִי אִיכָּא?

§ The Gemara asks: Upon receiving a belated report of a close relative's passing, **does one rend** his garment **or does he not rend** it?[N] **Rabbi Mani said: He does not rend** it, whereas **Rabbi Ḥanina said:** He does **rend** it.[H] **Rabbi Mani said to Rabbi Ḥanina: Granted,** it makes sense **that according to my** position this is consistent, **as I say** that **he does not rend** his garment, and **this is because there is no seven-**day period of **mourning. But according to you, who says** that **he does rend** his garment, **is there rending without a seven-**day period of **mourning** afterward?[N]

וְלָא? וְהָתַנְיָא אִיסִי אֲבוּהּ דְּרַבִּי זֵירָא, וְאָמְרִי לַהּ אֲחוּהּ דְּרַבִּי זֵירָא קַמֵּיהּ דְּרַבִּי זֵירָא: מִי שֶׁאֵין לוֹ חָלוּק לִקְרוֹעַ, וְנִזְדַּמֵּן לוֹ בְּתוֹךְ שִׁבְעָה – קוֹרֵעַ; לְאַחַר שִׁבְעָה – אֵינוֹ קוֹרֵעַ.

The Gemara asks: Is there **not? But isn't it taught** in a *baraita* reported by **Isi, father of Rabbi Zeira, and some say** it was taught by **the brother of Rabbi Zeira before Rabbi Zeira:**[P] If at first **one did not have** his own **garment**[N] **to rend,**[H] **and he acquired** one **during the seven-**day period of mourning, he should **rend** it then. But if he acquired it only **after the seven-**day period of mourning, **he does not rend** it.

עָנֵי רַבִּי זֵירָא בָּתְרֵיהּ: בַּמֶּה דְּבָרִים אֲמוּרִים – בַּחֲמִשָּׁה מֵתֵי מִצְוָה, אֲבָל עַל אָבִיו וְעַל אִמּוֹ – קוֹרֵעַ וְהוֹלֵךְ!

Rabbi Zeira explained the *baraita* **after him,** filling in a missing element: **In what** case **is this statement** that one does not rend his garment after the seven-day period of mourning **said?** In the case of **the** other **five close relatives** over whose **death** it is **a mitzva** to mourn, i.e., son, daughter, brother, sister, and spouse. **But for one's father or mother, one continues** to be obligated **to rend** his garment if he receives the garment after the seven-day mourning period as well. This apparently contradicts Rabbi Mani's statement that there is no rending without seven days of mourning.

כִּי תַּנְיָא הַהִיא – לִכְבוֹד אָבִיו וְאִמּוֹ.

The Gemara answers: **When that** *baraita* **is taught,** it is referring to a symbolic act meant **to honor his father or mother.**[N] It is for one's father or mother that he must rend his garment, even if it becomes available only after the seven-day period of mourning. Essentially, however, the obligation to rend one's garments applies only when it is followed by a seven-day period of mourning.

NOTES

Does one rend it or does he not rend it – **קוֹרֵעַ אוֹ אֵינוֹ קוֹרֵעַ**: Most authorities explain that the question applies to any type of distant tidings (Rif; Ramban; Rosh; Ritva). However, others explain that this applies only to one who received these tidings on a day when he is prohibited from mourning, and they became distant tidings afterward (*Tosafot*; *Talmid Rabbeinu Yeḥiel of Paris*; see *Tosefot HaRosh*).

Rending without a seven-day period of mourning – **קְרִיעָה בְּלָא שִׁבְעָה**: There is a *halakha* that one is required to rend his clothes at the death of his teacher or the *Nasi* of the Sanhedrin, despite the fact that this is not followed by seven days of mourning. Still, the question here is referring specifically to mourning over family members (*Tosefot HaRosh*; Ritva).

One did not have his own garment – **מִי שֶׁאֵין לוֹ חָלוּק**: *Tosafot* explain that this person was wearing a borrowed garment, which he cannot rend (see *Talmid Rabbeinu Yeḥiel of Paris*). Some explain that this refers to a case where one was wearing an outer garment, which is not torn (Rabbeinu Yehonatan of Lunel). The Ramban explain that this refers either to one who was half naked or to one who was wearing a garment that was already torn.

To honor his father or mother – **לִכְבוֹד אָבִיו וְאִמּוֹ**: Some say that this means that since the mourning over one's father and mother is more serious, one is required to rend his garments even after the seven-day mourning period, as long as it is still within thirty days of the burial (Ra'avad). Others explain that after seven days, rending is no longer obligatory but only a mark of respect. Therefore, it does not apply to the case of distant tidings (Commentary on *Moed Katan*; Ramban; *Sefer HaMeorot*).

PERSONALITIES

Rabbi Zeira – **רַבִּי זֵירָא**: Born in Babylonia, Rabbi Zeira, known in the Jerusalem Talmud as Rabbi Ze'eira, became one of the great third-generation *amora'im* in Eretz Yisrael. His father was a tax collector for the Persian government and was praised as one of the few who filled that position properly.

When Rabbi Zeira emigrated to Eretz Yisrael, he wanted to immerse himself completely in the Torah of Eretz Yisrael. The Gemara relates that he observed one hundred fasts in order to forget the Torah that he had studied in Babylonia.

Rabbi Zeira was famous for his sharp intellect and was the author of incisive *halakhot*. He was also known as an extremely God-fearing man and the Gemara records several stories related to his distinction in that area. He did not even want to be ordained with the title Rabbi, due to his modesty. He relented only after he was told that with ordination comes atonement for his sins.

The Gemara relates that he observed one hundred additional fasts so that the fire of Gehenna would not harm him, and he would periodically check whether the fasts worked by entering a fiery furnace. On one occasion, his legs were scorched, and from then on he was called: The little man with the scorched legs.

He was a contemporary of Rav Ḥisda, Rav Sheshet, and Rabba in Babylonia and one of the disciples of Rabbi Yoḥanan in Eretz Yisrael, and he engaged in extensive halakhic discourse with them. Apparently, he was a flax merchant in Eretz Yisrael, and it is conceivable that he had occasion in the course of his business to return to Babylonia several times.

The text of the beginning of the eulogy for Rabbi Zeira is preserved in the Talmud: The land of Shinar, Babylonia, conceived and gave birth; the land of splendor, Eretz Yisrael, raised her plaything. Woe unto her, said Reket, Tiberias, for she has lost her beloved vessel.

He had a son, Rabbi Ahava, who was also an *amora*.

תָּנוּ רַבָּנַן: כׇּל הָאָמוּר בְּפָרָשַׁת כֹּהֲנִים, שֶׁכֹּהֵן מִיטַּמֵּא לָהֶן – אָבֵל מִתְאַבֵּל עֲלֵיהֶן. וְאֵלּוּ הֵן: אִשְׁתּוֹ, אָבִיו, וְאִמּוֹ, אָחִיו, וַאֲחוֹתוֹ, בְּנוֹ, וּבִתּוֹ. הוֹסִיפוּ עֲלֵיהֶן אָחִיו וַאֲחוֹתוֹ הַבְּתוּלָה מֵאִמּוֹ, וַאֲחוֹתוֹ נְשׂוּאָה בֵּין מֵאָבִיו בֵּין מֵאִמּוֹ.

§ **The Sages taught:** With regard to **all** of the relatives **mentioned in the** Torah in the **passage** referring to **priests,**[N] **for which a priest becomes impure, a mourner must mourn for them. And they are: His wife, his father, and his mother, his brother and his** unmarried **sister** from the same father, **his son, and his daughter.**[H] The Sages **added** other relatives **to** this list: **His** maternal **brother and his unmarried sister from the same mother, and his married sister, whether from the same father or from the same mother.** One mourns for these relatives, **although** a priest would not become impure for them.

וּכְשֵׁם שֶׁמִּתְאַבֵּל עֲלֵיהֶם – כָּךְ מִתְאַבֵּל עַל שְׁנִיִּים שֶׁלָּהֶם, דִּבְרֵי רַבִּי עֲקִיבָא. רַבִּי שִׁמְעוֹן בֶּן אֶלְעָזָר אוֹמֵר: אֵינוֹ מִתְאַבֵּל אֶלָּא עַל בֶּן בְּנוֹ וְעַל אֲבִי אָבִיו. וַחֲכָמִים אוֹמְרִים: כׇּל שֶׁמִּתְאַבֵּל עָלָיו – מִתְאַבֵּל עִמּוֹ.

Just as one mourns for them, so too he mourns for their relatives' relatives, who are his **second-degree relatives.**[N] That is to say, just as one is required to mourn over his close relatives, so too he is required to mourn over his relatives' close relatives, which are known as second-degree relatives. For example, if his father's father, his son's son, his brother's son, or the like passed away, he must join his relatives in their mourning; this is **the statement of Rabbi Akiva. Rabbi Shimon ben Elazar says: He mourns only over his son's son and his father's father,** but not over the other relatives of his relatives. **And the Rabbis say: Any** relative **over whom one would mourn** if that person died, **one mourns with him** when he is in mourning.[NH]

חֲכָמִים הַיְינוּ תַּנָּא קַמָּא! אִיכָּא בֵּינַיְיהוּ עִמּוֹ בַּבַּיִת. כִּי הָא דַּאֲמַר לֵיהּ רַב לְחִיָּיא בְּרֵיהּ, וְכֵן אֲמַר לֵיהּ רַב הוּנָא לְרַבָּה בְּרֵיהּ: בְּאַפָּהּ – נְהוֹג אֲבֵילוּתָא; בְּלָא אַפָּהּ – לָא תִּינְהוֹג אֲבֵילוּתָא.

The Gemara asks: The statement of **the Rabbis is** identical to the statement of the **first** ***tanna***, Rabbi Akiva. What does their statement add? The Gemara answers: The practical difference **between them** is with regard to whether one mourn **with him** only **in the** same **house.** According to the Rabbis, one is required to mourn with his relative only while he is with him in the same house, whereas according to Rabbi Akiva, he is required to observe mourning even when he is not with him. This is **like what Rav said to his son, Ḥiyya, and** it is **similarly** like what **Rav Huna said to his son Rabba,** when the latter's wife was in mourning: **In her presence practice**[N] **mourning,** but **out of her presence do not practice mourning.**

מָר עוּקְבָא שְׁכִיב לֵיהּ בַּר חֲמוּהּ. סָבַר לְמֵיתָב עֲלֵיהּ שִׁבְעָה וּשְׁלֹשִׁים. עָל רַב הוּנָא לְגַבֵּיהּ, אַשְׁכְּחֵיהּ. אֲמַר לֵיהּ: צוּדָנִיָּיתָא בָּעֵית לְמֵיכַל? לֹא אָמְרוּ לִכְבוֹד אִשְׁתּוֹ אֶלָּא חָמִיו וַחֲמוֹתוֹ.

It is related that **the son of Mar Ukva's father-in-law,** i.e., Mar Ukva's brother-in-law, **died,** and Mar Ukva **thought to sit** in mourning **over him for the seven- and thirty-**day periods of mourning. **Rav Huna went into his** house, **found him** observing the rites of mourning, and **said to him: Do you desire to eat mourners' food** [***tzudaniyyata***]?[L] The Sages **said** that one should observe mourning **in honor of his wife only** when she is in mourning over the death **of his father-in-law or his mother-in-law.**

NOTES

All those mentioned in the passage of priests – כׇּל הָאָמוּר בְּפָרָשַׁת כֹּהֲנִים: It is stated in the passage: "Except for his close relatives, for his mother, and for his father, and for his son, and for his daughter, and for his brother; and for his virgin sister, that is near unto him, that has had no husband, for her he may make himself impure" (Leviticus 21:2–3). The Sages understand that the brother mentioned in the verse is referring to the priest's paternal brother, who inherits from him, and not to a maternal brother. With regard to his wife, the Sages derive the requirement to become impure for her from the expression: "Except for his close relatives."

However, many of the early authorities had a version of the Gemara text that did not include his wife in the list of permitted relatives. Some explain that the reason for this is because certain distinctions are made depending on the status of his wife, e.g., whether he was betrothed to her or married and whether she was permitted to marry a priest or not. Similarly, with regard to mourning over her relatives, she is not listed with the others (see Ritva). According to the Rambam, one's wife is considered one of his close family members by rabbinic decree.

Their second-degree relatives – שְׁנִיִּים שֶׁלָּהֶם: Some say that the second-degree relatives mentioned are the generations above and below, such as a father's father or a son's son (*Tosefot HaRosh*). Others hold that this category applies only to relatives with whom one has a blood relationship, but not to those to whom he is related through marriage, whether his marriage or his relatives' marriage. Alternatively, this *halakha* applies only to relatives on his father's side, to whom the *halakhot* of inheritance apply (see Ramban).

One mourns with him – מִתְאַבֵּל עִמּוֹ: The reason for this is due to their relationship and the desire to maintain peace within the home (Rabbeinu Yehonatan of Lunel). Based on this, the early authorities write that if a one's relatives are not concerned whether he mourns with them or not, they may forgo this honor. The common practice nowadays is to assume that everyone forgoes this honor, and no one observes these customs.

In her presence practice – בְּאַפָּהּ נְהוֹג: This does not mean that he is required to observe customs of mourning only when she is looking, for acting in this manner would make the issue seem trivial. Instead, this means that he is required to observe the mourning customs only when he is actually with her (Ramban; Ritva).

LANGUAGE

Mourners' food [*tzudaniyyata*] – צוּדָנִיָּיתָא: Many different versions of this word exist, and many different sources are used in order to offer an explanation for it. The version of the word in the Gemara appears to be related to the word *tzeida*, meaning provisions. In this context, the word means food prepared for a specific purpose, such as *tzeida laderekh*, provisions for a journey.

HALAKHA

Over whom does one mourn – עַל מִי מִתְאַבְּלִים: One is required to mourn over all relatives for which a priest becomes ritually impure, including one's father, mother, son, daughter, paternal brother, unmarried paternal sister, and wife. The Sages added that one should also mourn over his maternal brother and his sister, whether she is married or unmarried and whether they share the same father or mother. Just as a man mourns for his wife, so a woman is required to mourn for her husband (*Shulḥan Arukh*, *Yoreh De'a* 374:4).

Any relative over whom one would mourn, one mourns with him – כׇּל שֶׁמִּתְאַבֵּל עָלָיו, מִתְאַבֵּל עִמּוֹ: One is required to mourn with any family member over whom he would mourn if they were to die. This applies when they are in his presence. However, outside of their presence one is not required to observe mourning practices, in accordance with the opinion of the Rabbis.

Although a man is required to mourn for his wife, he mourns with her only over the death of her father or mother. Similarly, she is required to mourn with him only when one of his parents dies, but not when he loses another close family member.

The Rema writes that nowadays the custom is to be lenient with regard to this type of mourning, and one does not observe mourning practices for second-degree relatives (see *Tur*, citing Ramban and Rosh). This has become the common practice, and one who is stringent with regard to this issue is considered to be acting in a peculiar manner.

It is generally accepted that one practices certain customs of mourning during the first week after the death of a relative who is not one of those for whom one is required to mourn formally. This includes all those whose family relationship would prohibit giving joint testimony. In such circumstances, one does not bathe or change clothes, and in some places other customs of mourning are observed as well. This applies specifically to recent tidings.

One who wishes may act stringently and mourn formally for a person for whom he is not required to mourn or wear black clothes for him (*Shulḥan Arukh*, *Yoreh De'a* 374:6).

BACKGROUND

To paint [*koḥelet*] **her eyelids** – **לִהְיוֹת כּוֹחֶלֶת:** The Hebrew term refers to kohl, a dark blue or black color that is extracted from the sulfide mineral stibnite, Sb_2S_3, sometimes referred to as antimonite. In antiquity, the crystals of the mineral were ground up and used by women for painting their eyelashes, eyebrows, and eyelids, thereby accenting their eyes and giving the impression that their eyes were larger than they actually were. Kohl was also used for healing the eyes.

Stibnite crystal

Ancient Egyptian kohl tube

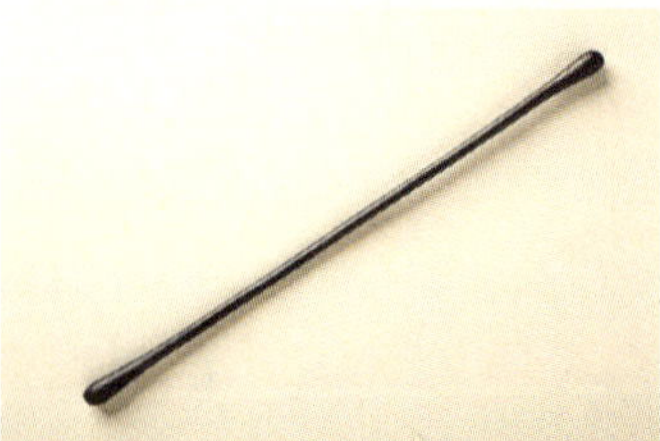

Ancient kohl applicator

LANGUAGE

Rouge [*pokeset*] – **פּוֹקֶסֶת:** From the Greek φῦκος, *fukos*, meaning the color red. See also LANGUAGE, p. 53.

דְּתַנְיָא: מִי שֶׁמֵּת חָמִיו אוֹ חֲמוֹתוֹ – אֵינוֹ רַשַּׁאי לָכוֹף אֶת אִשְׁתּוֹ לִהְיוֹת כּוֹחֶלֶת וְלִהְיוֹת פּוֹקֶסֶת. אֶלָּא כּוֹפֶה מִטָּתוֹ, וְנוֹהֵג עִמָּהּ אֲבֵילוּת. וְכֵן הִיא שֶׁמֵּת חָמִיהָ אוֹ חֲמוֹתָהּ – אֵינָהּ רַשָּׁאָה לִהְיוֹת כּוֹחֶלֶת וְלִהְיוֹת פּוֹקֶסֶת, אֶלָּא כּוֹפָה מִטָּתָהּ וְנוֹהֶגֶת עִמּוֹ אֲבֵילוּת.

As it is taught in a *baraita*: **One whose father-in-law or mother-in-law died may not force his wife to paint** [*koḥelet*] her eyelids[B] **or put rouge** [*pokeset*][L] on her face while she is in mourning. **Rather, he should overturn his bed, and observe** the rites of **mourning with her. And similarly, when her father-in-law or mother-in-law dies, she may not paint** her eyelids **or put rouge** on her face. **Rather, she should overturn her bed and practice** the rites of **mourning with him.**

וְתַנְיָא אִידָּךְ: אַף עַל פִּי שֶׁאָמְרוּ אֵינוֹ רַשַּׁאי לָכוֹף אֶת אִשְׁתּוֹ לִהְיוֹת כּוֹחֶלֶת וְלִהְיוֹת פּוֹקֶסֶת, בֶּאֱמֶת אָמְרוּ: מוֹזֶגֶת לוֹ אֶת הַכּוֹס, וּמַצַּעַת לוֹ מִטָּה, וּמַרְחֶצֶת לוֹ פָּנָיו יָדָיו וְרַגְלָיו. קַשְׁיָין אַהֲדָדֵי!

And it was taught in another *baraita*: **Even though** the Sages **said that** a husband **may not force his wife to paint** her eyelids **or put rouge** on her face when she is in mourning, i.e., that she may not treat her mourning lightly, **actually, they said** that **she may pour his cup**[N] of wine, **make his bed, and wash his face, hands, and feet,**[H] as these activities are expressions of affection between husband and wife rather than unnecessary adornment or a belittlement of the mourning. These two *baraitot* **contradict each other:** The first *baraita* indicates that the husband must practice the rites of mourning together with his wife, whereas the second one bars him only from forcing her to treat her own mourning lightly.

אֶלָּא לָאו שְׁמַע מִינָּהּ: כָּאן – בְּחָמִיו וַחֲמוֹתוֹ, כָּאן – בִּשְׁאָר קְרוֹבִים? שְׁמַע מִינָּהּ. תַּנְיָא נַמִי הָכִי: לֹא אָמְרוּ לִכְבוֹד אִשְׁתּוֹ – אֶלָּא חָמִיו וַחֲמוֹתוֹ בִּלְבַד.

Rather, must one **not conclude from this** as follows: **Here,** where one is required to observe the *halakhot* of mourning together with his wife, the *baraita* is referring to the death **of his father-in-law or mother-in-law. There,** where one is not required to mourn, the *baraita* is referring to the death of his wife's **other relatives** for whom she is required to mourn. The Gemara summarizes: **Conclude from this** that this is the case. **This is also taught** in a *baraita*: The Sages **said** that one is required to observe the rites of mourning **in honor of his wife only** when she is in mourning over **his father-in-law or his mother-in-law.**

אַמֵּימָר שְׁכִיב לֵיהּ בַּר בְּרֵיהּ, קְרַע עִילָּוֵיהּ. אֲתָא בְּרֵיהּ – קְרַע בְּאַפֵּיהּ. אִידְּכַר דִּמְיוּשָּׁב קְרַע – קָם קְרַע מְעוּמָּד.

It was further related that **the son of Ameimar's son died,** and Ameimar **rent** his garment **over him. His son came** before him, and **he rent** his garments again **in the presence of his** son,[N] as an expression of empathy with the his son's pain and grief. Later, **he remembered** that when he rent his garments in his son's presence **he rent** them while **sitting,** and therefore **he stood up** and **rent** his garment again while **standing.**

אֲמַר לֵיהּ רַב אַשִׁי לְאַמֵּימָר: קְרִיעָה דִּמְעוּמָּד מְנָלַן? דִּכְתִיב: ״וַיָּקָם אִיּוֹב וַיִּקְרַע אֶת מְעִילוֹ״.

With regard to this issue, the Gemara reports that **Rav Ashi said to Ameimar: From where do we** derive that **rending** must be done while **standing?** He responded: **As it is written** about the deaths of Job's sons: **"Then Job arose, and rent his coat"** (Job 1:20).

NOTES

She may pour his cup, etc. – **מוֹזֶגֶת לוֹ אֶת הַכּוֹס וכו׳:** This list includes tasks that were customarily performed by a wife for her husband. Although all of these actions increase affection between the couple, and therefore a woman may not perform them when she is impure due to menstruation, the Sages did not prohibit them when she is in mourning (*Talmid Rabbeinu Yeḥiel of Paris*, based on tractate *Ketubot*).

There are several explanations as to how the act of the wife pouring wine for her husband shows that he does not observe mourning practices with his wife. Some say that based on the statement that she may make his bed, it is implied that he is not required to overturn it (Rashi). Alternatively, this is derived by the fact that such a requirement is not stated explicitly (Ra'avad). Others suggest that since she may wash his face, with hot water according to some, he is clearly not observing the practices of mourning (see Commentary on *Moed Katan* and *Sefat Emet*).

His son came and he rent his garments in the presence of his son – **אֲתָא בְּרֵיהּ, קְרַע בְּאַפֵּיהּ:** Some explain that Ameimar forgot and rent his garments while sitting, and his son did not wish to tell him that he had acted incorrectly, out of respect for his father. Instead, he rent his garment while standing, and then Ameimar realized that he had rent his garment incorrectly (*Talmid Rabbeinu Yeḥiel of Paris*; see *Tosefot HaRosh* and *Tosafot*).

HALAKHA

One's wife in mourning – **אֵשֶׁת אִישׁ בִּזְמַן אֲבֵלָהּ:** When the close relative of a married woman dies, she is not permitted to wear makeup, and her husband cannot force her to do so. However, she may make his bed and pour him a cup of wine, or any other similar act. A married woman is permitted to wear makeup after the seven-day mourning period, so that she will not appear ugly to her husband (*Shulḥan Arukh, Yoreh De'a* 381:6).

אֶלָּא מֵעַתָּה – ״וְעָמַד וְאָמַר לֹא חָפַצְתִּי לְקַחְתָּהּ״ הָכָא נַמִי? וְהָא תַּנְיָא: בֵּין יוֹשֵׁב בֵּין עוֹמֵד בֵּין מוּטֶּה!

Rav Ashi challenged him: **However, if** that is **so,** one should be required to stand while performing the ritual through which the brother-in-law frees the *yevama* of her levirate bonds [*ḥalitza*], as the verse states: **"And if he stands and he says: I do not wish to take her"** (Deuteronomy 25:8). **Here** must he **also** stand for the ceremony? **But isn't it taught** in a *baraita* that *ḥalitza* may be performed **whether** the man is **sitting,**[H] **or standing,**[N] **or reclining?**

אֲמַר לֵיהּ: הָתָם לָא כְּתִיב ״וְיַעֲמֹד וְיֹאמַר״; הָכָא כְּתִיב ״וַיָּקָם וַיִּקְרַע״.

He said to him: There, in the case of *ḥalitza,* **it is not written: And he will stand**[N] **and he will say,** which would imply an obligation to stand; whereas **here,** in the case of rending, **it is written:** "**Then** Job **arose, and rent** his coat" (Job 1:20).

אָמַר רָמִי בַּר חָמָא: מִנַּיִן לִקְרִיעָה שֶׁהִיא מְעוּמָּד? שֶׁנֶּאֱמַר: ״וַיָּקָם אִיּוֹב וַיִּקְרַע״. דִּלְמָא מִילְּתָא יְתֵירְתָּא הוּא דַּעֲבַד? דְּאִי לָא תֵּימָא הָכִי – ״וַיָּגָז אֶת רֹאשׁוֹ״ הָכִי נַמִי?

Rami bar Ḥama said: From where is it derived **that rending must be** performed while **standing?**[H] **As it is stated: "Then Job arose, and tore** his coat" (Job 1:20). The Gemara asks: **Perhaps he did something extra** beyond what is required, and actually there is no obligation to stand; **as, if you do not say** that he did more than what was required of him, then how do you explain the continuation of the verse: **"And he shaved his head"** (Job 1:20)? Is every mourner required to act in **this** manner **also** and shave his head?

אֶלָּא מֵהָכָא: ״וַיָּקָם הַמֶּלֶךְ וַיִּקְרַע אֶת בְּגָדָיו״. וְדִלְמָא מִילְּתָא יְתֵירְתָּא עֲבֵיד? דְּאִי לָא תֵּימָא הָכִי – ״וַיִּשְׁכַּב אָרְצָה״ הָכִי נַמִי?

The Gemara concludes: **Rather,** this source must be rejected, and instead the *halakha* is derived **from here,** the verse that describes David's mourning over his son: **"Then the king arose, and rent his garments"** (II Samuel 13:31). The Gemara asks: But **perhaps he** too **did something extra** beyond what is required, and he was not actually obligated to stand; **as, if you do not say** that he did more than what was required of him, then how do you explain the continuation of the verse: **"And he lay on the earth"** (II Samuel 13:31)? Is every mourner required to act in **this** manner **also?**

וְהָתַנְיָא: יָשַׁב עַל גַּבֵּי מִטָּה, עַל גַּבֵּי כִּסֵּא, עַל גַּבֵּי אוּדְיָינֵי גְּדוֹלָה, עַל גַּבֵּי קַרְקַע – מִכּוּלָּן לֹא יָצָא יְדֵי חוֹבָתוֹ. וְאָמַר רַבִּי יוֹחָנָן: שֶׁלֹּא קִיֵּים כְּפִיַּית הַמִּטָּה.

But isn't it taught in a *baraita*: If a mourner **sat on a bed, on a chair, on a large mortar** [*udyanei*],[NL] **or on the ground, he does not fulfill his obligation through any of them.**[H] **And Rabbi Yoḥanan said:** This is **because he did not fulfill** his obligation to **overturn his bed,** even if he lay on the ground. This indicates that there is no requirement whatsoever to lie on the ground.

אֲמַר לֵיהּ: כְּעֵין אַרְצָה.

Ameimar **said to** Rav Ashi: The verse does not mean that David actually lay on the ground. Rather, it was **as if** he were **on the ground,** since he overturned his bed and brought it closer to the ground. If this is the case, then Ameimar acted correctly, and a mourner should rend his garments while standing.

NOTES

Whether sitting or standing – בֵּין יוֹשֵׁב בֵּין עוֹמֵד: The question is not with regard to the obligation to rend garments *ab initio*, as it is also clear that it is preferable to perform both rending and *ḥalitza* while standing. Rather, the question concerns Ameimar's decision to rend his garment again, which implies that, even after the fact, if one was not standing the rending is invalid. Consequently, the Gemara asks what the difference is between rending and *ḥalitza*, since the word standing is used in reference to both (Ramban).

It is not written: And he will stand – לָא כְּתִיב וְיַעֲמֹד: This derivation is based not on the difference in tense but on the structure of the verses. If the word "stand" had been stressed, this would have indicated that there is a specific requirement to stand. However, in the verses of *ḥalitza* all the actions are written in the same form, thereby conveying some degree of continuity, and the word "stand" is not stressed (Ritva).

Alternatively, some explain that the phrase: "And if he stands," does not mean that one is actually required to stand. Instead, it means: Come forward, or: Prepare yourself to perform a certain act (*Tosafot*; *Talmid Rabbeinu Yeḥiel of Paris*).

Large mortar – אוּדְיָינֵי גְּדוֹלָה: Some explain that this refers to a large mortar (Rashi; Rabbeinu Ḥananel), which people could sit on by placing it upside down. However, others say that this refers to a covering for a pit (Rashi, from manuscript; Rashbam). There are also those who claim that this means an overturned kneading bowl or a bathtub (see Ran).

HALAKHA

Ḥalitza while sitting – חֲלִיצָה בִּישִׁיבָה: During all parts of the *ḥalitza* ceremony, the judges sit, while the man and woman performing the ceremony stand. If the man is old or weak he may lean on a cane (*Be'er Heitev*). If he is incapable of standing at all, he may sit (*Shulḥan Arukh, Even HaEzer* 169:12, and in the comment of Rema).

Rending while standing – קְרִיעָה שֶׁהִיא מְעוּמָּד: Rending garments as a sign of mourning must be done while standing. If one performed this while sitting, he is required to rend the garments a second time (*Shulḥan Arukh, Yoreh De'a* 340:1).

The mitzva of overturning the bed – מִצְוַת כְּפִיַּית הַמִּטָּה: It is not enough for one simply to overturn his bed; he must sleep on the overturned bed in order to fulfill his obligation. Therefore, if one slept on a chair, wardrobe, or the ground, then has not fulfilled this obligation (Rambam *Sefer Shofetim, Hilkhot Evel* 5:18). However, nowadays the custom is not to overturn beds at all (*Shulḥan Arukh, Yoreh De'a* 387:2).

LANGUAGE

Mortar [*udyanei*] – אוּדְיָינֵי: Several different versions of this word exist, and therefore there are also many different interpretations of its meaning. Some say that it is related to the Aramaic *udna*, meaning handle or ear, and in this context it refers to a vessel with a handle.

Large mortar

NOTES

These are the activities that a mourner is prohibited from engaging in – וְאֵלּוּ דְּבָרִים שֶׁאָבֵל אָסוּר בָּהֶן: *Tosafot* note that not all of the activities that are prohibited to a mourner are mentioned here, and they explain why only some of these prohibitions are mentioned (see Ran). All the activities that are prohibited to a mourner are detailed in tractate *Semaḥot*.

He is prohibited from reading in the Torah, etc. – אָסוּר לִקְרוֹת בַּתּוֹרָה וכו׳: The Ramban discusses whether the fact that learning Torah is a mitzva is sufficient to permit a mourner to study Torah in certain situations; or perhaps it is permitted after the first day, similar to donning phylacteries; or perhaps since it gives pleasure it is not permitted for the entire week. In the Jerusalem Talmud, it is explained that one is permitted to study a Torah text that he is unfamiliar with, because this is not as enjoyable as other study. Similarly, it is stated there that one who is intensely passionate about Torah study may learn Torah, since refraining from Torah study would be a form of affliction, and one is not required to afflict himself when in mourning.

תָּנוּ רַבָּנַן, וְאֵלּוּ דְּבָרִים שֶׁאָבֵל אָסוּר בָּהֶן: אָסוּר בִּמְלָאכָה, וּבִרְחִיצָה, וּבְסִיכָה, וּבְתַשְׁמִישׁ הַמִּטָּה, וּבִנְעִילַת הַסַּנְדָּל, וְאָסוּר לִקְרוֹת בַּתּוֹרָה וּבַנְּבִיאִים וּבַכְּתוּבִים, וְלִשְׁנוֹת בַּמִּשְׁנָה, בַּמִּדְרָשׁ וּבַהֲלָכוֹת וּבַתַּלְמוּד וּבָאֲגָדוֹת. וְאִם הָיוּ רַבִּים צְרִיכִין לוֹ – אֵינוֹ נִמְנָע. וּמַעֲשֶׂה וּמֵת בְּנוֹ שֶׁל רַבִּי יוֹסֵי בְּצִיפּוֹרִי, וְנִכְנַס לְבֵית הַמִּדְרָשׁ וְדָרַשׁ כָּל הַיּוֹם כּוּלּוֹ.

§ **The Sages taught: These are the activities that a mourner is prohibited from** engaging **in:**[N] **He is prohibited from working, and from bathing, and from anointing** himself with oil, **and from engaging in sexual relations, and from wearing shoes. And he is prohibited from reading in the Torah,**[NH] **and in the Prophets, and in the Writings, and from studying in the Mishna, in the midrash, and in the *halakhot*, and in the Talmud, and in the *aggadot*. But if the public needs him** to teach them these things, **he need not refrain** from doing so. **There was an incident that the son of Rabbi Yosei**[P] **died in Tzippori, and** Rabbi Yosei **entered the study hall and expounded** there **for the entire day.**

רַבָּה בַּר בַּר חָנָה אִיתְרְעָא בֵּיהּ מִילְּתָא. סָבַר דְּלָא לְמֵיפַּק לְפִירְקָא. אֲמַר לֵיהּ רַבִּי חֲנִינָא: אִם הָיוּ רַבִּים צְרִיכִין לוֹ – אֵינוֹ נִמְנָע. סָבַר לְאוֹקְמֵי אָמוֹרָא עֲלֵיהּ – אֲמַר לֵיהּ רַב, תַּנְיָא: וּבִלְבַד שֶׁלֹּא יַעֲמִיד תּוּרְגְּמָן.

It was related that **a calamity,** i.e., a death in the family, once **befell Rabba bar bar Ḥana, and he thought not to go out to** deliver **his exposition. Rabbi Ḥanina said to him:** Is it not taught that **if the public needs him** to teach them these things, **one need not refrain** from doing so? **He** then **thought to place an interpreter**[B] **alongside him,** who would sound his words to the public, as was normally done for such an exposition. **Rav said to him: It is taught** in a *baraita* similarly: **Provided that he does not place the disseminator** alongside him.

HALAKHA

Torah study while in mourning – לִימּוּד תּוֹרָה בְּאֵבֶל: A mourner is prohibited from studying Torah for all seven days of the mourning period, but he may read the book of Lamentations, prophecies about catastrophic events, and the *halakhot* of mourning. If the community requires it, a mourner is permitted to expound in public. However, if he expounds through an interpreter then there must be an intermediary between him and the interpreter, in order to deviate from his ordinary way of speaking. A scholar who is in mourning may give a halakhic ruling to an individual who asks him a question. However, he may not teach a *halakha* to his students. This is the common practice; however, some are lenient with regard to this (*Shulḥan Arukh*, *Yoreh De'a* 384:1, and in the comment of Rema).

PERSONALITIES

Rabbi Yosei – רַבִּי יוֹסֵי: This is Rabbi Yosei ben Ḥalafta, one of the greatest of the *tanna'im*. He lived in the generation prior to the redaction of the Mishna, and the influence of his teachings is evident throughout tannaitic literature. His father, known as Abba Ḥalafta, was also considered one of the great Sages of his generation. According to one tradition, his family was descended from Jehonadab, son of Rechab (see II Kings 10:15).

In addition to studying with his father, Rabbi Yosei was also an outstanding student of Rabbi Akiva. Rabbi Yosei and his contemporaries, Rabbi Meir, Rabbi Yehuda, Rabbi Shimon bar Yoḥai, and other students of Rabbi Akiva, formed the center of talmudic creativity of that entire generation. In his halakhic approach, as in his way of life, Rabbi Yosei was moderate, and he refrained from taking extreme opinions on halakhic issues. A well-known principle in the *halakha* is that Rabbi Yosei's opinions are based on sound reasoning, and therefore the *halakha* is always in accordance with his opinion.

In addition to being a great master of *halakha*, Rabbi Yosei was also famous for his piety. The Talmud relates many stories about his modesty, humility, and holiness. It is related that Elijah the Prophet would appear to him every day, and several conversations between Elijah and Rabbi Yosei are recorded in the Talmud. Rabbi Yosei was the primary redactor of a series of *baraitot* on the history of the Jewish people known as *Seder Olam*. For many years, he lived in Tzippori in the Galilee and earned his living as a tanner.

Many of the prominent Sages of the following generation, including Rabbi Yehuda HaNasi, the redactor of the Mishna, were his students. But his main students were his five sons, all of whom were Sages in their generation. The most famous of them were Rabbi Eliezer, son of Rabbi Yosei, one of the great masters of *aggada*, and Rabbi Yishmael, son of Rabbi Yosei.

BACKGROUND

Interpreter [*amora*] – אָמוֹרָא: In this context, the word *amora*, literally speaker, has the same meaning as the word *meturgeman*, disseminator, used in the Mishna. This disseminator of the Sages' expositions was often a scholar himself, sometimes even an important Sage, whose job it was to translate the exposition from Hebrew to Aramaic and to project it so that it could be heard by everyone. Sometimes, there was more than one disseminator if the speech needed to be projected to a large group. Often, the disseminator would not only translate but also explain the exposition, as the Sage would say the most basic ideas, and the disseminator would expand and develop them. For this reason, the Sages of the talmudic period describe themselves as *amora'im*, as they saw their job as being similar to that of these interpreters for the Sages of the Mishna.

וְאֶלָּא הֵיכִי עָבֵיד? כִּי הָא דְּתַנְיָא: מַעֲשֶׂה וּמֵת בְּנוֹ שֶׁל רַבִּי יְהוּדָה בַּר אִילְעַאי, וְנִכְנַס לְבֵית הַמִּדְרָשׁ. וְנִכְנַס רַבִּי חֲנַנְיָה בֶּן עֲקַבְיָא וְיָשַׁב בְּצִדּוֹ, וְלָחַשׁ הוּא לְרַבִּי חֲנַנְיָה בֶּן עֲקַבְיָא, וְרַבִּי חֲנַנְיָה בֶּן עֲקַבְיָא לְתוּרְגְּמָן, וְתוּרְגְּמָן הִשְׁמִיעַ לָרַבִּים.

The Gemara asks: **But how,** then, should he **act** so that he can be heard? The Gemara answers: It is **like that which is taught** in a *baraita*: There was **an incident and the son of Rabbi Yehuda bar Ilai died, and** Rabbi Yehuda **entered the study hall. And Rabbi Ḥananya ben Akavya** entered after him and **sat by his side.** Rabbi Yehuda bar Ilai then **whispered** his lecture **to Rabbi Ḥananya ben Akavya, and Rabbi Ḥananya ben Akavya** whispered it **to the disseminator, and the disseminator sounded to the public** what had been told to him. In this way, it became known that Rabbi Yehuda bar Ilai was in mourning.

תָּנוּ רַבָּנַן: אָבֵל, שְׁלֹשָׁה יָמִים הָרִאשׁוֹנִים אָסוּר לְהָנִיחַ תְּפִילִּין. מִשְּׁלִישִׁי וְאֵילָךְ, וּשְׁלִישִׁי בִּכְלָל – מוּתָּר לְהָנִיחַ תְּפִילִּין. וְאִם בָּאוּ פָּנִים חֲדָשׁוֹת – אֵינוֹ חוֹלֵץ, דִּבְרֵי רַבִּי אֱלִיעֶזֶר. רַבִּי יְהוֹשֻׁעַ אוֹמֵר: אָבֵל, שְׁנֵי יָמִים הָרִאשׁוֹנִים – אָסוּר לְהָנִיחַ תְּפִילִּין. מִשֵּׁנִי וְשֵׁנִי בִּכְלָל – מוּתָּר לְהָנִיחַ תְּפִילִּין. וְאִם בָּאוּ פָּנִים חֲדָשׁוֹת – חוֹלֵץ.

§ **The Sages taught** the following *baraita*: For **the first three days, a mourner is prohibited from donning phylacteries.**[H] **From the third** day **and on, and including the third** day, **he is permitted to don phylacteries. And if new faces,**[N] i.e., people who had not yet come to console him, **come, he need not remove** them, although these people may falsely conclude that he had also donned phylacteries during the first two days of his mourning; this is **the statement of Rabbi Eliezer. Rabbi Yehoshua says: For the first two days, a mourner is prohibited from donning** phylacteries. **From the second** day, **and including the second** day, **he is permitted to wear** phylacteries. **But if new faces come in** to console him, **he must remove** his phylacteries.

אָמַר רַב מַתָּנָה: מַאי טַעְמָא דְּרַבִּי אֱלִיעֶזֶר? דִּכְתִיב: ״וַיִּתְּמוּ יְמֵי בְכִי אֵבֶל מֹשֶׁה״. אָמַר רַב עֵינָא: מַאי טַעְמָא דְּרַבִּי יְהוֹשֻׁעַ? דִּכְתִיב: ״וְאַחֲרִיתָהּ כְּיוֹם מָר״.

Rav Mattana said: What is the reason of Rabbi Eliezer?[N] **As it is written: "And the days of weeping and mourning for Moses ended"** (Deuteronomy 34:8). The plural term "days" implies a minimum of two, and it indicates that the main portion of the mourning period is the first two full days. **Rav Eina said: What is the reason of Rabbi Yehoshua? As it is written:** "And I will make it as the mourning for an only son, **and its end as a bitter day"** (Amos 8:10), i.e., a single "day."

וְרַבִּי יְהוֹשֻׁעַ נַמִי, הָא כְּתִיב: ״וַיִּתְּמוּ יְמֵי״ וגו׳! אָמַר לָךְ: שָׁאנֵי מֹשֶׁה, דְּתַקִּיף אֶבְלֵיהּ. וְרַבִּי אֱלִיעֶזֶר נַמִי, הָא כְּתִיב: ״וְאַחֲרִיתָהּ כְּיוֹם מָר״! עִיקַּר מְרִירָא חַד יוֹמָא הוּא.

The Gemara asks: **But also** for **Rabbi Yehoshua, isn't it written** in the Torah: **"And the days** of weeping and mourning for Moses **ended,"** thereby implying that this period lasts for two days? The Gemara answers: He could have **said to you** that **Moses was different, because the mourning for him was more intense,** and the people mourned for him longer than usual. The Gemara asks: **But also** for **Rabbi Eliezer, isn't it written** in the Torah: **"And its end as a bitter day"?** The Gemara answers: He could have said to you that **the main bitterness is** only **one day,** but the severity of the mourning lasts for two days.

אָמַר עוּלָּא: הֲלָכָה כְּרַבִּי אֱלִיעֶזֶר בַּחֲלִיצָה, וַהֲלָכָה כְּרַבִּי יְהוֹשֻׁעַ בַּהֲנָחָה.

Ulla said: The *halakha* is in accordance with the opinion of **Rabbi Eliezer with regard to the removal** of phylacteries. A mourner need not remove them when new people come in to console him. **And the *halakha* is in accordance with** the opinion of **Rabbi Yehoshua with regard to the donning** of phylacteries, and so a mourner may already don phylacteries on the second day.

אִיבַּעְיָא לְהוּ: בְּשֵׁנִי לְעוּלָּא, חוֹלֵץ אוֹ אֵינוֹ חוֹלֵץ?

A dilemma was raised before the scholars: **According** to **Ulla,** who rules in accordance with Rabbi Yehoshua that a mourner may don phylacteries **on** his **second day** of mourning, is the mourner required to **remove** them if new people arrive on that day, **or** is he **not** required to **remove** them?

תָּא שְׁמַע, אָמַר עוּלָּא: חוֹלֵץ וּמֵנִיחַ אֲפִילּוּ מֵאָה פְּעָמִים. תַּנְיָא נַמִי הָכִי, יְהוּדָה בֶּן תֵּימָא אוֹמֵר: חוֹלֵץ וּמֵנִיחַ אֲפִילּוּ מֵאָה פְּעָמִים.

The Gemara answers: **Come** and **hear** what **Ulla said** explicitly: **One removes** his phylacteries when new people come to console him, **and he dons** them again when they leave, **even** if he must don and remove them **a hundred times. This is also taught** in a *baraita*: **Yehuda ben Teima says: He removes** his phylacteries **and dons** them again, **even** if he must do so **a hundred times.**

רָבָא אָמַר: כֵּיוָן שֶׁהֵנִיחַ – שׁוּב אֵינוֹ חוֹלֵץ. וְהָא רָבָא הוּא דְּאָמַר: הֲלָכָה כְּתַנָּא דִּידַן, דְּאָמַר: שְׁלֹשָׁה!

Rava said: Once he dons his phylacteries, **he does not remove** them **again.** The Gemara asks: **But wasn't it Rava** himself who **said: The *halakha* is in accordance with** the opinion of **the *tanna* of our** mishna, who **said** that the most serious period of mourning is **three** days? How then does he rule in accordance with the *baraita* that a mourner may don phylacteries during these days?

HALAKHA

A mourner is prohibited from donning phylacteries – אָבֵל...אָסוּר לְהָנִיחַ תְּפִילִּין: A mourner is prohibited from wearing phylacteries on his first day of mourning, but he is required to wear them from the second day and onward. This ruling is in accordance with the opinion of Rabbi Yehoshua, as the *halakha* is in accordance with his opinion in disputes with Rabbi Eliezer. It is also in accordance with the opinion of Rava (*Shulḥan Arukh, Yoreh De'a* 388:1).

NOTES

New faces – פָּנִים חֲדָשׁוֹת: Most commentaries explain here, similar to the case with the seven-day period following marriage, that the phrase new faces refers to people who have not yet come to visit. Others explain that the term refers to other mourners who are joining this mourning (Rabbeinu Yehonatan of Lunel). There are also those who understand that the term refers to additional relatives who die while the mourner is still in mourning (Rabbi Shlomo ben HaYatom).

Some explain that the reason for removing the phylacteries is lest new people come, see him wearing phylacteries, and think that he is doing so on the first day of mourning and thereby acting disrespectfully toward the laws of mourning (*Talmid Rabbeinu Yeḥiel of Paris*; Ran; Meiri).

Others say that when new people come and begin speaking about the mourner's deceased relative, the mourner's pain will be renewed, and therefore the sadness becomes like that on the first day (Ritva). This is similar to the explanation of the *ge'onim*, mentioned by the Ramban, according to which a mourner may not wear phylacteries because one wearing phylacteries is prohibited from taking his mind off them. When the new guests weep and eulogize the deceased, the mourner may forget that he is wearing phylacteries.

The reasons of Rabbi Eliezer and Rabbi Yehoshua – טַעֲמָם שֶׁל רַבִּי אֱלִיעֶזֶר וְרַבִּי יְהוֹשֻׁעַ: It is mentioned in the name of the Ra'avad that Rabbi Eliezer's opinion can be explained as follows: "The days…ended" indicates that they were completed, and if this is the case then there were two full days of mourning. A part of the third day was added according to rabbinic law (see *Talmid Rabbeinu Yeḥiel of Paris*). Although the verse is describing events that happened thirty days after Moses' death, the derivation is based on the expression: "Days of weeping," i.e., the first two days of weeping before the rest of the days of mourning (see Ritva). With regard to the verse: "Its end as a bitter day," the expression "as…a day" also means a little more than a complete day, and therefore includes part of the second day.

מִצְוָה שָׁאנֵי.

The Gemara answers: **A mitzva is different,**[N] and since it is a mitzva to put on phylacteries, the mourner is required to do so, even during the first three days.

תָּנוּ רַבָּנַן: אָבֵל, שְׁלֹשָׁה יָמִים הָרִאשׁוֹנִים – אָסוּר בִּמְלָאכָה, וַאֲפִילּוּ עָנִי הַמִּתְפַּרְנֵס מִן הַצְּדָקָה. מִכָּאן וְאֵילָךְ – עוֹשֶׂה בְּצִינְעָא בְּתוֹךְ בֵּיתוֹ. וְהָאִשָּׁה טוֹוָה בְּפֶלֶךְ בְּתוֹךְ בֵּיתָהּ.

§ **The Sages taught** the following *baraita*: **During the first three days** after his bereavement, **a mourner is prohibited from working,**[NH] **even if he is a poor person who is supported by charity. From this** point **forward, he may do work privately in his** own **home** if he needs to do so. **And** similarly **a woman may spin** thread **on a spindle**[N] **in her** own **home** when she is mourning.

תָּנוּ רַבָּנַן: אָבֵל, שְׁלֹשָׁה יָמִים הָרִאשׁוֹנִים – אֵינוֹ הוֹלֵךְ לְבֵית הָאָבֵל; מִכָּאן וְאֵילָךְ – הוֹלֵךְ, וְאֵינוֹ יוֹשֵׁב בִּמְקוֹם הַמְנַחֲמִין אֶלָּא בִּמְקוֹם הַמִּתְנַחֲמִין.

The Sages taught in another *baraita*: **A mourner during the first three days** after his bereavement **may not go to** another **mourner's house**[N] to console him.[H] **From this point forward, he may go, but he may not sit among the consolers, but rather in the place of those being consoled,**[N] i.e., with the mourners in that house.

תָּנוּ רַבָּנַן: אָבֵל, שְׁלֹשָׁה יָמִים הָרִאשׁוֹנִים – אָסוּר בִּשְׁאִילַת שָׁלוֹם; מִשְּׁלֹשָׁה וְעַד שִׁבְעָה – מֵשִׁיב וְאֵינוֹ שׁוֹאֵל; מִכָּאן וְאֵילָךְ – שׁוֹאֵל וּמֵשִׁיב כְּדַרְכּוֹ.

§ **The Sages taught** in yet another *baraita*: **A mourner, during the first three days** after his bereavement, **is prohibited from extending greetings** to others. **From the third** day **to the seventh** day, **he may respond** when other people address him, **but he may not extend greetings**[N] to them. **From this point forward, he may extend greetings and respond in his usual manner.**"[H]

שְׁלֹשָׁה יָמִים הָרִאשׁוֹנִים אָסוּר בִּשְׁאִילַת שָׁלוֹם? וְהָתַנְיָא: מַעֲשֶׂה וּמֵתוּ בָּנָיו שֶׁל רַבִּי עֲקִיבָא, נִכְנְסוּ כָּל יִשְׂרָאֵל וְהִסְפִּידוּם הֶסְפֵּד גָּדוֹל.

The Gemara asks: Is he really **prohibited** from extending **greetings during the first three** days of mourning? **But isn't it taught** in a *baraita*: There was **an incident and the sons of Rabbi Akiva**[P] **died, and all the Jews entered to eulogize them with a great eulogy.**

NOTES

A mitzva is different – מִצְוָה שָׁאנֵי: Some have a version of the text that reads: The mitzva of phylacteries is different. This means that since the mitzva to wear phylacteries is from the Torah, it takes precedence over mourning, which is rabbinic (Rabbi Shlomo ben HaYatom; see Ritva).

The first three days a mourner is prohibited from working – אָבֵל, שְׁלֹשָׁה יָמִים הָרִאשׁוֹנִים אָסוּר בִּמְלָאכָה: Some write that the prohibition against working, and similarly the permission to work in private after the first three days, applies to everyone, although in practice, one who does not require the money is unlikely to perform work. Still, there is an opinion that one who needs the money is permitted to do so and others are similarly permitted (Rid). This opinion is not accepted by most commentaries and halakhic authorities, who say that only poor people with nothing to eat may work during the seven-day mourning period (see Riaz).

A woman may spin on a spindle – הָאִשָּׁה טוֹוָה בְּפֶלֶךְ: Most commentaries explain that this specifically refers to a poor woman, and the Sages permitted her to perform this type of work in her house because she needs to earn a livelihood. If she is unable to support herself with this work, then she may perform other types of work (see Ramban). There are those who write that any woman may do this work and not just a poor woman (Radbaz).

Go to another mourner's house – הוֹלֵךְ לְבֵית הָאָבֵל: Some say this means that he may go to a mourner's house only when he is related to the deceased, and this is why he sits with the other mourners, but he may not go to visit other mourners (Rabbeinu Yehonatan of Lunel; see Ran). However, most halakhic authorities hold that there is no distinction.

He sits in the place of those being consoled – יוֹשֵׁב בִּמְקוֹם הַמִּתְנַחֲמִים: Based on this, some halakhic authorities rule that a mourner is permitted to go to the synagogue on the Ninth of Av, as at that time the synagogue is a place of mourners, and everyone is considered to be like the consoled (see *Tosafot*). The *halakha* follows this opinion (*Shulḥan Arukh*, *Oraḥ Ḥayyim* 568:6).

He may respond but he may not extend greetings – מֵשִׁיב וְאֵינוֹ שׁוֹאֵל: The reason for this is explained in tractate *Berakhot*, where it is noted that people must be very careful to respond when a person extends greetings toward them, so as not to insult the greeter. The great people of every generation would respond to every person when greeted, regardless of his status. Therefore, the Sages permitted a mourner to respond when greeted, even when it would not be permitted for him to extend greetings to someone else. Even when it is not permitted for him to respond, he is still required to explain that he is not responding because he is mourning.

HALAKHA

A mourner is prohibited from working – אָבֵל...אָסוּר בִּמְלָאכָה: A mourner is prohibited from working during the first three days of mourning, even if he is poor and must take his livelihood from charity. From then onward, if he has nothing to eat he may perform work in the privacy of his own home (*Shulḥan Arukh*, *Yoreh De'a* 380:2).

Going to the house of another mourner – הֲלִיכָה לְבֵית הָאָבֵל: A mourner during the first three days of mourning may not attend a funeral unless there is no one else who can appropriately accompany the deceased or bury him. After the first three days of mourning, one may go to the funeral of someone from his neighborhood who has passed away, and may also visit a house of mourning. However, instead of sitting among the consolers he should sit with the mourners.

The Rema writes that today it is customary for the mourner not to leave his house for all seven days, even if he wishes to go to another house of mourning (*Shulḥan Arukh*, *Yoreh De'a* 393:1).

Greeting during mourning – שְׁאִילַת שָׁלוֹם בְּאֵבֶל: For the first three days, a mourner may not extend greetings to anyone. If people do not know that he is mourning and extend greetings to him, he should not respond to them. Instead, he should inform them that he is mourning.

From the third to the seventh day, he should not initiate extending greetings. However, if someone extends greetings to him then he may respond. From the seventh to the thirtieth days, he may extend greetings to others and respond. However, one should not extend greetings toward him.

After thirty days he is treated as any other person, if he is mourning for relatives other than his parents. One who is mourning for his father or mother may extend greetings to others after seven days, but others should not extend greetings to him until twelve months have passed. In order to show respect to a group he may say: Go in peace. Some permit extending greetings nowadays. However, this does not appear to be an appropriate custom unless he uses different wording and does not use the word: *Shalom* (*Shulḥan Arukh*, *Yoreh De'a* 385:1; Rema; *Shakh*).

PERSONALITIES

Rabbi Akiva – רַבִּי עֲקִיבָא: Akiva ben Yosef was one of the greatest of the *tanna'im*. He lived from just after the destruction of the Second Temple until the bar Kokheva revolt. He was one of the leading Sages at the time of Rabban Gamliel II in Yavne.

According to legend, Rabbi Akiva began his studies at the age of forty, when Rachel, the daughter of the wealthy Kalba Savua, agreed to marry him on condition that he went to study Torah. Rabbi Akiva became the student of Rabbi Eliezer ben Hyrcanus and Rabbi Yehoshua ben Ḥananya. Ultimately, he became a great scholar with twenty-four thousand students.

Among Rabbi Akiva's first students were Shimon ben Azzai and Shimon ben Zoma, with whom he entered the orchard (see *Hagiga* 14b), studying esoteric elements of the Torah. Subsequently, Rabbi Meir and Rabbi Shimon bar Yoḥai, among others, became his students.

He was a staunch supporter of bar Kokheva's revolt against Rome, and even declared him the Messiah. During the period of the Roman Emperor Hadrian's decrees, Torah study was prohibited, but Rabbi Akiva continued convening assemblies and teaching Torah. Ultimately, he was apprehended and executed, and he is one of the ten martyrs whose execution is described in liturgy.

Rabbi Akiva collected early rabbinic teachings and worked to organize the Oral Torah. The work done by Rabbi Akiva and his students served as the basis for the Mishna that was edited by Rabbi Yehuda HaNasi and his disciples.

בִּשְׁעַת פְּטִירָתָן עָמַד רַבִּי עֲקִיבָא עַל סַפְסָל גָּדוֹל וְאָמַר: אַחֵינוּ בֵּית יִשְׂרָאֵל שִׁמְעוּ! אֲפִילּוּ שְׁנֵי בָּנִים חֲתָנִים – מְנוּחָם הוּא בִּשְׁבִיל כָּבוֹד שֶׁעֲשִׂיתֶם. וְאִם בִּשְׁבִיל עֲקִיבָא בָּאתֶם – הֲרֵי כַּמָּה עֲקִיבָא בַּשּׁוּק. אֶלָּא כָּךְ אֲמַרְתֶּם: "תּוֹרַת אֱלֹהָיו בְּלִבּוֹ" וְכָל שֶׁכֵּן שֶׁשְּׂכַרְכֶם כָּפוּל. לְכוּ לְבָתֵּיכֶם לְשָׁלוֹם.

When they were about to take leave, **Rabbi Akiva stood on a large bench**[L] **and said: Our brothers, the house of Israel, listen! Even had my two sons been bridegrooms, I would have been consoled on account of the honor you have shown** them. **If you came** to console **for the sake of Akiva, there are many Akivas in the marketplace** whom the Jews do all not come to console. **Rather,** certainly **this is what you said** to yourselves: **"The Torah of his God is in his heart"** (Psalms 37:31), and you wished to show your respect for the Torah. **All the more so is your reward doubled,** for you have consoled mourners and shown respect for the Torah. **Return** now **to your homes in peace.** This indicates that a mourner may greet other people even on the first day of his mourning.

כְּבוֹד רַבִּים שָׁאנֵי.

The Gemara answers: Showing **respect for the public is different.** Rabbi Akiva was permitted to greet them to demonstrate courtesy and respect.

מִשְּׁלֹשָׁה וְעַד שִׁבְעָה – מֵשִׁיב וְאֵינוֹ שׁוֹאֵל; מִכָּאן וְאֵילָךְ – שׁוֹאֵל וּמֵשִׁיב כְּדַרְכּוֹ.

§ It was taught in the aforementioned *baraita*: **From the third** day **to the seventh** day, **he may respond** when other people address him, **but he may not extend greetings** to them. **From this** point **forward, he may extend greetings and respond in his** usual **manner.**

וּרְמִינְהוּ: הַמּוֹצֵא אֶת חֲבֵירוֹ אָבֵל, בְּתוֹךְ שְׁלֹשִׁים יוֹם – מְדַבֵּר עִמּוֹ תַּנְחוּמִין וְאֵינוֹ שׁוֹאֵל בִּשְׁלוֹמוֹ; לְאַחַר שְׁלֹשִׁים יוֹם – שׁוֹאֵל בִּשְׁלוֹמוֹ וְאֵינוֹ מְדַבֵּר עִמּוֹ תַּנְחוּמִין.

And the Gemara **raises a contradiction** from another *baraita* that states: **One who finds another in mourning during the** first **thirty days** of that person's bereavement **may** still **speak words of consolation to him, but he should not extend greetings toward him.** If he finds him **after thirty days, he may extend greetings toward him, but he should not speak words of consolation to him,** so as not to remind him of his pain.

מֵתָה אִשְׁתּוֹ וְנָשָׂא אִשָּׁה אַחֶרֶת – אֵינוֹ רַשַּׁאי לִיכָּנֵס לְבֵיתוֹ לְדַבֵּר עִמּוֹ תַּנְחוּמִין. מְצָאוֹ בַּשּׁוּק – אוֹמֵר לוֹ בְּשָׂפָה רָפָה וּבְכוֹבֶד רֹאשׁ!

If it was the mourner's **wife** who **died and he married another woman**[N] within thirty days of his first wife's death, **one may not enter his house to speak words of consolation with him,** so as not to offend his new wife. If, however, **he finds him** alone **in the marketplace, he may speak to him with gentle words and in a serious manner.** This indicates that the prohibition against extending greetings lasts for thirty days and not just seven.

אָמַר רַב אִידִי בַּר אָבִין: הוּא שׁוֹאֵל בִּשְׁלוֹם אֲחֵרִים – שֶׁאֲחֵרִים שְׁרוּיִין בְּשָׁלוֹם; אֲחֵרִים אֵין שׁוֹאֲלִין בִּשְׁלוֹמוֹ – שֶׁהוּא אֵינוֹ שָׁרוּי בְּשָׁלוֹם.

Rav Idi bar Avin said: The two *baraitot* refer to different situations: The first *baraita* is referring to the mourner **himself, who may extend greetings** [*shalom*] **to others** after the completion of his seven days of mourning, **as the others are at peace** [*shalom*]. The second *baraita*, which speaks of a prohibition that lasts thirty days, is referring to **other people, who may not extend greetings to him, as he,** the mourner, **is not at peace.**

וְהָא מִדְּקָתָנֵי מֵשִׁיב מִכְּלָל דְּשָׁיְילִינַן לֵיהּ! דְּלָא יָדְעִי.

The Gemara challenges: **But from** the fact **that it teaches** in a *baraita* that after the third day of his bereavement, the mourner may **respond** when other people address him, **by inference** others **may extend greetings to him.** The Gemara answers: This is referring to a case where people **did not know** that he was in mourning and unknowingly extended greetings to him.

אִי הָכִי, הָתָם נַמִּי! הָתָם מוֹדַע לְהוּ, וְלָא מְהַדַּר לְהוּ; הָכָא – לָא צָרִיךְ לְאוֹדוּעִינְהוּ.

The Gemara asks: **If so,** if the *baraita* speaks of a case where the people who greeted him were unaware that he was in mourning, then **there also,** during the first three days of his bereavement, he should be permitted to respond when other people address him. The Gemara answers: **There,** during the first three days, **he must inform them** that he is in mourning **and not respond** to their greetings. **Here,** after the first three days, **he need not inform them** about his bereavement, but rather he may respond to their greetings.

וּרְמִינְהוּ: הַמּוֹצֵא אֶת חֲבֵרוֹ אָבֵל, בְּתוֹךְ שְׁנֵים עָשָׂר חֹדֶשׁ – מְדַבֵּר עִמּוֹ תַּנְחוּמִין וְאֵינוֹ שׁוֹאֵל בִּשְׁלוֹמוֹ; לְאַחַר שְׁנֵים עָשָׂר חֹדֶשׁ – שׁוֹאֵל בִּשְׁלוֹמוֹ וְאֵינוֹ מְדַבֵּר עִמּוֹ תַּנְחוּמִין, אֲבָל מְדַבֵּר עִמּוֹ מִן הַצַּד.

And the Gemara **raises a contradiction** from another *baraita* that states: **One who finds another in mourning during** his **twelve months** of bereavement **may** still **speak words of consolation to him, but he should not extend greetings toward him.** If he finds him **after twelve months, he may extend greetings toward him, and he should not speak words of consolation to him. He may, however, speak to him indirectly,** i.e., he may say to him: May you be consoled, without mentioning the name of the deceased.

LANGUAGE

Bench [*safsal*] – סַפְסָל: The origin of this word is the Latin *subsellium*, meaning low seat or bench. Often this word was used to refer to the seats of judges or other leaders. Some say that the origin of the word is from the Hebrew word *sefel*, meaning mug, or at least influenced to some degree by the Hebrew, as it was common for people to sit on large overturned mugs.

Ancient figurine of a person sitting on a large overturned mug

NOTES

The mourner's wife died and he married another woman – מֵתָה אִשְׁתּוֹ וְנָשָׂא אִשָּׁה אַחֶרֶת: The commentaries explain that one may marry another woman this soon after the death of his first wife only if he has not yet fulfilled the mitzva of procreation or if he has small children who need a mother to take care of them. It is in these situations that one must be careful not to offend his second wife by mentioning the previous one.

אָמַר רַבִּי מֵאִיר: הַמּוֹצֵא אֶת חֲבֵרוֹ אָבֵל לְאַחַר שְׁנֵים עָשָׂר חֹדֶשׁ, וּמְדַבֵּר עִמּוֹ תַּנְחוּמִין, לְמָה הוּא דּוֹמֶה? לְאָדָם שֶׁנִּשְׁבְּרָה רַגְלוֹ וְחָיְתָה, מְצָאוֹ רוֹפֵא וְאָמַר לוֹ: כַּלֵּךְ אֶצְלִי, שֶׁאֲנִי שׁוֹבְרָהּ וַאֲרַפְּאֶנָּה, כְּדֵי שֶׁתֵּדַע שֶׁסַּמְמָנִין שֶׁלִּי יָפִין!

Rabbi Meir said: One who finds another in mourning after twelve months and speaks to him words of consolation, to what may this situation **be likened? To a person who broke his leg and it healed,** and afterward a physician **found him and said to him: Come to me, for I will break it** a second time **and** then **I will heal it, so that you may know how good my medicines are** and how well they work. One who consoles his friend after so much time has passed acts in a similar fashion, stirring up an old wound and then trying to heal it. In any event, it appears that one must not extend greetings to a mourner during the entire twelve-month mourning period.

לָא קַשְׁיָא: הָא – בְּאָבִיו וְאִמּוֹ; הָא – בִּשְׁאָר קְרוֹבִים.

The Gemara answers: **This is not difficult. This** *baraita*, which says that one must not extend greetings to a mourner for twelve months, is referring to one who lost **his father or mother. That** *baraita*, which teaches that a mourner may be greeted after seven days,[H] is referring to one who is in mourning over **other relatives.**

הָתָם נַמִי יְדַבֵּר עִמּוֹ תַּנְחוּמִין מִן הַצַּד! אִין, הָכִי נַמִי. וּמַאי אֵינוֹ מְדַבֵּר עִמּוֹ תַּנְחוּמִין? כְּדַרְכּוֹ, אֲבָל מְדַבֵּר עִמּוֹ מִן הַצַּד.

The Gemara asks: **There too,** in the case of other relatives after thirty days, **let him speak words of consolation to him indirectly.** Why does the *baraita* say that after thirty days he should not speak words of consolation to him at all? The Gemara answers: **Yes, it is indeed so. And what** is meant by the words: **He should not speak words of consolation to him?** This means that he may not console him **in his** usual **manner, but he may speak to him indirectly.**

תָּנוּ רַבָּנַן: אָבֵל, שְׁלֹשָׁה יָמִים הָרִאשׁוֹנִים בָּא מִמָּקוֹם קָרוֹב – מוֹנֶה עִמָּהֶן; בָּא מִמָּקוֹם רָחוֹק – מוֹנֶה לְעַצְמוֹ. מִכָּאן וְאֵילָךְ, אֲפִילּוּ בָּא מִמָּקוֹם קָרוֹב – מוֹנֶה לְעַצְמוֹ. רַבִּי שִׁמְעוֹן אוֹמֵר: אֲפִילּוּ בָּא בַּיּוֹם הַשְּׁבִיעִי מִמָּקוֹם קָרוֹב – מוֹנֶה עִמָּהֶן.

§ **The Sages taught** the following *baraita*: If **a mourner comes** to the house of mourning **from a nearby place**[N] **during the first three days** of mourning, **he counts** his days of mourning **with** the other mourners from the time of the burial and completes his mourning with them. This is the case even if he may end up observing mourning for only five or six days. But if **he came from a distant place, he counts on his own** seven complete days from the time that he was informed of his relative's death. **From this** point **forward,** i.e., after the first three days of mourning, **even if he came from a nearby place, he counts** seven days **on his own. Rabbi Shimon says: Even if he came on the seventh day from a nearby place, he counts** and completes the seven-day period of mourning **with** the other mourners.[H]

אָמַר מָר: שְׁלֹשָׁה יָמִים הָרִאשׁוֹנִים, בָּא מִמָּקוֹם קָרוֹב – מוֹנֶה עִמָּהֶן. אָמַר רַבִּי חִיָּיא בַּר אַבָּא אָמַר רַבִּי יוֹחָנָן: וְהוּא שֶׁיֵּשׁ גְּדוֹל הַבַּיִת בַּבַּיִת.

The Master said, citing the *baraita*: If **a mourner comes** to the house of mourning **from a nearby place during the first three days** of mourning, **he counts** his days of mourning **with** the other mourners and completes his mourning with them. **Rabbi Ḥiyya bar Abba said that Rabbi Yoḥanan said: This is** in a case **where the principal** member **of the household**[N] **is in the house,** and therefore all the other family members follow his mourning. If, however, it is the principal member of the family who comes home, he certainly does not follow the other members, but rather he counts seven days on his own.

אִיבַּעְיָא לְהוּ:

A dilemma was raised before the scholars:

HALAKHA

Consoling mourners after seven days – נִחוּם אֲבֵלִים לְאַחַר שִׁבְעָה: One who meets a mourner within the latter's thirty-day period of mourning should speak words of consolation to him and should not extend greetings. After thirty days, he may extend greetings toward him, but he may not speak words of consolation to him explicitly. However, he may say: You should be consoled, without mentioning the name of the deceased.

If a man's wife passes away and he marries another woman, one should not enter his house to console him. If he finds him on the street then he may say in an undertone: You should be consoled. If he did not marry another wife, then one may console him until three pilgrimage Festivals have passed.

One may speak words of consolation to a mourner whose father or mother has passed away within the last twelve months, and afterward he may console him without mentioning the name of the deceased (*Shulḥan Arukh, Yoreh De'a* 385:2).

How does one join the counting of seven – כֵּיצַד מִצְטָרֵף לְמִנְיַן שִׁבְעָה: In a case where one's close family member died and he did not know until he reached the place of the mourners, if he came from a nearby place, which is less than ten parasangs away, then he joins with the other mourners, even if he arrives on the seventh day. Nowadays, a nearby place is defined as any distance that one can reach in a single day's travel using modern forms of transportation (*Arukh HaShulḥan*). One joins the mourners if he still finds people who came to console the principal member of the household, even if they have stood up to leave. Similarly, such a person also counts the thirty-day period of mourning with this group. If he does not find consolers, there then he observes seven days of mourning on his own. Similarly, one who comes from a distant place counts his own seven- and thirty-day periods of mourning from the day on which he arrived, even if he arrives on the second day of mourning (*Shulḥan Arukh, Yoreh De'a* 375:8).

NOTES

One who comes from a nearby place – בָּא מִמָּקוֹם קָרוֹב: There is a tradition in the name of the *ge'onim* that a distant place refers to one that is more than a day's travel away from the place of the other mourners. The Rif explains that within this distance it is possible for a messenger to reach this relative and for him to arrive within the first three days after the death. As mentioned above, three days is referred to as the main portion of the mourning, and as long as one is close enough to the other mourners to reach them in this time period, he is joined together with the other mourners.

The principal member of the household – גְּדוֹל הַבַּיִת: Some commentaries explain that this term does not refer to a specific person, e.g., the oldest brother. Rather, it refers to the most important member of that family, whom everyone else follows with regard to mourning. This is the case even if he is a son or the youngest of the brothers (Rabbi Yitzḥak ibn Giat).

הָלַךְ גְּדוֹל הַבַּיִת לְבֵית הַקְּבָרוֹת מַהוּ?

If **the principal** member **of the household went**[N] with the remains of the deceased **to the cemetery** and did not return for several days,[H] **what is the** *halakha*? If another mourner came to the house of mourning during his absence, does he follow the principal member of the household and count from the time of the burial, or does he count from the time that the funeral procession departed, like the other members of the household?

תָּא שְׁמַע, דְּאָמַר רַבִּי חִיָּיא בַּר אַבָּא אָמַר רַבִּי יוֹחָנָן: אֲפִילּוּ הָלַךְ גְּדוֹל הַבַּיִת לְבֵית הַקְּבָרוֹת מוֹנֶה עִמָּהֶן. מוֹנֶה עִמָּהֶן? וְהָתַנְיָא מוֹנֶה לְעַצְמוֹ!

The Gemara answers: **Come and hear that which Rabbi Ḥiyya bar Abba said that Rabbi Yoḥanan said: Even** if the **principal** member **of the household went to the cemetery,** the mourner who comes home during his absence **counts with them,** i.e., the other members of the household who did not go to the cemetery. The Gemara asks: Does **he** really **count** and complete his mourning **with them? But isn't it taught** otherwise in a *baraita*, that **he counts** seven days **on his own?**

לָא קַשְׁיָא: הָא – דַּאֲתָא בְּגוֹ תְּלָתָא, וְהָא – דְּלָא אֲתָא בְּגוֹ תְּלָתָא. כִּי הָא דַּאֲמַר לְהוּ רַב לִבְנֵי הַצְלְפּוֹנִי: דְּאָתוּ בְּגוֹ תְּלָתָא – לִימְנוּ בַּהֲדַיְיכוּ; דְּלָא אָתוּ בְּגוֹ תְּלָתָא – לִימְנוּ לְנַפְשַׁיְהוּ.

The Gemara answers: **This is not difficult. This** statement, that he counts with them, is referring to a case **where** the principal member of the household **came** home **within three** days. **And the other** ruling, that he counts on his own, is referring to a case **where he did not come** home **within three** days. This conclusion is **similar to** what **Rav said to the sons of Hatzleponi**[N] when they were in mourning: **Those who come** home **within three** days **should count with you;** whereas **those who do not come** home **within three** days **should count on their own.**

אֲמַר לְהוּ רָבָא לִבְנֵי מְחוֹזָא: אַתּוּן דְּלָא אָזְלִיתוּ בָּתַר עַרְסָא, מִכִּי מְהַדְרִיתוּ אַפַּיְיכוּ מִבָּבָא דְּאַבּוּלָא – אַתְחִילוּ מְנוּ.

Rava said to the people of Meḥoza:[B] Those **of you who do not follow the coffin** all the way to the place of interment **should begin counting** your days of mourning **from when you turn your faces**[H] **from the city gates**[N] to return home. Since the dead were commonly transported long distances and buried far away, most of the mourners did not accompany their deceased relatives to the actual site of burial.

״רַבִּי שִׁמְעוֹן אוֹמֵר אֲפִילּוּ בָּא בַּיּוֹם הַשְּׁבִיעִי מִמָּקוֹם קָרוֹב מוֹנֶה עִמָּהֶן״. אָמַר רַבִּי חִיָּיא בַּר גַּמְדָא אָמַר רַבִּי יוֹסֵי בֶּן שָׁאוּל אָמַר רַבִּי: וְהוּא שֶׁבָּא וּמָצָא מְנַחֲמִין אֶצְלוֹ.

§ The Gemara cites the *baraita* taught above: **Rabbi Shimon says: Even** if one of the mourners **came on the seventh day from a nearby place, he counts with** the other mourners and completes the seven-day period of mourning with them. **Rabbi Ḥiyya bar Gamda said that Rabbi Yosei ben Shaul said that Rabbi** Yehuda HaNasi **said: And this is** the *halakha*, provided that **he came and found consolers** still present **in the house.**

בָּעֵי רַב עָנָן: נִנְעֲרוּ לַעֲמוֹד וְלֹא עָמְדוּ, מַהוּ? תֵּיקוּ.

§ **Rav Anan asks:** If the consolers **had** already **stirred** themselves **to stand up** and leave but **did not** yet actually **stand up** and leave, **what is the** *halakha*? Is it considered as if the consolers have already left or not? This question was not answered, and the dilemma **stands** unresolved.

HALAKHA

The principal member of the household went – הָלַךְ גְּדוֹל הַבַּיִת: Some say that in a case where a person arrives and finds that the principal member of the household has gone to tend to the needs of the dead, then if the principal member returns within three days, it is as though he was home when this person arrived, and this person is considered to be one of the members of the household. Therefore, he counts the days of his mourning period with this group (Rema; *Shulḥan Arukh, Yoreh De'a* 375:8).

When you turn your faces – מִכִּי מְהַדְרִיתוּ אַפַּיְיכוּ: In places where the deceased are carried to another city in order to be buried, those who remain in the city should begin counting the seven-day period of mourning once they turn away from the funeral procession. Those who accompany the deceased and those relatives who live near the place of burial begin to observe their mourning after the burial itself.

If the principal member of the household accompanies the deceased, then even those who stay at home must wait until the deceased has been buried to start counting the seven days of mourning. Everyone follows the principal member of the household, regardless of whether he is the eldest member or if he is young, though some say that he must be at least thirteen years old. When a married woman is the deceased, her husband is considered to be the principal member of the household (*Shakh*, citing Rashba; *Shulḥan Arukh, Yoreh De'a* 375:2).

BACKGROUND

Meḥoza – מְחוֹזָא: A city on the Tigris, located near the Malka River, Meḥoza was a large commercial city and most of its inhabitants were Jews. Unlike most other Jewish communities, the Jews of Meḥoza generally earned their living from commerce. The Jewish community included a large number of converts as well as Jews from many different countries. After Neharde'a was destroyed in 259 CE the Neharde'a yeshiva relocated to Meḥoza. Meḥoza became the Torah center of leading scholars such as Rav Naḥman; Rav Sheshet; Rava, who later became head of the Meḥoza Yeshiva; Ameimar; and Rav Kahana, who was Rav Ashi's teacher. After the death of Abaye in 338 CE, the Pumbedita yeshiva, which was then headed by Rava, also moved for a period to Meḥoza.

NOTES

The principal member of the household went, etc. – הָלַךְ גְּדוֹל הַבַּיִת וכו׳: The early authorities disagree about how to understand this *halakha*, and their dispute is based on, among other issues, whether this statement and those after it are a continuation of what was previously stated or separate from it.

Some explain that the question of the Gemara concerns the principal member of the household himself. If he accompanied the deceased to the cemetery and was not home when the rest of the family began their mourning, then the issue is whether he joins with their mourning or not. The conclusion is that if he returns within three days, then he joins with them; if not, he counts on his own (Rashi, from manuscript; Ra'avad; Rabbeinu Yehonatan of Lunel).

According to this explanation, the Babylonian Talmud contradicts the principle stated in the Jerusalem Talmud, that all mourning is based on the principal member of the family. In the Jerusalem Talmud, it is maintained that if the principal member remains in that place, the other mourners count with him; if he goes to accompany the dead, then they count with him after the burial.

However, others understand this as a continuation of the previous case, where a person comes and joins other mourners. This issue depends on the principal member of the household, and this case concerns the *halakha* when the principal member of the household is not present at that time that this other person came to the house of mourning. For example, if the principal member of the household went to accompany the deceased and returns within three days, it is as though he were there the entire time. Therefore, the newly arrived mourner joins with the rest of the mourners in that household (Rabbeinu Gershom Meor HaGola; *Talmid Rabbeinu Yeḥiel of Paris*; Rabbi Shlomo ben HaYatom).

There is another entirely different explanation, which understands the phrase: The principal member of the household went to the cemetery, to mean that the principal member of the household passed away. According to this explanation, the Gemara asks if the mourners follow the principal person who remains, or if the *halakha* of the principal member of the household no longer applies (Rashi, from manuscript; Commentary on *Moed Katan*).

Hatzleponi – הַצְלְפּוֹנִי: Some explain this to be the name of a place, while others understand it to be a family name (Rashi, from manuscript). There are also those who hold that this was the name of their father who passed away (*Talmid Rabbeinu Yeḥiel of Paris*).

The city gates – בָּבָא דְּאַבּוּלָא: Rabbeinu Gershom Meor HaGola explains that this refers to the gate in the house of mourning, and some have a version of the text that reflects this explanation.

גְּמִירִי חַבְרֵיהּ דְּרַבִּי אַבָּא בַּר חִיָּיא מֵרַבִּי אַבָּא, וּמַנּוּ – רַבִּי זֵירָא, וְאָמְרִי לַהּ: חַבְרֵיהּ דְּרַבִּי זֵירָא מֵרַבִּי זֵירָא, וּמַנּוּ – רַבִּי אַבָּא בְּרֵיהּ דְּרַבִּי חִיָּיא בַּר אַבָּא, אָמַר רַבִּי יוֹחָנָן: הֲלָכָה כְּרַבָּן שִׁמְעוֹן בֶּן גַּמְלִיאֵל בִּטְרֵיפוֹת, וַהֲלָכָה כְּרַבִּי שִׁמְעוֹן בְּאֵבֶל.

The Gemara relates that **a colleague of Rabbi Abba bar Ḥiyya learned** the following principle as a tradition **from Rabbi Abba.** The Gemara asks: **And who was** this colleague? It was **Rabbi Zeira. And some say** a different version of this tradition: **A colleague of Rabbi Zeira** learned a tradition **from Rabbi Zeira.** The Gemara asks: **And who is this** colleague? It was **Rabbi Abba, son of Rabbi Ḥiyya bar Abba: Rabbi Yoḥanan said: The *halakha* is in accordance with** the opinion of **Rabban Shimon ben Gamliel with regard to** an animals that is unsuitable for human consumption because of severe organic disease or congenital defect, making it **a *tereifa*, and the *halakha* is in accordance with** the opinion of **Rabbi Shimon with regard to** the *halakhot* of **mourning.**

כְּרַבִּי שִׁמְעוֹן בְּאֵבֶל – הָא דַּאֲמַרַן. כְּרַבָּן שִׁמְעוֹן בֶּן גַּמְלִיאֵל בִּטְרֵיפוֹת – דִּתְנַן: בְּנֵי מֵעַיִם שֶׁנִּיקְּבוּ וְלֵיחָה סוֹתַמְתָּן – כְּשֵׁרָה, דִּבְרֵי רַבָּן שִׁמְעוֹן בֶּן גַּמְלִיאֵל.

The Gemara explains: The *halakha* is **in accordance with** the opinion of **Rabbi Shimon with regard to mourning, concerning that which we** just **said** about a mourner who arrives on the seventh day. The *halakha* is **in accordance with** the opinion of **Rabban Shimon ben Gamliel with regard to** defects in animals that render them ***tereifa*** concerning **that which we learned** in a *baraita*: If the animal's **intestines became perforated, but** the hole **was stopped up by mucus,**[H] so that nothing comes out of this hole, the animal is **fit.** Unlike an ordinary hole in the intestines, this hole does not render the animal a *tereifa* and make it unfit for consumption. This is **the statement of Rabban Shimon ben Gamliel.**

מַאי לֵיחָה? אֲמַר רַב כַּהֲנָא: שִׁירְקָא דְּמֵעֲיָא דְּנָפֵיק אַגַּב דּוּחֲקָא. אָמַר מַאן דְּהוּא: אִיזְכֵּי וְאַסֵּיק וְאַגְמְרָא לִשְׁמַעְתָּא מִפּוּמֵּיהּ דְּמָרֵיהּ.

The Gemara asks: **What is this mucus? Rav Kahana said: The fat** [*shirka*][L] **of the intestines**[BN] **that comes out under pressure. Someone** whose name was not given **said: May I merit to go up** to Eretz Yisrael **and learn this *halakha* from the mouth of its author.**

כִּי סְלֵיק אַשְׁכְּחֵיהּ לְרַבִּי אַבָּא בְּרֵיהּ דְּרַבִּי חִיָּיא בַּר אַבָּא, אֲמַר לֵיהּ: אֲמַר מָר הֲלָכָה כְּרַבָּן שִׁמְעוֹן בֶּן גַּמְלִיאֵל בִּטְרֵיפוֹת? אֲמַר לֵיהּ: אֲנָא ״אֵין הֲלָכָה״ אֲמָרִי.

When he went up from Babylonia to Eretz Yisrael, **he found Rabbi Abba, son of Rabbi Ḥiyya bar Abba,** and **said to him: Did the Master say** that **the *halakha* is in accordance with** the opinion of **Rabban Shimon ben Gamliel with regard to** defects that render the animal **a *tereifa*? He said to him: I said** just the opposite, namely, that **the *halakha* is not** in accordance with Rabban Shimon ben Gamliel, and therefore such a hole in the animal's intestine makes it unfit for eating.

כְּרַבִּי שִׁמְעוֹן בְּאֵבֶל מַאי? אֲמַר לֵיהּ: פְּלוּגְתָּא נִינְהוּ. דְּאִיתְּמַר, רַב חִסְדָּא אָמַר: הֲלָכָה; וְכֵן אָמַר רַבִּי יוֹחָנָן: הֲלָכָה; רַב נַחְמָן אָמַר: אֵין הֲלָכָה.

He asked him again: **What** about the other ruling reported in your name, that the *halakha* **is in accordance with** the opinion of **Rabbi Shimon with regard to mourning?** Is this accurate? **He said to him:** This issue is **subject to dispute, as it was stated: Rav Ḥisda said: The *halakha*** is in accordance with the opinion of Rabbi Shimon, **and similarly Rabbi Yoḥanan said:** It is the ***halakha.*** But **Rav Naḥman said: It is not the *halakha.***

וְאֵין הֲלָכָה כְּרַבָּן שִׁמְעוֹן בֶּן גַּמְלִיאֵל בִּטְרֵיפוֹת. וַהֲלָכָה כְּרַבִּי שִׁמְעוֹן בְּאֵבֶל. דְּאָמַר שְׁמוּאֵל: הֲלָכָה כְּדִבְרֵי הַמֵּיקֵל בְּאֵבֶל.

The Gemara concludes: **The *halakha* is not in accordance with** the opinion of **Rabban Shimon ben Gamliel with regard to** the aforementioned issue of ***tereifa*, and the *halakha* is in accordance with Rabbi Shimon with regard to mourning, as Shmuel stated** a principle: **The *halakha* follows the opinion of the** more **lenient** authority **in** matters relating to **mourning.**

עַל כָּל הַמֵּתִים כּוּלָּן, מְדַחֶה מִטָּתוֹ – הֲרֵי זֶה מְשׁוּבָּח; עַל אָבִיו וְעַל אִמּוֹ – הֲרֵי זֶה מְגוּנֶּה. הָיָה עֶרֶב שַׁבָּת, אוֹ עֶרֶב יוֹם טוֹב – הֲרֵי זֶה מְשׁוּבָּח, שֶׁאֵינוֹ עוֹשֶׂה אֶלָּא לִכְבוֹד אָבִיו וְאִמּוֹ.

§ It was taught in a *baraita*: **With regard to all** other **deceased** relatives, it **is praiseworthy** for **one** to be **quick** in taking **the bier**[NH] out for burial. But **in the case of one's father or mother,** acting in this manner **is condemnable,** as one should draw out the period of acute mourning for his parent. If, however, **it was Friday**[N] **or the eve of a Festival,** then **one is praiseworthy** for expediting his parent's burial because **he does this only out of respect for his father or mother,** as he does not want them to remain unburied for the duration of Shabbat or the Festival.

עַל כָּל הַמֵּתִים כּוּלָּן, רָצָה מְמַעֵט בְּעִסְקוֹ, רָצָה אֵינוֹ

With regard to all other **dead,** if the mourner **wishes** he may **reduce his business**[NH] due to mourning. If, however, **he wishes** not to do so, he **need not**

HALAKHA

Intestines became perforated, but the hole was stopped up by mucus – נִקְבוּ הַדַּקִּים וְלֵיחָה סוֹתַמְתָּן: A hole in the small intestine qualifies an animal as a *tereifa*; even if liquid sticks to this hole and blocks it the animal may not be eaten. As is stated in the Gemara, the *halakha* is not in accordance with the opinion of Rabban Shimon ben Gamliel (*Shulḥan Arukh, Yoreh De'a* 46:1).

One to be quick in taking the bier – מְדַחֶה מִיטָּתוֹ: For most deceased relatives, it is praiseworthy to complete the burial as quickly as possible. However, in the case of one's father or mother, this is considered to be disrespectful, unless it is Friday, the eve of a Festival, or it is raining and the corpse will get wet. In these situations, it is preferable to conduct the burial quickly, out of respect for one's parents (*Shulḥan Arukh, Yoreh De'a* 357:2).

He may reduce his business – מְמַעֵט בְּעִסְקוֹ: One who is mourning over a close relative may choose whether or not to limit his involvement in business activities. However, one who is mourning over his father or mother is required to lessen his involvement in these activities (*Shulḥan Arukh, Yoreh De'a* 380:24).

LANGUAGE

Fat [*shirka*] – שִׁירְקָא: Apparently from the Middle Iranian širak, referring to secreted fatty liquid.

BACKGROUND

The fat of the intestines – שִׁירְקָא דְּמֵעֲיָא: This refers to the mucus membrane that covers the intestines, the *muscosa tunica*, which contains protrusions that enter into the intestines. This soft membrane is not considered to be enough of a protection if the intestine is punctured, as even if it manages to close the intestine for a short period of time the food in the intestines will eventually leave the intestinal tract from this hole.

NOTES

The fat of the intestines – שִׁירְקָא דְּמֵעֲיָא: Some say that this is a soft membrane that covers the intestines (Commentary on *Moed Katan*). It is said in the name of Rav Hai Gaon that this refers to the soft layer of fat that covers the walls of the intestines. Others claim that it refers to food that has not been entirely digested (see Commentary on *Moed Katan*).

One to be quick in taking the bier – מְדַחֶה מִיטָּתוֹ: Since one does not speak a lengthy eulogy over other relatives, it is preferable not to delay the burial unless it is for their honor (Rabbeinu Yehonatan of Lunel). Some say that one who buries the deceased quickly shows that he has accepted Heaven's decree with love, and that he is not challenging God's judgment (*Talmid Rabbeinu Yeḥiel of Paris*).

Friday, etc. – עֶרֶב שַׁבָּת וכו׳: It is preferable to show respect toward Shabbat or a Festival, which require preparation, rather than spend time eulogizing the dead. Similarly, there is also concern that if the burial is delayed there may not be time to complete the burial, causing the deceased to remain unburied for an additional day, in violation of the *halakha* (*Talmid Rabbeinu Yeḥiel of Paris*).

He may reduce his business – מְמַעֵט בְּעִסְקוֹ: Rav Hai Gaon explains that one who spends all day in his business must work for fewer hours. In the Jerusalem Talmud it explains that one who is mourning over his father or mother may not leave his home for business endeavors, even after thirty days, until such time as his colleagues rebuke him.

מְמַעֵט; עַל אָבִיו וְעַל אִמּוֹ – מְמַעֵט.

reduce it. In the case of **his father or mother,** he must always **reduce** his business.

עַל כׇּל הַמֵּתִים כּוּלָּן, רָצָה – חוֹלֵץ, רָצָה – אֵינוֹ חוֹלֵץ. עַל אָבִיו וְעַל אִמּוֹ – חוֹלֵץ.

With regard to all other **deceased** relatives, if the mourner **wishes, he may remove**[N] his garment from one of his shoulders,[BH] and if **he wishes** not to remove it, **he need not remove** it. However, in the case of **his father or mother, he** must always **remove** his garment from one of his shoulders.

וּמַעֲשֶׂה בִּגְדוֹל הַדּוֹר אֶחָד שֶׁמֵּת אָבִיו וּבִיקֵּשׁ לַחֲלוֹץ, וּבִיקֵּשׁ גְּדוֹל הַדּוֹר אַחֵר שֶׁעִמּוֹ לַחֲלוֹץ – וְנִמְנַע וְלֹא חָלַץ.

There was **an incident when the father of a leading authority of** his **generation died, and** the authority **wished to remove** his garment from one shoulder. **Another leading authority of the generation** also **wished to remove** his own garment together **with him,** in order to join him in his mourning, **but** due to this the first person **refrained and did not remove**[N] his garment, so that his colleague would not remove his garment as well.

אָמַר אַבָּיֵי: גְּדוֹל הַדּוֹר – רַבִּי; גְּדוֹל הַדּוֹר שֶׁעִמּוֹ – רַבִּי יַעֲקֹב בַּר אַחָא. וְאִיכָּא דְּאָמְרִי: גְּדוֹל הַדּוֹר – רַבִּי יַעֲקֹב בַּר אַחָא; גְּדוֹל הַדּוֹר שֶׁעִמּוֹ – רַבִּי.

Abaye said: The leading authority of the generation mentioned here is **Rabbi** Yehuda HaNasi, and **the leading authority of the generation** who was **with him** was **Rabbi Ya'akov bar Aḥa. And some say: The leading authority of the generation** was **Rabbi Ya'akov bar Aḥa,** and **the leading authority of the generation** who was **with him** was **Rabbi** Yehuda HaNasi.

בִּשְׁלָמָא לְמַאן דְּאָמַר גְּדוֹל הַדּוֹר שֶׁעִמּוֹ רַבִּי – הַיְינוּ דְּנִמְנַע וְלֹא חָלַץ.

The Gemara examines this issue: **Granted, according to the one who said** that **the leading authority of the generation** who was **with him was Rabbi** Yehuda HaNasi, **this is** the reason that **he refrained and did not remove** his garment from his shoulder. That is to say, Rabbi Ya'akov bar Aḥa refrained from doing so because he did not wish to cause the *Nasi* to remove his own garment.

אֶלָּא לְמַאן דְּאָמַר רַבִּי יַעֲקֹב בַּר אַחָא – אַמַּאי נִמְנַע וְלֹא חָלַץ? רַבָּן שִׁמְעוֹן בֶּן גַּמְלִיאֵל נָשִׂיא הֲוָה, וְכוּלֵּי עָלְמָא מִיחַיְּיבִי לְמִיחְלַץ! קַשְׁיָא.

But according to the one who said that it is **Rabbi Ya'akov bar Aḥa** who was the leader of the generation with him, **why did** Rabbi Yehuda HaNasi **refrain and not remove** his garment from his shoulder? **Rabban Shimon ben Gamliel,**[P] the father of Rabbi Yehuda HaNasi, was also **the *Nasi*, and everyone is required to remove** his garment from his shoulder for him, as was the accepted practice. Therefore, Rabbi Ya'akov bar Aḥa would also have been required to bare his shoulder. Why, then, did Rabbi Yehuda HaNasi prevent him from doing so? The Gemara concludes: Indeed **this** is **difficult.**

NOTES

He may remove [*holetz*] – חוֹלֵץ: The *ge'onim* explain that this means removing the garment from one's shoulder and exposing the shoulder. There is also support for this explanation from several places in the Talmud (Ramban). However, some explain slightly differently, maintaining that one is required to rend his garment until he exposes his shoulder (Rashi, from manuscript; *Talmid Rabbeinu Yeḥiel of Paris*). Others understand that this means removing one's outer garment, like a person who shows that he is about to engage in an act that requires physical exertion. By doing so, this mourner demonstrates that he is putting effort into showing honor for the deceased (Ramban; Ran citing *Tosefot of Rabbi Shimshon of Saens*). There are also those who understand that the word *ḥoletz* in this context means removing one's shoes, and that a mourner is required to remove his shoes and walk barefoot in order to honor the dead, not as an act of mourning. Therefore, one performs this act before the requirements of mourning take effect, when he is accompanying the body on the way to burial (see Rosh).

He refrained and did not remove – נִמְנַע וְלֹא חָלַץ: Although there is a mitzva to remove one's garment in order to show respect for the deceased, maintaining the honor of a Torah scholar of this stature is a greater mitzva and takes precedence. Perhaps one of the reasons that the custom of exposing the shoulder is no longer practiced is that there is concern that in the Diaspora it will cause the mourners to be treated disrespectfully by their gentile neighbors (Ramban).

BACKGROUND

Removal of the garment from one's shoulder – חֲלִיצַת כָּתֵף: Removing the garment from one's shoulder is similar to a symbolic rending of one's garment, and doing so is considered like removing one's garment in mourning. As is stated in the Gemara, the more one wishes to emphasize the mourning, and the more honor one wishes to show the deceased, the more he removes his garment.

Garment removed from the shoulder

HALAKHA

Removing a garment from the shoulder for a mourner – חֲלִיצַת כָּתֵף לְאָבֵל: One is required to remove his garment while walking with the bier of his father or mother, until the burial has been completed. If the mourner is an important person and it would be seen as dishonorable for him to remove his garment, then he is not required to do so. For all other deceased relatives, he is not required to remove his garment from his shoulder if he does not want to. The Rema writes, based on the *Kolbo*, that nowadays it is customary not to remove one's garment at all (*Shulḥan Arukh*, *Yoreh De'a* 340:16–17).

PERSONALITIES

Rabban Shimon ben Gamliel – רַבָּן שִׁמְעוֹן בֶּן גַּמְלִיאֵל: Rabban Shimon ben Gamliel II was head of the Sanhedrin following the bar Kokheva revolt. He was a member of the dynasty of Hillel the Elder. His grandfather, Rabban Shimon ben Gamliel the Elder, headed the Sanhedrin at the time of the destruction of the Temple and was one of the Ten Martyrs killed by the Romans.

Rabban Shimon ben Gamliel II was a young man studying in Beitar at the time of the bar Kokheva revolt. He escaped from the city before it was destroyed. When the Sanhedrin was reconstituted in Usha, he was chosen to preside there in place of his late father. The Talmud records that he studied Greek philosophy, and it appears that he was knowledgeable in a wide range of scholarly disciplines, including science and medicine.

He tended to be lenient in his halakhic rulings, often stating his concern that people not be overly inconvenienced. All of his rulings were accepted as *halakha*, with only three exceptions. His teachings included attempts to limit arguments and disputes. One example is his statement that no court can nullify the ruling of another court unless it is greater in wisdom and number. In tractate *Avot* (1:17), the following maxim is cited in his name: On three things the world is sustained: On truth, on judgment, and on peace.

עַל כָּל הַמֵּתִים כּוּלָּן מִסְתַּפֵּר לְאַחַר שְׁלֹשִׁים יוֹם; עַל אָבִיו וְעַל אִמּוֹ – עַד שֶׁיְּגַעֲרוּ בּוֹ חֲבֵרָיו. עַל כָּל הַמֵּתִים כּוּלָּן – נִכְנָס לְבֵית הַשִּׂמְחָה לְאַחַר שְׁלֹשִׁים יוֹם; עַל אָבִיו וְעַל אִמּוֹ – לְאַחַר שְׁנֵים עָשָׂר חֹדֶשׁ.

§ The Gemara returns to the continuation of the *baraita*: **With regard to all deceased** relatives except for parents, **one may cut his hair after thirty days. In the case of one's father or mother,** one may not cut his hair **until his colleagues have rebuked him** for his hair being too long.[H] **With regard to all** other **deceased** relatives, **he may enter a place** where **a joyous** celebration is taking place **after thirty days; in the case of his father or mother,** he may enter such a place only **after twelve months.**

אָמַר רַבָּה בַּר בַּר חָנָה: וּלְשִׂמְחַת מְרֵיעוּת. מֵיתִיבִי: וּלְשִׂמְחָה וְלִמְרֵיעוּת שְׁלֹשִׁים יוֹם! קַשְׁיָא.

Rabba bar bar Ḥana said: The ruling that a mourner may enter a house of joy after thirty days applies specifically **to a joyous social gathering,** that is to say, to the joyous meals that a group of friends would eat together, each taking a turn hosting. But this ruling does not apply to a large joyous occasion, such as a wedding feast. The Gemara **raises an objection** from a *baraita* which adds: **And also for joyous social gatherings, thirty days.**[N] This implies that when the *baraita* speaks of joyous celebrations without further specification, it is not referring to joyous social gatherings, but even to weddings and other joyous occasions. The Gemara concludes: Indeed, **it is difficult.**

אַמֵימָר מַתְנֵי הָכִי: אָמַר רַבָּה בַּר בַּר חָנָה, וּלְשִׂמְחַת מְרֵיעוּת – מוּתָּר לִיכָּנֵס לְאַלְתַּר. וְהָא תַּנְיָא: לְשִׂמְחָה שְׁלֹשִׁים, וְלִמְרֵיעוּת שְׁלֹשִׁים!

Ameimar taught the previous discussion **as follows: Rabba bar bar Ḥana said** an alternative version of the discussion: **For a joyous social gathering one is permitted to enter immediately.** The Gemara poses a question: **But isn't it taught** in a *baraita*: **For joyous celebrations and for joyous social gatherings,** one must wait **thirty** days?

לָא קַשְׁיָא; הָא בַּאֲרִיסוּתָא; הָא – בְּפוּרְעָנוּתָא.

The Gemara answers: **This is not difficult. This** ruling, of the *baraita*, is referring **to an initial** gathering,[N] when the mourner is the first in the group of friends to host. The *baraita* teaches that in such a situation the mourner is required to wait thirty days before doing so. **That** ruling, of Rabba bar bar Ḥana, is referring **to a reciprocal** gathering. The mourner's friends have already hosted these gatherings, and now it is his turn to host. Since he is required to host such a gathering for his colleagues, he need not postpone it. Rather, he may host the group immediately.[H]

עַל כָּל הַמֵּתִים כּוּלָּן – קוֹרֵעַ טֶפַח; עַל אָבִיו וְעַל אִמּוֹ – עַד שֶׁיְּגַלֶּה אֶת לִבּוֹ. אָמַר רַבִּי אַבָּהוּ: מַאי קְרָא? ״וַיַּחֲזֵק דָּוִד בִּבְגָדָיו וַיִּקְרָעֵם״, וְאֵין אֲחִיזָה פָּחוֹת מִטֶּפַח.

The *baraita* continues: **With regard to all** other **deceased** relatives, **one rends** his garment the length **of a handbreadth,** and that suffices. **In the case of his father or mother,** he must rend his garment **until he reveals his heart.**[NH] **Rabbi Abbahu said: What is the verse** that teaches that the rent must be a handbreadth? **"And David took hold of his clothes and rent them"** (II Samuel 1:11), **and taking hold cannot** be done for a garment **less than a handbreadth.**

NOTES

A joyous social gathering and other types of joyous celebrations – שִׂמְחַת מְרֵעוּת וְשִׂמְחָה אַחֶרֶת: The differences between the two versions in the Talmud are based on the issue of which is more likely to be prohibited to a mourner: Should a joyous social gathering be delayed until after thirty days because it is purely social and not a mitzva? Or, perhaps the celebration for a mitzva, such as a wedding, must be postponed. Since the joy is greater, a mourner should not take part until after this time. This issue is the subject of a disagreement between the early authorities.

Initial gathering [*arisuta*] – אֲרִיסוּתָא: According to most early authorities, the correct version of the text is *arishuta* or *rashuta*, which are derived from the Aramaic *rashu*, meaning creditor. These meals are considered like a form of a loan that must be repaid to one's friends by hosting them. Therefore, if the mourner is begins a cycle of social meals, he must postpone hosting because he does not yet owe anyone the invitation. However, when others have already hosted him and it is his turn to repay the debt, he is permitted to host the meal. Some have asked why the mourner cannot host the meal or repay the loan without actually taking part himself. They answer that to do so would be insulting for his friends, since they would be eating in his house without him present.

Until he reveals his heart – עַד שֶׁיְּגַלֶּה אֶת לִבּוֹ: In the Jerusalem Talmud, it is explained that by performing this act the mourner expresses his pain that the mitzva to honor one's father and mother no longer applies to him.

HALAKHA

Haircut for a mourner – תִּסְפּוֹרֶת לְאָבֵל: One who is mourning a deceased relative other than his parents may cut his hair after thirty days. After the death of his mother or father, he mourner must wait to cut his hair until his colleagues rebuke him, and a Festival does not interrupt this aspect of mourning. There is dispute with regard to the amount of rebuke he must receive, and the accepted practice is to wait three months to cut the hair on one's head. However, a man may trim his beard before this (*Pitḥei Teshuva*, citing *Noda Bihuda*). In some places, it is customary for a mourner not to cut his hair for twelve months, if it is not absolutely necessary to do so (*Shulḥan Arukh, Yoreh De'a* 390:4, and in the comment of Rema).

A mourner with regard to a party – אָבֵל לְעִנְיַן מִשְׁתֶּה: One who is mourning for a deceased relative may go to a celebration after thirty days, but one who is mourning over his father or mother is required to wait twelve months before doing so. In a leap year, which has an additional month, the mourner is required to wait for twelve months, not a full year. If one is required to host a social gathering to repay those who have hosted him in the past, he may do so after the seven-day mourning period has ended. However, one mourning for his father or mother may not host such a gathering under any circumstances for twelve months. With regard to a joyous mitzva celebration, if there is a concern that the event will not take place at all if he will not attend, such as when two orphans get married, then he may go, provided it takes place after the thirty-day mourning period.

A mourner may take part in a mitzva feast that is not especially joyful, such as a meal after a circumcision or for the redemption of the first born, even during the seven days of mourning, provided he does not have to leave his house. However, the custom is for a mourner not to take part in any feast outside of his house for twelve months.

If one's son is being circumcised or if the mourner is performing the circumcision, he may wear Shabbat clothes and join the feast, provided that it occurs after the thirty-day period of mourning (Rema). Some permit one mourning his parents to join a feast within twelve months, provided that he helps prepare the wedding or serves those in attendance in some way (*Shulḥan Arukh, Yoreh De'a* 391:2).

Rending – קְרִיעָה: One who is mourning a deceased relatives other than a parent is required to rend only his outer garment one handbreadth; if he tore his inner garment, it is acceptable after the fact (*Pitḥei Teshuva*, citing *Keneset HaGedola*), although others disagree and require him to tear his outer garment (Rabbi Akiva Eiger, citing *Torat Ḥayyim*). At the death of one's father or mother, he is required to tear all of his garments until he exposes his heart. It is also the accepted practice to rend one's garment on the left side over one's father or mother and on the right side for other deceased relatives (*Shakh*, citing Maharshal).

There is a dispute with regard to the term *apikarsuto*: Some say that it refers to an undergarment that is worn directly against the skin, and others say that it refers to an outer garment. The accepted practice is never to rend an outer cloak; however an undergarment should be rent. The Rema writes that the Ashkenazic custom is to tear neither one's outer garment nor one's innermost garment. Instead, one is required to tear his second outermost garment over a deceased relatives; over one's father or mother, he must rend all the middle garments between the outer one and the one closest to his body (*Shulḥan Arukh, Yoreh De'a* 340:9–10).

על כל המתים כולן, אפילו לבוש עשרה חלוקין – אינו קורע אלא עליון. על אביו ועל אמו – קורע את כולן, ואפיקרסותו אינה מעכבת,

The *baraita* teaches further: **With regard to all** other deceased relatives, **even if he is wearing ten garments,** one on top of the other, **he rends only** his **outer** garment. But **in the case of his father or mother, he must rend them all.** Failure to rend **his undergarment,**[NL] however, **does not invalidate** the fulfillment of the mitzva.

אחד האיש ואחד אשה. רבי שמעון בן אלעזר אומר: האשה קורעת את התחתון, ומחזירתו לאחוריה, וחוזרת וקורעת את העליון.

Both a man and a woman are required to rend their garments. **Rabbi Shimon ben Elazar says: A woman** first **rends** her **inner** garment **and turns** it **around,** so that the tear is **on her back. And** only **afterward** does **she rend** her **outer** garment, so that she does not expose her chest.[H]

על כל המתים כולן רצה – מבדיל קמי שפה שלו, רצה – אינו מבדיל. על אביו ועל אמו – מבדיל.

With regard to all other **deceased** relatives, if **one wishes he may rip apart** his garment **on the hem,**[NH] rather than merely expanding the neck hole, so that the tear stands out distinctly from the opening of the garment. If he **wishes** not to do this, **he does not rip apart** the hem in this manner. That is to say, one may simply enlarge the neck hole, although rending a garment in this way makes the tear less prominent. **In the case of one's father or mother,** however, **he must** always **rip apart** the hem.

רבי יהודה אומר: כל קריעה שאינו מבדיל קמי שפה שלו – אינו אלא קרע של תיפלות. אמר רבי אבהו: מאי טעמא דרבי יהודה? דכתיב: "ויחזק בבגדיו ויקרעם לשנים קרעים". ממשמע שנאמר "ויקרעם" איני יודע שהן לשנים? אלא: שנראין קרועים כשנים.

Rabbi Yehuda says: Any rending that does not rip apart his garment **on the hem** of the garment **is nothing other than a frivolous rent** of no significance, as it must be evident that one has rent his garment in mourning and that the rent is not merely an imperfection in the garment. **Rabbi Abbahu said: What is the reason for Rabbi Yehuda's opinion? As it is written: "And he took hold of his own clothes and he rent them in two pieces"** (II Kings 2:12). **From that which is stated: "And he rent,"** do **I not know that** he rent them **in two? Rather,** these words teach **that** the rent clothes must **appear as if they were torn into two** pieces, i.e., the tear must be obvious and visible.

על כל המתים כולן – שולל לאחר שבעה, ומאחה לאחר שלשים. על אביו ועל אמו – שולל לאחר שלשים, ואינו מאחה לעולם. והאשה שוללתו לאלתר, מפני כבודה.

The *baraita* continues: **With regard to all** other **deceased** relatives, **one may tack** the tear with rough stitches **after seven days, and one may join** the edges more carefully **after thirty** days. But **in** the case **of one's father or mother, he may tack** the tear only **after thirty days, and he may never** again **join** the edges more carefully. **A woman,** however, **may tack** the tear **immediately, due to her honor,** for it would be dishonorable for her to be seen with torn garments.[H]

כי אתא רבין אמר רבי יוחנן: על כל המתים, רצה – קורע ביד, רצה – קורע בכלי. על אביו ועל אמו – ביד.

When Ravin came from Eretz Yisrael to Babylonia, **he said that Rabbi Yohanan said: With regard to all** other **deceased** relatives, **if one wishes, he may rend** his garment **with his hand;** and if **he wishes, he may rend it with a utensil** in a way that will preserve it. But **in the case of his father or mother,** he must rend his garment **with his hand** in a manner that will utterly ruin it.[H]

NOTES

Undergarment – אפיקרסותו: According to the *ge'onim*, cited by the *Arukh* and the Ramban, this word refers to undergarments worn directly on one's skin, which are not important enough to have the same status as other clothes. Others explain this term as having the opposite meaning, i.e., it refers to an outer garment or a type of cloak that was worn only for honor, and therefore it was not considered to be an ordinary garment (Ra'avad; *Sefer HaMeorot*; Ritva; Meiri). There are also those who hold that this refers to a turban whose ends rests on the neck (Rashi, from manuscript; *Tosefot HaRosh*).

On the hem [*safa*] – קמי שפה: Some explain that the *safa* mentioned here is the opening of the garment around the neck, and the phrase: On the hem, means in front of it. In other words, according to this understanding one should not rend his garment from the neck, since he appears to be enlarging this opening. Instead, he should rend his garment near this opening, so that the rending will be more apparent (Rabbeinu Gershom Meor HaGola; Rashi). Others explain that the expression refers to the hem itself, which if not torn will leave the top of the tear closed. In that case, the tear will appear more like a hole and the garment will not look like it has been torn (Rid; *Talmid Rabbeinu Yehiel of Paris*; Ran).

LANGUAGE

Undergarment [*apikarsuto*] – אפיקרסותו: Apparently from the Greek ἐπικάρσιον, *epikarsiyon*, meaning a striped garment. The Sages generally use the word to refer to an undergarment.

HALAKHA

How does a woman rend her garment – כיצד קורעת אשה: A woman is required to rend all of her garments, in accordance with the opinion of Rabbi Shimon ben Elazar. However, these tears should not be one directly under the another in a manner that exposes her body. If a woman cannot turn some of her garments around, then she is not required to tear all of them (*Arukh HaShulhan*; *Shulhan Arukh, Yoreh De'a* 340:11).

Ripping apart on the hem – מבדיל קמי שפה: Some say that over deceased relatives one is not required to rip on the hem, in accordance with the opinion of the first *tanna*, and therefore one may leave the hem of the garment intact and tear only below it. However, for one's father or mother one is required to tear the edge of the garment. Others say that the *halakha* is in accordance with Rabbi Yehuda, and one must tear the hem of the garment for any relative (*Mordekhai*). This opinion is the basis for the common practice (*Shulhan Arukh, Yoreh De'a* 340:12 and in the comment of Rema).

Sewing the tear – תפירת הקרע: After the death of a man's mother or father, he may tack the tear rent in his garment only after thirty days, and he may never mend it. A woman may tack the tear immediately, due to her honor. For other deceased relatives, one may tack the tear with loose stitches after seven days, and he may mend it properly after thirty days. In some places, it is customary not to tack the tear within thirty days, even for rents torn for a relative other than a parent. In such a place, the ends of the tear may not be attached even with a safety pin (*Shulhan Arukh, Yoreh De'a* 340:15, and in the comment of Rema).

Rending by hand or with a utensil – קריעה ביד או בכלי: Over deceased relatives, one may tear the garment by hand or with a utensil, but over one's father or mother one must tear the garment by hand (*Shulhan Arukh, Yoreh De'a* 340:14).

וְאָמַר רַבִּי חִיָּיא בַּר אַבָּא אָמַר רַבִּי יוֹחָנָן: עַל כָּל הַמֵּתִים כּוּלָּן – מִבִּפְנִים; עַל אָבִיו וְעַל אִמּוֹ – קוֹרֵעַ מִבַּחוּץ. אָמַר רַב חִסְדָּא: וְכֵן לְנָשִׂיא.

And Rabbi Ḥiyya bar Abba said that Rabbi Yoḥanan said: With regard to all other **deceased** relatives, one rends his garment **on the inside,** meaning, he rends his inner garment and not necessarily his outermost garment. **In the case of one's father or mother,** however, **he must rend** the garment **on the outside,** i.e., the outermost garment.[NH] **Rav Ḥisda said: And likewise, over a *Nasi*,** one is required to rend his garment as he does over his father.

מֵיתִיבִי: לֹא הוּשְׁווּ לְאָבִיו וּלְאִמּוֹ אֶלָּא לְאִיחוּי בִּלְבַד.

The Gemara **raises an objection** from a *baraita* in which it was taught: The *halakhot* of rending for the death of other people referred to in the *baraita*, e.g., a *Nasi*, a president of the court, or one's teacher, **were likened to** the *halakhot* of rending for **one's father or mother only with regard to** the issue of carefully **rejoining** the edges of the rent, as in all of these cases it is prohibited to mend one's garment with precise stitches.

מַאי לָאו – אֲפִילּוּ לְנָשִׂיא? לָא, לְבַר מִנָּשִׂיא.

What, is this *baraita* **not** also referring **even** to one who rends his garment **for the *Nasi*?** The Gemara rejects this: **No,** the *baraita* is referring to the other people, **aside** from one who rends his garment for the *Nasi*, as rending for the *Nasi* is the same as rending for one's father with regard to all aspects of the rending.[H]

נְשִׂיאָה שְׁכֵיב. אֲמַר לֵיהּ רַב חִסְדָּא לְרַב חָנָן בַּר רָבָא: כְּפֵי אָסִיתָא וְקוּם עֲלָהּ, וְאַחֲוֵי קְרִיעָה לְעָלְמָא.

It was related that the ***Nasi* died,** and **Rav Ḥisda said to Rav Ḥanan bar Rava: Turn the mortar over and stand on it, and show** the **rent to everyone.** Everyone will then rend his garment in this manner, as everyone is required to rend his garment over the death of the *Nasi*.

עַל חָכָם חוֹלֵץ מִיָּמִין; עַל אַב בֵּית דִּין מִשְּׂמֹאל; עַל נָשִׂיא – מִכָּאן וּמִכָּאן.

§ It was further taught: **For** mourning **a Sage, one removes** his garment **from the right** shoulder. **For the president of the court**[B] he removes his garment **from the left** shoulder. **For the *Nasi*** he removes his garment **from here and from here,** from both shoulders.[N]

תָּנוּ רַבָּנַן: חָכָם שֶׁמֵּת – בֵּית מִדְרָשׁוֹ בָּטֵל; אַב בֵּית דִּין שֶׁמֵּת – כָּל בָּתֵּי מִדְרָשׁוֹת שֶׁבְּעִירוֹ בְּטֵילִין, וְנִכְנָסִין לְבֵית הַכְּנֶסֶת, וּמְשַׁנִּין אֶת מְקוֹמָן: הַיּוֹשְׁבִין בַּצָּפוֹן – יוֹשְׁבִין בַּדָּרוֹם, הַיּוֹשְׁבִין בַּדָּרוֹם – יוֹשְׁבִין בַּצָּפוֹן. נָשִׂיא שֶׁמֵּת – בָּתֵּי מִדְרָשׁוֹת כּוּלָּן בְּטֵילִין, וּבְנֵי הַכְּנֶסֶת נִכְנָסִין לְבֵית הַכְּנֶסֶת,

The Sages taught the following *baraita*: When **a Sage dies, his study hall ceases** its regular study[N] as a sign of mourning over him. When **the president of the court dies, all of the study halls in his city cease** their regular study, and everyone **enters the synagogue and changes their places** there as a sign of mourning over him. **Those who** ordinarily **sit in the north** should **sit in the south, and those who** ordinarily **sit in the south** should **sit in the north.** When **a *Nasi* dies, all study halls cease** their regular study. On Shabbat, **the members of the synagogue enter the synagogue** for public Torah reading, which requires a congregation of ten,[H]

NOTES

On the inside and on the outside – מִבִּפְנִים וּמִבַּחוּץ: Some explain that the term outside in this context means in public, and the term inside means that one may rend his garment even inside his house (Rashi, from manuscript; Commentary on *Moed Katan*). Others explain that the term inside means under his other garments, and in this case one is not required to make the tear noticeable on the outside (Rabbeinu Gershom Meor HaGola; Rabbi Yitzhak ibn Giat). Rabbeinu Yehonatan of Lunel, the Rambam, and the Meiri give both explanations for these terms.

Removal from the right and the left – חֲלִיצָה מִיָּמִין וּמִשְּׂמֹאל: Removing one's garment from the right shoulder does not appear to be a display of mourning, as sometimes a person will do so when carrying a load or performing another type of work. However, if one removes the left side of his garment, and even more so if he removes both sides, then it is clear that he is doing so as a sign of mourning (Rabbeinu Yehonatan of Lunel; *Talmid Rabbeinu Yeḥiel of Paris*).

His study hall ceases its regular study – בֵּית מִדְרָשׁוֹ בָּטֵל: The early authorities disagree as to whether this is done as a sign of mourning and is therefore practiced only for one day, like other acts of mourning for one's teacher (*Talmid Rabbeinu Yeḥiel of Paris*), or if it is done so that longer eulogies will be given and the public mourning will not be lessened in order to return to their studies. If the reason is the latter, the custom should apply for the entire seven-day mourning period, during which the deceased is spoken about and praised (Ramban; *Tosefot HaRosh*).

HALAKHA

Rending on the inside and on the outside – קְרִיעָה מִבִּפְנִים וּמִבַּחוּץ: Over deceased relatives, one may tear his garments in private. As the tear need not be visible to others, the inside of the garment may be torn. However, over one's father or mother, one must tear the garment in public. The tear should be on the outside of the garment, so that it will be visible to others (*Shulḥan Arukh, Yoreh De'a* 340:13).

Rending over the *Nasi* – קְרִיעָה עַל נָשִׂיא: One has the same obligations for one's father and for a *Nasi* with regard to removing one's garment from one's shoulder, having the tear visible to others, and mending the tear (*Shulḥan Arukh, Yoreh De'a* 340:17).

Mourning over the leaders of the generation – אֵבֶל עַל גְּדוֹלֵי הַדּוֹר: When a Sage dies, his study hall ceases its regular study, and he is spoken about and praised for seven days. Even after the eulogy, his students may not gather in the study hall. Instead, they study in pairs at home. However, other study halls are active, even during the time of these eulogies. When the president of the court dies, all the study halls in that city cease their regular study, and the members of these study halls change their seats in the synagogue. If the *Nasi* dies, then all the study halls in which he is eulogized cease their regular study. Even after the eulogies, they do not enter the study hall, but study in pairs at home. The residents of the city pray in the mourner's house; however, they come to the synagogue for Torah reading. Today, when there is no *Nasi* and no Sanhedrin, these mourning customs are not practiced (*Arukh HaShulḥan*; *Shulḥan Arukh, Yoreh De'a* 344:18).

BACKGROUND

A Sage [*Hakham*] and the president of the court – חָכָם וְאַב בֵּית דִּין: When used as a specific title, and not just as an ordinary honorific term, the word *ḥakham* can have either of two meanings. In certain cases, it refers to the rabbi of a city or of a specific synagogue. However, in the context of this Gemara, the term seems relate to the basic structure of the court, which replaced the Sanhedrin after the destruction of the Temple, and could therefore be translated as court officer.

The head of the court was the *Nasi*, who was a descendent of Hillel the Elder. In addition to being the head of the court, he was a political leader for the Jews in Eretz Yisrael and represented them to the foreign authorities. The *Nasi* could trace his lineage back to the Davidic line, and the position therefore represented the kingship of the house of David. Similarly, the Exilarch in Babylonia, who also descended from the Judean kings, was a reminder of the Davidic kingship, and the *halakhot* of mourning a *Nasi* applied to him as well. The honor shown to the *Nasi* was not only due to his Torah knowledge and his character traits, but also, to a large extent, because he represented independent Jewish rule.

The president of the court [*av beit din*] was considered to be second to the *Nasi* in terms of honor. His job was to actually head the central court. After the generation of Rabbi Yehuda HaNasi, the president of the court was also the head of the central study hall, and he was therefore the spiritual leader of that generation.

The *Ḥakham* mentioned in the Gemara refers to the third in command in the Sanhedrin. The *Ḥakham* was often one of the brightest scholars, but did not have the official position as the head of the study hall. The Gemara relates that these positions, and the honors associated with each one, were established during the time of Rabban Shimon ben Gamliel II, and, with slight modifications, they continued to exist for many generations.

וְקוֹרִין שִׁבְעָה וְיוֹצְאִין. רַבִּי יְהוֹשֻׁעַ בֶּן קָרְחָה אוֹמֵר: לֹא שֶׁיֵּלְכוּ וִיטַיְּילוּ בַּשּׁוּק, אֶלָּא יוֹשְׁבִין וְדוֹמְמִין.

and seven people **read**[N] from the Torah. **And** then **they leave** and pray on their own. **Rabbi Yehoshua ben Korḥa says:** It is **not that they stroll** afterward **in the marketplace,** but **rather they sit** at home **in silent** mourning.

וְאֵין אוֹמְרִים שְׁמוּעָה וְאַגָּדָה בְּבֵית הָאָבֵל. אָמְרוּ עָלָיו עַל רַבִּי חֲנַנְיָה בֶּן גַּמְלִיאֵל שֶׁהָיָה אוֹמֵר שְׁמוּעָה וְאַגָּדָה בְּבֵית הָאָבֵל.

And furthermore, **one may not speak** about ***halakha***[N] **or** ***aggada*** **in a house of mourning,** as this is an activity that brings people joy.[H] **It was said of Rabbi Ḥananya ben Gamliel**[N] **that he would speak about** ***halakha*** **and** ***aggada*** **in a house of mourning.**

תָּנוּ רַבָּנַן: אָבֵל, שַׁבָּת רִאשׁוֹנָה – אֵינוֹ יוֹצֵא מִפֶּתַח בֵּיתוֹ; שְׁנִיָּה – יוֹצֵא וְאֵינוֹ יוֹשֵׁב בִּמְקוֹמוֹ; שְׁלִישִׁית – יוֹשֵׁב בִּמְקוֹמוֹ וְאֵינוֹ מְדַבֵּר; רְבִיעִית – הֲרֵי הוּא כְּכׇל אָדָם.

§ **The Sages taught** the following *baraita*: During the **first week** after his bereavement, **the mourner may not go out**[N] **of the opening of his house.**[N] During the **second** week, **he may go out, but he may not sit in his** usual **place**[N] in the synagogue. During the **third** week, **he may sit in his** usual **place but he may not speak.** During the **fourth** week, **he is like any** other **person.**[H]

רַבִּי יְהוּדָה אוֹמֵר: לֹא הוּצְרְכוּ לוֹמַר שַׁבָּת רִאשׁוֹנָה לֹא יֵצֵא מִפֶּתַח בֵּיתוֹ – שֶׁהֲרֵי הַכֹּל נִכְנָסִין לְבֵיתוֹ לְנַחֲמוֹ. אֶלָּא: שְׁנִיָּה – אֵינוֹ יוֹצֵא מִפֶּתַח בֵּיתוֹ; שְׁלִישִׁית – יוֹצֵא וְאֵינוֹ יוֹשֵׁב בִּמְקוֹמוֹ; רְבִיעִית – יוֹשֵׁב בִּמְקוֹמוֹ וְאֵינוֹ מְדַבֵּר; חֲמִישִׁית – הֲרֵי הוּא כְּכׇל אָדָם.

Rabbi Yehuda says: They did not need to say that **during the first week** the mourner **may not go out of the opening of** his house. This teaches us nothing new, **as** at that time **everyone goes into his house to console him. Rather,** during the **second** week, he may **not go out of the opening of his house.** During the **third** week, **he may go out, but he may not sit in** his usual **place** in the synagogue. During the **fourth** week, **he may sit in his** usual **place, but he may not speak.** During the **fifth** week, **he is like any** other **person.**

NOTES

And seven read – וְקוֹרִין שִׁבְעָה: Some write that they would each pray alone at home (Rabbeinu Gershom Meor HaGola, Rashi; *Talmid Rabbeinu Yeḥiel of Paris*; Commentary on *Moed Katan*). Others say that they would pray in the mourner's house, but they would go to read the Torah in the synagogue (Ritva; see *Divrei David*).

One may not speak about *halakha* – אֵין אוֹמְרִים שְׁמוּעָה: This refers to the weekdays during the mourning period. However, many understand that *halakha* should not be discussed even on Shabbat. The Ran explains that the reason is that if people become engaged in Torah study they may forget about their mourning. A similar explanation is offered by the Ramban and Rabbeinu Yehonatan of Lunel. The Ritva mentions an explanation based on tractate *Semaḥot*, according to which this statement is a continuation of what was stated above with regard to the death of a *Nasi*.

Rabbi Ḥananya ben Gamliel, etc. – רַבִּי חֲנַנְיָה בֶּן גַּמְלִיאֵל וכו׳: It appears that this applies specifically to Shabbat, and Rabbi Ḥanina's practice was in accordance with the opinion that mourning does not apply on Shabbat at all (Jerusalem Talmud). This is discussed in 23b as well.

During the first week [*shabbat*] the mourner may not go out, etc. – אָבֵל, שַׁבָּת רִאשׁוֹנָה אֵינוֹ יוֹצֵא וכו׳: Some explain that in this context the word *shabbat* means week (Rashi; *Talmid Rabbeinu Yeḥiel of Paris*). However, others say that the word *shabbat* here refers to Shabbat itself, and during the other days of the week a mourner may leave his house if he needs to do so (Rabbeinu Yehonatan of Lunel; Ra'avad; Ran).

May not go out of the opening of his house – אינו יוצא מפתח ביתו: With regard to this issue, there are different customs for the residents of Babylonia and Eretz Yisrael. In Babylonia, it was the practice for the mourners to go to the synagogue every day. However, in Eretz Yisrael the custom was for mourners not to attend synagogue but to host a prayer group in their home. This is the common practice today (see Meiri).

He may not sit in his place – אֵינוֹ יוֹשֵׁב בִּמְקוֹמוֹ: This *halakha* applies in any place with assigned seats, e.g., the synagogue and the study hall (*Talmid Rabbeinu Yeḥiel of Paris*).

HALAKHA

One may not speak about *halakha* – אֵין אוֹמְרִים שְׁמוּעָה וכו׳: One may not speak about *halakha* or *aggada* in the house of a mourner (*Shulḥan Arukh, Yoreh De'a* 378:7).

First and second week, etc. – שָׁבוּעַ רִאשׁוֹן וְשֵׁנִי וכו׳: During the first week of mourning, a mourner may not leave his house, even to attend a wedding or circumcision ceremony. Some are lenient and permit him to go out at night if there is a reasonable need to do so. The prohibition against leaving the house applies only to one who goes to stroll or to engage in business. However, one who goes at the order of the ruler or in other cases of great need is permitted to leave, and this is the common practice (Rema).

During the second week, the mourner may leave his house. However, he may neither sit in his ordinary seat nor may he speak. During the third week he may sit in his regular seat, but may not speak. Alternatively, he may choose not to sit in his regular seat and is then permitted to speak. It is the accepted practice that a mourner does not sit in his ordinary seat for the entirety of the thirty-day period of mourning over a relative; when mourning one's father or mother this practice lasts for twelve months. Although this custom has no basis in the Gemara, it is not proper to deviate from the local custom (Rema). During the fourth week, the mourner is like everyone else.

For the purposes of these *halakhot*, the weeks are not counted from the beginning of the mourning, but rather from the beginning of the week, e.g., the Sunday after the third week ends is counted as the beginning of the fourth week (*Shulḥan Arukh, Yoreh De'a* 393:2).

תָּנוּ רַבָּנַן: כׇּל שְׁלֹשִׁים יוֹם לְנִישּׂוּאִין. מֵתָה אִשְׁתּוֹ – אָסוּר לִישָּׂא אִשָּׁה אַחֶרֶת, עַד שֶׁיַּעַבְרוּ עָלָיו שְׁלֹשָׁה רְגָלִים. רַבִּי יְהוּדָה אוֹמֵר: רֶגֶל רִאשׁוֹן וְשֵׁנִי – אָסוּר, שְׁלִישִׁי – מוּתָּר.

§ **The Sages taught** another *baraita*: During **the entire thirty-day** period of mourning, it is prohibited **to marry.**[H] **If one's wife died, it is prohibited to marry another wife until three Festivals pass**[N] since her death.[H] **Rabbi Yehuda says:** Until the **first and second** Festivals have passed, **he is prohibited** from marrying; before the **third** Festival, however, he is **permitted** to do so.

וְאִם אֵין לוֹ בָּנִים – מוּתָּר לִישָּׂא לְאַלְתַּר, מִשּׁוּם בִּיטּוּל פְּרִיָּה וּרְבִיָּה. הִנִּיחָה לוֹ בָּנִים קְטַנִּים – מוּתָּר לִישָּׂא לְאַלְתַּר, מִפְּנֵי פַּרְנָסָתָן.

And if he does not have children, he is permitted to marry another wife **immediately due to** the need to not **neglect** the mitzva to **be fruitful and multiply.** Since he has not yet fulfilled the mitzva of procreation, he is still required to marry a wife. Any delay might result in a lost opportunity for marriage. Similarly, if his wife died and **left him young children, he is permitted to marry** another wife **immediately, so that** she might **take care of them.**

מַעֲשֶׂה שֶׁמֵּתָה אִשְׁתּוֹ שֶׁל יוֹסֵף הַכֹּהֵן, וְאָמַר לַאֲחוֹתָהּ בְּבֵית הַקְּבָרוֹת: לְכִי וּפַרְנְסִי אֶת בְּנֵי אֲחוֹתֵיךְ. וְאַף עַל פִּי כֵן לֹא בָּא עָלֶיהָ אֶלָּא לִזְמַן מְרוּבֶּה. מַאי לִזְמַן מְרוּבֶּה? אָמַר רַב פָּפָּא: לְאַחַר שְׁלֹשִׁים יוֹם.

There was **an incident when the wife of Yosef the Priest died, and he said to her sister at the cemetery** immediately after the funeral: **Go and care for your sister's children.** In other words, he alluded that he wished to marry her immediately. **But even though** he married her immediately, **he did not engage in sexual relations with her for a long time** afterward. The Gemara asks: **What is** the meaning of the term: **A long time? Rav Pappa said: After thirty days.**

תָּנוּ רַבָּנַן: כׇּל שְׁלֹשִׁים יוֹם לְגִיהוּץ, אֶחָד כֵּלִים חֲדָשִׁים וְאֶחָד כֵּלִים יְשָׁנִים יוֹצְאִין מִתּוֹךְ הַמַּכְבֵּשׁ. רַבִּי אוֹמֵר: לֹא אָסְרוּ אֶלָּא כֵּלִים חֲדָשִׁים בִּלְבַד. רַבִּי אֶלְעָזָר בְּרַבִּי שִׁמְעוֹן אוֹמֵר: לֹא אָסְרוּ אֶלָּא כֵּלִים חֲדָשִׁים לְבָנִים בִּלְבַד.

§ **The Sages taught** yet another *baraita*: During **the entire thirty-day** period of mourning, it is prohibited **to wear ironed**[B] garments, **whether they are new garments or old garments taken out of the press,**[HB] as ironed garments appear to be new. **Rabbi** Yehuda HaNasi disagrees and **says:** The Sages **prohibited** wearing **only new garments. Rabbi Elazar, son of Rabbi Shimon, says: They prohibited** wearing **only new white garments.**

NOTES

It is prohibited to marry…until three Festivals pass – אָסוּר לִישָּׂא...עַד שֶׁיַּעַבְרוּ עָלָיו שְׁלֹשָׁה רְגָלִים: Several reasons for this decree are mentioned by *Tosafot*: This decree is either so that the mourner will not forget his first wife or so that when he is with his new wife he will not still be thinking about his previous wife. Rabbeinu Yehonatan of Lunel and the Ramban explain similarly.

It is also suggested that the mourner must wait this amount of time so that he will not constantly tell his new wife about his previous wife's actions. Some explain that since the Sages said that one's wife dies over unfulfilled vows, the mourning period lasts for three Festivals in order to correspond to vows, which remain in effect for the same amount of time (see Ramban).

Others explain that the mourner will forget his previous wife due to the joy of the three Festivals. This is the basis for those who say that these three Festivals do not refer specifically to the pilgrimage Festivals, but to any days that interrupt the mourning.

The early authorities write that this *halakha* applies specifically to a man. When a woman's husband dies, she is not required to wait for three Festivals to pass before she remarries. Several explanations are offered for this difference. Some explain that it is the ordinary way of the world for a man to pursue a woman and not the opposite. Therefore, when a woman finds someone who wishes to marry her, it is preferable not to delay the marriage, since she does not know when her next opportunity will arise (Rabbeinu Yehonatan of Lunel; see *Shakh* on *Yoreh De'a* 392:2).

BACKGROUND

Ironing – גִּיהוּץ: The origin of this word is unclear, and it has been compared to similar words in other languages, yet no exact match has been found. There are different opinions as to exactly which activity this is. It is clear that it involved taking a worn, dirty garment and making it look as though it were new. This includes laundering the garment with specific substances, e.g., soap, laundering soda, or the like, and pressing it flat with a stone or piece of metal.

Press – מַכְבֵּשׁ:

Fresco of a laundry press from Pompeii during the time of the Mishna

HALAKHA

Marriage of a mourner – נִישּׂוּאִין שֶׁל אָבֵל: It is prohibited for a mourner to remarry during the thirty-day mourning period. After thirty days, he may marry and have a wedding feast, even if he is mourning for his father or mother. Some say that one may even betroth a woman on the day of the death itself, as long as he does not prepare a feast. However, others say that a mourner may not betroth a woman within thirty days, and this is the accepted opinion (Rema, citing Rosh and Ramban). It is permitted to arrange a marriage within thirty days (*Shakh*; *Baḥ*; *Shulḥan Arukh*, *Yoreh De'a* 392:1).

Marriage after his wife's death – נִישּׂוּאִין לְאַחַר מוֹת אִשְׁתּוֹ: If a man's wife dies then he is not permitted to remarry until three Festivals have passed; the Eighth Day of Assembly is considered to be its own Festival in this regard (*Dagul Merevava*). Similarly, some say that Rosh HaShana and Yom Kippur are also considered to be Festivals for this purpose (*Taz*), however others disagree (*Arukh HaShulḥan*).

If one has not yet fulfilled the mitzva to procreate, or if he has young children, or if he needs someone to care for him, then he may betroth a woman immediately and marry her after seven days. However, some say that betrothing is also prohibited until the initial seven days of mourning have passed (*Shakh*). In such a case, he should not engage in sexual relations with his second wife until the thirty-day period of mourning has concluded, unless he has not fulfilled the mitzva of procreation.

Some say that even if one is wealthy and can hire many servants, he may marry before the established time if he is lonely without a wife. It is then considered as if he has no one to care for him. This is the basis for the common practice for people to remarry before the established time. However, one who is able to wait should be strict with himself (Rema).

A woman whose husband dies is not required to wait for three Festivals. Instead, with regard to the laws of mourning, she is permitted to marry even within thirty days. However, she is required to wait three months in case she is pregnant, in order to determine the father of the child (*Shakh*, citing the Rif; *Shulḥan Arukh*, *Yoreh De'a* 392:2).

Ironed garment – בֶּגֶד מְגוֹהָץ: For thirty days, a mourner is prohibited from wearing or spreading underneath himself a white, new, ironed garment, even if it is made of linen. This ruling is in accordance with the opinion of Rabbi Elazar, son of Rabbi Shimon (*Shulḥan Arukh*, *Yoreh De'a* 389:5).

אַבַּיֵי נָפֵיק בְּגַרְדָּא דְּסַרְבְּלָא, כְּרַבִּי. רָבָא נָפֵיק בְּחִימוּצְתָּא רוֹמִיתָא סוּמָקְתָּא חַדְתִּי, כְּרַבִּי אֶלְעָזָר בְּרַבִּי שִׁמְעוֹן.

The Gemara relates that **Abaye went out** while he was in mourning **in an old white garment, in accordance with** the opinion of **Rabbi** Yehuda HaNasi. **Rava,** on the other hand, **went out in a new, red Roman cloak,**[NL] as he acted **in accordance with** the opinion of **Rabbi Elazar, son of Rabbi Shimon.**

״מִפְּנֵי שֶׁאָמְרוּ שַׁבָּת עוֹלָה וְאֵינָהּ מַפְסֶקֶת״. בְּנֵי יְהוּדָה וּבְנֵי גְּלִילָא – הָנֵי אָמְרִי:

It was taught in the mishna: This is **because** the Sages **said** that **Shabbat counts** as one of the days of mourning, **but it does not interrupt** the mourning period, which continues after Shabbat. It is stated that with regard to mourning on Shabbat, there is a difference in practice between **the residents of Judea and the residents of the Galilee.**[B] **These say:**

NOTES

Cloak – חִימוּצְתָּא: Some explain that this refers to a type of shirt (Rashi; *Talmid Rabbeinu Yeḥiel of Paris*). Others claim that it is a garment made of silk or another similar material (Rabbi Shlomo ben HaYatom).

BACKGROUND

The residents of Judea and the residents of the Galilee – בְּנֵי יְהוּדָה וּבְנֵי גְּלִילָא: In the times when the Jewish community was well established in Eretz Yisrael, it was divided into three parts: Judea, the Galilee, and the East Bank of the Jordan, each of which had its own geography, climate, and traditions.

LANGUAGE

Cloak [*ḥimutzeta*] – חִימוּצְתָּא: This word appears to be Semitic and is similar to the Arabic خميصة, *ḥamīṣa*, a type of robe that is decorated around the edges.

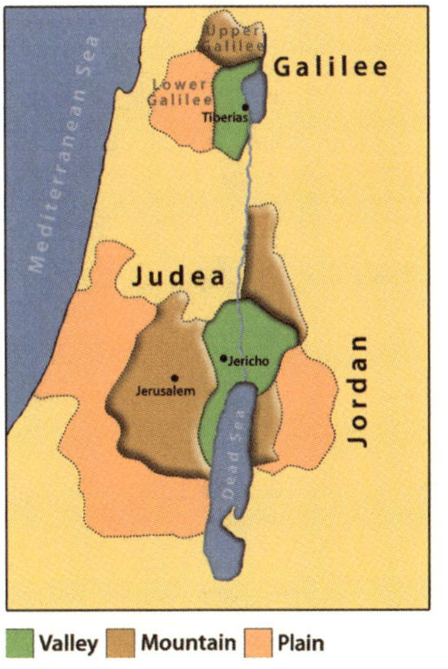

Map of the three regions of Eretz Yisrael

Perek **III**
Daf **23** Amud **b**

יֵשׁ אֲבֵילוּת בְּשַׁבָּת, וְהָנֵי אָמְרִי: אֵין אֲבֵילוּת בְּשַׁבָּת.

There is some **mourning on Shabbat,** i.e., with regard to mourning rites that can be observed privately in the mourner's home and will go unnoticed by other people; **whereas those say: There is no mourning on Shabbat**[N] at all.

מַאן דְּאָמַר יֵשׁ אֲבֵילוּת בְּשַׁבָּת – דְּקָתָנֵי: עוֹלָה. מַאן דְּאָמַר אֵין אֲבֵילוּת בְּשַׁבָּת – דְּקָתָנֵי: אֵינָהּ מַפְסֶקֶת.

The Gemara explains: **The ones who said** that **there is** some **mourning on Shabbat** rely on **that** which is **taught,** that Shabbat **counts** as one of the days of mourning, implying that some degree of mourning applies on that day. **The ones who said** that **there is no mourning on Shabbat** at all base this on **that** which is **taught** that Shabbat **does not interrupt** the mourning period.

NOTES

Mourning on Shabbat – אֲבֵילוּת בְּשַׁבָּת: The early authorities disagree about the meaning of the expression: There is mourning on Shabbat. There are those who say that this means that all of the *halakhot* of mourning, in their entirety, apply on Shabbat as they do during weekdays (Ramban). The Ra'avad holds that the customs of mourning do not obligate one to mourn Shabbat. Some hold that mourning is voluntary on Shabbat, while others have a custom that mourning is prohibited.

However, most of the early authorities hold that the disagreement in the Gemara is only whether mourning applies to what is done in private on Shabbat (*Tosafot*; Ritva). With regard to the source of this *halakha*, some early authorities write that on a Festival there is a mitzva to be joyous, but on Shabbat the mitzva is to delight, which is of lesser intensity (see *She'iltot*). Therefore, it is possible for the mourner to mourn in his heart while still delighting in Shabbat. Alternatively, it is stated in the Jerusalem Talmud, with regard to the verse: "The blessing of the Lord makes rich, and toil [*etzev*] adds nothing to it," (Proverbs 10:22) that "the blessing of the Lord" is Shabbat, which God blessed when He created the world. "And toil [*etzev*] adds nothing to it," means that one does not makes one's self sad [*lehitatzev*] on Shabbat at all.

אִי סָלְקָא דַעְתָּךְ יֵשׁ אֲבֵילוּת בְּשַׁבָּת – הַשְׁתָּא אֲבֵילוּת נָהֲגָא, אִפְסוּקֵי מִיבַּעְיָא?

The latter argue as follows: **If it should enter your mind** to say that **there** is some **mourning on Shabbat**, there is a difficulty, for **now** that it has been stated that actual **mourning applies** on Shabbat, **is it necessary** to teach us that this day does not **interrupt** the mourning period? Rather, the conclusion must be that there is no mourning on Shabbat whatsoever.

וְאֶלָּא הָא קָתָנֵי עוֹלָה! אַיְּידֵי דְּקָבָעֵי לְמִיתְנָא סֵיפָא אֵינָן עוֹלִים, תָּנָא רֵישָׁא עוֹלָה.

The Gemara asks: **But isn't it taught** in the mishna that Shabbat **counts**[N] as one of the days of mourning, implying that it is just like the other days of mourning, and at least some mourning rites are practiced on it? The Gemara answers: **Since** the mishna **wished to teach** in **the latter clause** that the days of a Festival **do not count** toward the requisite days of mourning, **it taught** also **in the first clause** that Shabbat **counts** as one of the days of mourning, although no mourning rites are practiced on it.

וּלְמַאן דְּאָמַר יֵשׁ אֲבֵילוּת בְּשַׁבָּת, הָא קָתָנֵי אֵינָהּ מַפְסֶקֶת! מִשּׁוּם דְּקָבָעֵי לְמִיתְנָא סֵיפָא מַפְסִיקִין – תָּנָא רֵישָׁא אֵינָהּ מַפְסֶקֶת.

The Gemara asks: **And according to the ones who said** that **there is** some **mourning on Shabbat, isn't** it **taught** in the mishna that **it does not interrupt** the mourning period, which would have been unnecessary to say if the mourning rites are practiced on it? The Gemara answers: This was not necessary for itself, but **due to** the fact that the since the mishna **wished to teach** in **the latter clause** that the Festivals **interrupt** the mourning, **it taught** also **in the first clause** that Shabbat **does not interrupt** it.

לֵימָא כְּתַנָּאֵי: מִי שֶׁמֵּתוֹ מוּטָל לְפָנָיו – אוֹכֵל בְּבַיִת אַחֵר. אֵין לוֹ בַּיִת אַחֵר – אוֹכֵל בְּבֵית חֲבֵרוֹ. אֵין לוֹ בֵּית חֲבֵרוֹ – עוֹשֶׂה לוֹ מְחִיצָה עֲשָׂרָה טְפָחִים. אֵין לוֹ דָּבָר לַעֲשׂוֹת מְחִיצָה – מַחֲזִיר פָּנָיו וְאוֹכֵל.

The Gemara asks: **Let us say** that this is **parallel to** a dispute between ***tanna'im*** with regard to whether or not some mourning rites are observed even on Shabbat, for it was taught in a *baraita*: **One whose deceased** relative **is laid out before him**[NH] **eats in another room. If he does not have another room, he eats in the house of a friend. If he does not have a friend's house** available, **he makes a partition ten handbreadths** high between him and the deceased, so that he may eat. If **he does not have material with which to make a partition, he averts his face** from the dead **and eats.**

וְאֵינוֹ מֵיסֵב וְאוֹכֵל, וְאֵינוֹ אוֹכֵל בָּשָׂר, וְאֵינוֹ שׁוֹתֶה יַיִן, וְאֵין מְבָרֵךְ, וְאֵין מְזַמֵּן, וְאֵין מְבָרְכִין עָלָיו, וְאֵין מְזַמְּנִין עָלָיו, וּפָטוּר מִקְּרִיאַת שְׁמַע, וּמִן הַתְּפִלָּה, וּמִן הַתְּפִילִּין, וּמִכָּל מִצְוֹת הָאֲמוּרוֹת בַּתּוֹרָה.

And in any case, **he does not recline while he eats**, as reclining is characteristic of a festive meal; **and he neither eats meat**[N] **nor drinks wine; and he does not recite a blessing**[N] before eating to exempt others from their obligation; **and he does not** recite the formula to **invite** the participants in the meal to join together in the Grace after Meals, **and they do not recite a blessing over him**[N] **nor do others invite him** to join in the Grace after Meals, as he cannot be a member of the three required to recite the formula. **And he is exempt from the recitation of *Shema*,**[N] **and from** the *Amida* **prayer, and from** donning **phylacteries, and from** performing **all of the mitzvot mentioned in the Torah.**

NOTES

But isn't it taught that Shabbat counts [*ola*] – וְאֶלָּא הָא קָתָנֵי עוֹלָה: The proofs brought in this discussion, which are based on close readings of the language of the mishna, are not entirely clear. The early authorities attempt to explain them in several different ways (see *Tosafot*) but many of them have difficulty explaining this sentence. The Rid goes so far as to say that the sentence is an error and should be erased from the text. This also appears to be the opinion of the Ra'avad.

However, there are those who explain that the word *ola*, counted, has two different meanings. It either means that Shabbat is counted as one of the days of mourning, and all the *halakhot* of mourning apply on it, or it means that Shabbat is counted in the mourning period, even though mourning is not practiced on it. Based on this distinction, it would have been more correct to state explicitly that it counts toward the number [*ola min haminyan*]. However, since the expression: Do not count [*ainam olim*], is used in the end of the mishna, the *tanna* did not wish to alter the style. This is the opinion of *Talmid Rabbeinu Yeḥiel of Paris*, and a similar statement is made in *Tosefot HaRosh* in the name of Rabbeinu Tam.

One whose deceased relative is laid out before him – מִי שֶׁמֵּתוֹ מוּטָל לְפָנָיו: There are two types of mourning recognized by *halakha*: One type is known as acute mourning, which applies from the time of death until the burial. It appears that the *halakhot* of acute mourning are meant to enable the mourner to properly prepare for and organize the burial. Since it is a mitzva to arrange the burial, the mourner is exempt from all other mitzvot. Alternatively, the rationale for the acute mourner's exemption from mitzvot is that it is not appropriate for the relatives to continue their lives in an ordinary manner before the deceased has been buried. These two reasons are discussed explicitly in the Jerusalem Talmud. The second type of mourning is the ordinary period of mourning that begins once the deceased has been buried, and it includes all the ways that the mourner expresses pain over his deceased relative.

And he neither eats meat, etc. – וְאֵינוֹ אוֹכֵל בָּשָׂר וכו׳: The Ran writes that the food restrictions are so that he will not get carried away with his eating and delay the burial. Since the *halakhot* of mourning do not yet apply to him, the prohibition against eating meat is not a sign of mourning.

And he does not recite a blessing – וְאֵין מְבָרֵךְ: Some say that this statement means that the acute mourner should not recite a blessing before eating his food because he is exempt from performing mitzvot (Rashi, from manuscript; Rashi on tractate *Berakhot*; Ran). Others write that the mourner is required to recite a blessing before eating, as it is not appropriate for him to benefit from the world without doing so (*Kolbo*). Instead, this phrase in the *baraita* means that he may not recite a blessing on behalf of others (Rabbeinu Gershom Meor HaGola; Rashi). Others claim that it refers specifically to the Grace after Meals, which he does not recite (*Talmid Rabbeinu Yeḥiel of Paris*).

And they do not recite a blessing over him – וְאֵין מְבָרְכִין עָלָיו: *Tosefot HaRosh* explain that no blessing may be recited on his behalf, for not only should he not recite a blessing, but others should not even fulfill his obligation for him.

And he is exempt from the recitation of *Shema* – וּפָטוּר מִקְּרִיאַת שְׁמַע: In the Jerusalem Talmud, in tractate *Berakhot*, an allusion is offered for this based on the verse: "So that you remember the day you left Egypt all the days of your life" (Deuteronomy 16:3). This means that you are obligated to remember the Exodus and recite *Shema* only on days during which you are involved in life, and not when you are occupied with the dead.

HALAKHA

One whose deceased relative is laid out before him – מִי שֶׁמֵּתוֹ מוּטָל לְפָנָיו: If one's relative has died but has not yet been buried, then he is referred to as an acute mourner. During this time he may not eat in the same room as the body. Instead, he must eat in a different room. If he does not have another room, he should eat in the house of a friend. If he does not have a friend with a house, then he should make a partition, even out of a sheet, and then he may eat. If he has nothing with which to make a partition, he should avert his face, and then he may eat.

Until the deceased is buried, an acute mourner may not recline and eat, he may not eat meat, and he may not drink wine. He does not recite the blessing before eating bread. Other people may not recite a blessing on his behalf or invite him to join them in Grace after Meals, and he is exempt from all the mitzvot stated in the Torah. This is the case even if the acute mourner is not required to make preparations for the burial, and even when he is in a different city from the deceased. However, if there is a group of people in that city who are responsible for the burial of the dead and the preparations for burial, known today as the *ḥevra kadisha*, then once he gives over the body to them he immediately becomes obligated in all mitzvot (*Peri Megadim*; *Ḥokhmat Adam*; *Sha'arei Teshuva*; *Derekh HaḤayyim*; *Mishna Berura*).

One who is an acute mourner on Shabbat or a Festival may eat meat or drink wine if he wishes (Rema). Similarly, on Shabbat he recites blessings, is obligated in all the mitzvot, and goes to pray in the synagogue. However, he may not engage in sexual relations. If he sets out on Shabbat to walk to the city limit, so that he can prepare for the burial immediately once Shabbat ends, then the prohibitions pertaining to acute mourning apply to him immediately, even though Shabbat has not yet ended. Similarly, if he wishes to hire gentile workers to perform the burial on the first day of a Festival, and all the more so on the second day of the Festival in the Diaspora, then all the *halakhot* of acute mourning apply to him. Some say that if a rabbi dies and has not yet been buried, his student is prohibited to eat meat or to drink wine on weekdays (*Shulḥan Arukh, Yoreh De'a* 341:1, and in the comment of Rema).

וּבְשַׁבָּת – מֵיסֵב וְאוֹכֵל, וְאוֹכֵל בָּשָׂר, וְשׁוֹתֶה יַיִן, וּמְבָרֵךְ, וּמְזַמֵּן, וּמְבָרְכִין וּמְזַמְּנִין עָלָיו, וְחַיָּיב בִּקְרִיאַת שְׁמַע וּבִתְפִלָּה וּבִתְפִילִּין וּבְכׇל מִצְוֹת הָאֲמוּרוֹת בַּתּוֹרָה. רַבָּן גַּמְלִיאֵל אוֹמֵר: מִתּוֹךְ שֶׁנִּתְחַיֵּיב בְּאֵלּוּ – נִתְחַיֵּיב בְּכוּלָּן.

But on Shabbat he reclines at the meal, as per his custom, **and eats; and he eats meat and drinks wine; and he recites blessings** to exempt others from their obligation; **and** he recites the formula to **invite** the participants in the meal to join together in the Grace after Meals, **and others may recite blessings on his behalf and invite** him to join in the Grace after Meals. **And he is** also **obligated in the recitation of *Shema*, and in** the *Amida* **prayer, and in** the mitzva of **phylacteries,**[N] **and in all the mitzvot mentioned in the Torah. Rabban Gamliel says: Since he is obligated** to fulfill **these** mitzvot associated with Shabbat, **he is obligated** to fulfill **all**[N] of the mitzvot on Shabbat.

וְאָמַר רַבִּי יוֹחָנָן: תַּשְׁמִישׁ הַמִּטָּה אִיכָּא בֵּינַיְיהוּ.

Rabban Gamliel's statement is vague. The following clarifies it: **Rabbi Yoḥanan said:** The practical difference **between them,** the opinion of the anonymous first *tanna* and Rabbi Yoḥanan's opinion, is with regard to **sexual relations.** According to Rabban Gamliel, the acute mourner is obligated in the mitzva to engage in marital intercourse with his wife on Shabbat, just as he is obligated in all the other mitzvot.

מַאי לָאו בְּהָא קָא מִיפַּלְגִי; דְּמָר סָבַר: יֵשׁ אֲבֵילוּת בְּשַׁבָּת, וּמָר סָבַר: אֵין אֲבֵילוּת בְּשַׁבָּת.

The Gemara asks: **What, is it not with regard to this** issue that **they disagree:**[N] Is it not **that** one **Sage,** the anonymous first *tanna,* **holds** that **there is** some **mourning on Shabbat** with regard to private issues, and therefore the mourner does not engage in sexual relations; **and** one **Sage,** Rabban Gamliel, **holds** that **there is no mourning on Shabbat** at all?

מִמַּאי? דִּלְמָא עַד כָּאן לָא קָאָמַר תַּנָּא קַמָּא הָתָם – אֶלָּא מִשּׁוּם דְּמֵתוֹ מוּטָל לְפָנָיו, אֲבָל הָכָא דְּאֵין מֵתוֹ מוּטָל לְפָנָיו – לָא.

The Gemara rejects this argument: **From where** do you reach this conclusion? **Perhaps the first *tanna* is saying** that it is prohibited for the grieving relative to engage in sexual relations in the case dealt with **only there, because his deceased** relative **is laid out before him** and has not yet been buried. **But here,** with regard to the period of mourning, when **his dead** has been buried and **is no** longer **laid out before him,** sexual relations are **not** prohibited.

וְעַד כָּאן לָא קָאָמַר רַבָּן גַּמְלִיאֵל הָתָם – דְּאַכַּתִּי לָא חָל אֲבֵילוּת עֲלֵיהּ, אֲבָל הָכָא דְּחָל אֲבֵילוּת עֲלֵיהּ – הָכִי נָמֵי.

And alternatively, perhaps **Rabban Gamliel is saying** that the grieving relative is permitted to engage in sexual relations **only there,** where the *halakhot* of **mourning have not** yet **taken effect,** as mourning begins only after the burial. **But here,** where the *halakhot* of **mourning** have already **taken effect,** he may **also** prohibit sexual relations.

NOTES

And he is obligated in phylacteries – **וְחַיָּיב בִּתְפִילִּין:** The early authorities ask how one can be obligated to wear phylacteries on Shabbat when phylacteries are not worn by anyone on Shabbat. Because of this difficulty, some explain that this expression should be erased (Rashi, from manuscript). Others say that this obligation is mentioned only here because the *baraita* is speaking in general terms. Yet others say that it teaches the *halakha* for the intermediate days of a Festival (*Talmid Rabbeinu Yeḥiel of Paris; Magen Avraham*). Alternatively, this statement may be in accordance with the opinion of those *tanna'im* who hold that phylacteries may be worn on Shabbat and Festivals.

He is obligated to fulfill all – **נִתְחַיֵּיב בְּכוּלָּן:** The early authorities explain that this expression does not describe a true obligation. Instead, this expression in this context means that performing mitzvot on Shabbat is permitted (*Talmid Rabbeinu Yeḥiel of Paris*). However, there are those who say that even the first *tanna* does not believe that any of these actions are prohibited. They explain that, according to the first *tanna*, these activities are permitted, and according to Rabban Gamliel there is an obligation to perform them (Rabbi Zeraḥya HaLevi).

What, is it not with regard to this issue that they disagree – **מַאי לָאו בְּהָא קָא מִיפַּלְגִי:** This question is based on the assumption that the *halakha* of acute mourning is included within the *halakhot* of ordinary mourning, and everything stated with regard to ordinary mourning applies also to acute mourning. The Gemara rejects this comparison and states that these are two separate concepts. One cannot derive the halakhot of one from other, neither to be lenient nor to be stringent (Ritva).

Perek **III**
Daf **24** Amud **a**

בְּעָא מִינֵּיהּ רַבִּי יוֹחָנָן מִשְּׁמוּאֵל: יֵשׁ אֲבֵילוּת בְּשַׁבָּת אוֹ אֵין אֲבֵילוּת בְּשַׁבָּת? אֲמַר לֵיהּ: אֵין אֲבֵילוּת בְּשַׁבָּת.

Rabbi Yoḥanan asked of Shmuel: Is there some **mourning on Shabbat or is there no mourning on Shabbat** at all?[H] **He said to him: There is no mourning on Shabbat** at all.

HALAKHA

Mourning on Shabbat – **אֲבֵילוּת בְּשַׁבָּת:** On Shabbat, the restrictions of mourning apply in private. This is the opinion of Rabbi Yoḥanan, and the *halakha* is in accordance with him, even when he argues against Rav and Shmuel. This is also the *halakha* according to a similar discussion in tractate *Ketubot*.

Therefore, a mourner is prohibited from engaging in sexual relations or bathe even on Shabbat. However, he may not show any public signs of mourning, and therefore he may not wrap his head in mourning like the Ishmaelites (Rema). He wears shoes, sets his bed upright, and does not wear a torn garment. If he has no other garment, then he should reverse the garment so that the tear is in the back.

Torah study is prohibited, as it is considered a private matter. However, he may read the Torah portion twice and its translation once, as this type of study is considered to be similar to the recitation of the *Shema*. If the mourner is called to the Torah, he should go up to the Torah, for not going is a public display of mourning. Similarly, one who is called to the Torah every week or a priest in a synagogue where there are no other priests may also read from the Torah (*Shulḥan Arukh, Yoreh De'a* 400:1, and in the comment of Rema).

יתבי רבנן קמיה דרב פפא וקאמרי משמיה דשמואל: אבל ששימש מטתו בימי אבלו – חייב מיתה. אמר ליה רב פפא: אסור איתמר, ומשמיה דרבי יוחנן איתמר.

The Sages sat before Rav Pappa and said in the name of Shmuel: A mourner who engaged in sexual relations during his days of mourning is liable to receive **the death penalty**[N] at the hand of Heaven. **Rav Pappa said to them: It was said** that sexual relations are **prohibited,** but not that the offender is guilty of a capital crime. **And** the ruling **was said in the name of Rabbi Yoḥanan,** and not in the name of Shmuel.

ואי שמיעא לכו משמיה דשמואל – הכי שמיע לכו: אמר רב תחליפא בר אבימי אמר שמואל: אבל שלא פרע ושלא פירם – חייב מיתה, שנאמר: "ראשיכם אל תפרעו ובגדיכם לא תפרומו ולא תמותו" וגו׳, הא אחר שלא פרע ושלא פירם – חייב מיתה.

And if you heard a statement on this issue **in the name of Shmuel,** then **you heard as follows: Rav Taḥlifa bar Avimi said** that **Shmuel said: A mourner who did not let** his hair **grow wild and did not rend** his garments[H] **is liable** to receive **the death penalty** at the hand of Heaven, **as it is stated** following the deaths of Nadab and Abihu concerning the surviving sons of Aaron: **"Let not the hair of your heads go loose, neither rend your clothes, that you not die"** (Leviticus 10:6). They were instructed not to mourn, so as not to interfere with the dedication of the Tabernacle. From here it may be deduced **that** any **other** mourner[N] **who did not let** his hair **grow wild or rend** his clothes **is liable** to receive **the death penalty.**

אמר רפרם בר פפא, תנא באבל רבתי: אבל אסור לשמש מטתו בימי אבלו. ומעשה באחד ששימש מטתו בימי אבלו, ושמטו חזירים את גוייתו.

Rafram bar Pappa said: A Sage **taught in *Evel Rabbati*,**[B] a separate tractate devoted to the *halakhot* of mourning: **A mourner is prohibited from engaging in sexual relations during his days of mourning.** There was **an incident with one who engaged in sexual relations during his days of mourning and** he was punished, for after his death **pigs dragged away his corpse.**[N]

אמר שמואל: פח״ז – חובה; נת״ר – רשות.

Shmuel offered a mnemonic device with regard to the observance of mourning rites on Shabbat, and **said: *Peh, ḥet, zayin* are obligatory.**[N] These letters combine to create a mnemonic standing for: Uncovering the head [*periat rosh*], reversing the torn garment [*ḥazarat kera*], and standing the bed upright [*zekifat hamitta*]. However, ***nun, tav, reish,*** which stand for: Wearing shoes [*ne'ilat hasandal*], marital relations [*tashmish hamitta*], and hand washing [*reḥitzat yadayim*], **are optional.**

פריעת הראש, חזרת קרע לאחוריו, זקיפת המטה – חובה. נעילת הסנדל, תשמיש המטה, רחיצת ידים ורגלים בחמין ערבית – רשות. ורב אמר: אף פריעת הראש רשות.

This is explained: **Uncovering the head,** i.e., removing the head covering usually worn by a mourner; **reversing the tear to the back,** so that it will not be visible; and **standing the bed upright** in the usual position, so that it is not overturned, are all **obligatory** for the mourner to uphold in honor of Shabbat. However, **wearing shoes, engaging in sexual relations, and washing one's hands and feet in hot water in the evening are optional** activities on Shabbat. If a mourner wishes to refrain from them he may do so. **And Rav said: Uncovering the head is also an optional** activity.

NOTES

Liable to receive the death penalty – חַיָּיב מִיתָה: The early authorities write that this phrase does not mean that such a mourner who engaged in sexual relations would actually be executed at the hand of Heaven, for doing so is not listed in tractate *Sanhedrin* among the sins that are punishable by death. Instead, it is meant to be a harsh expression that emphasizes the seriousness of the sin. This is similar to what is stated elsewhere: Anyone who transgresses the words of the Sages is liable to receive the death penalty (Ramban). All such cases are based on the verse: "One who breaks through a fence, a serpent shall bite him" (Ecclesiastes 10:8), as rabbinic law is considered a fence meant to protect the Torah (*Talmid Rabbeinu Yeḥiel of Paris*).

That you not die…any other mourner, etc. – וְלֹא תָמוּתוּ...הָא אַחֵר וכו׳: The Ramban, in his glosses to *Sefer HaMitzvot* and in his commentary on the Torah, writes that the phrase: "That you not die," can be understood in two different ways. It can be understood either as a simple statement, or as a warning.

As a statement, it means the following: You are not required to practice mourning. Despite the general principle that one who is obligated to mourn and does not do so will receive the death penalty, you will not die because God commanded you not to mourn. Based on this, the Gemara concludes that others who are required to practice mourning and do not do so are liable to receive the death penalty. However, if it is a warning, it means: You are prohibited from practicing mourning, for if you practice mourning you will die.

His corpse – גְּוִייָתוֹ: Some explain that this word means his corpse; others say that it refers to his penis (Rashi, from manuscript; Rabbi Shlomo ben HaYatom). According to this second explanation, this man was punished measure for measure; he both sinned and was punished through the same body part (*Talmid Rabbeinu Yeḥiel of Paris*).

***Peh, ḥet, zayin* are obligatory – פח״ז חוֹבָה:** On Shabbat, a distinction is made between mourning practices that are public and those that are private. Alternatively, the distinction is between those actions that make it obvious to others that one is mourning and those actions that are not noticeable signs of mourning (Ritva).

HALAKHA

The obligation to rend – חִיּוּב קְרִיעָה: A mourner is obligated to rend his garment over a deceased relative. This *halakha* is alluded to in the Bible but is a rabbinic enactment (Rambam *Sefer Shofetim, Hilkhot Evel* 8:1).

BACKGROUND

***Evel Rabbati* – אֵבֶל רַבָּתִי:** This is referring to one of the minor tractates not included in the six orders of Mishna. These tractates are primarily collections of *baraitot* organized according to topic. *Evel Rabbati* has fourteen chapters, though the early authorities apparently had a longer version. It deals with people who are near death, the *halakhot* of funerals, rending garments, eulogizing, and mourning. The tractate is called *Evel Rabbati* in order to distinguish it from *Evel Zutarti*, which mostly deals with one who is dangerously ill. The tractate *Evel Rabbati* is found in most versions of the Talmud with the other minor tractates, at the end of the order of *Nezikin*. Most early authorities refer to it euphemistically as the *Tractate of Joys*.

וּשְׁמוּאֵל, מַאי שְׁנָא נְעִילַת הַסַּנְדָּל דִּרְשׁוּת? דְּלָאו כּוּלֵּי עָלְמָא עֲבִידִי דְּסַיְּימִי מְסָאנַיְיהוּ; פְּרִיעַת הָרֹאשׁ נַמִּי לָאו כּוּלֵּי עָלְמָא עֲבִידִי דְּמְגַלּוּ רֵישַׁיְיהוּ!

The Gemara asks: **According to Shmuel, what is different about wearing shoes** that it is **optional?** His reasoning presumably is that **not everyone wears shoes** at all times, and therefore not wearing shoes will not be perceived by others as a sign of mourning. If so, the same thing may be said about **uncovering the head also,** i.e., **not everyone uncovers his head** at all times, as some people always walk around with their heads wrapped. This, too, should not be seen as a clear display of mourning, and therefore uncovering one's head should also be treated as optional.

שְׁמוּאֵל לְטַעְמֵיהּ, דְּאָמַר שְׁמוּאֵל: כָּל קֶרַע שֶׁאֵינוֹ בִּשְׁעַת חִימּוּם – אֵינוֹ קֶרַע, וְכָל עֲטִיפָה שֶׁאֵינָהּ כַּעֲטִיפַת יִשְׁמְעֵאלִים – אֵינָהּ עֲטִיפָה. מַחְוֵי רַב נַחְמָן עַד גּוּבֵי דְּדִיקְנָא.

The Gemara answers: **Shmuel** conforms **to his** standard line of **reasoning,** for **Shmuel said: Any rending** of garments **that is not** done **at the time of** the **most intense** grief, i.e., the time of death, **is not** considered proper **rending** of garments.[H] **And any wrapping** of the head **that is not** done **in the manner of the wrapping of the Ishmaelites,**[B] who wrap their heads on all sides, **is not** considered proper **wrapping.**[H] Since Shmuel requires that a mourner wrap his head in this special manner, one who acts in this way on Shabbat openly displays his mourning, as people do not ordinarily wrap their heads in this manner. What is this wrapping? **Rav Naḥman demonstrated** the procedure by covering up his face to the **sides of the beard,**[N] leaving only the center of his face exposed.

אָמַר רַבִּי יַעֲקֹב אָמַר רַבִּי יוֹחָנָן: לֹא שָׁנוּ אֶלָּא שֶׁאֵין לוֹ מִנְעָלִים בְּרַגְלָיו, אֲבָל יֵשׁ לוֹ מִנְעָלִים בְּרַגְלָיו – מִנְעָלָיו מוֹכִיחִין עָלָיו.

Rabbi Ya'akov said that **Rabbi Yoḥanan said: They taught** that a mourner is required to remove his head covering on Shabbat **only when he has no shoes on his feet,** so that he not appear too obviously to be in mourning. **But if he has shoes on his feet,** then **his shoes prove** that **he** is not observing the rites of mourning on Shabbat.

BACKGROUND

Wrapping of the Ishmaelites – עֲטִיפַת יִשְׁמְעֵאלִים: Wrapping a shawl so that one side of the shawl rests on the shoulder is called Ishmaelite wrapping because nomadic Arabs would wrap themselves in this manner as protection from the cold or sand.

Ishmaelite wrapping

HALAKHA

Rending garments at the time of most intense grief – קֶרַע בִּשְׁעַת חִימּוּם: The primary mitzva for the mourner to rend his garments applies from the time of death until the burial. If one did not rend his garments during this time he may rend them anytime during the seven-day mourning period, as this entire time falls into the category of the most intense moment of grief. However, if did not rend his garments during the seven days either, he should not do so afterward. Over one's father or mother one is required to rend garments in their honor, even after this time, if he has not already done so (*Shulḥan Arukh, Yoreh De'a* 340; see *Arukh HaShulḥan*).

Wrapping for mourners – עֲטִיפַת אֲבֵלִים: A mourner is required to wrap his head with a scarf or shawl, and one corner should reach across his mouth and his nose. The mourner must keep this wrapping in place for the entire day, except for when others come to console him. At that time, he removes it as a sign of respect toward those who have come to visit him. The Rema writes that this is not the accepted practice in European regions, and one does not deviate from the local custom to act in a more stringent manner. However, it is appropriate to perform an act similar to wrapping, such as lowering one's hat over one's face slightly (*Shakh*; *Taz*; *Shulḥan Arukh, Yoreh De'a* 386:1).

NOTES

Sides of the beard – גּוּבֵי דְּדִיקְנָא: Rashi and others explain that this refers to the indentations in the jaw slightly below the mouth. Rav Hai Gaon explains that this refers to the hair on the cheeks. The halakhic authorities disagree with regard to how and where this wrapping is performed: If it extends below the mouth or not and whether or not the nose must be covered. Although for many generations it has not been the common practice to perform this wrapping as a sign of mourning, this style of wrapping still has practical ramifications with regard to the manner in which one must wrap one's prayer shawl.

כָּל קֶרַע שֶׁאֵינוֹ בִּשְׁעַת חִימּוּם אֵינוֹ קֶרַע. וְהָא אָמְרוּ לֵיהּ לִשְׁמוּאֵל: נָח נַפְשֵׁיהּ דְּרַב. קְרַע עֲלֵיהּ תְּרֵיסַר מָנֵי, אֲמַר: אֲזַל גַּבְרָא דַּהֲוָה מִסְתְּפִינָא מִינֵּיהּ. אֲמַר לֵיהּ לְרַבִּי יוֹחָנָן: נָח נַפְשֵׁיהּ דְּרַבִּי חֲנִינָא. קְרַע עֲלֵיהּ תְּלֵיסַר אִצְטְלֵי מִלְתָא, אֲמַר: אֲזַל גַּבְרָא דַּהֲוָה מִסְתְּפִינָא מִינֵּיהּ!

The Gemara returns to Shmuel's statement that **any rending** of garments **that is not** done **at the time of most intense** grief and pain **is not** considered proper **rending** of garments. The Gemara poses a question: **But when they said to Shmuel** that **Rav had passed away, he rent twelve garments on account of him,**[N] **and said: The man of whom I was in fear,**[N] owing to his great learning, **has gone** and died. Similarly, when **they told Rabbi Yoḥanan**[P] that **Rabbi Ḥanina**[P] **had passed away, he rent thirteen** expensive **wool** [*mileta*][L] **garments** [*itztelei*][L] **on account of him, and said: The man of whom I was in fear has gone.** When each of these Sages received the news that their distinguished colleague had died, it was no longer the time of the most intense grief, i.e., the time of death, and yet they rent their garments.

שָׁאנֵי רַבָּנַן, דְּכֵיוָן דְּכׇל שַׁעְתָּא מִדְּכָּרִי שְׁמַעְתַּיְיהוּ – כִּשְׁעַת חִימּוּם דָּמֵי.

The Gemara answers: **The Sages are different. Since their teachings are mentioned all the time,** every time they are mentioned **is like the time of most intense** grief, as the pain over their death is once again renewed.

אֲמַר לֵיהּ רָבִין בַּר אַדָּא לְרָבָא: אָמַר תַּלְמִידָךְ רַב עַמְרָם, תַּנְיָא: אָבֵל, כׇּל שִׁבְעָה – קוֹרְעוֹ לְפָנָיו; וְאִם בָּא לְהַחֲלִיף – מַחֲלִיף, וְקוֹרֵעַ. בְּשַׁבָּת – קוֹרְעוֹ לַאֲחוֹרָיו; וְאִם בָּא לְהַחֲלִיף – מַחֲלִיף, וְאֵינוֹ קוֹרֵעַ.

Ravin bar Adda said to Rava: Your student, Rav Amram, said that **it is taught** in a *baraita* as follows: For **all seven days** of mourning, a **mourner** must keep **the tear** in his garment **before him** so that it will be seen. **And if he comes to change** clothing,[N] **he changes and rends** the new garment. **On Shabbat,** he turns **the tear to his back, and if he comes to change** clothing, **he changes but does not tear** the second garment. From here it seems that there is an obligation to rend garments during the entire week of mourning, not only at the most intense moment of grief.

כִּי תַּנְיָא הַהִיא – בִּכְבוֹד אָבִיו וְאִמּוֹ.

The Gemara answers: **When that** *baraita* **is taught,** it is referring to the specific case of rending one's garment **in honor of his father or mother.** Owing to the special honor due to one's parents, it is inappropriate for the child to wear a garment that is not torn. Consequently, if he changes clothing, he must tear the new garment, even if it is no longer the most intense time of grief.

אוֹתָן קְרָעִין מִתְאַחִין אוֹ אֵין מִתְאַחִין? פְּלִיגִי בָּהּ אֲבוּהּ דְּרַב אוֹשַׁעְיָא וּבַר קַפָּרָא. חַד אָמַר: אֵין מִתְאַחִין, וְחַד אָמַר: מִתְאַחִין.

The Gemara asks: **Those** additional **tears** that are made in honor of one's father or mother, **may they be** properly **mended** at the end of the son's period of mourning, **or may they not be** properly **mended,** like the tear made for one's father or mother at the most intense moment of grief? The Gemara answers: **They disagree about** this issue, **the father of Rav Oshaya and bar Kappara. One said: They may not be mended, and one said: They may be mended.**[H]

NOTES

He rent twelve garments on account of him – קְרַע עֲלֵיהּ תְּרֵיסַר מָנֵי: A similar story is related in the Jerusalem Talmud, where it is added that Rabbi Yoḥanan took out his Shabbat clothes and tore them over the death of Rabbi Ḥanina. Apparently, many of the commentaries understood that he tore his clothes in this manner for many days. Each time he needed a new garment, he would tear it first (see Rashi, from manuscript; *Haggahot Maimoniyyot*).

Of whom I was in fear – דַּהֲוָה מִסְתְּפִינָא מִינֵּיהּ: Rashi and others explain that Shmuel was afraid of the challenges that Rav raised against his opinions. Rabbi Shlomo ben HaYatom writes that he was awed and ashamed before him, due to Rav's greatness and wisdom. The Ra'avad explains that as long as Rav was alive, Shmuel felt that he needed to be precise with his speech, as Rav, who was greater than him, would critique everything he said. Now that Rav passed away, Shmuel was afraid that he would err.

The Maharsha describes a different type of fear, and writes that Shmuel said that Rav was the perfect Torah scholar, and the Sages said that one is required to fear Torah scholars, as fear of them is compared to the fear of Heaven.

And if he comes to change clothing – וְאִם בָּא לְהַחֲלִיף: The Ra'avad writes that a mourner may change into another garment only if the first one requires laundering. The Meiri writes that one may change from a lightweight garment to a warmer one if the weather changes. This implies that a mourner may change garments only if there is a reason to do so.

LANGUAGE

Wool [*mileta*] – מִילְתָא: Apparently from the Greek μηλωτή, *mèlotè*, meaning wool. However, there are those who say that this word is related to the city of Miletus, which was a center for wool trading.

Garments [*itztelei*] – אִצְטְלֵי: From the Greek στολά, *stola*, meaning garment or cloak.

HALAKHA

Tears that may not be mended – קְרָעִים שֶׁאֵינָם מִתְאַחִים: A garment that was torn in mourning over one's father or mother may never be mended, even if it was not torn at the time of most intense grief. This is in accordance with the opinion of Rabbi Oshaya and based on a ruling in the Jerusalem Talmud (Rosh; *Shulḥan Arukh*, *Yoreh De'a* 340:14).

PERSONALITIES

Rabbi Yoḥanan – רַבִּי יוֹחָנָן: Rabbi Yoḥanan bar Nappaḥa was one of the greatest *amora'im*. His teachings are fundamental components of both the Babylonian and the Jerusalem Talmud. He resided in Tiberias and lived to an advanced age. Almost nothing is known of his family background. He was orphaned at a young age and, although his family apparently owned considerable property, he spent virtually all of his resources in his devotion to the study of Torah and eventually became impoverished.

In his youth, he had the privilege of studying under Rabbi Yehuda HaNasi, the redactor of the Mishna, but most of his Torah learning came from Rabbi Yehuda HaNasi's students: Ḥizkiya ben Ḥiyya, Rabbi Oshaya, Rabbi Ḥanina, and Rabbi Yannai, who lavished praise upon him. In time, he became the head of the yeshiva in Tiberias, at which point his fame and influence increased greatly.

For a long time, Rabbi Yoḥanan was the leading rabbinic scholar in the entire Jewish world, not only in Eretz Yisrael, but in Babylonia as well, where he was respected by the Babylonian Sages. Many of them came to Eretz Yisrael and became his outstanding students. He was a master of both *halakha* and *aggada*, and his teachings in both disciplines are found throughout both the Babylonian and the Jerusalem Talmud. In recognition of his intellectual and spiritual stature, the *halakha* is ruled in accordance with his opinion in almost every case, even when Rav or Shmuel, the preeminent *amora'im* of Babylonia, whom he treated deferentially, disagreed with him. Only in disputes with his teachers in Eretz Yisrael, such as Rabbi Yannai and Rabbi Yehoshua ben Levi, is the *halakha* not ruled in accordance with his opinion.

Rabbi Ḥanina – רַבִּי חֲנִינָא: This is Rabbi Ḥanina bar Ḥama, who lived in the transitional generation between the *tanna'im* and *amora'im*. Rabbi Ḥanina was born in Babylonia but emigrated to Eretz Yisrael at a very young age, where he studied Torah from Rabbi Yehuda HaNasi. His teacher was very fond of him, saying that Rabbi Ḥanina was not a human being but an angel. Rabbi Ḥanina also studied under Rabbi Yehuda HaNasi's greatest students, in particular Rabbi Ḥiyya. At the time of his death, Rabbi Yehuda HaNasi appointed Rabbi Ḥanina as head of the yeshiva, but in his humility, Rabbi Ḥanina refused to accept the position during the lifetime of his older colleague, Rabbi Afes.

Rabbi Ḥanina lived in the city of Tzippori, where he dealt in the honey trade, from which he grew wealthy. He used his money to build a large study hall. Rabbi Ḥanina is considered one of the cleverest scholars of his generation and was also renowned for his righteousness and kindness.

Rabbi Ḥanina's halakhic and aggadic statements abound both in the Jerusalem and Babylonian Talmud. He enjoyed a long and healthy life and taught many students over several generations. Rabbi Yehoshua ben Levi was his student and colleague, and he was also privileged to teach Rabbi Yoḥanan for many years. The *amora* Rabbi Ḥama, son of Rabbi Ḥanina, was possibly his son.

תסתיים דאבוה דרב אושעיא דאמר אין מתאחין, דאמר רב אושעיא, אין מתאחין. ממאן שמיע ליה? לאו מאבוה? לא, מבר קפרא רביה שמיע ליה.

The Gemara comments: **Conclude that** it was **Rav Oshaya's father** who **said** that such rents **may not be** properly **mended, for Rav Oshaya said:** Such rents **may not be** properly **mended. From whom did he hear** this *halakha*? Was it **not from his father?** The Gemara rejects this argument: **No,** this cannot be offered as a proof, as perhaps **he heard it from bar Kappara,** who was **his teacher.**

אמר רבא: אבל מטייל באונקלי בתוך ביתו. אביי אשכחיה לרב יוסף דפריס ליה סודרא ארישיה, ואזיל ואתי בביתיה. אמר ליה: לאו סבר לה מר אין אבילות בשבת? אמר ליה: הכי אמר רבי יוחנן: דברים שבצינעא נוהג.

§ **Rava said: A mourner may walk about his house in** a torn **robe [*unkali*]**[NL] on Shabbat, since he is not doing so in public. It was related that **Abaye found Rav Yosef walking back and forth in his house** on Shabbat when he was in mourning **with a scarf spread over his head** in the manner of mourning. **He said to him: Master, do you not maintain** that **there is no mourning on Shabbat? He said to him: This is what Rabbi Yoḥanan said: Matters that are in private apply,** and so when one is in his house he must observe the rites of mourning even on Shabbat.

"רבי אליעזר אומר משחרב בית המקדש עצרת כשבת" וכו'. אמר רב גידל בר מנשיא אמר שמואל: הלכה כרבן גמליאל.

§ The mishna taught: **Rabbi Eliezer says: Since the Temple was destroyed, *Shavuot* is like Shabbat** with regard to mourning. Rabban Gamliel says: Even Rosh HaShana and Yom Kippur are considered like Festivals. The Gemara comments that **Rav Giddel bar Menashya said** that **Shmuel said: The *halakha* is in accordance** with the opinion **of Rabban Gamliel.**

ואיכא דמתני להא דרב גידל בר מנשיא אהא: כל שלשים יום תינוק יוצא בחיק, ונקבר באשה אחת ושני אנשים, אבל לא באיש אחד ושתי נשים.

And some teach this ruling **of Rav Giddel bar Menashya** as referring **to the following** case: It is taught in a *baraita*: Within the first **thirty days** after birth, **an infant** that dies **is taken out** for burial **in** one's **bosom,**[N] that is to say, he is carried to his grave in one's arms, not in a coffin. **And he is buried by one woman and two men,** there being no need for a quorum of ten men. **But** he should **not** be taken out **by one man and two women,**[N] because it is prohibited for one man to seclude himself with two women.

NOTES

Robe [*unkali*] – אונקלי: Many commentaries explain that *unkali* refers to a garment that is worn directly on one's skin. They explain that Rava permits a mourner to wear a torn undergarment within his home on Shabbat, if the mourner does not wish to change his garments (Rabbeinu Gershom Meor HaGola; Rashi). Rabbeinu Ḥananel explains that *unkali* refers to a type of turban that would cover the head of a mourner while he was mourning. This explanation is based on the opinion that holds that a mourner is not required to wrap his head specifically in the manner of the Ishmaelites. Some explain that the word *unkali* means a hook or clasp, and it refers to a torn garment that is held together by a clasp (Ramban; Ran).

Within the first thirty days an infant that dies is taken out for burial in one's bosom – כל שלשים יום תינוק יוצא בחיק: The reason for this is that until a baby has survived for thirty days, it is not considered viable. As a result, mourning for the death of such an infant is not as intense as for an older child or an adult. The early authorities write that these *halakhot* do not apply to a stillborn child.

One man and two women – איש אחד ושתי נשים: In tractate *Kiddushin*, it is stated that one man may not be alone with two women due to the prohibition of seclusion. According to the first *tanna*, there is no distinction between a time of mourning and any other time, because the case is one in which the child died within thirty days. Therefore, the grief is less intense, and it is possible that the mourners will come to sin (Rashi, from manuscript; Commentary on *Moed Katan*).

LANGUAGE

Robe [*unkali*] – אונקלי: From the Greek ἀνάκωλος, *anakolos*, meaning short or cut off. It is used in reference to a lower garment that reached the knees.

Perek **III**
Daf **24** Amud **b**

אבא שאול אומר: אף באיש אחד ושתי נשים. ואין עומדין עליו בשורה, ואין אומרים עליו ברכת אבלים ותנחומי אבלים.

Abba Shaul says: The infant may be taken out **even by one man and two women,**[N] for there is no concern with regard to seclusion in a time of mourning. **And for** such an infant, people **do not stand in a line** to offer their condolences to the mourners, as is ordinarily done after a burial; **nor do** others **recite over him the mourners' blessing,**[N] which is recited in the courtyard of the graveyard after the burial; **nor** is the usual formula for the **consolation of mourners** recited during the seven days of mourning.

NOTES

Even by one man, etc. – אף באיש אחד וכו': *Tosafot* explain: Although there is generally concern about the seclusion of one man with two women, Abba Shaul holds that one's sexual desire are not as strong during mourning. It can also be deduced from this Gemara that although there is no requirement for ten people to take part in a burial, there must be at least three people present (Ran).

Nor do others recite over him the mourners' blessing – ואין אומרים עליו ברכת אבלים: This implies that there is no public mourning for a small child who dies. However, it is not clear whether the relatives are required to mourn for their child. There was a difference in practice between the residents of the Diaspora and the residents of Eretz Yisrael. In the Diaspora, the custom was not to mourn for a baby unless it had survived for at least thirty days; whereas the residents of Eretz Yisrael mourned over any baby, even if it lived for only one day. This custom was based on a mishna (*Nidda* 5:3) concerning mourning that states that a newborn baby is to his father, his mother, and all of his relatives like a fully grown groom.

בֶּן שְׁלֹשִׁים יוֹצֵא בִּדְלוּסְקְמָא. רַבִּי יְהוּדָה אוֹמֵר: לֹא דְלוּסְקְמָא הַנִּיטֶּלֶת בְּכָתֵף, אֶלָּא הַנִּיטֶּלֶת בָּאֲגַפַּיִים. וְעוֹמְדִין עָלָיו בְּשׁוּרָה, וְאוֹמְרִים עָלָיו בִּרְכַּת אֲבֵלִים וְתַנְחוּמֵי אֲבֵלִים.

A thirty-day-old infant that dies **is taken out** for burial **in a coffin** [*deluskema*].[HL] **Rabbi Yehuda says: Not** in a small **coffin that is carried on** one's **shoulder, but rather** in a coffin that is carried **in the arms** of two people. **And for** such an infant, people **stand in a line** to offer their condolences to the mourners. **And** others **recite the mourners' blessing** at the cemetery. **And** people recite **the consolation of mourners** during the week of mourning.

בֶּן שְׁנֵים עָשָׂר חֹדֶשׁ – יוֹצֵא בְּמִטָּה. רַבִּי עֲקִיבָא אוֹמֵר: הוּא בֶּן שָׁנָה וְאֵבָרָיו כְּבֶן שְׁתַּיִם, הוּא בֶּן שְׁתַּיִם וְאֵבָרָיו כְּבֶן שָׁנָה – יוֹצֵא בְּמִטָּה.

A twelve-month-old infant **is taken out** for burial **on a bier,** just as an adult is. **Rabbi Akiva says:** This *halakha* applies if the infant that dies **is one year old and his limbs are like** those of **a two year old,** so that he looks older, or if **he is two years old and his limbs are like** those of **a one-year-old.** Only then **he is taken out on a bier.**

רַבִּי שִׁמְעוֹן בֶּן אֶלְעָזָר אוֹמֵר: הַיּוֹצֵא בְּמִטָּה – רַבִּים מִצְטַהֲבִין עָלָיו. אֵינוֹ יוֹצֵא בְּמִטָּה – אֵין רַבִּים מִצְטַהֲבִין עָלָיו. רַבִּי אֶלְעָזָר בֶּן עֲזַרְיָה אוֹמֵר: נִיכָּר לָרַבִּים – רַבִּים מִתְעַסְּקִים עִמּוֹ; אֵינוֹ נִיכָּר לָרַבִּים – אֵין רַבִּים מִתְעַסְּקִים עִמּוֹ.

Rabbi Shimon ben Elazar says: For one that is taken out on a bier, the public should grieve [*matzhivin*].[L] **For one that is not taken out on a bier, the public need not grieve. Rabbi Elazar ben Azarya says:** The *halakha* is as follows: If the infant was **known to the public,** because he regularly left the house and many people knew him, **the public must occupy themselves with him** and participate in his burial. **If he was not known to the public, the public need not occupy themselves with him.**

וּמַה הֵן בְּהֶסְפֵּד? רַבִּי מֵאִיר בְּשֵׁם רַבִּי יִשְׁמָעֵאל אוֹמֵר: עֲנִיִּים – בְּנֵי שָׁלֹשׁ; עֲשִׁירִים – בְּנֵי חָמֵשׁ. רַבִּי יְהוּדָה אוֹמֵר מִשְּׁמוֹ: עֲנִיִּים – בְּנֵי חָמֵשׁ; עֲשִׁירִים – בְּנֵי שֵׁשׁ. וּבְנֵי זְקֵנִים כִּבְנֵי עֲנִיִּים.

And what is the status of deceased infants **with regard to eulogy?**[N] **Rabbi Meir said in the name of Rabbi Yishmael:** The children of **the poor**[N] are eulogized from **the age of three,** whereas the children of **the wealthy** are eulogized from **the age of five.** This is because a child is the sole source of joy for the poor, and so the pain and grief of the poor over the death of a child is greater than that of the wealthy. **Rabbi Yehuda said in the name of** Rabbi Yishmael: The children of **the poor** are eulogized from **the age of five,** whereas the children of **the wealthy** are eulogized from **the age of six.**[H] **And the children of the elderly**[N] **are** treated **like the children of the poor,** for the death of a child is particularly painful for an older person.[H]

אָמַר רַב גִּידֵּל בַּר מְנַשְּׁיָא אָמַר רַב: הֲלָכָה כְּרַבִּי יְהוּדָה שֶׁאָמַר מִשּׁוּם רַבִּי יִשְׁמָעֵאל.

Rav Giddel bar Menashya said that **Rav said: The** ***halakha*** **is in accordance with** the opinion of **Rabbi Yehuda, who stated it in the name of Rabbi Yishmael.**

NOTES

What is the status with regard to eulogy – מַה הֵן בְּהֶסְפֵּד: It is stated in a *baraita* in tractate *Semaḥot* that if it is possible to praise the child and his deeds, then he should be eulogized in the merit of his deeds. If this is not the case, then he should be eulogized in the merits of his forefathers.

The children of the poor – בְּנֵי עֲנִיִּים: Rashi explains, and before him Rav Hai Gaon explained, that the poor do take pleasure from what they have, and consequently they feel more pain when their one joy, their child, dies. Others say that they are more pained by their children's death because they rely on them for financial support once they grow older (Rashi, from manuscript). Others write that since the poor must eat sparingly in order to provide for their children, they become more attached to them (Ran). There are also those who suggest that this decree was made because the poor are constantly living in pain and suffering, and if they do not eulogize their children there is a concern that people will suspect that they are not showing honor for their child because of their poverty (Rabbi Shlomo ben HaYatom).

The children of the elderly [*zekenim*] – בְּנֵי זְקֵנִים: Most commentaries note that this is because the elderly no longer have hope that they will have other children, and therefore their pain is greater (Rabbi Shlomo ben HaYatom; Ran). Or, it is possible that the reason for this is because they hope that their child will care for them in their old age. Others write that the word *zekenim*, literally Elders, refers to Sages, and more honor should be shown for Torah scholars.

HALAKHA

Less than thirty days old – פָּחוֹת מִבֶּן שְׁלֹשִׁים: A baby who dies within thirty days of birth is carried to burial in one's hands and there is no requirement to bury him in a coffin (*Shakh*, citing *Or Zarua*). The baby should be buried by one woman and two men, but not by one man and two women, due to the prohibition of seclusion, as mentioned by the first *tanna*. There is no requirement for others to stand in a line to comfort the mourners after his death (*Shakh*, citing Rashi). Similarly, the mourners' blessing and the consolation of mourners are not said after the baby's death, even when it is clear that the infant was not a stillbirth but was fully formed baby (*Shulḥan Arukh, Yoreh De'a* 353:3).

The burial of a child – קְבוּרַת יֶלֶד: If a child dies more than thirty days after his birth, he is carried to burial in a coffin that is held by two people. People stand in a line to comfort the mourners over his death, and the mourners' blessing and the consolation of mourners are said after his death. If the child was more than twelve months old then, he is carried for burial on a bier, just as an adult. Anyone who is carried on a bier should be mourned by the public. The public is involved with the funeral of any child that is known to them, and if he is not known to them they are not involved in his funeral, in accordance with the opinions of Rabbi Shimon ben Elazar and Rabbi Elazar ben Azarya (*Shulḥan Arukh, Yoreh De'a* 353:5).

Eulogies over children – הֶסְפֵּד עַל יְלָדִים: The children of the wealthy are eulogized if they are older than six, and the children of the poor or the elderly are eulogized from the age of five. The *Shulḥan Arukh* holds that the blessing: The true Judge and the mourners' prayer are recited from the age of thirty days in all cases. The Rema disagrees and writes that the custom is to recite this only if the child was at least twelve months old (*Shakh*; *Shulḥan Arukh, Yoreh De'a* 344:4).

LANGUAGE

Coffin [*deluskema*] – דְּלוּסְקְמָא: From the Greek γλωσσόκομος, *glossokomos*, meaning case. Originally, it referred specifically to a case in which to keep mouthpieces of wind-instruments. The meaning was expanded so that it referred to any box or crate, including a coffin or ossuary.

Ossuary

Grieve [*matzhivin*] – מִצְטַהֲבִין: The meaning of this word and its root, *tz-h-v*, are possibly related to the color *tzahov*, which in modern Hebrew means yellow, but in the Gemara can also refer to a more reddish color. The meaning of the word here is to make one's face redden with emotion, either with grief or anger.

דָּרַשׁ רַבִּי עֲנָנִי בַּר שָׂשׂוֹן אַפִּיתְחָא דְּבֵי נְשִׂיאָה: יוֹם אֶחָד לִפְנֵי עֲצֶרֶת וַעֲצֶרֶת – הֲרֵי כָּאן אַרְבָּעָה עָשָׂר. שְׁמַע רַבִּי אַמִּי וְאִיקְּפַד. אֲמַר: אַטּוּ דִּידֵיהּ הִיא? דְּרַבִּי אֶלְעָזָר אָמַר רַבִּי אוֹשַׁעְיָא הִיא!

Rabbi Anani bar Sason taught at the entrance to the house of the *Nasi*: If one suffered the loss of a close relative shortly before the festival of *Shavuot*, his **one day** of mourning **before *Shavuot*[H] and *Shavuot*** itself together count as **fourteen** days. The day before the Festival counts as seven full days of mourning because the Festival interrupts the seven-day period of mourning, and the Festival itself is counted as a seven-day Festival. Even though it is a one-day Festival, it is counted as seven days because it has the same *halakha* as the other Festivals. After *Shavuot*, then, only sixteen days are left to complete the thirty-day mourning period. **Rabbi Ami heard** this **and became angry** with him. **He said: Is that to say** that it is **his own** opinion?[N] **It is** the opinion **that Rabbi Elazar said** that **Rabbi Oshaya** said.

דָּרַשׁ רַבִּי יִצְחָק נַפָּחָא אַקִּילְעָא דְּרֵישׁ גָּלוּתָא: יוֹם אֶחָד לִפְנֵי עֲצֶרֶת, וַעֲצֶרֶת – הֲרֵי כָּאן אַרְבָּעָה עָשָׂר. שְׁמַע רַב שֵׁשֶׁת אִיקְּפַד, אֲמַר: אַטּוּ דִּידֵיהּ הִיא? דְּרַבִּי אֶלְעָזָר אָמַר רַבִּי אוֹשַׁעְיָא הִיא.

Similarly **Rabbi Yitzḥak Nappaḥa taught in the pavilion** [*kila*][L] **of the Exilarch:** If one's relative died shortly before the festival of *Shavuot*, his **one day** of mourning **before *Shavuot*** **and *Shavuot*** itself count as **fourteen** days. **Rav Sheshet heard and became angry.** He **said: Is that to say** that it is **his own** opinion? **It is** the opinion **that Rabbi Elazar said** that **Rabbi Oshaya** said.

דְּאָמַר רַבִּי אֶלְעָזָר אָמַר רַבִּי אוֹשַׁעְיָא: מִנַּיִן לַעֲצֶרֶת שֶׁיֵּשׁ לָהּ תַּשְׁלוּמִין כׇּל שִׁבְעָה? שֶׁנֶּאֱמַר: ״בְּחַג הַמַּצּוֹת וּבְחַג הַשָּׁבֻעוֹת״ – מַה חַג הַמַּצּוֹת יֵשׁ לָהּ תַּשְׁלוּמִין כׇּל שִׁבְעָה – אַף חַג הַשָּׁבוּעוֹת יֵשׁ לָהּ תַּשְׁלוּמִין כׇּל שִׁבְעָה.

In both of these cases, a Sage presented an opinion as their own, without attributing it to the original Sage who stated it, **for Rabbi Elazar said** that **Rabbi Oshaya said: From where** is it derived **that the *Shavuot*** offerings **have redress all seven** subsequent **days?**[H] That is to say, if someone failed to bring the Festival offering on the Festival itself, he has six more days to bring it. **As it is stated:** "Three times a year shall all your males appear before the Lord your God in the place that He shall choose; **on the festival of Passover, and on the festival of *Shavuot*,** and on the festival of *Sukkot*" (Deuteronomy 16:16). **Just as** the offerings of **the festival of Passover have redress all seven** days, as Passover is seven days long, **so too** the offerings of **the festival of *Shavuot* have redress all seven** days, during the week following *Shavuot*. From this we learn that *Shavuot* is treated like a seven-day Festival for all halakhic purposes.

אַדְבְּרֵיהּ רַב פַּפָּא לְרַב אָוְיָא סָבָא, וְדָרַשׁ: יוֹם אֶחָד לִפְנֵי רֹאשׁ הַשָּׁנָה, וְרֹאשׁ הַשָּׁנָה – הֲרֵי כָּאן אַרְבָּעָה עָשָׂר. אָמַר רָבִינָא: הִלְכָּךְ, יוֹם אֶחָד לִפְנֵי הֶחָג, וְחַג, וּשְׁמִינִי שֶׁלּוֹ – הֲרֵי כָּאן עֶשְׂרִים וְאֶחָד יוֹם.

Rav Pappa granted permission[B] **to Rav Avya the Elder** to speak **and he taught** the following in public: If one's relative died shortly before Rosh HaShana, his **one day** of mourning **before Rosh HaShana**[NH] **and Rosh HaShana** itself together count as **fourteen** days, because Rosh HaShana is treated like a seven-day Festival. **Ravina said: Therefore,** if a one's relative died shortly before *Sukkot*, his **one day** of mourning **before the Festival** of *Sukkot*,[H] **and the Festival** of *Sukkot* itself, which is seven days, **and its Eighth** day of Assembly, which is considered to be a separate Festival, count as **twenty-one** days, and he must observe only nine more days of mourning to complete the thirty-day period of mourning.

HALAKHA

One day before *Shavuot* – **יוֹם אֶחָד לִפְנֵי עֲצֶרֶת:** One who observed mourning practices for at least one day before *Shavuot* is considered as though he observed mourning for seven days, and *Shavuot* itself is counted as another seven days. Therefore, after the Festival he has only sixteen days of mourning left. The second day of the Festival that is observed in the diaspora is included in this number, in accordance with the opinions of Rabbi Anani bar Sason and Rabbi Oshaya (*Shulḥan Arukh, Yoreh De'a* 399:8).

Redress for the offerings of *Shavuot* – **תַּשְׁלוּמֵי עֲצֶרֶת:** One who did not bring the Festival peace-offerings on *Shavuot* may bring them for an additional six days after the Festival and thereby fulfills his obligation (Rambam *Sefer Korbanot, Hilkhot Ḥagiga* 1:7).

One day before Rosh HaShana – **יוֹם אֶחָד לִפְנֵי רֹאשׁ הַשָּׁנָה:** If one observed mourning practices for a deceased relative for even an hour before Rosh HaShana, then Rosh HaShana cancels the seven-day period of mourning. The thirty-day period of mourning is canceled by Yom Kippur, and one may cut his hair on the day before Yom Kippur, in accordance with the opinion of Rav Pappa (*Shulḥan Arukh, Yoreh De'a* 399:9).

One day before the Festival of *Sukkot* – **יוֹם אֶחָד לִפְנֵי הֶחָג:** If one observed mourning for a short time before the Festival of *Sukkot*, it is considered to be seven days of mourning. The Festival itself counts as an additional seven days, and the Eighth Day of Assembly also counts as seven days. Therefore, he needs to complete only nine days of mourning after the Festival, in order to finish his thirty-day period of mourning. In the Diaspora, *Simḥat Torah* counts as one day towards this number (*Shulḥan Arukh, Yoreh De'a* 399:11).

LANGUAGE

Pavilion [*kila*] – **קִילְעָא:** This word refers to any temporary structure built from screens or panels. Therefore, it means a tent or any other temporary partition.

BACKGROUND

Granted permission – **אַדְבְּרֵיהּ:** The expression refers to the granting of permission to teach *halakha* in public. Occasionally, this means that the Sage granting the permission also gave his approval to the teaching. There are a number of instances in the Gemara in which a Sage gave permission to different people from the house of the Exilarch to give these types of public lessons.

NOTES

Is that to say that it is his own opinion – **אַטּוּ דִּידֵיהּ הִיא:** Some say that Rabbi Ami became angry because one must be careful to cite words of Torah in the name of the person who originally said them, as is noted in numerous places in the Gemara. This is important both in terms of determining the *halakha* and also to honor the speaker and his Torah. Numerous stories are told both in the Jerusalem and the Babylonian Talmud about how the Sages were careful to quote statements they heard in the name of those who originally said them (Rabbi Shlomo ben HaYatom).

The Ramban holds that Rabbi Ami became angry because he thought that Rabbi Anani bar Sason based his statement incorrectly on what Rabbi Oshaya said. This is because Rabbi Oshaya's statement applies only when the Temple stood, as he refers to offerings when he discusses their redress. Therefore, this statement cannot be used as a basis for mourning practices after the destruction of the Temple.

One day before Rosh HaShana, etc. – **יוֹם אֶחָד לִפְנֵי רֹאשׁ הַשָּׁנָה:** The early authorities question the purpose of this *halakha*, as Yom Kippur is also considered to be a Festival (Ra'avad; *Tosafot*). Therefore, if someone begins mourning on the day before Rosh HaShana, the seven days ends with Rosh HaShana, and Yom Kippur itself should end the thirty-day mourning period. For what purpose is it necessary to state that the day before Rosh HaShana together with Rosh HaShana count as fourteen days? The *Ba'al Halakhot Gedolot* explains that since one leniency is applied to this period of mourning with regard to Rosh HaShana, another leniency cannot be applied in the case of Yom Kippur. Therefore, the latter is not also counted as seven days.

Tosafot also state in the name of Rabbeinu Yitzḥak and Rabbeinu Shimshon that after Rosh HaShana, the mourner is considered to already be in his third week of mourning, and therefore he may sit in his place in synagogue.

רָבִינָא אִיקְלַע לְסוּרָא דִּפְרָת. אֲמַר לֵיהּ רַב חֲבִיבָא מִסּוּרָא דִּפְרָת לְרָבִינָא: אָמַר מָר יוֹם אֶחָד לִפְנֵי רֹאשׁ הַשָּׁנָה וְרֹאשׁ הַשָּׁנָה הֲרֵי כָּאן אַרְבָּעָה עָשָׂר? אֲמַר לֵיהּ: אֲנָא מִסְתַּבְרָא כְּרַבָּן גַּמְלִיאֵל הוּא דְּאָמֵינָא.

It was related that **Ravina happened** to come **to** the city of **Sura on the Euphrates** River. **Rav Ḥaviva from Sura on the Euphrates said to Ravina:** Did the **Master say** that **one day** of mourning **before Rosh HaShana and Rosh HaShana** itself count **as fourteen** days? **He said to him: I said that it stands to reason** that this is so **according to Rabban Gamliel,**[N] who maintains that Rosh HaShana is treated like a pilgrimage Festival. But I did not rule in accordance with this opinion.

מתני׳ אֵין קוֹרְעִין, וְלֹא חוֹלְצִין, וְאֵין מַבְרִין, אֶלָּא קְרוֹבָיו שֶׁל מֵת. וְאֵין מַבְרִין אֶלָּא עַל מִטָּה זְקוּפָה.

MISHNA Mourners **do not rend**[N] their garments during the intermediate days of a Festival[H] **and do not remove** their garments from their shoulders. **And** others **do not provide them with a meal**[N] [*mavrin*][L] after the burial, **except for close relatives of the deceased. And** the consolers **provide the** first **meal** after the burial **only** while the mourner is sitting **on an upright bed,** and not on one that is overturned.

NOTES

It stands to reason according to Rabban Gamliel – מִסְתַּבְרָא כְּרַבָּן גַּמְלִיאֵל: It is explained that Ravina did not rule in this manner explicitly. Instead, he said that since the *halakha* is in accordance with Rabban Gamliel, that Rosh HaShana is considered to interrupt mourning like the Festivals, it is should also be considered to be like a Festival and count as seven days. He did not mean that the *halakha* is in accordance with Rabban Gamliel's opinion; rather, he was just explaining his reasoning.

According to the Rambam, Ravina did not agree with this ruling. Although the *halakha* is in accordance with Rabban Gamliel, that Rosh HaShana interrupts mourning, Ravina did not agree that Rosh HaShana should count as seven days. This is because it is not a pilgrimage Festival at all, and the comparison between *Shavuot* and *Sukkot* cannot be applied to Rosh HaShana. Other halakhic authorities hold that Rosh HaShana is considered to be like a pilgrimage Festival because all Festivals are compared to each other.

Mourners do not rend, etc. – אֵין קוֹרְעִין וכו׳: Most of the early authorities explain that this entire mishna specifically discusses the *halakhot* of mourning during the intermediate days of the Festival. However, this implies that on non-festive days mourners must rend their clothes (*ge'onim*; Ra'avad; Ramban). This also appears to be the conclusion in the Jerusalem Talmud. However, there are some who understand this mishna to be dealing with mourning during weekdays, and according to their explanation it is entirely prohibited to rend their garments (Rashi).

Others do not provide them with a meal, etc. – אֵין מַבְרִין: According to those who understand the mishna to be speaking of the intermediate days of the Festival, a mourner is not required to overturn his bed because mourning does not apply during this time. According to those who understand that this *halakha* was said with regard to regular weekdays, there are those who understand it to mean that the consolers sit on an upright bed, and not with the mourner on an overturned bed (Rashi; Rabbeinu Gershom Meor HaGola; Rabbeinu Yehonatan of Lunel). However, others explain that both out of respect for the consolers and so that they will not have to sit in separate place, the Sages even permitted the mourner to eat the feast after the burial on an upright bed (Ra'avad; Ramban).

HALAKHA

Rending during the Festival – קְרִיעָה בַּמּוֹעֵד: One may rend his garment over a death during the intermediate days of the Festival only when rending the garment is required according to *halakha*. Some disagree and say that one may not rend garments at all during the intermediate days of the Festival. It is the Ashkenazic custom for one to rend his garments during the intermediate days of the Festival only when mourning his father or mother. When mourning any other relatives one rends his garments after the Festival (Rema). However, in Poland it was customary to rend one's garments when mourning all relatives (*Magen Avraham*). The Sephardic communities of Jerusalem, Izmir, and Thessaloniki, had a similar custom to the Ashkenazic one; however, every place should act in accordance with the local custom there (*Kaf HaḤayyim*; *Shulḥan Arukh*, *Oraḥ Ḥayyim* 547:6).

LANGUAGE

Provide a meal [*mavrin*] – מַבְרִין: The root *v-r-h* means to eat and is found several times in the Bible (see II Samuel, chapter 13). The custom for mourners to eat their first meal after the burial from other people's food is very ancient and is first mentioned in the book of II Samuel: "And the people came to feed David bread" (3:35). Similarly, the custom is mentioned when Ezekiel the prophet is prohibited from acting like an ordinary mourner: "And people's bread you shall not eat" (Ezekiel 24:17–22). This meal is referred to as the *se'udat havra'a*, meaning the meal at which the mourners are fed.

גמ׳ וַאֲפִילּוּ חָכָם? וְהָתַנְיָא: חָכָם שֶׁמֵּת – הַכֹּל קְרוֹבָיו.

GEMARA The mishna teaches that only the relatives of the deceased rend their clothes. The Gemara asks: **And** is this the case **even** if the deceased was a Torah **Sage? But isn't it taught** otherwise in a *baraita*: When a Torah **scholar dies, everyone is his relative.**[H]

הַכֹּל קְרוֹבָיו סָלְקָא דַּעְתָּךְ?! אֶלָּא: הַכֹּל כִּקְרוֹבָיו – הַכֹּל קוֹרְעִין עָלָיו, וְהַכֹּל חוֹלְצִין עָלָיו, וְהַכֹּל מַבְרִין עָלָיו בָּרְחָבָה! לָא צְרִיכָא דְּלָאו חָכָם הוּא.

The Gemara clarifies: **Does it enter your mind** to say that **everyone is his relative? Rather,** this *baraita* should be understood as follows: **Everyone is** considered to be **like his relative** in the sense that **everyone rends his** garment in anguish **over him, and everyone bares**[H] his shoulder **over him** in mourning, **and everyone eats the mourner's meal over him**[H] **in the public square** as mourners do. The death of a Torah scholar is a personal loss for every Jew. So why is the mishna limited to only relatives? The Gemara answers: **No,** it is **necessary** for the mishna to teach this *halakha* in a case **where** the deceased **is not a** Torah **scholar.**

וְאִי אָדָם כָּשֵׁר הוּא – חִיּוּבֵי מִיחַיַּיב לְמִיקְרַע, דְּתַנְיָא: מִפְּנֵי מָה בָּנָיו וּבְנוֹתָיו שֶׁל אָדָם מֵתִים כְּשֶׁהֵן קְטַנִּים – כְּדֵי שֶׁיִּבְכֶּה וְיִתְאַבֵּל עַל אָדָם כָּשֵׁר.

The Gemara asks: **And if** the deceased **was an upright person** who feared Heaven and performed good deeds, then aren't all those present at his death **obligated to rend** their garments over his death?[H] **As it is taught** in a *baraita*: **For what reason do a person's sons and daughters die when they are young?** They die **so that he will cry and mourn** over the death of **an upright person.**

יִבְכֶּה וְיִתְאַבֵּל? עַרְבוֹנָא קָא שָׁקֵיל מִינֵּיהּ?! אֶלָּא: מִפְּנֵי שֶׁלֹּא בָּכָה וְהִתְאַבֵּל עַל אָדָם כָּשֵׁר. שֶׁכָּל הַבּוֹכֶה וּמִתְאַבֵּל עַל אָדָם כָּשֵׁר – מוֹחֲלִין לוֹ עַל כׇּל עֲוֹנוֹתָיו בִּשְׁבִיל כָּבוֹד שֶׁעָשָׂה לוֹ! דְּלָאו אָדָם כָּשֵׁר הוּא.

The Gemara questions the formulation: They die so that **he will cry and mourn? Is security,** i.e., his children, **taken from him** in advance to ensure that in the future he will mourn over the death of an upright person? **Rather** the *baraita* means as follows: His children died **because he did not cry or mourn over an upright person**[N] who died. **As** with regard to **anyone who cries and mourns over an upright person** who died, **they forgive him** for **all his transgressions because of the honor he accorded** to the deceased. If this is the case, one also rends his clothes over an upright person. The Gemara answers: Rather, the mishna is referring only to one **who** was **not an upright person.**

NOTES

Because he did not cry…over an upright person – מִפְּנֵי שֶׁלֹּא בָּכָה...עַל אָדָם כָּשֵׁר: In punishment for not crying over an upright person, this person will cry over the death of his children, who were certainly upright because they were not yet old enough to sin. Therefore, the punishment is tailored to the sin (Maharsha).

HALAKHA

Rending garments over a Torah scholar – קְרִיעָה עַל חָכָם: When a Torah scholar dies, everyone rends his garment over him on the day of burial or when they hear of his death, provided it is within thirty days of his passing. Additionally, one rends his garment over him at the time of the eulogy if the eulogy is within thirty days of the death (*Shakh*; *Baḥ* citing Rosh and Ra'avad). If one did not rend his garment on the day when he heard the news or during the eulogy, then he may no longer rend his garment (Rema). In this context anyone who is asked questions about *halakhot* and knows the answers is called a Torah scholar. When rendering garments over one's own rabbi, one tears until he exposes his chest. When rending one's garments over other Torah scholars, even if they are equal in wisdom to the mourner, the tear is one handbreadth in length. Some say that one rends his garments only over his rabbi or over one who taught him Torah. The common practice is to be lenient and not rend a garment over one's rabbi (*Shulḥan Arukh*, *Yoreh De'a* 340:7, and in the comment of Rema).

Everyone bares – הַכֹּל חוֹלְצִין: When one's rabbi dies he should uncover his garment from his shoulder, similar to the practice over the passing of his father or mother. Some say that this act of mourning is no longer performed, and this is the common practice (*Shulḥan Arukh*, *Yoreh De'a* 340:17).

Everyone eats the mourner's meal over him – הַכֹּל מַבְרִין עָלָיו: Everyone eats the mourner's meal over the death of a Torah scholar in the public square, even during the intermediate days of a Festival, because everyone is considered to be like his relative (*Shulḥan Arukh*, *Yoreh De'a* 401:4).

Rending garments over an upright person – קְרִיעָה עַל אָדָם כָּשֵׁר: When an upright person dies, one rends his garment between the time of death and burial as a sign of mourning. An upright person is one who is not suspected of committing grave sins or avoiding performance of any mitzva, even if he is not knowledgeable in Torah. Some say that a person does not fall into this category unless he is well known for his acts of kindness (*Shakh*, *Baḥ* citing Rabbeinu Yona and Ramban). Torah scholars are not required to rend their garments over such a person; however, some Torah scholars are strict and rend their garments nevertheless (*Shakh*, citing Ra'avad and Rosh).

Others say that only one who is present at the time of the departure of the soul is required to rend his garment over an upright person, however one is required to cry and mourn over him in every case. It is the accepted practice to be lenient and not to rend one's garment (*Shulḥan Arukh*, *Yoreh De'a* 340:6 and in the comment of Rema).

אִי דְּקָאֵי הָתָם בִּשְׁעַת יְצִיאַת נְשָׁמָה – חַיּוּבֵי מִיחַיַּיב, דְּתַנְיָא, רַבִּי שִׁמְעוֹן בֶּן אֶלְעָזָר אוֹמֵר: הָעוֹמֵד עַל הַמֵּת בִּשְׁעַת יְצִיאַת נְשָׁמָה – חַיָּיב לִקְרוֹעַ. לְמָה זֶה דּוֹמֶה? לְסֵפֶר תּוֹרָה שֶׁנִּשְׂרַף, שֶׁחַיָּיב לִקְרוֹעַ!

The Gemara challenges: But **if one was standing there at the time of the soul's departure,** i.e., at the time of death, he **is also obligated** to rend his clothes. **As it is taught** in a *baraita*: **Rabbi Shimon ben Elazar says: One who stands over the deceased at the time of the soul's departure is obligated to rend** his clothes.[H] **To what may this be likened? To a Torah scroll that is burned,**[N] for which anyone present **is obligated to rend** his clothes.

דְּלָא קָאֵי הָתָם בִּשְׁעַת יְצִיאַת נְשָׁמָה.

The Gemara answers: The mishna must be referring to a person **who was not standing there at the time of the soul's departure** but who heard that someone who is not a close relative died, and the deceased was neither a Torah scholar nor an upright person.

כִּי נָח נַפְשֵׁיהּ דְּרַב סָפְרָא לָא קְרָעוּ רַבָּנַן עֲלֵיהּ. אָמְרִי: לָא גָּמְרִינַן מִינֵּיהּ. אֲמַר לְהוּ אַבַּיֵּי: מִי תַּנְיָא הָרַב שֶׁמֵּת? חָכָם שֶׁמֵּת תַּנְיָא. וְעוֹד: כָּל יוֹמָא שְׁמַעְתְּתֵיהּ בְּפוּמִין בְּבֵי מִדְרָשָׁא.

§ The Gemara relates that **when Rav Safra**[P] **passed away the** other **Sages did not rend** their garments **over him.**[N] **They said: We did not learn from him,** as he did not disseminate his Torah knowledge to the public. **Abaye** berated them and **said to them: Is it taught** in the *baraita*: If one's **teacher died? It is taught:** If a **Torah scholar died,** and Rav Safra was certainly a Torah scholar. **And furthermore, every day his teachings are in our mouths in the study hall,** so that even if we did not learn directly from him, we should still be considered his students.

סְבוּר: מַה דַּהֲוָה – הֲוָה. אֲמַר לְהוּ אַבַּיֵּי, תָּנֵינָא: חָכָם, כָּל זְמַן שֶׁעוֹסְקִין בְּהֶסְפֵּד – חַיָּיבִין לִקְרוֹעַ. סְבוּר לְמִיקְרַע לְאַלְתַּר. אֲמַר לְהוּ אַבַּיֵּי, תַּנְיָא: חָכָם כְּבוֹדוֹ בְּהֶסְפֵּידוֹ.

The other Sages **thought that what was** done **was** done, and it was now too late for them to rend their garments. **Abaye said to them: We learned:** With regard to a Torah **scholar, as long as they are engaged in eulogizing** him, then people **are obligated to rend** their garments, even after the time of his death. **They** then **thought to rend** their garments **immediately. Abaye said to them: It is taught** in a *baraita*: **A Torah scholar's honor is at** the time of **his eulogy,** and so you should wait until the time of the eulogy before rending your garments.

כִּי נָח נַפְשֵׁיהּ דְּרַב הוּנָא, סְבוּר לְאוֹתוּבֵי סֵפֶר תּוֹרָה אַפּוּרְיֵיהּ. אֲמַר לְהוּ רַב חִסְדָּא: מִילְּתָא דִּבְחַיֵּיהּ לָא סְבִירָא לֵיהּ, הָשְׁתָּא לֵיקוּם לֵיהּ לִיעֲבַד לֵיהּ? דְּאָמַר רַב תַּחְלִיפָא: אֲנָא חֲזִיתֵיהּ לְרַב הוּנָא דְּבָעֵי לְמֵיתַב אַפּוּרְיֵיהּ, וַהֲוָה מַנַּח סֵפֶר תּוֹרָה עֲלֵיהּ, וְכָף כַּדָּא אַאַרְעָא וְאוֹתִיב סֵפֶר תּוֹרָה עִילָּוֵיהּ. אַלְמָא קָסָבַר: אָסוּר לֵישֵׁב עַל גַּבֵּי מִטָּה שֶׁסֵּפֶר תּוֹרָה מוּנָּח עָלֶיהָ.

§ The Gemara relates another incident: **When Rav Huna**[P] **died they thought to place a Torah scroll on his bier,** as was commonly done after the death of a Torah scholar, as if to say that the deceased fulfilled everything written in the scroll. **Rav Ḥisda said to them:** This is **a practice that he did not hold with during his lifetime; now should we stand up and do** it **for him** when he is dead? **As Rav Taḥlifa said: I myself saw Rav Huna, who wished to sit on his bed, and there was a Torah scroll placed on it. And he turned a jug over and placed the Torah scroll on it** so that he could then sit on the bed. **Apparently he holds** that **it is prohibited to sit on a bed upon which a Torah scroll lies.**[H] Therefore, it would be inappropriate to lay a Torah scroll next to his body after he died.[H]

HALAKHA

Rending garments at the time of the soul's departure – קְרִיעָה בִּשְׁעַת יְצִיאַת נְשָׁמָה: One who is in the presence of a Jew whose soul departs is required to rend his garment. This applies whether the deceased is a man or a woman, but does not apply to a minor who has died (*Shakh*, citing Maharshal), unless he has already studied Torah (*Shakh*, citing *Baḥ*). This applies even if he was not an upright person, and it is known that he occasionally sinned due to his desires or was negligent and did not trouble himself to perform a certain mitzva. However, one does not rend his garment over one who habitually sins, and even more so over an apostate (*Shulḥan Arukh*, *Yoreh De'a* 340:5).

A Torah scroll on the bier of a Torah scholar's – סֵפֶר תּוֹרָה עַל מִיטַּת חָכָם: A Torah scroll is not placed on the bier of a Torah scholar who died, as demonstrated in the incident with Rav Huna (*Shulḥan Arukh*, *Yoreh De'a* 353:2).

Sitting in a place on which a Torah scroll is resting – יְשִׁיבָה בְּמָקוֹם שֶׁמּוּנָּח סֵפֶר תּוֹרָה: It is prohibited to sit on a chair or bench on which a Torah scroll is resting. It is appropriate to be stringent and to raise the Torah ten handbreadths from where one is sitting, or at least three (*Shakh*, citing *Beit Yosef*), but after the fact, one handbreadth is sufficient (*Shakh*; *Shulḥan Arukh*, *Yoreh De'a* 282:7).

NOTES

To a Torah scroll that is burned – לְסֵפֶר תּוֹרָה שֶׁנִּשְׂרַף: The early authorities offer several explanations for this comparison. Rashi and Rabbeinu Gershom Meor HaGola explain that as one's soul and a Torah scroll are both likened to a candle of God, the mourning for both should be the same. The text of Rashi printed alongside the Rif, and cited in Rashi's name by the Ran, states that since the deceased could have studied more Torah during his lifetime but did not succeed in doing so, it is comparable to a Torah scroll that was burned.

The Ramban writes that just as one rends his garment for a Torah scroll that is burned, so too one rends them over a person who observes the Torah's mitzvot. He similarly explains that the relationship between the body and the soul is similar to that between the parchment and the letters. Once a scroll is burned the letters leave the page, just like the soul departs from the body. Others write that one rends his garment because of the sanctity of the soul that departs from the body (Commentary on *Moed Katan*). Rashi writes in tractate *Shabbat* that since even the most ignorant Jew is filled with mitzvot, every person is similar to a Torah scroll.

The Sages did not rend their garments over him – לָא קְרָעוּ רַבָּנַן עֲלֵיהּ: The early authorities ask: Even if Rav Safra was not their teacher, he was certainly an upright person, so why did they not rend their clothes over him? Some say that rending garments over an upright person is only done between the death and the burial. Since this discussion occurred after the burial the Sages thought that they did not need to rend their garments (Ra'avad). Others write that Torah scholars do not rend their garments over an upright person unless he is a Torah scholar of their stature (Ramban).

PERSONALITIES

Rav Safra – רַב סָפְרָא: Rav Safra was an *amora* from the third and fourth generation of *amora'im* in Babylonia. The Talmud records that Rav Safra discussed halakhic matters as a disciple-colleague of the greatest Sages of the third generation of *amora'im*, such as Rabba and Rav Yosef, and continued to flourish into the time of their students Abaye and Rava. Apparently Rav Safra was a merchant, and visited Eretz Yisrael, where he interacted with Sages such as Rabbi Abba and Rabbi Abbahu. He was primarily knowledgeable about *halakha*, and devoted less attention to the study of *aggada* or Bible. Rav Safra was also well known for his character traits, particularly with regard to his desire to entirely avoid falsehood. Because Rav Safra traveled from place to place he did not have his own academy and he was often absent from the study hall. Therefore, some Sages thought that he did not qualify as a Sage for whom everyone mourns.

Rav Huna – רַב הוּנָא: One of the greatest second-generation of *amora'im* in Babylonia, Rav Huna succeeded his primary teacher, Rav, as the head of the academy in Sura. After Shmuel passed away Rav Huna was considered by all to be the most learned scholar in Babylonia.

Under his tenure, the yeshiva of Sura experienced significant growth, both in the number of its students and in their quality. Almost all of the Sages of the next generation were considered Rav Huna's students to a certain degree. This included Rav Ami and Rav Asi, who studied from Rav Huna in Babylonia. Even after they moved to Eretz Yisrael and were recognized as the leading Sages there, they considered themselves subordinate to Rav Huna.

According to a tradition recorded by the *ge'onim*, Rav Huna was from the family of the Exilarch. Nonetheless, he was very poor in his youth, but he studied Torah despite his poverty. He became wealthy later in life (see 27b). The Talmud recounts numerous anecdotes about Rav Huna's piety (see *Ta'anit* 20b), and his wisdom was legendary.

Rav Huna lived for over eighty years, and after his death he was brought with great honor to Eretz Yisrael, where he was buried next to the great Sage Rabbi Ḥiyya.

Rav Huna's son, Rabba bar Rav Huna, was among the most prominent *amora'im* of the next generation.

לָא הֲוָה נָפֵיק פּוּרְיָא מִבָּבָא, סְבוּר לְשַׁלְשׁוּלֵי דֶּרֶךְ גַּגִּין. אֲמַר לְהוּ רַב חִסְדָּא: הָא גְּמֵירְנָא מִינֵּיהּ: חָכָם כְּבוֹדוֹ דֶּרֶךְ פֶּתַח.

When they tried to remove his corpse from his house for the burial, **the bier would not** fit **through the** narrow **door. They** then **thought to lower** the bier **from the roof. Rav Ḥisda said to them: This I learned from him,** Rav Huna himself: **A scholar's honor** is for him to be taken out **through the** main **opening,** and not in any other manner.

סְבוּר לְאַשְׁנוּיֵי מִפּוּרְיָא לְפוּרְיָא. אֲמַר לְהוּ רַב חִסְדָּא, הָכִי גְּמֵירְנָא מִינֵּיהּ: חָכָם, כְּבוֹדוֹ בְּמִטָּה רִאשׁוֹנָה. דַּאֲמַר רַב יְהוּדָה אָמַר רַב: מִנַּיִן לְחָכָם שֶׁכְּבוֹדוֹ בְּמִטָּה רִאשׁוֹנָה? שֶׁנֶּאֱמַר: ״וַיַּרְכִּיבוּ אֶת אֲרוֹן הָאֱלֹהִים אֶל עֲגָלָה חֲדָשָׁה״. פְּרוּס בָּבָא, וְאַפְּקוּהָ.

They then **thought to move him from** his **bier to** a narrower **bier** so that it would fit through the door. But **Rav Ḥisda said to them: I learned from him,** Rav Huna himself, **as follows: A scholar's honor is** for him to be taken out **on the first bier.**[H] **As Rav Yehuda said that Rav said: From where is** it derived that **a scholar's honor is** for him to be taken out **on the first bier? As it is stated: "And they set the Ark of God upon a new cart"** (II Samuel 6:3).[N] When taking the Ark to Jerusalem, King David had it placed back on the cart upon which it had been returned by the Philistines, and a Torah scholar is considered to be similar to the Ark of the Covenant. When they saw that there was nothing else that they could do, **they broke the doorway and took him out** through it.

פְּתַח עֲלֵיהּ רַבִּי אַבָּא: רָאוּי הָיָה רַבֵּינוּ שֶׁתִּשְׁרֶה עָלָיו שְׁכִינָה, אֶלָּא שֶׁבָּבֶל גָּרְמָה לֵיהּ.

Rabbi Abba opened his eulogy for **him: Our Rabbi was worthy that the Divine Presence should rest upon him, except** for the fact **that Babylonia caused it** not to rest. In other words, it was only because he lived in Babylonia and not in Eretz Yisrael that the Divine Presence did not rest upon him.

מְתִיב רַב נַחְמָן בַּר חִסְדָּא, וְאָמְרִי לַהּ רַב חָנָן בַּר חִסְדָּא: ״הָיֹה הָיָה דְבַר ה׳ אֶל יְחֶזְקֵאל בֶּן בּוּזִי הַכֹּהֵן בְּאֶרֶץ כַּשְׂדִּים״!

Rav Naḥman bar Ḥisda raised an objection against this, **and** some say that it was **Rav Ḥanan bar Ḥisda:** Is it not stated: **"The word of the Lord came** [*hayo haya*] **to Ezekiel the priest, son of Buzi, in the land of the Chaldeans"** (Ezekiel 1:3), thereby implying that a prophet can prophesy outside of Eretz Yisrael?

טְפַח לֵיהּ אֲבוּהּ בְּסַנְדְּלֵיהּ. אֲמַר לֵיהּ: לָאו אָמֵינָא לָךְ לָא תִּיטְרוֹד עָלְמָא? מַאי ״הָיָה״? שֶׁהָיָה כְּבָר.

His father tapped him with his sandal on his foot, thereby hinting to him that he should be quiet. **He said to him: Have I not told you not to trouble everyone** with questions in the middle of a eulogy? The Gemara answers the question: **What** is the meaning of the doubling of the word **"came** [*hayo haya*]"? It implies **that it had already come** before,[N] i.e., that Ezekiel had already begun to prophesy in Eretz Yisrael, and his prophecy in Babylonia was merely a continuation of that prophecy.

כִּי אַסְּקוּהּ לְהָתָם אֲמַרוּ לֵיהּ לְרַבִּי אַמִי וּלְרַבִּי אַסִּי: רַב הוּנָא אָתֵי. אֲמַרוּ: כִּי הָוֵינַן הָתָם לָא הֲוָה לָן לְדַלּוּיֵי רֵישִׁין מִינֵּיהּ, הַשְׁתָּא אָתֵינַן הָכָא אֲתָא בַּתְרִין?

§ The Gemara relates that **when they took** Rav Huna **there,** to Eretz Yisrael, for burial **they said to Rabbi Ami and Rabbi Asi: Rav Huna has come,** and they misunderstood and thought that he was still alive. **They said: When we were there,** in Babylonia, we **did not have strength to lift our heads before him. Now** that **we have come here, has he come after us?**

אֲמָרוּ לֵיהּ: אֲרוֹנוֹ בָּא. רַבִּי אַמִי וְרַבִּי אַסִי נְפוּק, רַבִּי אִילָא וְרַבִּי חֲנִינָא לָא נְפוּק. אִיכָּא דְּאָמְרִי: רַבִּי אִילָא נְפַק, רַבִּי חֲנִינָא לָא נְפַק.

They said to them: His coffin has come. Rabbi Ami and Rabbi Asi went out to meet his funeral procession. **Rabbi Ila and Rabbi Ḥanina did not go out. Some say that Rabbi Ila went out,** but **Rabbi Ḥanina did not go out.**

HALAKHA

A scholar's honor is on the first bier – **חָכָם, כְּבוֹדוֹ בְּמִטָּה רִאשׁוֹנָה**: It accords honor to a deceased Torah scholar to take his body out of his house through the doorway and not by lowering him from the roof. Similarly he should not be moved from one bier to another. Nowadays people are not particular about this (*Arukh HaShulḥan*; *Shulḥan Arukh, Yoreh De'a* 353:3).

NOTES

And they set…upon a new cart – **וַיַּרְכִּבוּ...אֶל עֲגָלָה חֲדָשָׁה**: Rashi explains that the cart mentioned here is the one on which the Philistines returned the Ark (I Samuel, chapter 6). See also Rabbeinu Gershom Meor HaGola and the Commentary on *Moed Katan*. The early authorities ask with regard to Rashi's explanation: It is stated explicitly (I Samuel 6:14) that this cart was destroyed and its wood was used to burn the cows that dragged the cart, as a burnt offering. There are some who explain that the cart was not entirely destroyed. However, this explanation is implausible. Some explain that the new cart refers to a different cart that was constructed in order to transport the ark (*Tosefot HaRosh*; see *HaKotev* on *Ein Ya'akov*). The Meiri adds to this explanation that the fact that Uzza died as a punishment (II Samuel 6:7) shows that moving the Ark to a new cart, and not transporting it on the original, was itself a transgression.

That it had already come – **שֶׁהָיָה כְּבָר**: Although there were prophets who prophesied outside of Eretz Yisrael, that happened only before the Jewish people entered their land, and from that point onward prophets prophesied only in Eretz Yisrael (*HaKotev* in *Ein Ya'akov*). The explanation that Ezekiel was a prophet even before he was exiled to Babylonia, which is mentioned in Rashi, is also mentioned in *midrashim* (see Maharsha). The *Kuzari* explains Ezekiel's prophecy differently, and notes that Ezekiel was able to prophesy in the Diaspora because he did so for the sake of Eretz Yisrael.

דִּנְפַק מַאי טַעֲמֵיהּ? דְּתַנְיָא: אָרוֹן הָעוֹבֵר מִמָּקוֹם לְמָקוֹם – עוֹמְדִים עָלָיו בְּשׁוּרָה, וְאוֹמְרִים עָלָיו בִּרְכַּת אֲבֵלִים וְתַנְחוּמֵי אֲבֵלִים. דְּלָא נְפַק מַאי טַעֲמָא? דְּתַנְיָא: אָרוֹן הָעוֹבֵר מִמָּקוֹם לְמָקוֹם – אֵין עוֹמְדִין עָלָיו בְּשׁוּרָה, וְאֵין אוֹמְרִים עָלָיו בִּרְכַּת אֲבֵלִים וְתַנְחוּמֵי אֲבֵלִים.

The Gemara asks: Those who **went out, what is the reason** that they went? **As it is taught** in a *baraita*: When a **coffin is passing from place to place,**[H] the people **stand in a line** to show respect **for** the deceased, **and they recite the mourners' blessing and the consolation of the mourners over it.** Those **who did not go out, what is the reason** that they did not? **As it is taught** in another *baraita*: When a **coffin is passing from place to place, they do not stand in a line** to show respect **for** the deceased, **and they do not recite the mourners' blessing** or the **consolation of the mourners for him.**

קַשְׁיָין אַהֲדָדֵי! לָא קַשְׁיָא, כָּאן – שֶׁשִּׁלְדּוֹ קַיֶּימֶת; כָּאן – בְּשֶׁאֵין שִׁלְדּוֹ קַיֶּימֶת. וְרַב הוּנָא שִׁלְדּוֹ קַיֶּימֶת הֲוָה. דְּלָא נְפַק – לָא סַיְּימוּהּ קַמֵּיהּ.

The Gemara asks: If so, **these** two tannaitic statements **contradict each other.** The Gemara answers: **It is not difficult: Here,** the *baraita* is referring to a case **where the skeleton** of the deceased **is still intact,** and the mourning practices must be observed. **And there** the *baraita* is referring to a case **where the skeleton** of the deceased **is no longer intact,** and it is not necessary to observe the customs of mourning. **And Rav Huna's skeleton was** still **intact.** The reason that the **one** Sage **did not go out** was that **they did not confirm for him** that the skeleton was still intact.

אָמְרִי: הֵיכָא נִינְחֵיהּ? רַב הוּנָא רִיבֵּץ תּוֹרָה בְּיִשְׂרָאֵל וְרַבִּי חִיָּיא רִיבֵּץ תּוֹרָה בְּיִשְׂרָאֵל הֲוָה.

The Sages of Eretz Yisrael **said: Where shall we bury him?** They concluded: **Rav Huna disseminated Torah to** the people of **Israel, and** similarly **Rabbi Ḥiyya disseminated Torah to** the people of **Israel;** therefore, it is appropriate to bury Rav Huna next to Rabbi Ḥiyya.

מַאן מְעַיֵּיל לֵיהּ? אֲמַר לְהוּ רַב חַגָּא: אֲנָא מְעַיֵּילְנָא לֵיהּ, דְּאוֹקַמְתֵּיהּ לְתַלְמוּדַאי כִּי הֲוֵינָא בַּר תְּמָנֵי סְרֵי שְׁנִין וְלָא חֲזֵי לִי קֶרִי, וּמְשַׁמַּע לֵיהּ קַמֵּיהּ וְיָדְעִי בְּעוֹבָדֵיהּ. דְּיוֹמָא חַד אִתְהַפִּיכָא לֵיהּ רְצוּעָה דִּתְפִילִּין, וִיתֵיב עֲלָהּ אַרְבָּעִין תַּעֲנְיָתָא.

They asked: **Who will take him in**[N] to Rabbi Ḥiyya's burial cave, as few are fit to enter it? **Rav Ḥagga**[P] **said to them: I will take him into** the cave, **for I presented my studies** before him **when I was** just **eighteen, never having experiencing a seminal emission. And** so too **I attended to him and knew his** great **deeds.** For example, **one day one of the straps of his phylacteries turned around,**[N] the unpainted side being turned outward, **and he observed forty fasts for this,** as he had acted negligently, allowing the black side to face inward.

עַיְּילֵיהּ, הֲוָה גָּנֵי יְהוּדָה מִימִינֵיהּ דַּאֲבוּהּ, וְחִזְקִיָּה מִשְּׂמָאלֵיהּ. אֲמַר לֵיהּ יְהוּדָה לְחִזְקִיָּה: קוּם מִדּוּכְתִּיךְ, דְּלָאו אוֹרַח אַרְעָא דְּקָאִים רַב הוּנָא. בַּהֲדֵי דְּקָאִים קָם בַּהֲדֵיהּ עַמּוּדָא דְּנוּרָא, חַזְיֵיהּ רַב חַגָּא, אִיבְעִית, זְקַפֵּיהּ לַאֲרוֹנֵיהּ וּנְפַק, אֲתָא. וְהַאי דְּלָא אִיעֲנַשׁ עָנַשׁ – מִשּׁוּם דִּזְקַפֵּיהּ לַאֲרוֹנֵיהּ דְּרַב הוּנָא.

Rav Ḥagga **took him in.** The body of Rabbi Ḥiyya's son **Yehuda lay** buried **to the right of his father, and** the body of his other son **Ḥizkiyya** lay **to his left.** The spirit of **Yehuda said to** the spirit of **Ḥizkiyya: Rise from your place,** as it is **not proper conduct** to remain lying when the body of **Rav Huna is standing here. When** Ḥizkiyya's corpse **stood up, a pillar of fire rose with him.** When **Rabbi Ḥagga saw this, he was frightened** by what he saw, and so **he stood up** Rav Huna's **coffin**[N] **and went away.** The Gemara comments: **And he was not punished** or harmed by this pillar of fire **because he set up Rav Huna's coffin** as protection for himself.

כִּי נָח נַפְשֵׁיהּ דְּרַב חִסְדָּא סְבוּר לְאוֹתוּבֵי סֵפֶר תּוֹרָה אַפּוּרְיֵיהּ. אֲמַר לְהוּ רַבִּי יִצְחָק: מִילְּתָא דִּלְרַבֵּיהּ לָא סְבִירָא לֵיהּ, אֲנַן נֵיקוּם נַעֲבֵיד לֵיהּ?

§ The Gemara relates another story about the burial of one of the Sages: **When Rav Ḥisda died they thought to place a Torah scroll on his bier. Rabbi Yitzḥak said to them:** This is a **practice that this Rabbi did not hold with during his lifetime; should we stand up and do it for him** now that he is dead?

HALAKHA

A passing coffin – אָרוֹן מֵתִים הָעוֹבֵר: When a coffin is passing from place to place, if the skeleton of the deceased is still intact and there are mourners in that place then they stand in a line to honor the deceased and say the mourners' blessing and the consolation of mourners. If the skeleton is no longer intact then there is no need to do so (*Shulḥan Arukh, Yoreh De'a* 345:8).

NOTES

Who will take him in – מַאן מְעַיֵּיל לֵיהּ: Tractate *Bava Metzia* describes the great respect with which Rabbi Ḥiyya's grave was treated. Only a few unique individuals were able to enter and exit safely. The pillar of fire that accompanied Rabbi Ḥiyya is also mentioned there. Similarly, the sanctity of Rabbi Ḥiyya and his sons is compared to that of the Patriarchs. In the Jerusalem Talmud it is told that the Sages suspected that Rav Ḥagga, who was already old, wished to enter the grave so that he himself would also die in this holy burial place. The qualifications Rav Ḥagga presented are sufficient to explain why he was fit to enter and exit that cave.

One of the straps of his phylacteries turned around – אִתְהַפִּיכָא לֵיהּ רְצוּעָה דִּתְפִילִּין: Some explain that the strap turned over so that the black side, which should face outward, could not be seen (Rabbeinu Gershom Meor HaGola). Others say it was not the straps that turned over, but the letters of God's name, which are formed by the straps of the phylacteries, that were turned over. According to those who explain the passage in this manner, Rav Huna fasted so much because he was concerned that he had not properly fulfilled the mitzva and thought that this might have been a desecration of God's name. There are also those who explain that Rav Huna thought that if this happened to him it must be because he had accidentally sinned in another matter (Commentary on *Moed Katan*).

He stood up Rav Huna's coffin – דִּזְקַפֵּיהּ לַאֲרוֹנֵיהּ דְּרַב הוּנָא: Many of the early authorities had a version of this text that states that because of this action the Exilarch is never fully punished by Heaven for his sins. Rabbeinu Ḥananel explains that through the merit of Rav Huna, who was descended from the family of the Exilarch, and through the symbolic act of standing up the coffin, all of his family were privileged to enjoy greatness, even though they did not always deserve it.

PERSONALITIES

Rav Ḥagga – רַב חַגָּא: Rav Ḥagga was a Babylonian *amora* who moved to Eretz Yisrael and was active there. Rav Ḥagga was apparently a disciple-colleague of Rav Huna, as this is consistent with the chronological calculation. In the Jerusalem Talmud, where he is known by the name Rabbi Haggai, it is told that when Rav Ḥagga brought Rav Huna for his burial he was already eighty years old, and it is known that he lived for a time afterward. In Eretz Yisrael he interacted with the students of Rabbi Yoḥanan, although he also transmitted statements from the Sages of previous generations. It appears that he served as a judge in his city and several stories about his activity there are related in the Jerusalem Talmud and in the *midrashim*. The Sages of the following generations received numerous traditions in his name, and he became known as one of the leaders of his generation.

סבור דלא למישלל קרעייהו. אמר להו רבי יצחק בר אמי: חכם, כיון שהחזירו פניהם מאחורי המטה – שוללין.

They then **thought not to tack,** i.e., sew up, **the tears** that they had made in their clothes. **Rabbi Yitzḥak bar Ami said to them:** When the deceased is **a Torah Sage, they** may **tack** the tears **once they turn their faces from the bier.**[H]

כי נח נפשיה דרבה בר הונא ורב המנונא אסקינהו להתם,

The Gemara relates that **when Rabba bar Huna and Rav Hamnuna died, they took them** both **up there,** to Eretz Yisrael.

HALAKHA

Tacking a tear made over the death of a Sage – שלילת קרע על חכם: A tear made in mourning for the death of a Sage may be tacked and mended once one has turned his face from the coffin of the deceased (*Shulḥan Arukh, Yoreh De'a* 340:17).

Perek **III**
Daf **25** Amud **b**

כי מטו אגישרא קמו גמלי. אמר להו ההוא טייעא: מאי האי? אמרו ליה: רבנן דקא עבדי יקרא אהדדי. מר אמר: מר ניעול ברישא, ומר אמר: מר ניעול ברישא. אמר: דינא הוא דרבה בר הונא ליעול ברישא. חליף גמליה דרבה בר הונא, נתור כביה ושניה דההוא טייעא.

When they reached a bridge that could be crossed only in single file, **the camels** carrying the two Sages **stood** in their places and would not cross the bridge. **A certain Arab** [*Tayya'a*][L] who witnessed what was happening **said to them: What is this** phenomenon that the camels have stopped moving? **They said to him: The** deceased **Sages are showing honor to each other.** It is as if one **Sage is saying: The Master should go** and cross the bridge **first,** while at the same time the other **Sage is saying: The Master should go** and cross **first.** The Arab **said: By law**[N] **Rabba bar Huna should go first,** since he is the son of a great man, and **the camel** carrying **Rabba bar Huna** then **passed** first. Shortly thereafter, **the molars and** other **teeth of that Arab fell out** due to the disrespect he showed Rav Hamnuna.

פתח עליה ההוא ינוקא: "גזע ישישים עלה מבבל ועמו ספר מלחמות. קאת וקפוד הוכפלו, לראות בשוד ושבר הבא משנער. קצף על עולמו וחמס ממנו נפשות, ושמח בהם ככלה חדשה. רוכב ערבות שש ושמח בבא אליו נפש נקי וצדיק".

When they reached Tiberias **a certain child opened** his eulogy saying as follows: **The shoot of an ancient line,** i.e., Rabba bar Rav Huna, who was the descendant of great people, **has ascended from Babylonia, and with him is the book of wars,** i.e., Rav Hamnuna, who was great in Torah, which is referred to as the book of the Wars of the Lord (Numbers 21:14). **The curses** of the **pelican and the bittern,** which are symbols of the destruction of the Temple (Isaiah 34:11), **have been doubled,**[N] **to see the ruin and brokenness that has come from Shinar,** i.e., Babylonia. The Lord **became angry with His world and seized souls from it, and He rejoices over them** when they come to Him **like a new bride.** God **who rides upon the clouds is joyous and happy when an innocent and righteous soul comes to Him.**

כי נח נפשיה דרבינא פתח עליה ההוא ספדנא: "תמרים הניעו ראש על צדיק כתמר, נשים לילות כימים" – על משים לילות כימים.

§ The Gemara continues recounting other famous eulogies. **When Ravina**[P] **passed away, a certain eulogizer opened** his eulogy **for him** with the following words: **Date-palms, hang your heads** in sadness **over the righteous man who may be likened to a date-palm. Women,** make your **nights like days** in weeping, **over** a man who **made** his **nights like days** studying the Torah.

LANGUAGE

Arab [*Tayya'a*] – טייעא: The origin of this word appears to be the name of a specific Arab tribe called الطائي, *al-ṭāī*. The Arab tribes that resided in the desert area between Arabia and Babylonia would come to trade even as far as Babylonia.

PERSONALITIES

Ravina – רבינא: Ravina was a sixth generation Babylonian sage, whose major work was assisting Rav Ashi in editing the Babylonian Talmud. In his youth he studied under the direction of Rava. He passed away in the year 422. Ravina and Rav Ashi discuss matters of *halakha* in many places throughout the Talmud.

NOTES

By law [*dina hu*], etc. – דינא הוא וכו׳: Most versions of the talmudic text read: In my judgment [*bedina didi*], i.e., in my opinion, the great man who is also the son of a great man should go in front, before Rav Hamnuna who was not the son of a great man. This Arab was punished because it was not appropriate for him to offer his opinion on the issue, especially since there were people far more learned than him present at the time (*Iyyun Ya'akov*).

The curses of the pelican and the bittern have been doubled [*hukhpalu*] – קאת וקפוד הוכפלו: Several explanations are offered for this poetic expression. Rashi explains that the pelican and bittern are mentioned as signs of a curse, and therefore this means that the curse was doubled, as two great people died. Some explain that *hukhpalu* should be related to as an Aramaic word, meaning to strive. According to this, the expression means that even these birds made an effort to attend the funeral of the righteous men (*Arukh*; Rabbeinu Gershom Meor HaGola; Commentary on *Moed Katan*; Ran). Some understand this as a reference to the Arabs who joined them on the funeral procession (Maharsha). The Meiri explains that the pelican and bittern are symbolic and allude to the increase of weeping and eulogies.

אֲמַר לֵיהּ רַב אַשִׁי לְבַר קִיפּוֹק: הַהוּא יוֹמָא מַאי אָמְרַתְּ? אֲמַר לֵיהּ, אָמִינָא: אִם בַּאֲרָזִים נָפְלָה שַׁלְהֶבֶת – מַה יַּעֲשׂוּ אֵיזוֹבֵי קִיר, לִוְיָתָן בְּחַכָּה הוּעֲלָה – מַה יַּעֲשׂוּ דְּגֵי רְקָק, בְּנַחַל שׁוֹטֵף נָפְלָה חַכָּה – מַה יַּעֲשׂוּ מֵי גְּבִים.

The Gemara relates that prior to Ravina's death, **Rav Ashi**[P] **said to bar Kippok**, who was a famous eulogizer: **On that day** when Ravina will die, **what will you say?**[N] **He said to him: I shall** begin my eulogy and **say** as follows: **If the cedars went up in flame, what shall the hyssop of the wall do? If the leviathan was lifted by a hook, what shall the** tiny **fish of the marsh do? If a fish hook was cast into the flowing river, what can the water of the puddles do?**

אֲמַר לֵיהּ בַּר אָבִין: חַס וְשָׁלוֹם דְּחַכָּה וְשַׁלְהֶבֶת בְּצַדִּיקֵי אָמִינָא. וּמַאי אָמְרַתְּ? אָמִינָא: בְּכוּ לַאֲבֵלִים וְלֹא לַאֲבֵידָה, שֶׁהִיא לִמְנוּחָה וְאָנוּ לַאֲנָחָה.

Bar Avin, who was also a eulogizer, **said to him: God forbid** that the words **hook and flame** should be **said with regard to the righteous**, as these are not expressions of honor. Rav Ashi asked him: **And what will you say?** He said to him: **I shall say: Cry for the mourners and not for that which was lost,** as that which was lost, i.e., the soul of Ravina, has gone **to** its eternal **rest, while we,** the mourners, are left with our **sighs.**

חֲלַשׁ דַּעְתֵּיהּ עֲלַיְיהוּ, וְאִתְהַפּוּךְ כַּרְעַיְיהוּ. הַהוּא יוֹמָא לָא אָתוּ לְאַסְפּוּדֵיהּ. וְהַיְינוּ דְּאָמַר רַב אַשִׁי: לָא בַּר קִיפּוֹק חָלֵיץ, וְלָא בַּר אָבִין חָלֵיץ.

Rav Ashi **was offended by them,**[N] as their words of praise for Ravina might have been understood as a show of disrespect to Rav Ashi, since they likened Ravina to a cedar and the other Sages, Rav Ashi included, to hyssops of the wall. Due to Rav Ashi's anger, **their feet turned** inward and became crooked. **On that day** when Ravina actually died, **neither** of them **came to eulogize him. This is** what **Rav Ashi said** using a metaphor to describe this incident: **Neither bar Kippok can perform *ḥalitza*, nor can bar Avin perform *ḥalitza*,** because their feet are crooked and so their shoes cannot be removed from their feet in the proper manner.

רָבָא, כִּי הֲוָה אֲתָא לְדִגְלַת אֲמַר לֵיהּ לְבַר אָבִין: קוּם אֵימָא מִילְּתָא. קָאֵי וְאָמַר: בָּאוּ רוֹב שְׁלִישִׁית בַּמַּיִם, זְכוֹר וְרַחֵם. תָּעִינוּ מֵאַחֲרֶיךָ כְּאִשָּׁה מִבַּעֲלָהּ, אַל תַּזְנִיחֵנוּ כְּאוֹת מֵי מָרָה.

When Rava once **came to the Tigris**[N] River, and he was concerned that he might be swept away by the water, **he said to bar Avin: Rise** and **say** a prayer on our behalf. **He rose and said: Most of the third,** a poetic reference to the Jewish people (Isaiah 19:24), **has come**[N] **in the water,** implying that Rava was equal in importance to the majority of the Jewish people. **Remember** then **and have mercy** on us. Although **we have strayed from you like an** unfaithful **woman** strays **from her husband, do not forsake** and punish **us like the sign of the bitter water,** with which a woman suspected of adultery is tested. That is to say, do not punish us with water.

חָנִין יוֹחָנָן זֵירָא אַבָּא יַעֲקֹב יוֹסֵי שְׁמוּאֵל חִיָּיא מְנַחֵם – סִימָן.

Apropos eulogies for righteous men, the Gemara presents the names: **Ḥanin, Yoḥanan, Zeira, Abba, Ya'akov, Yosei, Shmuel, Ḥiyya,** and **Menaḥem;** this is a **mnemonic device** for the stories that follow.

רַבִּי חָנִין חֲתָנֵיהּ דְּבֵי נְשִׂיאָה הֲוָה. לָא קָא הָווּ לֵיהּ בָּנֵי, בְּעָא רַחֲמֵי וְהָווּ לֵיהּ. הַהוּא יוֹמָא דַּהֲוָה לֵיהּ – נָח נַפְשֵׁיהּ. פְּתַח עֲלֵיהּ הַהוּא סַפְדָּנָא: "שִׂמְחָה לְתוּגָה נֶהֶפְכָה, שָׂשׂוֹן וְיָגוֹן נִדְבָּקוּ, בְּעֵת שִׂמְחָתוֹ נֶאֱנַח, בְּעֵת חֲנִינָתוֹ אָבַד חֲנִינוֹ". אַסִּיקוּ לֵיהּ חָנָן עַל שְׁמֵיהּ.

It was related that **Rabbi Ḥanin was a son-in-law in the house of the *Nasi*.** At first **he did not have** any **children,** but **he prayed** that God have **mercy** on him, **and** then **had** a child. **On the** same **day** that a son was born **to him,** he himself **passed away. A certain eulogizer opened** his eulogy **for him** with the following words: **Happiness has been turned into sorrow; joy and suffering have become joined together.**[N] **At the moment of his happiness he sighed** his dying breath. **At the moment he was graced** with a son, **his** own **grace was lost. And they named** the child **Ḥanan after** his father.

NOTES

On that day what will you say – הַהוּא יוֹמָא מַאי אָמְרַתְּ: Some explain that Rav Ashi asked: What will the eulogizers say when our older colleague Ravina passes away? (Rabbeinu Ḥananel; Rashi, from manuscript). Others explain that he asked what the eulogizer would say when Rav Ashi himself died (Rashi; Rabbi Shlomo ben HaYatom; Ran).

Rav Ashi was offended by them – חֲלַשׁ דַּעְתֵּיהּ עֲלַיְיהוּ: According to those who understand this to be describing a eulogy for Ravina, the reason that he was offended is because the eulogizer implied that all other Sages, including Rav Ashi himself, were of lesser stature than Ravina.

Those who understand this to be a description of the eulogy for Rav Ashi explain that the wording of the eulogy made it seem as though the death of the righteous person was an accident, and not the result of Divine providence (see Maharsha). Rabbi Shlomo ben HaYatom explains simply that Rav Ashi was insulted because they should have first reassured him that he will live for a very long time, so that it would not appear as though they were already ready to eulogize him.

When Rava once came to the Tigris – רָבָא כִּי הֲוָה אֲתָא לְדִגְלַת: Most of the early authorities explain that this prayer was said when the Tigris River began to overflow (Rashi). According to other versions of the text, Rava requested that bar Avin pray that he would not drown in the river (see Commentary on *Moed Katan* in the *Ein Ya'akov* and Rashi there).

Most of the third has come – בָּאוּ רוֹב שְׁלִישִׁית: As the verse says: "And Israel shall be the third [*shelishiyya*]" (Isaiah 19:24), some explain that the term third, *shelishit*, refers to the Jewish people (Rashi; Rashi, from manuscript). Others explain that this term refers to the settled third of the world, and the flood was threatening to overtake a portion of the settled region. Alternatively, it is possible that the Tigris River itself is called the third because it is the third river listed in Genesis, chapter 2. The prayer means that this third river threatens to flood everything with its water (Ran).

Joy and suffering have become joined together – שָׂשׂוֹן וְיָגוֹן נִדְבָּקוּ: The Maharsha writes that the days of celebration over the birth of the child were exactly the same as the days of mourning over the father: The day of Rav Ḥanin's death was the day that the child was born, the day of his circumcision was on the seventh day of mourning, counting from the day of the funeral. The redemption of the firstborn was at the end of the thirty-day mourning period for Rav Ḥanin.

PERSONALITIES

Rav Ashi – רַב אַשִׁי: Rav Ashi was a sixth generation Babylonian sage whose major work was editing the Babylonian Talmud, together with Ravina. He was born in the year 352 and studied with Rav Kahana. Rav Ashi reestablished the academy in Sura, which had not functioned since the days of Rav Ḥisda, and he led that yeshiva for sixty years.

Rav Ashi and Ravina were not the first ones to edit the oral traditions, as there are many discussions in the Talmud whose language and style show that they were prepared long before Rav Ashi. Rav Ashi arranged the material that he received from previous generations, which emanated from different academies and was written in different styles, to produce an organized and uniform Talmud.

Various factors helped Rav Ashi undertake this great project, which ultimately was completed over a period of several hundred years. It is likely that Rav Ashi was assisted by a committee of scholars who gathered in the academy in Sura. It was due to the unique political environment and economic conditions at that time that a mission of this scope could be launched. The Babylonian king Yazdegerd I treated all of his citizens fairly and showed particular interest in the Jewish community, whose Sages he respected. Under his reign, the economic situation of the Jews of Babylonia was excellent, and they enjoyed relative freedom. These conditions allowed the Babylonian Sages to commit themselves to this the vast enterprise of redacting the Gemara.

כִּי נָח נַפְשֵׁיהּ דְּרַבִּי יוֹחָנָן פְּתַח עֲלֵיהּ רַבִּי יִצְחָק בֶּן אֶלְעָזָר: קָשֶׁה הַיּוֹם לְיִשְׂרָאֵל כְּיוֹם בֹּא הַשֶּׁמֶשׁ בַּצׇּהֳרַיִם, דִּכְתִיב: ״וְהָיָה בַּיּוֹם הַהוּא וְהֵבֵאתִי הַשֶּׁמֶשׁ בַּצׇּהֳרָיִם״. וְאָמַר רַבִּי יוֹחָנָן: זֶה יוֹמוֹ שֶׁל יֹאשִׁיָּהוּ.

When Rabbi Yoḥanan passed away, Rabbi Yitzḥak ben Elazar opened his eulogy for him as follows: Today is as difficult for the Jewish people as the day that the sun set at noon, as it is written: "And it shall come to pass on that day, says the Lord God, that I will cause the sun to go down at noon, and I will darken the earth in the clear day. And I will turn your feasts into mourning, and all your songs into lamentation; and I will bring up sackcloth upon all loins, and baldness upon every head; and I will make it as the mourning for an only son, and its end like a bitter day" (Amos 8:9–10). And Rabbi Yoḥanan said: This was the day on which King Josiah was killed (see II Chronicles 35:20–24). This demonstrates that the most righteous person of the generation is described as the sun.

כִּי נָח נַפְשֵׁיהּ דְּרַבִּי יוֹחָנָן יְתֵיב רַבִּי אַמִי שִׁבְעָה וּשְׁלֹשִׁים. אָמַר רַבִּי אַבָּא בְּרֵיהּ דְּרַבִּי חִיָּיא בַּר אַבָּא: רַבִּי אַמִי דַּעֲבַד – לְגַרְמֵיהּ הוּא דַּעֲבַד. דְּהָכִי אָמַר רַבִּי חִיָּיא בַּר אַבָּא אָמַר רַבִּי יוֹחָנָן: אֲפִילּוּ רַבּוֹ שֶׁלִּימְּדוֹ חׇכְמָה – אֵינוֹ יוֹשֵׁב עָלָיו אֶלָּא יוֹם אֶחָד.

It was further related that when Rabbi Yoḥanan passed away, Rabbi Ami sat in mourning for him for seven days and for thirty days as though he had lost a close relative. Rabbi Abba, son of Rabbi Ḥiyya bar Abba, said: What Rabbi Ami did, he did on his own, but this practice does not reflect the *halakha*. For Rabbi Ḥiyya bar Abba said that Rabbi Yoḥanan said as follows: Even for the death of his teacher who taught him wisdom, one sits in mourning over him for only one day and no more.[H]

כִּי נָח נַפְשֵׁיהּ דְּרַבִּי זֵירָא, פְּתַח עֲלֵיהּ הַהוּא סַפְדָּנָא: ״אֶרֶץ שִׁנְעָר הָרָה וְיָלְדָה אֶרֶץ צְבִי גִּידְּלָה שַׁעֲשׁוּעֶיהָ. אוֹי נָא לָהּ אָמְרָה רַקַּת, כִּי אִבְּדָה כְּלִי חֶמְדָּתָהּ״.

The Gemara tells of another incident about a eulogy: When Rabbi Zeira died, a certain eulogizer opened his eulogy for him saying: The land of Shinar conceived and gave birth to him, as he was originally Babylonian, but the land of beauty, i.e., Eretz Yisrael, raised the darling of Babylonia, as he later moved to Eretz Yisrael and grew up there. Woe to her, said Rakkath, a poetic name for Tiberias, for her dearest vessel has been lost.

כִּי נָח נַפְשֵׁיהּ דְּרַבִּי אַבָּהוּ אַחִיתוּ עַמּוּדֵי דְּקֵסָרִי מַיָּא; דְּרַבִּי יוֹסֵי – שָׁפְעוּ מַרְזְבֵי דְּצִיפּוֹרִי דְּמָא; דְּרַבִּי יַעֲקֹב – אִתְחַמִיאוּ כּוֹכָבֵי בִּימָמָא; דְּרַבִּי אַסִי – אִיעַקְרוּ כׇּל אִילָנַיָּא; דְּרַבִּי חִיָּיא – נְחִיתוּ כֵּיפֵי דְּנוּרָא מֵרְקִיעָא; דְּרַבִּי מְנַחֵם בְּרַבִּי יוֹסֵי – אִישְׁתָּעוּ צַלְמָנַיָּא וְהָווּ לְמֶחְלָצַיָּא;

The Gemara continues to discuss the death of the righteous: When Rabbi Abbahu passed away, the pillars of Caesarea, his city, ran with water[N] as if they were shedding tears over him. When Rabbi Yosei passed away, the gutters of Tzippori, his city, flowed with blood. When Rabbi Ya'akov passed away, the stars were visible during the day. When Rabbi Asi passed away, all the trees were uprooted in a storm. When Rabbi Ḥiyya passed away, fiery stones fell from the sky. When Rabbi Menaḥem, son of Rabbi Yosei, passed away, the faces of the statues became smooth as if they had been smoothed with a plasterer's trowel [*meḥlatzaya*].[L]

דְּרַבִּי תַּנְחוּם בַּר חִיָּיא – אִיתְקַצְּצוּ כׇּל אַנְדַּרְטַיָּא; דְּרַבִּי אֶלְיָשִׁיב – אִיחַתְרוּ שִׁבְעִין מַחְתַּרְתָּא בִּנְהַרְדְּעָא; דְּרַב הַמְנוּנָא – נְחִיתוּ כֵּיפֵי דְּבַרְדָּא מֵרְקִיעָא; דְּרַבָּה וְרַב יוֹסֵף – נְשׁוּק כֵּיפֵי דִּפְרָת אַהֲדָדֵי; דְּאַבַּיֵּי וְרָבָא – נְשׁוּק כֵּיפֵי דִּדְגְלַת אַהֲדָדֵי; כִּי נָח נַפְשֵׁיהּ דְּרַבִּי מְשַׁרְשְׁיָא טְעוּן דִּיקְלֵי שִׁיצֵי.

When Rabbi Tanḥum bar Ḥiyya passed away, every statue [*andartaya*][L] of the king were mutilated. When Rabbi Elyashiv passed away, seventy tunnels of thieves were dug[N] in Neharde'a, because as long as he was alive there were no thieves in the town due to his merit. When Rav Hamnuna passed away, hail stones fell from the sky. When Rabba and Rav Yosef passed away, the tops of the bridges of the Euphrates collapsed and touched each other. When Abaye and Rava passed away, the tops of the bridges of the Tigris collapsed and touched each other. When Rabbi Mesharshiyya passed away, the palm trees became laden with thorns [*shitzei*].[L]

תָּנוּ רַבָּנַן:

§ The Gemara returns to the subject of tearing garments in mourning: The Sages taught the following *baraita*:

NOTES

The pillars of Caesarea ran with water – אַחִיתוּ עַמּוּדֵי דְּקֵסָרִי מַיָּא: Rav Hai Gaon writes that the events described here were miraculous occurrences that happened in those days so that everyone would recognize what was lost when the righteous person passed away. However, the Meiri explains that all of these statements do not refer to actual events and instead are portions of eulogies, with each description being a colorful explanation of mourning for the death (see Ran). In any event, there is a relationship between what is stated here and the personalities of those who passed away. For example, for Rabbi Abbahu, who was the leader of the Jewish people and based in Caesarea, even the pillars of Caesarea shed tears. When the stars were visible during the day it was because the sky became dark in the middle of the day. When the faces of the statues were smoothed it was because Rabbi Menaḥem bar Yosei would not look at any image, even if there was only a slight concern that it was used for idol worship. Similarly, when the bridges collapsed, it was because bridges represent something that holds a community together.

Tunnels of thieves were dug – אִיחַתְרוּ...מַחְתַּרְתָּא: Some explain that this means that the number of thieves increased greatly, as during his life they were kept in check due to his merit. Others explain that these tunnels were holes that opened by themselves in the ground, alluding to the same idea (Commentary on *Moed Katan*).

LANGUAGE

Plasterer's trowel [*meḥlatzaya*] – מֶחְלָצַיָּא: Some explain that this word means plasterer's trowel, and in this context it means that the statues' faces were so smooth it was as though they had been smoothed over with a trowel. Others explain that the word means reed mats [*maḥatzalot*], and in this case the statues' faces were covered by mats. This also appears to be the meaning in other, parallel, sources.

Statue [*andartaya*] – אַנְדַּרְטַיָּא: Apparently from the Greek ἀνδριάντος, *andriantos*, meaning a statue of a person.

Thorns [*shitzei*] – שִׁיצֵי: This Aramaic word is ordinarily used to describe the hardened branches of a palm tree, which become quite sharp and thorny after several years.

Thorny palm branch

HALAKHA

Mourning over the death of a teacher – אֵבֶל עַל מוֹת הָרַב: One rends all of his garments in mourning when his primary Torah teacher dies. Similarly, a convert rends his garments over the death of the rabbi who accepted him as a convert (*Pitḥei Teshuva*, citing *Sha'arei Efrayim*). Some say that he rends only one handbreadth of his garment, but he may never mend this tear. In addition he should practice all the customs of mourning for a portion of the day on the day of death or the day on which he receives news of the death (*Shulḥan Arukh, Yoreh De'a* 242:25).

HALAKHA

Rending garments over one's teacher – **קריעה על רבו**: If one's teacher dies, from whom he had learned the majority of his Torah, whether it be Bible, Mishna, or Gemara, he must rend his garments until his heart is revealed, and some say that he is required to rend only one handbreadth of his garments. These tears may never be sewn, even if they were made upon hearing of the death only some time later. However, if one did not acquire most of his knowledge from this teacher, then he rends his garment over his death as he would over other relatives for whom he is required to mourn. Even if one learned only one thing from his teacher, he should rend his garments over this teacher's death. Some say that even a tear made over a teacher who was not one's primary teacher may not be sewn (Rema). Some say that colleagues who study with each other treat each other as their primary teacher, and some say that they treat each other like other teachers. There are also those who say that rending garments over a colleague or over a teacher from whom one learned a single thing is merely a stringency. Therefore, the common practice is to be lenient (*Shulḥan Arukh, Yoreh De'a* 340:8).

Rending garments over bad tidings – **קריעה על שמועות רעות**: Upon hearing bad tidings, e.g., a large part of the community went out to war, one makes a tear that may never be mended, even if only a few people died or were taken captive (Rema). In addition, this tear may be tacked only on the day following hearing the news (*Shakh*, citing *Beit Yosef*). This ruling is in accordance with the *baraita* and the Gemara's conclusion (*Shulḥan Arukh, Yoreh De'a* 340:36).

ואלו קרעין שאין מתאחין: הקורע על אביו, ועל אמו, ועל רבו שלימדו תורה, ועל נשיא, ועל אב בית דין, ועל שמועות הרעות, ועל ברכת השם, ועל ספר תורה שנשרף, ועל ערי יהודה, ועל המקדש, ועל ירושלים. וקורע על מקדש ומוסיף על ירושלים.

And these are the rents of mourning **that may never be** properly mended: **One who rends** his garments **for the death his father, or for his mother, or for his teacher who taught him Torah, or for the** *Nasi*, **or for the president of the court; or upon** hearing **evil tidings; or** hearing God's **name being blessed,** which is a euphemism for hearing God's name being cursed; **or when a Torah scroll has been burned; or upon** seeing **the cities of Judea** that were destroyed **or the** destroyed **Temple or Jerusalem** in ruins. This is the way one conducts himself when approaching Jerusalem when it lies in ruin: **He** first **rends** his garments **for the Temple and** then **extends** the rent **for Jerusalem.**

אביו ואמו ורבו שלימדו תורה מנלן? דכתיב: "ואלישע ראה והוא מצעק אבי אבי רכב ישראל ופרשיו". "אבי אבי" – זה אביו ואמו; "רכב ישראל ופרשיו" – זה רבו שלימדו תורה.

The Gemara elaborates upon the *halakhot* mentioned in this *baraita*: **From where do we** derive that one must rend his clothing for **his father, his mother, and his teacher who taught him Torah?**[H] **As it is written** with regard to the prophet Elijah, when he ascended to Heaven in a tempest: **"And Elisha saw it, and he cried, My father, my father, the chariots of Israel and their horsemen"** (II Kings 2:12). The Gemara interprets this verse as follows: **"My father, my father"; this** comes to teach that one must rend his garments for the death of **his father or mother. "The chariots of Israel and their horsemen"; this** comes to include also **one' teacher who taught him Torah.**

מאי משמע? כדמתרגם רב יוסף: רבי רבי, דטב להון לישראל בצלותיה מרתיכין ופרשין.

The Gemara asks: **From where** may it **be inferred** that this is referring to one's teacher? The Gemara explains: **As the verse was translated by Rav Yosef:**[N] **My teacher, my teacher, who was better for** the protection of the **Jewish people with his prayers than** an army with **chariots and horsemen.**

ולא מתאחין מנלן? דכתיב: "ויחזק בבגדיו ויקרעם לשנים קרעים". ממשמע שנאמר "ויקרעם" איני יודע שלשנים?! אלא, מלמד שקרועים ועומדים לשנים לעולם.

And from where do we derive that these rents **are never** to be properly **mended? As it is written: "And he took hold of his own clothes, and rent them in two pieces"** (II Kings 2:12). **From the fact that it is stated: "And he rent them," do I not know that** he rent them **in two** pieces? **Rather,** when the verse adds that they were torn into two pieces, **it teaches that they must remain torn in two** pieces **forever.** Accordingly, this rent must never be properly mended.

אמר ליה ריש לקיש לרבי יוחנן: אליהו חי הוא! אמר ליה: כיון דכתיב: "ולא ראהו עוד" – לגבי דידיה כמת דמי.

Reish Lakish said to Rabbi Yoḥanan: But isn't **Elijah** still **alive?** Why, then, did Elisha rend his garments for him? **He said to him: Since it is written: "And he saw him no more"** (II Kings 2:12), Elijah was **considered dead from** Elisha's perspective, and so Elisha rent his clothing for him.

נשיא ואב בית דין ושמועות הרעות מנלן? דכתיב: "ויחזק דוד בבגדיו ויקרעם, וגם כל האנשים אשר אתו. ויספדו ויבכו ויצומו עד הערב על שאול ועל יהונתן בנו ועל עם ה׳ ועל בית ישראל, כי נפלו בחרב".

§ **From where do we** derive that one must rend his clothing for the death of the *Nasi* or the **president of the court and** upon hearing **evil bad tidings?**[H] **As it is written,** when David heard about the defeat of Israel and the death of Saul and his sons: **"Then David took hold of his clothes, and rent them; and likewise all the men that were with him: And they mourned, and wept, and fasted until evening, for Saul and for Jonathan his son, and for the people of the Lord, and for the house of Israel; because they were fallen by the sword"** (II Samuel 1:11–12).

"שאול" – זה נשיא; "יהונתן" – זה אב בית דין; "על עם ה׳ ועל בית ישראל" – אלו שמועות הרעות.

The Gemara explains how the aforementioned *halakhot* are derived from the verse: **"Saul"; this is** a reference to the *Nasi*, as Saul was king of Israel. **"Jonathan"; this is** a reference to the **president of the court. "For the people of the Lord, and for the house of the Israel"; these are** a reference to **evil tidings.**

NOTES

As it was translated by Rav Yosef, etc. – **כדמתרגם רב יוסף וכו׳**: This explanation is necessary because without it we would think that Elisha rent his garments over the death of Elijah because Elijah was a prophet. We learn from this translation that Elisha rent his garments over him because Elijah was his teacher (Ritva).

אֲמַר לֵיהּ רַב בַּר שַׁבָּא לְרַב כָּהֲנָא: וְאֵימָא עַד דְּהָווּ כּוּלְּהוּ! אֲמַר לֵיהּ: "עַל" "עַל" הִפְסִיק הָעִנְיָן.

Rav bar Shaba said to Rav Kahana: But perhaps you can **say** that one need not rend his clothing **until all these** calamities occur together, and that rending clothing is performed only over a tragedy of this magnitude. **He said to him:** The repetition of the word "for": **"For** Saul," **"for** Jonathan," and "for the people of the Lord" **divides the matter** and teaches that each individual misfortune is sufficient cause to rend one's garments.

וּמִי קָרְעִינַן אַשְּׁמוּעוֹת הָרָעוֹת? וְהָא אֲמָרוּ לֵיהּ לִשְׁמוּאֵל: קְטַל שָׁבוֹר מַלְכָּא תְּרֵיסַר אַלְפֵי יְהוּדָאֵי בִּמְזִיגַת קֵסָרִי, וְלָא קְרַע! לֹא אָמְרוּ אֶלָּא בְּרוֹב צִבּוּר, וּכְמַעֲשֶׂה שֶׁהָיָה.

The Gemara asks: **But do we** actually **rend** our clothing upon hearing **evil tidings? But didn't they say to Shmuel: King Shapur killed twelve thousand Jews in Mezigat[L] Caesarea,[B] and** Shmuel **did not rend** his clothing? The Gemara answers: **They said** that one must rend his clothing upon hearing evil tidings **only** in a case where the calamity involved **the majority of the community** of Israel **and resembles the incident that occurred** when Saul was killed and the entire nation of Israel suffered defeat.

וּמִי קְטַל שָׁבוֹר מַלְכָּא יְהוּדָאֵי? וְהָא אֲמַר לֵיהּ שָׁבוֹר מַלְכָּא לִשְׁמוּאֵל: תֵּיתֵי לִי, דְּלָא קְטַלִי יְהוּדִי מֵעוֹלָם! הָתָם אִינְהוּ גָּרְמִי לְנַפְשַׁיְיהוּ. דְּאָמַר רַבִּי אַמִי: לְקַל יְתֵירֵי דִּמְזִיגַת קֵסָרִי פְּקַע שׁוּרָא דְּלוּדְקְיָא.

The Gemara tangentially asks: **Did King Shapur** really **kill Jews? But didn't King Shapur say to Shmuel: I have** a blessing **coming to me, for I have never killed a Jew?** The Gemara answers: King Shapur never instigated the killing of Jews; **there,** however, **they brought it upon themselves, as Rabbi Ami said** in an exaggerated manner: **Due to the noise of the** harp **strings of Mezigat Caesarea, the walls of Laodicea were breached,** for the residents of the city celebrated when they rebelled against King Shapur. Because they rebelled against him and threatened his rule, he was forced to kill them.

עַל בִּרְכַּת הַשֵּׁם מְנָלַן? דִּכְתִיב: "וַיָּבֹא אֶלְיָקִים בֶּן חִלְקִיָּה אֲשֶׁר עַל הַבַּיִת וְשֶׁבְנָא הַסּוֹפֵר וְיוֹאָח בֶּן אָסָף הַמַּזְכִּיר אֶל חִזְקִיָּהוּ קְרוּעֵי בְגָדִים".

§ The Gemara continues its analysis of the *baraita*: **From where do we** derive that one must rend his garments **upon** hearing God's **name being blessed,** i.e., cursed?[NH] **As it is written** with regard to the blasphemous words said by Rab-shakeh: **"Then came Eliakim, son of Hilkiya, who was over the household, and Shebna the scribe, and Joah, son of Asaph, the recorder, to Hezekiah with their clothes rent"** (II Kings 18:37).

תָּנוּ רַבָּנַן: אֶחָד הַשּׁוֹמֵעַ וְאֶחָד הַשּׁוֹמֵעַ מִפִּי הַשּׁוֹמֵעַ חַיָּיב לִקְרוֹעַ, וְהָעֵדִים אֵינָן חַיָּיבִין לִקְרוֹעַ, שֶׁכְּבָר קָרְעוּ בְּשָׁעָה שֶׁשָּׁמְעוּ.

The Sages taught a *baraita* with regard to this issue: Both **one who** actually **hears** the curse **and one who hears from the mouth of** the one **who heard** the curse **are obligated to rend** their garments. **But the witnesses** who testify against the person who uttered the blasphemy **are not obligated to rend** their clothing when they testify as to what they heard **because they already rent** their clothing **when they heard** the curse the first time.

בְּשָׁעָה שֶׁשָּׁמְעוּ מַאי הָוֵי? הָא קָא שָׁמְעִי הַשְׁתָּא! לָא סָלְקָא דַּעְתָּךְ, דִּכְתִיב: "וַיְהִי כִּשְׁמוֹעַ הַמֶּלֶךְ חִזְקִיָּהוּ וַיִּקְרַע אֶת בְּגָדָיו" – הַמֶּלֶךְ קָרַע, וְהֵם לֹא קָרְעוּ.

The Gemara asks: **What** difference **does** it make that they rent their garments **when they heard** the curse the first time? **Didn't they hear** it again **now?** The Gemara rejects this argument: **This will not enter your mind, as it is written: "And it came to pass, when King Hezekiah heard it, that he rent his clothes"** (II Kings 19:1). This indicates that **the king rent** his garments, **but** those who reported the blasphemy to him **did not rend** theirs, as they had already rent their garments the first time.

וְלָא מִתְאַחִין מְנָלַן? אָתְיָא קְרִיעָה קְרִיעָה.

And from where do we derive that these rents **may not be** properly **mended?**[N] **This is derived** by way of a verbal analogy between the verb **rending** used here with regard to Hezekiah and the verb **rending** used in the case of Elijah and Elisha.

LANGUAGE

Mezigat – מְזִיגַת: The variation *megizat* appears to be preferable, as it means passage or path and is similar to the Arabic مَجَاز, *majāz*.

BACKGROUND

King Shapur and Mezigat Caesarea – שָׁבוֹר מַלְכָּא וּמְזִיגַת קֵיסָרִי: The King Shapur mentioned here refers to the king of Persia, Shahpuhr the first, who ruled from 241–272 CE. He had especially close ties with the Sage Shmuel. King Shapur was the founder of the great Sassanid Empire, and he expanded its borders while waging numerous wars against the Romans. Through wartime journeys, he reached Anatolia and even Syria. Mezigat Caesarea appears to be the city of Kayseri in modern day Turkey, which was the capital of Cappadocia in that time. The residents of this place, including the Jewish residents, rebelled against the king. During the ensuing battle, the area changed hands many times. Due to the strategic importance of this area, this rebellion had an extremely great influence, and consequently, they said in an exaggerated manner that the walls of Laodicea, which was hundreds of kilometers away, shook due to this rebellion. Because of its strategic importance, the rebellion was strongly crushed by King Shapur, even though he ordinarily had warm relations with the Jews.

Bas-relief sculpture depicting the triumph of Shapur I over the Roman emperor Valerian

NOTES

From where do we upon hearing God's name being blessed, i.e., cursed – עַל בִּרְכַּת הַשֵּׁם מְנָלַן: Although it is not explicitly stated that God's name was cursed, Rab-Shakeh's statement implied disrespect toward God, for he compared the Holy One, Blessed be He, to the gods of others nations, and this is considered to be like a curse (Rashi on II Kings 18:37; see Maharsha).

And from where do we derive that these rents may not be properly mended – וְלָא מִתְאַחִין מְנָלַן: The Rosh disagrees with this derivation by means of verbal analogy. He prefers a textual variation mentioned by the Ra'avad: It is stated: "With torn garments" (II Kings 18:37). It is derived from this statement that the garments must remain torn forever.

HALAKHA

Rending garments over the cursing of God's name – קְרִיעָה עַל בִּרְכַּת הַשֵּׁם: One who hears a Jew curse God's name, even if the blasphemer uses another term to refer to God or speaks in a foreign language (Rema), is required to rend his garments. One who hears the Tetragrammaton being cursed is required to rend his garments, even if it is uttered by a gentile (*Shakh*, citing Ramban). However, one is not required to rend his garments upon hearing a gentile curse God's name more generally. Some say that today an apostate is considered to be like a gentile in this regard (Rema). If a Jew came and said that he heard a certain curse, then one who hears this report is required to rend his garments. Even when one hears from the witnesses in court who testify that so-and-so cursed God's name, he is required to rend his garments. Some say that if the witnesses do not explicitly state the curse, then one is not required to rend their garments (*Pitḥei Teshuva*, citing Rambam and *Semag*). The witnesses themselves, who have already rent their garments, are not required to do so a second time (*Shulḥan Arukh*, *Yoreh De'a* 340:37).

סֵפֶר תּוֹרָה שֶׁנִּשְׂרַף מְנָלַן? דִּכְתִיב: ״וַיְהִי כִּקְרֹא יְהוּדִי שָׁלֹשׁ דְּלָתוֹת וְאַרְבָּעָה וַיִּקְרָעֶהָ בְּתַעַר הַסֹּפֵר וְהַשְׁלֵךְ אֶל הָאֵשׁ אֲשֶׁר אֶל הָאָח״ וגו׳. מַאי ״שָׁלֹשׁ דְּלָתוֹת וְאַרְבָּעָה״?

§ **From where do we** derive that one must rend his garments when **a Torah scroll has been burned?**[H] **As it is written: "And it came to pass, that when Jehudi had read three or four leaves, he would cut it with a penknife, and cast it into the fire that was in the brazier"** (Jeremiah 36:23). With regard to the verse itself the Gemara asks: **What is meant by "three or four leaves,"** and why did he cut the book only at that point?

אֲמָרוּ לֵיהּ לִיהוֹיָקִים: כָּתַב יִרְמְיָה סֵפֶר קִינוֹת. אֲמַר לְהוּ: מַה כְּתִיב בֵּיהּ? ״אֵיכָה יָשְׁבָה בָדָד״. אֲמַר לְהוּ: אֲנָא מַלְכָּא. אֲמַר לֵיהּ ״בָּכוֹ תִבְכֶּה בַּלַּיְלָה״. אֲנָא מַלְכָּא. ״גָּלְתָה יְהוּדָה מֵעֹנִי״ – אֲנָא מַלְכָּא. ״דַּרְכֵי צִיּוֹן אֲבֵלוֹת״ – אֲנָא מַלְכָּא.

The Gemara explains: **They said to Jehoiakim: Jeremiah has written a book of Lamentations** over the future downfall and destruction of Jerusalem. **He said to them: What is written in it?** They read him the first verse: **"How does the city sit solitary"** (Lamentations 1:1). **He said to them: I am king,** and this does not apply to me. **They read him** the second verse: **"She weeps sore in the night"** (Lamentations 1:2). He said to them: **I am king,** and this does not apply to me. They read him the third verse: **"Judah is gone into exile due to affliction"** (Lamentations 1:3). He said to them: **I am king.** They read to him: **"The ways of Zion do mourn"** (Lamentations 1:4). He said to them: **I am king.** These are the four leaves, or verses, that he read first.

״הָיוּ צָרֶיהָ לְרֹאשׁ״ – אֲמַר לְהוּ: מַאן אֲמָרָהּ? ״כִּי ה׳ הוֹגָהּ עַל רֹב פְּשָׁעֶיהָ״. מִיָּד קָדַר כָּל אַזְכָּרוֹת שֶׁבָּהּ וּשְׂרָפָן בָּאֵשׁ. וְהַיְינוּ דִּכְתִיב: ״וְלֹא פָחֲדוּ וְלֹא קָרְעוּ אֶת בִּגְדֵיהֶם״, מִכְּלָל דְּבָעוּ לְמִיקְרַע.

They read him an additional verse: **"Her adversaries have become the chief"** (Lamentations 1:5), i.e., the reigning king will be removed from power. Once he heard this, **he said to them: Who said** this? They said to him: This is the continuation of the verse: **"For the Lord has afflicted her**[N] **for the multitude of her transgressions"** (Lamentations 1:5). **Immediately, he cut out all the names** of God **from** the book **and burned them in fire. This is as it is written: "Yet they were not afraid, nor rent their garments,** neither the king, nor any of his servants that heard all these words" (Jeremiah 36:24). **By inference,** this shows **that** they **were required to rend** their clothing[N] when they saw this.

אֲמַר לֵיהּ רַב פַּפָּא לְאַבַּיֵּי: אֵימַר מִשּׁוּם שְׁמוּעוֹת הָרָעוֹת! אֲמַר לֵיהּ: שְׁמוּעוֹת רָעוֹת בְּהַהִיא שַׁעְתָּא מִי הָווּ?

Rav Pappa said to Abaye: Perhaps you can **say** that they should have rent their garments **due to the evil tidings** contained in the scroll and not because of the destruction of the book? Abaye **said to him: Were they evil tidings at that time?** This was a prophecy and not an account of current events.

אֲמַר רַבִּי חֶלְבּוֹ אָמַר רַב הוּנָא: הָרוֹאֶה סֵפֶר תּוֹרָה שֶׁנִּקְרַע חַיָּיב לִקְרוֹעַ שְׁתֵּי קְרִיעוֹת: אֶחָד עַל הַגְּוִיל וְאֶחָד עַל הַכְּתָב, שֶׁנֶּאֱמַר: ״אַחֲרֵי שְׂרֹף הַמֶּלֶךְ אֶת הַמְּגִלָּה וְאֶת הַדְּבָרִים״.

Rabbi Ḥelbo said that **Rav Huna said: One who sees a Torah scroll that was torn is obligated to make two rents, one for the parchment** that was damaged **and one for the writing, as it is stated:** "Then the word of the Lord came to Jeremiah, **after the king had burned the scroll and the words"** (Jeremiah 36:27). This implies that a separate rent must be made for each of them, both the parchment and the writing.

רַבִּי אַבָּא וְרַב הוּנָא בַּר חִיָּיא הָווּ יָתְבִי קַמֵּיהּ דְּרַבִּי אַבָּא. בְּעָא לְאִפַּנּוֹיֵי, שְׁקַלֵיהּ לְטוֹטַפְתֵּיהּ אַחְתֵּיהּ אַבֵּי סָדְיָא. אֲתַאי בַּת נַעֲמִיתָא בְּעָא לְמִיבְלְעֵיהּ.

It was related that **Rabbi Abba and Rav Huna bar Ḥiyya were sitting before Rabbi Abba.**[N] Rabbi Abba **needed to relieve himself. He removed his phylacteries** from his head **and placed them on the cushion** on which he was sitting. **An ostrich**[B] **came and wanted to swallow** the phylacteries.

אֲמַר: הַשְׁתָּא אִיחַיְּיבִין לִי שְׁתֵּי קְרִיעוֹת. אֲמַר לֵיהּ: מְנָא לָךְ הָא? וְהָא בְּדִידִי הֲוָה עוּבְדָּא, וַאֲתַאי לְקַמֵּיהּ דְּרַב מַתָּנָה וְלָא הֲוָה בִּידֵיהּ, אֲתַאי לְקַמֵּיהּ דְּרַב יְהוּדָה, וַאֲמַר לִי: הָכִי אֲמַר שְׁמוּאֵל, לֹא אָמְרוּ אֶלָּא בְּזָרוֹעַ, וּכְמַעֲשֶׂה שֶׁהָיָה.

He said: Now, had it succeeded to swallow it, **I would have been obligated to make two rents. He said to him: From where do you** derive **this? There was an incident in which I** was involved **and I came before Rav Mattana** asking what to do, **but he did not have** an answer readily available. I then **came before Rav Yehuda, and he said to me: Shmuel said as follows: They said** that one is obligated to rend his clothing **only** when a Torah scroll or some other sacred book is torn **by force, and it resembles the incident that occurred**[N] with Jehoiakim.

HALAKHA

Rending garments over the burning of the Torah – קְרִיעָה עַל שְׂרֵיפַת הַתּוֹרָה: One is required to rend his garments twice upon seeing a Torah scroll, phylacteries, or even a scroll of Prophets or Writings being burned, erased, or torn by force, in order to destroy it (*Shulḥan Arukh, Yoreh De'a* 340:37).

NOTES

For the Lord has afflicted her [*hoga*] – כִּי ה׳ הוֹגָהּ: Some explain that the word *hoga* can be read as *haga*, uttered, meaning that it was the Lord who said this (Rashi, from manuscript).

By inference they were required to rend their clothing – מִכְּלָל דְּבָעוּ לְמִיקְרַע: The Rosh comments that the derivation mentioned here does not imply that it is prohibited to mend a tear made for a burned Torah scroll. Instead, he holds that it is possible to derive this through an *a fortiori* inference. If one rends his garments and may never mend them over the deaths of those who study the Torah, i.e., one's teachers, shouldn't this be the case all the more for the Torah itself?

Sitting before Rabbi Abba – יָתְבִי קַמֵּיהּ דְּרַבִּי אַבָּא: Some change the text of the Gemara, removing the phrase: Were sitting before, as how could Rabbi Abba sit before himself? Rav Betzalel Ronsburg explains that there is no need to alter the text, for there were several *amora'im* known as Rabbi Abba.

By force and it resembles the incident that occurred – בְּזָרוֹעַ וּכְמַעֲשֶׂה שֶׁהָיָה: Some explain that this term means specifically with violence and not by accident. One rends his garments only when the destruction occurs through human action and in a situation where the person seeing the burning cannot prevent it. However, one is not required to rend his garments if it occurred through an accident (Rashi, from manuscript). Some say that this applies only when the tearing was specifically done in order to anger God. Some of the later authorities suggest that one is required to rend his garments only when the act is performed by a Jew by force, as was the case with Jehoiakim (see *Tal Ḥayyim*).

BACKGROUND

Ostrich – בַּת נַעֲמִיתָא: The bird mentioned here is among those ordinarily found in the desert. However, elsewhere ostriches were also raised domestically, apparently for their feathers. These birds are well known for their inclination to swallow almost anything, even objects normally considered to be inedible.

עָרֵי יְהוּדָה מְנָלַן? דִּכְתִיב: ״וַיָּבֹאוּ אֲנָשִׁים מִשְּׁכֶם מִשִּׁילוֹ וּמִשֹּׁמְרוֹן שְׁמֹנִים אִישׁ מְגֻלְּחֵי זָקָן וּקְרֻעֵי בְגָדִים וּמִתְגֹּדְדִים וּמִנְחָה וּלְבוֹנָה בְּיָדָם לְהָבִיא בֵּית ה׳״ וגו׳.

§ From where do we derive that one must rend his garments upon seeing **the cities of Judea** in ruin?[NH] **As it is written: "There came certain men from Shechem, from Shiloh, and from Samaria, eighty people, their beards shaven, and their clothes rent, and having cut themselves, with offerings and incense in their hand, to bring to the house of the Lord"** (Jeremiah 41:5). This indicates that they rent their garments upon seeing the destruction.

אָמַר רַבִּי חֶלְבּוֹ אָמַר עוּלָּא בִּירָאָה אָמַר רַבִּי אֶלְעָזָר, הָרוֹאֶה עָרֵי יְהוּדָה בְּחוּרְבָּנָן – אוֹמֵר: ״עָרֵי קָדְשְׁךָ הָיוּ מִדְבָּר״, וְקוֹרֵעַ. יְרוּשָׁלַיִם בְּחוּרְבָּנָהּ – אוֹמֵר: ״צִיּוֹן מִדְבָּר הָיָתָה יְרוּשָׁלַיִם שְׁמָמָה״, וְקוֹרֵעַ. בֵּית הַמִּקְדָּשׁ בְּחוּרְבָּנוֹ – אוֹמֵר ״בֵּית קָדְשֵׁנוּ וְתִפְאַרְתֵּנוּ אֲשֶׁר הִלְלוּךָ אֲבוֹתֵינוּ הָיָה לִשְׂרֵפַת אֵשׁ וְכָל מַחֲמַדֵּינוּ הָיָה לְחָרְבָּה״, וְקוֹרֵעַ.

Rabbi Ḥelbo said that **Ulla Bira'a said** that **Rabbi Elazar said: One who sees the cities of Judea in their desolation says: "Your sacred cities are become a wilderness"** (Isaiah 64:9), **and then rends** his garments. One who sees **Jerusalem in its desolation says: "Zion is a wilderness, Jerusalem a desolation"** (Isaiah 64:9), **and then rends** his garments. One who sees **the Temple in its desolation says: "Our sacred and our beautiful house, where our fathers praised You, is burned with fire; and all our pleasant things are laid waste"** (Isaiah 64:10), **and then rends** his garments.

״קוֹרֵעַ עַל מִקְדָּשׁ וּמוֹסִיף עַל יְרוּשָׁלַיִם״. וּרְמִינְהוּ: אֶחָד הַשּׁוֹמֵעַ וְאֶחָד הָרוֹאֶה, כֵּיוָן שֶׁהִגִּיעַ לַצּוֹפִים – קוֹרֵעַ, וְקוֹרֵעַ עַל מִקְדָּשׁ בִּפְנֵי עַצְמוֹ וְעַל יְרוּשָׁלַיִם בִּפְנֵי עַצְמָהּ!

It was taught in the *baraita*: **He** first **rends** his garments **for the Temple and** then **extends** the rent **for Jerusalem. And they raise a contradiction** from another *baraita* that states: Both **one who hears** that Jerusalem is in ruin **and one who sees** the destruction, **once he reaches** Mount Scopus [*Tzofim*],[B] **rends** his garments. **And he rends** his garments **for the Temple separately and for Jerusalem separately.**

לָא קַשְׁיָא: הָא – דִּפְגַע בְּמִקְדָּשׁ בְּרֵישָׁא, הָא – דִּפְגַע בִּירוּשָׁלַיִם בְּרֵישָׁא.

The Gemara answers: **This is not difficult. This** *baraita*, which states that instead of making a separate rent for Jerusalem one may extend the first rent that he had made for the Temple, is referring to the case where **one reached the Temple first,** before seeing the rest of Jerusalem, and saw it in ruin. **That** *baraita*, which states that one must make separate rents for Jerusalem and for the Temple, is referring to the case where **one reached Jerusalem first,** and only afterward the Temple.

תָּנוּ רַבָּנַן: וְכוּלָּן רַשָּׁאִין לְשׁוֹלְלָן, וּלְמוֹלְלָן, וּלְלוֹקְטָן וְלַעֲשׂוֹתָן כְּמִין סוּלָּמוֹת, אֲבָל לֹא לְאַחוֹתָן.

§ **The Sages taught** the following *baraita*: **And all of these** rents, **one may tack them** together with loose stitches,[H] **and hem them,**[N] **and gather them, and fix them** with imprecise **ladder-like** stitches.[B] **But one may not mend them** with precise stitches.

אָמַר רַב חִסְדָּא:

Rav Ḥisda said:

NOTES

From where do we derive that one must rend his garments upon seeing the cities of Judea in ruin – עָרֵי יְהוּדָה מְנָלַן: The Gemara does not mention the cities of the kingdom of Israel is because in Judah it was known which cities had always been Jewish. However, in the Galilee, which was only partially settled by those who returned from Babylonia, they were unsure which cities were considered to be Jewish cities (Maharsha).

Tack them [*sholelan*] and hem them [*molelan*], etc. – לְשׁוֹלְלָן וּלְמוֹלְלָן: Several explanations are offered with regard to the details of these actions. Rabbeinu Yehonatan of Lunel explains that the words *shelila* and *melila* refer to types of tying without the use of a needle. However, when the Gemara refers to gathering them and fixing them with ladder-like stitches it means using an imprecise type of stitch, which does not fall into the category of sewing. Rashi explains that *sholelan* refers to tacking with wide stitches, *molelan* refers to binding the two edges of a tear together with two stitches, and gathering [*loktan*] refers to sewing a tear from top to bottom with proper stitching (Rashi, from manuscript).

HALAKHA

Rending garments over the cities of Israel and the Temple – קְרִיעָה עַל עָרֵי יִשְׂרָאֵל וְהַמִּקְדָּשׁ: If one sees the cities of Judea in their destroyed state, as he approaches he says: "Your sacred cities have become a wilderness" (Isaiah 64:9), and rends his garments. Even if the cities are inhabited by Jews, they are still considered to be destroyed as long as they are under foreign, gentile rule. As one approaches Jerusalem and reaches Mount Scopus [*Tzofim*], he recites the verse: "Zion has become a wilderness, Jerusalem a desolation" (Isaiah 64:9), and rends his garments. Some say that *tzofim* refers to a specific place, while others understand it to be any place from which Jerusalem is visible (see *Magen Avraham*). Practically speaking, since the area surrounding Jerusalem is built up one does not rend his garments before seeing the walls of the Old City (*Kaf HaḤayyim*). Afterward, when he sees the site where the Temple stood, he says: "Our holy and our beautiful Temple, where our fathers praised You, is burned with fire; and all our pleasant things are laid waste" (Isaiah 64:10), and he rends his garments a second time. These tears should be at least one handbreadth in length. If one arrives from the east and sees the ruins of the Temple first, then he should rend his garments over the Temple and extend this tear over Jerusalem. Anyone who has not seen the destroyed cities or the ruins of the Temple for thirty days must rend his garments again (*Shulḥan Arukh, Oraḥ Ḥayyim* 561:1–2 and Rema).

Tacking the tears – לְשׁלוֹל הַקְּרָעִים: Tears made over the death of one's father or Torah teacher, bad tidings, the burning of the Torah, the cities of Judea, or the Temple may never be sewn. However, they may be tacked and closed up in a different manner on the following day (*Shulḥan Arukh, Yoreh De'a* 340:39).

BACKGROUND

Tzofim – צוֹפִים: Some people explain that the word *tzofim* refers to a specific place, perhaps what is referred to today as Mount Scopus, from which one could see Jerusalem and the Temple. Others say that *tzofim* more generally refers to any place from which one can see the city of Jerusalem.

View of Jerusalem from Mount Scopus

View of Mount Scopus from Jerusalem

Ladder-like stiches – כְּמִין סוּלָּמוֹת: Connecting a tear with parallel stitches creates a ladder-like form

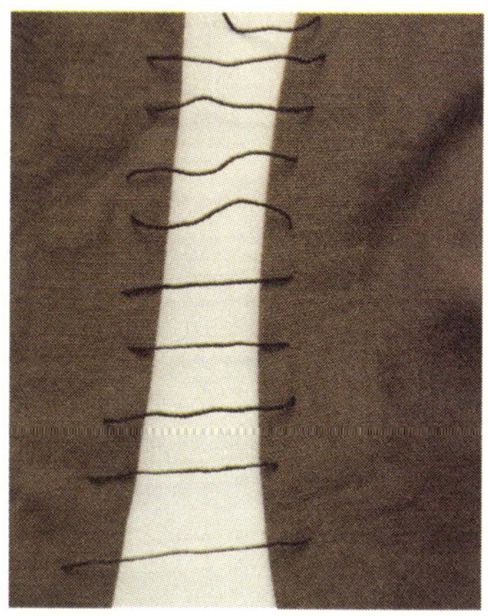

Ladder-like stitching

וּבְאִיחוּי אֲלֶכְּסַנְדְּרִי.

And the reference here is **to** the **Alexandrian** method of **mending,**[BNH] a type of sewing performed in Alexandria, which is considered to be of exceptional quality and after which the tear is no longer visible.

תָּנוּ רַבָּנַן: הַקּוֹרֵעַ מִתּוֹךְ הַשְּׁלָל, מִתּוֹךְ הַמְּלָל, מִתּוֹךְ הַלֶּקֶט, מִתּוֹךְ הַסּוּלָּמוֹת – לֹא יָצָא. מִתּוֹךְ הָאִיחוּי – יָצָא. אָמַר רַב חִסְדָּא: וּבְאִיחוּי אֲלֶכְּסַנְדְּרִי.

The Sages taught the following *baraita*: **One who rends** his garment in a place **that had been** loosely **tacked** together, or **from the hem of the garment,**[H] or **on the gathering,** or **on the ladder-like stiches has not fulfilled** his obligation to rend it. But if he rends it in a place **that had been** carefully **mended, he has fulfilled** his obligation, because such a garment is regarded as whole. **Rav Ḥisda said: And** here, too, the reference is **to the Alexandrian** method of **mending** and not to ordinary sewing.

תָּנוּ רַבָּנַן: רַשַּׁאי לְהוֹפְכוֹ לְמַטָּה וּלְאַחוֹתוֹ. רַבִּי שִׁמְעוֹן בֶּן אֶלְעָזָר אוֹסֵר לְאַחוֹתוֹ. וּכְשֵׁם שֶׁהַמּוֹכֵר אָסוּר לְאַחוֹתוֹ – כָּךְ הַלּוֹקֵחַ אָסוּר לְאַחוֹתוֹ. וּלְפִיכָךְ מוֹכֵר צָרִיךְ לְהוֹדִיעוֹ לַלּוֹקֵחַ.

The Sages taught another *baraita*: One is **permitted to turn** a garment that was rent on the upper edge **upside down and** then **mend** it in a precise fashion. **Rabbi Shimon ben Elazar prohibits** careful **mending** in this case as well. **And** if one wishes to sell a garment that he had previously rent in mourning, **just as the seller,** who had rent the garment, **is prohibited from** carefully **mending** the garment, **so too the buyer,** who purchases it from him, **is prohibited from mending it. The seller must therefore inform the buyer** that the rent was made on account of mourning and may not be mended.[H]

תָּנוּ רַבָּנַן: תְּחִילַּת קְרִיעָה טֶפַח, וְתוֹסֶפֶת שָׁלֹשׁ אֶצְבָּעוֹת, דִּבְרֵי רַבִּי מֵאִיר. רַבִּי יְהוּדָה אוֹמֵר: תְּחִילַּת קְרִיעָה שָׁלֹשׁ אֶצְבָּעוֹת, וְתוֹסֶפֶת כָּל שֶׁהוּ.

The Sages taught a *baraita*: **The initial rending is a handbreadth** in length, **and the extension,** if one is obligated to rend his garment for other deceased relatives and he wishes to use the same rent for this purpose, **is three fingerbreadths;** this is **the statement of Rabbi Meir. Rabbi Yehuda says:** The **initial rending is three fingerbreadths**[N] in length, **and** its **extension is any amount,** with no minimum measure.[H]

אָמַר עוּלָּא: הֲלָכָה כְּרַבִּי מֵאִיר בִּקְרִיעָה, וַהֲלָכָה כְּרַבִּי יְהוּדָה בְּתוֹסֶפֶת. תַּנְיָא נַמִי הָכִי, רַבִּי יוֹסֵי אוֹמֵר: תְּחִילַּת קְרִיעָה טֶפַח וְתוֹסֶפֶת כָּל שֶׁהוּ.

Ulla said: The ***halakha* is in accordance with** the opinion of **Rabbi Meir that** the initial **rending** is one handbreadth in length, **and the *halakha* is in accordance with** the opinion of **Rabbi Yehuda that an extension** can be any length. The Gemara comments: **That is also taught** in a *baraita*: **Rabbi Yosei says:** The **initial rending** is **one handbreadth, and the** size of the **extension is any** minimal **amount.** By tradition, the *halakha* is in accordance with the opinion of Rabbi Yosei when he disagrees with any one of his colleagues.

BACKGROUND

Alexandrian mending – **אִיחוּי אֲלֶכְּסַנְדְּרִי**: This refers to the city of Alexandria in Egypt. In ancient times, it was the center of science and technology in the Middle East, and perhaps in the entire world. Items of high quality were named for the city, and consequently the highest quality of sewing is referred to as Alexandrian sewing.

NOTES

Alexandrian mending – **אִיחוּי אֲלֶכְּסַנְדְּרִי**: Some say that this refers to precise sewing, in which the stitching is straight and smooth on the outer side of the garment, although it protrudes from the inner side of the garment (Ra'avad; Rabbeinu Yehonatan of Lunel). Others say that this refers to a type of mending through which the torn threads are removed and replaced and new threads are woven into the garment (Rabbeinu Ḥananel; Ramban; see Jerusalem Talmud). The Ritva writes that since the definition of Alexandrian sewing disputed, one should act stringently in accordance with both opinions. Therefore, it is prohibited for a mourner to mend a garment from one side. Conversely, only a garment that is properly mended may be rent in mourning. Some write that Alexandrian sewing refers to strong stitching, as opposed to tacking, which is imprecise, temporary stitching (Commentary on *Moed Katan*; Rabbi Shlomo ben HaYatom; Meiri).

The initial rending is three fingerbreadths – **תְּחִילַּת קְרִיעָה שָׁלֹשׁ אֶצְבָּעוֹת**: *Tosafot* ask how this measure is derived. Earlier (22b) the Gemara cited the verse "and he took hold" (II Kings 2:12) as a source. Some explain that this does not refer to holding with the entire hand, as it would then be a handbreadth; rather, it refers to the way people ordinarily hold a garment, with three fingers (Ritva).

HALAKHA

With Alexandrian mending – **בְּאִיחוּי אֲלֶכְּסַנְדְּרִי**: If a tear may not be mended, this prohibition includes Alexandrian sewing, in accordance with the opinion of Rav Ḥisda (Rambam *Sefer Shofetim, Hilkhot Evel* 9:3).

One who rends…from the hem, etc. – **הַקּוֹרֵעַ...מִתּוֹךְ הַמְּלָל וכו׳**: One who rends his garment in mourning from within a hem, or in a similar manner, does not fulfill his obligation to rend his garment. However, if he rends something that was attached with Alexandrian sewing, i.e., stitching that is not noticeable from the outside, then he fulfills his obligation in accordance with the opinion of Rav Ḥisda (*Shulḥan Arukh, Yoreh De'a* 340:20).

Tears that may not be sewn – **קְרָעִים שֶׁאֵינָם מִתְאַחִים**: All tears in this category may never be sewn, even if one turns the garment upside down so that the torn portion is on the bottom. Similarly, it is prohibited to purchase such a garment in order to sew it; therefore, one who sells a garment that was rent in mourning must inform the buyer (*Shulḥan Arukh, Yoreh De'a* 340:19).

The measure of the tear – **שִׁיעוּר קְרִיעָה**: One must tear his garment one handbreadth as a sign of mourning. If his garment was already torn and he heard within seven days of the death that another family member died, then he extends this tear one handbreadth. If the second death occurred more than seven days after the first death, then he may add any amount to the first tear. This ruling is in accordance with the opinion of Rabbi Yosei. However, it applies only to mourning over other relatives; for a father and mother, one is required to rend his garment until he reaches the point in the garment that covers his heart (*Shulḥan Arukh, Yoreh De'a* 340:3).

תָּנוּ רַבָּנַן: אָמְרוּ לוֹ מֵת אָבִיו, וְקָרַע, מֵת בְּנוֹ, וְהוֹסִיף, תַּחְתּוֹן מִתְאַחֶה, עֶלְיוֹן אֵינוֹ מִתְאַחֶה.

The Sages taught the following *baraita*: If **they** first **said to** a person that **his father died, and he rent** his garment, and afterward they told him that **his son died, and he added** to the same rent, in such a case the **lower** portion of the rent that had been made for his son **may be mended.** The is because, after completing the period of mourning, one is permitted to mend a rent made for relatives other than one's parents. However, the **upper** portion of the rent **may not be mended,** as a tear made for one's father may never be carefully sewn back together.

מֵת בְּנוֹ וְקָרַע, מֵת אָבִיו וְהוֹסִיף, עֶלְיוֹן מִתְאַחֶה, תַּחְתּוֹן אֵינוֹ מִתְאַחֶה.

If, on the other hand, they said to him first that **his son died, and he rent** his garment, and afterward they told him that **his father died, and he added** to the same rent, then in that case the **upper** portion of the rent, which that had been made for his son, **may be mended,** but **the lower** portion of the rent, which had been made for his father, **may not be mended.**

מֵת אָבִיו, מֵת אִמּוֹ, מֵת אָחִיו, מֵתָה אֲחוֹתוֹ, קוֹרֵעַ קֶרַע אֶחָד לְכוּלָּן. רַבִּי יְהוּדָה בֶּן בְּתֵירָה אוֹמֵר: עַל כּוּלָּן קֶרַע אֶחָד, עַל אָבִיו וְאִמּוֹ קֶרַע אֶחָד, לְפִי שֶׁאֵין מוֹסִיפִין עַל קֶרַע אָבִיו וְאִמּוֹ.

If they said to him all at one time that **his father died, his mother died, his brother died, and his sister died,** then **he may make one rent for all of them. Rabbi Yehuda ben Beteira says: For all** of his other relatives he makes **one rent,** and **for his father and mother** he makes **another rent, as one must not add** to a rent made **for his father and mother.**[H]

מַאי טַעְמָא? אָמַר רַב נַחְמָן בַּר יִצְחָק: לְפִי שֶׁאֵינָן בְּתוֹסֶפֶת.

The Gemara asks: **What is the reason** for Rabbi Yehuda ben Beteira's opinion that one may not add to the rent torn for a mother or father? **Rav Naḥman bar Yitzḥak said: Because they cannot be added;**[N] one has only one father and one mother and cannot add others.

אָמַר שְׁמוּאֵל: הֲלָכָה כְּרַבִּי יְהוּדָה בֶּן בְּתֵירָה. וּמִי אָמַר שְׁמוּאֵל הָכִי? וְהָאָמַר שְׁמוּאֵל: הֲלָכָה כְּדִבְרֵי הַמֵּיקֵל בְּאֵבֶל! אֲבֵילוּת לְחוּד, קְרִיעָה לְחוּד.

Shmuel said: The ***halakha*** **is in accordance with** the opinion of **Rabbi Yehuda ben Beteira.** The Gemara asks: **And did Shmuel** actually **say this? But didn't Shmuel say** the principle is that **the** ***halakha*** **is in accordance with the statement** of the **lenient** Sage with regard to **mourning;** yet here he rules in accordance with the more stringent opinion. The Gemara answers: The *halakhot* of **mourning are discrete** and the *halakhot* of **rending are discrete,**[N] and it is only with regard to the *halakhot* of mourning that Shmuel rules consistently in accordance with the lenient opinion.

עַד הֵיכָן קוֹרֵעַ? עַד טִיבּוּרוֹ, וְיֵשׁ אוֹמְרִים: עַד לִבּוֹ. אַף עַל פִּי שֶׁאֵין רְאָיָה לַדָּבָר – זֵכֶר לַדָּבָר, שֶׁנֶּאֱמַר: "וְקִרְעוּ לְבַבְכֶם וְאַל בִּגְדֵיכֶם".

It was taught in a *baraita*: **Until where** may **he rend** his garment,[H] if he continues to rend the same garment for additional relatives? **He may continue rending until** the point where the garment covers **his navel. Some say: Until** the point where the garment covers **his heart. Although there is no** absolute **proof for the matter** that one may rend the garment until this point, there is **an allusion to this matter, as it is stated: "And rend your hearts, and not your garments"** (Joel 2:13), thereby intimating that one may extend the rent in his garment only until he reaches the point where the garment covers his heart.

HALAKHA

Extending a tear – תּוֹסֶפֶת קְרִיעָה: If one rends his garment in mourning over his mother or father, and after seven days another one of his relatives dies, and he extends this tear, then the upper portion of the tear may never be sewn but the lower portion may be sewn. However, if one rends his garment over one of his other relatives and afterward hears that his father or mother died, then he should make a new tear and not extend the first one. The latter ruling is in accordance with the opinion of Rabbi Yehuda ben Beteira (Ramban; Rabbeinu Yeruḥam; *Shulḥan Arukh, Yoreh De'a* 340:22).

Until where may he rend his garment – עַד הֵיכָן קוֹרֵעַ: One who rent his garment in mourning and then extended this tear for other relatives may continue extending the tear until it reaches the point on the garment that covers his navel. If he becomes obligated to rend his garment again, then he must rend it from the edge of the garment three fingerbreadths away from the first tear. If the garment has tears in the front, then he may turn it around and rend it from the portion of the garment that is now in front of him. If the upper portion is torn, he may turn the garment over and rend what was formerly the bottom. If every portion of the garment is torn, then he is considered like one who has no garment and he does not rend it (*Shulḥan Arukh, Yoreh De'a* 340:21).

NOTES

Because they cannot be added – לְפִי שֶׁאֵינָן בְּתוֹסֶפֶת: Some explain that due to the honor one must show toward his parents, it is not appropriate for him to extend the tear rent over them as mourning for another relative (see Rashi). Others explain that because a mourner must make a longer tear for his father and mother, with no maximum size, any extension will not be noticeable (Ra'avad; Rid; Rosh). Rabbi Yitzḥak ibn Giat explains that one is required to rend his garment for his father and mother until he reaches the point on the garment which covers his navel, and since one may not tear below this, it is impossible to extend the tear (see Ramban and Ritva).

There are also those who understand this not as a halakhic statement but as a moral explanation for this ruling. One will never have another father or mother, and therefore it is not appropriate to add to the tear made as a sign of mourning for one's parents (*Tal Torah*). One may, however, have relatives in other categories in the future, e.g., children or even half siblings from his surviving parent.

Halakhot **of mourning are discrete and** ***halakhot*** **of rending are discrete – אֲבֵילוּת לְחוּד, קְרִיעָה לְחוּד:** Some say that this is because rending garments is a Torah law, as derived from the verses concerning the sons of Aaron, while the *halakhot* of mourning are of rabbinic origin (Ra'avad; see *Tosefot HaRosh*). The Ramban writes that the mitzva of rending is not itself a Torah law. Rather, it is a rabbinic law with supporting verses from the Torah. The *Nimmukei Yosef* writes simply that these two practices do not fall into the same category. Rending is performed before the mourning actually begins, and therefore Shmuel's principle that the *halakha* is ruled in accordance with the opinion of the lenient Sage with regard to mourning does not apply to it.

NOTES

The High Priest may tear his garment at the bottom – כֹּהֵן גָּדוֹל פּוֹרֵם מִלְּמַטָּה: Although a High Priest is prohibited from rending his garment as a sign of grief (Leviticus 21:10), he may perform a symbolic act that does not fall into the category of actual rending (Rashi, from manuscript).

הִגִּיעַ לְטִיבּוּרוֹ, מַרְחִיק שָׁלֹשׁ אֶצְבָּעוֹת וְקוֹרֵעַ. נִתְמַלֵּא מִלְּפָנָיו – מַחֲזִירוֹ לַאֲחוֹרָיו. נִתְמַלֵּא מִלְמַעְלָה – הוֹפְכוֹ מִלְּמַטָּה. וְהַקּוֹרֵעַ מִלְּמַטָּה וּמִן הַצְּדָדִין לֹא יָצָא. אֶלָּא שֶׁכֹּהֵן גָּדוֹל פּוֹרֵם מִלְּמַטָּה.

If **he** tore his garment until he **reached** the point where it covers **his navel,** he should not continue rending in the same place. Instead, **he should move away** a space of **three fingerbreadths** from the first rent **and make** a new **rent.** If the garment **became full** of rents **in the front, he should turn** the garment **front to back** and make a rent on the other side. If **it became full** of rents **above, he should turn it** top to bottom and make a rent on what used to be **the bottom. But one who rends** his garment **at the bottom or at the sides has not fulfilled** his obligation, as rending may be done only at the top of the garment.[H] **The High Priest, however,** who is prohibited from rending his garments in mourning, **may tear** his garment **at the bottom**[N] to mark his mourning in a symbolic manner.[H]

פְּלִיגוּ בָּהּ רַב מַתָּנָה וּמַר עוּקְבָא, וְתַרְוַיְיהוּ מִשְּׁמֵיהּ דַּאֲבוּהּ דִּשְׁמוּאֵל וְלֵוִי; חַד אָמַר: כָּל שִׁבְעָה קוֹרֵעַ, לְאַחַר שִׁבְעָה מוֹסִיף. וְחַד אָמַר: כָּל שְׁלֹשִׁים קוֹרֵעַ, לְאַחַר שְׁלֹשִׁים מוֹסִיף.

Rav Mattana and Mar Ukva disagreed about the following issue, **and both of them** stated their respective opinions **in the name of Shmuel's father and Levi. One said:** During **all seven** days of mourning, if the mourner hears that another relative of his passed away, **he makes** a new **rent; after seven** days of mourning **he** merely **adds** to the first one. **And one said:** During **all** of the first **thirty days he makes** a new rent; **after thirty** days **he** merely **adds** to the first one.

מַתְקִיף לַהּ רַבִּי זֵירָא: מַאן דְּאָמַר כָּל שִׁבְעָה קוֹרֵעַ, אַמַּאי? דְּלֹא נִיתָּן לְשׁוֹלְלוֹ. אֶלָּא הָא דְּאָמַר מָר: הָאִשָּׁה שׁוֹלַלְתּוֹ לְאַלְתַּר, הָכָא נַמִי?

Rabbi Zeira strongly objects to this: According to **the one who said** that during **all seven** days of mourning **he makes** a new **rent, why** is it not enough to add to the first one? It is because **he may not tack it** until the end of the seven-day period of mourning, and therefore if he adds to the rent it will look like a continuation of the previous tear. **But** then, with regard to **that which the Master said** in the *baraita*: After **a woman** rends her garment, she **may tack** the tear **immediately,** would you say that **here also** she may add to the first rent for a new bereavement during the seven-day period of mourning?

הָתָם מִשּׁוּם כְּבוֹד אִשָּׁה הוּא.

The Gemara answers: **There** the woman is permitted to tack the rent **due to the woman's honor,** as it would be dishonorable for her to be seen wearing torn garments. However, halakhically the rent is considered as if it still exists, and therefore she must make a new rent for a new bereavement and not merely add to the previous one.

מַאן דְּאָמַר כָּל שְׁלֹשִׁים קוֹרֵעַ, אַמַּאי? דְּלֹא נִיתָּן לְאַחוֹתוֹ. אֶלָּא לְאָבִיו וּלְאִמּוֹ, דְּלֹא נִיתָּן לְאַחוֹתוֹ לְעוֹלָם, הָכִי נַמִי?

Rabbi Zeira asked further: According to **the one who said** that **all thirty days** of mourning **one must make** a new **rent** rather than add to the existing tear, **why** does he say this? It is because during the thirty days **one is not given** permission to properly **mend** the garment, and so it still appears to be torn. **But** then, in a case of a rent made **for one's father or mother,** for **which** he **is not given** permission to **ever** properly **mend it,** would you say that he should **so too** be forever barred from adding to the rent for a new bereavement and is instead obligated to make a new rent?

הָתָם מִשּׁוּם כְּבוֹד אָבִיו וְאִמּוֹ הוּא.

The Gemara answers: **There** he may not properly mend the rent **due to the honor due to his father and mother.** Essentially, however, the tear is considered as if it had been sewn up after the thirty-day period, and therefore the son may extend it in the case of a new bereavement.

HALAKHA

The place of the rending – מְקוֹם הַקְּרִיעָה: Rending may be performed on any part of the front of a garment, from the neck. One who rends the garment from the bottom or from the sides does not fulfill his obligation. Others hold that one can fulfill his obligation by rending from the sides of the garment. It is customary to rely on this lenient opinion when rending over the dead to whom one is not related, e.g., when one is present at the time when the soul departs (*Shakh*). However, one who rends his garment over relatives for whom he is required to rend it must do so from the neckline (*Shulḥan Arukh*, *Yoreh De'a* 340:2, and in the comment of Rema).

Rending of a High Priest – קְרִיעַת כֹּהֵן גָּדוֹל: A High Priest, who is prohibited from rending his garment, may tear the bottom of his garment near his feet (Rambam *Sefer Avoda*, *Hilkhot Kelei HaMikdash* 5:6).

תָּנוּ רַבָּנַן: הַיּוֹצֵא בְּבֶגֶד קָרוּעַ לִפְנֵי הַמֵּת הֲרֵי זֶה גּוֹזֵל אֶת הַמֵּתִים וְאֶת הַחַיִּים.

The Sages taught the following *baraita*: **One who goes out before the deceased in a rent garment** that he had previously torn[H] over another bereavement, thereby giving the appearance of having rent his garment for him, **steals from the dead,**[N] as he did not rend a garment for him. **And** he similarly steals **from the living,** who see him and think that he made the tear in honor of the deceased, when in reality he is deceiving them.

רַבָּן שִׁמְעוֹן בֶּן גַּמְלִיאֵל אוֹמֵר, הָאוֹמֵר לַחֲבֵירוֹ: ״הַשְׁאִילֵנִי חֲלוּקְךָ וְאֵלֵךְ וַאֲבַקֵּר אֶת אַבָּא שֶׁהוּא חוֹלֶה״, וְהָלַךְ וּמְצָאוֹ שֶׁמֵּת – קוֹרֵעַ, וּמְאַחוֹ. וּכְשֶׁיָּבֹא לְבֵיתוֹ מַחֲזִיר לוֹ חֲלוּקוֹ וְנוֹתֵן לוֹ דְּמֵי קִרְעוֹ. וְאִם לֹא הוֹדִיעוֹ – הֲרֵי זֶה לֹא יִגַּע בּוֹ.

Rabban Shimon ben Gamliel says: In the case of **one who says to his fellow: Lend me your cloak and I will go and visit my father because he is sick, and he goes and finds that** his father **has died, he rends** the cloak **and** may then **mend it** in the proper manner. **And when he returns home, he returns the cloak** to his fellow **and pays him the value of the rent,** i.e., the depreciation in the value of the cloak that resulted from the tear. The assumption is that the lender considered the possibility that the sick father might die, and lent the garment anyway, understanding that he might have to tear it. **But if one did not inform** his fellow that he was going to visit his sick father, **he must not touch it,** as he was not granted permission to tear the garment belonging to someone else.[H]

תָּנוּ רַבָּנַן: חוֹלֶה שֶׁמֵּת לוֹ מֵת – אֵין מוֹדִיעִין אוֹתוֹ שֶׁמֵּת, שֶׁמָּא תִּטָּרֵף דַּעְתּוֹ עָלָיו. וְאֵין מַקְרִעִין בְּפָנָיו, וּמַשְׁתִּיקִין אֶת הַנָּשִׁים מִפָּנָיו.

The Sages taught the following *baraita*: When a relative **of a sick person dies,**[H] those around him **do not inform him that** this relative **died, lest he lose control of his mind** due to his emotional state and his grief exacerbate his physical health. **And** other people **may not rend** their garments **in his presence,** so that he will not know that one of his relatives passed away. **And we silence the women** who weep **in his presence,** so that he will not know that his relative is no longer alive.

וּמַקְרִעִין לְקָטָן מִפְּנֵי עָגְמַת נֶפֶשׁ. וְקוֹרְעִין עַל חָמִיו וְעַל חֲמוֹתוֹ מִפְּנֵי כְּבוֹד אִשְׁתּוֹ.

And the relatives **rend** the garment **of a minor child** when there is mourning in his family **in order to arouse grief. Although** a minor is not required to rend his garments, this will add to the grief of those who see that even the garments of children are rent. **And one rends** his garment **for his father-in-law or mother-in-law, although** he is not required to mourn for them, **due to the honor of his wife,** to show her that he joins in her mourning.[H]

וְאָמַר רַב פַּפָּא, תָּנָא בְּאֵבֶל רַבָּתִי: אָבֵל לֹא יָנִיחַ תִּינוֹק בְּתוֹךְ חֵיקוֹ מִפְּנֵי שֶׁמְּבִיאוֹ לִידֵי שְׂחוֹק, וְנִמְצָא מִתְגַּנֶּה עַל הַבְּרִיּוֹת.

And Rav Pappa said: A Sage **taught in** ***Evel Rabbati*****: A mourner should not place** a young **child in his lap because** the child **will bring him to laughter, and he will be disgraced in** the eyes of **other people** because he laughed while in mourning.[H]

״וְאֵין מַבְרִין עַל מִטּוֹת זְקוּפוֹת״. תָּנוּ רַבָּנַן: הַהוֹלֵךְ לְבֵית הָאָבֵל, אִם הָיָה לִבּוֹ גַּס בּוֹ – יַבְרוּהוּ עַל מִטּוֹת כְּפוּיוֹת; וְאִם לָאו – יַבְרוּהוּ עַל מִטּוֹת זְקוּפוֹת.

§ The mishna taught: **And** the consolers **provide the** first **meal** after the burial **only** while the mourner sits **on an upright bed** and not on one that is overturned. **The Sages taught** in a *baraita*: With regard to **one who goes to the house of the mourner, if he is confident** in his friendship **with him**[N] because they are close friends, **they provide him with the meal of comfort** while both he and the mourner sit **on overturned beds. And if** he is **not** confident in his friendship with him, both **he** and the mourner **should be fed on upright beds.**

רָבָא אִיתְרַע בֵּיהּ מִילְּתָא. עָל לְגַבֵּיהּ אַבָּא בַּר מַרְתָּא, דְּהוּא אַבָּא בַּר מִנְיוֹמִי. רָבָא – זְקֵיף, אַבָּא בַּר מַרְתָּא – כָּפֵי. אֲמַר: כַּמָּה לֵית בֵּיהּ דַּעְתָּא לְהַאי צוּרְבָא מֵרַבָּנַן.

The Gemara relates that **something** unpleasant **happened to Rava,** i.e., one of his close relatives died, and **Abba bar Marta, who** was also known as **Abba bar Minyomi, entered** to visit **him. Rava stood** the bed **upright,** treating him like any other person who came to comfort him. **Abba bar Marta overturned** the bed because he saw himself as being on very familiar terms with Rava. Rava **said: How lacking in sense**[N] **is this Torah scholar.** Rava had shown from the outset that he did not consider Abba bar Marta to be a close friend, yet the latter ignored this message and viewed himself as being exceptionally close to Rava.

תָּנוּ רַבָּנַן: הַהוֹלֵךְ מִמָּקוֹם לְמָקוֹם,

The Sages taught a *baraita*: If **one who was going from place to place**[H] learned of the death of a close relative, so that he must now observe the rites of mourning,

HALAKHA

One who goes out in a rent garment that he had previously torn – הַיּוֹצֵא בְּבֶגֶד קָרוּעַ: One who goes out before the dead in a garment that was previously torn in order to make it appear as though he rent this garment in honor of the deceased is considered as though he has stolen both from the living and from the dead (*Shulḥan Arukh, Yoreh De'a* 340:33).

Rending a borrowed garment – קְרִיעַת בֶּגֶד שָׁאוּל: One who is wearing a borrowed garment when one of his relatives dies may not rend it, and one who does rend such a garment does not fulfill his obligation (*Shakh*). However, if one told the lender that he was going to visit the sick relative, then the borrower may rend the borrowed garment and pay the owner for the damage, in accordance with the opinion of Rabban Shimon ben Gamliel (*Shulḥan Arukh, Yoreh De'a* 340:34).

When a relative of a sick person dies – חוֹלֶה שֶׁמֵּת לוֹ מֵת: When the relative of a sick person's dies, even if it is not a close relative, he should not be informed of the death, lest his grief makes his condition worsen. Similarly, he does not rend his garment, and he is not told to rend it even if he knows about the death. Others should not cry or eulogize the deceased in his presence (*Shulḥan Arukh, Yoreh De'a* 337:1, see *Shakh* and *Baḥ*).

One rends his garment for his father-in-law or mother-in-law – קוֹרְעִין עַל חָמִיו וַחֲמוֹתוֹ: Both men and women should rend their garments over their father- and mother-in-law. However, the custom nowadays is not to rend the garment in such a case (*Shulḥan Arukh, Yoreh De'a* 340:4, and in the comment of Rema).

A mourner is prohibited from being joyous – אָבֵל אָסוּר בְּשִׂמְחָה: A mourner should not place a child on his lap for all seven days of mourning, lest the child take his mind off of his mourning. When a mourner recites *havdala*, he should not recite the verses of joy. Rather, he should begin from the blessings (*Pitḥei Teshuva*; *Shulḥan Arukh, Yoreh De'a* 391:1).

Who was going from place to place – הַהוֹלֵךְ מִמָּקוֹם לְמָקוֹם: With regard to one who was traveling when he heard news of a death, if he can entirely avoid doing business in that place then this is preferable. However, if business transactions are unavoidable because if he does not make a purchase there he will not be able to find food elsewhere, then he should purchase the minimal essentials for the rest of his journey (*Shulḥan Arukh, Yoreh De'a* 380:23).

NOTES

Steals from the dead – גּוֹזֵל אֶת הַמֵּתִים: If one was obligated to rend his garment and did not do so, he stole the honor due to the deceased (see Rabbeinu Yehonatan of Lunel). Rav Hai Gaon writes, based on *Evel Rabbati*, that stealing from the dead is very serious because one cannot ask forgiveness from the deceased, as he can with a living person whom he has dishonored.

If he is confident in his friendship with him – אִם הָיָה לִבּוֹ גַּס בּוֹ: Some explain that this means that the mourner is close to the consoler. Since they are so familiar with each other the mourner does not need to honor the consoler. The mourner is not required to turn the bed upright as a sign of respect for the guest because he knows that the guest will not be offended (Ramban). Others write that the consoler might see sitting on an overturned bed as a bad omen, and if he is not a regular visitor to this place then the mourners must take care not to upset him (Rabbeinu Yehonatan of Lunel; see *Nimmukei Yosef*).

Alternatively, this expression refers to the mourner. If the mourner is so friendly that he becomes happy, then the consolers must also overturn their beds in order to reach his heart and remind him of his mourning (Rashi, from manuscript).

How lacking in sense – כַּמָּה לֵית בֵּיהּ דַּעְתָּא: Some explain this to mean that Rava acted appropriately and stood up both beds, yet his guest overturned his own one. He thereby put Rava in an inappropriate situation where he, a mourner, was sitting on an upright bed while his guest was sitting on an overturned bed (Rabbi Shlomo ben HaYatom).

אם יכול למעט בעסקו – ימעט; ואם לאו – יגלגל עמהן.

if he can reduce his business, he should reduce it; **and if not, he may carry on with them,**[N] i.e., his business partners. He may act in partnership with the members of the group with which he is traveling, but he may not engage in business independently.

תנו רבנן: מאימתי כופין את המטות? משיצא מפתח ביתו, דברי רבי אליעזר. רבי יהושע אומר: משיסתם הגולל.

§ **The Sages taught** the following *baraita*: **From when do** the mourners **overturn** their **beds?**[N] **From when** the corpse **is taken out of the opening of his house;** this is **the statement of Rabbi Eliezer. Rabbi Yehoshua says: From when the** tomb **is sealed** with **the grave cover.**[BH]

מעשה שמת רבן גמליאל הזקן. כיון שיצא מפתח ביתו אמר להם רבי אליעזר: כפו מטותיכם. וכיון שנסתם הגולל, אמר להם רבי יהושע: כפו מטותיכם. אמרו לו: כבר כפינו על פי זקן.

There was **an incident in which** the *Nasi* **Rabban Gamliel the Elder**[P] **died,** and **once** his body **left the opening of his house, Rabbi Eliezer said to** the members of the household: **Overturn your beds. And once the** tomb **was sealed** with **the grave cover, Rabbi Yehoshua said to them: Overturn your beds. They** then **said to him: We already overturned** them **in accordance with the Elder,** i.e., Rabbi Eliezer.

תנו רבנן: מאימתי זוקפין את המטות בערב שבת? מן המנחה ולמעלה. אמר רבה בר הונא: אף על פי כן, אינו יושב עליה עד שתחשך. ולמוצאי שבת, אף על פי שאין לו לישב אלא יום אחד – חוזר וכופה.

The Sages taught in a *baraita*: **From when do** the mourners **stand** their **beds upright on Friday;**[H] as the rites of mourning are not observed on Shabbat, and the beds must be returned to their ordinary position beforehand? **From** ***minḥa*** time **onward. Rabba bar Huna said: Even so, one may not sit down on** his upright bed immediately. Rather, he must wait **until it becomes dark** to do so. **And at the conclusion of Shabbat, even if he has** only **one** more **day to sit** in mourning, i.e., his period of mourning concludes on Sunday, **he must** once **again overturn** his bed.

תנו רבנן: הכופה מטתו, לא מטתו בלבד הוא כופה, אלא כל מטות שיש לו בתוך ביתו הוא כופה. ואפילו יש לו עשר מטות בעשרה מקומות כופה את כולן. ואפילו חמשה אחין ומת אחד – כולן כופין.

The Sages taught in a *baraita*: With regard to **one who** is in mourning and must **overturn his bed,**[N] **he overturns not only his** own **bed, but rather he overturns all the beds he has**[N] **in his house. And even if he has ten beds**[N] **in ten** different **places, he overturns them all. And even** if there are **five brothers and one** of them **died, all of them overturn** their beds wherever they live.[H]

NOTES

He should reduce his business…and he may carry on with them – ימעט בעסקו...ויגלגל עמהן: Two explanations are offered for this expression. Some say that the phrase: He should reduce, means that he should not engage in business at all, and if he absolutely must do so he may purchase only the minimal amount to eat on the journey home (Rabbeinu Ḥananel; Rosh). Some explain the expression: He may carry on with them, to mean that he should not perform business on his own at all. Instead, he should join in partnership with others or others may engage in business on his behalf (Rashi; Rabbeinu Gershom Meor HaGola; Rabbeinu Yehonatan of Lunel).

From when do they overturn their beds – מאימתי כופין את המטות: Overturning the bed signifies the beginning of all of the mourning practices. Since the activities of removing shoes or wrapping the head are not applicable to all, the Gemara referred to overturning the bed because it applies equally to all (*Tosefot HaRosh*).

Overturning of the bed – כפיית המיטה: The early authorities mention a statement in the Jerusalem Talmud that a guest in an inn does not overturn his bed because the gentiles there are likely to think that he is engaging in witchcraft. Based on this, they explain why it is no longer customary for a mourner to overturn his bed. When the Jewish people are in exile, it is as though they are always residing in temporary accommodations. Additionally, it is explained that modern beds have pieces that protrude upward, and overturning them would not be noticeable or practical; therefore, it became customary not to overturn one's bed at all (see Rosh).

All the beds he has – כל מיטות שיש לו: Some of the early authorities explain that a mourner must overturn all of the beds in his house, whether they belong to him, to the members of his household, or to others. However, guests who are not mourners stand these beds upright when they wish to use them (Ramban). According to the Ra'avad, a mourner is required to overturn only the beds belonging to the members of his household (see Rosh).

And even if he has ten beds, etc. – ואפילו יש לו עשר מיטות וכו׳: Rabbeinu Yehonatan of Lunel writes that the principle behind this *halakha* is that the obligation to overturn one's bed does not apply specifically to the house where the person died. Rather, it is the obligation of every mourner. Therefore, if the mourner sleeps in several different places, he is required to overturn his bed in each place. Similarly, brothers who are each mourning in their own homes are required to overturn their beds.

BACKGROUND

Grave cover – גולל: The grave cover was a large stone that was rolled onto the grave to seal it. In burial caves, these stones, which cover the entrance to the cave, are considered like large stone wheels that are not susceptible to ritual impurity and that can be rolled away when people wish to enter the cave.

Stone used to seal a burial cave

HALAKHA

When is the beginning of mourning – מאימתי תחילת אבילות: Mourning begins when the deceased is buried and the grave is covered with dirt, in accordance with the opinion of Rabbi Yehoshua. At this point, the mourner is also required to wrap his head. However, he does not remove his shoes until he reaches his house. Nowadays, it is customary to remove one's shoes immediately after the grave has been sealed. If one thought that the grave had been sealed and he began mourning, and it later became known to him that he had made a mistake, then he should count his mourning period from the time of the actual burial (*Shulḥan Arukh, Yoreh De'a* 375:1, and in the comment of Rema).

The time of the standing up of the bed – זמן זקיפת המיטה: A mourner stands his bed upright on Friday from the time of the afternoon prayer and onward. However, he should not sit on an upright bed until it becomes dark. At the conclusion of Shabbat, he again overturns the bed, even if he has only one day of mourning left (*Shulḥan Arukh, Yoreh De'a* 400:1).

Which beds are overturned – אלו מטות כופים: A mourner who is required to overturn his bed is required to overturn not only his own bed, but also all the beds in his house. If he has many houses in various places, then he must overturn all of the beds in each house. This obligation applies to all of the mourners. However, the obligation applies only to beds intended for lying on. A bed that has been designated for storing garments or for some other use need not be overturned. Similarly, a bed with large posts need not be overturned. With regard to a *dargash*, one should untie its loops rather than overturning it (Rambam *Sefer Shofetim, Hilkhot Evel* 5:18). Nowadays, the custom is not to overturn beds at all (*Shulḥan Arukh, Yoreh De'a* 387:2).

PERSONALITIES

Rabban Gamliel the Elder – רבן גמליאל הזקן: Rabban Gamliel is referred to as the Elder to distinguish him from his grandson, whose name was also Rabban Gamliel, and who was referred to as Rabban Gamliel of Yavne. He was a grandson of Hillel the Elder and served as the head of the Sanhedrin for many years during the Temple period.

It seems that Rabban Gamliel was the first to receive the honorary title Rabban because he was accepted by all the Sages of the Jewish people. Many of his rulings were cited in subsequent generations. He enacted many important rulings, e.g., that a woman may remarry based on the testimony of a single witness that her previous husband has died. He enacted other rulings as well, in order to improve public welfare. During his time, people would study Torah only while standing, but that practice ceased when he died. Therefore, it is said that when Rabban Gamliel died, honor for the Torah ceased (Sota 49a).

His son was Rabban Shimon ben Gamliel, who led the Jewish people during the era of the Great Revolt and who was later executed by the Romans.

וְאִם הָיְתָה מִטָּה הַמְיוּחֶדֶת לְכֵלִים – אֵין צָרִיךְ לְכוֹפוֹתָהּ. דַּרְגָּשׁ – אֵין צָרִיךְ לְכוֹפוֹתוֹ, אֶלָּא זוֹקְפוֹ. רַבָּן שִׁמְעוֹן בֶּן גַּמְלִיאֵל אוֹמֵר: דַּרְגָּשׁ, מַתִּיר אֶת קַרְבִּיטָיו וְהוּא נוֹפֵל מֵאֵלָיו.

If, however, it is a bed designated for the storage of **garments** and not for sleeping, **he is not required to overturn it. It is also not necessary to overturn a *dargash*,**[N] **but rather he stands it upright. Rabban Shimon ben Gamliel says: With regard to a *dargash*, one loosens its loops [*karbitav*],**[L] which hold up the pillows, **and it falls on its own.**

מַאי דַּרְגָּשׁ? אֲמַר עוּלָּא: עַרְסָא דְּגַדָּא.

The Gemara asks: **What** is the meaning of the word ***dargash*? Ulla said:** It is a good-**luck** [*gada*] **bed,** as it was common to have ornamental beds for good luck, which were not used for sleeping.

אֲמַר לֵיהּ רַבָּה: אֶלָּא מֵעַתָּה גַּבֵּי מֶלֶךְ, דִּתְנַן: כָּל הָעָם מְסוּבִּים עַל הָאָרֶץ וְהוּא מֵיסֵב עַל הַדַּרְגָּשׁ, מִי אִיכָּא מִידֵּי דְּעַד הָאִידָּנָא לָא אוֹתְבִינֵיהּ – וְהָשְׁתָּא מוֹתְבִינַן לֵיהּ?

Rabba said to him: However, if that is **so,** then the following statement **with regard to a king** is difficult, **as we learned** in a mishna (*Sanhedrin* 20a): When the mourner's meal is served to the king and his family, **all the people recline on the ground, and he,** the king, due to his honor, **reclines on a *dargash*.**[H] **Is there anything upon which we would not have seated him until now,** when he was not a mourner, **but now,** specifically during the mourning period, **we seat him on it?**

מַתְקִיף לָהּ רַב אַשִׁי: מַאי קוּשְׁיָא? מִידֵּי דַּהֲוָה אַאֲכִילָה וּשְׁתִיָּה, דְּעַד הָאִידָּנָא – לָא אוֹכְלִינֵיהּ וְלָא אַשְׁקִינֵיהּ, הָשְׁתָּא – אוֹכְלִינֵיהּ וְאַשְׁקִינֵיהּ!

Rav Ashi strongly objects to this: What is the difficulty raised by Rabba? One can answer: The *halakha* is **just as it is in** the case **of eating and drinking,** that **until now,** before one became a mourner, **we did not feed him or give him drink,** but **now** that he is a mourner **we feed him and give him drink** during the first meal after the burial.

אֶלָּא, אִי קַשְׁיָא – הָא קַשְׁיָא: דִּתְנַן: דַּרְגָּשׁ אֵינוֹ צָרִיךְ לְכוֹפוֹתוֹ אֶלָּא זוֹקְפוֹ, וְאִי עַרְסָא דְּגַדָּא – אַמַּאי אֵינוֹ צָרִיךְ לְכוֹפוֹתוֹ? הָא תְּנַן: הַכּוֹפֶה מִטָּתוֹ – לֹא מִטָּתוֹ בִּלְבַד הוּא כּוֹפֶה, אֶלָּא כָּל מִטּוֹת שֶׁיֵּשׁ לוֹ בְּתוֹךְ בֵּיתוֹ כּוֹפֶה!

Rather, if it is difficult, this is difficult, as **we learned** in a *baraita*: **It is not necessary to overturn a *dargash*, but rather he stands it upright. But if it is a** good-**luck bed, why is it not necessary to overturn it? Didn't we learn: One who** is in mourning and must **overturn his bed overturns not only his own bed, but rather he overturns all the beds in his house,** including this good luck bed?

וּמַאי קַשְׁיָא? מִידֵּי דַּהֲוָה אַמִּטָּה הַמְיוּחֶדֶת לְכֵלִים, דְּתַנְיָא: אִם הָיְתָה מִטָּה הַמְיוּחֶדֶת לְכֵלִים – אֵינוֹ צָרִיךְ לְכוֹפוֹתָהּ!

The Gemara rejects this: **And what is difficult** in this? One can answer: The *halakha* is **just as it is in** the case of **a bed designated for** the storage of **garments, as it is taught** in a *baraita*: **If it is a bed designated for** the storage of **garments,** and not for sleeping, **one is not required to overturn it.** So too, one is not required to overturn a *dargash*, as it is a bed that is not used for sleeping.

אֶלָּא, אִי קַשְׁיָא הָא קַשְׁיָא: רַבָּן שִׁמְעוֹן בֶּן גַּמְלִיאֵל אוֹמֵר: דַּרְגָּשׁ, מַתִּיר קַרְבִּיטָיו וְהוּא נוֹפֵל מֵאֵלָיו. וְאִי סָלְקָא דַּעְתָּךְ עַרְסָא דְּגַדָּא – מַאי קַרְבִּיטִין אִית לֵיהּ?

Rather if it is **difficult, this is the difficulty:** It was taught in a *baraita*: **Rabban Shimon ben Gamliel says:** With regard to a ***dargash*, one loosens the loops** that hold up the pillows, **and it falls on its own. And if it enters your mind** to say that a *dargash* is a good-**luck bed,** it is like other beds, so **what loops does it have?**

כִּי אֲתָא רָבִין אֲמַר לֵיהּ הַהוּא מֵרַבָּנַן, וְרַב תַּחֲלִיפָא בַּר מַעַרְבָא שְׁמֵיהּ, דַּהֲוָה שְׁכִיחַ בְּשׁוּקָא דְּגִילְדָאֵי: מַאי דַּרְגָּשׁ? עַרְסָא דִּצְלָא.

When Ravin came from Eretz Yisrael to Babylonia, **one of the Sages, whose name was Rav Taḥalifa from the West,** and who **was frequently** found **in the market of leather workers, said to him: What is a *dargash*?** It is **a leather bed.**

אִיתְּמַר נַמִּי, אָמַר רַבִּי יִרְמְיָה: דַּרְגָּשׁ – סֵירוּגוֹ מִתּוֹכוֹ; מִטָּה – סֵירוּגָהּ עַל גַּבָּהּ.

It was also stated that **Rabbi Yirmeya said: A *dargash* has its interlacing from the inside,**[B] i.e., attached to loops that go through holes that are made in the bed frame itself; whereas **a bed** has **its interlacing from the outside,**[B] i.e., the strapping itself is looped around the wood of the frame, and therefore it cannot be loosened.

אָמַר רַבִּי יַעֲקֹב בַּר אַחָא אָמַר רַבִּי יְהוֹשֻׁעַ בֶּן לֵוִי: הֲלָכָה כְּרַבָּן שִׁמְעוֹן בֶּן גַּמְלִיאֵל. אִיתְּמַר נַמִּי, אָמַר רַבִּי יַעֲקֹב בַּר אַחָא אָמַר רַבִּי אַסִּי: מִטָּה שֶׁנַּקְלִיטֶיהָ יוֹצְאִין – זוֹקְפָהּ, וְדַיּוֹ.

Rabbi Ya'akov bar Aḥa said in the name of Rabbi Yehoshua ben Levi: The *halakha* is in accordance with the opinion of **Rabban Shimon ben Gamliel** with regard to a *dargash*. **It was also stated** that **Rabbi Ya'akov bar Aḥa said in the name of Rabbi Asi: A bed whose posts [*naklitin*]**[NLB] **extend,** meaning that they are very long so that the bed will remain high off the ground even if it is overturned, **may be stood upright and that is sufficient.** That is to say, one is not required to overturn such a bed.

NOTES

It is not necessary to overturn a *dargash* – דַּרְגָּשׁ, אֵין צָרִיךְ לְכָפוֹתוֹ: According to the Meiri, this is because it is not readily apparent if the *dargash* is overturned, since it is always low to the ground. The Ritva writes that because a *dargash* is made of expensive leather, there is concern that it will be damaged if it is overturned, and therefore it is sufficient to stand it on its side as a sign of mourning.

Whose posts extend – נַקְלִיטֶיהָ יוֹצְאִין: Rabbeinu Yehonatan of Lunel writes that the posts are two poles that stick out from the middle of the ends of the bed. Therefore, it is impossible to overturn such a bed.

LANGUAGE

Loops [*karbitin*] – קַרְבִּיטִין: From the Greek κράββατος, *krabatos*, meaning mattress, cushion, or interlacing of the bed.

Posts [*naklitin*] – נַקְלִיטִין: Probably from the Greek ἀνάκλιτα, *anaklita*, or ἀνάκλιτος, *anaklitos*, meaning leaning back in a bed or chair.

HALAKHA

The first meal for a king after the burial – סְעוּדַת הַבְרָאָה לַמֶּלֶךְ: When a king eats the first meal after the burial of his relative, everyone else sits on the ground and he sits on a *dargash* (Rambam *Sefer Shofetim*, *Hilkhot Evel* 7:8).

BACKGROUND

Interlacing from the inside – סֵירוּגוֹ מִתּוֹכוֹ:

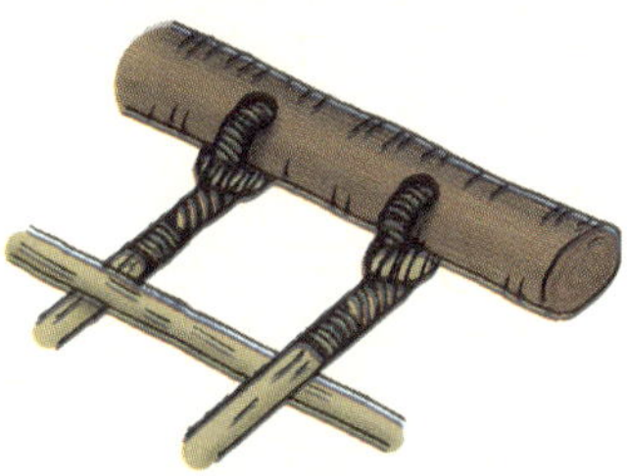

Interlacing from the outside – סֵירוּגָהּ עַל גַּבָּהּ:

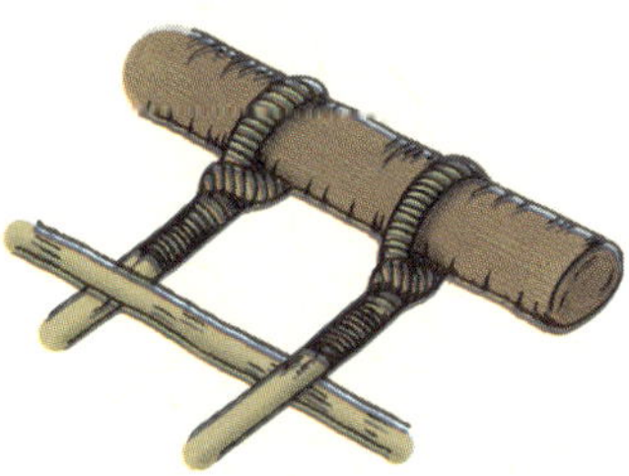

Bed and bedpost – מִטָּה וְנַקְלִיטִין: On the bed depicted in the image, the supports at the head and the foot, which may be the posts referred to by the Gemara, extend from the bed, and therefore it is difficult to overturn it. Furthermore, overturning it would not be immediately noticeable.

Ancient Roman bed from mishnaic period

תָּנוּ רַבָּנַן: יָשֵׁן עַל גַּבֵּי כִּסֵּא, עַל גַּבֵּי אוּדְיָינֵי גְּדוֹלָה, עַל גַּבֵּי קַרְקַע – לֹא יָצָא יְדֵי חוֹבָתוֹ. אָמַר רַבִּי יוֹחָנָן: שֶׁלֹּא קִיֵּים כְּפִיַּית הַמִּטָּה.

The Sages taught the following *baraita*: If the mourner **sleeps on a chair,** or **on a large** overturned **mortar,** or **on the ground, he does not fulfill his obligation,** even though he is uncomfortable while sleeping. **Rabbi Yoḥanan said:** This is **because he did not fulfill** the mitzva of **overturning the bed.**[H]

תָּנוּ רַבָּנַן: מְכַבְּדִין וּמְרַבִּיצִין בְּבֵית הָאֵבֶל, וּמְדִיחִין קְעָרוֹת וְכוֹסוֹת וּצְלוֹחִיּוֹת וְקִיתוֹנִיּוֹת בְּבֵית הָאֵבֶל, וְאֵין מְבִיאִין אֶת הַמּוּגְמָר וְאֶת הַבְּשָׂמִים לְבֵית הָאֵבֶל.

The Sages taught another *baraita*: **One may sweep and sprinkle** water[H] on a dirt floor **in the house of a mourner, and one may wash bowls, cups, jugs, and pitchers in the house of a mourner. But one may not bring incense** or fragrant **spices into the house of a mourner.**

אִינִי: וְהָא תָּנֵי בַּר קַפָּרָא: אֵין מְבָרְכִין לֹא עַל הַמּוּגְמָר וְלֹא עַל הַבְּשָׂמִים בְּבֵית הָאֵבֶל. בְּרוּכֵי הוּא דְּלָא מְבָרְכִין, הָא אַתּוּיֵי – מַיְיתִינַן!

The Gemara asks: **Is that so? But doesn't bar Kappara teach** the following *baraita*: **One may not recite a blessing either over incense or over fragrant spices in the house of a mourner?** From this one may infer that **one may not recite a blessing** over these incense or spices, **but one may bring them** into the house of the mourner. This appears to contradict the previous *baraita*.

לָא קַשְׁיָא; הָא – בְּבֵית הָאֵבֶל, הָא – בְּבֵית הַמְנַחֲמִין.

The Gemara explains: **It is not difficult. Here,** the *baraita* is referring **to the house of a mourner,** into which spices should not be taken; **there,** the *baraita* that states that one may not recite a blessing over them, is referring **to the house of the consolers,** his relatives, into which spices may be brought.[N]

מתני׳ אֵין מוֹלִיכִין לְבֵית הָאֵבֶל לֹא בְּטַבְלָא וְלֹא בְּאִסְקוּטְלָא וְלֹא בְּקָנוֹן, אֶלָּא בְּסַלִּים. וְאֵין אוֹמְרִים בִּרְכַּת אֲבֵלִים בַּמּוֹעֵד, אֲבָל עוֹמְדִין בְּשׁוּרָה, וּמְנַחֲמִין, וּפוֹטְרִין אֶת הָרַבִּים.

MISHNA **One does not bring**[N] the first meal after the burial **to the house of mourning on a small tray** [*tavla*],[L] **in a bowl** [*iskutla*],[NL] **or in a narrow-mouthed basket** [*kanon*],[L] **but rather in** ordinary **baskets. And the mourners' blessing is not recited on** the intermediate days of **a Festival, but** the consolers may **stand in a row** when the mourners leave the cemetery **and console** them. **And** the mourners **dismiss the many** consolers,[N] by telling them that they may return home after they have fulfilled the mitzva of consoling the mourners.[H]

אֵין מַנִּיחִין אֶת הַמִּטָּה בָּרְחוֹב שֶׁלֹּא לְהַרְגִּיל אֶת הַהֶסְפֵּד. וְלֹא שֶׁל נָשִׁים לְעוֹלָם, מִפְּנֵי הַכָּבוֹד.

The bier of the deceased **is not set down in the street** during the intermediate days of a Festival[H] **so as not to encourage eulogies.** On an ordinary weekday, people would gather in the street around the bier to eulogize the deceased, but this should be avoided during the intermediate days of the Festival. **And the** biers **of women** are **never** set down, even if it is not the intermediate days of a Festival, **due to their honor.** Blood might drip from their bodies, and it would cause them dishonor if their blood stained the street.

HALAKHA

Sleeping on an overturned bed – שֵׁינָה עַל מִיטָּה כְּפוּיָה: It is not enough for a mourner to overturn his bed; he must sleep on it overturned as well (Rambam *Sefer Shofetim, Hilkhot Evel* 5:18).

Sweep and sprinkle water – מְכַבְּדִין וּמְרַבִּיצִין: It is permitted to sweep and sprinkle water on the dirt floor in a mourners' house. Similarly, one may wash dishes there as well. However, one should not bring any type of fragrant spices there. Spices may be taken into a house in which a dead body is present, but one does not recite a blessing over those spices (*Shulḥan Arukh, Yoreh De'a* 378:7).

Customs of mourning during the intermediate days of the Festival – מִנְהַג אֲבֵילוּת בַּמּוֹעֵד: The mourners' blessing is not recited in open areas during the intermediate days of a Festival. However, the consolers stand in a line and the mourners dismiss the masses (*Tur, Yoreh De'a* 401).

Placing a bier during the intermediate days of the Festival – הֲנָחַת הַמִּיטָּה בַּמּוֹעֵד: The bier is not placed in the street during the intermediate days of a Festival, so as not to encourage eulogizing at that time. On these days, eulogies are given only in honor of a Torah scholar. A bier is not taken for burial during the intermediate days of the Festival until the grave has already been prepared (*Shulḥan Arukh, Yoreh De'a* 401:1).

LANGUAGE

Tray [*tavla*] – טַבְלָא: From the Greek τάβλα, *tabla*, which is borrowed from the Latin tabula. Ordinarily, it refers to a tablet that was used for writing or on which objects were placed. By extension, the word is used here in reference to a flat tray that is similar to a tablet. See also LANGUAGE, p. 54.

Bowl [*iskutla*] – אִסְקוּטְלָא: From the Latin scutella, meaning flat dish.

Narrow-mouthed basket [*kanon*] – קָנוֹן: From the Greek κάνεον, *kaneon*, or κανῶν, *kanon*, meaning breadbasket, or a basket in which items were taken as gifts or to be sacrificed as offerings. According to the description in the Talmud, this basket had a narrow opening.

NOTES

The house of the mourner and the house of the consolers – בֵּית הָאֵבֶל וּבֵית הַמְנַחֲמִין: The authorities disagree with regard to the meaning of the expression: House of the mourner. Some say that the house of the mourner refers to a house where the mourner alone is present, and the house of the consolers refers to the place where people come to comfort him (Ra'avad; Rabbeinu Yehonatan of Lunel).

Others explain that the house of the mourner refers to a house that still contains the body of the deceased, and the more correct name would be the house of the mourning; whereas the house of the consolers is the room that no longer contains the body of the deceased, where others come to console the mourners (Rosh).

Similarly, there is a dispute with regard to the *halakha*, as there are those who say that it is permitted to bring fragrant spices into a house where the body of the deceased is present, to remove any unpleasant odor, however such spices may not be brought to a place where there is no dead body (Rabbi Yitzḥak ibn Giat; Ritva; Meiri). Some say that in a house where only the mourner is present one may not bring fragrant spices because it is not appropriate for the mourner to take pleasure while he is mourning. However, in honor of the consolers one may bring such spices (Rabbeinu Ḥananel).

One does not bring – אֵין מוֹלִיכִין: Some say that this mishna refers to the intermediate days of the Festival. Despite the honor of the intermediate days of the Festival, one may not take food to the mourner's house in elaborately decorated vessels. This is all the more so prohibited on an ordinary weekday (Ritva).

In a bowl – בְּאִסְקוּטְלָא: Some explain that this refers to a type of large bowl (Rashi) or that it was a gold or silver bowl (*Arukh*). Others understand it to be a small table (Rabbeinu Yehonatan of Lunel), or a fine tablecloth (Rabbi Shlomo ben HaYatom).

And dismiss the many consolers – וּפוֹטְרִים אֶת הָרַבִּים: Some explain that the mourners would dismiss the consolers immediately, telling them that they have not fulfilled their obligation since they cannot recite the mourners' blessing (Rabbeinu Yehonatan of Lunel). Those who came to console were also exempt after the Festival from reciting the mourners' blessing (Ra'avad). Some say that in honor of the Festival it is permitted to tell the consolers: Go in peace (Ran).

גמ׳ תָּנוּ רַבָּנַן: בָּרִאשׁוֹנָה הָיוּ מוֹלִיכִין בְּבֵית הָאֵבֶל, עֲשִׁירִים – בְּקָלָתוֹת שֶׁל כֶּסֶף וְשֶׁל זָהָב, וַעֲנִיִּים – בְּסַלֵּי נְצָרִים שֶׁל עֲרָבָה קְלוּפָה. וְהָיוּ עֲנִיִּים מִתְבַּיְּישִׁים, הִתְקִינוּ שֶׁיְּהוּ הַכֹּל מְבִיאִין בְּסַלֵּי נְצָרִים שֶׁל עֲרָבָה קְלוּפָה, מִפְּנֵי כְּבוֹדָן שֶׁל עֲנִיִּים.

GEMARA **The Sages taught** the following *baraita*: **At first,** the meal after the burial **would be brought to the house of the mourner** in various ways. **The wealthy** would bring the meal **in baskets of silver and gold, and the poor** would bring it in **baskets of peeled willow branches. And the poor were embarrassed,**[N] as everyone would see that they were poor. The Sages **instituted that everyone should bring** the meal **in baskets of peeled willow branches,**[H] **due to the honor of the poor.**

תָּנוּ רַבָּנַן: בָּרִאשׁוֹנָה הָיוּ מַשְׁקִין בְּבֵית הָאֵבֶל, עֲשִׁירִים – בִּזְכוּכִית לְבָנָה, וַעֲנִיִּים – בִּזְכוּכִית צְבוּעָה, וְהָיוּ עֲנִיִּים מִתְבַּיְּישִׁין. הִתְקִינוּ שֶׁיְּהוּ הַכֹּל מַשְׁקִין בִּזְכוּכִית צְבוּעָה, מִפְּנֵי כְּבוֹדָן שֶׁל עֲנִיִּים.

The Sages taught a similar *baraita*: **At first, they would serve** wine **in the house of the mourner** during the first meal after the burial; the **wealthy** would do so **in** cups made from **white glass, and the poor** would serve this wine **in** cups of **colored glass.**[B] **And the poor were embarrassed,** as everyone would see that they were poor. The Sages **instituted that all should serve** drinks in the house of the mourner **in colored glass** cups, **due to the honor of the poor.**

בָּרִאשׁוֹנָה הָיוּ מְגַלִּין פְּנֵי עֲשִׁירִים, וּמְכַסִּין פְּנֵי עֲנִיִּים, מִפְּנֵי שֶׁהָיוּ מוּשְׁחָרִין פְּנֵיהֶן מִפְּנֵי בַּצּוֹרֶת, וְהָיוּ עֲנִיִּים מִתְבַּיְּישִׁין. הִתְקִינוּ שֶׁיְּהוּ מְכַסִּין פְּנֵי הַכֹּל, מִפְּנֵי כְּבוֹדָן שֶׁל עֲנִיִּים.

Furthermore, **at first they would uncover the faces of the wealthy**[N] who passed away **and cover the faces of the poor, because their faces were blackened by famine. And the poor were embarrassed** because they were buried in a different manner. The Sages **instituted that everyone's face should be covered, due to the honor of the poor.**[H]

בָּרִאשׁוֹנָה הָיוּ מוֹצִיאִין עֲשִׁירִים בְּדַרְגָּשׁ, וַעֲנִיִּים

Additionally, **at first the wealthy would take** the deceased **out** for burial **on a** ***dargash*****, and the poor** would take the deceased out

HALAKHA

Baskets of peeled willow branches – סַלֵּי נְצָרִים שֶׁל עֲרָבָה קְלוּפָה: Food for the first meal after burial may be transferred only in simple willow baskets (Rambam *Sefer Shofetim*, *Hilkhot Evel* 13:7).

Covering the faces of the dead – כִּיסּוּי פְּנֵי הַמֵּת: The faces of the deceased should be covered, regardless of whether they were wealthy or poor, in accordance with the enactment of the Sages (*Shulḥan Arukh*, *Yoreh De'a* 353:1).

NOTES

Would be brought…and the poor were embarrassed – הָיוּ מוֹלִיכִין...וְהָיוּ עֲנִיִּים מִתְבַּיְּישִׁים: There is a dispute as to whether the concern is for the honor of the mourners or the consolers. According to one opinion, people would use inexpensive vessels to bring food to the mourners who were from poor households, and the Sages were concerned about the honor of the poor. Alternatively, this ordinance was instituted because the poor consolers would bring simple utensils, and the Sages were concerned about the honor of the consolers (Rabbeinu Yehonatan of Lunel; see *Nimmukei Yosef*).

Uncover the faces of the wealthy – מְגַלִּין פְּנֵי עֲשִׁירִים: Uncovering the face was done to increase the eulogies because people would be pained when they saw the face of the deceased. Or perhaps those present, when seeing the deceased, would realize that despite how beautiful he had once been his body will nevertheless soon become dirt and decay. This leads to an understanding of the frailty of life (Rabbeinu Yehonatan of Lunel).

BACKGROUND

Colored glass – זְכוּכִית צְבוּעָה:

Roman glassware in various colors

Perek **III**
Daf **27** Amud **b**

בִּכְלִיכָה, וְהָיוּ עֲנִיִּים מִתְבַּיְּישִׁין. הִתְקִינוּ שֶׁיְּהוּ הַכֹּל מוֹצִיאִין בִּכְלִיכָה, מִפְּנֵי כְּבוֹדָן שֶׁל עֲנִיִּים.

on a plain bier made from poles that were strapped together, **and the poor were embarrassed.** The Sages **instituted that everyone should be taken out** for burial **on a plain bier, due to the honor of the poor.**

בָּרִאשׁוֹנָה הָיוּ מַנִּיחִין אֶת הַמּוּגְמָר תַּחַת חוֹלֵי מֵעַיִם מֵתִים, וְהָיוּ חוֹלֵי מֵעַיִם חַיִּים מִתְבַּיְּישִׁין, הִתְקִינוּ שֶׁיְּהוּ מַנִּיחִין תַּחַת הַכֹּל, מִפְּנֵי כְּבוֹדָן שֶׁל חוֹלֵי מֵעַיִם חַיִּים.

Similarly, **at first they would place incense under** the beds of **those who died with an intestinal disease,** because the body emitted an especially unpleasant odor. **And those who were alive with an intestinal disease were embarrassed** when they understood that they, too, would be treated in this manner after their death, and that everyone would know the cause of their death. The Sages **instituted that incense should be placed under everyone, due to the honor of those with an intestinal disease who were still living.**

בָּרִאשׁוֹנָה הָיוּ מַטְבִּילִין אֶת הַכֵּלִים עַל גַּבֵּי נִדּוֹת מֵתוֹת, וְהָיוּ נִדּוֹת חַיּוֹת מִתְבַּיְּישׁוֹת. הִתְקִינוּ שֶׁיְּהוּ מַטְבִּילִין עַל גַּבֵּי כָּל הַנָּשִׁים, מִפְּנֵי כְּבוֹדָן שֶׁל נִדּוֹת חַיּוֹת. בָּרִאשׁוֹנָה מַטְבִּילִין עַל גַּבֵּי זָבִין מֵתִים, וְהָיוּ זָבִין חַיִּים מִתְבַּיְּישִׁין. הִתְקִינוּ שֶׁיְּהוּ מַטְבִּילִין עַל גַּב הַכֹּל, מִפְּנֵי כְּבוֹדָן שֶׁל זָבִין חַיִּים.

Moreover, **at first they would** ritually **immerse** all **the utensils** that had been used **by** women who **died** while **menstruating,** which had thereby contracted ritual impurity. **And** due to this, **the living menstruating women were embarrassed.** The Sages **instituted that** the utensils that had been used **by all** dying **women must be immersed, due to the honor of living menstruating women.** And, **at first they would** ritually **immerse** all **the utensils** that had been used by ***zavin***, men suffering from gonorrhea, **who died,** as the utensils had thereby contracted ritual impurity. **And** due to this **the living** ***zavin*** **felt embarrassed.** The Sages **instituted that** the utensils that had been used **by all** men **must be immersed, due to the honor of the living** ***zavin*****.**

בָּרִאשׁוֹנָה הָיְתָה הוֹצָאַת הַמֵּת קָשָׁה לִקְרוֹבָיו יוֹתֵר מִמִּיתָתוֹ, עַד שֶׁהָיוּ קְרוֹבָיו מַנִּיחִין אוֹתוֹ וּבוֹרְחִין. עַד שֶׁבָּא רַבָּן גַּמְלִיאֵל וְנָהַג קַלּוּת רֹאשׁ בְּעַצְמוֹ וְיָצָא בִּכְלֵי פִשְׁתָּן, וְנָהֲגוּ הָעָם אַחֲרָיו לָצֵאת בִּכְלֵי פִשְׁתָּן. אָמַר רַב פַּפָּא: וְהָאִידָּנָא נְהוּג עָלְמָא אֲפִילּוּ בִּצְרָדָא בַּר זוּזָא.

Likewise, **at first taking the dead out** for burial **was more difficult for the relatives than the** actual **death,** because it was customary to bury the dead in expensive shrouds, which the poor could not afford. The problem grew **to the point that relatives would** sometimes **abandon** the corpse **and run away.** This lasted **until Rabban Gamliel came and acted**[N] **with frivolity,** meaning that he waived his dignity, by leaving instructions that he be **taken out** for burial **in linen garments. And the people** adopted this **practice after him** and had themselves **taken out** for burial **in linen garments.**[H] **Rav Pappa said: And nowadays, everyone follows the practice** of taking out the dead for burial **even in** plain **hemp garments** [*tzerada*][L] that cost only **a dinar.**[N]

״אֵין מַנִּיחִין אֶת הַמִּטָּה בָּרְחוֹב״. אָמַר רַב פַּפָּא: אֵין מוֹעֵד בִּפְנֵי תַלְמִיד חָכָם, וְכׇל שֶׁכֵּן חֲנוּכָּה וּפוּרִים.

It is taught in the mishna: **The bier** of the deceased **is not set down in the street** during the intermediate days of a Festival, **so as not to encourage eulogies. Rav Pappa said:** There are **no** restrictions on eulogizing on the intermediate days of **a Festival in the presence** of a deceased **Torah scholar,**[H] and therefore he may be eulogized in the ordinary manner during the Festival week. **And all the more so** a Torah scholar may be eulogized on the days of **Hanukkah and Purim,** which have less sanctity than the intermediate days of a Festival.

וְהָנֵי מִילֵּי – בְּפָנָיו, אֲבָל שֶׁלֹּא בְּפָנָיו – לֹא. אִינִי? וְהָא רַב כָּהֲנָא סַפְדֵיהּ לְרַב זְבִיד מִנְּהַרְדְּעָא בְּפוּם נַהֲרָא! אָמַר רַב פַּפִּי: יוֹם שְׁמוּעָה הֲוָה, וְכִבְפָנָיו דָּמֵי.

The Gemara comments: **But this** allowance to eulogize a Torah scholar during the intermediate days of a Festival **applies only** when the eulogy is **in the presence** of the deceased, before the bier. **However,** giving a eulogy that is **not in his presence** is **not** permitted. The Gemara asks: **Is that so? But didn't Rav Kahana eulogize Rav Zevid from Neharde'a in** his city **Pum Nahara** during the intermediate days of a Festival? **Rav Pappa said: It was the day** on which Rav Kahana received the **news** of Rav Zevid's death, **and** a eulogy in such a situation **is considered as** if it is **in his presence.**

אָמַר עוּלָּא: הֶסְפֵּד עַל לֵב, דִּכְתִיב: ״עַל שָׁדַיִם סוֹפְדִים״; טִיפּוּחַ – בַּיָּד; קִילּוּס – בָּרֶגֶל.

The Gemara continues its discussion of the *halakhot* of mourning: **Ulla said:** Although *hesped* usually refers to a eulogy, strictly speaking, ***hesped*** is referring to striking oneself **on the heart, as it is written: "Striking** [*sofedim*] **the breasts"** (Isaiah 32:12). The term ***tipuaḥ*** is referring to striking **with** one **hand** against the other hand, i.e., clapping. The term ***killus***[L] is referring to stomping **with** one's **foot**[N] on the ground.

תָּנוּ רַבָּנַן: הַמְקַלֵּס – לֹא יְקַלֵּס בְּסַנְדָּל, אֶלָּא בְּמִנְעָל, מִפְּנֵי הַסַּכָּנָה.

The Sages taught a *baraita*: **One who stomps his foot on the ground** as a sign of mourning **should not stomp with a sandal,**[N] **but rather** he should do so wearing **a shoe, due to the danger** of being hurt. Because a sandal is easily torn, it is possible that something sharp on the ground will puncture his foot, or that he will suffer some other injury.

אָמַר רַבִּי יוֹחָנָן: אָבֵל, כֵּיוָן שֶׁנִּיעְנַע רֹאשׁוֹ – שׁוּב אֵין מְנַחֲמִין רַשָּׁאִין לֵישֵׁב אֶצְלוֹ.

Rabbi Yoḥanan said: Once a mourner nods his head[NH] to show that his grief has slightly diminished, **the consolers may no longer sit next to him,** as with his action the mourner shows that he no longer desires their presence.

NOTES

Rabban Gamliel came and acted – בָּא רַבָּן גַּמְלִיאֵל וְנָהַג: He was remembered for this practice throughout the generations, since he did it for the sake of the masses. It was such an important act that when people would drink cups of wine in the house of the mourner, as was the custom then, they would also drink an extra cup in honor of Rabban Gamliel (*Ketubot* 8b).

Hemp garments that cost one dinar – צְרָדָא בַּר זוּזָא: Some explain that this is a simple thick garment (Rabbi Shlomo ben HaYatom).

Killus is referring to stomping with one's foot – קִילּוּס בָּרֶגֶל: This custom is mentioned in the Bible as a mourning custom, as it is stated: "Stamp your feet and say: Alas!" (Ezekiel 6:11). This custom continued for a long time as a sign of mourning in Eretz Yisrael (Rabbi Shlomo ben HaYatom; *Tosefot HaRosh*).

Should not stomp with a sandal – לֹא יְקַלֵּס בְּסַנְדָּל: One version of the text inverts the statement and says: One should not stomp with a shoe, because it has a soft sole and one may injure himself. On the other hand, a sandal has a hard sole, which was made from wood (Rashi manuscript). There is another version that reads: Not with a shoe and not with a sandal, lest one become distracted and be injured.

Once a mourner nods his head – אָבֵל, כֵּיוָן שֶׁנִּיעְנַע רֹאשׁוֹ: Some explain that when a mourner nods his head he displays that he has already been somewhat consoled, and it is no longer necessary to sit with him and trouble him with conversation (Rabbeinu Gershom Meor HaGola; Rabbeinu Yehonatan of Lunel). Some say that since he is sitting with his face wrapped and he is required to sit quietly, if he wishes to hint that he is tired or that it is difficult for him to be in the company of others, then he should do so only with a nod of his head (Rav Hai Gaon).

LANGUAGE

Hemp garments [*tzerada*] – צְרָדָא: According to most commentaries this refers to a simple linen or hemp garment. It is apparently related to the Middle Persian čādur, meaning a veil.

Killus – קִילּוּס: Apparently a Greek word, although there is dispute with regard to its precise origin. Some say that it is derived from κλῆσις, *klēsis*, meaning to raise one's voice or to call.

HALAKHA

The people adopted…burial in linen garments – ...נָהֲגוּ הָעָם בִּכְלֵי פִשְׁתָּן: It is customary not to bury the dead in expensive shrouds, even if he was a great person (*Shulḥan Arukh, Yoreh De'a* 352:1).

There are no restrictions of a Festival in the presence of a deceased Torah scholar – אֵין מוֹעֵד בִּפְנֵי תַלְמִיד חָכָם: When a Torah scholar dies, even during the intermediate days of a Festival, and all the more so on Hanukkah, Purim, or a New Moon, he is eulogized as he would be during a weekday, as a sign of respect. The eulogy must be delivered in the presence of his body, and if the body is not present it is prohibited to eulogize the deceased. One may also eulogize a Torah scholar on the day one hears about his death, even if it is not in the presence of his body. The custom today is to eulogize the deceased during the intermediate days of a Festival or on holidays only if the deceased is a Torah scholar and it is in his presence (*Arukh HaShulḥan*; *Shulḥan Arukh, Yoreh De'a* 401:5).

Once a mourner nods his head – אָבֵל, כֵּיוָן שֶׁנִּיעְנַע רֹאשׁוֹ: Once the consolers see that the mourner wants them to leave then they must leave, even if he does not say so explicitly. For example, they should leave even if he simply nods his head or motions in any other way (see *Arukh HaShulḥan*; *Shulḥan Arukh, Yoreh De'a* 376:1).

וְאָמַר רַבִּי יוֹחָנָן: הַכֹּל חַיָּיבִין לַעֲמוֹד מִפְּנֵי נָשִׂיא, חוּץ מֵאָבֵל וְחוֹלֶה. וְאָמַר רַבִּי יוֹחָנָן: לַכֹּל אוֹמְרִים לָהֶם ״שְׁבוּ״ חוּץ מֵאָבֵל וְחוֹלֶה.

Rabbi Yoḥanan further said: All are obligated to stand in **the presence of the** ***Nasi*****, except for a mourner**[H] **and one who is sick. Rabbi Yoḥanan said: To all** who stand before a great person **one says: Be seated,**[NH] and only then may they sit down, **except for a mourner and one who is sick.** If they stood up they do not need permission to sit down, but rather they may do so if they wish.

אָמַר רַב יְהוּדָה אָמַר רַב: אָבֵל, יוֹם רִאשׁוֹן – אָסוּר לֶאֱכוֹל לֶחֶם מִשֶּׁלּוֹ, מִדְּאָמַר לֵיהּ רַחֲמָנָא לִיחֶזְקֵאל: ״וְלֶחֶם אֲנָשִׁים לֹא תֹאכֵל״. רַבָּה וְרַב יוֹסֵף מְחַלְּפֵי סְעוּדָּתַיְיהוּ לַהֲדָדֵי.

Rav Yehuda said in the name of Rav: A mourner on the **first** day of his mourning **is prohibited from eating of his own bread.**[NH] From where is this derived? **From what the Merciful One says to Ezekiel** when the latter is in mourning: **"Nor eat the bread of men"** (Ezekiel 24:17), which indicates that other mourners must eat bread made by others. It was related that when **Rabba and Rav Yosef** were in mourning they **would exchange their meals**[N] **with each other.**

וְאָמַר רַב יְהוּדָה אָמַר רַב: מֵת בָּעִיר – כָּל בְּנֵי הָעִיר אֲסוּרִין בַּעֲשִׂיַּית מְלָאכָה.

And Rav Yehuda said in the name of Rav: When a person **dies in a city,**[N] **all of the residents of that city are prohibited from performing work** until he has been buried.[H]

רַב הַמְנוּנָא אִיקְלַע לְדָרוּמָתָא. שְׁמַע קוֹל שִׁיפּוּרָא דְּשָׁכְבָא. חֲזָא הָנָךְ אֱינָשֵׁי דְּקָא עָבְדִי עֲבִידְתָּא, אֲמַר לְהוּ: לֶיהֱווֹ הָנָךְ אֱינָשֵׁי בְּשַׁמְתָּא! לָא שָׁכְבָא אִיכָּא בְּמָתָא? אֲמַרוּ לֵיהּ: חֲבוּרָתָא אִיכָּא בְּמָתָא. אֲמַר לְהוּ: אִי הָכִי – שַׁרְיָא לְכוּ.

The Gemara relates that when **Rav Hamnuna** once **happened** to come **to** a place called **Darumata he heard the sound of a** ***shofar*** announcing that a person **had died** in the town. When **he saw some people doing work he said to them: Let these people be under an excommunication. Is there not a dead** person **in town? They said to him: There are** separate **groups in the town,** each one responsible for its own dead. Knowing that the deceased was not from our group, we continued our work. **He said to them: If so, it is permitted** to you,[N] and he revoked his excommunication.

וְאָמַר רַב יְהוּדָה אָמַר רַב: כָּל הַמִּתְקַשֶּׁה עַל מֵתוֹ יוֹתֵר מִדַּאי – עַל מֵת אַחֵר הוּא בּוֹכֶה. הַהִיא אִיתְּתָא דַּהֲוַת בְּשֵׁיבָבוּתֵיהּ דְּרַב הוּנָא, הָווּ לָהּ שִׁבְעָה בְּנֵי. מֵת חַד מִינַּיְיהוּ, הֲוַות קָא בָּכְיָא בִּיתֵירְתָּא עֲלֵיהּ. שְׁלַח לָהּ רַב הוּנָא: לָא תַּעַבְדִי הָכִי! לָא אַשְׁגַּחָה בֵּיהּ. שְׁלַח לָהּ: אִי צַיְיתַּתְּ – מוּטָב; וְאִי לָא – צְבִית זַוְודָתָא לְאִידָּךְ מֵית. וּמִיתוּ כּוּלְּהוּ. לַסּוֹף אֲמַר לָהּ: תִּיגּוֹשׁ זַוְודָתָא לְנַפְשִׁיךְ, וּמִיתָא.

And Rav Yehuda said further in the name of Rav: Anyone who grieves excessively over his dead[NH] and does not allow himself to be consoled **will** in the end **weep for another** person.[N] The Gemara relates that **a certain woman** who lived **in the neighborhood of Rav Huna had seven sons. One of them died and she wept for him excessively. Rav Huna sent** a message **to her: Do not do this.** But **she took no heed of him. He** then **sent** another message **to her: If you listen to me, it is well, but if not, prepare shrouds for another death.** But she would not listen **and they all died. In the end,** when she continued with her excessive mourning, **he said to her:** Since you are acting in this way, **prepare shrouds for yourself,** and soon thereafter **she died.**

NOTES

To all who stand one says, Be seated – לַכֹּל אוֹמְרִים שְׁבוּ: The early authorities write that saying: Be seated, to a mourner is a bad omen, as if saying to him that he should remain in mourning. *Tosefot HaRosh* writes that in the Bible the word sitting means remaining and continuing. Some say that this custom applies only during the time of the ritual sitting and standing after the burial, when one may not say to the mourners: Be seated (Rabbeinu Yehonatan of Lunel). Others explain that if mourners stand before an important person he should not say to them: Be seated, but should instead use different language that does not contain a bad omen (see Ran).

Is prohibited from eating of his own – אָסוּר לֶאֱכוֹל...מִשֶּׁלּוֹ: The early authorities write that it is implied in the Jerusalem Talmud that if a mourner does not wish to eat or to accept assistance from other people then he may fast for the first day.

Exchange their meals – מְחַלְּפֵי סְעוּדָּתַיְיהוּ: Some explain that this refers to a case in which they were both mourning at the same time (Commentary on *Moed Katan*).

When a person dies in a city – מֵת בָּעִיר וכו׳: Some explain that the *halakha* that all residents of a city must refrain from work in order to involve themselves in the burial applies specifically to a corpse with no one to bury it [*met mitzva*], whom everyone is obligated to bury (*Be'er Halakhot Gedolot*). However, most of the early authorities do not accept this explanation and state that the obligation to refrain from working refers to whenever there is any dead person in the city.

It is permitted to you – שַׁרְיָא לְכוּ: Some explain this expression to mean that you are permitted to act in accordance with your custom, while others say that it means that the excommunication that he had just declared was nullified (Rashi manuscript).

One who grieves excessively [*hamitkashe*] over his dead – הַמִּתְקַשֶּׁה עַל מֵתוֹ יוֹתֵר מִדַּאי: Some, including Rashi in the manuscript, have a version that reads: Passionately eulogizes [*hamakshir*] or [*hamitkashir*], which is understood to mean that he excessively eulogizes his dead, as in the expression: Tied eulogy [*hesped kashur*] (Jerusalem Talmud, *Yevamot* 16:4), which refers to the custom of tying something to the doorway of a house so that passersby would know it was a house of mourning (*Korban HaEda*).

Will in the end weep for another person – עַל מֵת אַחֵר הוּא בּוֹכֶה: The early authorities explain this statement in two different ways. Perhaps he will continue to weep because he shows that he does not accept God's judgment upon himself. If so, his punishment corresponds to his transgression in that he is punished by having to mourn again. Alternatively, it is possible that he is punished for a similar reason to when the Jewish people in the desert were punished for crying without cause upon hearing the report of the spies (see *Iyyun Ya'akov*).

HALAKHA

A mourner is not required to stand – אֵין אָבֵל חַיָּיב לַעֲמוֹד: A mourner, and similarly a sick person, is not required to stand in respect in the presence of the *Nasi* (*Shulḥan Arukh Yoreh De'a* 376:1, and in the comment of Rema).

To all who stand one says, Be seated – לַכֹּל אוֹמְרִים שְׁבוּ: One who wishes to honor his fellow should say to him: Be seated. However, one does not say this to a mourner or to a sick person (*Shulḥan Arukh, Yoreh De'a* 376:2).

The first meal after the burial – סְעוּדַּת הַבְרָאָה: During the first meal after the burial it is prohibited for the mourner to eat his own food, and it is a mitzva for his neighbors to bring him food to eat. However, if no one sends him food or he has no neighbors he may eat his own food and is not required to starve himself (*Taz*). It was the common practice in the time of the Gemara to prepare special foods as a sign of mourning, such as eggs or lentils, and in many places it is customary to serve the mourner a cup of wine. Nowadays there are many different customs. One may bring food to another when he is mourning and that person can return the favor and bring food to the first if he is subsequently in mourning, like Rabba and Rav Yosef, provided that this condition to repay the meal is not stated explicitly (*Shulḥan Arukh, Yoreh De'a* 378:1).

Prohibition against working when there is a dead person in the city – אִיסּוּר מְלָאכָה כְּשֶׁמֵּת בָּעִיר: When there is an unburied dead person in a city all of the residents of that city are prohibited from working until he is buried. Anyone who sees a funeral and does not join is deserving of excommunication. If there are assigned groups that care for the dead, then other people in this city may perform work. However, at the time when the deceased is taken out for burial everyone must refrain from working (Shulḥan Arukh, Yoreh De'a 343:1).

One who grieves excessively over his dead – הַמִּתְקַשֶּׁה עַל מֵתוֹ יוֹתֵר מִדַּאי: One should not excessively mourn over his dead. Instead there should be three days of mourning, seven days for eulogizing, and thirty days during which it is prohibited to cut one's hair or iron one's clothes (*Shulḥan Arukh, Yoreh De'a* 394:1).

"אַל תִּבְכּוּ לְמֵת וְאַל תָּנֻדוּ לוֹ" – "אַל תִּבְכּוּ לְמֵת" – יוֹתֵר מִדַּאי; "וְאַל תָּנֻדוּ לוֹ" – יוֹתֵר מִכְּשִׁיעוּר. הָא כֵּיצַד? שְׁלֹשָׁה יָמִים – לִבְכִי, וְשִׁבְעָה – לְהֶסְפֵּד, וּשְׁלֹשִׁים – לְגִיהוּץ וּלְתִסְפּוֹרֶת. מִכָּאן וְאֵילָךְ – אָמַר הַקָּדוֹשׁ בָּרוּךְ הוּא: אִי אַתֶּם רַחֲמָנִים בּוֹ יוֹתֵר מִמֶּנִּי.

The Sages taught in a *baraita* with regard to the verse that states: **"Weep not for the dead, neither bemoan him"** (Jeremiah 22:10): **"Weep not for the dead"** is referring to **excessive** mourning; **"neither bemoan him" more than the** appropriate **measure** of time. **How so?** What is the appropriate measure? **Three days for weeping, and seven for eulogizing, and thirty for** the prohibition against **ironing** clothing **and for** the prohibition against **cutting hair. From this** point **forward the Holy One, Blessed be He, says: Do not be more merciful with** the deceased **than I am.** If the Torah commands one to mourn for a certain period of time, then that suffices.

"בְּכוּ בָכוֹ לַהֹלֵךְ", אָמַר רַב יְהוּדָה: לַהוֹלֵךְ בְּלֹא בָּנִים. רַבִּי יְהוֹשֻׁעַ בֶּן לֵוִי לָא אָזֵיל לְבֵי אֲבִלָא אֶלָּא לְמַאן דְּאָזֵיל בְּלָא בְּנֵי, דִּכְתִיב: "בְּכוּ בָכוֹ לַהֹלֵךְ כִּי לֹא יָשׁוּב עוֹד וְרָאָה אֶת אֶרֶץ מוֹלַדְתּוֹ". רַב הוּנָא אָמַר: זֶה שֶׁעָבַר עֲבֵירָה וְשָׁנָה בָּהּ.

It is stated in the continuation of the verse: **"Weep sore for him that goes away." Rav Yehuda said:** This is referring **to one who leaves** the world **without children**[N] to survive him, since mourning for him is much more intense. It was related that **Rabbi Yehoshua ben Levi would go to a house of mourning only for one who passed away without children, as it is written: "Weep sore for him that goes away; for he shall return [*yashuv*] no more, nor see his native land"** (Jeremiah 22:10). **Rav Huna** disagreed with the interpretation of the verse and **said:** "Him that goes" **is one who committed a transgression**[N] **and** then **repeated it,** i.e., one who sins constantly and does not repent [*yashav*], and therefore loses his portion in the World-to-Come, his "native land."

רַב הוּנָא לְטַעְמֵיהּ, דְּאָמַר רַב הוּנָא: כֵּיוָן שֶׁעָבַר אָדָם עֲבֵירָה וְשָׁנָה בָּהּ – הוּתְּרָה לוֹ. הוּתְּרָה לוֹ סָלְקָא דַּעְתָּךְ?! אֶלָּא אֵימָא: נַעֲשֵׂית לוֹ כְּהֶיתֵּר.

The Gemara notes that **Rav Huna** conforms **to his** standard line of **reasoning,** as **Rav Huna said: Once a person commits a transgression and repeats it, it becomes permitted to him.** The Gemara questions the wording used here: **Does it enter your mind** that it is actually **permitted?** How could it possibly be permitted for him to sin? **Rather, say** instead: **It becomes as though it were permitted,** for after doing it twice he no longer relates to his action as the violation of a serious prohibition.

אָמַר רַבִּי לֵוִי: אָבֵל שְׁלֹשָׁה יָמִים הָרִאשׁוֹנִים – יִרְאֶה אֶת עַצְמוֹ כְּאִילּוּ חֶרֶב מוּנַּחַת לוֹ בֵּין שְׁתֵּי יְרֵיכוֹתָיו. מִשְּׁלֹשָׁה עַד שִׁבְעָה – כְּאִילּוּ מוּנַּחַת לוֹ כְּנֶגְדּוֹ בְּקֶרֶן זָוִית. מִכָּאן וְאֵילָךְ – כְּאִילּוּ עוֹבֶרֶת כְּנֶגְדּוֹ בַּשּׁוּק.

Rabbi Levi said: A mourner during **the first three days** of his mourning **should see himself as though a sword were lying between his two thighs,**[N] meaning that he too may be facing imminent death. During this period he should live in dread. **From the third to the seventh** days he should conduct himself **as if** the sword **were lying opposite him in the corner,** but still threatening him. **From this** point **forward it is as if** the sword **was moving before him in the marketplace,** and the fear is not as great.

"וְלֹא שֶׁל נָשִׁים לְעוֹלָם מִפְּנֵי הַכָּבוֹד". אָמְרִי נְהַרְדָּעֵי: לֹא שָׁנוּ

§ The mishna teaches: **And the** biers **of women** are **never** set down, **due to** their **honor.** The Sages **of Neharde'a say: They only taught** this

NOTES

To one who leaves the world without children – לַהוֹלֵךְ בְּלֹא בָּנִים: Some write that since, as the Sages say, one who does not have children is considered to be as though he is dead, it is as though this person died twice, once during his lifetime and once after his death. Therefore, the grief over his demise is much greater (*Iyyun Ya'akov*). This issue is explained in several other ways, based on both its simple meaning and the mystical meaning.

Rav Huna said this is one who committed a transgression – רַב הוּנָא אָמַר זֶה שֶׁעָבַר עֲבֵירָה: Many of the early authorities hold that Rav Huna does not dispute the first explanation of the verse. Rather, he bases his teaching on the second half of the same verse: "He shall return no more, nor see his native land," meaning that the sinner will not find a path of repentance for himself (see Ran; Meiri).

Between his two thighs – בֵּין שְׁתֵּי יְרֵכוֹתָיו: Many have a version of the text that reads: Between his shoulders, meaning that the mourner stands bowed over in the manner of one who stands in fear lest he be stabbed in the back with a sword, and must consequently be fearful and submissive at every moment (Rabbeinu Yehonatan of Lunel). *Tosafot* cite a parallel statement from the Jerusalem Talmud. It is also stated there that if a child is born within that family, it is a good sign that the family has been healed.

Perek **III**
Daf **28** Amud **a**

אֶלָּא חַיָּה, אֲבָל שְׁאָר נָשִׁים – מַנִּיחִין.

with regard to **a woman** who died **in childbirth,** and therefore continues to bleed. **But** the biers of **other women may be set down** in the street.

רַבִּי אֶלְעָזָר אָמַר: אֲפִילּוּ שְׁאָר הַנָּשִׁים, דִּכְתִיב: "וַתָּמׇת שָׁם מִרְיָם וַתִּקָּבֵר שָׁם" – סָמוּךְ לְמִיתָה קְבוּרָה.

Rabbi Elazar said: Even the biers of **other women**[N] must not be set down in the street,[H] **as it is written: "And Miriam died there and was buried there"** (Numbers 20:1), which teaches that **the** site of her **burial was close to** the place of her **death.** Therefore, it is preferable to bury a woman as close as possible to the place where she died.

NOTES

Even other women – אֲפִילּוּ שְׁאָר הַנָּשִׁים: Some say that not placing the bier of women in the street is a Torah law, as it is derived from the Torah's description of Miriam's death. Others say that it was due to the honor of the community (Meiri). Some suggest that it is done on account of the women's honor and that it is not appropriate for a woman to be displayed in burial shrouds before all (Rabbeinu Yehonatan).

HALAKHA

The bier of a woman in the street – מִיטַּת אִשָּׁה בָּרְחוֹב: The bier of a deceased woman is never placed in the street, even if she did not die in childbirth, in accordance with the opinion of Rabbi Elazar (*Shulḥan Arukh, Yoreh De'a* 355:ג).

וְאָמַר רַבִּי אֶלְעָזָר: אַף מִרְיָם בִּנְשִׁיקָה מֵתָה. אָתְיָא ״שָׁם״ ״שָׁם״ מִמֹּשֶׁה. וּמִפְּנֵי מָה לֹא נֶאֱמַר בָּהּ ״עַל פִּי ה׳״ – מִפְּנֵי שֶׁגְּנַאי הַדָּבָר לְאוֹמְרוֹ.

With regard to that same verse **Rabbi Elazar said** further: **Miriam also died by** the divine **kiss,** just like her brother Moses. What is the source for this? **This is derived** through a verbal analogy between the word **"there"** stated with regard to Miriam and the word **"there"**[N] mentioned **with regard to Moses.** With regard to Moses it says: "So Moses the servant of the Lord died there in the land of Moab by the mouth of the Lord" (Deuteronomy 34:5). **For what** reason **was it not** explicitly **stated with regard to her,** as it is stated with regard to Moses, that she died **"by the mouth of the Lord"?** It is **because it would be unseemly to say such a thing,** that a woman died by way of a divine kiss, and therefore it is not said explicitly.

אָמַר רַבִּי אַמִי: לָמָּה נִסְמְכָה מִיתַת מִרְיָם לְפָרָשַׁת פָּרָה אֲדוּמָּה? לוֹמַר לָךְ: מַה פָּרָה אֲדוּמָּה מְכַפֶּרֶת – אַף מִיתָתָן שֶׁל צַדִּיקִים מְכַפֶּרֶת. אָמַר רַבִּי אֶלְעָזָר: לָמָּה נִסְמְכָה מִיתַת אַהֲרֹן לְבִגְדֵי כְהוּנָּה? מַה בִּגְדֵי כְהוּנָּה מְכַפְּרִין – אַף מִיתָתָן שֶׁל צַדִּיקִים מְכַפֶּרֶת.

Rabbi Ami said: Why was the Torah portion that describes the **death of Miriam juxtaposed to the portion** dealing with **the red heifer? To tell you: Just as the red heifer atones** for sin, **so too, the death of the righteous atones** for sin. **Rabbi Elazar said: Why was** the Torah portion that describes the **death of Aaron juxtaposed to** the portion discussing **the priestly garments?** This teaches that **just as the priestly garments atone** for sin, **so too, the death of the righteous atones** for sin.[N]

תָּנוּ רַבָּנַן: מֵת פִּתְאוֹם – זוֹ הִיא מִיתָה חֲטוּפָה. חָלָה יוֹם אֶחָד וּמֵת – זוֹ הִיא מִיתָה דְּחוּפָה. רַבִּי חֲנַנְיָא בֶּן גַּמְלִיאֵל אוֹמֵר: זוֹ הִיא מִיתַת מַגֵּפָה, שֶׁנֶּאֱמַר: ״בֶּן אָדָם הִנְנִי לוֹקֵחַ מִמְּךָ אֶת מַחְמַד עֵינֶיךָ בְּמַגֵּפָה״ וּכְתִיב: ״וָאֲדַבֵּר אֶל הָעָם בַּבֹּקֶר וַתָּמָת אִשְׁתִּי בָּעֶרֶב״.

§ **The Sages taught** the following *baraita*: If one **dies suddenly** without having been sick, **this is death through snatching.** If he **became sick for a day and died, this is an expedited**[N] **death. Rabbi Ḥananya ben Gamliel says: This is death at a stroke, as it is stated: "Son of man, behold, I am about to take away from you the delight of your eyes at a stroke"** (Ezekiel 24:16). **And** when this prophecy is fulfilled **it is written: "So I spoke to the people in the morning and at evening my wife died"** (Ezekiel 24:18).

שְׁנֵי יָמִים וּמֵת – זוֹ הִיא מִיתָה דְּחוּיָה; שְׁלֹשָׁה – גְּעָרָה; אַרְבָּעָה – נְזִיפָה; חֲמִשָּׁה – זוֹ הִיא מִיתַת כָּל אָדָם.

If he was sick for **two days and died, this is a quickened death.** If he was sick for **three** days and died, this is a death of **rebuke.** If he died after being sick for **four** days, this is a death of **reprimand.** If one died after a sickness lasting **five** days, **this is the** ordinary **death of all people.**

אָמַר רַבִּי חָנִין: מַאי קְרָא? ״הֵן קָרְבוּ יָמֶיךָ לָמוּת״, ״הֵן״ – חַד; ״קָרְבוּ״ – תְּרֵי; ״יָמֶיךָ״ – תְּרֵי; הָא חֲמִשָּׁה. ״הֵן״ חַד – שֶׁכֵּן בִּלְשׁוֹן יְוָנִי קוֹרִין לְאַחַת ״הֵן״.

Rabbi Ḥanin said: What is the verse from which this is derived? It is stated: **"Behold, your days approach that you must die"** (Deuteronomy 31:14).[N] This verse is expounded in the following manner: **"Behold [*hen*]"** indicates **one; "approach [*karvu*],"** a plural term, indicates **two; "your days [*yamekha*],"** also a plural term, indicates another **two;** and therefore in total **this is five.** How does the word ***hen*** indicate **one? Because in the Greek language they call** the number **one *hen*.**[L]

מֵת בַּחֲמִשִּׁים שָׁנָה – זוֹ הִיא מִיתַת כָּרֵת; חֲמִשִּׁים וּשְׁתַּיִם שָׁנָה זוֹ הִיא מִיתָתוֹ שֶׁל שְׁמוּאֵל הָרָמָתִי; שִׁשִּׁים – זוֹ הִיא מִיתָה בִּידֵי שָׁמַיִם.

The Gemara discusses the significance of death at different ages: If one **dies when** he is **fifty years** old, **this is death through *karet*,**[N] the divine punishment of excision, meted out for the most serious transgressions. If he dies when he is **fifty-two years** old, **this is the death of Samuel from Ramah.** If he dies at the age of **sixty, this is death at the hand of Heaven.**

אָמַר מָר זוּטְרָא: מַאי קְרָא? דִּכְתִיב: ״תָּבֹא בְכֶלַח אֱלֵי קָבֶר״. ״בְּכֶלַח״ בְּגִימַטְרִיָּא שִׁיתִּין הָווּ.

Mar Zutra said: What is the verse from which this is derived? **As it is written: "You shall come to your grave in a ripe age [*bekhelaḥ*]"** (Job 5:26). The word **"ripe age" [*bekhelaḥ*] has the numerical value of sixty,** and it is alluded to there that dying at this age involves a divine punishment.

שִׁבְעִים – שֵׂיבָה, שְׁמוֹנִים – גְּבוּרוֹת, דִּכְתִיב: ״יְמֵי שְׁנוֹתֵינוּ בָהֶם שִׁבְעִים שָׁנָה וְאִם בִּגְבוּרוֹת שְׁמוֹנִים שָׁנָה״. אָמַר רַבָּה: מֵחֲמִשִּׁים וְעַד שִׁשִּׁים שָׁנָה – זוֹ הִיא מִיתַת כָּרֵת. וְהַאי דְּלָא חָשֵׁיב לְהוּ – מִשּׁוּם כְּבוֹדוֹ שֶׁל שְׁמוּאֵל הָרָמָתִי.

One who dies at the age of **seventy** has reached **old age.** One who dies at the age of **eighty** dies in **strength, as it is written: "The days of our years are seventy, or if by reason of strength, eighty years"** (Psalms 90:10). **Rabba said:** Not only is death at the age of fifty a sign of *karet*, but even death **from fifty to sixty years** of age **is death by *karet*. And** the reason that **all of these years were not counted** in connection with *karet* is **due to the honor of Samuel from Ramah,** who died at the age of fifty-two.

NOTES

This is derived between the word there and there – אָתְיָא שָׁם שָׁם: In this version of the text the derivation is from the verses describing the death of Moses. However, there is a different version of the talmudic text in which the fact that Miriam died by divine kiss is derived through a verbal analogy to the verses describing Aaron's death. Rabbi Eliyahu Mizraḥi explains similarly (*Beit Moed*).

The death of Aaron and the priestly garments – בִּגְדֵי כְהוּנָּה וּמִיתַת אַהֲרֹן: See Rashi manuscript and *Tosafot*, who explain that the Torah describes Aaron's removal of his priestly garments before his death. This detail is unnecessary for the narrative, and is mentioned by the Torah only to teach that there is a relationship between these garments and Aaron's death. The atonement performed by the priestly garments is described in tractate *Zevaḥim*, and each individual garment atones for a specific sin. The Torah states explicitly that the frontplate of the High Priest atones for sin.

Snatching, expedited – חֲטוּפָה, דְּחוּפָה: The death of the wicked is sudden, as the verse states: "Like the passing of the storm, and there is no wickedness" (Proverbs 10:25), and therefore it is a bad sign when one dies in this manner. Death through snatching is extremely sudden, while expedited death is also quick, but not quite as sudden. Quickened death [*mita deḥuya*], literally, pushed death, is analogous to when one pushes something and it rolls away gradually. Expedited death [*mita deḥufa*] is analogous to pushing something which falls immediately and is lost (Rabbi Shlomo ben HaYatom).

Behold, your days approach that you must die – הֵן קָרְבוּ יָמֶיךָ לָמוּת: The early authorities question this, as the verse refers to Moses, who was not sick at all prior to his death. Some write that this was said to Moses in order to inform him that this is the way that a person ordinarily dies, but that one who is completely righteous like him does not require this (*Tosefot HaRosh*). Some say that the reason ordinary people die in this manner is to give them time to prepare for their death, and therefore God informed Moses that he should prepare himself (Ritva).

The age of fifty and *karet* – חֲמִשִּׁים מִיתַת כָּרֵת: A proof is offered in the Jerusalem Talmud based on the verses stated with regard to the Levites: "You shall not cut the staff of the families of the Kohathites" (Numbers 4:18), meaning that precautions should be taken that they not die while serving in the Temple. Because Levites served in the Temple until the age of fifty, it is deduced that anyone who dies up to this point dies through *karet*. See the Ran, who offers another reason for this statement: Since the lifespan of strength is eighty years, and the first twenty years, during which one is not punished by divine intervention, are removed from the equation, then one who does not live for half of these remaining years fits the description "They shall not live half of their days" (Psalms 55:24).

LANGUAGE

One [*hen*] – הֵן: From the Greek ἕν, *hen*, meaning one.

PERSONALITIES

Rabba – רבה: Rav Abba bar Naḥmani HaKohen, popularly referred to as Rabba throughout the Babylonian Talmud, was a third-generation Babylonian *amora*. Rabba was a student of Rav Huna, who himself was a student of Rav. Therefore, Rabba's opinions on *halakha* were in concert with Rav's teachings. Rabba was considered the sharpest among his peers, to the extent that he was referred to as one who uproots mountains, in contrast with his colleague Rav Yosef, whose expertise was in his broad knowledge, and who was consequently referred to as Sinai. In almost every disagreement between them, the ruling follows Rabba's opinion.

Rabba had many students, and virtually all of the Sages of the following generation studied under him. His personal life was one of great tragedy; it appears that his children died during his lifetime. He was poverty stricken his entire life, eking out a living from agricultural work. When his nephew Abaye became orphaned at a young age, Rabba took him in and raised him.

LANGUAGE

Finest flour [*semida*] – סמידא: This word is similar to the Greek σεμίδαλις, *semidalis*, meaning fine wheat flour.

רב יוסף, כי הוה בר שיתין עבד להו יומא טבא לרבנן. אמר: נפקי לי מכרת. אמר ליה אביי: נהי דנפק ליה מר מכרת דשני, מכרת דיומי מי נפיק מר? אמר ליה: נקוט לך מיהא פלגא בידך.

The Gemara relates that **when Rav Yosef turned sixty he made a holiday for the Sages.** Explaining the cause for his celebration, **he said: I have passed** the age of ***karet*****. Abaye said to him: Master, even though you have passed the *karet* of years, have you, Master, escaped the *karet* of days?** As previously mentioned, sudden death is also considered to be a form of *karet*. **He said to him: Grasp at least half in your hand,** for I have at least escaped one type of *karet*.

רב הונא נח נפשיה פתאום. הוו קא דייגי רבנן. תנא להו זוגא דמהדייב: לא שנו אלא שלא הגיע לגבורות, אבל הגיע לגבורות – זו היא מיתת נשיקה.

It was related that **Rav Huna died suddenly,** and **the Sages were concerned** that this was a bad sign. The Sage **Zuga**[N] **from Hadayeiv taught them** the following: They **taught** these principles **only when** the deceased **had not reached** the age of **strength,** i.e., eighty. **But if he had reached** the age of **strength** and then died suddenly, **this is death by way of a divine kiss.**

אמר רבא: חיי, בני ומזוני, לא בזכותא תליא מילתא, אלא במזלא תליא מילתא. דהא רבה ורב חסדא תרווייהו רבנן צדיקי הוו, מר מצלי ואתי מיטרא, ומר מצלי ואתי מיטרא.

Rava said: Length of **life, children, and sustenance do not depend on** one's **merit,**[N] **but rather they depend upon fate. As, Rabba**[P] **and Rav Ḥisda were both pious Sages;** one **Sage would pray** during a drought **and rain would fall, and** the other **Sage** would **pray and rain would fall.**

רב חסדא חיה תשעין ותרתין שנין – רבה חיה ארבעין. בי רב חסדא – שיתין הלולי; בי רבה – שיתין תיכלי.

And nevertheless, their lives were very different. **Rav Ḥisda lived for ninety-two years,** whereas **Rabba lived for** only **forty** years. **The house of Rav Ḥisda** celebrated **sixty wedding feasts,** whereas the **house of Rabba** experienced **sixty calamities.** In other words, many fortuitous events took place in the house of Rav Ḥisda and the opposite occurred in the house of Rabba.

בי רב חסדא – סמידא לכלבי ולא מתבעי; בי רבה – נהמא דשערי לאינשי, ולא משתכח.

In the house of Rav Ḥisda there was bread from **the finest flour** [*semida*][L] even **for the dogs, and it was not asked after,** as there was so much food. **In the house of Rabba,** on the other hand, there was coarse **barley bread** even **for people, and it was not found** in sufficient quantities. This shows that the length of life, children, and sustenance all depend not upon one's merit, but upon fate.

ואמר רבא: הני תלת מילי בעאי קמי שמיא, תרתי יהבו לי, חדא לא יהבו לי; חוכמתיה דרב הונא ועותריה דרב חסדא – ויהבו לי; ענותנותיה דרבה בר רב הונא – לא יהבו לי.

Apropos Rav Ḥisda's great wealth, the Gemara reports that **Rava said: These three things I requested from Heaven, two** of which **were given to me,** and **one was not given to me:** I requested the **wisdom of Rav Huna and the wealth of Rav Ḥisda and they were given to me.** I also requested the **humility of Rabba bar Rav Huna,** but **it was not given to me.**

רב שעורים אחוה דרבא הוה יתיב קמיה דרבא. חזייה דהוה קא מנמנם. אמר ליה: לימא ליה מר דלא לצערן! אמר ליה: מר לאו שושביניה הוא? אמר ליה: כיון דאימסר מזלא – לא אשגח בי. אמר ליה: ליתחזי לי מר. איתחזי ליה. אמר ליה: הוה ליה למר צערא? אמר ליה: כי ריבדא דכוסילתא.

The Gemara continues its discussion of the deaths of the righteous. **Rav Seorim, Rava's brother, sat before Rava,** and **he saw that** Rava **was dozing,** i.e., about to die. Rava **said to** his brother: **Master, tell him,** the Angel of Death, **not to torment me.** Knowing that Rava was not afraid of the Angel of Death, Rav Seorim **said to** him: **Master, are you not a friend of** the Angel of Death?[N] Rava **said to him: Since my fate has been handed over** to him, and it has been decreed that I shall die, the Angel of Death **no longer pays heed to me.** Rav Seorim said to Rava: **Master, appear to me** in a dream after your death. And Rava **appeared to him.** Rav Seorim **said to** Rava: **Master, did you have pain** in death? **He said to him: Like the prick** of the knife **when letting blood.**

NOTES

Zuga – זוגא: In an alternative version of the text his name appears as Zawa. Rashi in the manuscript understands that Zuga is not a name, but refers to a pair [*zug*] of Sages.

Do not depend on merit – לא בזכותא תליא: Some of the early authorities write that this opinion is rejected, as it is said elsewhere that Jews are not under the authority of fate (Meiri). However, others say that one's fortune depends not only upon his actions, but also on his fate, as although one's merit may change his fate, it does not always change it completely (Ran; Ritva; *Tosafot*).

Are you not a friend of the Angel of Death – לאו שושביניה הוא: Many stories are told in the Talmud about different Sages who engaged in discussions with various angels, including the Angel of Death (see *Berakhot* 51a, *Ḥagiga* 4b, and *Ketubot* 77b) The Angel of Death takes the righteous into account and does not kill them in a disgraceful manner.

רָבָא הֲוָה יָתֵיב קַמֵּיהּ דְּרַב נַחְמָן. חַזְיֵיהּ דְּקָא מְנַמְנֵם. אֲמַר לֵיהּ: לֵימָא לֵיהּ מָר דְּלָא לְצַעֲרַן. אֲמַר לֵיהּ: מָר לָאו אָדָם חָשׁוּב הוּא? אֲמַר לֵיהּ: מַאן חֲשִׁיב, מַאן סְפִין, מַאן רְקִיעַ?

It was similarly related that **Rava sat before Rav Naḥman, and he saw that** Rav Naḥman **was dozing,** i.e., slipping into death. Rav Naḥman **said to** Rava: **Master, tell** the Angel of Death **not to torment me. Rava said to him: Master, are you not an important person** who is respected in Heaven? Rav Naḥman **said to him:** In the supernal world **who is important? Who is honorable? Who is complete?**[N]

אֲמַר לֵיהּ: לִיתְחֲזֵי לִי מָר. אִתְחֲזֵי לֵיהּ. אֲמַר לֵיהּ: הֲוָה לֵיהּ לְמָר צַעֲרָא? אֲמַר לֵיהּ: כְּמִישְׁחַל בִּנִיתָא מֵחֶלְבָּא. וְאִי אֲמַר לִי הַקָּדוֹשׁ בָּרוּךְ הוּא זִיל בְּהַהוּא עָלְמָא כַּד הֲוֵית – לָא בָּעֵינָא, דְּנָפֵישׁ בִּיעֲתוּתֵיהּ.

Rava **said to** Rav Naḥman: **Master, appear to me** in a dream after your death. And **he appeared to him.** Rava **said to him: Master, did you have pain** in death? Rav Naḥman **said to him: Like the removal of hair from milk,** which is a most gentle process. But nevertheless, **were the Holy One, Blessed be He, to say to me: Go** back **to that world,** the physical world, **as you were, I would not want to go, for the fear of** the Angel of Death **is great.**[N] And I would not want to go through such a terrifying experience a second time.

רַבִּי אֶלְעָזָר הֲוָה קָאָכֵיל תְּרוּמָה, אִיתְחֲזֵי לֵיהּ. אֲמַר לֵיהּ: תְּרוּמָה קָא אָכֵילְנָא, וְלָאו קוֹדֶשׁ אִיקְרֵי? חָלְפָא לֵיהּ שַׁעֲתָא.

The Gemara relates that **Rabbi Elazar** was once **eating** ***teruma*****,** when the Angel of Death **appeared to him. He said to** the Angel of Death: **I am eating** ***teruma*****; is it not called sacred?** It would be inappropriate for me to die now and thereby defile this sacred *teruma*. The Angel of Death accepted his argument and left him. **The moment passed,** and he lived for some time afterward.

רַב שֵׁשֶׁת אִיתְחֲזֵי לֵיהּ בְּשׁוּקָא. אֲמַר לֵיהּ: בְּשׁוּקָא כִּבְהֵמָה? אִיתָא לְגַבֵּי בֵּיתָא.

It was similarly related that the Angel of Death once **appeared to Rav Sheshet in the marketplace.** Rav Sheshet **said to** the Angel of Death: Shall I die **in the market like an animal? Come to** my **house** and kill me there like a human being.

רַב אַשִׁי אִיתְחֲזֵי לֵיהּ בְּשׁוּקָא. אֲמַר לֵיהּ: אִיתְרַח לִי תְּלָתִין יוֹמִין, וְאַהַדְרִי לְתַלְמוּדַאי. דְּאָמְרִיתוּ: אַשְׁרֵי מִי שֶׁבָּא לְכָאן וְתַלְמוּדוֹ בְּיָדוֹ. בְּיוֹם תְּלָתִין אֲתָא. אֲמַר לֵיהּ: מַאי כּוּלֵּי הַאי? קָא דָּחֲקָא רַגְלֵיהּ דְּבַר נָתָן, וְאֵין מַלְכוּת נוֹגַעַת בַּחֲבֶירְתָּהּ אֲפִילּוּ כִּמְלֹא נִימָא.

So too, the Angel of Death **appeared to Rav Ashi in the marketplace.** Rav Ashi **said to** the Angel of Death: **Give me thirty days so that I may review my studies, for you say** above: **Fortunate is he who comes here** to Heaven **with his learning in his hand. On the thirtieth day** the Angel of Death **came** to take him. Rav Ashi **said to** the Angel of Death: **What is all of this?** Why are you in such a hurry to take me? Why can you not postpone my death? He said to him: **The foot of** Rav Huna **bar Natan**[P] **is pushing** you, as he is ready to succeed you as the leader of the generation, **and one sovereignty does not overlap with its counterpart, even by one hairbreadth.** Therefore, you cannot live any longer.

רַב חִסְדָּא לָא הֲוָה יָכֵיל לֵיהּ, דְּלָא הֲוָה שָׁתֵיק פּוּמֵּיהּ מִגִּירְסָא. סְלֵיק יְתֵיב בְּאַרְזָא דְּבֵי רַב. פְּקַע אַרְזָא וּשְׁתַק וְיָכֵיל לֵיהּ.

The Angel of Death **was unable** to take **Rav Ḥisda because his mouth was never silent from study.** So the Angel of Death **went** and **sat on the cedar** column that supported the roof of **the study hall of the Sages. The cedar cracked and** Rav Ḥisda **was silent** for a moment, as he was startled by the sound. At that point the Angel of Death was **able to take him.**

רַבִּי חִיָּיא לָא הֲוָה מָצֵי לְמִיקְרְבָא לֵיהּ. יוֹמָא חַד אִידַּמִּי לֵיהּ כְּעַנְיָא, אֲתָא טָרֵיף אַבָּבָא, אֲמַר לֵיהּ: אַפֵּיק לִי רִיפְתָּא. אַפִּיקוּ לֵיהּ. אֲמַר לֵיהּ: וְלָאו קָא מְרַחֵם מָר אַעַנְיָא? אַהַהוּא גַּבְרָא אַמַּאי לָא קָא מְרַחֵם מָר? גַּלֵּי לֵיהּ, אַחְוֵי לֵיהּ שׁוֹטָא דְנוּרָא, אַמְצֵי לֵיהּ נַפְשֵׁיהּ.

The Angel of Death **could not come near Rabbi Ḥiyya,** owing to his righteousness. **One day** the Angel of Death **appeared to him as a poor person. He came and knocked on the door. He said to** Rabbi Ḥiyya: **Bring out bread for me,** and **he took out** bread **for him.** The Angel of Death then **said** to Rabbi Ḥiyya: **Master, do you not have mercy on a poor person? Why, then, do you not have mercy upon that man,** i.e., upon me, and give me what I want? The Angel of Death then **revealed** his identity **to him,** and **showed him a fiery rod** in order to confirm that he was the Angel of Death. At this point Rav Ḥiyya **surrendered** himself **to him.**

PERSONALITIES

Bar Natan – בַּר נָתָן: Apparently bar Natan refers to Rav Huna bar Rav Natan. It was said that with regard to the combination of Torah and greatness in one place, he was second only to Rav Ashi himself (*Gittin* 59a). According to the tradition of Rav Sherira Gaon, Rav Huna bar Natan was the Exilarch in the time of Rav Ashi. However, due to Rav Ashi's greatness he was also submissive before him. It seems that he was Rav Pappa's student, and he studied Torah under the other leaders of that generation as well. Occasionally the Gemara records his discussions with Rav Ashi.

NOTES

Who is honorable [*sefin*], who is complete [*rekia*] – מַאן סְפִין, מַאן רְקִיעַ: Some explain that the word *sefin* means important or respected (Rabbi Shlomo ben HaYatom). Others say that the word *sefin*, similarly to the term afraid [*mistafina*], refers to one who is feared and is therefore respected (Rashi manuscript). Or perhaps the word means high (Rashi on *Ein Ya'akov*). *Tosefot HaRosh* explains that the word *sefin* is similar to what is stated with regard to Moses: "For there a portion of a ruler [*safun*] was reserved" (Deuteronomy 33:21).

The word *rekia* is explained by some to mean complete (*ge'onim*). Others claim that it means simple or smooth, and that this is an honorific adjective for a righteous person (Rabbi Shlomo ben HaYatom). Still others say that the word refers to one who ascends into the sky [*rakia*] like Moses (*Tosefot HaRosh*).

The fear…is great – נָפֵישׁ בִּיעֲתוּתֵיהּ: Most of the commentaries explain that Rav Naḥman was very fearful of the Angel of Death. This is also the version of the text in the *Ein Ya'akov*. Therefore, he did not wish to die a second time. However, others say that he was fearful of this world and its physical and spiritual dangers (Rabbi Shlomo ben HaYatom).

מתני׳ נָשִׁים בַּמּוֹעֵד מְעַנּוֹת, אֲבָל לֹא מְטַפְּחוֹת. רַבִּי יִשְׁמָעֵאל אוֹמֵר: הַסְּמוּכוֹת לַמִּטָּה מְטַפְּחוֹת.

MISHNA **On the intermediate days of a Festival women may wail**[H] in grief over the deceased, **but they may not clap** [***metapeḥot***] their hands in mourning. **Rabbi Yishmael says: Those who are close to the bier may clap.**

בְּרָאשֵׁי חֳדָשִׁים, בַּחֲנוּכָּה וּבְפוּרִים – מְעַנּוֹת וּמְטַפְּחוֹת, בָּזֶה וָזֶה – לֹא מְקוֹנְנוֹת. נִקְבַּר הַמֵּת – לֹא מְעַנּוֹת וְלֹא מְטַפְּחוֹת.

On New Moons, Hanukkah and Purim, which are not Festivals by Torah law, the women **may** both **wail and clap** their hands in mourning. **On both** the intermediate days of a Festival **and on** New Moons, Hanukkah and Purim **they may not lament. After the deceased has been buried they may neither wail nor clap.**

אֵיזֶהוּ עִינּוּי – שֶׁכּוּלָּן עוֹנוֹת כְּאַחַת; קִינָה – שֶׁאַחַת מְדַבֶּרֶת וְכוּלָּן עוֹנוֹת אַחֲרֶיהָ, שֶׁנֶּאֱמַר: ״וְלַמֵּדְנָה בְנוֹתֵיכֶם נֶהִי וְאִשָּׁה רְעוּתָהּ קִינָה״.

The mishna explains: **What is considered wailing?** This is **when they all wail together** simultaneously. And **what is considered a lament?** This is **when one speaks and they all answer after her** with a repeated refrain, **as it is stated: "And teach your daughters wailing and everyone her neighbor lamentation"** (Jeremiah 9:19).

אֲבָל לֶעָתִיד לָבֹא הוּא אוֹמֵר: ״בִּלַּע הַמָּוֶת לָנֶצַח וּמָחָה ה׳ אֱלֹהִים דִּמְעָה מֵעַל כׇּל פָּנִים״ וגו׳.

In order to conclude on a positive note, the mishna says: **But with regard to the future,**[N] the verse **states: "He will destroy death forever; and the Lord, God, will wipe away tears from off all faces** and the reproach of His people He will take away from off all the earth" (Isaiah 25:8).

גמ׳ מַאי אָמְרָן? אָמַר רַב: וַיי לְאָזְלָא, וַיי לַחֲבִילָא.

GEMARA **What do** the women who wail over the dead **say? Rav said:** They say: **Woe over him who is now departing; woe over** him who is now returning **the pledge,** i.e., his soul, which had been deposited in his hands all the years of his life.

אָמַר רָבָא, נְשֵׁי דְּשָׁכַנְצִיב אָמְרָן הָכִי: וַיי לְאָזְלָא, וַיי לַחֲבִילָא. וְאָמַר רָבָא, נְשֵׁי דְּשָׁכַנְצִיב אָמְרָן: גּוּד גַּרְמָא מִכַּכָּא, וְנִמְטֵי מַיָּא לְאַנְטִיכֵי.

Rava said: The women in the city of **Shekhantziv,**[NB] who were known for their wisdom, **would say as follows: Woe over him who** is now **departing; woe over** him who is now returning **the pledge.**[N] **And Rava said: The women of Shekhantziv would say** about an elderly person: **The bone has been removed from the jaw and the water returns to the kettle.**[N]

HALAKHA

On the intermediate days of a Festival women may wail – נָשִׁים בַּמּוֹעֵד מְעַנּוֹת: It is permitted to wail during the intermediate days of a Festival when everyone wails a single lament together; however, one may not clap. On New Moons, Hanukkah, and Purim they may wail and clap but not lament, in accordance with the opinion of the first *tanna*. All of this applies only in the presence of the deceased (*Shulḥan Arukh*, *Yoreh De'a* 401:5).

BACKGROUND

Shekhantziv – שָׁכַנְצִיב: It is believed that the city of Shekhantziv was on the banks of the Tigris River. It was an important center of Torah, and several Sages were active there.

The residents of this city were well known for their wit and even warned others to stay away from their sharp speech and scoffing. This Gemara demonstrates that the sayings of the women of Shekhantziv were complex and clever.

NOTES

But with regard to the future – אֲבָל לֶעָתִיד לָבֹא: *Tosafot* explain that this statement is made in order to conclude on a positive note, because according to their ordering of the tractates, *Moed Katan* is the final tractate in the order of *Moed*. However, according to the Rambam's order of the tractates, *Ḥagiga* is the final tractate. Even so, it is possible to say that the editors of the mishna also wished to conclude each tractate with more positive material (Rabbi Ovadya MiBartenura). Other tractates have similar endings as well.

The women of Shekhantziv – נְשֵׁי דְּשָׁכַנְצִיב: Rabbi Shlomo ben HaYatom writes that the women of Shekhantziv spoke through deep riddles. He offers explanations from the *ge'onim* but suggests that there may be alternative explanations. Many textual variations exist for these riddles, and different explanations are offered for each variation.

Woe over him who is departing, woe over the pledge [*laḥavila*] – וַיי לְאָזְלָא, וַיי לַחֲבִילָא: Some explain the word *laḥavila* to be a pledge, and they explain allegorically that a person's soul is a deposit or a security that must be returned upon his death (Rabbeinu Ḥananel). Others explain that they would say this when a person died in poverty, as his children and the members of his household would have to give security to repay their debts (*Tosefot HaRosh*; Meiri).

There are also those who say that the word *ḥavila* means destruction or pain, and consequently the expression means: Woe over the suffering one endures in death (*ge'onim*). Some explain that the word means load and the expression means: Woe over the load that one must carry (Rabbi Betzalel Ransburg, citing an earlier commentary). Still others say that the expression means: Woe over the package, and the knot that became undone (Commentary on *Moed Katan*).

The bone has been removed from the jaw and the water returns to the kettle [*antikhei*] – גּוּד גַּרְמָא מִכַּכָּא וְנִמְטֵי מַיָּא לְאַנְטִיכֵי: Some explain that this means that when the bone that one eats is uprooted from his mouth, i.e., he stops eating it, his temperature rises like water in a kettle (Rabbeinu Ḥananel). Others say it means: The teeth fall out of the mouth, and the hot water may be returned to the vessel, as one can no longer drink it (Commentary on *Moed Katan*).

Other commentaries have a version of the text that reads: The water is returned to Antioch [*la'Antokhia*], which was a city very far away. According to this version of the text, the statement means that the water can now go to a very distant place, as there is no longer any need for it. Some see this as an allusion to what happens after death; the women meant that when one dies the soul goes to the place where it was at first (Rabbi Shlomo ben HaYatom).

The *Tosefot HaRosh* understands the text differently, explaining that this refers to a case where one's son died, and the women told the father to remove one of his teeth so as to remember him in the future. Afterward he should heat water and wash the tooth, in order to increase the crying and the eulogizing (see Meiri). Elsewhere (*Berakhot* 5b) the Gemara relates that Rabbi Yoḥanan acted similarly, and kept a bone from his youngest son who had died.

וְאָמַר רָבָא, נְשֵׁי דִשְׁכַנְצִיב אָמְרָן: עֲטוֹף וּכְסוֹ טוּרֵי, דְּבַר רָמֵי וּבַר רַבְרְבֵי הוּא. וְאָמַר רָבָא, נְשֵׁי דִשְׁכַנְצִיב אָמְרָן: שַׁיּוּל אִצְטְלָא דְמֵלְתָא לְבַר חוֹרִין דִּשְׁלִימוּ זְוָדֵיהּ.

And Rava said: The women of Shekhantziv would say at a time of bereavement: **Wrap and cover the mountains**[N] in mourning, as the deceased is **the son of the high and distinguished. Rava said: The women of Shekhantziv would say: Lend** out **a cloak of fine wool**[N] to serve as a burial shroud **for a free man whose sustenance has been depleted.** In other words, a wealthy person who loses his fortune would rather die than live in poverty.

וַאֲמַר רָבָא, נְשֵׁי דִשְׁכַנְצִיב אָמְרָן: רָהֵיט וְנָפֵיל אַמַּעְבְּרָא, וְיזוֹפְתָא יָזֵיף. וַאֲמַר רָבָא, נְשֵׁי דִשְׁכַנְצִיב אָמְרָן: אַחֲנָא תַּגָּרֵי אַזְבְּזָגֵי מִיבַּדְקוּ. וַאֲמַר רָבָא, נְשֵׁי דִשְׁכַנְצִיב אָמְרָן: מוֹתָא כִּי מוֹתָא, וּמַרְעִין – חִיבּוּלַיָּא.

And Rava said: The women of Shekhantziv would say: A person **runs and tumbles at the ford**[N] and still **he borrows. And Rava said: The women of Shekhantziv would say: Our brothers, the merchants, will be examined**[N] **at their places** of business to see if they are honest businessmen. **And Rava said: The women of Shekhantziv would say: Death is like death,** as everyone must die, **and suffering is like interest.**[N]

תַּנְיָא, הָיָה רַבִּי מֵאִיר אוֹמֵר: "טוֹב לָלֶכֶת אֶל בֵּית אֵבֶל" וגו׳ עַד "וְהַחַי יִתֵּן אֶל לִבּוֹ" דְּבָרִים שֶׁל מִיתָה. דְּיִסְפַּד – יִסְפְּדוּנֵיהּ, דְּיִקְבַּר – יִקְבְּרוּנֵיהּ, דְּיִטְעַן – יִטְעֲנוּנֵיהּ. דְּיִדַּל – יִדְלוּנֵיהּ.

It is taught in a *baraita* that **Rabbi Meir would say** with regard to the verse **"It is better to go to the house of mourning** than to go to the house of feasting, for that is the end of all men; **and the living will lay it to his heart"** (Ecclesiastes 7:2): What should the living lay to his heart? **Matters relating to death.** And these matters are as follows: He **that eulogizes will be eulogized** by others. He **that buries** others **will be buried** by others. He **that loads** many words of praise and tribute into the eulogies that he delivers for others **will be** similarly **treated** by others. He **that raises** his voice in weeping over others **will** have others **raise** their voices **over him.**

וְאִיכָּא דְאָמְרִי: דְּלָא יָדֵל – יִדְלוּנֵיהּ, דִּכְתִיב: "כִּי טוֹב אֲמָר לְךָ עֲלֵה הֵנָּה" וגו׳.

And some say: One **who does not raise himself** with pride, but chooses his place among the lowly, **will be raised**[N] by others, **as it is written:** "Do not exalt yourself in the king's presence, and stand not in the place of great men. **For it is better to be told, step up here,** than to be degraded in the presence of the great" (Proverbs 25:6–7).

NOTES

Wrap [*atuf*] and cover the mountains – עֲטוֹף וּכְסוֹ טוּרֵי: Some explain that this is a poetic call for the mountains to wrap themselves in fine clothes in order to greet a great person. Alternatively, it may mean that many people should gather to accompany the deceased, thereby wrapping and concealing the mountains with their multitudes (Rabbeinu Ḥananel). Others explain similarly, but understand the verb *atuf* to mean darken, i.e., that the mountains should darken themselves (Rashi, Rabbeinu Gershom Meor HaGola).

Some understand this phrase as an allegory that means that the great people, who are referred to as mountains, should come to the funeral (Commentary on *Moed Katan*). Others say that this refers to one who was buried in a mountain cave, so that the mountains become his burial shroud (Ran).

Lend [*shayyul*] a cloak of fine wool, etc. – שַׁיּוּל אִצְטְלָא דְמֵלְתָא וכו׳: Some explain that this means that it is preferable for a formerly wealthy person who has no food to eat to find a burial shroud, as it is preferable for him to die and not be ashamed (Rabbeinu Ḥananel). Alternatively, it means that one should prepare fine clothes in order to join the funeral of a person from a wealthy family who died in poverty (Rabbeinu Ḥananel). Others suggest that it means that one should prepare a fine burial shroud for such a person (Rabbi Shlomo ben HaYatom). Rabbeinu Gershom Meor HaGola explains that the word *shayyul* is similar to the word *She'ol* meaning underworld or death, which is the best state for such a person.

Runs and tumbles at the ford [*amabra*] – רָהֵיט וְנָפֵיל אַמַּעְבְּרָא: Many different textual variations and explanations exist for this statement. Some explain that this was said about one who did not work during his life and now must borrow for the sake of the *mabarot*, the burial shrouds (*ge'onim*; see Ran and Maharsha). Others suggest that this refers to one who ran his entire life earning money but fell in with people who lost all of his money, and in the end he no longer had money at the ford, meaning for his burial (Rabbeinu Ḥananel).

Similarly, the passage is explained in many other ways, based on numerous textual variations that exist. One version reads: Run and go, son of divers, meaning that a diver who makes a living by swimming in deep waters must borrow money to pass over a small river at a ford (*Tosefot HaRosh*; see Meiri).

The merchants [*azavzagei*] will be examined – אַזְבְּזָגֵי מִיבַּדְקוּ: Another version of the text has the word purchases [*azbinei*], so that this means: The merchants will be examined not by their speech but by the way in which they conducted their business (Rabbeinu Ḥananel). Some explain that the merchants will be examined at the end of their lives to see how much they actually profited (Rabbi Betzalel Ransburg). Others have a version that reads *azla bazag*, meaning that the traveling merchants eventually go to the grave (Rabbi Shlomo ben HaYatom).

Suffering is like interest – וּמַרְעִין, חִיבּוּלַיָּא: Some explain: The length of one's sickness until he dies is like interest on the capital, i.e., death (Rabbeinu Ḥananel). Others explain that diseases are additional pain and suffering (Ran).

One who does not raise himself will be raised [*dela yiddal yidlunei*] – דְּלָא יָדֵל יִדְלוּנֵיהּ: Rabbeinu Ḥananel has a version that reads *la yiddal de'idlonei*, meaning that one should not raise himself, so that he will not be lifted and taken down from his place. Others explain, in accordance with our version of the text, that one who does not raise himself will either be raised through receiving honor (Commentary on *Moed Katan*), or other people will carry his bier and eulogize him with honor. Consequently, the verse is an allusion to the matter and the essence of the concept (Rabbi Shlomo ben HaYatom).

תָּנוּ רַבָּנַן: כְּשֶׁמֵּתוּ בָּנָיו שֶׁל רַבִּי יִשְׁמָעֵאל נִכְנְסוּ אַרְבָּעָה זְקֵנִים לְנַחֲמוֹ: רַבִּי טַרְפוֹן, וְרַבִּי יוֹסֵי הַגְּלִילִי, וְרַבִּי אֶלְעָזָר בֶּן עֲזַרְיָה, וְרַבִּי עֲקִיבָא. אָמַר לָהֶם רַבִּי טַרְפוֹן: דְּעוּ שֶׁחָכָם גָּדוֹל הוּא, וּבָקִי בְּאַגָּדוֹת, אַל יִכָּנֵס אֶחָד מִכֶּם לְתוֹךְ דִּבְרֵי חֲבֵירוֹ. אָמַר רַבִּי עֲקִיבָא: וַאֲנִי אַחֲרוֹן.

The Sages taught the following *baraita*: **When the sons of Rabbi Yishmael**[P] **died, four Elders entered to console him: Rabbi Tarfon, Rabbi Yosei HaGelili, Rabbi Elazar ben Azarya, and Rabbi Akiva. Rabbi Tarfon said to them: Know that** Rabbi Yishmael **is a great Sage**[N] **and well versed in *aggadot*. Let none of you interrupt the words of another,** but rather each person should say something novel of his own. **Rabbi Akiva said: And I** shall speak **last.**

פָּתַח רַבִּי יִשְׁמָעֵאל וְאָמַר: רַבּוּ עֲוֹנוֹתָיו, תְּכָפוּהוּ אֲבֵלָיו, הִטְרִיחַ רַבּוֹתָיו פַּעַם רִאשׁוֹנָה וּשְׁנִיָּה.

Rabbi Yishmael, the mourner, **opened and said** about himself: **Many are his sins.** Due to this, **his bereavements came in** quick **succession and he troubled his teachers once and** then **a second time** to come and console him.

נַעֲנָה רַבִּי טַרְפוֹן וְאָמַר: ״וַאֲחֵיכֶם כָּל בֵּית יִשְׂרָאֵל יִבְכּוּ אֶת הַשְּׂרֵפָה״, וַהֲלֹא דְּבָרִים קַל וָחוֹמֶר: וּמַה נָּדָב וַאֲבִיהוּא שֶׁלֹּא עָשׂוּ אֶלָּא מִצְוָה אַחַת, דִּכְתִיב: ״וַיַּקְרִיבוּ בְּנֵי אַהֲרֹן אֶת הַדָּם אֵלָיו״ – כָּךְ, בָּנָיו שֶׁל רַבִּי יִשְׁמָעֵאל – עַל אַחַת כַּמָּה וְכַמָּה.

Having been granted permission to speak, **Rabbi Tarfon answered and said:** With regard to the death of Aaron's sons it says: **"But let your brethren, the whole house of Israel, bewail the burning that the Lord has kindled"** (Leviticus 10:6). **Are these matters not** inferred ***a fortiori*: If, with regard to Nadav and Avihu, who had performed only one mitzva**[N] that is explicitly mentioned in the Bible, **as it is written: "And the sons of Aaron brought the blood to him"** (Leviticus 9:9), **this** was nevertheless stated about them, then with regard to **the sons of Rabbi Yishmael,** who were well known for their performance of many mitzvot, **all the more so** should the entire Jewish people bewail their death.

נַעֲנָה רַבִּי יוֹסֵי הַגְּלִילִי וְאָמַר: ״וְסָפְדוּ לוֹ כָּל יִשְׂרָאֵל וְקָבְרוּ אוֹתוֹ״. וַהֲלֹא דְּבָרִים קַל וָחוֹמֶר: וּמָה אֲבִיָּה בֶּן יָרָבְעָם שֶׁלֹּא עָשָׂה אֶלָּא דָּבָר אֶחָד טוֹב, דִּכְתִיב בֵּיהּ: ״יַעַן נִמְצָא בוֹ דָּבָר טוֹב״ – כָּךְ, בָּנָיו שֶׁל רַבִּי יִשְׁמָעֵאל – עַל אַחַת כַּמָּה וְכַמָּה.

Rabbi Yosei HaGelili answered and said: With regard to Abijah, son of King Jeroboam, the verse states: **"And all Israel shall mourn for him, and bury him"** (I Kings 14:13). **Are these matters not** inferred ***a fortiori*: If, with regard to Abijah, son of Jeroboam, who did only one good thing, as it is written: "Because in him there is found some good thing** toward the Lord God of Israel" (I Kings 14:13), i.e., he did only one good thing, and **this** was his reward, then with regard to **the sons of Rabbi Yishmael all the more so** should they be rewarded by having the entire Jewish people mourn for them and bury them.

מַאי דָּבָר טוֹב? רַבִּי זֵירָא וְרַבִּי חִינָּנָא בַּר פַּפָּא; חַד אָמַר: שֶׁבִּיטֵּל מִשְׁמַרְתּוֹ וְעָלָה לָרֶגֶל; וְחַד אָמַר: שֶׁבִּיטֵּל פַּרְדְּסָאוֹת שֶׁהוֹשִׁיב יָרָבְעָם אָבִיו עַל הַדְּרָכִים שֶׁלֹּא יַעֲלוּ יִשְׂרָאֵל לָרֶגֶל.

The Gemara asks: **What was this** one **good thing** that Abijah did? **Rabbi Zeira and Rabbi Ḥinnana bar Pappa** disagreed about this issue. **One said: He abandoned his guard post.** His father, Jeroboam, had assigned him to serve as one of the guards whose mission it was to prevent people from going up to Jerusalem on the pilgrimage Festivals. **And he** himself **went up** to Jerusalem **for the pilgrimage Festival. And one said: He removed the guards** [*pardesaot*][L] **that his father, Jeroboam, had placed along the roads so that** the people of **Israel would not go up** to Jerusalem **for the pilgrimage Festivals.**

נַעֲנָה רַבִּי אֶלְעָזָר בֶּן עֲזַרְיָה וְאָמַר: ״בְּשָׁלוֹם תָּמוּת וּבְמִשְׂרְפוֹת אֲבוֹתֶיךָ הַמְּלָכִים הָרִאשׁוֹנִים [אֲשֶׁר הָיוּ לְפָנֶיךָ כֵּן] יִשְׂרְפוּ לָךְ״. וַהֲלֹא דְּבָרִים קַל וָחוֹמֶר: וּמַה צִּדְקִיָּהוּ מֶלֶךְ יְהוּדָה, שֶׁלֹּא עָשָׂה אֶלָּא מִצְוָה אַחַת, שֶׁהֶעֱלָה יִרְמְיָה מִן הַטִּיט – כָּךְ, בָּנָיו שֶׁל רַבִּי יִשְׁמָעֵאל – עַל אַחַת כַּמָּה וְכַמָּה.

The *baraita* continues: **Rabbi Elazar ben Azarya answered and said:** With regard to King Zedekiah, the verse states: **"But you shall die in peace; and with the burnings of your fathers, the former kings that were before you, so shall they make a burning for you"** (Jeremiah 34:5). **Are these matters not** inferred ***a fortiori*: If, with regard to Zedekiah, king of Judea, who had performed** only **one mitzva** that is explicitly mentioned in the Bible, **for he had Jeremiah lifted out of the mire** (Jeremiah 38:10), **this** was nevertheless stated about him, then with regard to **the sons of Rabbi Yishmael all the more so** should they be rewarded by dying in peace.

נַעֲנָה רַבִּי עֲקִיבָא וְאָמַר: ״בַּיּוֹם הַהוּא יִגְדַּל הַמִּסְפֵּד בִּירוּשָׁלַיִם כְּמִסְפַּד הֲדַדְרִימּוֹן [בְּבִקְעַת מְגִידּוֹן]״. וְאָמַר רַב יוֹסֵף: אִלְמָלֵא תַּרְגּוּמֵיהּ דְּהַאי קְרָא לָא הֲוָה יָדַעְנָא מַאי קָאָמַר:

Rabbi Akiva answered and said: The verse states: **"On that day shall there be a great mourning in Jerusalem, like the mourning of Hadadrimmon in the valley of Megiddon"** (Zechariah 12:11). The Gemara comments: With regard to this verse, **Rav Yosef said: Had it not been for the** Aramaic **translation of this verse, we would not have known what it is saying,** as nowhere in the Bible do we find this incident involving Hadadrimmon.

PERSONALITIES

Rabbi Yishmael – רַבִּי יִשְׁמָעֵאל: Rabbi Yishmael ben Elisha II was the grandson of Rabbi Yishmael ben Elisha, the High Priest who served in the Temple at the end of the Second Temple period. The grandson is the *tanna* who is usually referred to simply as Rabbi Yishmael throughout the Talmud. As a young man, he was imprisoned by the Romans. He was redeemed by Rabbi Yehoshua and ultimately became his student. Later he became one of the renowned scholars in Yavne, where he was a close friend and intellectual adversary of Rabbi Akiva. Each of them developed a unique system of biblical hermeneutics. The thirteen principles of interpretation formulated by Rabbi Yishmael serve as the foundation for halakhic midrash, which derives Jewish *halakha* from the Torah. We find many of his teachings throughout the Mishna. There are many more in the Talmud, which are taught by his students under the rubric: It was taught in the school of Rabbi Yishmael.

It appears that Rabbi Yishmael passed away prior to the bar Kokheva revolt. The Talmud mentions his sons and daughters; it is likely that the *tanna* Rabbi Eliezer, son of Rabbi Yishmael, was among his children.

NOTES

Know that Rabbi Yishmael is a great Sage, etc. – דְּעוּ שֶׁחָכָם גָּדוֹל וכו׳: Therefore, each one of you should say something novel that Rabbi Yishmael has not yet heard. The phrase: Let none of you interrupt the words of another, means that you should not cite the statement of one of your colleagues and begin to discuss it. Consequently, Rabbi Akiva's choice to volunteer to say something novel after everyone else was the most difficult of the options (Ran). Some explain that the Sages were told not to discuss another's statement lest Rabbi Yishmael forget his mourning. It was best for them to speak in an orderly fashion so that Rabbi Yishmael would listen and not speak (Maharsha).

Who had performed only one mitzva – שֶׁלֹּא עָשׂוּ אֶלָּא מִצְוָה אַחַת: It is explained that this means that they performed only one mitzva, for which they earned merit, and through which they died (Commentary on *Moed Katan*). Others say that this means that they performed a mitzva that is relevant and applicable to all of Israel (Maharsha).

LANGUAGE

Guards [*pardesaot*] – פַּרְדְּסָאוֹת: From the Latin praesidia, meaning guards. In other tractates and other manuscripts this word is written as *peruzdaot*.

בְּעִידָּנָא הַהוּא יִסְגֵּי מִסְפְּדָא בִּירוּשָׁלַםִ כְּמִסְפְּדָא דְּאַחְאָב בַּר עָמְרִי דִּקְטַל יָתֵיהּ הֲדַדְרִימּוֹן בַּר טַבְרִימּוֹן, וּכְמִסְפֵּד דְּיֹאשִׁיָּה בַּר אָמוֹן דִּקְטַל יָתֵיהּ פַּרְעֹה חֲגִירָא בְּבִקְעַת מְגִידוֹ.

The Aramaic translation reads as follows: **At that time the mourning in Jerusalem will be as great as the mourning over Ahab, son of Omri, who was slain by Hadadrimmon, son of Tabrimmon, and like the mourning over Josiah, son of Amon, who was slain by Pharaoh the lame in the valley of Megiddon.**

וַהֲלֹא דְּבָרִים קַל וָחוֹמֶר: וּמָה אַחְאָב מֶלֶךְ יִשְׂרָאֵל, שֶׁלֹּא עָשָׂה אֶלָּא דָּבָר אֶחָד טוֹב, דִּכְתִיב: ״וְהַמֶּלֶךְ הָיָה מָעֳמָד בַּמֶּרְכָּבָה נֹכַח אֲרָם״ – כָּךְ, בָּנָיו שֶׁל רַבִּי יִשְׁמָעֵאל – עַל אַחַת כַּמָּה וְכַמָּה.

The *baraita* continues: Are these **matters not** inferred *a fortiori*: **If, with regard to Ahab, king of Israel, who did** only **one good thing** that is explicitly mentioned in the Bible, **as it is written: "And the king was propped up in his chariot facing Aram"** (I Kings 22:35), as he did not want the Jewish people to see that he was mortally wounded and flee, and **this,** that he was greatly mourned, was nevertheless stated about him, then **all the more so** will **the sons of Rabbi Yishmael** be greatly mourned.

אֲמַר לֵיהּ רָבָא לְרַבָּה בַּר מָרִי, כְּתִיב בֵּיהּ בְּצִדְקִיָּהוּ ״בְּשָׁלוֹם תָּמוּת״, וּכְתִיב ״וְאֶת עֵינֵי צִדְקִיָּהוּ עִוֵּר״! אֲמַר לֵיהּ: הָכִי אֲמַר רַבִּי יוֹחָנָן: שֶׁמֵּת נְבוּכַדְנֶאצַּר בְּיָמָיו.

The Gemara discusses issues in the aforementioned verses: **Rava said to Rabba bar Mari: It is written with regard to Zedekiah: "You shall die in peace," but** elsewhere **it is written: "And he put out Zedekiah's eyes"** (Jeremiah 39:7). Rabba bar Mari **said to him: Rabbi Yoḥanan said as follows:** The first verse: "You shall die in peace," means **that Nebuchadnezzar died in** Zedekiah's **lifetime** and consequently the latter died in peace, having seen the death of the wicked.

וַאֲמַר רָבָא לְרַבָּה בַּר מָרִי: כְּתִיב בֵּיהּ בְּיֹאשִׁיָּהוּ: ״לָכֵן הִנְנִי אוֹסִפְךָ עַל אֲבוֹתֶיךָ וְנֶאֱסַפְתָּ אֶל קִבְרוֹתֶיךָ בְּשָׁלוֹם״ וּכְתִיב: ״וַיּוֹרוּ הַיּוֹרִים לַמֶּלֶךְ יֹאשִׁיָּהוּ״, וְאָמַר רַב יְהוּדָה אָמַר רַב: שֶׁעֲשָׂאוּהוּ כִּכְבָרָה!

And Rava further **said to Rabba bar Mari: It is written with regard to Josiah: "Behold, therefore I will gather you unto your fathers, and you shall be gathered into your grave in peace"** (II Kings 22:20), **and** elsewhere **it is written: "And the archers shot at King Josiah;** and the king said to his servants, Get me away; for I am grievously wounded" (II Chronicles 35:23). **And** with regard to this verse **Rabbi Yehuda said** that **Rav said:** With their many arrows, **they made** his body **like a sieve.**

אֲמַר לֵיהּ, הָכִי אֲמַר רַבִּי יוֹחָנָן: שֶׁלֹּא חָרַב בֵּית הַמִּקְדָּשׁ בְּיָמָיו.

Rabba bar Mari **said to him: Rabbi Yoḥanan said as follows:** The words "in peace" stated with regard to King Josiah refer to the fact **that the Temple was not destroyed in his lifetime,** as the verse itself continues: "And your eyes shall not see all the evil that I will bring upon this place" (II Kings 22:20).

אָמַר רַבִּי יוֹחָנָן: אֵין מְנַחֲמִין רַשָּׁאִין לוֹמַר דָּבָר עַד שֶׁיִּפְתַּח אָבֵל, שֶׁנֶּאֱמַר: ״אַחֲרֵי כֵן פָּתַח אִיּוֹב אֶת פִּיהוּ״ וַהֲדַר ״וַיַּעַן אֱלִיפַז הַתֵּימָנִי״.

The Gemara returns to examining the *halakhot* of consolation. **Rabbi Yoḥanan said: The consolers are not permitted to speak words of** consolation **until the mourner opens** and speaks first.[H] **As it is stated:** "And they sat down with him upon the ground for seven days and seven nights, and none spoke a word to him; for they saw that his suffering was very great. **After this Job opened his mouth"** (Job 2:13–3:1). **And afterward: "And Eliphaz the Temanite answered** and said" (Job 4:1).

אָמַר רַבִּי אַבָּהוּ: מִנַּיִן לְאָבֵל שֶׁמֵּיסֵב בָּרֹאשׁ? שֶׁנֶּאֱמַר: ״אֶבְחַר דַּרְכָּם וְאֵשֵׁב רֹאשׁ וְאֶשְׁכּוֹן כְּמֶלֶךְ בַּגְּדוּד כַּאֲשֶׁר אֲבֵלִים יְנַחֵם״.

Rabbi Abbahu said: From where is it derived that **the mourner reclines at the head** [*rosh*] of the table? **As it is stated: "I chose out their way, and sat as chief** [*rosh*], **and dwelt as a king in the army, as one that comforts** [*yenaḥem*] **the mourners"** (Job 29:25). This indicates that the mourner sits at the head of the table, as the chief.

״יְנַחֵם״ אַחֲרִינֵי מַשְׁמַע! אָמַר רַב נַחְמָן בַּר יִצְחָק: יִנָּחֵם כְּתִיב.

The Gemara raises an objection: But the word *yenaḥem* **means that he comforts others,** thereby implying that one who comforts the mourners sits at the head of the table. **Rav Naḥman bar Yitzḥak said:** The word **is written** as *yinaḥem*,[N] meaning: Will be comforted, and therefore can be understood as referring to the mourner.

HALAKHA

The custom of the consolers – מִנְהַג מְנַחֲמִים: The consolers may not begin speaking until the mourner speaks first. However, this applies only when one eats in a mourner's house and not when he merely visits (*Arukh HaShulḥan*; *Shulḥan Arukh*, *Yoreh De'a* 376:1).

NOTES

It is written *yinaḥem* – יִנָּחֵם כְּתִיב: The early authorities have a version that reads: It is written *yenuḥam*, he who is consoled. They comment that this statement does not imply that the word is actually written in this manner; rather, it means that the word can be read in this way as well (Ritva).

LANGUAGE

Mirzaḥ – מַרְזֵחַ: The origin of this word is unclear, even in its Aramaic form, *marziḥa*. However, from the verse: "Enter not into the house of mourning [*mirzaḥ*]" (Jeremiah 16:5), it appears to mean a house of mourning. Some explain that the meaning of the root *r-z-ḥ* is to raise one's voice, whether in weeping or in joy.

HALAKHA

A priest at the head – כֹּהֵן בָּרֹאשׁ: When many people sit together to eat, the greatest person there should recite the blessing over the bread and cut it. If a groom is present and it is the day of his wedding, then he should cut the bread, even when there is a greater person there (*Magen Avraham*, citing *Beit Yosef*). If everyone is of equal stature and there is a priest present, then it is a mitzva for him to do so first. However, if the priest is an ignoramus and there is a Torah scholar present, then the Torah scholar cuts the bread first (*Magen Avraham*). If the priest is also a Torah scholar, he should be first, even if there is a greater scholar present, but this is not required (Rema). It is a mitzva to first present a priest who is a Torah scholar with any honor related to a mitzva. However, he may pass the honor to someone else in his place (Rema, citing *Smag*; *Shulḥan Arukh*, *Oraḥ Ḥayyim* 167:14, 201:2).

מָר זוּטְרָא אָמַר מֵהָכָא: ״וְסָר מִרְזַח סְרוּחִים״, מַרְזֵחַ – נַעֲשָׂה שַׂר לִסְרוּחִים.

Mar Zutra said: A proof may be derived **from here:** The verse **"And the revelry [*mirzaḥ*] of those who stretched themselves out shall pass away [*sar*]"** (Amos 6:7) means that ***mirzaḥ***,[L] he who is bitter [*mar*] and whose mind is overwrought [*zaḥ*] due to grief, **is made a prince [*sar*] over those who** sit beside him **stretched out** below him to comfort him.

אָמַר רַבִּי חָמָא בַּר חֲנִינָא: מִנַּיִן לֶחָתָן שֶׁמֵּיסֵב בָּרֹאשׁ? שֶׁנֶּאֱמַר: ״כֶּחָתָן יְכַהֵן פְּאֵר״, מָה כֹּהֵן בָּרֹאשׁ – אַף חָתָן בָּרֹאשׁ.

Rabbi Ḥama bar Ḥanina said: From where is it derived **that a groom reclines at the head** of the table? **As it is stated: "As a bridegroom decks himself [*yekhahen*] with a garland"** (Isaiah 61:10). **Just as a priest [*kohen*]** is **at the head** of the table, **so too, a bridegroom** is **at the head** of the table.

וְכֹהֵן גּוּפֵיהּ מְנָלַן? דְּתָנָא דְּבֵי רַבִּי יִשְׁמָעֵאל: ״וְקִדַּשְׁתּוֹ״ – לְכָל דָּבָר שֶׁבִּקְדוּשָּׁה, לִפְתּוֹחַ רִאשׁוֹן, וּלְבָרֵךְ רִאשׁוֹן, וְלִיטּוֹל מָנָה יָפָה רִאשׁוֹן.

The Gemara asks: **From where do we** derive that **the priest himself** sits at the head?[H] The Gemara answers: **As the school of Rabbi Yishmael taught:** With regard to a priest it says: **"You shall sanctify him,** for he offers the bread of your God" (Leviticus 21:8), meaning that you are to sanctify him **with regard to all matters of sanctity: To be first to begin** reading the Torah, **to be first to recite the** Grace after Meals, **and to be first to take a portion** during a meal.

אָמַר רַבִּי חֲנִינָא: קָשָׁה יְצִיאַת נְשָׁמָה מִן הַגּוּף

§ The Gemara returns to its discussion of death: **Rabbi Ḥanina said: The soul's departure from the body is as difficult**

Perek **III**
Daf **29** Amud **a**

LANGUAGE

Halyard [*pitirei*] – פִּטִירֵי: According to those who understand that this word means a kind of ship's rope, it is similar to the expression "knobs and open flowers [*peturei tzitzim*]" (I Kings 6:18), which Rashi explains to mean decorated ropes.

HALAKHA

One who departs from the deceased – הַנִּפְטָר מִן הַמֵּת: Based on the verse "and you shall go to your fathers in peace" (Genesis 15:15), those who have accompanied the deceased say after the burial: Go in peace (Rambam *Sefer Shofetim*, *Hilkhot Evel* 4:4).

כְּצִיפּוֹרִי בְּפִי הַוּוֹשֶׁט. רַבִּי יוֹחָנָן אָמַר: כִּפְטִירֵי בְּפִי וַושֶׁט.

as it is for a knotted rope [*tzippori*][N] **to pass through an eye** [*veshet*] in a ship's rigging. **Rabbi Yoḥanan said:** It is as difficult as it is **for a halyard [*pitirei*]**[L] **to pass through an eye [*veshet*].**[N]

וְאָמַר רַבִּי לֵוִי בַּר חַיְּתָא: הַנִּפְטָר מִן הַמֵּת לֹא יֹאמַר לוֹ ״לֵךְ לְשָׁלוֹם״ אֶלָּא ״לֵךְ בְּשָׁלוֹם״. הַנִּפְטָר מִן הַחַי לֹא יֹאמַר לוֹ ״לֵךְ בְּשָׁלוֹם״, אֶלָּא ״לֵךְ לְשָׁלוֹם״.

And Rabbi Levi bar Ḥayyata said: One who departs from the deceased[H] **should not say to him: Go to peace, but rather** he should say: **Go in peace.**[N] **One who departs from the living should not say to him: Go in peace, but rather** he should say: **Go to peace.**

הַנִּפְטָר מִן הַמֵּת לֹא יֹאמַר לוֹ ״לֵךְ לְשָׁלוֹם״ אֶלָּא ״לֵךְ בְּשָׁלוֹם״ – שֶׁנֶּאֱמַר: ״וְאַתָּה תָּבֹא אֶל אֲבוֹתֶיךָ בְּשָׁלוֹם״.

One who departs from the deceased should not say to him: Go to peace, but rather: Go in peace, as it is stated: "And you shall go to your fathers in peace; you shall be buried in a good old age" (Genesis 15:15).

NOTES

Like a knotted rope [*tzippori*] to pass through an eye [*veshet*] in a ship's rigging – כְּצִיפּוֹרִי בְּפִי הַוּוֹשֶׁט: Some explain that the word *tzippori* means: Like the knot of a rope (Rashi). Others explain that it refers to a rope made from the fibers of a coconut tree, which was used to tie ships (*Arukh*). Still others say that the word is related to the term "young goat [*tzefir izim*]" (Daniel 8:8) and means that death is as difficult as the birth of a firstborn goat (Rabbi Shlomo ben HaYatom).

There are some with a version of the text that reads: Like a bird [*tzippor*] caught in the esophagus [*veshet*]. They say that the expression refers to the difficulty of swallowing a bird in a single gulp (*ge'onim*). The Ran has a version that reads: Like a fingernail [*tzipporen*] caught in the esophagus, which would cause great pain. Most commentaries explain that the metaphor is meant to compare death to something that has become stuck in the esophagus [*veshet*] and can be swallowed only with difficulty and great pain.

As a halyard [*pitirei*] to pass through an eye – כִּפְטִירֵי בְּפִי וַושֶׁט: Most commentaries explain that the word *pitirei* is similar in meaning to the word *tzippori*, and it denotes a thick rope used on a ship. The *ge'onim* explain that it means mushroom [*pitria*], so that death is compared to one who swallows a mushroom whole (see Ran).

Go to peace…go in peace – לֵךְ לְשָׁלוֹם...לֵךְ בְּשָׁלוֹם: With regard to the difference between these expressions, some say that: Go in peace, means that this person should be in a place where there is peace, i.e., to the grave. Meanwhile, the phrase: Go to peace, refers to the person's direction. Using this time alludes to a person going towards greatness, symbolized by the letter *lamed*, which is the tallest of all the letters (Rabbi Shlomo ben HaYatom). The Ran explains that: Go in peace, means that one's journey should be in peace; however, it does not refer to his destination. Therefore, it is appropriate to say this only with regard to the dead and not the living.

The Ritva explains that the dead no longer need to be concerned about future calamities, and everything that will happen to them in the future depends on what they did in this world. Therefore, those present bless the dead with the words: Go in peace, meaning that this person's passing will be complete and in peace. However, with regard to the living, they have already left in peace and now need only a blessing that they should go peacefully to their future destination.

הַנִּפְטָר מִן הַחַי לֹא יֹאמַר לוֹ "לֵךְ בְּשָׁלוֹם" אֶלָּא "לֵךְ לְשָׁלוֹם", שֶׁהֲרֵי דָּוִד שֶׁאָמַר לְאַבְשָׁלוֹם "לֵךְ בְּשָׁלוֹם" – הָלַךְ וְנִתְלָה. יִתְרוֹ שֶׁאָמַר לְמֹשֶׁה "לֵךְ לְשָׁלוֹם" – הָלַךְ וְהִצְלִיחַ.

One who departs from the living[H] should not say to him: Go in peace, but rather: Go to peace, as David said to Absalom: "Go in peace" (II Samuel 15:9), and he subsequently went and was hanged; whereas Jethro said to Moses: "Go to peace" (Exodus 4:18), and he went and was successful.

וְאָמַר רַבִּי לֵוִי: כׇּל הַיּוֹצֵא מִבֵּית הַכְּנֶסֶת לְבֵית הַמִּדְרָשׁ, וּמִבֵּית הַמִּדְרָשׁ לְבֵית הַכְּנֶסֶת – זוֹכֶה וּמְקַבֵּל פְּנֵי שְׁכִינָה, שֶׁנֶּאֱמַר: "יֵלְכוּ מֵחַיִל אֶל חָיִל יֵרָאֶה אֶל אֱלֹהִים בְּצִיּוֹן".

And Rabbi Levi said: Anyone who leaves from the synagogue and goes **to the study hall**[NH] **or goes from the study hall to the synagogue,** i.e., he goes from the mitzva of prayer to the mitzva of Torah study or vice versa, **merits to receive the Divine Presence, as it is stated: "They go from strength to strength, every one of them appears before God in Zion"** (Psalms 84:8).

אָמַר רַב חִיָּיא בַּר אַשִׁי אָמַר רַב: תַּלְמִידֵי חֲכָמִים אֵין לָהֶם מְנוּחָה אֲפִילּוּ לָעוֹלָם הַבָּא, שֶׁנֶּאֱמַר: "יֵלְכוּ מֵחַיִל אֶל חָיִל יֵרָאֶה אֶל אֱלֹהִים בְּצִיּוֹן".

With regard to the same verse, **Rav Ḥiyya bar Ashi said** that **Rav said: Torah scholars have no rest,**[N] **even in the World-to-Come,** as even there they remain in constant movement and ascent, **as it is stated: "They go from strength to strength, every one of them appears before God in Zion."** Even when they are in the World-to-Come, they continue to go from strength to strength, until the final redemption will arrive in the end of days and God will appear in Zion.

הדרן עלך ואלו מגלחין
וסליקא לה מסכת מועד קטן

HALAKHA

One who departs from the living – הַנִּפְטָר מִן הַחַי: One should not say to his friend: Go in peace, rather he should say: Go to peace (*Magen Avraham*; *Shulḥan Arukh*, *Oraḥ Ḥayyim* 110).

From the synagogue to the study hall – מִבֵּית הַכְּנֶסֶת לְבֵית הַמִּדְרָשׁ: After leaving the synagogue, one should go to the study hall and set aside time to study. He must establish a regular time to study, so that he will not skip it, even if an opportunity arises during that time to make a large profit. Even one who does not know how to study Torah should go to the study hall so that he will receive reward for walking there (Rabbeinu Yona). One should establish a fixed place for himself in the study hall, so that he can study what he is capable of studying and contemplate his actions, so as to develop the fear of Heaven (*Shulḥan Arukh*, *Oraḥ Ḥayyim* 155:1, and in the comment of Rema).

NOTES

From the synagogue to the study hall – מִבֵּית הַכְּנֶסֶת לְבֵית הַמִּדְרָשׁ: By doing so, one shows that engaging in Torah and mitzvot is his primary intent and goal; however, in order to make a living he must also engage in other activities.

Have no rest – אֵין לָהֶם מְנוּחָה: This is a continuation of what is stated with regard to one who goes from the synagogue to the study hall. In the World-to-Come, there is no break, and he goes from strength to strength there as well (*Yad David*). The early authorities write that this is based on what is mentioned in many places in the Talmud, that in the supernal world souls engage in Torah study and understanding of the Creator (*Tosefot HaRosh*; Rabbi Shlomo ben HaYatom). The Rambam writes in *Sefer HaMadda* that the reward of the righteous will be that they will know the truth of the Creator, things that they could not know when they were in a body.

Summary of **Perek III**

Many different areas of *halakha* were discussed and ruled on in this chapter. With regard to the intermediate days of a Festival, it was explained that one who was prevented due to duress is permitted to cut his hair and wash his clothing on these days, whether the duress was due to an external factor, such as being locked up in prison, or whether due to his halakhic status, for example if he was a mourner or had been excommunicated. Similarly, even though it is normally prohibited to write on the intermediate days of a Festival, it is permitted to do so in cases of loss, or for the sake of dire financial need.

This chapter also discussed those *halakhot* and restrictions of the intermediate days of a Festival that are shared by a leper, a mourner, and one who is ostracized, e.g., haircutting, laundering, and greeting others. Similarly, they are prohibited from wearing leather shoes, from engaging in marital relations, and from donning phylacteries, and all are required to wrap their heads.

The Gemara explained that there is a difference between the more lenient form of ostracism and the more stringent excommunication, which are applied to those who transgress various prohibitions or who do not listen to the rulings of the court. The most stringent form of excommunication involves a higher degree of isolation from others, and contains an aspect of curse.

This chapter is the main source in the Talmud for the *halakhot* of mourning. It explained most of the *halakhot* of mourning, of rending garments, and of comforting mourners. There is a distinction made between rending at the time of death over any person, particularly an upright person, rending over a relative for whom one is obligated to mourn, and rending over a parent, a teacher, or the *Nasi*. For a relative other than one's parents there is a specific time to rend and a minimum size for the tear. For a mother, father, teacher, or *Nasi* one must make a tear that is more visible, and it may never be fully mended. The Gemara also discusses other times when one must rend one's garments as a sign of mourning.

The *halakhot* of the meal of comfort for the mourners were also explained in this chapter, as well as how one comforts the mourners, both during their mourning period and afterward.

The Gemara discussed the various degrees of mourning, which lessen with the passage of time. Acute mourning begins before the burial of the deceased; mourning is most stringent on the first day; for seven days the mourner must remain in his home, may not work, and must observe all the stringencies of mourning; for thirty days there are public signs of mourning for relatives; and for twelve months there are mourning practices observed after the death of a parent. The *halakhot* of distant tidings, i.e., if one hears of the death only after some time has passed, were also discussed.

The Gemara concluded that on Shabbat and Festivals there is no public mourning, and even during the intermediate days of a Festival one may not eulogize excessively or do other activities that lead to emotional pain. Furthermore, the days of a Festival sometimes cancel the mourning, or at least shorten the length of the mourning period.

Image **Credits**

My Notes

My Notes

My Notes

תלמוד בבלי

— מהדורת נאה —

מועד קטן חלק ב

Steinsaltz Center

ירושלים

KOREN

Please note that the number ranges that appear at the bottom of each daf of the Vilna pages indicate the corresponding pages of the Koren Talmud Bavli translation and commentary.

תלמוד בבלי

הוצאת קוֹרֵן ירושלים

— מהדורת נאה —

מסכת מועד קטן

דף יג: עד דף כט.

COMMENTARY BY

Rabbi Adin Even-Israel
Steinsaltz

EDITOR-IN-CHIEF

Rabbi Dr Tzvi Hersh Weinreb

EXECUTIVE EDITOR

Rabbi Joshua Schreier

•

STEINSALTZ CENTER
KOREN PUBLISHERS JERUSALEM

א ל מיי' שם הלכה יז יח טוש"ע שם סי' תקלא סעיף ד:

ב מ מיי' שם סמג לאוין עה טוש"ע שם סי' תקלד סעיף א:

ואלו מגלחין במועד. משום דתנא באידך פירקין דברים שעושין לצורך המועד, כמו מוכרי פירות דנעשים כדין – קתני נמי ואלו נעשים שלא כדין, לצורך המועד:

והיוצא מבית האסורים. שאינו יכול לגלח קודם המועד, שאין מניחין לו לגלח. ואפילו מניחין לו – אינו ערב לאדם לגלח בבית האסורין: [כ"ה בירושלמי]

ומנודה

וְאֵלּוּ מְגַלְּחִין בַּמּוֹעֵד: הַבָּא מִמְּדִינַת הַיָּם, וּמִבֵּית הַשִּׁבְיָה, וְהַיּוֹצֵא מִבֵּית הָאֲסוּרִין, וְהַמְנוּדֶּה שֶׁהִתִּירוּ לוֹ חֲכָמִים, וְכֵן מִי שֶׁנִּשְׁאַל לְחָכָם וְהוּתַּר, *וְהַנָּזִיר וְהַמְּצוֹרָע (א) מִטּוּמְאָתוֹ לְטָהֳרָתוֹ. וְאֵלּוּ מְכַבְּסִין בַּמּוֹעֵד: הַבָּא מִמְּדִינַת הַיָּם וּמִבֵּית הַשִּׁבְיָה, וְהַיּוֹצֵא מִבֵּית הָאֲסוּרִין, וּמְנוּדֶּה

וְאֵלּוּ מְגַלְּחִין בַּמּוֹעֵד הַבָּא מִמְּדִינַת הַיָּם כו'. בַּמּוֹעֵד, לְפִי שֶׁהָיָה אָנוּס, שֶׁלֹּא הָיָה יָכוֹל לְגַלֵּחַ קוֹדֶם: וּמִי שֶׁנִּשְׁאַל לְחָכָם. שֶׁנָּדַר שֶׁלֹּא לְגַלֵּחַ, וְשָׁאַל לְחָכָם בַּמּוֹעֵד: מִטּוּמְאָתוֹ לְטָהֳרָתוֹ. נָזִיר טָמֵא כְּשֶׁעָלָה מִטּוּמְאָתוֹ, וְשׁוּב אֵינוֹ מְשַׁמֵּר נִזְרוֹ, וּמְגַלֵּחַ. וְכֵן מְצוֹרָע שֶׁעָלָה מִטּוּמְאָתוֹ – מְגַלֵּחַ בָּרֶגֶל, לְפִי שֶׁלֹּא הָיָה לָהֶם פְּנַאי לְגַלֵּחַ קוֹדֶם הָרֶגֶל:

[לקמן יד:]

גנז'

הגהות הב"ח

(א) מתני' והמצורע הטהר מטומאתו:

וּמְנוּדֶּה שֶׁהִתִּירוּ לוֹ חֲכָמִים, וְכֵן מִי שֶׁנִּשְׁאַל לְחָכָם וְהוּתַּר. מִטְפְּחוֹת הַיָּדַיִם, וּמִטְפְּחוֹת הַסַּפָּרִים, וּמִטְפְּחוֹת הַסְּפָג, הַזָּבִין וְהַזָּבוֹת וְהַנִּדּוֹת וְהַיּוֹלְדוֹת, וְכָל הָעוֹלִין מִטּוּמְאָה לְטָהֳרָה — הֲרֵי אֵלּוּ מוּתָּרִין. וּשְׁאָר כָּל אָדָם אֲסוּרִין.§ **גמ'** וּשְׁאָר כָּל אָדָם מַאי טַעְמָא אֲסוּרִין? כִּדְתְנַן: *אַנְשֵׁי מִשְׁמָר וְאַנְשֵׁי מַעֲמָד אֲסוּרִין לְסַפֵּר וּלְכַבֵּס, וּבַחֲמִישִׁי מוּתָּרִין, מִפְּנֵי כְּבוֹד הַשַּׁבָּת. וְאָמַר *רַבָּה בַּר בַּר חָנָה אָמַר ר' אֶלְעָזָר: מ"ט — כְּדֵי שֶׁלֹּא יִכָּנְסוּ לְמִשְׁמַרְתָּן כְּשֶׁהֵן מְנוּוָּלִין. הָכָא נַמִי: כְּדֵי שֶׁלֹּא יִכָּנְסוּ לָרֶגֶל כְּשֶׁהֵן מְנוּוָּלִין. בָּעֵי ר' זֵירָא: אָבְדָה לוֹ אֲבֵידָה עֶרֶב הָרֶגֶל, כֵּיוָן דַּאֲנִיס — מוּתָּר, אוֹ דִלְמָא: כֵּיוָן דְּלָא מוּכְחָא מִילְּתָא — לָא? אָמַר אַבַּיֵי, *"יֹאמְרוּ: כָּל הַסְּרִיקִין אֲסוּרִין סְרִיקֵי בַּיְיתוֹס מוּתָּרִין"?! וּלְטַעְמִיךְ, הָא דְּאָמַר רַבִּי אַסִּי אָמַר רַבִּי יוֹחָנָן: *כָּל מִי שֶׁאֵין לוֹ אֶלָּא חָלוּק אֶחָד — מוּתָּר לְכַבְּסוֹ בְּחוּלּוֹ שֶׁל מוֹעֵד, הָתָם נַמִי: יֹאמְרוּ כָּל הַסְּרִיקִין אֲסוּרִין סְרִיקֵי בַּיְיתוֹס מוּתָּרִין! הָא אִתְּמַר עֲלַהּ, אָמַר מָר בַּר רַב אַשִׁי: אֵיזוֹרוֹ מוֹכִיחַ עָלָיו. רַב אַשִׁי מַתְנֵי: בָּעֵי ר' זֵירָא אוּמָּן שֶׁאָבְדָה לוֹ אֲבֵידָה עֶרֶב הָרֶגֶל מַהוּ? כֵּיוָן דְּאוּמָּן הוּא — מוּכְחָא מִילְּתָא, אוֹ דִלְמָא: כֵּיוָן דְּלָא מוּכְחָא מִילְּתָא כִּי הָנָךְ — לָא? תֵּיקוּ.§ "מִמְּדִינַת הַיָּם".§ מַתְנִיתִין דְּלָא כְּר' יְהוּדָה, דְּתַנְיָא, *ר' יְהוּדָה אוֹמֵר: הַבָּא מִמְּדִינַת הַיָּם — לֹא יְגַלֵּחַ, מִפְּנֵי שֶׁיָּצָא שֶׁלֹּא בִּרְשׁוּת. אָמַר רָבָא: לָשׁוּט — דִּבְרֵי הַכֹּל אָסוּר, לִמְזוֹנוֹת — דִּבְרֵי הַכֹּל מוּתָּר, לֹא נֶחְלְקוּ אֶלָּא לְהַרְוִיחָא. מָר מְדַמֵּי לֵיהּ כְּלָשׁוּט, וּמָר מְדַמֵּי לֵיהּ כִּלְמְזוֹנוֹת. מֵיתִיבִי, אָמַר ר' *נִרְאִין דִּבְרֵי ר' יְהוּדָה כְּשֶׁיָּצָא שֶׁלֹּא בִּרְשׁוּת, וְדִבְרֵי חֲכָמִים כְּשֶׁיָּצָא בִּרְשׁוּת. מַאי שֶׁלֹּא בִּרְשׁוּת? אִילֵּימָא לָשׁוּט — וְהָאָמַרְתְּ דִּבְרֵי הַכֹּל אָסוּר. וְאֶלָּא לִמְזוֹנוֹת — וְהָאָמַרְתְּ דִּבְרֵי הַכֹּל מוּתָּר! אֶלָּא פְּשִׁיטָא — לְהַרְוִיחָא, אֵימָא סֵיפָא: נִרְאִין דִּבְרֵי חֲכָמִים כְּשֶׁיָּצָא בִּרְשׁוּת. מַאי בִּרְשׁוּת? אִילֵּימָא לִמְזוֹנוֹת — הָא אָמַרְתְּ דִּבְרֵי הַכֹּל מוּתָּר, וְאֶלָּא לְהַרְוִיחָא — וְהָא אָמַרְתְּ נִרְאִין דִּבְרֵי רַבִּי יְהוּדָה בְּהָא! הָכִי קָאָמַר: נִרְאִין דִּבְרֵי ר' יְהוּדָה לְרַבָּנַן כְּשֶׁיָּצָא שֶׁלֹּא בִּרְשׁוּת, וּמַאי נִיהוּ — לָשׁוּט, שֶׁאֲפִילּוּ חֲכָמִים לֹא נֶחְלְקוּ עָלָיו אֶלָּא לְהַרְוִיחָא, אֲבָל לָשׁוּט — מוֹדוּ לֵיהּ. וְנִרְאִין דִּבְרֵי רַבָּנַן לְר' יְהוּדָה כְּשֶׁיָּצָא בִּרְשׁוּת, וּמַאי נִיהוּ — לִמְזוֹנוֹת, שֶׁאֲפִילּוּ רַבִּי יְהוּדָה לֹא נֶחֱלַק עֲלֵיהֶם אֶלָּא לְהַרְוִיחָא, אֲבָל לִמְזוֹנוֹת — מוֹדֶה לְהוּ. אָמַר שְׁמוּאֵל: קָטָן הַנּוֹלָד בַּמּוֹעֵד — מוּתָּר לְגַלֵּחַ בַּמּוֹעֵד, שֶׁאֵין לְךָ בֵּית הָאֲסוּרִין גָּדוֹל מִזֶּה. בַּמּוֹעֵד — אִין, מֵעִיקָּרָא — לָא, מְתִיב ר' פִּנְחָס: *כָּל אֵלּוּ שֶׁאָמְרוּ מוּתָּר לְגַלֵּחַ בַּמּוֹעֵד — מוּתָּר לְגַלֵּחַ בִּימֵי אֶבְלוֹ. הָא אָסוּר לְגַלֵּחַ בַּמּוֹעֵד — אָסוּר לְגַלֵּחַ בִּימֵי אֶבְלוֹ.

וְאִי

[פרש"י ע"ז לקמן יח. ותוס' שם ע"ב] · תענית טו: · [שם יז. ע"ש] · פסחים לו. חולין קז: · חולין שם [לקמן יח.] תענית כט: · [תוספ' פ"ב] · [תוספתא שם] · [לקמן יז: תוספתא פ"ב]

גמ' הָכִי גָּרְסִינַן: וּשְׁאָר כָּל אָדָם מַאי טַעְמָא אֲסוּרִין כִּדְתְנַן אַנְשֵׁי מִשְׁמָר כו' וְאָמַר רַבָּה בַּר בַּר חָנָה כו' עַד כְּשֶׁהֵן מְנוּוָּלִים. וּמַאן דְּמִתְרַשֵּׁל וְלֹא גִּילַּח מִקַּמֵּי רֶגֶל, וּמָטֵי זְמַן עֲלַיְיהוּ לְגַלֵּחַ בָּרֶגֶל – הֶחְמִירוּ רַבָּנַן, הוֹאִיל וְלָא מְזָרְזִי נַפְשַׁיְיהוּ לְסַפֵּר מִקַּמֵּי רֶגֶל, דְּלָא לֶהֱוֵי בָּרֶגֶל מְנוּוָּלִין – אִם הָיוּ מְגַלְּחִין בַּמּוֹעֵד לֹא הָיוּ מְגַלְּחִים לִפְנֵי הַמּוֹעֵד, וְנִכְנָסִין לָרֶגֶל כְּשֶׁהֵן מְנוּוָּלִין: **אָבְדָה לוֹ אֲבֵידָה.** שֶׁלֹּא הָיָה לוֹ פְּנַאי לְגַלֵּחַ קוֹדֶם הָרֶגֶל: **דְּלָא מוּכְחָא מִילְּתָא.** דְּלָא יָדְעִי כּוּלֵּי עָלְמָא דְּאָנוּס הָיָה, אֶלָּא יֹאמְרוּ: הוּא מְכַוֵּין לְהַשְׁהוֹת עַד הַמּוֹעֵד: **יֹאמְרוּ כָּל הַסְּרִיקִין אֲסוּרִין וכו'.** כְּלוֹמַר: דְּבַיְיתוֹס הָיָה יָכוֹל לִסְרוֹק חַלּוֹתָיו בְּלִי שָׁהוּת, לְפִי שֶׁהָיָה לוֹ דְּפוּס. וְאעפ"כ אָסְרוּ, מִשּׁוּם דְּאָמְרִי: כָּל הַסְּרִיקִים כו'. הָכָא נַמִּי, כֵּיוָן דְּלָא מִיגַּלְיָא לְכוּלֵּי עָלְמָא אוֹנְסֵיהּ – יֹאמְרוּ: כּוּלֵּי עָלְמָא אֲסוּרִין לְגַלֵּחַ, וְזֶה מוּתָּר: **מִי שֶׁאֵין לוֹ אֶלָּא חָלוּק אֶחָד.** נַמִּי לָאו מוּכְחָא מִילְּתָא לְכוּלֵּי עָלְמָא: **אֵיזוֹרוֹ מוֹכִיחַ עָלָיו.** דְּמִי שֶׁאֵין לוֹ אֶלָּא חָלוּק אֶחָד פּוֹשְׁטוֹ וּמִתְעַטֵּף בְּמִקְטוֹרְנוֹ וְחוֹגְרוֹ בְּאֵיזוֹרוֹ וְעוֹמֵד וּמְכַבֵּס הֶחָלוּק וּמוֹדִיעַ לַכֹּל שֶׁאֵין לוֹ אֶלָּא חָלוּק אֶחָד: **אוּמָּן.** כְּגוֹן סַפָּר, שֶׁהַכֹּל בָּאִים אֶצְלוֹ עֶרֶב הָרֶגֶל וְרוֹאִים שֶׁאָבְדָה לוֹ אֲבֵידָה, וְאָנוּס הוּא, וְאֵינוֹ יָכוֹל לְסַפֵּר עַצְמוֹ: **כִּי הָנָךְ.** דְּמַתְנִיתִין דְּקָתָנֵי מְגַלְּחִין, דְּמִידַּע לַכֹּל: **מִפְּנֵי שֶׁיָּצָא שֶׁלֹּא בִּרְשׁוּת.** כְּלוֹמַר: הוֹאִיל וְלֹא יָצָא בִּרְשׁוּת אֲחֵרִים, אֶלָּא בִּרְצוֹן עַצְמוֹ – לָאו אָנוּס הוּא: **לָשׁוּט.** אִם יָצָא שֶׁלֹּא לְצוֹרֶךְ, וְלֹא יָצָא אֶלָּא כְּדֵי לָשׁוּט בָּעוֹלָם וְלִרְאוֹתוֹ, וְחָזַר בַּמּוֹעֵד: **דִּבְרֵי הַכֹּל אָסוּר.** לְגַלֵּחַ בַּמּוֹעֵד: **לִמְזוֹנוֹת.** שֶׁיָּצָא לְחַזֵּר אַחַר מְזוֹנוֹת, שֶׁאֵין לוֹ מְזוֹנוֹת וְחִזֵּר בַּמּוֹעֵד אַחֲרֵיהֶן – דִּבְרֵי הַכֹּל מוּתָּר לְגַלֵּחַ בַּמּוֹעֵד, לְפִי שֶׁיָּצָא בְּאוֹנֶס: **לְהַרְוִיחָא.** שֶׁיֵּשׁ לוֹ נְכָסִים הַרְבֵּה, וְיוֹצֵא כְּדֵי לְהַרְוִיחַ יוֹתֵר: **נִרְאִין לִי דִּבְרֵי רַבִּי יְהוּדָה.** דְּאָסַר בְּגִילּוּחַ לַבָּא מִמְּדִינַת הַיָּם, כְּשֶׁיָּצָא שֶׁלֹּא בִּרְשׁוּת: **וְדִבְרֵי חֲכָמִים.** הַמַּתִּירִין – כְּשֶׁיָּצָא בִּרְשׁוּת: **אִילֵּימָא לָשׁוּט.** דְּקָאָמַר רַבִּי נִרְאִין דִּבְרֵי ר"י בְּיָצָא לָשׁוּט, דְּהַיְינוּ שֶׁלֹּא בִּרְשׁוּת – הָא אָמַרְתְּ וכו', וּמַאי נִרְאִין דִּבְרֵי רַבִּי יְהוּדָה? הֲלֹא שְׁנֵיהֶם מוֹדִים בָּהּ, אֶלָּא פְּשִׁיטָא – לְהַרְוָוחָא, וְאַשְׁמְעִינַן דְּנִרְאִין לוֹ דִּבְרֵי ר' יְהוּדָה שֶׁאוֹסֵר בְּגִילּוּחַ: **וְהָא נִרְאִין דִּבְרֵי רַבִּי יְהוּדָה בְּהָא.** וְקַשְׁיָא דְּרַבִּי אַדְּרַבִּי; דְּבְרֵישָׁא נִרְאֶה לוֹ דִּבְרֵי ר"י דְּאָסַר בְּהַרְוָוחָא, וּבְסֵיפָא נִרְאֶה לוֹ דִּבְרֵי חֲכָמִים דְּמַתִּירִין הַרְוָוחָא. אֶלָּא וַדַּאי אִיכָּא לְמִשְׁמַע מֵהָכָא דְּלָאו הָכִי הוּא כִּדְקָאָמַרְתְּ, דְּבְלָשׁוּט וּבִמְזוֹנוֹת פְּלִיגֵי: **ה"ק.** לָאו הֶיתֵּר דִּידֵיהּ אַשְׁמְעִינַן. וְלֹא רוֹאֶה אֲנִי קָאָמַר, אֶלָּא פְּלוּגְתַּיְיהוּ קמ"ל, בְּמַאי פְּלִיגֵי, נִרְאִין דִּבְרֵי ר"י הָאוֹסֵר לַחֲכָמִים וכו': **קָטָן הַנּוֹלָד בַּמּוֹעֵד.** וְלוֹ שְׂעָרוֹת גְּדוֹלִים, מוּתָּר לְגַלֵּחַ בַּמּוֹעֵד שְׂעַר רֹאשׁוֹ הַמְלוּכְלָךְ: **שֶׁאֵין לְךָ בֵּית הָאֲסוּרִין גָּדוֹל מִזֶּה.** מִמְּעֵי אִמּוֹ שֶׁהָיָה שָׁם, וְאָנוּס הוּא: **מֵעִיקָּרָא לָא.** דְּאִם נוֹלַד קוֹדֶם הָרֶגֶל – אֵינוֹ מְגַלֵּחַ בָּרֶגֶל, הוֹאִיל וְהָיָה יָכוֹל לְגַלֵּחַ קוֹדֶם הָרֶגֶל:

וְאִי

ומנודה וכו' ושנשאל. בירושל' מקשה: (א) הני למה התירו? והלא פשע, שלא בא לפני המועד לפני חכמים להתיר לו! ומשני: שכלו לו שלשים יום של נדוי במועד. דאין נדוי פחות משלשים יום. וכן מי שנשאל לחכם מוקי לה כשבא בחול המועד. א"י נמי: לפני המועד לא מצאו (ב) בו פתח. וגילוח הראש נמי אסור במועד, דהא אמר בגמ': שלא יכנסו לרגל מנוולין, ואין לך ניוול גדול מזה. ושמא לא קאי טעמא בגמרא אלא אשארא, אבל גילוח של ראשו – אסור משום מלאכה אפילו במקום אונס. ושאר גילוח דבעי בגמרא מאי טעמא אסורין – והיינו גילוח של יפוי, דהוה לן למישרי לצורך המועד, אע"פ שהיא מלאכה. אבל גילוח כל הראש – אסור משום מלאכה. והני (ג) כגון נזיר ומצורע הוא דשרי, משום מצוה. ולפי זה אסור לגלח ראשו במועד. ועוד יש לפרש: שנראה שמותר לגלח ראשו במועד, וא"ת: מאי קא משמע לן נזיר ומצורע? יש לומר: דס"ד דאסור, שלא ישהו קרבנותיהן – קא משמע לן דשרי. ואי מיירי הכא בשלא היה להן פנאי דוקא, והוא כדבעי למימר בגמרא – יש לומר דהכי קאמר: דנזיר ומצורע העולין מטומאה לטהרה – דוקא שעולין עתה, אבל עולין מטומאה לטהרה מקודם רגל – אסורין:

ושאר כל אדם מאי טעמא אסורין. אע"פ שהוא מלאכה – היה לנו להתירה לצורך המועד. (ד) א"נ: [אף] שיש מלאכות אסורות במועד שאין בהן טורח, כגון פרקמטיא, מכל מקום זה שהוא ליפוי ראוי להתיר לכבוד מועד. ויש מפרשים: דקאי על גילוח הראש, דאסרינן משום טירחא. מכל מקום מקשה: דהיה לו להתיר לצורך המועד. ואין זה (ה) נוטה לפי מה שפירש' המשנה דגילוח כל הראש מלאכה גמורה, ואסור!

שאין לו אלא חלוק אחד מותר לכבסו במועד. ואם תאמר: היאך יכבסנו במועד? אם כן ישאר במועד בלא חלוק בשעת כיבוס. כמו כן היה יכול לכבס קודם המועד, ויהיה בלא חלוק בשעת כיבוס! וכי תימא: כשכבסו קודם מועד, ומשום הכי מותר לכבסו במועד – א"כ, תרתי נמי אם יתלכלכו – למה נאסור לו והלא לא פשע! י"ל: דדי לו בשתי חלוקין, אחד ליו"ט ראשון ואחד לי"ט אחרון. בירושלמי אמרו: בגדי קטנים – מותר לכבסן במועד, דניכרים שהם קטנים ומלוכלכין, כמי שאין לו אלא חלוק אחד (ו):

אומן שאבדה לו אבידה ערב הרגל. פירש בקונטרס: דבאומן מבעי' ליה. אבל בני העיר, אע"פ שאין להם (ז) אומן אחר – לא מיבעיא ליה, דפשיטא דאסורים. יש להסתפק אם חלה ונתרפא, אם מותר לגלח, אם מוכחא מילתא כי הני:

מתני' דלא כר"י. תימה: לוקמא אפילו כר"י, ולמזונות אפי' רבי יהודה מודה! ושמא, כיון דקתני ר"י אומר הבא וכו' – משמע שבא לחלוק על המשנה:

אלא להרווחא והא אמרת נראין דברי ר"י בהא. נראה דל"ג ועוד, מכלל דפליגי רבנן אפילו למזונות. ובההיא פ"ק דשחיטת חולין (דף יב.): (ח) נראין דברי רבי יהודה שמלאה באשפה, ל"ג "ועוד":

עשה

עין משפט נר מצוה

ג א מיי' פ"ז מהלכות י"ט הלכה כא טוש"ע א"ח סי' תקלב סעיף א:

ד ב מיי' שם:

ה ג ד מיי' פ"ז מהל' כלי המקדש הלכה יא ופ"ז מהל' י"ט הל' יט ופ"א מהל' ביאת מקדש הלכה יב:

ו ה מיי' פ"ז מהלכות י"ט הל' יח טוש"ע א"ח סי' תקלא סעיף ד:

רבינו חננאל

ואלו מגלחין במועד הבא ממדינת הים ומבית השביה והיוצא מבית האסורין כו'. מ"ט כדתנן אנשי משמר ואנשי מעמד אסורין לספר ולכבס ואמרינן מה טעם שלא יכנסו למשמרתן מנוולין דכיון דיודעין דאסורין לכבס אף הן מספרין ומכבסין מקודם ונכנסין מתוקנין ומגוהצין. הכא נמי כדי שלא יכנסו לרגל מנוולין. בעי ר' ירמיה אבדה לו אבידה ערב הרגל כיון דטרוד הוא באבידתו אנוס הוא ומותר לספר ולכבס במועד או דלמא כיון דלא מוכחא מלתא כמו השביה ובית האסורים לא. ועלתה בתיקו. פירוש יאמרו כל הסריקין אסורין כו' הא לגבי מצה בפסח איתמר דאסרו רבנן לעשות מצות סרוקות מפני שהאשה שוהה עליהן ומחמצתן ואמרו בייתוס עושה בדפוס שאין שם שהייה אלא בפעם אחת קובעה בדפוס ונמצאת המצה מצויירת. ומתמהינן התם יאמרו כל הסריקין אסורין סריקי בייתוס מותרין מי יודע כי בדפוס נעשו הכא נמי יאמרו הכל אסורין לספר ולכבס וזה האיש מותר אבל מי שאין לו אלא חלוק אחד מותר לכבסו בחולו של מועד. כי איזורו מוכיח עליו כלומר כשרואין אדם ערום חגור איזור ורוחץ חלוקו כל רואיו יודעין שאין לו אלא חלוק אחד: הבא ממדינת הים. מתניתין דלא כר' יהודה דתניא ר' יהודה אומר הבא ממדינת הים לא יגלח מפני שיצא שלא ברשות אמר רבה לשוט פי' לשוט כמטייל וכמשתעשע כלומר שלא לצורך דברי הכל אסור למזונות כלומר יצא למדינת הים ודחוק לבקש מחיה דברי הכל מותר. כי פליגי ר"י וחכמים כשיצא להרויחא פירוש להתעשר כלומר לסחור ולהרויח. ר"י מדמי ליה לשוט דהא בכאן מחייתו מצויה ואסיר ורבנן מדמו לה ליוצא בבקשת מזון ומותבינן עליה. אמר ר' נראין דברי ר' יהודה שיצא שלא ברשות ונראין דברי חכמים שיצא ברשות ואי אמרינן לא פליגי אלא בהרויחא קשיא א) דר"י ואמר נראין דברי ר' יהודה בהרויחא מכלל דפליגי רבנן עליה ועוד נראין דברי חכמים אלא פליגי אפי' לשוט. והאמרת לשוט דברי הכל אסור. ופרקינן הכי קאמר נראין דברי ר' יהודה לחכמים. ומודה להו כשיצא שלא ברשות ומאי ניהו למזונות שאף ר' יהודה לא חלק אלא בהרויחא וקי"ל בסתמא דמתני' דשרי אפי' מאן דנפיק להרויחא וכן אמר הגאון זצ"ל. אמר שמואל קטן הנולד ברגל מגלחין אותו במועד אין לך בית אסורין גדול ממעי אמו. איני שאם נולד קודם המועד

א) נראה דל"ל קשיא דרבי אדרבי דברישא אמר נראין כו' ובסיפא אמר נראין דברי חכמים וכו'.

הגהות הב"ח

(א) תוס' ד"ה ומנודה כו' בירושלמי מקשה וא"ת הני למה התירו: (ב) בא"ד א"נ לפני המועד לא מצאו לו פתח וגילוח כל הראש נמי אסור כו' אבל גילוח של כל הראש אסור משום: (ג) בא"ד והני דוקא כגון נזיר ומצורע כו' אסור לגלח כל ראשו במועד כו' שמותר לגלח כל ראשו: (ד) ד"ה ושאר כו' א"נ אע"פ שיש דברים אסורות במועד שאין בהן מלאכה אלא טורח כגון פרקמטיא: (ה) בא"ד ואין זה נראה לפי מה שפי': (ו) ד"ה שאין כו' כמי שאין לו אלא חלוק אחד דמי הס"ד: (ז) ד"ה אומן כו' אע"פ שאין להם אלא אומן אחד לא מיבעיא ליה: (ח) ד"ה אלא כו' פ"ק דשחיטת חולין דקאמר נראין דברי ר' יהודה שמלאה באשפה נמי ל"ג ועוד:

ואי אמרת קטן אית ביה פלוגתא — נמצאת אבילות נוהגת בקטן. והתניא: מקרעין לקטן מפני עגמת נפש! אמר רב אשי, מי קתני: הא אסורין?! דלמא: יש מהן אסור, ויש מהן מותר. אמימר, ואי תימא רב שישא בריה דרב אידי, מתני הכי: אמר שמואל: קטן מותר לגלחו במועד, לא שנא נולד במועד ולא שנא נולד מעיקרא. אמר רב פנחס, אף אנן נמי תנינא: כל אלו שאמרו מותר לגלח במועד — מותר לגלח בימי אבלו, הא אסורין לגלח במועד — אסורין לגלח בימי אבלו. אי אמרת קטן אסור — נמצאת אבילות נוהגת בקטן. ותניא: מקרעין לקטן מפני עגמת נפש. אמר רב אשי, מי קתני: הא אסורין? דלמא: יש מהן אסור ויש מהן מותר. אבל אינו נוהג אבילותו ברגל, שנאמר: "ושמחת בחגך" (דברים טז). אי אבילות דמעיקרא הוא — אתי עשה דרבים, ודחי עשה דיחיד. ואי אבילות דהשתא הוא — לא אתי עשה דיחיד ודחי עשה דרבים. מנודה, מהו שינהוג נידויו ברגל? אמר רב יוסף, תא שמע: דנין דיני נפשות, ודיני מכות, ודיני ממונות. ואי לא צייית דינא — משמתינן ליה. ואי סלקא דעתך אינו נוהג נידויו ברגל — משומת ואתי מעיקרא — אתי רגל דחי ליה, השתא משמתינן ליה אנן?! א"ל אביי: ודלמא לעיוני בדיניה, דאי לא תימא הכי — דיני נפשות דקתני, ה"נ דקטלין ליה? והא קא מימנעי משמחת יום טוב. דתניא, ר"ע אומר: מנין לסנהדרין (שראו בא') שהרגו את הנפש שאין טועמין כל אותו היום — ת"ל "לא תאכלו על הדם" (ויקרא יט). אלא — לעיוני בדיניה, ה"נ — לעיוני בדיניה. א"ל: אם כן נמצאת מענה את דינו! אתו מצפרא ומעייני בדיניה, ועיילי ואכלי ושתו כולי יומא, והדר אתו בשקיעת החמה וגמרינן לדיניה, וקטלו ליה. אמר אביי, ת"ש: ומנודה שהתירו לו חכמים. אמר רבא: מי קתני שהתירוהו חכמים? שהתירו לו חכמים קתני, דאזל ופייסיה לבעל דיניה, ואתי קמי דרבנן, ושרו ליה. מצורע מהו שינהיג צרעתו ברגל? אמר אביי, תא שמע: והנזיר והמצורע (א) מטומאתו לטהרתו. הא בימי טומאתו — נהיג. לא מיבעיא קאמר; לא מיבעיא בימי טומאתו דלא נהיג, אבל לטהרתו — ניגזור שמא ישהה קרבנותיו, קמ"ל. אמר רבא, ת"ש: "והצרוע" (שם יג) — לרבות כהן גדול. והא כה"ג דכל השנה כרגל לכולי עלמא דמי, דתנן: כהן גדול מקריב אונן ואינו אוכל. שמע מינה: נוהג צרעתו ברגל, שמע מינה. אבל אסור בתספורת, מדקאמר להו רחמנא לבני אהרן "ראשיכם אל תפרעו" (שם י) — מכלל דכולי עלמא אסור.

מנודין

ואי אמרת בקטן אית ליה פלוגתא. חילוק, דנולד קודם הרגל — אינו מגלח ברגל. ואית לן למימר: הואיל ואסור לגלח ברגל — אסור לגלח נמי בימי אבלו. א"כ נמצאת אתה אומר אבילות אפילו בקטן: מקרעין לקטן. את בגדיו: מפני עגמת נפש. שיבכו הרואין, וירבו בכבוד המת, ולא מפני שהוא אבל: מי קתני הא אסורין. דמשמע: האסורין לגלח במועד אסורין לגלח באבל: יש מהן אסורין. בשאר כל אדם שאסורין לגלח במועד (ב) — אסורין לגלח בימי אבלן: ויש מהן מותרין. כגון קטן זה, שנולד קודם הרגל שאסור לגלח ברגל — מותר לגלח בימי אבלו: אתי עשה דרבים. "ושמחת": ודחי עשה דיחיד. אבל, דכתיב (ירמיה ו): "אבל יחיד עשי לך": דהשתא. שאירעו במועד: דנין דיני נפשות. במועד, אבל לא ביום טוב, שאסור משום שבות. ודייקינן מינה: מדדנין במועד — מכלל דאי לא ציית — נמי משמתינן ליה במועד: אתי רגל ודחי ליה. שאינו נוהג נדוי ברגל: דלמא לעיוני. הא דתני דדנין — לא אמרי' דלימא: "איש פלוני חייב איש פלוני זכאי". ואיכא למידק מינה, דאי לא ציית — משמתינן ליה. אלא מעייני בדין, ולא אמרי ליה כלום: מענה את דינו. דכי לא אמרו ליה דינו לאלתר, דעייני ביה — הוה ליה עינוי הדין: אלא. לעולם דנין דינו וגומרין ממש במועד. ואיכא למידק מינה: אי לא ציית — משמתינן ליה. ואיכא למשמע מינה דנוהג נמי ברגל, ודאמרת א"כ מימנע משמחת י"ט — הכא במאי עסקינן דאתו מצפרא כו': ת"ש מנודה שהתירו לו חכמים. קא סלקא דעתך: התירו לכל מנודה נידויו ברגל, דאין נידוי נוהג ברגל: דאזיל ופייסיה לבעל דיניה. ברגל, והתירו לו חכמים, ב"ד שבאותו דור: שינהיג צרעתו. שלא יבא אל תוך המחנה, ולא יגלח: הא בימי טומאתו נוהג. צרעתו ברגל: ניגזור. שלא יהא מגלח במועד, דכיון דגילח צריך להביא קרבן, ושמא משהה קרבנותיו עד יום טוב האחרון ומקריבן. ואסור להקריב קרבנות יחיד בי"ט: לרבות כ"ג. שנוהג בו צרעת: הא כהן גדול כל השנה לדידיה כרגל לכולי עלמא דמי. דתנן: כ"ג מקריב אונן. מדאמר לו אהרן למשה: "ואכלתי חטאת היום" (ויקרא י) ולא אמר למשה "והקרבתי" — מכלל דהקרבה באנינות. ולמדנו דכ"ג מקריב אונן. אבל כולי עלמא בשאר ימות השנה — אונן אינו משלח קרבנותיו, כדאמרינן לקמן (דף טו:): שלמים — בזמן שהוא שלם ולא בזמן שהוא אונן. וברגל משלח. וכהן גדול אונן מקריב כל השנה, אלמא: כל השנה לדידיה כרגל דמי, וקתני דנוהג בו צרעת. תיפשוט דכל מצורע נוהג צרעתו ברגל: אל תפרעו. גידול שער. והאי קרא גבי מיתת נדב ואביהוא כתיב, ומדאצטריך קרא למישרי להו — מכלל דאחריני אסורין: מצורעין. אע"ג דכתיב: "וראשו יהיה פרוע" — הא דריש ליה לקמן להאי פרוע למילתא אחריתי:

מנודין

עשה דיחיד. משמע דאבילות איכא עשה דאורייתא, מדלא קאמר ודחי עשה דרבנן. והאי דקאמר לעיל (דף יח:) לא מבעיא ימי אבלו דרבנן — היינו עשיית מלאכה, דנפקא לן (לקמן טו:) באסמכתא מ"והפכתי חגיכם לאבל". אבל גוף האבילות — דאורייתא. מיהו, נראה לי דשמחת הרגל נמי דרבנן, "ושמחת" — היינו בשלמי שמחה, כדאיתא בחגיגה (ח.): מהו שינהוג נידויו ברגל. א]והקשה הרב: הא ליכא אלא עשה,(ג) ואין עשה דוחה עשה! ואפילו עשה ליכא, אלא עזרא גזר, כדלקמן (דף טז.)! והא לאו קושיא היא, דהא נידוי דחי לאו דמקלל חברו, דאיכא לאו. ושמא מסוטה ילפינן. ועוד: כיון שעבר על דברי הדיינין — הרי יש כאן עשה דרבים: ואי לא צייית דינא משמתינן ליה. תימה: לימא דאי לא לית דינא — נחתינן לנכסיה!ב] מיהו, פריך שפיר: ממנעי משמחת י"ט. הקשה בתוס' הר"א: היכי קשה ליה, דהא ממנעי משמחת י"ט מאכילה ושתיה, וגוף ההריגה דהוא מלאכה לא חיישינן! ונראה לי מדאסר רחמנא הבערת בת כהן בשבת — מכלל דבמועד שרי. אי נמי: כיון שהיא מלוה — לצורך י"ט קרינא ביה: נמצאת אתה מענה את דינו. קשיא לן: דבפ' "אחד דיני ממונות" (סנהדרין דף לה.) בשמעתין דלפיכך אין דנין (*בשבת) מוכח דעינוי הדין לא שייך עד שילינוהו אחר שיגמור הדין. וכי תימא דלעיוני דהכא היינו גמר דין, ולא יהרגוהו עדיין עד אחר הרגל — א"כ אמאי פריך? לימא לעיוני בעלמא: בלא גמר דין, ולא יעשוהו גמר דין עד אחר המועד! וי"ל: דמשתכחי, אף על גב דאיכא סופרי דיינין הכותבים דברי כל אחד — מ"מ הסברא אשר בלב משתכח. ומהאי טעמא אמרינן (שם) דאין דנין בערב שבת, דליכא דאינשי אינשי: אמר אביי ת"ש מנודה שהתירו כו'. אביי לטעמיה דדחי ודלמא לעיוני, ואין חושב ראייה להוכחה דלעיל. ואע"ג דדחי דאי לא תימא דקאמ', לא חש באותו דיחוי,ג] ואפי' נראה דיחוי ה"נ מסתברא — מ"מ נוכל לומר לעיוני בלאו הכי נמי מסתברא: והא כ"ג דכל השנה כולה כרגל כו'. משמע דאם אין מנודה נוהג נידוי ברגל — הוא הדין כ"ג אינו נוהג נידוי כלל. וקשה: דהא *כ"ג דן ודנין אותו, ואי לא צייית דינא — (לא) משמתינן ליה, ולמאי דפרישית לעילד] דנוכל לומר למיחת לנכסיה — ניחא:

מנודין

ז א מיי' פ"ח מהל' אבל הלכה ד טוש"ע י"ד סי' שמ סעיף כז:
ח ב מיי' פ"ז מהלכות אבל הלכה יג טוש"ע א"ח סי' תקלא סעיף ו:
ט ג מיי' פ"ו מהלכות אבל הלכה ג ח טוש"ע א"ח סי' תקמח סעיף א:
י ד טוש"ע י"ד סי' שלד סעיף לח:
יא ה ו מיי' פ"ז מהל' י"ט הלכה יט טוש"ע א"ח סי' תקמה סעיף י:
יב ו מיי' פי"ג מהל' סנהדרין הלכה ד סמג לאוין רלב:
יג ז מיי' שם הלכה ה:
יד ח מיי' פ"י מהל' טומאת צרעת הל' ו סמג עשין רלה:
טו י מיי' פ"ב מהלכות ביאת המקדש הל' ו:
טז כ מיי' שם הל' ח:
יז ל מיי' פ"י מהל' טומאת צרעת הל' ו:
יח מ מיי' פ"ה מהל' אבל הל' א ב סמג עשין דרבנן ג טוש"ע י"ד סי' שפ סעיף א וסי' שצ סעיף א:

[לקמן כו.]
[גי' הערוך אגמת ע"ש]
[תוספתא פ"ב ע"ש]
סנהדרין סג. ע"ש
[אלא כל"ל וכ"ג רש"י]
[נ"ל תגמרי יעב"ץ]
[לעיל יג:]
[לקמן טו.]
יומא יג: הוריות יב: [ב"ק קי. זבחים צט.]

גליון הש"ס

הגהות הב"ח (א) גמ' ת"ש והנזיר והמצורע העולה מטומאתו: (ב) רש"י ד"ה יש מהן וכו' לגלח במועד יש מהן אסורין לגלח: (ג) תוס' ד"ה מהו כו' הא ליכא אלא עשה דיחיד ואין עשה דיחיד דוחה עשה דרבים ואפילו עשה ליכא:

הגהות מהר"ב רנשבורג

א] תוס' ד"ה מהו שינהיג וכו' והקשה הרב כו' אלא עזרא גזר כדלקמן. עיין ריטב"א דבור המתחיל מנודה: ב] ד"ה ואי לא צייית כו' מיהו פריך שפיר. עיין יד דוד: ג] ד"ה אמר אביי כו' אביי לטעמיה כו' ואפילו נראה דיחוי ה"נ מסתברא כו'. בספריהם היה הגירסא א"ל אביי ודלמא לעיוני ה"נ מסתברא דאי לא תימא הכי כו' וק"ל: ד] ד"ה והא כ"ג כו' ולמאי דפרישית לעיל בד"ה ואי לא צייית:

מנודין ומצורעין מה הן בתספורת? ת"ש: מנודין ומצורעין אסורין לספר ולכבס. מנודה שמת — ב"ד סוקלין את ארונו, ר' יהודה אומר: לא שיעמידו עליו גל אבנים כגלו של עכן, אלא: ב"ד שולחין ומניחין אבן גדולה על ארונו. *ללמדך שכל המתנדה ומת בנידויו ב"ד סוקלין את ארונו. אבל חייב בעטיפת הראש, מדקאמר ליה רחמנא ליחזקאל "ולא תעטה על שפם" — מכלל דכולי עלמא מיחייבי. מנודה מהו בעטיפת הראש? אמר רב יוסף, ת"ש: *והן מתעטפין ויושבין כמנודין וכאבלים עד שירחמו עליהם מן השמים. א"ל אביי: דלמא מנודה לשמים שאני דחמיר. מצורע מהו בעטיפת הראש? ת"ש: "ועל שפם יעטה" — מכלל שחייב בעטיפת הראש, ש"מ. *אבל אסור להניח תפילין, מדקאמר ליה רחמנא ליחזקאל: "פארך חבוש עליך" — מכלל דכ"ע אסור. א) מנודה מהו בתפילין? תיקו. מצורע מהו בתפילין? ת"ש: *"והצרוע" — לרבות כ"ג, "בגדיו יהיו פרומים" — שיהו מקורעים, "וראשו יהיה פרוע" — אין פריעה אלא גידול שער, דברי ר"א. ר"ע אומר: נאמרה הוייה בראש ונאמרה הוייה בבגד, מה הוייה האמורה בבגד — דבר שחוץ מגופו, אף הוייה בראש — דבר שחוץ מגופו. מאי לאו — אתפילין? אמר רב פפא: לא, ב) אכומתא וסודרא. אבל אסור בשאילת שלום, דקאמר ליה רחמנא ליחזקאל: "האנק דום", מנודה מהו בשאילת שלום? אמר רב יוסף: ת"ש: *ובשאילת שלום שבין אדם לחבירו, כבני אדם הנזופין למקום. א"ל אביי: דלמא מנודה לשמים שאני, דחמיר. מצורע מהו בשאילת שלום? ת"ש: "ועל שפם יעטה" — שיהו שפתותיו מדובקות זו בזו, שיהא כמנודה וכאבל, ואסור בשאילת שלום, ש"מ. ונפשוט מינה למנודה! אמר רב אחא בר פנחס משמיה דרב יוסף: מי קתני שאסור? שיהא כמנודה וכאבל [קתני] — במילי אחרנייתא, ואסור נמי בשאילת שלום. אבל אסור בדברי תורה, מדקאמר רחמנא ליחזקאל "דום", מנודה מהו בדברי תורה? אמר רב יוסף, ת"ש: מנודה — שונה ושונין לו, נשכר ונשכרין לו. מוחרם — לא שונה ולא שונין לו, לא נשכר ולא נשכרין לו, אבל שונה הוא לעצמו שלא יפסיק את למודו. ועושה לו חנות קטנה בשביל פרנסתו. ואמר רב: זבוני מיא בפקתא דערבות. שמע מינה. מצורע מהו בדברי תורה? ת"ש: *"והודעתם לבניך ולבני בניך יום אשר עמדת לפני ה' אלהיך בחורב", מה להלן באימה וביראה וברתת ובזיעה — מכאן אמרו: *הזבין והמצורעין ובועלי נדות מותרין לקרות בתורה ובנביאים ובכתובים, ולשנות במדרש ובהלכות ובאגדות, ובעלי קריין אסורין, ש"מ. אבל אסור *בתכבוסת, דכתיב: "וישלח יואב תקועה ויקח משם אשה חכמה ויאמר אליה התאבלי נא ולבשי נא בגדי אבל ואל תסוכי שמן והיית כאשה זה ימים רבים מתאבלת על מת". מנודין ומצורעין מה הן בתכבוסת? ת"ש: מנודין ומצורעין אסורין לספר ולכבס. ש"מ. אבל חייב בקריעה דקאמר להו רחמנא לבני אהרן: "לא תפרומו" — מכלל דכ"ע מיחייבי. מנודה מהו בקריעה? תיקו. מצורע מהו בקריעה? ת"ש: "בגדיו יהיו פרומים" — שיהו מקורעין, שמע מינה. אבל חייב בכפיית המטה, דתני בר קפרא:

דמות

רש"י

מנודין ומצורעין מהו. להכי קאמר להו בהדדי — משום דפשיט להו בהדדי: מנודה שמת וכו'. סיפא דברייתא היא: כגלו של עכן. דכתיב (יהושע ז) "ויקימו עליו גל אבנים גדול": והן מתעטפין. מפורש במסכת תענית, לאחר שהתענו שלש עשרה ת"צ: מנודה לשמים. כי הני שאני, דחמירי, ולהכי צריכי עטיפת הראש. אבל אחרים — אינן צריכין עטיפת הראש: יעטה. משמע עטיפת הראש: פארך. זה תפילין: דבר שהוא חוץ מגופו אף הוייה. האמורה בראש "ראשו יהיה פרוע" משמע מגולה, כענין דכתיב: "ופרע את ראש האשה" (במדבר ה) — דבר שהוא חוץ מגופו. ולא אמרינן משער, שהוא מגופו: מאי לאו. שיהא ראשו מגולה מתפילין: אכומתא וסודרא. כלומר שיהא ראשו מגולה מכומתא וסודרא, אבל תפילין מניח: דהא א"ל רחמנא ליחזקאל האנק דום. כלומר, כדבר זה תנהוג אבילות: שתדום ולא תשאל לשלום: ת"ש. דתני גבי תעניות: הן יושבין כמנודין ואבלים כו': שפם. משמע: שפתותיו מדובקות: מי קתני כמנודה. שאסור בשאילת שלום: מוחרם. שמחרימין בחרם לאחר ל' יום לאחר נידוי א]: בפקתא דערבות. בשוק של אותו מקום: בעלי קריין אסורין. לפי שבא להם מחמת שמחה וקלות ראש, וליכא אימה:

א) [עי' תוס' ישנים נדה ז: ד"ה הקשה ה"ר לאבי"ה וכו']
ב) [פי' כומתא מגבעה רבה שהיא כמלא הראש ואין עולה למעלה מן הראש. ערוך]

תוספות

מנודין ומצורעין מה הן בתספורת. ומ"ראשו יהיה פרוע" לא בעי לאוכוחי, דלית ליה דר"א, דמוקי לה לקמן בתספורת. תדע, דלקמן בעי לאוכוחי מינה הנחת תפילין כר"ע:

(*מנודה) מהו בעטיפת הראש אמר רב יוסף תא שמע. ולא נראה לו לדברי רב פפא דמוקי "ראשו יהיה פרוע" אכומתא וסודרא:

וראשו יהיה פרוע. צריך עיון אי פליגי הכי ב"ראשיכם אל תפרעו ובגדיכם לא תפרומו" דלעיל מייתי (א) עליה תספורת לאבל, ולא מייתי מיניה למצורע, דמשמע דסבר כר"ע, ופליג אדר' אליעזר, כדפרישית לעיל? ושמא ר"ע לא פליג אדרבי אליעזר, דפריעת הראש היינו גידול שער בין במצורע בין באבל, ותרוייהו דורש ר"ע. ולעיל דלא מייתי מיניה למצורע — משום דמשכח ברייתא בהדיא מייתי לה, ואע"ג דברישא דסוגיא מייתי אבל אינו נוהג אבילותו ברגל, ומניח המשנה דלקמן ומייתי קרא ד"ושמחת" — לפי שצריך לפרש מגלן מתני' דאבל אינו נוהג אבילותו ברגל. אבל ראשו יהיה פרוע, דמיירי בגידול שער, דומה לו דבר פשוט וניחא ליה לאתויי ברייתא:

אסור בשאילת שלום דקאמר ליה רחמנא ליחזקאל האנק דום. דמשמע שתיקה משאילת שלום. ומתלמוד תורה נמי משמע בסמוך מ"האנק דום". והא דהיה יחזקאל נוהג אבילות ב"האנק דום" ובכל שאר דברים לא היה עושה — שהיה צריך להראות בקצת דברים שהוא אבל, ולא היה נוהג דיני אבל אלא למשל:

שיהו שפתותיו מדובקות. לעיל דרשינן מיניה עטיפת הראש. ושמא תרוייהו משמע. א"נ: מדכתיב שפם ולא כתיב שפה:

ובועלי נדות מותרין. אחר שטבל לקרי, אבל לקריו — צריך טבילה. ולרבי יהודה משמע התם דלא צריך טבילה לדברי תורה לבעל קרי, היכא דלא נטהר ע"י טבילה זו. בפרק "מי שמתו" (ברכות דף כו.) במשמשת ורואה דם, ובעל קרי שראה זיבה — צריכין טבילה, ור' יהודה פוטר. והא דהכא בלא טבילה כרבי יהודה — צריך ליישב דאיירי רבי יהודה בסיפא דהך ברייתא בפ' "מי שמתו" (שם דף כב.), וקאמר רבי יהודה: שונה הוא בהלכות דרך ארץ. וליכא למימר דלרבי יהודה נמי בועלי נדות חייבין טבילה כמו בעל קרי בעלמא, דהשתא ומה בעל קרי שראה זיבה אחר כך, שהיה חייב כבר — פוטר רבי יהודה, בועל נדה לא כל שכן. מיהו, לכאורה נ"ל דלא פליגי רבי יהודה ורבנן אלא בהני טומאות דדומיא דקרי הוי, דהיינו דטומאה יוצאה עליו מגופו. אבל בטומאת שרצים — מודה רבי יהודה דבהדי קרי צריך טבילה. א"כ ה"נ בועל נדה מודה, דלא חשיב טומאה יוצאה מגופו. ואפילו מאן דבעי למימר בפרק "אלו דברים" בפסחים (דף סח.) ובפ"ק דיומא (דף ו.) דמשתלח חוץ לשתי מחנות כמו בעל קרי — מ"מ לא חשיב טומאה יוצאה מגופו. ורבי יהודה נמי הצריך טבילה לדברי תורה. בתוספ' פי': דכיון דטומאת בועל נדה מכח קרי — רבי יהודה מודה דצריך טבילה:

ה"ג **מנודין** ומצורעין מה הן בתכבוסת? ת"ש: מנודין ומצורעין אסורין לספר ולכבס. ובספר הרב לא היה כתוב כל זה. והיה קשה לרב: למה לא בעי ליה? ותירץ: דכבר אייתי לעיל הך ברייתא דגבי תספורת. והא הקשה לקמן גבי עשיית מלאכה קמיבעי, ומביא ברייתא דמתנייא לעיל ונשכרין! ותירץ: דאגב דמצורע קאי בתיקו, קא בעי מנודה, ומייתי לברייתא דלעיל.

ורחיצה

רבינו חננאל

מנודה וכן מצורע דתניא מנודין ומצורעין אסורין לספר ולכבס. מנודה שמת ב"ד סוקלין את ארונו. ר' יהודה אומר לא שיעמידו עליו גל אבנים כגל עכן. אלא ב"ד שולחין ומניחין אבן על ארונו כו'. אבל חייב בעטיפת הראש מדאמר ליה רחמנא ליחזקאל לא תעטה על שפם מכלל דכ"ע אסירי וכן מנודה דתנן והן מתעטפין ויושבין כמנודין ואבלין עד שירחמו עליהן מן השמים ודחי אביי ודלמא מנודה לשמים דחמיר חייב בעטיפת הראש אבל מנודה לבני אדם לא. ולקולא עבדינן. ולא מחייבינן למנודה בעטיפת הראש דהא איבעיא ולא איפשיטא. מצורע אסיקנא דחייב בעטיפת הראש. אבל אסור בתפלין מדכתיב ביחזקאל פארך חבוש עליך מכלל דכ"ע אסירי מנודה מהו בתפלין תיקו. מצורע מהו בתפלין ולא איפשיטא בהדיא אבל אסור בשאילת שלום מדכתיב ביחזקאל האנק דום אלא דבר מכלל דכ"ע אסירי. מנודה מאי ת"ש מנודה שונה ושונין לו נשכר ונשכרין לו מוחרם לא שונה ולא שונין לו [לא נשכר] ולא נשכרין לו אבל שונה לעצמו שלא יפסיד תלמודו ועושה לו חנות קטנה בפקתא דערבות שהיא ארץ ציה רחוקה מן הישוב לזבוני מיא כדי פרנסתו וכן מצורע מותר בדברי תורה אבל אסור בתכבוסת ובסיכה שנאמר וישלח יואב תקועה ויקח משם אשה חכמה ויאמר אליה התאבלי נא ולבשי נא בגדי אבל ואל תסוכי שמן והיית כאשה זו ימים רבים מתאבלת על מת. אבל אסור ברחיצה דרחיצה בכלל סיכה היא מנודה ומצורע ברחיצה לא איפשיטא בהדיא. אבל חייב בקריעת בגדיו מדכתיב בבני אהרן ובגדיכם לא תפרומו מכלל דכולי עלמא חייבי וכן מצורע מנודה מאי תיקו אבל חייב בכפיית המטה. מנודים ומצורעים מהו תיקו

עין משפט נר מצוה

יט א מיי' פ"ה מהלכות ת"ת הלכה ד סמג לאוין רח ועשין לג טוש"ע י"ד סי' שלד סעיף ב: ג' רש"ע מצורע:
כ ב מיי' פ"י מהלכות טומאת צרעת הלכה ו סמג עשין רלה:
כא ג מיי' פ"ה מהלכות ת"ת הלכה ד סמג עשין שם טוש"ע י"ד סי' שלד סעיף ג:
כב ד מיי' פ"ה מהל' אבל הלכה א יט סמג עשין דרבנן ג טוש"ע י"ד סי' שפ סעיף א:
כג ה מיי' פ"י מהלכות טומאת צרעת הלכה ו סמג עשין רלה:
כד ו מיי' פ"ה מהל' אבל הלכה ע סמג עשין דרבנן ג טוש"ע י"ד סי' שפ סעיף א וסי' שפח סעיף א וש"ע א"ח סי' לח ועי' ש"ך יו"ד סי' שלד ס"ק יב:
כה ז ח ט מיי' פ"י מהל' טומאת צרעת הלכה ו סמג עשין רלה:
כו י מיי' פ"ה מהל' אבל הלכה א כ סמג עשין דרבנן ג טוש"ע י"ד סי' שפ סעיף א וסי' שפה סעיף א:
כז כ מיי' פ"ג מהלכות תענית הל' ה ש"ע א"ח סי' תקעה סעיף ז:
כח ל מיי' פ"ז מהלכות ת"ת הל' ו סמג עשין לג:
כט מ מיי' פ"ה מהל' אבל הל' א יט סמג עשין דרבנן ג טוש"ע י"ד סי' שפ סעיף א וסי' שפד סעיף א:
ל נ ס ע פ מיי' פ"ז מהלכות ת"ת הל' ה טוש"ע י"ד סי' שלד סעיף ב:
לא צ מיי' פ"י מהל' טומאת צרעת הל' ו סמג עשין רלה:
לב ק מיי' פ"ד מהל' ק"ש הל' ח טוש"ע א"ח סי' פח:
לג ר מיי' פ"ה מהלכות אבל הלכה א ג סמג עשין דרבנן ג טוש"ע י"ד סי' שפ סעיף א וסי' שפט סעיף א:
לד ש מיי' פ"ח מהל' אבל הלכה א סמג עשין דרבנן ב טוש"ע י"ד סי' שמ סעיף א:
לה ת מיי' פ"י מהלכות טומאת צרעת הל' ו סמג עשין רלה:
לו א מיי' פ"ה מהלכות אבל הלכה א סמג עשין דרבנן ג טוש"ע י"ד סי' שפ סעיף א וסי' שפז סעיף א:

מסורת הש"ס

ברכות יט. עדיות פ"ה מ"ו
תענית יד:
סוכה כה. כתובות ו: ע"ש [מס' שמחות פ"ו ברכות יא. ע"ז]
[לעיל יד:]
תענית יד:
ס"א
ברכות כב.
[תוספתא דברכות פ"ב]
לקמן יז:
שמואל ב יד
ויקרא י
שם יג

הגהות מהר"ב רנשבורג

א] רש"י ד"ה מוחרם שמחרימין בחרם לאחר ל' יום לאחר נידוי. נ"ב לאחר ששים יום תניא לקמן דף טז ע"א ואולי כוונת רש"י אחרי שלשים השניים דהנידוי שם ושונין לאחר שלשים ומחרימין לאחר ששים:

הגהות הב"ח

(א) תוס' ד"ה וראשו כו' דלעיל מייתי מיניה איסור תספורת לאבל:

גליון הש"ס

תוס' ד"ה ובועלי נדות וכו' ובתוספ' פי' דכיון דטומאת בועל נדה. עיין משנה למלך פ"ג ה"ג מהל' ביאת מקדש:

לז א מיי' פ"י מהלכות טומאת צרעת הל' ו סמג עשין רלה:
לח ב מיי' פ"ה מהל' אבל הל' א ז טוש"ע י"ד סי' שפ סעיף א:
לט ג מיי' פ"ג מהלכות תענית הל' ד טוש"ע א"ח סי' תקעה סעיף ג:
מ ד מיי' פ"ה מהלכות אבל הלכה א ג סמג עשין דרבנן ג טוש"ע י"ד סי' שפ סעיף א:
מא ה מיי' פ"ג מהלכות תענית הל' ד טוש"ע א"ח סי' תקעה סעיף ג:
מב ו מיי' פ"י מהל' טומאת צרעת הל' ו:
מג ז מיי' פ"ה מהל' אבל הל' א ו טוש"ע י"ד סי' שפ סעיף א:
מד ח טוש"ע י"ד סי' שלד סעיף ב:
מה ט מיי' פ"ג מהל' תענית הלכה ד טוש"ע א"ח סי' תקעה סעיף ג:
מו י מיי' פ"י מהלכות טומאת צרעת הל' ו:
מז כ מיי' פ"ה מהלכות אבל הלכה א ה סמג עשין דרבנן ג טוש"ע י"ד סי' שפ סעיף א:
מח ל מיי' פ"י מהלכות טומאת צרעת הל' ו:
מט מ נ ס מיי' פ"ב מהלכות ביאת מקדש הלכה יא סמג לאוין שג:

תוספתא דתענית פ"א

[ועי' תוספות ד"ה וקרע ובת"י נקה ו: ד"ה הקשה ה"ר ראבי"ה]

דמות דיוקני נתתי בהן, ובעונותיהם הפכתיה – כפו מטותיהן עליה. מנודה [א]ומצורע מה הן בכפיית המטה? תיקו. [ב]אבל אסור בעשיית מלאכה, דכתיב: "והפכתי חגיכם לאבל" (עמוס ח) מה חג אסור במלאכה – אף אבל אסור במלאכה. מנודה מהו בעשיית מלאכה? אמר רב יוסף, ת"ש: *[ג]כשאמרו אסור בעשיית מלאכה – לא אמרו אלא ביום, אבל בלילה מותר. וכן אתה מוצא במנודה ובאבל. מאי לאו – אכולהו? לא, אשארא. ת"ש: מנודה שונה ושונין לו, נשכר ונשכרין לו. שמע מינה. מצורע מהו בעשיית מלאכה? תיקו. [ד]אבל אסור ברחיצה, דכתיב: "ואל תסוכי שמן" (שמואל ב יד), ורחיצה בכלל סיכה. מנודה מהו ברחיצה? אמר רב יוסף, ת"ש: *כשאמרו אסור ברחיצה – [ה]לא אמרו אלא כל גופו, אבל פניו ידיו ורגליו – מותר. וכן אתה מוצא במנודה ובאבל. מאי לאו אכולהו? לא, אשארא. [ו]מצורע מהו ברחיצה? תיקו. *[ז]אבל אסור בנעילת הסנדל, מדקאמר ליה רחמנא ליחזקאל: "ונעליך תשים ברגליך" (יחזקאל כד) – מכלל דכולי עלמא אסור. [ח]מנודה מהו בנעילת הסנדל? אמר רב יוסף, תא שמע: *כשאמרו אסור בנעילת הסנדל – [ט]לא אמרו אלא בעיר, אבל בדרך – מותר. ◦הא כיצד? יצא לדרך – נועל, נכנס לעיר – חולץ, וכן אתה מוצא במנודה ובאבל. מאי לאו אכולהו? לא, אשארא. [י]מצורע מהו בנעילת הסנדל? תיקו. *[כ]אבל אסור בתשמיש המטה, דכתיב: "וינחם דוד את בת שבע אשתו ויבא אליה" (שמואל ב יב) – מכלל דמעיקרא אסור. מנודה מהו בתשמיש המטה? אמר רב יוסף, ת"ש: כל אותן שנים שהיו ישראל במדבר מנודין היו, ושימשו מטותיהן. א"ל אביי: ודלמא מנודה לשמים שאני, דקיל? קיל?! והא אמרת חמיר! ספוקי מספקא ליה, זיל הכא – קמדחי ליה, וזיל הכא – קמדחי ליה. [ל]מצורע מהו בתשמיש המטה? ת"ש, דתניא: "וישב מחוץ לאהלו" (ויקרא יד) – שיהא כמנודה [א] וכאבל, *ואסור בתשמיש המטה. ואין אהלו אלא אשתו, שנא' "לך אמור להם שובו לכם לאהליכם" (דברים ה) – שמע מינה. וניפשוט נמי למנודה! אמר רב חונא בריה דרב פנחס משמיה דרב יוסף: מי קתני "שאסור"? שיהא כמנודה וכאבל – במילי אחרנייתא, ואסור נמי בתשמיש המטה. [מ]אבל אינו משלח קרבנותיו, דתניא, *ר"ש אומר: "שלמים" – בזמן שהוא שלם, ולא בזמן שהוא אונן. [נ]מנודה מהו שישלח קרבנותיו? אמר רב יוסף, ת"ש: כל אותן שנים שהיו ישראל במדבר מנודין היו, ושלחו קרבנותיהן. א"ל אביי: ודלמא מנודה לשמים שאני, דקיל? קיל?! והאמרת חמיר! ספוקי מספקא ליה, ומדחי ליה. מצורע מהו שישלח קרבנותיו? [ס]ת"ש, דתניא: "ואחרי טהרתו" (יחזקאל מד) – אחר פרישתו מן המת, "שבעת ימים יספרו לו" – אלו ז' ימי ספירו, "וביום באו אל הקודש אל החצר הפנימית לשרת בקודש יקריב חטאתו" (שם)

זו

ורחיצה בכלל סיכה. תימה: אדבעי מהו ברחיצה, אמאי לא בעי מהו בסיכה? **לא** אשארא. דמיירי התם בסוף פ"ק דתענית (דף יג.) בנעילת הסנדל ועשיית מלאכה. ואעשיית מלאכה לא קאי, דהא מנודה שרי במלאכה, אלא אנעילת סנדל. סוף פ"ק דתענית (שם) מסיק, הלכתא: אבל אסור בין בחמין בין בצונן, אבל לרחוץ פניו ידיו ורגליו בחמין – אסור, בצונן – מותר. ולסוך – אפילו כל שהוא אסור. ובתוס' הרב פי': קשיא ליה מאי שנא בט' באב ויוה"כ אסור לרחוץ אפילו אצבעות, כדמשמע בפרק בתרא דיומא (דף עז.): ומביאין לו מטפחת כו'. והא תרוייהו מסיכה נפקי, אבילות מ"ואל תסוכי שמן", יום הכפורים מ"וסוך לא סכתי" (דניאל י)! ובשם רשב"ס: דלפי המסקנא דמסיק בפ"ק דתענית דאבל מותר לרחוץ פניו ידיו ורגליו בצונן – הוא הדין ט' באב ויוה"כ. ותימה: אמאי לא מייתי בסוגיין דתענית ההיא דמטפחת כו'? ובשם רבינו תם שמעתי שהיה אוסר לרחוץ כלל בט' באב ויוה"כ חוץ מידיו שחרית, דחשיב להו כמו מלוכלכות בטיט ובואה. הואיל ואינו יכול ליגע בפיו ועיניו ◦משום בת מלך: **לא** אשארא. פי': לא קאי אנעילת סנדל אלא ארחילה. וזיל הכא קמדחי ליה, ◦וזיל הכא קמדחי ליה. דאעשיית מלאכה לא קאי, כדפרישית לעיל. וא"ת: ואמאי לא פשיט מר"א דסוף פרק "הזהב" (ב"מ דף נט:*): קרע את בגדיו וחלץ מנעליו! וי"ל: דשמא היה מחמיר על עצמו. אי נמי: מספקא ליה, כי היכי דמספקא לן: **ושמשו** מטותיהן. בכל הני דלעיל לא מייתי מבני המדבר, דלא ידעי היאך היו נוהגין. אלא הא פשיטא לן שהיו משמשים מטותיהן – שהרי הם היו פרים ורבים. וכן גבי שלחו קרבנות דבסמוך – שמא יש להוכיח הכי מן הפסוקים: **וישב** מחוץ לאהלו. פי': בימי ספרו. ובימי חלוטו פליגי בה לעיל (דף ז:). כי האי גוונא אמרינן אבל אסור להניח תפילין ולא כל ימי אבלו קאמרינן, אלא יום ראשון בלבד ושני, כדלקמן (דף כא.): **ואחרי** טהרתו. פי' בקונטרס: דבטומאת מת איירי. ז' ימים ימי הזאתו, "יספרו לו" – איירי בימי ספירו. וכמו מילתא אחריתי קמ"ל. וביום באו לעבודה יביא כהן הדיוט עשירית האיפה, "וחטאתו" – כמו חטוי, וקדושתו לעבודה – מילי מילי קאמר. וקשה: אמאי לא מפרש ליה בכהן גדול? ויש לומר: משום דבכהן הדיוט איירי, דכתיב: "כי אם לאב ולאם", ואילו כ"ג לא יטמא לאביו ולאמו. ולא ניחא ליה למימר כדאמרינן בקדושין (דף עח:): רישא בכהן גדול וסיפא בכהן הדיוט. ועוד: דלא הוה קמ"ל מידי. אבל כהן הדיוט ביום חינוכו – אינו כתיב בקרא בפירוש. מיהו, קשה לן: כיון דמילי מילי כתיב, אמאי ר"ש אומר בבאו מקריב – בזמן שראוי לביאה, (ב)וקשה: דבפרק "תמיד נשחט" (פסחים דף סב. ושם), דקאמרינן: כל הזבחים ערל וטמא משלחין קרבנותיהן! ועוד: דהכא נמי לא משמע דאיירי אלא במצורע, דהאי דבעי מצורע מהו שישלח קרבנותיו מייתי ליה! ונראה לי, דר"ש לאפוקי מצורע אתי, דרבי יהודה דריש "ביום באו" – ביום שמתחנך לעבודה, ור"ש מוקי ל"ביום באו" – דקאי אדלעיל, דאיירי במצורע, ולא איירי מידי בעשירית האיפה. אלא בא לומר דבמצורע דאיירי בקרא, כשיטהר ויכנס לעזרה, דהיינו לאחר ימי ספרו – אז יקריב חטאתו או שאר קרבנותיו. ובתוספות פי': דערל וטמא משלחין קרבנותיהן(ג) בטומאת שרץ, ולא בטומאה מגופו. והקשה על זה מהא דאמרינן במגילה פ"ק (דף ח.): מזובו ולא מנגעו. משמע, דאם יטהר מזובו – יביא קרבן, אע"פ שהוא מצורע! וכמו כן קשה למאי דפרישית! ותירץ: דלא איירי התם לענין קרבן אלא שיהא טהור מדין משכב ומושב, דחמירא הוה טפי מבמצורע. ול"ע: בפרק "כל הזבחים שנתערבו" (זבחים עד: ושם), ובפרק "כל הגט" (גיטין דף כח: ושם), *מפורש קצת דיני סמיכה שצריך בעלים, ואם כן אין טמא מביא קרבנותיו! [ועי' תוס' יבמות קד: ד"ה דאמר]:

דמות דיוקני. "בצלם אלהים עשה את האדם" (בראשית ט): [כשאמרו. חכמים גבי "עברו אלו ולא נענו" (תענית דף יג.) אסור במלאכה וכו' וכן אתה מוצא במנודה]: מאי לאו אכולהו. קאמר, דמנודה אסור: לא אשארא. דקתני (א) אעטיפת הראש, דאמרי' התם (דף יד:): בתענית צבור מתעטפין ויושבין כמנודין: ורחיצה בכלל סיכה. דכתיב: "ותבא כמים בקרבו וכשמן בעצמותיו" (תהלים קט): כשאמרו אסור ברחיצה. בתענית צבור: אכולהו. ארחילה נמי, דמנודה אסור: לא אשארא. קאמר, דמנודה אית ליה דין דהני דתעניות צבור: כשאמרו אסור בנעילת הסנדל. בתענית צבור: ויבא אליה. לאחר אבילות: מנודין היו. למקום: ספיקא הוא. אי קיל אי חמיר: זיל הכא ומדחי. דלקולא *אזלי בהדייהו: לפיכך נקראים שלמים בזמן שהוא שלם. בדעתו, שדעתו מיושבת עליו: יספרו לו. לעיל מיניה כתיב: "ואל מת אדם לא יבא לטמאה" ובכהן משתעי, ואחרי טהרתו – דהיינו מפרישתו מן המת, משפריש מן המת מונין שבעת ימי הזאתו שבעת ימים אחרים יספרו לו. מדאפקיה רחמנא בלשון ספירה ולא נקט הזאה – שמעינן: שבעת ימי ספירו אם נצטרע: וביום באו *ביום טהרתו. כתיב בכהן גדול:

זו

תענית יג. | [עי' ברא"ש ס"ס נא] | שם [פסחים נד:] | [לקמן כ:] | ביום חינוכו כתיב בכהן הדיוט כצ"ל כפי הסוגיא ופי' התוספות | [לקמן כה.] שמואל ב יב | ויקרא יד | דברים ה | [זבחים נט:] | יחזקאל מד | שם | [ובחגיגה טז:]

מתרינן

רבינו חננאל

אבל אסור בעשיית מלאכה שנאמר והפכתי חגיכם לאבל מה חג אסור בעשיית מלאכה אף אבל אסור. מצורע תיקו אבל מנודה מותר במלאכה. אבל אסור בנעילת הסנדל מדכתיב ביחזקאל ונעליך תשים ברגליך. מכלל דכ"ע אסירי. כשאמרו אסור בנעילת הסנדל לא אמרו אלא בעיר אבל בדרך מותר. יצא לדרך נועל. נכנס לעיר חולץ. וכן המנודה. מצורע תיקו. אבל אסור בתשמיש המטה שנאמר וינחם דוד את בת שבע אשתו ויבא אליה. מכלל דמעיקרא אסיר. מנודה מהו ת"ש כל השנים שהיו ישראל במדבר היו כמנודים והיו משמשין מטותיהן. ודלמא שאני מנודה לשמים דקיל והא אמרת מנודה לשמים חמור הוא ספוקי מספקא ליה אזיל הכא מדחי ליה אזיל הכא מדחי ליה. מצורע מהו בתשמיש המטה ולא איפשיטא בהדיא. אבל אינו משלח קרבנותיו שנאמר שלמים בזמן שהוא שלם ולא בזמן שהוא אונן מנודה מהו ולא איפשיטא מצורע מהו ת"ש

הגהות הגר"א

[א] גמ' כמנודה מביתו וכאבל כו' כצ"ל:

גליון הש"ס

גמ' הא כיצד יצא לדרך. עי' לקמן דף כז ע"א תוס' ד"ה אם יכול: **תוס'** ד"ה לא אשארא דמיירי כו' משום בת מלך. ע' שבת דף קנ ע"ב: **ד"ה** לא אשארא פי' לא קאי כו' וזיל הכא קמדחי. וכן כתבו כל הפוסקים ותמיה לי לפי ההלכה בתענית דף יג ע"א דבתענית צבור מותר ברחיצת כל גופו בצונן אם כן על כרחך הך ברייתא מיירי ברחיצת חמין וממילא וכן אתה מוצא במנודה וכאבל לא קאי על רחיצה דהא באבל אפילו אצבע אסור בחמין וכמבואר שם להדיא דקאי אשארא וא"כ מוכח דקאי אנעילת סנדל ונפסק דמנודה אסור בנעילת סנדל וצע"ג:

הגהות הב"ח

(א) רש"י ד"ה לא אשארא דקתני התם אעטיפת הראש: (ב) תוס' ד"ה ואחרי כו' בזמן שראוי לביאה כבפ' תמיד נשחט כו' כצ"ל ותיבת וקשה נמחק: (ג) בא"ד ובתוס' פי' כו' משלחין קרבנותיהן איירי בטומאת שרץ:

זו עשירית האיפה שלו. שמביא כהן הדיוט כשמחנכין אותו לעבוד תחילה, כדכתיב (ויקרא ו): "זה קרבן אהרן ובניו אשר יקריבו לה' ביום המשח אותו עשירית האיפה", ואמרינן (מנחות דף נא:): לרבות עשירית האיפה של כהן הדיוט לחינוך. ולאו אקראי דלעיל קאי, אלא מלות כהנים בעלמא הוא דקאמר יחזקאל. אלמא: שלא היה יכול להקריב קרבנו עשירית האיפה עד שנטהר מטומאת מת, והוא הדין מצרעתו: אמר רבא וכו'. אידי דאיירי במנודה מפרש להו: ומזמנינן ליה לדינא. לבעל דין: זימנא בתר זימנא. דאי לא אתי ההוא זימנא – קבעינן ליה זימנא אחריתי: קראו שם. שמתא. כלומר: שמתא לפרעה שהעביר המועד. כלומר שהעביר אותו מועד ששמו אחר מועד ראשון: דאי מתפקר בשליחא דרבנן. כלומר, שמירף שליח ב"ד, ושליח אמר: "מירפני": העיני האנשים ההם תנקר. אי לאו דשליח דא"ל למשה – משה לא הוה ידע: הכי סברא דגברא פלניא. דעת פלוני, שבא לנדות את פלוני, דצריך לנדותו משמו של אותו חכם: אמר מלאך ה'. ברק אמר לשמתו, שהוא שלוחו של מקום: ומחרימין. בארור: ופרטינן חטאיה. דאמרי לאנשי עירו: משום הכי והכי משמתינן ליה: כוכבא הוה. מנליה דקיסרא: דמפקרינן לנכסיה. דמאן דלא ציית להו לרבנן: יחרם (ג) הוא וכל רכושו. דהפקר ב"ד הפקר – מהכא נפקא לן בכל דוכתי*: ואריב עמם ואקללם. לאותם שהושיבו נשים גויות: דכפתינן. ידיו ורגליו: ואסרינן ליה. שקושרין אותו על העמוד להלקותו: הרדפה. קא מפרש רב יהודה בריה דרב שמואל לרודפו מיד, דכיון דלא ציית דינא – מנדין אותו: ושונין. ומנדין אותו פעם אחרת: לממונא. שחייב ממון לחבירו, ולא רצה לשלם ע"פ ב"ד: לאפקירותא. מבזה תלמידי חכמים: לא חל עליה שמתא ל' יום. ואין שמתא פחותה מל' יום: קא בעו רבנן למיעל. שצריכין לו: טוט אסר טוט שרי. כלומר: מצי למישרי ליה, אע"ג דלא חל עליה ל' יום. דאותו שופר שנדוהו יכול להתיר לו, ומישרי ליה בתוך ל' יום: לא אתו אחריני ושרו ליה. מדמהדר אינהו נפשייהו למישרי: שנידה לכבודו. ולא לשם שמים, אלא שהתריס נגדו ודאי, כיון דתני אין מנודה לרב – ודאי לא נידה אלא בשביל כבודו, דאי במילי דאיסורא – הוי כמי שמנודה לרב "דאין חכמה ואין עצה וגו'" (משלי כא). וקתני: אין מנודה לרב, אבל לכולי עלמא – מנודה: כל אחד מיפר חלקו. מדקתני: חלקו אינו מופר: לא אתו אחריני ושרו. מדקתני חלקו אינו מופר לעולם, אפי' שרו ליה אחריני: נזיפה. גערה, כדלקמן: נדוי שלנו. בני בבל: כנזיפה שלהן. ארץ ישראל: צריך רבי. רבי, אבוה דר"ש הוה: מה רבי אומר בדבר זה. אין רבי בעולם היודע דבר זה: א"ל לאבוה. לפי תומו, ולאו משום לישנא בישא: לאיתחזויי ליה. לבקר את רבי, שהיה חולה, שקבל עליו יסורין: אמר ליה בר קפרא איני מכירך. רמז לו שאינו רוצה לראותו: חמוקי ירכיך. כמו "חמק עבר" (שיר ה): אף

תורה אור

זו עשירית האיפה שלו, דברי רבי יהודה. ר"ש אומר: *"בבאו יקריב" (יחזקאל מד) – בזמן שראוי לביאה ראוי להקרבה, בזמן שאינו ראוי לביאה – אינו ראוי להקרבה. אמר רבא: (א) מנלן דמשדרין שליחא דבי דינא, ומזמנינן ליה לדינא – דכתיב: "וישלח משה לקרא לדתן ולאבירם בני אליאב" (במדבר טז). ומנלן דמזמנינן לדינא – דכתיב: "ויאמר משה אל קרח אתה וכל עדתך" (שם). לקמי גברא רבה – דכתיב: "לפני ה'", את ופלניא – דכתיב: "אתה והם ואהרן", דקבעינן זימנא – דכתיב: "מחר". זימנא בתר זימנא – דכתיב: "קראו שם פרעה מלך מצרים שאון העביר המועד" (ירמיה מו). ומנלן דאי מתפקר בשליחא דבי דינא, ואתי ואמר, לא מיתחזי כלישנא בישא – דכתיב: "העיני האנשים ההם תנקר" (במדבר טז). ומנלן דמשמתינן – דכתיב: "אורו מרוז" (שופטים ה), דהכי סברא דגברא *רבה, דכתיב: "אמר מלאך ה'". ומנלן דמחרמינן – דכתיב: "אורו ארור", דאכיל ושתי בהדיה וקאי בארבע אמות דידיה – דכתיב: "יושביה". ומנלן דפרטינן חטאיה בציבורא – דכתיב: "כי לא באו לעזרת ה'" (שם). ואמר עולא: *בד' מאה שיפורי שמתיה ברק למרוז. איכא דאמרי: גברא רבה הוה, ואיכא דאמרי: כוכבא הוה, שנאמר: "מן שמים נלחמו הכוכבים" (שם). ומנלן דמפקרינן נכסיה – דכתיב: "וכל אשר לא יבא לשלשת הימים בעצת השרים והזקנים יחרם כל רכושו והוא יבדל מקהל הגולה" (עזרא י). ומנלן דנצינן ולייטינן ומחינן ותלשינן שיער ומשבעינן – דכתיב: "ואריב עמם ואקללם ואכה מהם אנשים ואמרטם ואשביעם" (נחמיה יג). ומנלן דכפתינן ואסרינן ועבדינן הרדפה – דכתיב: "הן למות הן לשרושי הן לענש נכסין ולאסורין" (עזרא ז). מאי לשרושי? אמר אדא מרי אמר נחמיה בר ברוך אמר רב חייא בר אבין אמר רב יהודה: הרדפה. מאי הרדפה? אמר רב יהודה בריה דרב שמואל בר שילת משמיה דרב: מנדין לאלתר, ושונין לאחר ל' ומחרימין לאחר ששים. א"ל רב הונא בר חיננא, הכי אמר רב חסדא: מתרין ביה שני וחמישי ושני. ה"מ – לממונא. אבל לאפקירותא – לאלתר. ההוא טבחא דאיתפקר ברב טובי בר מתנה, אימנו עליה אביי ורבא ושמתוהו. לסוף אזל פייסיה לבעל דיניה. אמר אביי: היכי ליעביד? לישרי ליה – לא חל שמתא עליה תלתין יומין, לא לישרי ליה – קא בעו רבנן [א]למיעל! א"ל לרב אידי בר אבין: מידי שמיע לך בהא? א"ל: הכי אמר רב תחליפא בר אבימי אמר שמואל: *טוט אסר, וטוט שרי. אמר ליה: ה"מ – לממונא, אבל לאפקירותא – עד דחיילא שמתא עליה תלתין יומין. אלמא קסבר אביי: הני בי תלתא דשמיתו – לא אתו תלתא אחריני ושרו ליה. דאיבעיא להו: הני בי תלתא דשמיתו, מהו למיתי תלתא אחריני ושרו ליה? ת"ש: *מנודה לרב – מנודה לתלמיד, מנודה *לתלמיד – אינו מנודה לרב. מנודה לעירו – מנודה לעיר אחרת, מנודה לעיר אחרת – אינו מנודה לעירו. מנודה לנשיא – מנודה לכל ישראל, מנודה לכל ישראל – אינו מנודה לנשיא. רשב"ג אומר: אחד מן התלמידים שנידה ומת – חלקו אינו מופר. ש"מ תלת: שמע מינה: תלמיד שנידה לכבודו נידויו נידוי, וש"מ: כל אחד ואחד מיפר חלקו, וש"מ: הני בי תלתא דשמיתו – לא אתו תלתא אחריני ושרו ליה. אמר אמימר: הלכתא, הני בי תלתא דשמיתו – אתו בי תלתא אחריני ושרו ליה. א"ל רב אשי לאמימר: והא תניא רשב"ג אומר: אחד מן התלמידים שנידה ומת – חלקו אינו מופר. מאי לאו – אינו מופר כלל? לא, עד דאתו בי תלתא אחריני ושרו ליה. ת"ר: אין נידוי פחות מל' יום, ואין נזיפה פחות מז' ימים. ואף על פי שאין ראיה לדבר – זכר לדבר: שנאמר: "ואביה ירק ירק בפניה הלא תכלם שבעת ימים" (במדבר יב). אמר רב חסדא: נידוי שלנו כנזיפה שלהן. ונזיפה דידהו שבעה, ותו לא? והא ר"ש בר רבי ובר קפרא הוו יתבי וקא גרסי, קשיא להו שמעתא. א"ל ר"ש לבר קפרא: דבר זה צריך רבי. א"ל בר קפרא לר"ש: ומה רבי אומר בדבר זה? אזל א"ל לאבוה. איקפד. אתא בר קפרא לאיתחזויי ליה, אמר ליה: בר קפרא, איני מכירך מעולם. ידע דנקט מילתא בדעתיה, נהג נזיפותא בנפשיה תלתין יומין. שוב, פעם אחד גזר רבי שלא ישנו לתלמידים בשוק. מאי דרש – *"חמוקי ירכיך *)כמו חלאים" (שיר ז), מה ירך בסתר – אף

*) [כמו חלאים אין חלאים אלא רבנן כדגרסינן בנדרים מט. וכן שמתעסקין בתורה שהיא מעשה ידי אומן. ערוך בערך חמק]

מתרין בו שני וחמישי ושני. פירש בקונטרס: שני מתרין בו תחילה, ומנדין אותו, וכן בחמישי, ובשני אחר מחרימין. וא"ל שלשים יום. ויש מפרשים קודם שינדוהו כלל יתרו בו, וכן משמע בפרק "הגוזל בתרא" (ב"ק דף קיג.): וטרקיה

רבינו חננאל

ר"ש אומר כתיב כאן בבאו יקריב עצמו בזמן שראוי לבא בקדש יקריב בזמן שאינו ראוי לביאה אינו ראוי להקרבה. אמר רבא מנ"ל דמשדרינן שליחא מבי דינא ומזמנינן ליה לדינא לקמיה גברא רבה שנאמר ויאמר משה אל קרח אתה וכל עדתך היו לפני ה' ופלניא בעל דינך שנא' אתה והם ואהרן ומנ"ל דקבעינן להו זימנא שנאמר מחר. ומנ"ל דקבעינן זימנא בתר זימנא שנאמר קראו שם פרעה מלך מצרים שאון העביר המועד. העביר המועד שקבעו לו מועד ולא נענש עד אחר כן. מנ"ל דאי מתפקר בשליחא דבי דינא ואתי שליחא ומחוי ליתיה לישנא בישא שנאמר העיני האנשים ההם תנקר לא נעלה ומנ"ל דמשמתינן בהרמנא דגברא רבה שנאמר אורו מרוז אמר וגו' ומנ"ל דמחרמינן ליה נמי דכתיב אורו ארור ומנ"ל דמחרמינן על כל מאן דאכיל ושתי בהדיה וקאי בד' אמות דיליה שנאמר אורו ארור יושביה. ומנ"ל דפרטינן חטאיה שנאמר כי לא באו לעזרת ה' פי' לעזרת עם ה'. איכא דאמרי מרוז אדם גדול הוה ואיכא דאמרי כוכבא הוה והאי דכתיב יושביה כענין עייש על בניה תנחם. ומנ"ל דמאן דמתפקר אבי דינא מפקרינן נכסיה שנאמר וכל אשר לא יבא לשלשת הימים בעצת השרים והזקנים יחרם כל רכושו והוא יבדל מקהל הגולה. ומנ"ל דנצינן ולטינן ומחינן ומתלשינן שיער ומשבעינן דכתיב ואריב עמם ואקללם ואכה מהם אנשים ואמרטם ואשביעם וגו' ומנ"ל דכפתינן ואסרינן ועבדינן הרדפה שנאמר הן למות הן לשרושי הן לענוש נכסין ולאסורין. מאי לשרושי הרדפה. אמר רב יהודה משמיה דרב מנדין לאלתר דמתפקר ושונין לאחר שלשים ומחרימין לאחר ששים. אמרו משמיה דרב חסדא מתרינן ביה שני וחמישי ושני ואח"כ מנדין אותו. והני מילי לממונא אבל לאפקירותא מנדין לאלתר בלא התראה. ההוא טבחא דאתפקר ברב טובי אימנו אביי ורבא ושמתי' אזל פייסיה לרב טובי אמר אביי היכי נעביד נישרי ליה לא חל שמתא עליה שלשים יום נשבקיה בשמתיה קא בעו רבנן לאפטורי. א"ל רב אידי בר אבין הכי אמר שמואל טוט אסר וטוט שרי. כלומר תקיעת השופר היא השמתא הקול שמכריז בתקיעת שופר הוא האוסר הוא המתיר כלומר אינו צריך ימים לחול עליה שמתא א"ל ה"מ לממונא אבל לאפקירותא עד דחייל עליה שמתא שלשים יום. דייקינן מדקאמר אביי בעי רבנן לאפטורי קסבר תלתא דשמיתו לא אתו תלתא אחרינא ושרו מאי ת"ש מנודה לרב מנודה לתלמיד מנודה לתלמיד אינו מנודה לרב מנודה לעירו מנודה לעיר אחרת. מנודה לעיר אחרת אינו מנודה לעירו. מנודה לנשיא מנודה לכל ישראל מנודה לכל ישראל אינו מנודה לנשיא. רשב"ג אומר אחד מן התלמידים שנידה ומת חלקו אינו מופר ש"מ תלת ש"מ מדקתני אחד מן התלמידים שנידה ומת וקתני נמי מנודה לתלמיד אינו מנודה לרב דייקינן מינה לרב אינו מנודה הא לכ"ע מנודה ש"מ תלמיד שנידה לכבודו נידויו נידוי ומדקתני ומת חלקו אינו מופר ש"מ דכל אחד מיפר חלקו. ש"מ נמי דלא אתו אחריני ושרו חלקו א' אמימר הלכתא *) דמשמתי מופר עד דאתו תלתא אחריני ושרו ליה. ת"ר אין נדוי פחות משלשים יום ואין נזיפה פחות משבעה ואע"פ שאין ראיה לדבר זכר לדבר שנאמר ויאמר ה' אל משה ואביה ירק ירק בפניה הלא תכלם שבעת ימים. אמר רב חסדא נידוי שלנו כנזיפה שלהן ונזיפה דידהו שבעה איני והא בר קפרא בעידנא דאמר ליה ר' בר קפרא איני מכירך מעולם וכן כדאמר ליה ר' לר' חייא ראה מה קורא לך בחוץ ידעו דנקיט מילתא עלייהו נהגו נזיפתא בנפשייהו תלתין יומין. ואסיקנא נזיפותא דנשיא תלתין יומין. סוגיא דשמעתא כך גזר ר'

*) נ"ל בי תלתא דשמיתו אתו בי תלתא אחרינא ושרו ליה א"ל רב אשי לאמימר והא תניא וכו' חלקו אינו מופר לא אינו מופר עד דאתו וכו'.

עין משפט נר מצוה

נ א ב ג מיי' פכ"ה מהלכות סנהדרין הל' ח טוש"ע ח"מ סימן יא סעיף א:

נא ד מיי' שם הלכה ו סמג לאוין רח טוש"ע שם וסימן ח סעיף ה בהג"ה:

נב ה מיי' שם הלכה ח ופ"ו מהלכות ת"ת הלכה יד ופכ"ד מהלכות סנהדרין הלכה ז טוש"ע ח"מ סימן ב וטוש"ע י"ד סימן שלד סעיף מג:

נג ו מיי' פ"ז מהלכות ת"ת הלכה יג טוש"ע י"ד סי' שלד סעיף ט:

נד ז מיי' פכ"ד מהל' סנהדרין הלכה ז:

נה ח מיי' שם הלכה ו טוש"ע ח"מ סימן ב בהג"ה:

נו ט י מיי' שם הלכה ח והלכה ט:

ס"א פלניא שופטים ה

נז כ מיי' פ"ז מהלכות ת"ת הלכה ד טוש"ע י"ד סימן שלד סעיף א:

[שבועות לו.]

נח ל מיי' פכ"ה מהל' סנהדרין הלכה ח טוש"ע י"ד סימן שלד סעיף א בהג"ה וטוש"ע ח"מ סימן ק סעיף ג:

נט מ מיי' פ"ז מהלכות ת"ת הל' יג טוש"ע י"ד סימן שלד סעיף א:

ס נ מיי' שם הל' יב טוש"ע י"ד סי' שלד סעי' יג:

סא ס מיי' פ"ו שם הל' יג טוש"ע שם סעיף טו:

סב ע מיי' שם טוש"ע שם סעיף כ:

סג פ מיי' שם טוש"ע שם סעיף כח:

סד צ מיי' שם טוש"ע שם סעיף מה:

סה ק טוש"ע שם סעיף כו:

סו ר מיי' פ"ז שם הל' ט טוש"ע שם סעיף כה:

סז ש ת טוש"ע שם סעיף א:

מסורת הש"ס

[נ"ל וביום בואו]

[יבמות פט:]

[עי' תוספות מנחות לד: ד"ה טטו]

[לקמן יז.]

[עי' תוספות סנהדרין ח. ד"ה מפיקנא]

[סוכה מט: ע"ש]

הגהות הב"ח

(א) גמ' אמר רבא מנלן דקבעינן זוכתא ומשדרינן שליחא דבי דינא דכתיב וישלח כו' כצ"ל ותיבות ומזמנין ליה לדינא נמחק: (ג) רש"י ד"ה יחרם כל רכושו כו' ותיבת הוא נמחק:

הגהות הגר"א

[א] גמ' למיעל. נ"ב נ"א למיזל [ועיין ר"ן ופרש"י שברי"ף]:

סח א טוש"ע י"ד סימן שלב סעיף ח:

*אַף דִּבְרֵי תוֹרָה בְּסֵתֶר. יָצָא רַבִּי חִיָּיא וְשָׁנָה לִשְׁנֵי בְּנֵי אָחִיו בַּשּׁוּק, *לְרַב וּלְרַבָּה בַּר בַּר חָנָה. שָׁמַע ר' — אִיקְפַּד. אֲתָא ר' חִיָּיא לְאִיתְחֲזוּיֵי לֵיהּ, א"ל: *עִיָּיא, מִי קוֹרֵא לְךָ בַּחוּץ? יָדַע דִּנְקַט מִילְּתָא בְּדַעְתֵּיהּ, נְהַג נְזִיפוּתָא בְּנַפְשֵׁיהּ תְּלָתִין יוֹמִין. בְּיוֹם תְּלָתִין שְׁלַח לֵיהּ: תָּא, הֲדַר שְׁלַח לֵיהּ דְּלָא לֵיתֵי. מֵעִיקָּרָא מַאי סָבַר וּלְבַסּוֹף מַאי סָבַר? מֵעִיקָּרָא סָבַר: *מִקְצָת הַיּוֹם כְּכוּלּוֹ, וּלְבַסּוֹף סָבַר: לָא אָמְרִינַן מִקְצָת הַיּוֹם כְּכוּלּוֹ. לְסוֹף אֲתָא, א"ל: אַמַּאי אָתֵית? א"ל: דִּשְׁלַח לִי מָר דְּלֵיתֵי. וְהָא שְׁלַחִי לָךְ דְּלָא תֵּיתֵי? א"ל: זֶה רָאִיתִי, וְזֶה — לֹא רָאִיתִי. קְרֵי עֲלֵיהּ: °"בִּרְצוֹת ה' דַּרְכֵי אִישׁ גַּם אוֹיְבָיו יַשְׁלִים אִתּוֹ". מ"ט עֲבַד מָר הָכִי? א"ל: דִּכְתִיב: °"חָכְמוֹת בַּחוּץ תָּרֹנָּה". א"ל: *אִם קָרִיתָ — לֹא שָׁנִיתָ, וְאִם שָׁנִיתָ — לֹא שִׁילַּשְׁתָּ, וְאִם שִׁילַּשְׁתָּ, לֹא פֵּירְשׁוּ לְךָ. "חָכְמוֹת בַּחוּץ תָּרֹנָּה" — כִּדְרָבָא. דְּאָמַר רָבָא: כָּל הָעוֹסֵק בַּתּוֹרָה מִבִּפְנִים — תּוֹרָתוֹ מַכְרֶזֶת עָלָיו מִבַּחוּץ. וְהָא כְּתִיב: °"לֹא מֵרֹאשׁ בַּסֵּתֶר דִּבַּרְתִּי"! הַהוּא בְּיוֹמֵי דְּכַלָּה. וְר' חִיָּיא, הַאי "חַמּוּקֵי יְרֵכַיִךְ" מַאי עָבֵיד לָהּ? מוֹקֵי לָהּ בִּצְדָקָה וּבִגְמִילוּת חֲסָדִים. אַלְמָא, נְזִיפָה דִּידְהוּ תְּלָתִין יוֹמִין! נְזִיפַת נָשִׂיא שָׁאנֵי. [א]וּנְזִיפָה דִּידַן כַּמָּה הָוֵי? חַד יוֹמָא. כִּי הָא דִּשְׁמוּאֵל וּמָר עוּקְבָא, כִּי הָווּ יָתְבִי גָּרְסִי שְׁמַעְתָּא — הֲוָה יָתֵיב מָר עוּקְבָא קַמֵּיהּ דִּשְׁמוּאֵל בְּרָחוֹק ד' אַמּוֹת, וְכִי הָווּ יָתְבִי בְּדִינָא — הֲוָה יָתֵיב שְׁמוּאֵל קַמֵּיהּ דְּמָר עוּקְבָא בְּרָחוֹק ד' אַמּוֹת. וְהָווּ חָיְיקִי לֵיהּ דּוּכְתָּא לְמָר עוּקְבָא *בְּצִיפְתָּא וְיָתֵיב עִילָּוֵיהּ, כִּי הֵיכִי דְּלִישְׁתַּמְעַן מִילֵּיהּ. כָּל יוֹמָא הֲוָה מְלַוֵּי לֵיהּ מָר עוּקְבָא לִשְׁמוּאֵל עַד אוּשְׁפִּיזֵיהּ, יוֹמָא חַד אִיטְרִיד בְּדִינֵיהּ. הֲוָה אָזֵיל שְׁמוּאֵל בַּתְרֵיהּ, כִּי מְטָא לְבֵיתֵיהּ א"ל: לָא נְגַה לָךְ? לִישְׁרֵי לִי מָר בְּתִיגְרֵיהּ! יָדַע דִּנְקַט מִילְּתָא בְּדַעְתֵּיהּ, נְהַג נְזִיפוּתָא בְּנַפְשֵׁיהּ חַד יוֹמָא. הַהִיא אִיתְּתָא דַּהֲוָות יָתְבָה בִּשְׁבִילָא, הֲוָות פַּשְׁטָה כַּרְעָהּ וְקָא מְנִיפָה *חוּשְׁלָאֵי, וַהֲוָה חָלֵיף וְאָזֵיל צוּרְבָּא מֵרַבָּנַן, וְלָא אִיכַּנְעָה מִקַּמֵּיהּ. אֲמַר: כַּמָּה חֲצִיפָא הַהִיא אִיתְּתָא! אֲתַאי לְקַמֵּיהּ דְּר"נ, אֲמַר לָהּ: מִי שְׁמַעְתְּ שַׁמְתָּא מִפּוּמֵיהּ? אֲמַרָה לֵיהּ: לָא. אֲמַר לָהּ: זִילִי, נְהוֹגִי נְזִיפוּתָא חַד יוֹמָא בְּנַפְשִׁיךְ. זוּטְרָא בַּר טוֹבִיָּה הֲוָה קָפָסֵיק סִידְרָא קַמֵּיהּ דְּרַב יְהוּדָה, כִּי מְטָא לְהַאי פְּסוּקָא: °"וְאֵלֶּה דִּבְרֵי דָוִד הָאַחֲרֹנִים: א"ל: אַחֲרוֹנִים — מִכְּלָל דְּאִיכָּא רִאשׁוֹנִים, רִאשׁוֹנִים מַאי נִינְהוּ? שָׁתֵיק וְלָא אֲמַר לֵיהּ וְלָא מִידֵּי. הֲדַר א"ל: אַחֲרוֹנִים מִכְּלָל דְּאִיכָּא רִאשׁוֹנִים, רִאשׁוֹנִים מַאי הִיא? א"ל: מַאי דַּעְתָּךְ, דְּלָא יָדַע פֵּירוּשָׁא דְּהַאי קְרָא — לָאו גַּבְרָא רַבָּה הוּא? יָדַע דִּנְקַט מִילְּתָא בְּדַעְתֵּיהּ, נְהַג נְזִיפוּתָא בְּנַפְשֵׁיהּ חַד יוֹמָא. וּדְאָתַן עֲלָהּ, מִיהָא אַחֲרוֹנִים — מִכְּלָל דְּאִיכָּא רִאשׁוֹנִים, רִאשׁוֹנִים מַאי הִיא? °"וַיְדַבֵּר דָּוִד לַה' אֶת דִּבְרֵי הַשִּׁירָה הַזֹּאת בְּיוֹם הִצִּיל ה' אוֹתוֹ מִכַּף כָּל אֹיְבָיו וּמִכַּף שָׁאוּל". אָמַר לוֹ הקב"ה לְדָוִד: [י]דָּוִד, שִׁירָה אַתָּה אוֹמֵר עַל מַפַּלְתּוֹ שֶׁל שָׁאוּל? *אִלְמָלֵי אַתָּה שָׁאוּל וְהוּא דָּוִד אִיבַּדְתִּי כַּמָּה דָּוִד מִפָּנָיו. הַיְינוּ דִּכְתִיב: °"שִׁגָּיוֹן לְדָוִד אֲשֶׁר שָׁר לַה' עַל דִּבְרֵי כוּשׁ בֶּן יְמִינִי". וְכִי כּוּשׁ שְׁמוֹ? וַהֲלֹא שָׁאוּל שְׁמוֹ! אֶלָּא: מַה כּוּשִׁי מְשׁוּנֶּה בְּעוֹרוֹ — אַף שָׁאוּל מְשׁוּנֶּה בְּמַעֲשָׂיו. כַּיּוֹצֵא בַּדָּבָר אַתָּה אוֹמֵר: °"עַל אוֹדוֹת הָאִשָּׁה הַכֻּשִׁית אֲשֶׁר לָקָח", וְכִי כּוּשִׁית שְׁמָהּ? וַהֲלֹא צִיפּוֹרָה שְׁמָהּ! אֶלָּא: מַה כּוּשִׁית מְשׁוּנָּה בְּעוֹרָהּ — אַף צִיפּוֹרָה מְשׁוּנָּה בְּמַעֲשֶׂיהָ. כַּיּוֹצֵא בַּדָּבָר אַתָּה אוֹמֵר: °"וַיִּשְׁמַע עֶבֶד מֶלֶךְ הַכּוּשִׁי", וְכִי כּוּשִׁי שְׁמוֹ? וַהֲלֹא צִדְקִיָּה שְׁמוֹ! אֶלָּא: מַה כּוּשִׁי מְשׁוּנֶּה בְּעוֹרוֹ — אַף צִדְקִיָּה מְשׁוּנֶּה בְּמַעֲשָׂיו. כַּיּוֹצֵא בַּדָּבָר אַתָּה אוֹמֵר: °"הֲלוֹא כִבְנֵי כֻשִׁיִּים אַתֶּם לִי (*בֵּית) יִשְׂרָאֵל", וְכִי כּוּשִׁיִּים שְׁמָן? וַהֲלֹא יִשְׂרָאֵל שְׁמָן! אֶלָּא: מַה כּוּשִׁי מְשׁוּנֶּה בְּעוֹרוֹ — אַף יִשְׂרָאֵל מְשׁוּנִּין בְּמַעֲשֵׂיהֶן מִכָּל הָאוּמּוֹת. *א"ר שְׁמוּאֵל בַּר נַחְמָנִי א"ר יוֹנָתָן: מַאי דִּכְתִיב: °"נְאֻם דָּוִד בֶּן יִשַׁי וּנְאֻם הַגֶּבֶר הֻקַם עָל" — נְאֻם דָּוִד בֶּן יִשַׁי, שֶׁהֵקִים עוּלָּהּ שֶׁל תְּשׁוּבָה. °"אָמַר אֱלֹהֵי יִשְׂרָאֵל לִי דִבֶּר צוּר יִשְׂרָאֵל מוֹשֵׁל בָּאָדָם צַדִּיק מוֹשֵׁל יִרְאַת אֱלֹהִים", מַאי קָאָמַר? א"ר אַבָּהוּ, ה"ק, אָמַר אֱלֹהֵי יִשְׂרָאֵל: לִי דִּבֶּר צוּר יִשְׂרָאֵל, אֲנִי מוֹשֵׁל בָּאָדָם, מִי מוֹשֵׁל בִּי — צַדִּיק. שֶׁאֲנִי *גּוֹזֵר גְּזֵרָה וּמְבַטְּלָהּ. °"אֵלֶּה שְׁמוֹת הַגִּבֹּרִים אֲשֶׁר לְדָוִד יֹשֵׁב בַּשֶּׁבֶת" וגו' מַאי קָאָמַר? א"ר אַבָּהוּ, ה"ק, וְאֵלֶּה שְׁמוֹת גְּבוּרוֹתָיו שֶׁל דָּוִד: "יוֹשֵׁב בַּשֶּׁבֶת" — בְּשָׁעָה שֶׁהָיָה יוֹשֵׁב בִּישִׁיבָה לֹא הָיָה יוֹשֵׁב עַל גַּבֵּי כָּרִים וּכְסָתוֹת, אֶלָּא עַל גַּבֵּי קַרְקַע. דְּכָל כַּמָּה דַּהֲוָה רַבֵּיהּ עִירָא הַיָּאִירִי קַיָּים — הֲוָה מַתְנֵי לְהוּ לְרַבָּנַן עַל גַּבֵּי כָּרִים וּכְסָתוֹת, כִּי נָח נַפְשֵׁיהּ — הֲוָה מַתְנֵי דָּוִד לְרַבָּנַן, וַהֲוָה יָתֵיב עַל גַּבֵּי קַרְקַע. אֲמַרוּ לֵיהּ: לֵיתֵיב מָר אַכָּרִים וּכְסָתוֹת! לָא קַבֵּיל עֲלֵיהּ. "תַּחְכְּמֹנִי" — אָמַר רַב: אָמַר לוֹ הקב"ה, הוֹאִיל וְהִשְׁפַּלְתָּ עַצְמְךָ — תְּהֵא כָּמוֹנִי, שֶׁאֲנִי גּוֹזֵר גְּזֵרָה — וְאַתָּה מְבַטְּלָהּ. "רֹאשׁ הַשָּׁלִשִׁים" — תְּהֵא רֹאשׁ לִשְׁלֹשֶׁת אָבוֹת. °"הוּא עֲדִינוֹ הָעֶצְנִי" — כְּשֶׁהָיָה יוֹשֵׁב וְעוֹסֵק בַּתּוֹרָה — הָיָה מְעַדֵּן עַצְמוֹ כְּתוֹלַעַת, וּבְשָׁעָה שֶׁיּוֹצֵא לַמִּלְחָמָה — הָיָה מַקְשֶׁה עַצְמוֹ כְּעֵץ. "עַל שְׁמֹנֶה מֵאוֹת חָלָל בְּפַעַם אֶחָת" — שֶׁהָיָה זוֹרֵק חֵץ וּמַפִּיל שְׁמוֹנֶה מֵאוֹת חָלָל בְּפַעַם אַחַת, וְהָיָה מִתְאַנֵּחַ עַל מָאתַיִם. דִּכְתִיב: °"אֵיכָה יִרְדֹּף אֶחָד אֶלֶף". יָצְתָה בַּת קוֹל וְאָמְרָה: °"רַק בִּדְבַר אוּרִיָּה הַחִתִּי". אָמַר רַבִּי תַּנְחוּם בְּרֵיהּ דְּרַבִּי חִיָּיא אִישׁ כְּפַר עַכּוֹ אָמַר רַבִּי יַעֲקֹב בַּר אַחָא אָמַר ר' שִׂמְלַאי, וְאָמְרִי לָהּ אָמַר ר' תַּנְחוּם אָמַר רַב הוּנָא, וְאָמְרִי לָהּ אָמַר רַב הוּנָא לְחוּדֵיהּ:

תַּלְמִיד

רש"י

אַף דִּבְרֵי תוֹרָה בַּסֵּתֶר. דִּכְתִיב בְּסֵיפֵיהּ דִּקְרָא: "מַעֲשֵׂה יְדֵי אוּמָּן" — הַתּוֹרָה מַעֲשֵׂה אוּמָנוּתוֹ שֶׁל הַקָּדוֹשׁ בָּרוּךְ הוּא: (א) רַב בַּר אֲחוּהּ דְּרַבִּי חִיָּיא דַּהֲוָה בַּר אַחְתֵּיהּ, וְרַבָּה בַּר בַּר חָנָה בַּר אֲחוּהּ דְּרַבִּי חִיָּיא [דְּלָאו] בַּר אַחְתֵּיהּ, כִּדְאָמְרִינַן בְּסַנְהֶדְרִין*: עִיָּיא. כָּךְ כִּינָּה שְׁמוֹ שֶׁל ר' חִיָּיא, לְשׁוֹן גְּנַאי: רְאֵה מִי קוֹרֵא לְךָ. כְּלוֹמַר: לֹא מִכָּאן: תָּא. בּוֹא אֵלַי וְהָדַר שָׁלַח לֵיהּ: לָא תֵּיתֵי: וְזֶה. שָׁלִיחַ שֵׁנִי, לֹא רָאִיתִי: בִּרְצוֹת ה' דַּרְכֵי אִישׁ גַּם אוֹיְבָיו יַשְׁלִים אִתּוֹ. כִּי הוּא עַל כָּרְחוֹ בָּא: מַאי טַעְמָא עֲבַדְתְּ הָכִי. דְּשָׁנִיתָ בַּשּׁוּק: בְּיוֹמָא דְּכַלָּה. דְּרָשָׁה שֶׁהַכֹּל מְלוּיִין שָׁם: מוֹקִים לֵיהּ בִּצְדָקָה. דְּמִיבָּעֵי לְמֵיעֲבַד בַּסֵּתֶר: מָר עוּקְבָא. כְּתַלְמִיד לִשְׁמוּאֵל, דִּשְׁמוּאֵל גָּדוֹל בַּתּוֹרָה יוֹתֵר מִמָּר עוּקְבָא: כִּי יָתְבַן בְּדִינָא כו'. מִשּׁוּם דְּמָר עוּקְבָא הָיָה נָשִׂיא: חָיְיקִי לֵיהּ דּוּכְתֵּיהּ. מַנְמִיכִין לוֹ מָקוֹם כְּשֶׁיּוֹשֵׁב בַּדִּין: כִּי הֵיכִי דְּמִשְׁתַּמַּע לֵיהּ מִילֵּיהּ. דִּשְׁמוּאֵל רַבֵּיהּ בַּתּוֹרָה: אִיטְרִיד. מָר עוּקְבָא בְּדִינָא, שֶׁהָיָה מְחַשֵּׁב בַּדִּין, וְלָא אִידְּכַר לֵיהּ לְמֵיזַל בָּתַר שְׁמוּאֵל: לֹא נְגַה לָךְ. כְּלוֹמַר: לָא סַגִּי לָךְ דְּאָזֵילְנָא בַּתְרָךְ? לִישְׁרֵי לִי מָר בְּתִיגְרֵיהּ. הַב לִי רְשׁוּתָא לְמִיהְדַּר: יָדַע. מָר עוּקְבָא: דִּנְקַט. שְׁמוּאֵל בְּדַעְתֵּיהּ, מִשּׁוּם דְּאָזֵיל בַּתְרֵיהּ: מִי שָׁמְעַתְּ שַׁמְתָּא מִפּוּמֵיהּ. אִי שָׁמְעִית לָךְ: פָּסֵיק סִידְרָא. לִימֵּד פָּרָשִׁיּוֹת: מִכְּלָל דְּאִיכָּא רִאשׁוֹנִים. וַהֲלֹא לֹא מָצִינוּ שֶׁאָמַר דָּוִד 'דִּבְרֵי' אֶלָּא בְּמִקְרָא זֶה, דְּ'דִבְרֵי' לְשׁוֹן נְבוּאָה: אַתָּה שָׁאוּל. שֶׁנּוֹלַדְתָּ בְּמַזָּלוֹ: וְהוּא דָּוִד. שֶׁנּוֹלַד בְּמַזָּל שֶׁלְּךָ: אִבַּדְתִּי כַּמָּה דָּוִד. שֶׁהוּא צַדִּיק מִמְּךָ: שִׁגָּיוֹן. שְׁגָגָה הָיְתָה לוֹ: מְשׁוּנֶּה בְּמַעֲשָׂיו. צַדִּיק גָּמוּר: שֶׁהֵקִים עוּלָּהּ שֶׁל תְּשׁוּבָה. שֶׁהוּא שָׁב תְּחִלָּה, וְנָתַן דֶּרֶךְ לַשָּׁבִים. כִּדְאָמְרִינַן בְּפ"ק דַּע"ז (דף ד:): לֹא דָּוִד רָאוּי לְאוֹתוֹ מַעֲשֶׂה, אֶלָּא שֶׁאִם חָטָא יָחִיד — אוֹמְרִים לוֹ: כֵּלֵךְ אֵצֶל דָּוִד, שֶׁמָּחַל לוֹ הקב"ה אוֹתוֹ עָוֹן, אַף אַתָּה — חֲזוֹר בִּתְשׁוּבָה: צוּר יִשְׂרָאֵל. מוֹשֵׁל בָּאָדָם אֲנִי, מִי מוֹשֵׁל בִּי? צַדִּיק מוֹשֵׁל בִּי, וּמְבַטְּלָהּ: עִירָא הַיָּאִירִי. הֲוָה מַתְנֵי לְדָוִד *אַגַּב כָּרֵי וּכְסָתוֹת, וְדָוִד הֲוָה מַתְנֵי לְרַבָּנַן עַל גַּבֵּי קַרְקַע: רֹאשׁ לְג' אָבוֹת. שֶׁהוּא הוֹלֵךְ לִפְנֵיהֶם לָעוֹה"ב: מְעַדֵּן עַצְמוֹ. כּוֹפֵף עַצְמוֹ יָדָיו וְרַגְלָיו כְּיַחַד וְיוֹשֵׁב לָאָרֶץ: בִּדְבַר אוּרִיָּה הַחִתִּי. נָטְלוּ לוֹ מָאתַיִם:

תַּלְמִיד

תורה אור

רבינו חננאל

ר' שלא ישנו לתלמידים בשוק שנאמר חמוקי ירכיך כמו חלאים ואין חלאים אלא רבנן כדגרסינן בנדרים (מט.) מאן חולים רבנן והן שמתעסקים בתורה שהיא מעשה ידי אמן ואמר רבי מה ירך זה בסתר אף דברי תורה בסתר והני מילי בשאר ימות השנה. אבל ביומי דכלה לא שנאמר חכמות בחוץ תרונה ברחובות תתן קולה. ונזיפה דידן כמה הוי חד יומא כמר עוקבא כד ידע דנקיט שמואל מלתא בדעתיה נהג נזיפותא בנפשיה חד יומא וכרב נחמן דאמר להההיא דשמעה מפומיה דצורבא מרבנן כמה חציפא הא [אתתא זילי] נהוג בנפשיך חד יומא. מר זוטרא בר טוביה הוה פסיק סידריה קמיה דרב יהודה מטו להאי קרא ואלה דברי דוד האחרונים מכלל דאיכא ראשונים שאליה ולא הגיד ליה. א"ל אטו מאן דלא ידע פירושא דהאי פסוקא לאו גברא רבה הוא ידע דנקיט מילתא בדעתיה נהג נזיפותא בנפשיה חד יומא. פשטוה דראשונים הן דברי השיר אשר שר דוד ביום הציל ה' אותו מכף כל אויביו ומיד שאול. א"ל הקב"ה שירה אתה אומר על מפלתו של שאול כו'. כיון דידע דחטא חזר והודה כי שגג כדכתיב שגיון לדוד אשר שר לה' על דברי כוש בן ימיני ופי' כי כוש הוא שאול. ולפיכך אמר אלה דברי דוד האחרונים נאם דוד בן ישי נאם הגבר הוקם על שהקים עולה של תשובה. רוח ה' דבר בי ומלתו על לשוני. אמר אלהי ישראל לי דבר צור ישראל אמר לי הוא המושל באדם וצדיק הוא המושל ביראת אלהים הוא מושל בדברו כי מבטל בתחינתו גזירות של הקב"ה הרעות מלבוא על עמו ישראל. יושב בשבת תחכמוני כו' עדינו העצני

הגהות הב"ח

(א) רש"י ד"ה רב בר אחוה. נ"ב עיין לקמן בדף כ' ע"א:

גליון הש"ס

גמ' דוד שירה אתה אומר. עיין יומא דף כב ע"ב תוספות ד"ה והאמר: שם הוא עדינו העצני. עיין רש"י תענית דף כח ע"א ד"ה בני עדין הן הן:

מסורת הש"ס ומראה מקומות

[דף ה.] | סוכה מט: | פסחים ז. | [כריתות ח.] | משלי טז | שם ח | ישעיה מח | [פסחים ז. וש"נ] | נ"ל אגבי | [ברכות יח.]

מחאלת עיין רש"י שבת קמ: ד"ה אליפתא חדתא ובערוך ערך לפא ועיין מהרש"א בח"ה ובח"א

שטורין קלופין רש"י סנהדרין כז. ד"ה תולאלא והיא הויתה מניפה קליפתא מתוכן עיין מהרש"א

שמואל ב כג | שמואל ב כב | [עיין תוספות מגילה כח. ד"ה אלמלא] | תהלים ז | במדבר יב | ירמיה לח | עמוס ט | [נ"ל בני] | ע"ז ה. | שמואל ב כג | שם | [שבת סג. ב"מ פה.] | שם | דברים לב | מלכים א טו

תלמיד שנידה לכבודו – נדויו נידוי. דתניא: – *מנודה לרב – מנודה לתלמיד, מנודה לתלמיד – אינו מנודה לרב. לרב הוא דאינו מנודה, הא לכולי עלמא – מנודה. למאי? אי במילי דשמיא – "אין חכמה ואין תבונה ואין עצה לנגד ה'"! אלא לאו – לכבוד עצמו. אמר רב יוסף: צורבא מרבנן עביד דינא לנפשיה במילתא דפסיקא ליה. ההוא צורבא מרבנן דהוו סנו שומעניה. א"ר יהודה: היכי ליעביד? לשמתיה – צריכי ליה רבנן, לא לשמתיה – קא מיתחיל שמא דשמיא. א"ל לרבב"ח: מידי שמיע לך בהא, א"ל: הכי א"ר יוחנן, *מאי דכתיב: "כי שפתי כהן ישמרו דעת ותורה יבקשו מפיהו כי מלאך ה' צבאות הוא" אם דומה הרב למלאך ה' – יבקשו תורה מפיו, ואם לאו – אל יבקשו תורה מפיו. שמתיה רב יהודה. לסוף איחלש רב יהודה, אתו רבנן לשיולי ביה, ואתא איהו נמי בהדייהו. כד חזייה רב יהודה חייך אמר ליה: לא מסתייך דשמתיה לההוא גברא אלא אחוכי נמי חייך בי?! א"ל: לאו בדידך מחייכנא אלא דכי אזלינא לההוא עלמא בדיחא דעתאי דאפילו לגברא כוותך לא חניפי ליה. נח נפשיה דרב יהודה, אתא לבי מדרשא אמר להו: שרו לי! אמרו ליה רבנן: גברא דחשיב כרב יהודה ליכא הכא דלישרי לך, אלא זיל לגביה דר' יהודה נשיאה דלישרי לך, אזל לקמיה, א"ל לר' אמי: פוק עיין בדיניה, אי מיבעי למישרא ליה – שרי ליה. עיין ר' אמי בדיניה, סבר למישרא ליה. עמד ר' שמואל בר נחמני על רגליו ואמר: ומה שפחה של בית רבי לא נהגו חכמים קלות ראש בנידויה שלש שנים – יהודה חבירינו על אחת כמה וכמה! א"ר זירא: מאי דקמן דאתא האידנא האי סבא בבי מדרשא, דהא כמה שני לא אתא. ש"מ לא מיבעי למישרא ליה. לא שרא ליה. נפק כי קא בכי ואזיל, אתא זיבורא וטרקיה אאמתיה, ושכיב. עיילוהו למערתא דחסידי – ולא קיבלוהו, עיילוהו למערתא דדייני – וקיבלוהו. מ"ט? דעבד כר' אילעאי. דתניא, *ר' אילעאי אומר: אם רואה אדם שיצרו מתגבר עליו – ילך למקום שאין מכירין אותו, וילבש שחורים ויתעטף שחורים, ויעשה מה שלבו חפץ, ואל יחלל שם שמים בפרהסיא. שפחה של בית רבי מאי היא? דאמתא דבי רבי חזיתיה לההוא גברא דהוה מחי לבנו גדול, אמרה: ליהוי ההוא גברא בשמתא, דקעבר משום: "ולפני עור לא תתן מכשול". דתניא: "ולפני עור לא תתן מכשול" – במכה לבנו גדול הכתוב מדבר. ריש לקיש הוה מנטר פרדיסא, אתא ההוא גברא וקאכיל תאיני. רמא ביה קלא, ולא אשגח ביה. אמר: ליהוי ההוא גברא בשמתא. א"ל: אדרבה, ליהוי ההוא גברא בשמתא! אם ממון נתחייבתי לך – נידוי מי נתחייבתי לך? אתא לבי מדרשא. א"ל: שלו – נידוי, שלך – אינו נידוי. ומאי תקנתיה? זיל לגביה דלישרי לך. לא ידענא ליה. אמרו ליה: זיל לגבי נשיאה דלישרי לך, דתניא: נידוהו ואינו יודע מי נידהו – ילך אצל נשיא, ויתיר לו נדויו. אמר רב הונא, באושא התקינו: אב בית דין שסרח – אין מנדין אותו, אלא אומר לו: "הכבד ושב בביתך". חזר וסרח – מנדין אותו, מפני חילול השם. ופליגא דריש לקיש. *דאמר ריש לקיש: תלמיד חכם שסרח – אין מנדין אותו בפרהסיא, שנאמר: "וכשלת היום וכשל גם נביא עמך לילה" – כסהו כלילה. *מר זוטרא חסידא, כי מיחייב צורבא מרבנן שמתא – ברישא משמית נפשיה, והדר משמית לדידיה. כי הוה עייל באושפיזיה – שרי ליה לנפשיה והדר שרי ליה לדידיה. *אמר רב גידל אמר רב: ת"ח מנדה לעצמו, ומיפר לעצמו. אמר רב פפא: תיתי לי דלא שמיתי צורבא מרבנן מעולם. אלא, כי קא מיחייב צורבא מרבנן שמתא היכי עביד? כי הא, *דבמערבא מימנו אנגידא דצורבא מרבנן ולא מימנו אשמתא. מאי שמתא? אמר רב: שם מיתה, ושמואל אמר: שממה יהיה, ומהניא ביה כי טיחיא בתנורא. ופליגא דריש לקיש. דאמר ריש לקיש: כשם שנכנסת במאתים וארבעים ושמונה איברים כשהיא יוצאה – יוצאה ממאתים וארבעים ושמונה איברים. כשהיא נכנסת – דכתיב: "והיתה העיר חרם", "חרם" בגימטריא מאתים וארבעים ושמונה הוו. כשהיא יוצאה – דכתיב: "ברוגז רחם תזכור" "רחם" בגימטריא הכי הוו. אמר רב יוסף: שדי שמתא אגנובתא דכלבא – ואיהי דידה עבדה. דההוא כלבא דהוה אכיל מסאני דרבנן, ולא הוו קא ידעי מנו. ושמתוה ליה. איתלי ביה נורא בגנובתיה, ואכלתיה. ההוא אלמא דהוה קא מצער ליה לההוא צורבא מרבנן, אתא לקמיה דרב יוסף. א"ל: זיל שמתיה. א"ל: מסתפינא מיניה. אמר ליה: שקילי פתיחא עליה. א"ל: כל שכן דמסתפינא מיניה. א"ל: שקליה אחתיה בכדא, ואחתיה

משלי כא | מלאכי ב | חגיגה טו: | ויקרא יט | [לעיל טז.] | חגיגה טז. קדושין מ. | מלכים ב יד | מנחות לט: | הושע ד | [נדרים ז:] | פסחים נב. | יהושע ו | חבקוק ג

רש"י

תלמיד חכם שנידה לכבודו. כבר פירשתי למעלה: עביד (איניש) דינא לנפשיה. דאמר ליה: את מחייבת לי הכי והכי: דפסיקא ליה. שודאי הוא לו, ולא ספק: סנו שומעניה. שיוצאין עליו שמועות רעות: צריכי ליה רבנן. דאתריה, דהוה רבהון: ואם לאו אל יבקשו תורה. הואיל וסנו שומעניה, הא דצריכי ליה רבנן לאו כלום הוא, דמוטב דלא ילפי מיניה: אתא איהו. האי מנודה נמי בהדייהו: מאי דקמן. כלומר, היכי מתרמי דעל האי סבא, ר' שמואל בר נחמני, האידנא לבית המדרש: שמע מינה. דלהכי איתרמי דאתא האידנא לבי מדרשא, דלאו מזליה הוא דלישרי ליה: וטרקיה אאמתיה. נשכו למנודה באמתו: ולא קבלוהו. דהדרא עכנא למערתא, ולא פתחה פיה: דדייני. ראשי ב"ד. וחסידים עדיפי מינייהו: מאי טעמא קבלוהו: דעבד כרבי אילעאי וכו'. דהני שמועות רעות: מה שלבו חפץ. עבירה. והואיל ואין מכירין אותו שם ליכא חלול השם. (א) ואמר לן רבי משום רב האי גאון: ויעשה מה שלבו חפץ – רוצה לומר: דודאי כיון שלבוש שחורים וכו' – אני ערב בדבר שאינו חפץ מכאן ואילך בעבירה: דקא עבר משום ולפני עור לא תתן מכשול. דכיון דגדול הוא, שמא מבעט באביו, והוה ליה איהו מכשילו: שלך אינו נידוי. דלאו בדינא שמתיה: הכבד. בלשון הזה אומרים לו: עשה עצמך כאדם שכבד עליו ראשו, ושב בביתך. בלשון כבוד אומר לו. (ב) לישנא אחרינא: הכבד = התכבד, כבודך שתשב בביתך: כסהו. אל תבזה אותו בפרהסיא: כלילה. שחשיכה, ואין אדם רואה: משמית נפשיה. משום יקרא דההוא צורבא מדרבנן: מימנו אנגידא. מלקות, ומלקות יפה להם יותר משמתא, והוו מלקי להו: ומהניא כי טיחיא בתנורא. כשומן שטוחין את התנור ונבלע בתוכו, שאין יוצא לעולם. כלומר: מכה לכל מאן דמשמתינן ליה, דלא פסקא מיניה לעולם: ופליגא דר"ש ב"ל. דאמר: יוצאה: גנובתיה. זנב: דידה עבדא. ומלקי ליה: מסתפינא מיניה. דגברא אלמא הוא: שקיל פתיחא עליה. כתוב עליו שמתא: שקליה. לכתב שמתא: ואחתיה

תוספות

וטרקיה. נשכו אאמתו. ויש מפרשים: מדה כנגד מדה, משום דנחשד בזונות: ולא קיבלוהו. דהדרא ליה עכנא: דעבר אדרבי אילעאי. ולכך לא קיבלוהו, אע"פ שהיה תלמיד חכם. וי"ג: דעבד כר' אילעאי, ומשום הכי קיבלוהו דייני:

אם רואה אדם שיצרו מתגבר עליו. וכתב ר"ח: חס ושלום, לא הותר לו לעשות עבירה, אלא ע"י כך יכנע לבו. בפ"ק דקדושין (דף מ. ושם) פירשתי:*

נידוי מי נתחייבתי לך. אע"פ שמשמתין בעבור ממון, כדאמרינן לעיל (דף טז.): הני מילי לממונא – י"ל: שהיה לו לקרותו לב"ד תחילה, שמא יפרע. ועוד: דבב"ד נמי צריך שני וחמישי ושני, כדפירשתי לעיל, וכדמשמע בפרק "הגוזל בתרא" (ב"ק דף קיג.). ולא דמי לאיסורא (*דמכין) לאלתר, כדאמר *בההוא גברא דקאכל תמרי שנשרו בשבת, וכן [ריש] פרק "הדר" (עירובין דף סג.). ובשם רבינו תם שמעתי שהיו רגילין באותו מקום שאוכלין באילנות ונותן דמים, והשתא לא היו עוברים על הגזל:

משמית נפשיה. משום צער, שצריך לנדות ת"ח. א"נ: כדי שיהא זכור להתיר. והא דלא התיר לחבירו מתחילה – כדאמרינן בשבועות פרק קמא (דף יד.): יבא זכאי ויכפר על החייב, לכך טוב כשיתיר לחבירו – שיהא הוא מותר קודם: שלא

עין משפט נר מצוה

[סט] [א] מיי' פ"ו מהל' ת"ת הלכה יד טוש"ע י"ד סימן שלד סעיף יז:
סט א מיי' פ"ב מהל' סנהדרין הלכה יב טוש"ע ח"מ סימן ד:
ע ב מיי' פ"ו מהל' ת"ת הל' יד ופ"ז הלכה א טוש"ע י"ד ופ"ז הלכה א טוש"ע י"ד סימן שלד סעיף מב וסעיף מג: [ועי' תוס' חגיגה טז. ד"ה ויעשה וכו']
עא ג מיי' פ"ו מהלכות ת"ת שם ופ"ו מהל' ממרים הלכה ט טוש"ע י"ד סי' שלד סעיף מג:
עב ד מיי' פ"ו מהלכות ת"ת שם. טוש"ע שם סעיף לט וסעיף מג:
[נ"ל דמכדין]
[לא נמצא בשום מקום]
עג ה מיי' שם פ"ז הל' י:
עד ו מיי' שם הל' א טוש"ע שם סעי' מב:
עה ז מיי' שם הלכה יא טוש"ע שם סעי' לג:
עו ח מיי' שם הלכה א טוש"ע שם סעי' מב:

רבינו חננאל

העצני כו' עד רק בדבר אוריה החתי כולן פשוטין הן. עדינו שהיה מעדן עצמו להיות מיושב דעת בדברי תורה וכשיוצא למלחמה קשה כעץ. אמר רב הונא ת"ח שנידה לכבודו נידויו נידוי דדייק מדתניא מנודה לתלמיד אינו מנודה לרב לבדו הא לכ"ע מנודה והני מילי לכבוד עצמו אבל במילי דשמיא אין חכמה ואין תבונה לנגד ה'. אמר רב יוסף צורבא מרבנן עביד דינא לנפשיה. במלתא דפסיקא ליה. כגון הקורא לחבירו עבד יהא בנידוי וכיוצא בו. ההוא צורבא מרבנן דהוה סני שומעניה שהיה שם שמים מתחלל על ידו. כגון הא דגרסינן בסוף יוה"כ מי שיש בידו חילול השם. יצחק דבי ר' אמי אמר כל שחביריו מתביישין משמועתו היכי דמי דאמרי שרי ליה מריה לפלוני. אבל הא דאמר רב כגון אנא דשקילנא בישרא כו'. ודאמר ר' יוחנן כגון אנא דאי מסגינא ד' אמות בלא תורה ובלא תפילין על עצמן בלבד אמרו ולא על זולתם שהיו מחמירין הרבה על עצמם. הלא תראה שכל אחד כך אמר כגון אנא אבל כ"ע כדאמרן וכגון אלישע אחר שהיה מתעסק בספרי מינין ושותה במיני זמר דגרסינן זמר יוני לא פסק מביתו. אמרו עליו על אחר שהיה עומד מבית המדרש הרבה ספרי מינים היו נושרין לו מחיקו וגרסינן נמי השותה במיני זמר כו' וכל צורבא מרבנן דהכי עובדיה מתקריה סנו שומעניה. ואמר רב יהודה בההוא צורבא מרבנן דהוו סני שומעניה בדאמרן היכי נעביד ביה נשמתיה צריכי ליה רבנן לא נשמתיה קא מתחלל שם שמים. א"ל רבה בר בר חנה הכי אמר ר' יוחנן מ"ד כי שפתי כהן ישמרו דעת ותורה יבקשו מפיהו כי מלאך ה' צבאות הוא. אם דומה הרב למלאך ה' צבאות יבקשו תורה מפיהו ואם לאו אל יבקשו תורה מפיהו. שמתיה רב יהודה ולא שרייא לשמתיה לא הוא ולא ר' יהודה נשיאה ואמר רב יהודה בעידנא דשכיב בריתנא דאפילו לגברא רבא כי האי לא חניפי ליה ולא אשכח חד דשרי ליה עד דטרקיה זיבורא אאמתיה ושכיב עיילוה למערתא דחסידי ולא קיבלוה עיילוה למערתא דדייני וקיבלוה. מאי סני שומעניה דעבד כר' אילעאי דתניא ר' אילעאי הזקן אומר אם רואה אדם שיצרו מתגבר עליו פירוש מבקש לשתות במיני זמר ולשמוח בשמחה המרגילה לידי עבירה כגון זה אמר ילך למקום שאין מכירין אותו וילבש שחורין ויכסה שחורין ויעשה מה שלבו חפץ כגון אכילה ושתייה במיני זמר וכיוצא בהן אבל דבר עבירה שיש בה דין אדם או דין שמים ואפילו חייבי לאוין או חייבי עשה וכ"ש למעלה שאיסורן איסור עולם ח"ו שהתיר ר' אילעאי ואפילו בסתר אלא דבר שפירשנו למעלה הוא שאמר לעשות. ואפילו דברים הללו לא התירן לו אלא אמר כמשיא עצה לעשות כך כדי להבריח את יצרו להשלים תאותו וכיון שיראה עצמו לבוש שחורין ועטוף שחורין משתבר יצרו ונמנע ואינו עושה וזה צורבא מרבנן עשה כר' אילעאי ולבש שחורין ונתעטף ואחר זה כולן חזר לשתות במיני זמר כגון שהיה עושה [אלישע] ולפיכך שמתיה רב יהודה. תנא דבי ר' ישמעאל ולפני עור לא תתן מכשול זה המכה בנו הגדול שכיון שהוא גדול חוזר גם הוא ומכה אביו זה ונמצא כי אביו גורם לו והכשילו: ריש לקיש הוה מנטר פרדיסא אתא ההוא גברא אכיל תאיני רמא ביה קלא לא אשגח ביה אמר ליהוי ההוא גברא בשמתא. א"ל אדרבה ליהוי ההוא גברא בשמתא. אם ממון נתחייבתי לך נידוי מי נתחייבתי לך אתא שאיל לבי מדרשא [א"ל] שלו נידוי שלך אינו נידוי. זיל לגבי נשיאה דלישרי לך. דתנא נידוהו ואינו יודע מי נדהו ילך אצל נשיא ויפר לו. ירושלמי הדא אמרה המנדה למי שאינו צריך וחזר הוא ונידהו נידוי השני נידוי. אמר רב הונא באושא התקינו אב בית דין שסרח אין מנדין אותו אלא אומר לו הכבד ושב בביתך חזר וסרח מנדין אותו מפני חילול השם ריש לקיש אמר תלמיד חכם שסרח אין מבזין אותו בפרהסיא שנאמר וכשלת היום וכשל גם נביא עמך

וְאַחֲתֵיהּ בֵּי קִבְרֵי, וּקְרִי בֵּיהּ אַלְפָּא שִׁפּוּרֵי בְּאַרְבָּעִין יוֹמִין. אָזִיל עָבֵיד הָכִי. פְּקַע כַּדָּא, וּמִית אַלְמָא. מַאי שִׁפּוּרֵי? שֶׁנִּפְרָעִין מִמֶּנּוּ. מַאי תַּבְרָא? אָמַר רַב יִצְחָק בְּרֵיהּ דְּרַב יְהוּדָה: תַּבְרֵי בָּתֵּי רָמֵי. דְּתַנְיָא, *אָמַר רַבָּן שִׁמְעוֹן בֶּן גַּמְלִיאֵל: כָּל מָקוֹם שֶׁנָּתְנוּ חֲכָמִים עֵינֵיהֶם — אוֹ מִיתָה אוֹ עוֹנִי.§ "וְהַנָּזִיר וְהַמְּצוֹרָע מִטּוּמְאָתוֹ לְטָהֳרָתוֹ".§ בְּעָא מִינֵּיהּ רַבִּי יִרְמְיָה מֵרַבִּי זֵירָא: בְּשֶׁלֹּא הָיָה לָהֶם פְּנַאי, אוֹ דִּלְמָא אַף בְּשֶׁהָיָה לָהֶם פְּנַאי? אֲמַר לֵיהּ: תְּנֵינָא, [א]כָּל אֵלּוּ שֶׁאָמְרוּ מוּתָּרִין לְגַלֵּחַ בַּמּוֹעֵד — בְּשֶׁלֹּא הָיָה לָהֶם פְּנַאי, אֲבָל הָיָה לָהֶם פְּנַאי — אֲסוּרִים. [ב]נָזִיר וּמְצוֹרָע, אע"פ שֶׁהָיָה לָהֶם פְּנַאי — מוּתָּרִים, שֶׁלֹּא יַשְׁהוּ קָרְבְּנוֹתֵיהֶן. תָּנָא: הַכֹּהֵן וְהָאָבֵל מוּתָּרִין בְּגִילּוּחַ. הַאי אָבֵל הֵיכִי דָּמֵי? אִילֵימָא שֶׁחָל שְׁמִינִי שֶׁלּוֹ בְּעֶרֶב הָרֶגֶל — [ג]אִיבָּעֵי לֵיהּ לְגַלּוּחֵי בְּעֶרֶב הָרֶגֶל, אֶלָּא שֶׁחָל שְׁמִינִי שֶׁלּוֹ לִהְיוֹת בְּשַׁבָּת עֶרֶב הָרֶגֶל — [ד]אִיבָּעֵי לֵיהּ לְגַלּוּחֵי עֶרֶב שַׁבָּת, דְּאָמַר רַב חִסְדָּא אָמַר רָבִינָא בַּר שִׁילָא: *[ה]הֲלָכָה כְּאַבָּא שָׁאוּל, וּמוֹדִים חֲכָמִים לְאַבָּא שָׁאוּל בְּשֶׁחָל שְׁמִינִי שֶׁלּוֹ לִהְיוֹת בְּשַׁבָּת עֶרֶב הָרֶגֶל, שֶׁמּוּתָּר לְגַלֵּחַ בְּעֶרֶב שַׁבָּת! לָא צְרִיכָא, [ו]שֶׁחָל שְׁבִיעִי שֶׁלּוֹ לִהְיוֹת בְּשַׁבָּת עֶרֶב הָרֶגֶל. תַּנָּא בָּרָא סָבַר לָהּ כְּאַבָּא שָׁאוּל, דְּאָמַר *[ז]מִקְצָת הַיּוֹם כְּכוּלּוֹ, וְיוֹם שְׁבִיעִי עוֹלֶה לוֹ לְכָאן וּלְכָאן. וְכֵיוָן דְּשַׁבָּת הָוֵי — אָנוּס הוּא. תַּנָּא דִּידַן סָבַר לָהּ כְּרַבָּנָן, דְּאָמְרִי: לָא אָמְרִינַן מִקְצָת הַיּוֹם כְּכוּלּוֹ, וְאַכַּתִּי לָא שָׁלְמִים אֲבֵילוּת דְּשִׁבְעָה. הַאי כֹּהֵן הֵיכִי דָּמֵי? אִילֵימָא דִּשְׁלִים מִשְׁמַרְתּוֹ עֶרֶב הָרֶגֶל — אִיבָּעֵי לֵיהּ לְגַלּוּחֵי עֶרֶב הָרֶגֶל! לָא צְרִיכָא, [ח]דִּשְׁלִים מִשְׁמַרְתּוֹ בָּרֶגֶל. תַּנָּא דִּידַן סָבַר: כֵּיוָן *דִּתְנַן: [ט]בִּשְׁלֹשָׁה פְּרָקִים בַּשָּׁנָה הָיוּ כָּל הַמִּשְׁמָרוֹת שָׁווֹת בְּאֵימוּרֵי הָרְגָלִים וּבְחִילּוּק לֶחֶם הַפָּנִים. כְּמַאן דְּלָא שְׁלִים מִשְׁמַרְתּוֹ בָּרֶגֶל דָּמֵי. וְתַנָּא בָּרָא סָבַר: אע"ג דְּשַׁיֵּיךְ בַּהֲנָךְ מִשְׁמָרוֹת — מִשְׁמַרְתֵּיהּ מִיהָא שְׁלִימָא לֵיהּ. תָּנוּ רַבָּנַן: *כָּל אֵלּוּ שֶׁאָמְרוּ מוּתָּרִין לְגַלֵּחַ בַּמּוֹעֵד — מוּתָּרִין לְגַלֵּחַ בִּימֵי אֶבְלָן. וְהָתַנְיָא אֲסוּרִים! אָמַר רַב חִסְדָּא אָמַר רַב שִׁילָא: [י]כִּי תַּנְיָא הָכָא מוּתָּרִין — בְּשֶׁתְּכָפוּהוּ אֲבֵלָיו, אִי בְּשֶׁתְּכָפוּהוּ אֲבֵלָיו מַאי אִירְיָא כָּל אֵלּוּ שֶׁאָמְרוּ? אֲפִי' כּוּלֵּי עָלְמָא נַמִי! דְּתַנְיָא: *[כ]תְּכָפוּהוּ אֲבֵלָיו זֶה אַחַר זֶה, הִכְבִּיד שְׂעָרוֹ — מֵיקֵל בְּתַעַר, [ל]וּמְכַבֵּס כְּסוּתוֹ בְּמַיִם. הָא אִתְּמַר עֲלַהּ, אָמַר רַב חִסְדָּא: [מ]בְּתַעַר וְלֹא בְּמִסְפָּרַיִם. [נ]בְּמַיִם וְלֹא בְּנֶתֶר וְלֹא בְּאָהָל. אָמַר רַב חִסְדָּא: זֹאת אוֹמֶרֶת: *אָבֵל אָסוּר בְּתִכְבּוֹסֶת. ת"ר: *כְּשֵׁם שֶׁאָמְרוּ אָסוּר לְגַלֵּחַ בַּמּוֹעֵד — כָּךְ אָסוּר לִיטּוֹל צִפּוֹרְנַיִם בַּמּוֹעֵד, דִּבְרֵי ר' יְהוּדָה. [ס]וְרַבִּי יוֹסֵי מַתִּיר. וּכְשֵׁם שֶׁאָמְרוּ: אָבֵל אָסוּר לְגַלֵּחַ בִּימֵי אֶבְלוֹ — כָּךְ אָסוּר לִיטּוֹל צִפּוֹרְנַיִם בִּימֵי אֶבְלוֹ, דִּבְרֵי רַבִּי יְהוּדָה. וְרַבִּי יוֹסֵי מַתִּיר. אָמַר עוּלָּא: הֲלָכָה כְּרַבִּי יְהוּדָה בְּאָבֵל, וַהֲלָכָה כְּרַבִּי יוֹסֵי בַּמּוֹעֵד, שְׁמוּאֵל אָמַר: הֲלָכָה

רש"י

וְאַחֲתֵיהּ בְּכַדָּא. תָּקַע בְּתוֹךְ הַכַּד וְלֹא יִשְׁמְעוּ: בֵּי קִבְרֵי. דְּלָא שְׁכִיחִי תַּמָּן אֱינָשֵׁי: וּקְרִי בֵּיהּ. כְּלוֹמַר: תָּקַע בֵּיהּ אֲלָפִין שִׁיפּוּרֵי: מַאי תַּבְרֵי. לָמָּה תּוֹקְעִין תְּקִיעָה וּשְׁבָרִים? תַּבְרֵי בָּתֵּי רָמֵי. כְּלוֹמַר: שַׁמְתָּא מְשַׁבֵּר בָּתִּים גְּבוֹהִים: בְּשֶׁלֹּא הָיָה לָהֶן פְּנַאי. דְּדַוְקָא נָקַט שֶׁעָלוּ מִטּוּמְאָתָם בָּרֶגֶל — לְפִיכָךְ מְגַלְּחִין, שֶׁלֹּא הָיָה לָהֶן פְּנַאי לְגַלֵּחַ, דַּעֲדַיִין לֹא עָלוּ מִטּוּמְאָתָן: אוֹ דִּלְמָא אע"פ שֶׁהָיָה לָהֶם פְּנַאי. וְלֹא גִּילְּחוּ קוֹדֶם הַמּוֹעֵד, מוּתָּרִים לְגַלֵּחַ בַּמּוֹעֵד: שֶׁלֹּא יַשְׁהוּ קָרְבְּנוֹתֵיהֶן. בְּתִגְלַחְתָּן עַד לְאַחַר הָרֶגֶל, דְּנָזִיר וּמְצוֹרָע אֵין מְבִיאִין קָרְבְּנוֹתֵיהֶן עַד לְאַחַר גִּילּוּחַ, כִּדְכְתִיב בְּהוּ קְרָאֵי. הִלְכָּךְ לָא קָנְסִינַן לְהוּ כִּדְלָא עָבְדֵי מִקַּמֵּי רֶגֶל, דְּזִימְנִין דְּלָא עָבֵיד קַמֵּי רֶגֶל. (א)וּמִיתַּסְרֵי לְהוּ בַּמּוֹעֵד — נִמְצָא שֶׁמַּשְׁהִין הַקָּרְבָּנוֹת וְאֵינָן קְרֵיבִין בַּיּוֹם הַשְּׁמִינִי בִּזְמַנָּן. לְפִיכָךְ אָמְרוּ מְגַלֵּחַ בַּמּוֹעֵד, דְּמוּטָב לְקָרֵב זְמַן הַקְרָבָה וְלֹא לְאַחֵר: אִיבָּעֵי לֵיהּ לְגַלּוּחֵי עֶרֶב הָרֶגֶל. דִּתְנַן מַתְנִיתִין (לקמן דף יט.): הַקּוֹבֵר מֵתוֹ שְׁמוֹנָה יָמִים קוֹדֶם הָרֶגֶל — בָּטְלוּ מִמֶּנּוּ גְּזֵרַת ל' יוֹם, וּמוּתָּר בְּגִילּוּחַ. הוֹאִיל וּכְבָר הִתְחִיל יוֹם אֶחָד מִן הַשְּׁלֹשִׁים. וְזֶה, הוֹאִיל וְלֹא גִּילַּח עֶרֶב הָרֶגֶל — לֹא יְגַלַּח בָּרֶגֶל: בְּשַׁבָּת עֶרֶב הָרֶגֶל. וְהָוֵי אָנוּס, דְּלָא מָצֵי לְגַלֵּחַ בַּשְּׁמִינִי עֶרֶב הָרֶגֶל — לְהָכִי מְגַלֵּחַ בָּרֶגֶל: אִיבָּעֵי לֵיהּ לְגַלּוּחֵי עֶרֶב שַׁבָּת. שֶׁהוּא שְׁבִיעִי: הֲלָכָה כְּאַבָּא שָׁאוּל. דַּאֲפִילּוּ לֹא קָבַר אֶלָּא שִׁבְעָה יָמִים קוֹדֶם הָרֶגֶל — בָּטְלָה מִמֶּנּוּ גְּזֵרַת שְׁלֹשִׁים: וּמוֹדִים חֲכָמִים לְאַבָּא שָׁאוּל. אע"ג דִּבְעוּ שְׁמוֹנָה: בְּשֶׁחָל שְׁמִינִי לִהְיוֹת בְּשַׁבָּת עֶרֶב הָרֶגֶל. דְּהָוֵי אָנוּס: שֶׁמּוּתָּר לְגַלֵּחַ בְּעֶרֶב שַׁבָּת. שֶׁהוּא שְׁבִיעִי: הַאי תַּנָּא דִּבְרַיְיתָא. דְּתָנֵי: אָבֵל מְגַלֵּחַ בַּמּוֹעֵד: סָבַר כְּאַבָּא שָׁאוּל. דְּיוֹם שְׁבִיעִי עוֹלֶה לְכָאן וּלְכָאן, לְשִׁבְעָה וְלִשְׁלֹשִׁים. וְכֵיוָן דִּכְבָר הִתְחִילוּ שְׁלֹשִׁים — אִיבָּעֵי לֵיהּ לְגַלּוּחֵי קוֹדֶם הָרֶגֶל. אֶלָּא דְּשַׁבָּת הָוֵי, וְאָנוּס הוּא, לְהָכִי מְגַלֵּחַ בַּמּוֹעֵד: וְתַנָּא דִּידַן. דְּתָנֵי: אֵלּוּ מְגַלְּחִין בָּרֶגֶל, וְלֹא אָבֵל: סָבַר כְּרַבָּנָן דְּאָמְרִי לָא אָמְרִינַן מִקְצָת הַיּוֹם כְּכוּלּוֹ. אֶלָּא שִׁבְעָה שְׁלֵימִין בָּעֵינַן, וְאַכַּתִּי לָא שְׁלִים אֲבֵילוּת דְּשִׁבְעָה קוֹדֶם הָרֶגֶל, וְלָא הָוֵי אָנוּס. דַּאֲפִי' לָא הָוֵי שַׁבָּת — לָא מָצֵי לְגַלֵּחַ, לְהָכִי אֵינוֹ מְגַלֵּחַ בַּמּוֹעֵד: דִּשְׁלִים מִשְׁמַרְתּוֹ עֶרֶב הָרֶגֶל. בְּשַׁבָּת, דִּלְעוֹלָם לֹא שָׁלְמָה מִשְׁמָרָה אֶלָּא בְּשַׁבָּת: אִיבָּעֵי לֵיהּ לְגַלּוּחֵי עֶרֶב הָרֶגֶל. כְּלוֹמַר, בְּעֶרֶב שַׁבָּת שֶׁהוּא עֶרֶב הָרֶגֶל. דְּהָא אָמְרִינַן (לעיל דף יד.): אַנְשֵׁי מִשְׁמָר אֲסוּרִין בְּגִילּוּחַ, וּבַחֲמִישִׁי מוּתָּרִין מִפְּנֵי כְּבוֹד הַשַּׁבָּת: דִּשְׁלִים מִשְׁמַרְתּוֹ בָּרֶגֶל. כְּגוֹן דְּהָוֵי יוֹם חֲמִישִׁי יוֹם רִאשׁוֹן שֶׁל רֶגֶל — דְּלָא מָצֵי לְגַלֵּחַ דְּהָוֵי י"ט. וּשְׁלִים מִשְׁמַרְתּוֹ בַּשַּׁבָּת, שֶׁהוּא יוֹם שְׁלִישִׁי לָרֶגֶל: תַּנָּא דִּידַן. דְּקָאָמַר: אֵינוֹ מְגַלֵּחַ בַּמּוֹעֵד: סָבַר כֵּיוָן דִּתְנַן בִּשְׁלֹשָׁה פְּרָקִים. בִּשְׁלֹשָׁה רְגָלִים כָּל הַמִּשְׁמָרוֹת שָׁוִים, אַלְמָא, כְּמַאן דְּלָא שְׁלִים מִשְׁמַרְתּוֹ דָּמֵי, וַעֲדַיִין יֵשׁ לוֹ חֵלֶק בְּאֵימוּרֵי רְגָלִים, וְלָא שְׁלִים מִשְׁמַרְתּוֹ בְּכָל הָרֶגֶל, לְהָכִי אֵינוֹ מְגַלֵּחַ בָּרֶגֶל. כִּדְתְנַן: אַנְשֵׁי מִשְׁמָר אֲסוּרִין לְגַלֵּחַ: וְתַנָּא בָּרָא. דְּקָאָמַר: מוּתָּרִין לְגַלֵּחַ: אע"ג דְּשַׁיֵּיךְ בַּהֲנָךְ מִשְׁמָרוֹת. [שְׁלִים] עִיקַּר מִשְׁמַרְתּוֹ דִּידֵיהּ, לְהָכִי מוּתָּר בְּגִילּוּחַ: הָא אִתְּמַר עֲלַהּ. הָא דְּתָנֵי תְּכָפוּהוּ אֲבֵלָיו מֵיקֵל בְּתַעַר וְלֹא בְּמִסְפָּרַיִם, וְקָתָנֵי בְּרַיְיתָא דְּכָל הָנֵי שֶׁמּוּתָּרִין לְגַלֵּחַ בַּמּוֹעֵד — מוּתָּרִין לְגַלֵּחַ בִּימֵי אֶבְלוֹ, כְּשֶׁתְּכָפוּהוּ אֲבֵלָיו, וּמְגַלֵּחַ בְּמִסְפָּרַיִם: זֹאת אוֹמֶרֶת. מִדְּקָתָנֵי תְּכָפוּהוּ אֲבֵלָיו מְכַבֵּס כְּסוּתוֹ — מִכְּלָל דִּשְׁאָר אָבֵל אָסוּר בְּתִכְבּוֹסֶת:

הֲלָכָה

תוספות

שלא ישהו קרבנותיהן. אע"ג דתגלחת דנזיר לא מעכבא — *מכל מקום רגיל הוא לגלח, דמלוה הוא לגלח ולשלוח שערו תחת הדוד: **כשחל** שמיני בשבת. כגון שמע שמועה בשבת, דקבורתו לא היה בשבת, ובירושלמי מוקי לה כשגררתו חיה ונתייאשו לבקש, דמונין לו משעה שנתייאשו:

ותנא דידן סבר לה כרבנן. ואין להקשות: מ"מ יגלח ע"ש, כמו חל שבעה שלו בערב שבת ערב הרגל, דשרו רבנן לגלח, ואע"ג דלית להו מקצת היום ככולו באבילות? דהתם נשלם האבילות קודם יו"ט, אע"ג דמגלח קודם שנשלם, דהא לית להו מקצת היום ככולו באבילות, והכא מיהא אית להו, משום כבוד יו"ט, דאשכחן (יומא דף ו:) בזב וזבה דהויא מקצת היום ככולו, אבל כשיש עדיין ימי אבילות — לא. אבל תימה: (ב)דהיכי אסרינן מהאי דלא תני מתניתין האבל והכהן מותרים לגלח משום דלית ליה פנאי והא מיבעיא לעיל (דף יד.) באבדה לו אבידה, ולא פשיט מדלא תני לה, *דאיכא למימר תנא ושייר כמו כן הני — תני ושייר! ויש לומר: כיון דאשכחנא פלוגתא דאבא שאול ורבנן באבל — אית לן למימר דתנא דמתני' וברייתא בהכי פליגי, וכיון דבאבל פליגי — בכהן נמי פליגי:

זאת אומרת אבל אסור בתכבוסת. וא"ת: פשיטא, דהא אפי' שאר מלאכות אסור? וי"ל: משום דקתני לקמן (דף כא.): אלו דברים שאבל אסור בהן ולא קתני תכבוסת. אי נמי: תכבוסת (*חייב) קאמר:

ה"ג: **ושמואל** אמר הלכה כר' יוסי בזו ובזו, דאמר שמואל הלכה כדברי המיקל באבל. וא"ת: בעירובין (דף מו. ושם), דאמר *שמואל: הלכה כדברי המיקל בעירוב, ואמר נמי: הלכה כרבי יוחנן בן נורי. ומקשה התם: תרתי למה לי (ג)כו'! וי"ל: איצטריך הכא לאפוקי מדעולא. וא"ת: וכיון דאית ליה לשמואל רבי יהודה ור' יוסי הלכה כרבי יוסי, כדאמרינן פרק "מי שהוציאוהו" (שם:) למה ליה למימר הכא הלכה כרבי יוסי? וי"ל: לאפוקי מדעולא. ואעולא לא קשיא מידי מהתם, דהיכא דאתמר — אתמר, כדאמר התם:

רבינו חננאל

עמך לילה כסהו כלילה אמר רב תלמיד חכם מנדה לעצמו ומיפר לעצמו רב זוטרא חסידא כי הוה מתחייב ת"ח נידוי הוה משמית נפשיה ברישא והדר משמיה ל'ה. וכד הוה עייל לביתיה הוה א) שרי ליה ברישא והדר שרי לנפשיה. אמר רב פפא תיתי לי דלא שמיתנא צורבא מרבנן מעולם כי הא דבני מערבא מימנו אנגידא דצורבא מרבנן ולא מימנו אשמותיה אלא מכסין אותו. מאי שמתא. רב אמר שם מיתה כלומר מיתה בה ושמואל אמר שם תהא כלומר שם תיתי כדכתיב ובאה אל בית הגנב וגו'. אמר אבוה דשמואל ומהניא כי טחיה בתנורא כלומר אינה יוצאה משם לעולם. ופליגא דר"ל דאמר כשם שנכנס ברמ"ח איברים כדכתיב והיית חרם. חר"ם בגימטריא רמ"ח הוי כך יוצאה ברמ"ח איברים שנאמר ברוגז רחם תזכור. רח"ם בגימטריא רמ"ח הוי. אמר רב יוסף שדי שמתא אגנובתא דכלבתא והיא דידה עבדה ההוא כלבא דהוה אכיל מסאני דרבנן ולא הוה ידעי מאן דעבד הא מלתא ושמתו ליה ואתלי נורא בנגובתיה ואכלתיה ההוא אלמא דהוה מצער ההוא צורבא מרבנן כו'. והאידנא נמי מאן דבעי הכי כרב יוסף רשאי. מאי שיפורא אמר רבא שנפרעין ממנו מאי תברי תברי בתי. תניא אמר ר' שמעון בן גמליאל כל מקום שנתנו חכמים עיניהם בו או מיתה או עוני: **ירושלמי** ריב"ל זמין ליה לחד בר נש ג' זימני ולא אשגח ביה אמר אילולי דלא חרמית ב"נ מן יומא הוינא מחרים ליה. שעל כ"ד דברים מנדין על כבוד הרב וזה אחד מהן שנא' וכל אשר לא יבא לשלשת הימים וכתיב בו יבדל מקהל הגולה. א"ר יצחק אית סגי מינהון מבדרן במתני'. בתעניות (דף יט) שלח לו שמעון בן שטח צריך אתה נידוי נגזרה גזרה בשני אליהו כו'. בר"ה (דף כא) שלח לו ר"ג כל המעכב את הרבים מעשות מצוה ג) צריך נידוי בפסחים (דף נג) אילמלי תודוס אתה גוזרני עליך נידוי. תנא את מי נידו את אלעזר בטהרת ידים. הדא אמרה המפקפק אפי' בדבר מדברי סופרים צריך נידוי. בעדיות דכמה השקוה מהו דכמה. דכוותה. פי' גרים שכמותה השקוה. כלומר גינה שמעיה ואבטליון ונידוהו ומת ב ארונו הדא אמרה המבזה זקן אפילו לאחר מיתה צריך נידוי א"ר יוסי נמנו וגמרו לכשיחזור מקרבין אותו. אמתא חזא לחד ספר מהי ינוקא יותר מן צרכיה אמרה יהא ההוא גברא מוחרם. שאלו צריך למיחש על גרמיה הדא אמרה העושה דבר שלא כשורה צריך נידוי. ר' יעקב בן אבי בשם רב ששת נמנו באושא שלא לנדות זקן [ואתייא כי הא דאמר שמואל בשם ר'] (בר) אבהו דאמר זקן אין מורידין אותו מגדולתו אלא אומרים לו הכבד ושב בביתך. וזקן ששכח תלמודו מחמת אונסו נוהגין בו קדושת הארון ששימש הלוחות. ר' חייא בש"ר יוחנן זקן שנידה לעצמו אפי' כהלכה בימי ר' ירמיה אתת עקא על טבראי שלח בעי מנרתא דכספא גבי ר' יעקב ב"ר אבון שלח ליה עדיין לא שב ר' ירמיה מרעתו ובקש לנדותו. וא"ל ר' חייא בר יצחק עטושיא שמעתי שאין עשה כירבעם בן נבט וחביריו שהעמידו עגלים. אמר ליה מי שאמר דכמה השקוה ונידוהו כירבעם בן נבט עשה. ונדון אילין לאילין. וחששו אילין לאילין. וצרכין למשתריא אלין מן אילין:

פיסקא

עין משפט נר מצוה

עז א מיי' פ"ז מהלכות יו"ט הלכה יט סמג לאוין עה טוש"ע א"ח סי' תקלא סעי' ז:

עח ב מיי' שם:

עט ג ד ה מיי' פ"ו מהלכות אבל הל' ז טוש"ע י"ד סימן שצט סעיף ג:

פ ו ז מיי' שם ופ"ז מהלכות יו"ט הלכה יח טוש"ע א"ח סימן תקלא סעיף ד וטוש"ע י"ד סימן שצט סעיף ג:

פא ח מיי' פ"ז מהלכות יו"ט הלכה יט ופ"א מהלכות ביאת מקדש הלכה:

פב ט מיי' פ"ד מהל' כלי המקדש הלכה ה:

פג י כ מיי' פ"ו מהל' אבל הל' ב טוש"ע י"ד סימן שצ סעיף ג:

פד ל מיי' שם טוש"ע י"ד סימן שפא סעיף ה:

פה מ מיי' שם טוש"ע י"ד סי' שצ סעי' ג:

פו נ מיי' שם טוש"ע י"ד סימן שפא סעיף ה:

פז ס מיי' פ"ז מהלכות יו"ט הלכה כ טוש"ע א"ח סי' תקלב סעיף א:

מסורת הש"ס

[נזיר מו.] — חגיגה ה: נדרים ז: ע"ש סוטה מז. — לקמן יט: — [לעיל טז. פסחים ז. וש"נ] — סוכה נה: — [לעיל יז. תוספתא פ"ב] — תענית יז. — לעיל טו. — [תוספתא פ"ב] — רש"א — גי' רש"א מים — [ע"ש דאי' ריב"ל]

הגהות הב"ח

(א) רש"י ד"ה שלא ישהו כו' דלא עביד קמי רגל ולהו אסרינן להו במועד: (ב) תום' ד"ה ותנא כו' אבל תימה דהיכי פשיטא ליה דלתנא דידן שריין ממאי דלא קתני במתני' כו' באבדה לו אבדה ולא פשיטא ליה דלתנא מגלח מדלא תני לה: (ג) ד"ה ושמואל כו' ומקשה התם תרתי למה לי ה"ג קשיא תרתי למה לי וי"ל לאצטריך הכא:

גליון הש"ס

תום' ד"ה ותנא דידן וכו' דאיכא למימר תנא ושייר. עיין שבת קד ע"ב תוספות ד"ה חסר חסר וכתובות רפ"ג תוספות ד"ה ועל הכותית:

א) לפנינו הגי' להיפך דשרי ליה לנפשיה בתחלה ואמנם גירסת רבינו נכונה יותר ועי' בתוס' ד"ה משמית ודו"ק. ב) בירושלמי איתא שאילו נגזרה גזרה כשם שנגזרה בימי אליהו וכו'. ג) במשנה שלפנינו ליתא זה אכן בירושלמי משמע דגריס כן.

תורה אור

אהֲלָכָה כְּרַבִּי יוֹסֵי בַּמּוֹעֵד וּבְאָבֵל. *דְּאָמַר שְׁמוּאֵל: הֲלָכָה כְּדִבְרֵי הַמֵּיקֵל בְּאָבֵל. פִּנְחָס אֲחוּהּ דְּמָר שְׁמוּאֵל, אִיתְרַע (א) בֵּיהּ מִילְּתָא, עָל שְׁמוּאֵל לְמִישְׁאַל טַעְמָא מִינֵּיהּ. חֲזָנְהוּ לְטוּפְרֵי דְּהָווּ נְפִישָׁן, אֲמַר לֵיהּ: אַמַּאי לָא שָׁקְלַתְּ לְהוּ? אֲמַר לֵיהּ: אִי בְּדִידֵיהּ הֲוָה, מִי מְזַלְזְלַתְּ בֵּיהּ כּוּלֵּי הַאי? *הֲוַאי °"כִּשְׁגָגָה שֶׁיּוֹצָא מִלִּפְנֵי הַשַּׁלִּיט", וְאִיתְרַע בֵּיהּ מִילְּתָא בִּשְׁמוּאֵל. עָל פִּנְחָס אֲחוּהּ לְמִישְׁאַל טַעְמָא מִינֵּיהּ, שַׁקְלִינְהוּ לְטוּפְרֵיהּ חַבְטִינְהוּ לְאַפֵּיהּ, אֲמַר לֵיהּ: לֵית לָךְ *בְּרִית כְּרוּתָה לַשְּׂפָתַיִם? דְּאָמַר ר' יוֹחָנָן: מִנַּיִן שֶׁבְּרִית כְּרוּתָה לַשְּׂפָתַיִם — שֶׁנֶּאֱמַר: °"וַיֹּאמֶר אַבְרָהָם אֶל נְעָרָיו שְׁבוּ לָכֶם פֹּה עִם הַחֲמוֹר וַאֲנִי וְהַנַּעַר נֵלְכָה עַד כֹּה וְנִשְׁתַּחֲוֶה וְנָשׁוּבָה אֲלֵיכֶם" וְאִיסְתַּיְּעָא מִלְּתָא דַּהֲדוּר תַּרְוַיְיהוּ. סְבוּר מִינֵּיהּ: דְּיָד — אִין, דְּרֶגֶל — לָא. אָמַר רַב עָנָן בַּר תַּחְלִיפָא: לְדִידִי מְפָרְשָׁא לִי מִינֵּיהּ דִּשְׁמוּאֵל: לָא שְׁנָא דְּיָד, וְלָא שְׁנָא דְּרֶגֶל. אָמַר רַב חִיָּיא בַּר אַשִׁי אָמַר רַב: בוּבְגְנוּסְטְרָא אָסוּר. אָמַר רַב שֶׁמֶן בַּר אַבָּא: הֲוָה קָאֵימְנָא קַמֵּיהּ דְּר' יוֹחָנָן בֵּי מִדְרָשָׁא בְּחוּלּוֹ שֶׁל מוֹעֵד, וְשַׁקְלִינְהוּ לְטוּפְרֵיהּ בְּשִׁינֵּיהּ וְזַרְקִינְהוּ. שְׁמַע מִינָּהּ תְּלָת; שְׁמַע מִינָּהּ: מוּתָּר לִיטּוֹל צִפָּרְנַיִם בְּחוּלּוֹ שֶׁל מוֹעֵד, וּשְׁמַע מִינָּהּ: אֵין בָּהֶן מִשּׁוּם מִיאוּס, וּשְׁמַע מִינָּהּ: מוּתָּר לְזוֹרְקָן. אִינִי? וְהָתַנְיָא: *שְׁלֹשָׁה דְּבָרִים נֶאֶמְרוּ בְּצִפָּרְנַיִם: הַקּוֹבְרָן — צַדִּיק, שׂוֹרְפָן — *חָסִיד, זוֹרְקָן — רָשָׁע. טַעְמָא מַאי, שֶׁמָּא תַּעֲבוֹר עֲלֵיהֶן אִשָּׁה עוּבָּרָה וְתַפִּיל — אִשָּׁה בֵּי מִדְרָשָׁא לָא שְׁכִיחָא. וְכִי תֵּימָא: זִימְנִין דְּמִיכַּנְשִׁי לְהוּ וּשְׁדֵי לְהוּ אַבַּרַאי, כֵּיוָן דְּאִשְׁתַּנִּי — אִשְׁתַּנִּי. אָמַר רַב יְהוּדָה אָמַר רַב: זוּג בָּא מֵחַמָּתָן לִפְנֵי רַבִּי, וּמָר זוּטְרָא מַתְנֵי: זוּג בָּא מֵחַמָּתָן לִפְנֵי רַבִּי, וּבִקְּשׁוּ מִמֶּנּוּ צִפָּרְנַיִם — וְהִתִּיר לָהֶם, וְאִם בִּקְּשׁוּ מִמֶּנּוּ שָׂפָה — הִתִּיר לָהֶם. וּשְׁמוּאֵל אָמַר: אַף בִּקְּשׁוּ מִמֶּנּוּ שָׂפָה גוְהִתִּיר לָהֶם אָמַר אֲבִיטוּל סַפְרָא מִשְּׁמֵיהּ דְּרַב (*פַּפָּא:) שָׂפָה מִזָּוִית [א]לְזָוִית. אָמַר רַבִּי אַמִּי: וּבְשָׂפָה הַמְעַכֶּבֶת. א"ר נַחְמָן בַּר יִצְחָק: לְדִידִי כְּשָׂפָה הַמְעַכֶּבֶת דָּמֵי לִי. וְאָמַר אֲבִיטוּל סַפְרָא מִשְּׁמֵיהּ דְּרַב (*פַּפָּא:) פַּרְעֹה שֶׁהָיָה בִּימֵי מֹשֶׁה הוּא אַמָּה וּזְקָנוֹ אַמָּה, וּפַרְמַשְׁתָּקוֹ אַמָּה וָזֶרֶת, לְקַיֵּים מַה שֶּׁנֶּאֱמַר: °"וּשְׁפַל אֲנָשִׁים יָקִים עָלֶיהָ". וְאָמַר אֲבִיטוּל סַפְרָא מִשְּׁמֵיהּ דְּרַב (*פַּפָּא:) פַּרְעֹה שֶׁהָיָה בִּימֵי מֹשֶׁה אַמְגוּשִׁי הָיָה, שֶׁנֶּאֱמַר: °"הִנֵּה יוֹצֵא הַמַּיְמָה" וגו'. § "וְאֵלּוּ מְכַבְּסִין בַּמּוֹעֵד הַבָּא מִמְּדִינַת הַיָּם". § אָמַר רַב אַסִּי א"ר יוֹחָנָן: *) דמִי שֶׁאֵין לוֹ אֶלָּא חָלוּק אֶחָד — מוּתָּר לְכַבְּסוֹ בְּחוּלּוֹ שֶׁל מוֹעֵד. מְתִיב ר' יִרְמְיָה: אֵלּוּ מְכַבְּסִין בַּמּוֹעֵד, הַבָּא מִמְּדִינַת הַיָּם כו'. הָנֵי — אִין, מִי שֶׁאֵין לוֹ אֶלָּא חָלוּק אֶחָד — לָא! אֲמַר לֵיהּ ר' יַעֲקֹב לְר' יִרְמְיָה: אַסְבְּרָה לָךְ, מַתְנִי' — אע"ג דְּאִית לֵיהּ תְּרֵי וּמְטַנְּפִי. שְׁלַח רַב יִצְחָק בַּר יַעֲקֹב בַּר גִּיּוֹרֵי מִשְּׁמֵיהּ דְּר' יוֹחָנָן: הכְּלֵי פִשְׁתָּן מוּתָּר לְכַבְּסָן בְּחוּלּוֹ שֶׁל מוֹעֵד. מְתִיב רָבָא: *מִטְפְּחוֹת הַיָּדַיִם, מִטְפְּחוֹת הַסְּפָרִים

*) תענית כט: לעיל יז. חולין קז:

רש"י

הֲלָכָה כְּרַבִּי יוֹסֵי בַּמּוֹעֵד. דְּמַתִּיר: אִיתְרַע בֵּיהּ מִילְּתָא. בְּפִנְחָס אֲחוּהּ, *דְּפִנְחָס הֲוָה אָבֵל: עַיֵּיל שְׁמוּאֵל לִישְׁאַל בֵּיהּ טַעְמָא. לְדַבֵּר עַל לִבּוֹ דְּפִנְחָס: אִילּוּ בְּדִידֵיהּ הֲוָה. כְּלוֹמַר: אִילּוּ הָיִיתָ אָבֵל: מִי מְזַלְזַלְתְּ בֵּיהּ כּוּלֵּי הַאי. בַּאֲבֵילוּת, דְּשָׁקְלַתְּ לְטוּפְרָךְ: וְאִיתְרַע בֵּיהּ מִילְּתָא. אֲבֵילוּת: שַׁקְלִינְהוּ לְטוּפְרֵיהּ חַבְטִינְהוּ לְאַפֵּיהּ. זַרְקִינְהוּ מֵרוֹב כַּעַס. וַהֲדַר מְכַנֵּס לְהוּ, דְּזוֹרְקָן רָשָׁע: בְּרִית כְּרוּתָה לַשְּׂפָתַיִם. דִּכְתִיב: "וְנִשְׁתַּחֲוֶה וְנָשׁוּבָה אֲלֵיכֶם" וְכֵן הֲוָה, דְּחָזְרוּ תַּרְוַיְיהוּ: סְבוּר מִינֵּיהּ דְּיָד. מוּתָּר בִּימֵי אֶבְלוֹ מִשּׁוּם דְּמָאִיס, דְּרֶגֶל — לֹא: גִּינוּסְטְרֵי. מִסְפָּרַיִם: אֵין בָּהֶם מִשּׁוּם מִיאוּס. מִדְּשָׁקַל לֵיהּ בְּשִׁינֵּיהּ: וּשְׁדֵי לֵיהּ לְאַבְּרַאי. וְעָבְרָה עֲלַיְיהוּ אִיתְּתָא חַבְרָתִי: כֵּיוָן דְּאִישְׁתַּנֵּי. מֵהֵיכָא דַּהֲווּ מֵעִיקָּרָא — אִישְׁתַּנֵּי, וְלָא מַזִּיקֵי: וּמָר זוּטְרָא מַתְנֵי. בְּבָרַיְיתָא, דְּבִקְּשׁוּ מִמֶּנּוּ לְפָרְנַיִם בִּימֵי אֶבְלוֹ, וְלָאו מִשְּׁמֵיהּ דְּרַב יְהוּדָה: וְאִם בִּקְּשׁוּ מִמֶּנּוּ שָׂפָה הָיָה מַתִּיר לָהֶם. כְּלוֹמַר: אֲנָא חֲזֵינָא לְדַעְתֵּיהּ אִי שָׁאֲלוּ לְגַלֵּחַ הַשָּׂפָה — הָיָה מַתִּיר לָהֶם, דְּאֵין בָּהֶם מִשּׁוּם: "בַּל תַּשְׁחִית פְּאַת זְקָנֶךָ" (ויקרא יט): מִזָּוִית לְזָוִית. מִסּוֹף הַשָּׂפָה לְסוֹף הָאַחֵר מוּתָּר לְגַלֵּחַ, שֶׁהֲרֵי מְעַכֶּבֶת אֲכִילָה וּשְׁתִיָּה, וּמָאִיס: וּלְדִידִי. דַּאֲמֵינָא דַּעְתִּי — כָּל הַשָּׂפָה כְּשָׂפָה הַמְעַכֶּבֶת דָּמֵי, דַּאֲמֵינָא לִי דַּעְתִּי: פַּרְמַשְׁתָּקוֹ. אַמָּתוֹ: אַמְגוּשִׁי הֲוָה דִּכְתִיב הִנֵּה יוֹצֵא הַמַּיְמָה. מַחֲלוֹקֶת בְּמַסֶּכֶת שַׁבָּת (דף עה.), חַד אָמַר: חָרָשֵׁי, לְהָכִי יוֹצֵא לַיְאוֹר בִּשְׁבִיל מְכַשְּׁפוּת. וְאִידָךְ אָמַר: גִּידּוּפֵי, לְהָכִי יוֹצֵא, שֶׁאוֹמֵר: לִי יְאוֹרִי וַאֲנִי עֲשִׂיתִנִי: *מִטְפְּחוֹת יָדַיִם. שֶׁמְּנַגְּבִין בָּהֶן יָדַיִם, מִשּׁוּם דְּמָאִיס: *מִטְפְּחוֹת הַסְּפוֹג. שֶׁמְּנַגְּבִין בָּהֶן עַצְמָן כְּשֶׁיּוֹצְאִין מִבֵּית הַמֶּרְחָץ: וְשֶׁעָלוּ מִטּוּמְאָתָן. בַּמּוֹעֵד: מַתְנִי'. דְּקָתָנֵי "אֵלּוּ מְכַבְּסִין" — אע"ג דְּאִית לֵיהּ תְּרֵי וּמְטַנְּפִי. אֲבָל מִי שֶׁאֵין לוֹ אֶלָּא חָלוּק אֶחָד — דְּכוּלֵּי עָלְמָא שָׁרֵי: כְּלֵי

תוספות

ואיסתייעא מילתא דהדור. תימה: דלמא מדה טובה מרובה? והוה ליה לאתויי הא דאמר עולא בעלמא (ברכות דף יט. ע"ש): לעולם אל יפתח אדם פיו לשטן, שנאמר "שמעו דבר ה' קציני סדום" כו' (ישעיה א)! **ובגנוסטרי** אסור. פי' בערוך: * שהוא כלי המתוקן ליטול לפרנים וכך שמו. ומלשון דגנוסטרא אסור — משמע שהיה מתיר בין בתער בין במספרים, ולאו דוקא בשינים. מיהו, קאמר בגמרא רבי יוחנן דשקלינהו בשיניו — משמע דוקא בשיניו שרי. ותימה: דלעיל אמרינן הלכה כר' יוסי במועד לדברי הכל! ושמא רבי יוחנן סבר הלכה כר' יהודה, ומפרש טעמא דמחמרינן במועד טפי מבאבל, ● ולא כרב שישא בריה דרב אידי דאמר: דברים המותרין בחולו של מועד — אסורין בימי אבלו. ורבינו תם פירש: דכשם שמותר בשיניו — כך מותר ליטול לפרניו [בזו] מחבירתה, דכל זה חשוב שינוי לענין שבת בפ' "המצניע" (שבת דף צד:). ושמעתי בשם רבי שמשון בר אברהם שבחול המועד מותר ליטול לפרנים לנשים, דקתני בירושלמי גבי ועושה אשה תכשיטיה במועד, וחשיב נוטלת שערה ולפרניה, וצ"ע: בהלכות גדולות נמי אמרינן: והאשה מותרת בנטילת שער לאחר שבעה! ונראה דבאשה נשואה דוקא קאמר, ומיירי במעברת סרק על פניה וטופלה בסיד, שהוא משום תכשיט שלא תתגנה על בעלה, אבל בתספורת ממש — אסורה. וגם בשם רבינו חיים שמעתי שהיה מתיר נטילת לפרנים במועד. ובהלכות גדולות פוסק:(ב) שבעה — אסור בגנוסטרי, בשיניו — מותר, לאחר שבעה — מותר אף בגנוסטרי. ולא ידענא מנא ליה דברייתא איירי תוך שבעה? אי משום דקתני בימי אבלו — ה"נ קתני ימי אבלו גבי גילוח, והיינו כל שלשים. וקאמר: כשם שאסור לגלח בימי אבלו כך אסור ליטול לפרניו בימי אבלו — משמע: כל שלשים. ואי סברי כר' יוסי — יתירו לגמרי! וי"ל: דסברי כר' יוסי, ומסתבר להו דאפילו רבי יוסי היה אוסר בגנוסטרי תוך שבעה, דומיא דמועד או שמא(ג) מעשה דשמואל משמע קצת דשקלינהו לטופריה חבטינהו באפיה — דמיירי תוך שבעה דוקא, דבתוך שבעה היה, ובשיניו היה — מדקא אמרינן בתר הכי ובגנוסטרי אסור. משמע דשמואל לא היה בגנוסטרי, ולא אשכחנא דאסר רק תוך שבעה כשהלך רב פנחס לנחמו: **בקשו** ממנו שפה. יש לפרש: על ידי שינוי, דומיא דלפרנים. ונראה דהכא פירוש דוקא לאחר שבעה: **אע"ג** דאית ליה תרי ומטנפי. מדלא משני הכא במאי עסקינן בשלא כיבסו לפני הרגל, דלא שרינן מי שאין לו אלא חלוק אחד אלא היכא דכבסו לפני הרגל, אבל לא כבסו דפשע — לא שרי. משמע דמי שאין לו אלא חלוק אחד — שרי לכבסו במועד אפילו פשע ולא כבסו לפני המועד, כך נראה לי. ובתוספות מסופק בזה. ונראה לי דהכי משמע, מדלא מפליג. ונראה דגבי אבל לא שרינן כשאין לו אלא חלוק אחד, דהא אפילו אם היו לו מכובסין אסור ללבוש, מה שאין כן ברגל. נ"ע בכהן ששלמה משמרתו ברגל אם מותר לכבס לתנא דלעיל, (דף יז:) דתנא: כהן ואבל. אפילו לתנא דידן, אם חל שלישי להיות בעי"ט, שאסור ברחילה עד הערב. ופירש בקונטרס: עד הלילה בלונן, או עד חול המועד בחמין, ואינו מותר לרחוץ מבעי"ט. מיהו, כשחל שביעי שלו בערב הרגל דאסור לכבס ולרחוץ כל היום — מותר לכבס ברגל. וצ"ע: אם אמת הוא שמותר — מאי טעמא לא תני?

רבינו חננאל

א)פיסקא דנזיר והמצורע מטומאתו לטהרתו. אוקימנא כדתניא כל אלו שאמרו מותרים לגלח במועד. בשלא היה להן פנאי. אבל היה להן פנאי לגלח ולא גילחו אסורין והנזיר והמצורע אע"פ שהיה להן פנאי לגלח ולא גילחו מותרין שלא ישהו קרבנותיהם. תנא האבל והכהן מותרין לגלח במועד. אוקימנא באבל שחל שביעי שלו להיות בשבת ערב הרגל. תנא ברא סבר לה כאבא שאול דאמר מקצת היום ככולו. ויום שביעי עולה לו לכאן ולכאן. וכיון דשבת הואי אנוס הוא לפיכך מגלח במועד. ותנא דידן סבר לה כרבנן כו'. כהן נמי כגון דשלים ליה משמרתו ברגל כו'. ופשוטה היא: ת"ר תכפוהו אבליו זה אחר זה. פי' קודם שישלים ימי אבל זה מת לו מת אחר וכן עוד בתוך ימי אבל זה מת לו מת אחר הכביד שערו מיקל בתער ומכבס כסותו במים. ואמר רב חסדא נוטל שערו בתער ולא במספריים. מכבס במים לבדם ולא בנתר ולא בחול. זאת אומרת אבל אסור בתכבוסת: ת"ר כשם שאסור לגלח במועד כך אסור ליטול צפרנים. ור' יוסי מתיר ליטול צפרנים במועד ובאבל. ואסיקנא כשמואל דאמר הלכתא כדברי המיקל באבל. דאמר שמואל הלכתא כר' יוסי במועד ובאבל ל"ש צפרנים דיד ל"ש צפרנים דרגל. אמר רב ובגנוסטרא אסור. אמר רב שמן הוה קאימנא קמיה דר' יוחנן בבי מדרשא ושקלינהו לטופריה בשיניה וזרקינהו. ש"מ תלת. ש"מ מותר ליטול צפרנים במועד וש"מ מדשקלינהו בשיניה אין בהם משום מיאוס. וש"מ מדזרקינהו מותר לזורקן. והתניא ג' דברים נאמרו בצפרנים קוברן צדיק שורפן חסיד זורקן רשע. מ"ט שמא תעבור אשה עוברה עליהן ותפיל. ופרקינן אשה בי מדרשא לא שכיחא. וכי תימא זמנין דמכנשו ושדי להו לבראי כיון דאשתני אישתני. אמר רב יהודה אמר רב זוג בא לפני רבי ובקשו ממנו מהו ליטול צפרנים והתיר להם. ושמואל אמר גם עשיית שפה בקשו ממנו והתיר להם. ואסיקנא עשיית שפה מזוית לזוית. כלומר אם צריכה כולה תקון שרי. אבל מקצתה לא. ב) הנחה כל שהיא מעכבת. פי' אם עשה שפמו והניח מקצתו שאינו עשוי מותר ליטלו כי מעכבתו באכילתו. ג) וכיוצא בה אמר רב נחמן לדידי שפה כי הנחה מעכבת דמי לי. ואלו כולם שאמרו בתוך שלשים יום. אבל בשבעת ימי האבל אסור בכולן. שמואל נכנס לבקר פנחס אחיו בימי אבלו וראה צפרניו גדולים. אמר ליה אמאי [לא שקלית] להו. א"ל אילו בך היה מי הוית מזלזל כולי האי. הואי כשגגה שיוצא מלפני השליט. ואירע אבל לשמואל נכנס פנחס אחיו לבקרו שקלינהו לטופריה חבטינהו באפיה. א"ל לית לך ברית כרותה לשפתים שנאמר ואני והנער נלכה עד כה ונשתחוה ונשובה אליכם. ואסתייעא מלתא והדרי תרווייהו ואתו. פרעה שהיה בימי משה הוא אמה וזקנו אמה ופרמשתקו אמה וזרת לקיים הכתוב ושפל אנשים יקים עליה: **מתני'** ואלו מכבסין במועד הבא ממדינת הים כו'. א"ר אסי א"ר יוחנן מי שאין לו אלא חלוק אחד מותר לכבסו בחולו של מועד. איני והתנינן אלו מכבסין במועד הבא ממדינת הים כו' וחשיב להו כל מי שהתירו לו חכמים לכבס במועד. ולא תני מי שאין לו אלא חלוק אחד בהדייהו. ופרקינן [מתני'] אע"ג דאית ליה תרי ומטנפי] שרי לכבסינהו לכולהו. משמיה דר' יוחנן אמרו כלי פשתן מותר לכבסן במועד. והני מטפחות דתנינן במתני' דלאו

א) מכאן עד ואסיקנא כשמואל דאמר הלכתא כדברי המיקל שייך לעיל דף יז ע"ב. ב) פי' הגי' בה"ג ולפ"ז גי' רבינו יותר נכונה. ג) נ"ל דאסר בדברי רבינו כי' אמי אמר שפה נמי כל שמעכבת וכיוצא בה וכו'.

מסורת הש"ס

נ"א דשמואל

עירובין מו. לקמן יט: [כ. כג. כתובות מו. חולין נ.]

[כתובות כג. סב: ב"מ סח.]

[סנהדרין קב. ע"ש]

[שייך למתני' לעיל יז.]

[נ"ז שייך שם]

[בכה"ש ליתא]

[בילקוט וכע"י ליתא]

[לעיל ד]

[בע"י וגם בתוס' שבת עה. ד"ה אמגושי כו' מוכח דהוא משמי' דרב]

לעיל יד.

הגהות הב"ח

(א) גמ' אחוה דמר שמואל איתרע ליה מילתא: (ב) תוס' ד"ה ובגנוסטרי כו' וכה"ג פוסק תוך שבעה אסור: (ג) בא"ד או שמא ממעשה דשמואל משמע קצת מדשקלינהו לטופריה כו' אסור משמע דמעשה דשמואל לא היה:

הגהות הגר"א

[א] גמ' לזוית. נ"ב הנחה כל שמעכבת ר' אמי וכשפה המעכבת. כ"ה גירסת בה"ג ועי' רא"ש מש"כ. (ועמש"כ רבינו בא"ח סי' תקל"א):

גליון הש"ס

גמ' אשה עוברה ותפיל. עי' סנהדרין דף ק ע"א תוס' ד"ה ובגנוסטרי וכו' ולא כרב שישא בריה דרב אידי. לעיל דף יז ע"ב.

עין משפט נר מצוה

פח א ב מיי' פ"ה מהל' אבל הלכה ב סמג עשין דרבנן ג טוש"ע י"ד סי' שצ סעיף ז:

[וכעין גנסטר וגרסתו אמר רב ובגנוסטרי אסור וע"ש שהאריך]

פט ג מיי' פ"ז מהלכות יו"ט הלכה כ טור ש"ע א"ח סי' תקלא סעיף ח:

צ ד מיי' שם הלכה כה סמג לאוין סה טור ש"ע א"ח סי' תקלד סעיף ל:

צא ה מיי' וסמג שם טוש"ע שם סעיף ב:

[עי' פי' שכתבו תוס' נדה יז. ד"ה שורפן וכו' בשם הערוך]

הַסַּפָּרִים. הָנֵי — אִין, כְּלֵי פִּשְׁתָּן — לָא! אֲמַר לֵיהּ אַבַּיֵי: מתני' אֲפִילּוּ דִּשְׁאָר מִינֵי. אֲמַר בַּר הֶדְיָא: לְדִידִי חֲזֵי לִי יַמָּה שֶׁל טְבֶרְיָה, דְּמַפְּקִי לָהּ מְשִׁיכְלֵי דְּמָנֵי כִּיתָּנָא בְּחוּלָּא דְּמוֹעֲדָא. מַתְקִיף לָהּ אַבַּיֵי: *מַאן לֵימָא לָן דִּבִרְצוֹן חֲכָמִים עָבְדִי? דִּלְמָא שֶׁלֹּא בִּרְצוֹן חֲכָמִים עָבְדִי.§ **מתני'** [א]וְאֵלּוּ כּוֹתְבִין בַּמּוֹעֵד: קִדּוּשֵׁי נָשִׁים, וְגִיטִּין, וְשׁוֹבְרִין, דְּיַיתֵּיקִי, מַתָּנָה, וּפְרוֹזְבּוּלִין, אִיגְּרוֹת שׁוּם, וְאִיגְּרוֹת מָזוֹן, שִׁטְרֵי חֲלִיצָה, וּמֵיאוּנִים, וְשִׁטְרֵי בֵּירוּרִין, גְּזֵרוֹת בֵּית דִּין, וְאִיגְּרוֹת שֶׁל רְשׁוּת.§ **גמ'** אָמַר שְׁמוּאֵל: [ב]מוּתָּר לְאָרֵס אִשָּׁה בְּחוּלּוֹ שֶׁל מוֹעֵד, שֶׁמָּא יְקַדְּמֶנּוּ אַחֵר. לֵימָא מְסַיַּיע לֵיהּ: וְאֵלּוּ כּוֹתְבִין בַּמּוֹעֵד: קִדּוּשֵׁי נָשִׁים. מַאי לָאו שִׁטְרֵי קִדּוּשִׁין מַמָּשׁ? *לָא, שִׁטְרֵי פְּסִיקְתָּא, וּכְדְרַב גִּידֵּל אָמַר רַב. *דְּאָמַר רַב גִּידֵּל אָמַר רַב: [ג]"כַּמָּה אַתָּה נוֹתֵן לִבְנְךָ" — כָּךְ וְכָךְ, "כַּמָּה אַתָּה נוֹתֵן לְבִתְּךָ" — כָּךְ וְכָךְ. עָמְדוּ וְקִדְּשׁוּ — קָנוּ. הֵן הֵן הַדְּבָרִים הַנִּקְנִין בַּאֲמִירָה. לֵימָא מְסַיַּיע לֵיהּ: *אֵין נוֹשְׂאִין נָשִׁים בַּמּוֹעֵד, לֹא בְּתוּלוֹת וְלֹא אַלְמָנוֹת, וְלֹא מְיַבְּמִין, מִפְּנֵי שֶׁשִּׂמְחָה הִיא לוֹ. הָא לְאָרֵס — שָׁרֵי! לָא מִיבַּעְיָא קָאָמַר; לָא מִיבַּעְיָא לְאָרֵס — דְּלָא קָעָבֵיד מִצְוָה, אֶלָּא אֲפִילּוּ לִישָּׂא נַמִי, דְּקָא עָבֵיד מִצְוָה — אָסוּר. תָּא שְׁמַע, דְּתָנָא דְּבֵי שְׁמוּאֵל: מְאָרְסִין אֲבָל לֹא כּוֹנְסִין, [ד]וְאֵין עוֹשִׂין סְעוּדַּת אֵירוּסִין, וְלֹא מְיַבְּמִין, מִפְּנֵי שֶׁשִּׂמְחָה הִיא לוֹ. ש"מ. וּמִי אָמַר שְׁמוּאֵל שֶׁמָּא יְקַדְּמֶנּוּ אַחֵר? וְהָאָמַר רַב יְהוּדָה אָמַר שְׁמוּאֵל: *בְּכָל יוֹם וָיוֹם בַּת קוֹל יוֹצֵאת וְאוֹמֶרֶת: בַּת פְּלוֹנִי לִפְלוֹנִי, שְׂדֵה פְלוֹנִי לִפְלוֹנִי! אֶלָּא: שֶׁמָּא יְקַדְּמֶנּוּ אַחֵר בְּרַחֲמִים. כִּי הָא דְּרָבָא שַׁמְעֵיהּ לְהַהוּא גַּבְרָא דְּבָעֵי רַחֲמֵי וְאָמַר: תִּזְדַּמֵּן לִי פְּלָנִיתָא. א"ל: לָא תִּיבָּעֵי רַחֲמֵי הָכִי. אִי חַזְיָא לָךְ — לָא אָזְלָא מִינָּךְ, וְאִי לָא — כָּפַרְתְּ בַּה'. בָּתַר הָכִי שַׁמְעֵיהּ דְּקָאָמַר: אוֹ אִיהוּ לֵימוּת מִקַּמָּהּ אוֹ אִיהִי תָּמוּת מִקַּמֵּיהּ. א"ל: לָאו אָמֵינָא לָךְ לָא תִּיבָּעֵי עֲלַהּ דְּמִילְּתָא? הָכִי אָמַר רַב מִשּׁוּם רַבִּי רְאוּבֵן בֶּן אִצְטְרוֹבִילִי: מִן הַתּוֹרָה וּמִן הַנְּבִיאִים וּמִן הַכְּתוּבִים מֵה' אִשָּׁה לְאִישׁ. מִן הַתּוֹרָה — דִּכְתִיב: °"וַיַּעַן לָבָן וּבְתוּאֵל וַיֹּאמְרוּ מֵה' יָצָא הַדָּבָר", מִן הַנְּבִיאִים — דִּכְתִיב: °"וְאָבִיו וְאִמּוֹ לֹא יָדְעוּ כִּי מֵה' הִיא". מִן הַכְּתוּבִים — דִּכְתִיב: °"בַּיִת וָהוֹן נַחֲלַת אָבוֹת וּמֵה' אִשָּׁה מַשְׂכָּלֶת". וְאָמַר רַב מִשּׁוּם רַבִּי רְאוּבֵן בֶּן אִצְטְרוֹבִילִי, וְאָמְרִי לָהּ בְּמַתְנִיתָא תָּנָא, א"ר רְאוּבֵן בֶּן אִצְטְרוֹבִילִי: אֵין אָדָם נֶחְשָׁד בְּדָבָר אֶלָּא א"כ עֲשָׂאוֹ, וְאִם לֹא עָשָׂה כּוּלּוֹ — עָשָׂה מִקְצָתוֹ, וְאִם לֹא עָשָׂה מִקְצָתוֹ — הִרְהֵר בְּלִבּוֹ לַעֲשׂוֹתוֹ, וְאִם לֹא הִרְהֵר בְּלִבּוֹ לַעֲשׂוֹתוֹ — רָאָה אֲחֵרִים שֶׁעָשׂוּ, וְשָׂמַח. מְתִיב רַבִּי יַעֲקֹב: °"וַיְחַפְּאוּ בְנֵי יִשְׂרָאֵל דְּבָרִים אֲשֶׁר לֹא כֵן עַל ה' אֱלֹהֵיהֶם" — הָתָם לְהַכְעִיס הוּא דַּעֲבוּד. *תָּא שְׁמַע: °"וַיְקַנְאוּ לְמֹשֶׁה בַּמַּחֲנֶה לְאַהֲרֹן קְדוֹשׁ ה'", רַב שְׁמוּאֵל בַּר יִצְחָק אָמַר: מְלַמֵּד שֶׁכָּל אֶחָד קִינֵּא לְאִשְׁתּוֹ מִמֹּשֶׁה! הָתָם מִשּׁוּם שִׂנְאָה הוּא דַּעֲבוּד. ת"ש: אָמַר רַבִּי יוֹסֵי: *יְהֵא חֶלְקִי עִם מִי שֶׁחוֹשְׁדִין אוֹתוֹ בְּדָבָר וְאֵין בּוֹ. וְאָמַר רַב פַּפָּא: לְדִידִי חַשְׁדוּן וְלָא הֲוָה בִּי! לָא קַשְׁיָא; הָא — בְּקָלָא דְּפָסֵיק, הָא — בְּקָלָא דְּלָא פָּסֵיק. וְקָלָא דְּלָא פָּסֵיק עַד כַּמָּה? *אָמַר אַבַּיֵי: אָמְרָה לִי אֵם: *דּוּמֵי דְּמָתָא יוֹמָא וּפַלְגָא. וְהָנֵי מִילֵּי — דְּלָא פָּסַק בֵּינֵי בֵּינֵי, אֲבָל פָּסַק בֵּינֵי בֵּינֵי — לֵית לָן בָּהּ. וְכִי פָּסַק בֵּינֵי בֵּינֵי — לָא אֲמָרַן אֶלָּא דְּלָא פָּסַק מֵחֲמַת יִרְאָה, אֲבָל פָּסַק מֵחֲמַת יִרְאָה — לָא. [א]וְלָא אֲמָרַן אֶלָּא דְּלָא הָדַר נָבַט, אֲבָל הָדַר נָבַט — לָא. וְלָא אֲמָרַן אֶלָּא דְּלֵית לֵיהּ אוֹיְבִים, אֲבָל אִית לֵיהּ אוֹיְבִים — אוֹיְבִים הוּא דְּאַפְּקוּהָ לְקָלָא.§ **מתני'** *[ה]אֵין כּוֹתְבִין שִׁטְרֵי חוֹב בַּמּוֹעֵד. וְאִם אֵינוֹ מַאֲמִינוֹ, אוֹ שֶׁאֵין לוֹ מַה יֹּאכַל — הֲרֵי זֶה יִכְתּוֹב. [ו]אֵין כּוֹתְבִין סְפָרִים תְּפִילִּין וּמְזוּזוֹת בַּמּוֹעֵד, וְאֵין מַגִּיהִין אוֹת אַחַת אֲפִילּוּ בְּסֵפֶר עֶזְרָא. רַבִּי יְהוּדָה אוֹמֵר: [ז]כּוֹתֵב אָדָם תְּפִילִּין וּמְזוּזוֹת לְעַצְמוֹ, וְטוֹוֶה

רש"י

*כְּלֵי פִּשְׁתָּן. דְּלָא נָפֵישׁ טִירְחָא: מְטַפְּחוֹת הַסַּפָּרִים. שֶׁל פִּשְׁתָּן: הָנֵי אִין. אֲבָל שְׁאָר כְּלֵי פִּשְׁתָּן לָא: אֲפִילּוּ דִּשְׁאָר מִינֵי. כְּלוֹמַר, מְטַפְּחוֹת דִּשְׁאָר מִינִין, כְּגוֹן דְּצֶמֶר, אע"ג דִּנְפִישׁ טִירְחָא — שָׁרֵי לְכַבֵּס, אֲבָל שְׁאָר כֵּלִים דִּשְׁאָר מִינִין — לָא. אֲבָל כְּלֵי פִּשְׁתָּן שָׁרֵי לְכַבֵּס: מְשִׁיכְלֵי. סְפָלִים: **מתני'** קִדּוּשֵׁי נָשִׁים. שֶׁכָּתַב בִּשְׁטָר: הֲרֵי אַתְּ מְקוּדֶּשֶׁת לִי. דְּאִשָּׁה נִקְנֵית בִּשְׁטָר: דְּיַיתֵּיקִי. שְׁטָר לְצַוָּואָה: פְּרוֹזְבּוּלִין. שֶׁכּוֹתֵב מַלְוֶה בִּשְׁטָר שֶׁאֵינוֹ מְשַׁמֵּט, וְלָא מַשְׁמִיט לֵיהּ שְׁמִיטָּה: אִיגְּרוֹת שׁוּם. כָּךְ שָׁמוּ בֵּית דִּין שָׂדֶה זוֹ, וְנָתְנוּ לָאַחִים כָּךְ וְכָךְ נֶגְדּוֹ: אִיגְּרוֹת מָזוֹן. פְּלוֹנִי קִבֵּל לָזוּן בַּת אִשְׁתּוֹ: שִׁטְרֵי בֵּירוּרִים. בֵּירְרוּ ב"ד חֵלֶק זֶה לָזֶה וְחֵלֶק זֶה לָזֶה: גְּזֵרוֹת ב"ד. פִּסְקֵי דִּינִין: וְאִיגְּרוֹת שֶׁל רְשׁוּת. לִוּוּי וְקִיּוּס שֶׁל שִׁלְטוֹן: **גמ'** כִּדְרַב גִּידֵּל. שֶׁכּוֹתֵב תְּנָאֵי זֶה בִּשְׁטָר: נִיקְנִין בַּאֲמִירָה. בְּלָא קִנְיָן: דְּקָא עָבֵיד מִצְוָה. דְּעוֹסֵק בִּפְרִיָּה וּרְבִיָּה: כָּפַרְתְּ בַּה'. בְּאֱמוּנָה, דְּקָאָמַר דְּלָא מְסַיַּיע לְגוּתָא כְּלוּם, הוֹאִיל וְלָא מְזַמְּנָא(א) לֵיהּ. כְּלוֹמַר, הַשְׁתָּא נָלֵינָא עֲלַהּ וְלָא אַסְתַּיְּעָא מִילְּתָא: אָמַר. אִי לָא מִנְסְבָא — אוֹ אִיהִי תָּמוּת מִקַּמַּאי, דְּלָא אֶיחֱזֵי כַּד מִנְסְבָא לְאַחֵר וְאֶצְטַעֵר בָּהּ: אוֹ אִיהוּ. עַצְמוֹ יָמוּת מִקַּמֵּי דְּתִינְסְבָא אִיהִי לְאִידָךְ. וּלְהָכִי מְאָרֵס בַּמּוֹעֵד, שֶׁלֹּא יְקַדְּמֶנּוּ אַחֵר בְּרַחֲמִים שֶׁתָּמוּת הִיא: נֶחְשָׁד בְּדָבָר. עֲבֵירָה: לְהַכְעִיס עֲבוּד. וְיָדְעִי דְּלָא הָיָה: בְּקָלָא דְּפָסֵיק. לֹא הָיָה בֵּיהּ: קָלָא דְּלָא פָּסֵיק. הָיָה בֵּיהּ: דּוּמֵי. חֲשָׁד. כְּמוֹ: לֹא יִשָּׂא בַּת דּוּמָה (סוטה דף כז.): אֲבָל הָדַר נָבַט. דְּבָתַר דְּפָסֵיק הִתְחִיל קָלָא. נָבַט = נִשְׁמַע. דִּמְיוֹן כְּמוֹ בְּמַסֶּכֶת תַּעֲנִית (דף ז.): הַאי צוּרְבָּא מֵרַבָּנָן דָּמֵי לְפַרְצִידָא דְּתוּתֵי קָלָא, כֵּיוָן דְּנָבַט נָבַט. וּפֵי' זֶה וָזֶה — לְשׁוֹן צֶמַח: **מתני'** וְאִם אֵינוֹ מַאֲמִינוֹ. הַמַּלְוֶה לַלֹּוֶה: אוֹ שֶׁאֵין לוֹ מַה יֹּאכַל. לַסּוֹפֵר: אֲפִילּוּ בְּסֵפֶר עֶזְרָא. ס"ת שֶׁל עֲזָרָה. וַאֲנִי שָׁמַעְתִּי עֲזָרָה בְּה', וּפֵי': סֵפֶר מוּגָּה הָיָה בָּעֲזָרָה, שֶׁמִּמֶּנּוּ הָיוּ מַגִּיהִים כָּל סִפְרֵי גוֹלָה: לְעַצְמוֹ. לְקַיֵּים זֶה הַמִּצְוָה. אֲבָל לִגְבּוֹר, לִמְכּוֹר, דְּדֶרֶךְ שְׂכִירוּת הֲוָה — חֲשִׁיב מְלָאכָה, כְּדְאָמְרִינַן לְעֵיל (דף יב.). *אוֹנַכְלָה, דְּכֵיוָן דְּלָאו אַגְרָא קָשְׁקֵיל — שְׁרַשׁוּיֵי בְּעָלְמָא הוּא, וְשָׁרֵי: וְטוֹוֶה

תוספות

*הַסַּפָּרִים. פירוש להסתפר, ובמסתפר לכל אותם שהתירו חכמים. וי"ג: הַסְּפָרִים, ומטפחת *הספגנין, ובירושלמי קאמר עלה: מטפחת הספרים [אין] מכבסין אותן במי רגלים *מפני הכבוד. ואין נראה לי להביא ראיה דאיירי בכתבי הקדש, דאפילו דאיירי באומן המספר — שייך כבוד המסתפרים, שנותנין אותן בפניהם, וכשמסתפרין אין כבוד להם במטונפין:

*הָעוֹלִים מטומאה לטהרה. במצורע איירי, דהא מצורע אסור לכבס, כדאמר לעיל (דף טו.). ומסופק אם נאמר כן בעולה מטומאת מת ונבילה שצריך לכבס בגדיו, או אמרינן דוקא מצורע, הואיל ואסור לכבס כל בגדיו שלו. מיהו, מה שפירש דבמצורע איירי — קשיא לן: אי אמרינן דמצורע אינו נוהג צרעתו ברגל — א"כ מאי איריא עולים מטומאה לטהרה? אפילו בימי צרעתו נמי מותר לכבס ברגל! דלא מצי למימר לא מיבעיא קאמר, כדלעיל (דף יד:) — דאם כן לא שייך שמא ישהו קרבנותיהן. דבשלמא גילוח הוא בשעת קרבן, אבל כיבוס לא שייך לקרבן! ויש לומר: דכיבוס נמי שייך לקרבן:

מַתְקִיף לה אביי מאן לימא לן. ואע"ג דאביי גופיה שני לעיל מתני' אליבא דרבי יוחנן — אינו סובר כן: וְאֵלּוּ כותבין במועד. נראה דכל הני הוו דבר האבד, פן ימות הנותן או העדים או ב"ד, או ילכו למדינת הים:

וְאִיגְּרוֹת רשות. בירושלמי מפרש: פריסת שלום. ויש מפרשים: ליווי השלטון, כמו: אל תתודע לרשות (אבות פ"א מ"י):

אֵין כותבין שטרי חוב. פירשו בתוספות: הוא הדין שטר מכירה, דהא בהדי אלו כותבין במועד לא חשיב שטר מכירה. ולי נראה: דהא דלא קתני — משום דאין כותבין שטר מכירה אלא על הקרקע, ואמרינן לעיל (דף יג.): אין *מוכרין בתים אלא לצורך המועד. ולצורך המועד פשיטא דשרי. והוא הדין אם מכר קודם המועד ועתה רוצה לכתוב — דשרי במועד, דהא נמי דבר האבד. רק אם היה לו אונס ולא יכול לכתוב קודם המועד:א) הֵן הן דברים הנקנין באמירה. גפ' "הנושא" (כתובות דף קב:) מפורש: *וּמִי אמר שמואל שמא יקדמנו אחר. תימה לי: אמאי לא משני: הא — בזוג שני, הא בזוג ראשון, כדמשני פרק שני דסנהדרין (דף כב.) ובפרק קמא דסוטה (דף ב. ושם):

וטווה

(ל"ל מוקמי) (ג"ז שייך לעיל)

רבינו חננאל

כלי פשתן אלא צמר ושל שאר מינין זולתי. אמר בר הדיא אנא חזיתי ים טבריא דמפקי לה משיכלי ומכבסי בהו מאני דכיתנא בחולי דמועדא. א"ל אביי ומאן לימא לן דברצון חכמים עבוד דלמא שלא ברצון חכמים עביד: **ירושלמי** תני מטפחות ספרים אין מכבסין אותן במי רגלים מפני הכבוד אלא מכבסין אותן בנתר ובורית: **מתני'** אלו כותבין [במועד] קדושי נשים גיטין ושוברין דיתיקאות מתנות פרוזבולין איגרות שום איגרות מזון שטרי חליצה ומיאונין שטרי ברורין וזירות ב"ד איגרות רשות: **ירושל'** (שטרי חוב) [ושוברין] אומי לוגיאום. ואיגרות של רשות. איגרות שאילת שלום. איגרות שום. שום היתומים. איגרות מזון מזונות אלמנה של (רשות כו') עד גזירות ב"ד. אלו גזרי דינין (ואיגרות של רשות זו שאילת שלום) קידושי נשים. אוקימנא שטרי פסיקתא. כמה אתה נותן לבנך. כמה אתה נותן לבתך כך וכך ועמדו וקדשו הן הן הדברים הנקנין באמירה: **ירושלמי** איגרות של רשות זו שאילת שלום. אמר שמואל מותר ליארס בחולו של מועד שמא יקדמנו אחר. איני והא איהו דאמר מ' יום קודם יצירת הולד בכל יום ב"ק יוצאת ומכרזת בת פלוני לפלוני כו'. ופרקינן שמא יקדמנו אחר בתפלה. תנא דבי מנשה מארסין במועד ואין כונסין ואין עושין סעודת אירוסין ולא מייבמין מפני ששמחה היא לו. אבל מחזיר גרושתו. אמר רב מן התורה ומן הנביאים ומן הכתובים מה' אשה לאיש. מן התורה שנאמר מה' יצא הדבר. מן הנביאים שנאמר ואביו [ואמו] לא ידעו כי מה' היה הדבר. מן הכתובים דכתיב בית והון נחלת אבות ומה' אשה משכלת. ואמר רב אין אדם נחשד בדבר אלא אם כן עשאו או כולו או מקצתו או הרהר בלבו לעשותו או ראה אחרים שעשאוהו וייטב בעיניו. איני והכתיב ויחפאו בני ישראל דברים אשר לא כן על ה' אלהיהם. ופרקינן התם להכעיס הוא דעבוד. והכתיב וישמע משה ויפול על פניו. ואמר ר' יוחנן שחשדוהו באשת איש. וכתיב ויקנאו למשה במחנה מלמד שכל אחד ואחד קינא על אשתו. ופרקינן התם משום שנאה עשו כך. ת"ש דא"ר יוסי יהא חלקי עם מי שחושדין אותו בדבר ואין בו. ואמר רב פפא לדידי חשדו לי ולא הוה בי ואסיקנא בקלא דלא פסיק ובאתרא דלית ליה אויבים. אבל היכא דאית ליה אויבים מעיקרא לאו מלתא היא דאויבים הוא דאפקוה לקלא: **מתני'** אין כותבין שטרי חוב במועד אם אינו מאמינו או שאין לו מה יאכל. שאין לו *) הרי זה יכתוב. אין כותבין סתו"מ. ואין מגיהין אות אחת ואפילו בספר העזרה כו'.

*) אולי צ"ל שאין לו משות לקטת.

ת"ר

א) שייך לעיל קודם ד"ה אין כותבין.

עין משפט נר מצוה

[שייך לעיל יז. במשנה] עיין מהרש"א [ע"ש הלכה כ]

צב א מיי' פ"ז מהלכות י"ט הלכה יב סמג לאוין עה טוש"ע א"ח סי' תקמה סעיף ה:

שייך לדף יז. במתני'

צג ב מיי' פ"ז מהלכות י"ט הלכה עז סמג לאוין עה טוש"ע א"ח סי' תקמו סעיף א:

צד ג מיי' פכ"ג מהל' אישות הלכה יג ופ"ז מהל' זכייה ומתנה הלכה יז סמג עשין מח טוש"ע אה"ע סי' נח:

צה ד מיי' פ"ז מהלכות י"ט הלכה עז טור ש"ע א"ח סי' תקמו סעיף ה:

צו ה מיי' פ"ז מהלכות י"ט הלכה יב סמג לאוין עה טוש"ע א"ח סי' תקמה סעיף ה:

צז ו ז מיי' שם הלכה יג טוש"ע שם סעיף א ב:

מסורת הש"ס

שייך לע"ח | [גיטין מה.] | כתובות קב. | ג"ז שם קדושין ט: | לעיל ח: | סנהדרין כב. ע"ש סוטה ב. ע"ש | [אבוגדי כל"ל] | בראשית כד | שופטים יד | משלי יט | מלכים ב יז | סנהדרין קי. תהלים קו | שבת קיח: | [קידושין לה: וש"נ] | יבמות כה. | [לעיל יג.]

הגהות הב"ח

(א) רש"י ד"ה כפרת כו' הואיל ולא מזמנה לך כלומר:

גליון הש"ס

גמ' מאן לימא לן דברצון חכמים. עיין תשובת מהרי"ט ח"א סי' פג:

הגהות מהר"ב רנשבורג

א] גמ' ולא אמרן אלא דלא הדר נבט. כלומר דלא יצא עכ"ל הערוך בערך נבט ועי' בפרש"י דמפרש מלשון צמח. ואיך שיהיה הפי' דלא הדר שוב ונשמע כדפרש"י מעיקרא נבט נשמע וכו' ולפענ"ד דברי הש"ס אלו קא מהדרי אדלעיל דקא מסיינין ל"ק הא בקלא דפסיק וכו' וקא מפרש הש"ס בתחילה עד כמה הוי קלא דלא פסיק וכל דיני ותלוקי קלא דלא פסיק והשתא קא מהדר תו ק לא אמרן אלא דלא הדר נבט כו' ודוק היטב. דלפ"ז הוי ג' חלוקים בדבר דבקלא דלא פסיק יומא ופלגא אית בי' ודאי משכא. וקלא דפסיק לגמרי דלא הדר נביט לית בי' שום ממש. וקלא דפסיק דהדר נבט אף דלא הוי מיומא ופלגא נהי דלא הוי בי' גמור הוא דאית בי' ממש עכ"פ איכא לספוקי ביה ולא נפיק מתורת חשדא. אולי אית בי'. כנלענ"ד ברור ודוק היטב. וראיי' גמורה מצאתי לפירושי הזה. דביבמות דף כ"ה ע"א ליתא להך ולא אמרן בתרא יעוש"ה ולדברינו מיושב משום דלענין להוציא אשה מבעלה מיירי ואספיקא לא מפקינן והדר נבט רק ספיקא הוי ודו"ק היטב כי נכון הוא:

וְטוֹוֶה עַל יְרֵיכוֹ תְּכֵלֶת לְצִיצִיתוֹ.§ **גמ'** ת"ר: כּוֹתֵב אָדָם תְּפִילִּין וּמְזוּזוֹת לְעַצְמוֹ, וְטוֹוֶה עַל יְרֵיכוֹ תְּכֵלֶת לְצִיצִיתוֹ, וְלַאֲחֵרִים בְּטוֹבָה, דִּבְרֵי רַבִּי מֵאִיר. ר' יְהוּדָה אוֹמֵר מַעֲרִים וּמוֹכֵר אֶת שֶׁלּוֹ, וְחוֹזֵר וְכוֹתֵב לְעַצְמוֹ. ר' יוֹסֵי אוֹמֵר: כּוֹתֵב וּמוֹכֵר כְּדַרְכּוֹ כְּדֵי פַּרְנָסָתוֹ. אוֹרֵי לֵיהּ רַב לְרַב חֲנַנְאֵל, וְאָמְרִי לָהּ רַבָּה בַּר בַּר חָנָה לְרַב חֲנַנְאֵל: הֲלָכָה, כּוֹתֵב וּמוֹכֵר כְּדַרְכּוֹ כְּדֵי פַּרְנָסָתוֹ.§ "וְטוֹוֶה עַל יְרֵיכוֹ תְּכֵלֶת".§ ת"ר: טוֹוֶה אָדָם עַל יְרֵיכוֹ תְּכֵלֶת לְצִיצִיתוֹ, אֲבָל לֹא בְּאֶבֶן, דִּבְרֵי ר' אֱלִיעֶזֶר. וַחֲכָמִים אוֹמְרִים: אַף בְּאֶבֶן. ר' יְהוּדָה אוֹמֵר מִשְּׁמוֹ: בְּאֶבֶן, אֲבָל לֹא בְּפֶלֶךְ. וַחֲכָמִים אוֹמְרִים: בֵּין בְּאֶבֶן בֵּין בְּפֶלֶךְ. אָמַר רַב יְהוּדָה אָמַר שְׁמוּאֵל, וְכֵן א"ר חִיָּיא בַּר אַבָּא א"ר יוֹחָנָן: הֲלָכָה, בֵּין בְּאֶבֶן בֵּין בְּפֶלֶךְ. וַהֲלָכָה: כּוֹתֵב כְּדַרְכּוֹ וּמוֹכֵר כְּדֵי פַּרְנָסָתוֹ.§ **מתני'** *הַקּוֹבֵר אֶת מֵתוֹ שְׁלֹשָׁה יָמִים קוֹדֶם לָרֶגֶל – בָּטְלָה הֵימֶנּוּ גְּזֵרַת שִׁבְעָה, שְׁמוֹנָה – בָּטְלוּ הֵימֶנּוּ גְּזֵרַת שְׁלֹשִׁים. מִפְּנֵי שֶׁאָמְרוּ: שַׁבָּת עוֹלָה וְאֵינָהּ מַפְסֶקֶת, רְגָלִים – מַפְסִיקִין וְאֵינָן עוֹלִין, ר' אֱלִיעֶזֶר אוֹמֵר: מִשֶּׁחָרַב בֵּית הַמִּקְדָּשׁ *עֲצֶרֶת כְּשַׁבָּת. רַבָּן גַּמְלִיאֵל אוֹמֵר: רֹאשׁ הַשָּׁנָה וְיוֹם הַכִּפּוּרִים כִּרְגָלִים. וַחֲכָמִים אוֹמְרִים: *לֹא כְּדִבְרֵי זֶה וְלֹא כְּדִבְרֵי זֶה, אֶלָּא: עֲצֶרֶת – כִּרְגָלִים, רֹאשׁ הַשָּׁנָה וְיוה"כ – כְּשַׁבָּת.§ **גמ'** אָמַר רַב: גְּזֵרַת – בָּטְלוּ, יָמִים – לֹא בָּטְלוּ. וְכֵן א"ר הוּנָא: גְּזֵרַת – בָּטְלוּ, יָמִים – לֹא בָּטְלוּ. וְרַב שֵׁשֶׁת אָמַר: אֲפִילּוּ יָמִים נַמִּי בָּטְלוּ. מ"ט יָמִים לֹא בָּטְלוּ? שֶׁאִם לֹא גִּילַּח עֶרֶב הָרֶגֶל – אָסוּר לְגַלֵּחַ אַחַר הָרֶגֶל.

וְהָתַנְיָא

רש"י

וְטוֹוֶה עַל יְרֵיכוֹ. הַחוּטִין, אֲבָל לֹא בְּיָדוֹ בֵּין אֶצְבְּעוֹתָיו, וּבְפֶלֶךְ, כְּדֶרֶךְ חוֹל: **גמ'** לַאֲחֵרִים בְּטוֹבָה. וְלֹא בְּשָׂכָר: מַעֲרִים וּמוֹכֵר שֶׁלּוֹ. כֵּן עוֹשֶׂה כָּל יְמוֹת הֶחָג: כְּדֵי פַּרְנָסָתוֹ. בְּהַרְוָוחָה. וְלָא מַיְירֵי בְּמִי שֶׁאֵין לוֹ מַה יֹּאכַל: אֲבָל לֹא בְּאֶבֶן. שֶׁתּוֹלֶה בְּחוּט, כְּדֵי שֶׁיּוּכַל לְשׁוֹזְרוֹ יָפֶה: **מתני'** הַקּוֹבֵר מֵתוֹ שְׁלֹשָׁה יָמִים קוֹדֶם הָרֶגֶל. הוֹאִיל וְעִיקַּר אֲבֵילוּת אֵינוֹ אֶלָּא שְׁלֹשָׁה יָמִים: בָּטְלָה מִמֶּנּוּ גְּזֵרַת שִׁבְעָה. דִּלְאַחַר הָרֶגֶל אֵינוֹ צָרִיךְ לִמְנוֹת יוֹתֵר: שְׁמוֹנָה יָמִים. קוֹדֶם הָרֶגֶל – בָּטְלָה מִמֶּנּוּ גְּזֵרַת שְׁלֹשִׁים. דְּהוֹאִיל וְהִתְחִיל יוֹם אֶחָד מִן הַשְּׁלֹשִׁים – אֵינוֹ צָרִיךְ לִשְׁמוֹר כְּלוּם לְאַחַר הָרֶגֶל דִּין שְׁלֹשִׁים, אֶלָּא מוּתָּר לַאֲלְתַּר בְּתִכְבּוֹסֶת, בְּגִיהוּץ וְתִסְפּוֹרֶת: שַׁבָּת עוֹלָה. אֵירַע שַׁבָּת בִּימֵי אֶבְלוֹ – עוֹלָה לְמִנְיַן שִׁבְעָה: וְאֵינָהּ מַפְסֶקֶת. דִּלְאַחַר שַׁבָּת צָרִיךְ לְהַשְׁלִים שִׁבְעָה יְמֵי אֲבֵלוּת, עִם הַשַּׁבָּת: וְהָרְגָלִים מַפְסִיקִין. דְּכִי קָבַר מֵתוֹ שְׁלֹשָׁה יָמִים קוֹדֶם הָרֶגֶל – מַפְסִיק הָאֲבֵילוּת לְגַמְרֵי, וּלְאַחַר הָרֶגֶל אֵין מַשְׁלִים כְּלוּם: וְאֵין עוֹלִין. דְּכִי קָבַר מֵתוֹ בְּתוֹךְ הָרֶגֶל, דְּלֹא בָּטְלָה מִמֶּנּוּ גְּזֵרַת ז' – אֵין יְמֵי הָרֶגֶל עוֹלִין לְמִנְיַן ז' יְמֵי אֲבֵילוּת, אֶלָּא לְאַחַר הָרֶגֶל צָרִיךְ לֵישֵׁב ז' יְמֵי אֲבֵילוּת – זוֹ הִיא סְבָרָתִי. אֲבָל בְּהֶעְתֵּק מָצָאתִי: וְאֵין עוֹלִין – דְּכִי קָבַר אֶת מֵתוֹ שְׁנֵי יָמִים לִפְנֵי הָרֶגֶל דְּלֹא בָּטְלָה מִמֶּנּוּ גְּזֵרַת שִׁבְעָה – אֵין יְמֵי הָרֶגֶל עוֹלִין לְמִנְיַן שִׁבְעַת יְמֵי אֶבְלוֹ, אֶלָּא לְאַחַר הָרֶגֶל צָרִיךְ לֵישֵׁב ה' יְמֵי אֲבֵלוּת לְהַשְׁלִים לִשְׁנֵי יָמִים שֶׁנָּהַג לִפְנֵי הָרֶגֶל. (א) וַאֲנִי אוֹמֵר כִּי טָעוּת סוֹפֵר הוּא, דְּמַה שֶּׁנִּזְכַּר שְׁלֹשָׁה יָמִים לִפְנֵי הָרֶגֶל – לָאו דַּוְקָא, וַאֲפִילּוּ שָׁעָה אַחַת לִפְנֵי הָרֶגֶל – בָּטְלָה מִמֶּנּוּ גְּזֵרַת שִׁבְעָה, דְּהָרֶגֶל מַפְסִיק: מִשֶּׁחָרַב בֵּית הַמִּקְדָּשׁ. שֶׁאֵין לַעֲצֶרֶת תַּשְׁלוּמִין כָּל ז', וְאֵינוֹ אֶלָּא יוֹם אֶחָד: כְּשַׁבָּת. וְדִינוֹ כַּשַּׁבָּת, דְּעוֹלָה וְאֵינָהּ מַפְסֶקֶת: רֹאשׁ הַשָּׁנָה כְּשַׁבָּת. הוֹאִיל וְאֵינוֹ אֶלָּא יוֹם אֶחָד: **גמ'** גְּזֵרַת. שְׁלֹשִׁים בָּטְלוּ, אֲבָל יָמִים לֹא בָּטְלוּ. שְׁלֹשִׁים יוֹם לֹא בָּטְלוּ, דַּעֲדַיִין תְּלוּיִין וְעוֹמְדִים: מַאי טַעְמָא יָמִים לֹא בָּטְלוּ. כְּלוֹמַר: בְּאֵיזֶה עִנְיָן לֹא בָּטְלוּ יָמִים? שֶׁאִם לֹא גִּילַּח עֶרֶב הָרֶגֶל. דְּכִי בָּטְלוּ גְּזֵרַת שְׁלֹשִׁים, וְאִיבָּעֵי לֵיהּ לְגַלּוֹחֵי עֶרֶב הָרֶגֶל וְלֹא גִּילַּח: אָסוּר לְגַלֵּחַ אַחַר הָרֶגֶל. כָּל שְׁלֹשִׁים יוֹם:

וְהָתַנְיָא

תוספות

וטווה על ירכו תכלת לציציתו. פירוש: ע"י שינוי. אבל בתפילין אי אפשר בשינוי, שצריך כתיבה תמה. ובעשיית תפילין וציצית לא איירי במתני'. ושמא אין איסור כי אם בכתיבה וטוייה. ומה שנהגו לכתוב בעוגל – לא מצינו היתר. (ב) וכן פירש בתוספות הרב בשם רבו. ואפילו על ידי הדחק, על יהודי אחד שתפוש היה – התירו בדוחק. גם על ידי היפוך, שהוא נקרא מלך אחר, לא היו מתירין. וגם אי לא אסור משום מלאכה – הא אסרינן ⊕אפילו טירחא דלאו מלאכה בפרק קמא (דף ד.). מיהו נהגו לומר דמתני' לא איירי על ידי היפוך. ויש כותבין על ידי חילוק האות, וכן היה עושה רבי זקני. והיו"ד שאי אפשר – היה כותב בכתב הפוך: **רבי** יהודה **אומר** מערים. לכאורה מחמיר יותר מרבי מאיר שהתיר לאחרים. ובתוספות פירשו דרבי מאיר אינו מתיר אלא בהערמה, ולא הבנתי: **רבי** יוסי **אומר** כותב ומוכר כדי פרנסתו. דשרי לגמרי לאחרים בשכר, ודוקא כדי פרנסתו. ולכאורה מיקל מכולהו, וכן פ' הר"א. עוד פי': דכולהו הוי שרי כדי פרנסתו דאין לו מה יאכל. ולא איירי אלא כשיש לו מה יאכל, ומחמיר רבי יוסי יותר מכולהו. ולישנא לא משמע הכי, דהוה ליה למימר: אינו כותב אלא כדי פרנסתו. מיהו, במילתא דרבי יהודה קשה נמי קצת: דהוה ליה למימר אינו כותב אלא כדי פרנסתו על ידי אחרים, או על ידי הערמה. והשתא מתני' אתיא כרבי מאיר. ויש מפרשים: דכדי פרנסתו נמי לא משמע דאין לו מה יאכל *שרי, דהואיל דצורך מלוה – מותר להשתכר בה, דבחנם לא ירצה לעשות כן. ומתניתין פירש בתוספות הרב דפליגא אכולהו, ותנא אחר הוא. וה"ר יונה פירש: דאתיא כתנא קמא, והכי פירושו: אין כותבין ספרים תפילין ומזוזות כדי למוכרם או כדי להניחם. ועוד פי': דאתיא כרבי יוסי, לפי מה שפירש שרבי יוסי מחמיר. ואין ראיה מכאן שמותר להניח תפילין, דדלמא רבי מאיר ורבי יהודה לטעמייהו, דסבירא להו פרק "המוצא תפילין" (עירובין דף צו: ושם) שבת זמן תפילין. [ורבה בר בר חנה נמי הכי מלי סברי. ואע"ג דכולהו אמוראי דפרק "הקומץ רבה" (מנחות דף לו: ושם) משמע דאית להו שבת לאו זמן תפילין הוא. אבל ר' יצחק בן אברהם היה מביא מן הירושלמי להתיר להניח, דאמר בירושלמי: חד בר נש אובד תפילוי בחולא דמועדא, אתא לקמיה דרב חננאל. פי': שיכתוב לו, לפי שהיה סופר, כדאיתא במגילה (דף יח:). שלחיה לקמיה דרבה בר בר חנה, אמר ליה: זיל הב ליה תפילך, ואת כתב לך. דתנן: כותב אדם תפילין לעצמו. אתא לקמיה דרב, אמר ליה: כתוב ליה. פירוש: בלא הערמה. מתני' פליגא על רב: כותב אדם תפילין ומזוזה לעצמו, הא לאחר – לא. רב פתר לה בכותב להניח. פירוש: רב מעמיד המשנה להניחם אחר המועד, אבל להניחם במועד – שרי. ובהלכות גדולות פסק דאסור להניח תפילין בחולו של מועד. ולטעם שממעט שבתות וימים טובים מ"ימים ימימה" – מסתבר שפיר דממעט חולו של מועד. ולמאן דדריש (מנחות דף לו:) מ"לְךָ לאות" יצאו שבתות וימים טובים שהן בעצמן אות – יש לומר לפי שאין עושין מלאכה כי אם בדבר האבד. אבל קשיא למאי דפרישית לעיל (דף ג. ד"ה מסקין) דמלאכה דחול המועד מדרבנן, היכי ממעט להו? יש לומר: הואיל ואוכל מצה ויושב בסוכה – אין צריך אות. ואם הוא אמת דבחול המועד חייב בתפילין – יש לומר: הואיל ועושין מלאכה בו – אין אות, ו"מימים ימימה" נמי לא ממעט אלא יום טוב, דחלוק משאר ימים: **הקובר** את מתו. להכי נקט קובר, דאבילות מתחלת משעת סתימת הגולל, כדאמרינן לקמן (דף כז.): **שלשה** ימים. כך הוא עיקר אבילות לכמה מילי. ואמרינן לקמן (שם:): שלשה ימים לבכי: **מאי** טעמא לא בטלו. הכא הוה ניחא טפי לגרוס ימים לענין מאי לא בטלו, ואין צריך להגיה, דהיא היא: **שאם** לא גילח ערב הרגל כו'. ונראה לי דה"ה לא כיבס ולא רחץ ערב הרגל, אם מותר לרחוץ ולכבס מבערב יו"ט, ולא כיבס ולא רחץ – לא יכבס ברגל. והשתא ניחא הא דקתני: גזרת שבעה בטלו, הא ימים לא בטלו. ומיהו, קשיא לן: דקאמר בסמוך שכשם שמצות שלשה מבטלת גזרת שבעה, אפילו לתנא קמא – דמבטלת אפילו ימים, שמביא אבא שאול ראיה למצות שלשים שבטלו לגמרי, אפילו ימים. והרי"ן פי': דדוקא לא גילח, אבל לא כיבס – לא, דמותר לכבס אפילו לא כיבס, שהוא צורך גדול יותר. ואין נראה לי טעמו, דאם הוא צורך גדול – כ"ש שיש לנו לקנסו בשלא עשה קודם הרגל ונכנס ברגל. ולפירוש הקונטרס, דמפרש לקמן שאם חל שלישי להיות ערב הרגל שאסור ברחילה עד הערב – והו עד שחשכה. אם כן לא שייך לקנסו במה שלא רחץ ולא כבס. וא"כ, ימים לענין מאי לא בטלו גבי שבעה? מיהו, יש לומר: דאם לא רחץ ברגל – אסור לרחוץ אחר הרגל. ועוד יש לומר: אגב דנקט סיפא גזרת נקט ברישא גזרת. ועוד נראה לי: דרישא ה"פ: שלשה ימים בטלה גזרת שבעה, הא שני ימים – לא בטלה גזרת. מ"מ, פי' אמת, מדקאמר בסמוך: שכשם שגזרת שלשה מבטלת גזרת ז' כו', משמע שזה פשוט אפילו לת"ק. והשתא תימה לי: דכי משני שאם לא גילח בו, תינח סיפא אבל ברישא, דקאמר בטלה הימנו גזרת ז' – אמאי נקט גזרת ולענין מאי קאמר ימים לא בטלו? וי"ל: דאגב דנקט סיפא גזרת – תנא נמי רישא גזירת. ועוד נראה לי, דרישא ה"פ: שלשה ימים בטלה גזרת ז', הא שני ימים – בטלו גזרת, הא ימים – לא בטלו, לענין דנוהג דברים שבצינעא:

והתניא

עין משפט נר מצוה

צח א ב מיי' פ"ז מהלכות י"ט הלכה יג טוש"ע א"ח סי' תקמה סעיף ג:

צט ג מיי' פ"י מהל' אבל הלכה ח סמג עשין ב טוש"ע י"ד סי' תא סעיף א:

ק ד מיי' שם הלכה ג טוש"ע שם סי' שצט סעיף ב:

קא ה מיי' שם טור ש"ע שם סעיף ו:

קב ו מיי' שם טוש"ע שם סעיף ח:

אלא כדי פרנסתו היינו בהרווחה שרי וכו' כן הוא גירסת מהרש"א

רבינו חננאל

ת"ר כותבין תפילין ומזוזות לעצמן ולאחרים בטובה דברי ר' מאיר ר' יהודה אומר מערים ומוכר וחוזר וכותב לעצמו ר' יוסי אומר כותב ומוכר כדרכו כדי פרנסתו. אורי ליה רב לרב חננאל הלכה כותב ומוכר כדרכו כדי פרנסתו: וטווה אדם על יריכו תכלת לציציתו אסיקנא אמר רב יהודה אמר שמואל וכן א"ר חייא בר אבא א"ר יוחנן טווה אדם בין באבן בין בפלך. והלכה כותב ומוכר כדי פרנסתו: **מתני'** הקובר את מתו ג' ימים קודם לרגל בטלה הימנו גזירת שבעה. קברו קודם לרגל שמונה ימים בטלה הימנו גזירת שלשים מפני שאמרו שבת עולה ואינה מפסקת. רגלים מפסיקין ואינן עולין כו'. אמר רב גזרת בטלו ימים לא בטלו. פי' גזרת בטלו נדחו גזירת האבילות גבי הרגל שיש לו לגלח ותולתי זה מגזירת האבילות. ואם לא גילח ערב הרגל אסור לו לגלח אחר הרגל. כי ימים לא בטלו

מסורת הש"ס

נזיר טו.

[ע' תוס' לקמן כד. ד"ה עולת]

תוספ' ע"ז לקמן כד.

הגהות הב"ח

(א) רש"י ד"ה ואין עולין כו' (ואני אומר כי טעות סופר הוא וכו' הרגל מפסיק) תא"מ ונ"ב הדבר פשוט שהיה תלמיד טועה כתבו בגליון דהא מוכח לקמן דף כ לתנא דידן (דוקא שלשה ימים): (ב) תוס' ד"ה וטווה כו' לא מצינו היתר בזה וכן פירש כו' ואפילו ע"י הדחק אסור על יהודי אחד:

גליון הש"ס

רש"י ד"ה שמונה ימים וכו' מותר לאלתר בתכבוסת. עי' יבמות דף מג ע"א ברש"י ד"ה מקום שנהגו ועיין לקמן דף כג ע"א תוס' ד"ה כל שלשים: ד"ה ואין עולין וכו' ג"י לאו דוקא. קשה לי הא בהדיא מבואר לקמן דף כ ע"א דלתנא דמתני' דהכא ג"י דוקא כדאמרינן שם הלכה כתנא דידן דאמר שלשה וכו': תוס' ד"ה וטווה וכו' אפי' טירחא דלאו מלאכה. עי' לעיל דף יב ע"ב תוס' ד"ה מכניסים:

קג א ב ג מיי' פ"ו מהלכות אבל הלכה ה ו ז טוש"ע י"ד סי' שצט סעיף א:
קד ד מיי' שם ה"ט סמג עשין דרבנן ב טור ש"ע שם סי' שצט סעיף ה:
קה ה מיי' פ"ג מהל' נזירות הלכה יג סמג לאוין רכ:
קו ו מיי' פ"ו מהלכות אבל הלכה ו טוש"ע א"ח סי' תקמח סעיף י וטוש"ע י"ד סי' שצט סעיף ה:

שהרי כשחל שמיני שלו בשבת ערב הרגל מגלח בע"ש ואילו חל שלשים כו' כצ"ל וכ"ה בירושלמי ור"ל אפי' אבא שאול כן ס"ל הא דה"ל מוכח הטעמים הוא משום כבוד הרגל. העתק מחילופי גרסאות

וְהָתַנְיָא: *הַקּוֹבֵר אֶת מֵתוֹ שְׁלֹשָׁה יָמִים קוֹדֶם לָרֶגֶל — בָּטְלָה הֵימֶנּוּ גְּזֵרַת שִׁבְעָה, שְׁמוֹנָה יָמִים קוֹדֶם לָרֶגֶל — בָּטְלָה הֵימֶנּוּ גְּזֵרַת שְׁלֹשִׁים. וּמְגַלֵּחַ עֶרֶב הָרֶגֶל, אִם לֹא גִּילַּח עֶרֶב הָרֶגֶל — אָסוּר לְגַלֵּחַ אַחַר הָרֶגֶל. אַבָּא שָׁאוּל אוֹמֵר: [א]מוּתָּר לְגַלֵּחַ אַחַר הָרֶגֶל. שֶׁכְּשֵׁם שֶׁמִּצְוַת שְׁלֹשָׁה מְבַטֶּלֶת גְּזֵרַת שִׁבְעָה — כָּךְ מִצְוַת שִׁבְעָה מְבַטֶּלֶת גְּזֵרַת שְׁלֹשִׁים. שִׁבְעָה? וְהָאֲנַן שְׁמוֹנָה תְּנַן! *קָסָבַר אַבָּא שָׁאוּל: מִקְצָת הַיּוֹם כְּכוּלּוֹ, וְיוֹם שְׁבִיעִי עוֹלֶה לוֹ לְכָאן וּלְכָאן. *אָמַר רַב חִסְדָּא אָמַר רָבִינָא בַּר שִׁילָא: [ב]הֲלָכָה כְּאַבָּא שָׁאוּל. וּמוֹדִים חֲכָמִים לְאַבָּא שָׁאוּל [ג]כְּשֶׁחָל שְׁמִינִי שֶׁלּוֹ לִהְיוֹת בְּשַׁבָּת עֶרֶב הָרֶגֶל, שֶׁמּוּתָּר לְגַלֵּחַ בְּעֶרֶב שַׁבָּת. כְּמַאן אָזְלָא הָא דְּאָמַר רַב עַמְרָם אָמַר רַב: אָבֵל, כֵּיוָן שֶׁעָמְדוּ מְנַחֲמִין מֵאֶצְלוֹ — מוּתָּר בִּרְחִיצָה. כְּמַאן — כְּאַבָּא שָׁאוּל. אָמַר אַבַּיֵי: הֲלָכָה כְּאַבָּא שָׁאוּל בְּיוֹם שִׁבְעָה, וּמוֹדִים חֲכָמִים לְאַבָּא שָׁאוּל בְּיוֹם שְׁלֹשִׁים, דְּאָמְרִינַן: מִקְצָת הַיּוֹם כְּכוּלּוֹ. רָבָא אָמַר: הֲלָכָה כְּאַבָּא שָׁאוּל בְּיוֹם שְׁלֹשִׁים, וְאֵין הֲלָכָה כְּאַבָּא שָׁאוּל בְּיוֹם שִׁבְעָה. וּנְהַרְדְּעֵי אָמְרִי: [ד]הֲלָכָה כְּאַבָּא שָׁאוּל בְּזוֹ וּבְזוֹ. *דְּאָמַר שְׁמוּאֵל: הֲלָכָה כְּדִבְרֵי הַמֵּיקֵל בְּאֵבֶל. שְׁלֹשִׁים יוֹם מְנָלַן? יָלֵיף "פֶּרַע" "פֶּרַע" מִנָּזִיר: כְּתִיב הָכָא: °"רָאשֵׁיכֶם אַל תִּפְרָעוּ" וּכְתִיב הָתָם: °"גַּדֵּל פֶּרַע שְׂעַר רֹאשׁוֹ", מַה לְּהַלָּן שְׁלֹשִׁים — אַף כָּאן שְׁלֹשִׁים. וְהָתָם מְנָלַן? *אָמַר רַב מַתָּנָה: [ה]סְתָם נְזִירוּת שְׁלֹשִׁים יוֹם. מַאי טַעְמָא — אָמַר קְרָא: °"קָדוֹשׁ יִהְיֶה". "יִהְיֶה" בְּגִימַטְרִיָּא תְּלָתִין הָווּ. אָמַר רַב הוּנָא בְּרֵיהּ דְּרַב יְהוֹשֻׁעַ: הַכֹּל מוֹדִין [ו]כְּשֶׁחָל שְׁלִישִׁי שֶׁלּוֹ לִהְיוֹת עֶרֶב הָרֶגֶל — שֶׁאָסוּר בִּרְחִיצָה עַד הָעֶרֶב. אָמַר רַב נְחֶמְיָה בְּרֵיהּ דְּרַב יְהוֹשֻׁעַ: אַשְׁכַּחְתִּינְהוּ לְרַב פַּפִּי וּלְרַב פַּפָּא דְּיָתְבִי וְקָאָמְרִי: הֲלָכָה כְּרַב הוּנָא בְּרֵיהּ דְּרַב יְהוֹשֻׁעַ. אִיכָּא דְּאָמְרִי, אָמַר רַב נְחֶמְיָה בְּרֵיהּ דְּרַב יוֹסֵף: אַשְׁכַּחְתִּינְהוּ לְרַב פַּפִּי וּלְרַב פַּפָּא וּלְרַב הוּנָא בְּרֵיהּ דְּרַב יְהוֹשֻׁעַ דְּיָתְבִי וְקָאָמְרִי: הַכֹּל מוֹדִים שֶׁאִם חָל שְׁלִישִׁי שֶׁלּוֹ לִהְיוֹת עֶרֶב הָרֶגֶל שֶׁאָסוּר בִּרְחִיצָה עַד הָעֶרֶב. בְּעָא מִינֵּיהּ אַבַּיֵי (*מֵרַבָּא:) קְבָרוֹ בָּרֶגֶל, רֶגֶל עוֹלֶה לוֹ לְמִנְיַן שְׁלֹשִׁים אוֹ אֵין רֶגֶל עוֹלֶה לוֹ לְמִנְיַן שְׁלֹשִׁים? °לְמִנְיַן שִׁבְעָה לָא קָמִיבַּעְיָא לִי — דְּלָא נָהֲגָא מִצְוַת שִׁבְעָה בָּרֶגֶל. כִּי קָא מִיבַּעְיָא לִי — לְמִנְיַן שְׁלֹשִׁים, דְּקָא נָהֲגָא מִצְוַת שְׁלֹשִׁים בָּרֶגֶל. מַאי? א"ל: אֵינוֹ עוֹלֶה. אֵיתִיבֵיהּ: *הַקּוֹבֵר אֶת מֵתוֹ שְׁנֵי יָמִים קוֹדֶם הָרֶגֶל — נוֹהֵג חֲמִשָּׁה יָמִים אַחַר הָרֶגֶל, וּמְלַאכְתּוֹ נַעֲשֵׂית ע"י אֲחֵרִים, וַעֲבָדָיו וְשִׁפְחוֹתָיו עוֹשִׂים בְּצִינְעָא בְּתוֹךְ בֵּיתוֹ, וְאֵין רַבִּים מִתְעַסְּקִין עִמּוֹ, שֶׁכְּבָר

תורה אור: ויקרא י; במדבר ו; שם

רש"י

וְהָתַנְיָא. סַיַּיעְתָּא: שֶׁכְּשֵׁם (א)שֶׁגְּזֵרַת שְׁלֹשָׁה מְבַטֶּלֶת שִׁבְעָה. דְּכִי קָבַר מֵתוֹ שְׁלֹשָׁה יָמִים לִפְנֵי הָרֶגֶל אֵינוֹ יוֹשֵׁב לְאַחַר הָרֶגֶל כְּלוּם: כָּךְ (ב)גְּזֵרַת שִׁבְעָה מְבַטֶּלֶת גְּזֵרַת שְׁלֹשִׁים. דְּכִי קָבַר מֵתוֹ שִׁבְעָה יָמִים קוֹדֶם הָרֶגֶל — בָּטְלָה מִמֶּנּוּ גְּזֵרַת שְׁלֹשִׁים, דַּאֲפִילּוּ לֹא גִּילַּח עֶרֶב הָרֶגֶל — מְגַלֵּחַ אַחַר הָרֶגֶל: וְיוֹם (ג) שִׁבְעָה עוֹלֶה לְכָאן וּלְכָאן. דְּחָשֵׁיב נַמִּי שְׁמִינִי: כֵּיוָן שֶׁעָמְדוּ מְנַחֲמִים מֵאֶצְלוֹ. הַיְינוּ בְּיוֹם ז': כְּמַאן כְּאַבָּא שָׁאוּל. דְּאָמַר: עוֹלֶה לְכָאן וּלְכָאן, דְּחָשֵׁיב נַמִּי שְׁמִינִי דִּמְבַטֵּל מִמֶּנּוּ גְּזֵרַת שְׁלֹשִׁים: וּמוֹדִים הֵן לְאַבָּא שָׁאוּל. בְּיוֹם שְׁלוֹשִׁים לִקְבוּרַת מֵתוֹ דְּמוּתָּר לְגַלֵּחַ, דְּלָא בָּעִינַן שְׁלֹשִׁים שְׁלֵימִין, דְּאָמְרִינַן: מִקְצָת הַיּוֹם כְּכוּלּוֹ: מְנָלַן. דִּשְׁלֹשִׁים יוֹם אָסוּר בְּגִילּוּחַ: רָאשֵׁיכֶם אַל תִּפְרָעוּ. הָא שְׁאָר אֲבֵלִים — חַיָּיבִים מַשְׁמַע: הַכֹּל מוֹדִים. אֲפִילּוּ אַבָּא שָׁאוּל, דְּאָמַר: מִקְצָת הַיּוֹם כְּכוּלּוֹ: שֶׁאָסוּר בִּרְחִיצָה עַד הָעֶרֶב. דְּוַדַּאי שָׁלֹשׁ שְׁלֵימִין בָּעִינַן עַד הָעֶרֶב, וְלָעֶרֶב רוֹחֵץ בְּצוֹנֵן, אוֹ יַמְתִּין עַד חוּלּוֹ שֶׁל מוֹעֵד וְיִרְחַץ בְּחַמִּין: לְמִנְיַן שִׁבְעָה לָא קָמִבַּעְיָא לִי. דְּוַדַּאי אֵינוֹ עוֹלֶה, דְּוַדַּאי לָא נָהֲגָא מִצְוַת שִׁבְעָה בָּרֶגֶל, דְּהָא אֵינוֹ אָסוּר בִּנְעִילַת הַסַּנְדָּל, וְאֵינוֹ נוֹהֵג בִּכְפִיַּית הַמִּטָּה: דְּהָא נָהֲגָא מִצְוַת שְׁלֹשִׁים בָּרֶגֶל. דְּהָא בָּרֶגֶל נַמִּי אָסוּר בְּגִיהוּץ וּבְתִסְפּוֹרֶת כִּשְׁלֹשִׁים: וְאֵין רַבִּים מִתְעַסְּקִין עִמּוֹ. כְּלוֹמַר: אֵין צְרִיכִין לְנַחֲמוֹ אַחַר הָרֶגֶל, שֶׁכְּבָר נִחֲמוּהוּ שִׁבְעָה יָמִים בָּרֶגֶל: כָּל

תוספות

והתניא. בניחותא הקובר את מתו כו'. הקשה בתוספות הרב: אמאי לא קאמר כתנאי, ורב ששת כאבא שאול, ורב הונא כתנא קמא? א]ושמא משום דברייתא מזכיר לשון בטלו, וקאמר לדידיה ימים לא בטלו — א"כ לא סבירא הברייתא כרב ששת, דרב ששת קאמר ימים נמי בטלו, משום דלשון בטלו משמע בכולו, כן נראה לי:

הלכה כאבא שאול. נראה דהלכה כמותו בכל מאי דפליג אתנא קמא, בין במקצת היום ככולו, בין לענין אם לא גילח. מדלא מפליג בהלכה כאבא שאול במקצת היום ככולו ולא בגילח, הרי"ן. בירושלמי מקשה לרבנן דאבא שאול: מה בין יום שלשים ליום שמיני. דקאמר מקצת היום ככולו ומגלח ערב הרגל, ויום שלשים לא אמר מקצת היום ככולו שיהא מגלח בו? ומשני, משום כבוד הרגל התירו. תדע, *שהרי חל שמיני שלו בערב הרגל, מגלח ערב הרגל ואילו חל שלשים בשבת — אינו מגלח בערב שבת:

אתיא פרע פרע מנזיר. יש שאומרים שאסור לאבל להיות סורק ראשו לאחר שבעה, משום דאמרינן (נזיר דף מב.): נזיר חופף ומפספס, אבל לא סורק, ואנן ילפינן מנזיר. ואין נראה כלל, דהא בנזיר אסור ודאי, שאפילו תלש שערו אסור. אבל לענין אבילות, שהוא משום יפוי — לא. ובשעת מעשה שאלתי ממורי ריב"א והתיר לי. והר"ר יום טוב פירש: כיון דקיימא לן מקצת יום שבעה ככולו ועולה לכאן ולכאן — מקצת היום ככולו, ויכול לגלח ביום עשרים ותשעה.ב] ובתוספות הרב לא פירש כן, דלא אמרינן שיהא יום שבעה לשני ימים לענין שלשים יום:

תלתין הוו. ולבר פדא דאמר בנזיר בפ"ק (דף ה.) "נזיר להזיר" כ"ט אסור, שלשים שרי. ונזירות הוא עשרים ותשעה יום לדידיה — א"כ סבר על כרחך כדפירש אבא שאול. מיהו, יש לומר: לכתחילה אינו מגלח בנזיר עד שלשים יום מדרבנן, כדמשמע הכא. ובירושלמי מקשה מן המשנה (שם דף טז.) דאמר: גלח ביום שלשים — יצא! ומשני: תמן — לשעבר, הכא — מתחילה, והיינו כדפרישית:

שאסור ברחיצה עד הערב. פי' בקונטרס: ולערב יכול לרחוץ גופו בצונן. אי נמי: פניו, ידיו ורגליו, אבל כל גופו בחמין — לא, דאסור לרחוץ בי"ט. א"נ יש לפרש: בחמי טבריא. א"נ: לשטוף מותר, כדאי' פרק "כירה" (שבת דף לט: ושם). אי נמי: בחמין שהוחמו בקרקע. ואמר בפרק "כירה": מחלוקת בחמין שהוחמו בכלי. וא"ת: מאי שנא דלא אמרינן מקצת היום ככולו בשלישי ובשביעי לרבנן, °ובשביעי לאבא שאול שרינן על ידי מקצת היום ככולו? וכי תימא משום דאפשר לרחוץ ביו"ט, ולא יהא ניוול — תינח רחילה, אלא כיבוס מאי איכא למימר? ואין נראה לר"י דכיבוס שרי בשלישי! וי"ל: דבאבילות שבעה חמיר טפי. בה"ג מפרש: הוא הדין רביעי וחמישי אסור, עד הערב, ע"כ פי' בתוספות. °והרי"ט פירש: עד הערב — היינו *מבערב י"ט, ולאפוקי דלא שרי מן הבקר, ונראה דהוא הדין בכיבוס — מותר לערב מעי"ט. ולפירושו נראה דשבעה קודם הרגל אליבא דרבנן — מותר מבערב י"ט. *ומדקאמר הכל מודים — פירוש: אפילו אבא שאול דשרי בשביעי מן הבקר — הכא מודה לרבנן דלא שרי מן הבקר, אלא יש לו דין שביעי לרבנן: **קברו** ברגל רגל עולה לו מן המנין שלשים או אינו עולה. פירש בתוספות: דהוא הדין דמיבעיא לן בקברו שני ימים קודם הרגל. וקשיא לן: דהא בסמוך משמע דפשיטא בקברו שני ימים קודם הרגל, דקאמרינן: מאי לאו אסיפא — לא, ארישא. משמע, דברישא ניחא ליה! ושמא היה הרב רוצה לומר דתרוייהו מיבעי ליה, וכי פשיט — בעי למיפשט הכל. ומשני דלא תיפשוט הכל: **דלא** נוהגין מצות שבעה ברגל. ומיהו, דברים שבצינעא נוהגין, כדמשמע פ"ק דכתובות (דף ד. ושם) דקאמרינן: כל אותן הימים הוא ישן בין האנשים והיא ישינה בין הנשים, מסייע ליה לרבי יוחנן. וכן פירש הרב בשם רבו. ממתני' מאי למיפשט דאינו עולה למנין שבעה, דקתני: מפסיקין ואין עולין. ולכל הפחות איירי לענין שבעה. ומיהו, יש לומר: דנותן טעם מנין לו פשוט דמתניתין איירי שאינו עולה למנין שבעה, אימא לענין שלשים: **ומלאכתו** נעשית ע"י אחרים. אפילו בביתו. °אע"ג דאמר לעיל בפ"ב (דף יא:) היתה מלאכתו ביד אחרים, בתוך ביתו — אסור לעשות, בבתיהם — מותר! וי"ל: דהכא מיירי בדבר האבד:

שכבר

רבינו חננאל

ומקשינן עליה והתניא הקובר את מתו קודם לרגל ג' ימים בטלה הימנו גזירת שבעה. ח' ימים קודם לרגל בטלה הימנו גזירת שלשים ומגלח ערב הרגל א) אסור לגלח אחר הרגל. אבא שאול אומר אף מגלח אחר הרגל. שכשם שמצות שלשה מבטלת גזירת שבעה. כלומר כיון שקיים מצות אבלות דיי לו. כן מצות ז' מבטלת גזירת שלשים. ומקשינן כך מצות שבעה והאנן שמונה תנן. ופרקינן אבא שאול סבר מקצת היום ככולו ב) ויום השביעי עולה לו למנין שבעה. ושאר יום השביעי כולו עולה לו למנין שלשים. וכיון שקיים מצות שלשים במקצת היום דיי לו. ומגלח ערב הרגל ואם לא גילח ערב הרגל מגלח לאחר הרגל. ואמרו הלכתא כאבא שאול. קשיא לרב דאמר ימים לא בטלו. ג) ופריק רב כי קאמרינן הלכתא כאבא שאול בשבעה ואין צריך שמונה כרבנן דפליגי עליה. ומודים חכמים לאבא שאול ביום ל' שמקצת היום ככולו ואסיקנא הלכתא כאבא שאול בין ביום שביעי בין ביום שלשים דמקצת היום ככולו. והני מילי בתשלום שבעה ובתשלום שלשים. אבל בזמן שהרגל מפסיק האבלות לא כרב הונא בריה דרב יהושע דאמר הכל מודים שאם חל שלישי שלו להיות ערב הרגל שאסור ברחיצה עד הערב. ואמרינן הלכתא כרב הונא בריה דרב יהושע. ד) בעא מיניה אביי מרבה קברו ברגל עולה לו הרגל למנין שלשים או לא. ודאי למנין שבעה אינו עולה דהא לא נהג ביה מצות אבלות דהא פסח"ז נת"ר רשות כי תיבעי לך שלשים דהא קיים בה מצות גילוח שהיא מצות שלשים א"ל אין עולה לו אפילו למנין שלשים. ושקלינן וטרינן ודברים פשוטים הן. ומסקנא דשמעתא הלכה למעשה הקובר אפילו שעה אחת קודם לרגל בטלה הימנו גזירת אבלות. אבל הנקבר ברגל לא חיילא עליה אבלות אלא אחר הרגל ונוהג שבעת ימי אבלות מ"ט האחרון שהוא י"ט שני ואע"ג דלא נהיג ביה אבל עולה למנין שבעה ועצרת ור"ה ויוה"כ מפסיקין אבלות כרגלים כדפסק רבינא. והלכתא

הגהות הב"ח

(א) רש"י ד"ה שכשם שמצות שלשה מבטלת גזירת שבעה דכי קבר מתו: (ב) ד"ה כך מצות שבעה מבטלת: (ג) ד"ה ויום שביעי עולה.

מסורת הש"ס

[נזיר טו.] מס' שמחות פ"ז ע"ש; [לעיל יז: פסחים ז. וש"נ]; לעיל יז.; לעיל יח. וש"נ עירובין מו.; נזיר ה. לט. תענית יז. [סנהדרין כב:]; [נ"ל מרבה]; [תוספתא פ"ב]; מבערב כצ"ל וכ"ה בערב י"ט כצ"ל; נ"ל ודקאמר

א) נראה דצ"ל ואם לא גילח ערב הרגל אסור לגלח אחר הרגל וכו'. ב) נראה דמה שהיה לו גירסא אחרת בסוגיא ולפי גרסתו זו משמע דהלכה כרב דאמר ימים לא בטלו וכו'. ג) חולי דצ"ל ומקצת יום השביעי עולה. ד) והדין למחרינן במגמרא למעדים חכמים לאבא שאול כשחל שמיני שלו וכו'.

גליון הש"ס

גמ' למנין שבעה לא קמיבעיא לי דלא נהגא מצות שבעה ברגל. עי' לקמן דף כג ע"ב תוס' ד"ה יש אבילות בשבת. תוס' ד"ה שאסור ברחיצה וכו' ובשביעי לאבא שאול. נ"ל ובשמיני. עי' לקמן דף כג ע"א תוס' ד"ה ואמר לאחותה: ד"ה ומלאכתו וכו' אע"ג דאמר לעיל. תמוה לי הא הכא מקילי רק באחר שאלמלי ז' ימים ממתחילה לאבילות וצ"ע:

הגהות מהר"ב רנשבורג

א] תוס' ד"ה והתניא כו' ושמא משום דברייתא מזכיר לשון בטלו וקאמר לדידיה ימים לא בטלו כו'. כוונתם דמש"ה לא קאמר הש"ס כתנאי דניחא ליה לומר דבלשון ובהתניא מיבעי ליה לעיל... ד"ה ומלאכתו וכו' [illegible]

שכבר נתעסקו בו ברגל. כללו של דבר: כל שהוא משום אבל — רגל מפסיקו, וכל שהוא משום עסקי רבים — אין רגל מפסיקו. קברו שלשה ימים בסוף הרגל — מונה שבעה אחר הרגל. ארבעה ימים הראשונים — רבים מתעסקין בו, שלשה ימים האחרונים — אין רבים מתעסקין בו, שכבר נתעסקו ברגל, ורגל עולה לו. מאי לאו אסיפא? לא, ארישא. איתיביה: רגל עולה לו למנין שלשים, כיצד? קברו בתחילת הרגל — מונה שבעה אחר הרגל, [א]ומלאכתו נעשית על ידי אחרים, ועבדיו ושפחותיו עושין בצנעא בתוך ביתו, ואין רבים מתעסקין בו, שכבר נתעסקו בו ברגל, ורגל עולה לו! תיובתא. כי אתא רבין אמר רבי יוחנן: [ב]אפילו קברו ברגל. וכן אורי ליה ר' אלעזר לרבי פדת בריה: אפילו קברו ברגל. ת"ר: *קיים כפיית המטה שלשה ימים קודם הרגל — אינו צריך לכפותה אחר הרגל, דברי רבי אליעזר. וחכמים אומרים: אפי' יום אחד, ואפי' שעה אחת. א"ר אלעזר בר' שמעון: הן הן דברי ב"ש, הן הן דברי בית הלל. שבית שמאי אומרים: שלשה ימים, וב"ה אומרים: אפי' יום אחד. אמר רב הונא אמר ר' חייא בר אבא אמר ר' יוחנן, ואמרי לה אמר(א) (*ליה) ר' יוחנן לר' חייא בר אבא ולרב הונא: אפי' יום אחד, אפי' שעה אחת. רבא אמר: *הלכה כתנא דידן, דאמר שלשה. רבינא איקלע לסורא דפרת, א"ל רב חביבא לרבינא: הלכתא מאי? אמר ליה אפי' יום אחד, [ג]ואפילו שעה אחת. יתיב רבי חייא בר אבא ורבי אמי ור' יצחק נפחא אקילעא דרבי יצחק בן אלעזר, נפק מילתא מבינייהו: מנין לאבילות שבעה? דכתיב: (עמוס ח) "והפכתי חגיכם לאבל" מה חג שבעה — אף אבילות שבעה. ואימא עצרת, דחד יומא! ההוא מיבעי ליה לכדריש לקיש, דאמר ר"ל משום ר' יהודה נשיאה: מנין לשמועה רחוקה שאינה נוהגת אלא יום אחד — דכתיב: "והפכתי חגיכם לאבל" ואשכחן עצרת דאיקרי חד יומא חג. *ת"ר: שמועה קרובה נוהגת שבעה ושלשים, שמועה רחוקה אינה נוהגת אלא יום אחד. [ד]איזו היא קרובה ואיזו היא רחוקה? קרובה — בתוך שלשים, רחוקה — לאחר שלשים, דברי ר"ע. וחכמים אומרים: אחת שמועה קרובה ואחת שמועה רחוקה — נוהגת שבעה ושלשים. אמר רבה בר בר חנה א"ר יוחנן: *כל מקום שאתה מוצא יחיד מקיל ורבים מחמירין — הלכה כרבים, חוץ מזו, שאע"פ שרבי עקיבא מקיל וחכמים מחמירין — [ה]הלכה כרבי עקיבא. *דאמר שמואל: הלכה כדברי המקיל באבל. רב חנינא אתיא ליה שמועה דאבוה מבי חוזאי, אתא לקמיה דרב חסדא. אמר ליה: שמועה רחוקה אינה נוהגת אלא יום אחד. רב נתן בר אמי אתא ליה שמועה דאימיה מבי חוזאי, אתא לקמיה דרבא. אמר ליה: הרי אמרו: שמועה רחוקה אינה נוהגת אלא יום אחד בלבד. איתיביה: במה דברים אמורים — בחמשה מתי מצוה, אבל על אביו ועל אמו — שבעה ושלשים! אמר ליה: יחידאה היא, ולא סבירא לן כוותיה. דתניא: מעשה ומת אביו של רבי צדוק בגינזק, והודיעוהו לאחר שלש שנים, ובא ושאל את אלישע בן אבויה וזקנים שעמו, ואמרו: נהוג שבעה ושלשים. וכשמת בנו של רבי אחיה בגולה ישב עליו שבעה ושלשים. איני? והא *רב, בר אחוה דרבי חייא, דהוא בר אחתיה דר' חייא. כי סליק להתם, אמר ליה: אבא קיים? אמר

רש"י

כל שהוא משום אבל רגל מפסיקו. שצריך להשלימו אחר הרגל. כיון דכי ישב שני ימים לפני הרגל — צריך להשלים ולישב חמשה ימים אחר הרגל: כל שהוא משום עסקי רבים. כלומר, תנחומי רבים — אין רגל מפסיקו [כדי] שיהא צריך להשלים ולעסוק בו אחר הרגל, אלא מתעסקין בו ברגל: ארבעה ימים הראשונים. של אחר הרגל רבים מתעסקים בו, ומשלימין לשלשה שנתעסקו ברגל, שכבר נתעסקו בו ברגל שלשה ימים: ורגל עולה. למנין שלשים: מאי לאו אסיפא. הא דתני דרגל עולה למנין שלשים — היינו אסיפא, אקברו ברגל. ותיפשוט מינה דכי קברו ברגל — עולה למנין שלשים, וקשיא לרבא, דאמר: אינו עולה: לא, ארישא. קא מהדר, אקברו שני ימים קודם הרגל — רגל עולה לו למנין שלשים. דהתם ודאי עולה לו, הואיל וכבר התחיל באבילות. אבל קברו ברגל — לא ידענא: בתחילת הרגל. ביום ראשון של רגל, וקשיא לרבא: שכבר נתעסקו ברגל. כל שבעה: אפילו קברו ברגל. רגל עולה למנין שלשים, ולא מיבעיא קברו קודם הרגל: תנא דידן. היינו תנא א] (*דברייתא): במה דברים אמורים. שאינה נוהגת אלא יום אחד: אלא חמשה. מהני שבעה מתי מלוה דכתיב בקרא (ויקרא כא): בנו ובתו אחיו ואחותו ואשתו: יחידאה היא. ולא ר' עקיבא. דלר"ע לא שנא אביו ואמו, לא שנא שאר קרוביו: בגינזק. מקום: רב בר אחוה דר' חייא דהוא בר אחתיה דר' חייא. דרבי אחא מכפרי נשא לאה, והוליד ממנה אייבו, מתה ונשא רחל ולה בת מאיש אחר, וממנה נולד רבי חייא. ונשא אייבו הבת, ונולד להן רב. ונמצא: רב בר אייבו בר אחוה דרבי חייא מאבוה, ובר אחתיה מאמיה: כי סליק. רב מעירו דבבל לא"י, שהיה רבי חייא שם: א"ל. רבי חייא לרב: אבא קיים. ר"ל: אייבו אביך, קיים הוא? א"ל

תוספות

שכבר נתעסקו בו ברגל. תנחומין וברכה בשורה. והרי"ט דפירש לענין הבראה חולק על מחזור מויטר"י, שפירש בשם רש"י, שהיה אומר שאין עושים הבראה ברגל, הואיל וליכא אבילות. ולאחר הרגל — נמי לא יעשוה, הואיל ובטלה סעודה ראשונה. פי': דמספקא ליה לרש"י אי הבראה במועד אי לאחר המועד, דשמא הבראה אינו עסקי רבים הואיל ויחיד יכול לעשות. ועל הבראה פירש לקמן, כל יום ראשון אסור לאכול משלו, אפי' אוכל שתי פעמים ביום. דהא לא קאמר גמרא סעודה ראשונה, אלא יום ראשון:

שלשה ימים אחרונים אין רבים מתעסקין בו. פירש בתוספות: דהוא הדין דמלאכתו נעשית ע"י אחרים: אמר רבי יוחנן אפילו יום אחד אפי' שעה אחת. קשיא לי: דהא אית ליה לר' יוחנן* הלכה כסתם משנה!

מה חג שבעה. ובירושלמי דייק: אימא שמונה כשמונה דחג? ומשני: שמיני — רגל בפני עצמו הוא, ומ"ויעש לאביו אבל שבעת ימים" (בראשית נ) לא מצי לאתויי, דהתם קודם קבורה היה. ובירושלמי משני דאין למידין מקודם מתן תורה, והתם בירושלמי מייתי קראי טובא:

כל מקום שאתה מוצא יחיד מקיל ורבים מחמירין. והוא הדין יחיד מחמיר ורבים מקילין — הלכה כרבים, ומשום דהכא איירי ביחיד מקיל נקיט הכי. וכל מקום לאו דוקא, דבהרבה מקומות פוסק כדברי היחיד, והיכא דאתמר אתמר. ועוד: דבעירובין אומר הלכה כדברי המקיל אפי' לגבי רבים. מיהו, התם היינו ריב"ל ולא רבי יוחנן, פר' "מי שהוציאוהו" (עירובין מו.):

יחידאה היא. ואף על גב דלעיל נקיט "וחכ"א":

*אייבו קיים. עדיין לא השיבותיך על אייבו. כך פי' בקונטרס. וקשה: שהיה לר' חייא לומר אמך קיימת, ולא "אימא" דמשמע אמו של ר' חייא? ועוד: דרב היה לו להשיב אבא, ולא היה לו לקרות אביו בשם אייבו? ונראה שר"ח גורס: א"ל: אבא קיים? א"ל: אבא קיים. אימא קיימת? א"ל: אימא קיימת. פירש: ר' חייא היה שואל על אביו ואמו, ורב היה משיב לו על אביו ואם שלו. ואין לנו להקשות: מה לנו לומר דרב בר אחוה דרבי חייא ובר אחתיה? בשלמא לפירוש ראשון — הביאו לומר מה היה חושש ר' חייא על אביו ועל אמו של רב. כי לפירוש זה נמי י"ל דהוצרך יפה, שלא תאמר מה היה לו לרב להשיב על אביו ואמו שלו — כמו כן היה לו להשיב שאר בני אדם קיימין. אבל השתא קמ"ל שהיה משיב לו, לפי שהיה אחיו של ר' חייא ונוח לו להשמיעו חדשות טובות, דלא לימא נא ובשר לקרובים. כדאמרינן בריש פסחים (דף ג: ושם): לא ובשר לסוסים ולחמורים. וי"ג: אמר ליה אבא קיים, אמר ליה אימא קיימת. א"ל: אימא קיימת, אמר ליה: אבא קיים. וכפר"ח. וכענין שפירש ר"ח לגירסת ר"ח. (ג)ורבי חייא היה שואל על אביו ואמו שלו, והוא משיב על אביו ואמו של עצמו. ומה שלא משיב לו כמו גירסת ר"ח – שאם היה משיב לו אבא קיים כשהיה שואל על אביו שלו – משום דהוה משמע שהיה משיב לו על אביו של רבי חייא, שהיה רגיל לקרות אבי אביו אבא:

עולה

עין משפט נר מצוה

קז א טוש"ע י"ד סימן שצט סעיף ב:

קח ב מיי' פ"י מהלכות אבל הלכה ח טוש"ע שם:

קט ג מיי' שם הלכה ג סמג עשין דרבנן ב ובלאוין עה טוש"ע שם סעיף א:

קי ד ה מיי' שם פ"ז הלכה א סמג שם טוש"ע י"ד סימן תב סעיף א:

רבינו חננאל

והלכתא אפילו יום אחד או שעה אחת נמצאת אומר מי שמת לו מת תוך הרגל נקיט שבעה מיו"ט שני של יו"ט האחרון ואף על פי שיו"ט שני אין נוהג בו אבילות ונקיט ל' מההוא יומא דמית ביה ומאן דשכיב ליה שכבא ביו"ט שני של יו"ט האחרון או ביו"ט שני דעצרת *) נהיג אבל בו ביום דהוא יום קבורה והוא מדאורייתא דכתיב ואכלתי חטאת היום וכתיב נמי ואחריתה כיום מר והוא יום המיתה הלכך יום מיתה מדאורייתא ויו"ט שני מדרבנן אתי דאורייתא ומבטל דרבנן ונהיג ביה אבלות כשאר יומי. מניין לאבלות שהיא שבעה שנאמר והפכתי חגיכם לאבל. מה חג שבעה אף אבלות שבעה. ומניין לשמועה רחוקה שאינה נוהגת אלא יום אחד כבר הקיש הכתוב האבל לחג ומצאנו עצרת שהוא חג והוא יום אחד: ת"ר שמועה קרובה נוהגת שבעה ושלשים שמועה רחוקה אינה נוהגת אלא יום אחד איזו היא קרובה ואיזו היא רחוקה קרובה בתוך ששים לקבורתו רחוקה לאחר שלשים דברי ר' עקיבא וחכמים אומרים אחת זו ואחת זו נוהגת שבעה ושלשים. אמר רבה בר בר חנה אמר רבי יוחנן כל מקום שאתה מוצא יחיד מקיל ורבים מחמירין הלכה כמחמירין חוץ מזו. שאע"פ שר' עקיבא מקיל וחכמים מחמירין הלכה כר' עקיבא דאמר שמואל הלכה כדברי המקיל באבל. והא דתניא בד"א כי שמועה רחוקה אינה נוהגת אלא יום אחד בה' מתי מצוה פי' בחמשה שמצוה להתאבל עליהן. והן בנו ובתו ואחיו ואחותו ואשתו. אבל על אביו ועל אמו אפי' שמועה רחוקה נוהגת שבעה ושלשים לית הלכתא כוותיה דהא יחידאה היא כלומר אלישע בן אבויה וח' זקנים שהיו עמו והורו בשמועה רחוקה לנהוג שבעה ושלשים יחידים הן ולא סבירא לן כוותייהו דהא רב חסדא ורבה הורו על אביו ועל אמו בשמועה רחוקה שלא לנהוג אלא יום

*) כל דברי רבינו אלו הובא בא"ז בא"ב סימן תל"ב בשמו וכן דעת בה"ג ורב אלפס ז"ל וע"ש בא"ז וברא"ש מש"כ על זה.

הגהות הב"ח

(א) גמ' ואמרי לה אמר ליה ר' יוחנן לר' חייא בר אבא ור' חייא בר אבא לרב הונא אפילו יום אחד: (ב) תום' ד"ה אייבו כו' לגירסת ר"ח דר' חייא היה שואל כו' כשהיה שואל על אביו שלו הוה משמע כו' כנ"ל ותיבת משום נמחק:

גליון הש"ס

גמ' אורי ליה רבי אלעזר לרבי פדת בריה. עיין נדה דף ח ע"א תוס' ד"ה ואמר ר' פדת: שם הן הן כעין זה כתובות דף ס ע"ב: תום' ד"ה שכבר כו' שאין עושין הבראה ברגל. עי' לקמן דף כד ע"ב תוס' ד"ה אלא:

מסורת הש"ס

תורה אור

[תוספ' פ"ב]

[נ"ל דמשנה]

[נ"ל להו]

[לקמן כא.]

עירובין מו.

[שם]

לעיל יח. יעו' לקמן כב. כו: עירובין מו. [בכורות מט. חולין ג.]

נזיר מד. שמחות פי"ב

פסחים ד. [סנהדרין ה.]

הגהות מהר"ב רנשבורג

א] רש"י ד"ה תנא דידן היינו תנא דברייתא. נ"ב תנא דמתני' נמי קאמר שלשה ימים קודם הרגל ונ"ע ונלע"ד דרש"י אתי שפיר לשיטתו שפי' במתניתין דלהמשנה לאו דוקא שלשה ימים אלא אפילו שעה אחת והיינו מדקתני במשנה דרגלים מפסיקין משא"כ הכא בברייתא שלשה ימים דוקא דהא לא קתני פסיקין ועוד דפליגי נמי חכמים עלה ולרש"י מיושב קושית התוס' בד"ה אמר ר' יוחנן והתוספות לשיטתם מקשים דפירשו לעיל במשנה כהיש מפרשים דשלשה ימים דוקא וקצת מזה כוונתי לבעל יד דוד וכ"כ בעל שושנים לדוד:

אֲמַר לֵיהּ: אִימָּא קַיֶּימֶת? אֲמַר לֵיהּ: אִימָּא קַיֶּימֶת? א"ל: אַבָּא קַיָּים?! אֲמַר לֵיהּ לְשַׁמָּעֵיהּ: חֲלוֹץ לִי מִנְעָלַי, °וְהוֹלֵךְ אַחֲרַי כֵּלַי לְבֵית הַמֶּרְחָץ. שְׁמַע מִינָּהּ תְּלָת: שְׁמַע מִינָּהּ: *אָבֵל אָסוּר בִּנְעִילַת הַסַּנְדָּל, וּשְׁמַע מִינָּהּ: שְׁמוּעָה רְחוֹקָה אֵינָהּ נוֹהֶגֶת אֶלָּא יוֹם אֶחָד, וּשְׁמַע מִינָּהּ: *[א]מִקְצָת הַיּוֹם כְּכוּלּוֹ?! רַבִּי חִיָּיא — לְחוּד, רַבִּי אַחִיָּיה — לְחוּד. אָמַר רַבִּי יוֹסֵי בַּר אָבִין: [ב]שָׁמַע שְׁמוּעָה קְרוֹבָה בָּרֶגֶל, וּלְמוֹצָאֵי הָרֶגֶל נַעֲשֵׂית רְחוֹקָה — עוֹלָה לוֹ, וְאֵינוֹ נוֹהֵג אֶלָּא יוֹם אֶחָד. תָּנֵי רַבִּי אַדָּא דְּמִן קֵסָרִי קַמֵּיהּ דְּר' יוֹחָנָן: [ג]שָׁמַע שְׁמוּעָה קְרוֹבָה בְּשַׁבָּת, וּלְמוֹצָאֵי שַׁבָּת נַעֲשֵׂית רְחוֹקָה — אֵינוֹ נוֹהֵג אֶלָּא יוֹם אֶחָד. קוֹרֵעַ אוֹ אֵינוֹ קוֹרֵעַ? רַבִּי מָנִי אָמַר: [ד]אֵינוֹ קוֹרֵעַ. רַבִּי חֲנִינָא אָמַר: קוֹרֵעַ. אָמַר לֵיהּ רַבִּי מָנִי לְר' חֲנִינָא: בִּשְׁלָמָא לְדִידִי, דְּאָמִינָא אֵינוֹ קוֹרֵעַ, הַיְינוּ דְּלָא אִיכָּא אֲבֵילוּת שִׁבְעָה. אֶלָּא לְדִידָךְ דְּאָמְרַתְּ קוֹרֵעַ, קְרִיעָה בְּלֹא שִׁבְעָה מִי אִיכָּא? וְלָא? וְהָתַנְיָא אִיסִי אֲבוּהּ דְּרַבִּי זֵירָא, וְאָמְרִי לָהּ אֲחוּהּ דְּרַבִּי זֵירָא קַמֵּיהּ דְּר' זֵירָא: °[ה]מִי שֶׁאֵין לוֹ חָלוּק לִקְרוֹעַ, וְנִזְדַּמֵּן לוֹ בְּתוֹךְ שִׁבְעָה — קוֹרֵעַ, לְאַחַר שִׁבְעָה — אֵינוֹ קוֹרֵעַ. עָנֵי ר' זֵירָא בַּתְרֵיהּ: בַּמֶּה דְּבָרִים אֲמוּרִים — בַּחֲמִשָּׁה מֵתֵי מִצְוָה, [ו]אֲבָל עַל אָבִיו וְעַל אִמּוֹ — קוֹרֵעַ וְהוֹלֵךְ! כִּי תַּנְיָא הַהִיא — לִכְבוֹד אָבִיו וְאִמּוֹ. ת"ר: [ז]כָּל הָאָמוּר בְּפָרָשַׁת כֹּהֲנִים, שֶׁכֹּהֵן מִיטַּמֵּא לָהֶן — אָבֵל מִתְאַבֵּל עֲלֵיהֶן, וְאֵלּוּ הֵן: אִשְׁתּוֹ, אָבִיו, וְאִמּוֹ, אָחִיו, וַאֲחוֹתוֹ, בְּנוֹ, וּבִתּוֹ. א]הוֹסִיפוּ עֲלֵיהֶן אָחִיו וַאֲחוֹתוֹ הַבְּתוּלָה מֵאִמּוֹ, וַאֲחוֹתוֹ נְשׂוּאָה בֵּין מֵאָבִיו בֵּין מֵאִמּוֹ. *וּכְשֵׁם שֶׁמִּתְאַבֵּל עֲלֵיהֶם — כָּךְ מִתְאַבֵּל עַל שְׁנִיִּים שֶׁלָּהֶם, דִּבְרֵי ר"ע. רַבִּי שִׁמְעוֹן בֶּן אֶלְעָזָר אוֹמֵר: אֵינוֹ מִתְאַבֵּל אֶלָּא עַל בֶּן בְּנוֹ וְעַל אֲבִי אָבִיו. וְחכ"א: [ח]כָּל שֶׁמִּתְאַבֵּל עָלָיו — מִתְאַבֵּל עִמּוֹ. חֲכָמִים הַיְינוּ תַּנָּא קַמָּא! אִיכָּא בֵּינַיְיהוּ עִמּוֹ [ט]בַּבַּיִת. *כִּי הָא דַּאֲמַר לֵיהּ רַב לְחִיָּיא בְּרֵיהּ, וְכֵן א"ל רַב הוּנָא לְרַבָּה בְּרֵיהּ: בְּאַפַּהּ — נְהוֹג אֲבֵילוּתָא, בְּלָא אַפַּהּ — לָא תִּינְהוֹג אֲבֵילוּתָא. מָר עוּקְבָא שְׁכִיב לֵיהּ בַּר חֲמוּהּ, סָבַר לְמֵיתַב עֲלֵיהּ שִׁבְעָה וּשְׁלֹשִׁים. עָל רַב הוּנָא לְגַבֵּיהּ, אַשְׁכְּחֵיהּ. אֲמַר לֵיהּ: צוּדָנִיָּיתָא בָּעֵית לְמֵיכַל? לֹא אָמְרוּ לִכְבוֹד אִשְׁתּוֹ [י]אֶלָּא חָמִיו וַחֲמוֹתוֹ. דְּתַנְיָא: מִי שֶׁמֵּתָה חָמִיו אוֹ חֲמוֹתוֹ — [כ]אֵינוֹ רַשַּׁאי לָכוֹף אֶת אִשְׁתּוֹ לִהְיוֹת כּוֹחֶלֶת וְלִהְיוֹת פּוֹקֶסֶת. אֶלָּא כּוֹפֶה מִטָּתוֹ, וְנוֹהֵג עִמָּהּ אֲבֵילוּת. וְכֵן הִיא שֶׁמֵּת חָמִיהָ אוֹ חֲמוֹתָהּ — אֵינָהּ רַשָּׁאָה לִהְיוֹת כּוֹחֶלֶת וְלִהְיוֹת פּוֹקֶסֶת, אֶלָּא כּוֹפָה מִטָּתָהּ וְנוֹהֶגֶת עִמּוֹ אֲבֵילוּת. וְתַנְיָא אִידָךְ: *אַף עַל פִּי שֶׁאָמְרוּ אֵינוֹ רַשַּׁאי לָכוֹף אֶת אִשְׁתּוֹ לִהְיוֹת כּוֹחֶלֶת וְלִהְיוֹת פּוֹקֶסֶת, בֶּאֱמֶת אָמְרוּ: מוֹזֶגֶת לוֹ אֶת הַכּוֹס, וּמַצַּעַת לוֹ מִטָּה, וּמַרְחֶצֶת לוֹ פָּנָיו יָדָיו וְרַגְלָיו. קַשְׁיָין אַהֲדָדֵי! אֶלָּא לָאו שְׁמַע מִינָּהּ: כָּאן — בְּחָמִיו וַחֲמוֹתוֹ, כָּאן — בִּשְׁאָר קְרוֹבִים, שְׁמַע מִינָּהּ. תַּנְיָא נַמִּי הָכִי: לֹא אָמְרוּ לִכְבוֹד אִשְׁתּוֹ — אֶלָּא חָמִיו וַחֲמוֹתוֹ בִּלְבַד. אַמֵימָר שְׁכִיב לֵיהּ בַּר בְּרֵיהּ, קָרַע עִילָּוֵיהּ. אֲתָא בְּרֵיהּ — קָרַע בְּאַפֵּיהּ, אִידְּכַר דִּמְיוּשָּׁב קָרַע — קָם קָרַע מְעוּמָּד. אֲמַר לֵיהּ רַב אַשִׁי לְאַמֵימָר: קְרִיעָה [ל]דִּמְעוּמָּד *) מְנָלַן? דִּכְתִיב: °"וַיָּקָם אִיּוֹב וַיִּקְרַע אֶת מְעִילוֹ". אֶלָּא

*) [עי' תוספות סנהדרין ס. ד"ה אתיא וכו' מה שהניחו סוגי' דהכא בתימה]

רש"י

א"ל אִימָּא קַיֶּימֶת. בִּלְשׁוֹן שְׁאֵלָה הוּא. כְּלוֹמַר,(א) שֶׁאַתָּה שׁוֹאֵל עַל אָבִי — שְׁאַל עַל אִמִּי, שֶׁאַף הִיא אֲחוֹתְךָ: א"ל. ר' חִיָּיא: וְאִמְּךָ אֲחוֹתִי קַיֶּימֶת הִיא? א"ל. רַב: אַבָּא קַיָּים, עֲדַיִין לֹא הִשְׁכַּבְתִּיךְ עָלָיו, וּמִמֵּילָא הֵבִין. וְיֵשׁ אוֹמְרִים: בִּנְיחוּתָא הָיָה רַב מְשִׁיבוֹ עַל מִי שֶׁאֵינוֹ שׁוֹאֵל, כְּדֵי שֶׁיָּבִין מִן הַכְּלָל. וְקָשֶׁה בְּעֵינַי לוֹמַר שֶׁרַב יוֹצִיא דְּבַר שֶׁקֶר מִפִּיו: חֲלוֹץ מִנְעָלַי. לְהִתְאַבֵּל עַל אָחִי וַאֲחוֹתִי: וְהוֹלֵךְ כֵּלַי אַחֲרַי לְבֵית הַמֶּרְחָץ. לְלַמֵּד הֲלָכָה(ב) נִתְכַּוֵּין, שֶׁאֵין שְׁמוּעָה רְחוֹקָה לְאַחַר שְׁלֹשִׁים נוֹהֶגֶת אֶלָּא יוֹם אֶחָד, וּמִקְצָת הַיּוֹם כְּכוּלּוֹ: לְמוֹצָאֵי הָרֶגֶל נַעֲשֵׂית רְחוֹקָה. דַּהֲוֵי שְׁלֹשִׁים יוֹם: אֵינָהּ נוֹהֶגֶת אֶלָּא יוֹם אֶחָד. אע"פ דְּכִי שָׁמַע עֲדַיִין הָיְתָה קְרוֹבָה — עוֹלֶה הָרֶגֶל לְהַשְׁלִים שְׁלֹשִׁים, דַּהֲוֵי שְׁמוּעָה רְחוֹקָה: אֵינוֹ קוֹרֵעַ. עַכְשָׁיו, דְּנוֹהֵג יוֹם אֶחָד לִשְׁמוּעָה רְחוֹקָה: הַיְינוּ דְּלֵיכָּא אֲבֵילוּת שִׁבְעָה. כְּלוֹמַר, מִשּׁוּם דְּלֵיכָּא שִׁבְעָה אֵינוֹ קוֹרֵעַ: קוֹרֵעַ וְהוֹלֵךְ. אַחַר שִׁבְעָה, אע"ג דְּלֵיכָּא שִׁבְעָה: אָבֵל מִתְאַבֵּל עֲלֵיהֶן. עַל אוֹתָן קְרוֹבִים: אָחִיו מֵאִמּוֹ. שֶׁלֹּא מֵאָבִיו, דִּקְרָא מַשְׁמַע מֵאָבִיו שֶׁלֹּא מֵאִמּוֹ: אֲחוֹתוֹ נְשׂוּאָה בֵּין מֵאָבִיו בֵּין מֵאִמּוֹ. דִּבִקְרָא לָא אַשְׁכְּחַן אֶלָּא בְּתוּלָה: עַל שְׁנִיִּים שֶׁלָּהֶן. אֲבִי אָבִיו, וְעַל בֶּן בְּנוֹ, וְעַל בֶּן בִּתּוֹ, וְעַל בֶּן אֲחוֹתוֹ: כָּל שֶׁמִּתְאַבֵּל עָלָיו מִתְאַבֵּל עִמּוֹ. כְּלוֹמַר, מִתְאַבֵּל עִם אָבִיו כְּשֶׁהוּא מִתְאַבֵּל עַל אָב שֶׁלּוֹ — נִמְצָא זֶה מִתְאַבֵּל עַל אֲבִי אָבִיו. וְכֵן כָּל שֶׁמִּתְאַבֵּל עָלָיו, כְּגוֹן שֶׁמִּתְאַבֵּל עַל בְּנוֹ — מִתְאַבֵּל עִמּוֹ, כְּלוֹמַר מִתְאַבֵּל עִם בְּנוֹ כְּשֶׁהוּא מִתְאַבֵּל (ג)פי' עַל בֵּן שֶׁלּוֹ, וְנִמְצָא זֶה מִתְאַבֵּל עַל בֶּן בְּנוֹ: הַיְינוּ תַּנָּא קַמָּא. שֶׁל רַבִּי שִׁמְעוֹן: עִמּוֹ בַּבַּיִת. דְּתַנָּא קַמָּא לָא בָּעֵי שֶׁיְּהֵא אָבִיו אוֹ (בֶּן) בְּנוֹ עִמּוֹ בַּבַּיִת וְיוֹשֵׁב עִמּוֹ, וַחֲכָמִים בָּעוּ עִמּוֹ בַּבַּיִת: כִּי הַאי. עִנְיָן דְּא"ל רַב לְר' חִיָּיא וכו': בְּאַפַּהּ. דְּאִיתְּתָךְ, כְּשֶׁהִיא אֲבֵילָה. דְּהַאי נַמִּי כָּל שֶׁמִּתְאַבֵּל עָלָיו, כְּגוֹן אִשְׁתּוֹ — מִתְאַבֵּל עִמּוֹ בְּפָנָיו: צִידוֹנִיָּיתָא. סְעוּדוֹת דְּאָבֵל: קַשְׁיָין אַהֲדָדֵי. דְּהָכָא קָתָנֵי: מַצַּעַת לוֹ מִטָּתוֹ, וְהָכָא קָתָנֵי: כּוֹפֶה מִטָּתוֹ: בִּשְׁאָר קְרוֹבֵי אִשְׁתּוֹ. מַצַּעַת לוֹ מִטָּתוֹ: אֲתָא בְּרֵיהּ. הָדַר אַמֵימָר קָרַע בְּאַפֵּיהּ דִּבְרֵיהּ: קָם קָרַע. פַּעַם שְׁלִישִׁית:

אוֹדְיֵינִי

תוספות

עולה לו. פירוש הרגל עולה לו למנין שאינו נוהג אלא יום אחד:

קורע או אינו קורע. דוקא כענין זה מיבעי ליה, לפי שהיה חייב לקרוע בשעת שמועה. אבל שמע שמועה רחוקה בחול — אינו קורע כלל, ואפי' על אביו ואמו. וכן קאמר נמי בסמוך: כי תניא ההיא — בכבוד אביו ואמו. והכי משמע לעיל דלא מצינו לר' חייא שקרע, אע"פ שהיה אביו ואמו לגירסת ר"ת. וא"ת: אי מהא משמע דאינו קורע על אביו ואמו, אמאי לא קאמר ש"מ דאינו קורע? יש לומר: דאינו מביא ש"מ כי אם ממה שראינו שעשה, אבל ממה שלא ראינו — אינו מביא ראיה. מכל מקום, מדלא קבעי התלמוד כלל אם רבי חייא קרע — משמע א"צ לקרוע. ובתשובת רבינו זקיני פי': דאינו קורע על שמועה רחוקה אפי' על אביו ואמו. והרי"ן וגם בתוס' הרב מסופק. והא דאמר בסמוך מי שאין לו חלוק וכו' — מיירי כגון שהיה שאול מחבירו, או נתמלא קרעים. ונראה לי שיש לסמוך יותר על ה"ג מרב נמה גאון דאין קורעים לאחר ל' יום אלא על אביו ואמו בלבד. וברכת אבלים נחלקו בה"ג אם שמע בשבת, אם חייב לברך ברכת אבלים. דיש מפרשים דנקרא דברים שבצינעא, וי"א: כיון דמברכין בג' או בעשרה — לאו דברים שבצינעא הוא:

ואחותו נשואה בין מאביו בין מאמו. לא מיבעי מאביו, אלא אפי' מאמו נמי:

על שניים שלהם. פי': הנולדים מהן. אבל באחיהם ובנשותיהם — היה מסופק בתוספות הרב בשם רבו. ולא ידענא מאי שנא:

על אבי אביו ועל בן בנו. פירוש בתוספות הרב בשם רבו: דהוא הדין אבי אמו ובת בתו:

באפה נהוג אבילות. פירוש בתוספות: בכל דיני אבלות, נעילת הסנדל ורחילה וסיכה וכולן, כל זמן שהוא בפניה. ובפ"ק דכתובות (דף ד:) קאמר: עמו בבית. ושמא באפיה דוקא, או שמא) בכל הבית:

ומרחצת לו פניו ידיו ורגליו. בחמין קאמר, דאילו בצונן — היא נמי מותרת: **אלא** בחמיו וחמותו. והוא הדין היא נוהגת עמו בחמיה וחמותה. והא דקתני לעיל כל שמתאבל עליו מתאבל עמו — בכל שאר קרובים קאמר. אבל אשתו, יש חילוק בין חמיו וחמותו לשאר קרובים:

אתא בריה קרע באפיה. להיות נוהג עמו אבילות. ותימה: כיון דקרע כבר, וכי צריך לקרוע כלל לפני הקרובים? ושמא לאשמועינן דבאפיה נוהג אבילות. והר"א פירש: אתא בריה קרע באפיה, לפי שאמימר קרע מיושב, ואתא בנו להזכירו שהוא טעה לקרוע מיושב, והקריעה זה עשה בנו של אמימר, ועל ידי כך נזכר אמימר, וקרע פעם שניה מעומד:

אלא

עין משפט נר מצוה

קיא א מיי' פ"ז מהל' אבל הלכה א סמג עשין דרבנן ב טוש"ע י"ד סימן תב סעיף א:

קיב ב ג מיי' שם הלכה ג וסמג שם טוש"ע י"ד שם סעיף ה:

קיג ד מיי' שם הל' א טוש"ע שם סעי' ד:

קיד ה ו מיי' פ"ח שם הלכה ו טוש"ע י"ד סימן שמ סעיף יח:

קטו ז מיי' שם פ"ב הלכה א סמג שם טוש"ע י"ד סימן שעד סעיף ד:

קטז ח ט י מיי' שם הלכה ד ה טוש"ע שם סעיף ו:

קיז כ מיי' שם הל' ה טוש"ע שם וסימן שפא סעיף ו:

קיח ל מיי' שם פ"ח הלכה א סמג שם טוש"ע י"ד סימן שמ סעיף א:

רבינו חננאל

אחד. ועוד ר' חייא נהג על אביו ועל אמו בשמועה רחוקה יום אחד ולמדנו ממנו ג' דברים. למדנו כי האבל אסור בנעילת הסנדל. וכי שמועה רחוקה אינה נוהגת אלא יום אחד. וכי מקצת היום ככולו תני ר' אדא קמיה דר' יוחנן שמע שמועה קרובה בשבת ולמו"ש נעשה רחוקה עולה לו ואינה נוהגת אלא יום אחד. וכן א"ר יוסי בר אבין שמע שמועה קרובה ברגל ולמוצאי הרגל נעשית רחוקה אינה נוהגת אלא יום אחד כללו של דבר כל יום שמועה שאינו נוהג בו אבלות כאילו עדיין לא שמע. השומע שמועה רחוקה ברגל קורע או אינו קורע ר' מני אמר אינו קורע ר' חנינא אמר קורע ר' מני אמר אינו קורע דכל היכא דליכא עליה אבלות שבעה אינו קורע איני והא תני איסי אבוה דר' זירא מי שאין לו (אלא חלוק אחד) [חלוק לקרוע] ונזדמן לו חלוק בתוך שבעה קורע לאחר שבעה אינו קורע. הנה קורע בתוך שבעה ואע"פ שאינו נוהג אחר הקריעה שבעה. וכי תימא משום דהיא בתוך שבעה ועוד הא תני ר' זירא בתריה בד"א בה' מתי מצוה פי' חמשה מכלל השבעה שהוא מצוה להתאבל עליהם. אבל על אביו ועל אמו קורע והולך. הנה שאין שם אבלות קורע ופרקינן כי תניא היא דר' זירא לכבוד אביו ואמו: ת"ר כל האמור בפרשת כהנים כהן מיטמא להם אבל מתאבל עליהם.

ואלו הן אביו ואמו בנו ובתו אחיו ואחותו ואשתו הוסיפו עליהן אחיו ואחותו בתולה מאמו ואחותו נשואה מאביו וכשם שמתאבל עליהן כך מתאבל על שניים שלהם דברי ר"ע ר"ש בן אלעזר אומר אינו מתאבל אלא על [אבי] אביו ועל בן בנו. וחכמים אומרים כל שמתאבל עליו מתאבל עליהן. וקיי"ל כחכמים. ואוקימנא עמו בבית כגון ראובן שמת לו בן נוהג יעקב אביו עמו בבית בלבד. וכי הא דאמר ליה רב לחייא בריה. ורב הונא אמר לרבה בריה חמיך וחמותך שמתו ואשתך מתאבלת עליהן באפה כלומר בבית עמה נהוג אבלות שלא בפניה לא תנהוג כלל מפני כבוד אשתו א"ל רב הונא למר עוקבא לא אמרו לכבוד אשתו אלא חמיו וחמותו בלבד ותניא כוותיה וכדתניא מי שמת חמיו או חמותו כופה מטתו ונוהג אבלות עמה וכן אם מת חמיה או חמותה אינה רשאה להיות כוחלת ופוקסת אלא כופה מטתה

מסורת הש"ס

[לעיל טו:]

[לעיל טז: פסחים ד. וש"נ]

[שמחות פ"ז]

כתובות ד:

ג"ז שם

ג"ז שם

איוב א

הגהות הב"ח

(א) רש"י ד"ה א"ל אימא כו' כלומר עד שאתה שואל (ב) ד"ה והולך כו' ללמד הלכה לתלמידים נתכוין (ג) ד"ה כל שמתאבל וכו' כשהוא מתאבל על בן ש ותיבת פי' נמחק:

גליון הש"ס

גמ' והולך אחרי כלי. עי' לקמן דף כד ע"ב תוספ ד"ה אלא קרובין: **שם** מי שאין לו חלוק. עיין לקמן דף כד ע' תוספות ד"ה וכל קר ובתוספות ד"ה כי תניא:

הגהות מהר"ב רנשבורג

א] גמ' הוסיפו עליהן אח ואחותו הבתולה מאמו ואחותו נשואה כו'. ע' עיין ריטב"א:

אֶלָּא מֵעַתָּה — °"וְעָמַד וְאָמַר לֹא חָפַצְתִּי לְקַחְתָּהּ" ה"נ? וְהָא תַּנְיָא: אבֵּין יוֹשֵׁב בֵּין עוֹמֵד בֵּין מוּטֶּה! א"ל: הָתָם לָא כְּתִיב "וַיַּעֲמֹד וַיֹּאמֶר" הָכָא כְּתִיב "וַיָּקָם וַיִּקְרַע". אָמַר רָמִי בַּר חָמָא: מִנַּיִן לִקְרִיעָה שֶׁהִיא מְעוּמָּד — שֶׁנֶּאֱמַר: °"וַיָּקָם אִיּוֹב וַיִּקְרַע". דִּלְמָא מִילְּתָא יְתֵירְתָּא הוּא דַּעֲבַד? דְּאִי לָא תֵּימָא הָכִי — °"וַיָּגָז אֶת רֹאשׁוֹ" ה"נ? אֶלָּא מֵהָכָא: °"וַיָּקָם הַמֶּלֶךְ וַיִּקְרַע אֶת בְּגָדָיו". •וְדִלְמָא מִילְּתָא יְתֵירְתָּא עֲבֵיד? דְּאִי לָא תֵּימָא הָכִי — °"וַיִּשְׁכַּב אָרְצָה" ה"נ? וְהָתַנְיָא: בישַׁב עַל גַּבֵּי מִטָּה, עַל גַּבֵּי כִּסֵּא, עַל גַּבֵּי *אוּדְיָינֵי (*גְּדוֹלָה, ע"ג קַרְקַע — מְכוּלָּן) לֹא יָצָא יְדֵי חוֹבָתוֹ, וְא"ר יוֹחָנָן: שֶׁלֹּא קִיֵּים כְּפִיַּית הַמִּטָּה. א"ל: כְּעֵין אַרְצָה. ת"ר, (*וְאֵלּוּ) דְּבָרִים שֶׁאָבֵל גאָסוּר בָּהֶן: *אָסוּר בִּמְלָאכָה, *וּבִרְחִיצָה, וּבְסִיכָה, וּבְתַשְׁמִישׁ הַמִּטָּה, וּבִנְעִילַת הַסַּנְדָּל, דוְאָסוּר לִקְרוֹת בַּתּוֹרָה וּבַנְּבִיאִים וּבַכְּתוּבִים, וְלִשְׁנוֹת בַּמִּשְׁנָה, בַּמִּדְרָשׁ וּבַהֲלָכוֹת וּבַתַּלְמוּד וּבָאַגָּדוֹת. הוְאִם הָיוּ רַבִּים צְרִיכִין לוֹ — אֵינוֹ נִמְנָע. וּמַעֲשֶׂה וּמֵת בְּנוֹ שֶׁל ר' יוֹסֵי בְּצִיפּוֹרִי, וְנִכְנַס לְבֵית הַמִּדְרָשׁ וְדָרַשׁ כָּל הַיּוֹם כּוּלּוֹ. רַבָּה בַּר בַּר חָנָה אִיתְרַעָא בֵּיהּ מִילְּתָא, סָבַר דְּלָא לְמִיפַּק לְפִירְקָא. א"ל ר' חֲנִינָא: אִם הָיוּ רַבִּים צְרִיכִין לוֹ — אֵינוֹ נִמְנָע. סָבַר לְאוֹקְמֵי אָמוֹרָא עֲלֵיהּ — א"ל רַב, ותַּנְיָא: וּבִלְבַד שֶׁלֹּא יַעֲמִיד תּוּרְגְּמָן. וְאֶלָּא הֵיכִי עָבֵיד? כִּי הָא דְּתַנְיָא: מַעֲשֶׂה וּמֵת בְּנוֹ שֶׁל ר' יְהוּדָה בַּר אִילְעַאי, וְנִכְנַס לְבֵית הַמִּדְרָשׁ. וְנִכְנַס ר' חֲנַנְיָה בֶּן עֲקַבְיָא וְיָשַׁב בְּצִדּוֹ, זוְלָחַשׁ הוּא לְר' חֲנַנְיָה בֶּן עֲקַבְיָא, וְר' חֲנַנְיָה בֶּן עֲקַבְיָא לְתוּרְגְּמָן, וְתוּרְגְּמָן הִשְׁמִיעַ לָרַבִּים. ת"ר: אָבֵל, ג' יָמִים הָרִאשׁוֹנִים אָסוּר לְהָנִיחַ תְּפִילִּין. *מִשְּׁלִישִׁי וְאֵילָךְ, וּשְׁלִישִׁי בִּכְלָל — מוּתָּר לְהָנִיחַ תְּפִילִּין. וְאִם בָּאוּ פָּנִים חֲדָשׁוֹת — אֵינוֹ חוֹלֵץ, דִּבְרֵי ר"א. ר' יְהוֹשֻׁעַ אוֹמֵר: אָבֵל, ב' יָמִים הָרִאשׁוֹנִים — אָסוּר לְהָנִיחַ תְּפִילִּין, *מִשֵּׁנִי וְשֵׁנִי בִּכְלָל — מוּתָּר לְהָנִיחַ תְּפִילִּין, וְאִם בָּאוּ פָּנִים חֲדָשׁוֹת — חוֹלֵץ. אָמַר רַב מַתָּנָה: מַאי טַעְמָא דר"א — דִּכְתִיב: °"וַיִּתְּמוּ יְמֵי בְכִי אֵבֶל מֹשֶׁה". אָמַר רַב עֵינָא: מ"ט דְּר' יְהוֹשֻׁעַ — דִּכְתִיב: °"וְאַחֲרִיתָהּ כְּיוֹם מָר". וְרַבִּי יְהוֹשֻׁעַ נַמִּי, הָא כְּתִיב: "וַיִּתְּמוּ יְמֵי" וגו'! אָמַר לָךְ: שָׁאנֵי מֹשֶׁה, דְּתַקִּיף אֶבְלֵיהּ. וְר"א נַמִּי, הָא כְּתִיב: "וְאַחֲרִיתָהּ כְּיוֹם מָר"! עִיקַּר מְרִירָא חַד יוֹמָא הוּא. אָמַר עוּלָּא: הֲלָכָה כְּר"א בַּחֲלִיצָה, וַהֲלָכָה כְּר' יְהוֹשֻׁעַ חבַּהֲנָחָה. אִיבַּעְיָא לְהוּ: בְּשֵׁנִי לְעוּלָּא, חוֹלֵץ אוֹ אֵינוֹ חוֹלֵץ? ת"ש, אָמַר עוּלָּא: חוֹלֵץ וּמֵנִיחַ אפי' מֵאָה פְּעָמִים. תַּנְיָא נַמִּי הָכִי, יְהוּדָה בֶּן תֵּימָא אוֹמֵר: חוֹלֵץ וּמֵנִיחַ אפי' מֵאָה פְּעָמִים. רָבָא אָמַר: כֵּיוָן שֶׁהֵנִיחַ — שׁוּב אֵינוֹ חוֹלֵץ. וְהָא רָבָא הוּא דְּאָמַר: *הֲלָכָה כְּתַנָּא דִּידַן, דְּאָמַר: שְׁלֹשָׁה —

מִצְוָה

דברים כה | איוב א | שם | שמואל ב יג | שם | [שמחות פ"ו] | [פי' בה"ג] | דברים לד | עמוס ח | לעיל כ.

אוּדְיָינֵי. מַכְתֶּשֶׁת גְּדוֹלָה: מִכּוּלָּם. אָמְרוּ אֲפִי' יָשֵׁן ע"ג קַרְקַע לֹא יָצָא — עַד שֶׁיִּכְפֶּה מִטָּתוֹ וְיֵשֵׁב עָלֶיהָ: כְּעֵין אַרְצָה. כְּלוֹמַר, שֶׁכָּפָה מִטָּתוֹ וְיָשַׁב עָלֶיהָ. וּלְעוֹלָם קְרִיעָה מְעוּמָּד: וְאָסוּר לִקְרוֹת. כִּדְאָמְרִינַן לְעֵיל (דף טו.): מִדְּאָמַר רַחֲמָנָא לִיחֶזְקֵאל: הֵאָנֵק דּוֹם. וְהָא דְּאָמַר (סוכה דף כה.): אָבֵל חַיָּיב בְּכָל הַמִּצְוֹת הָאֲמוּרוֹת בַּתּוֹרָה חוּץ מִן הַתְּפִילִּין — הָתָם שְׁאָר מִצְוֹת בְּעָלְמָא, אֲבָל הָנֵי — אִית בְּהוּ שִׂמְחָה: רַבִּים צְרִיכִים לֵיהּ. לִדְרָשָׁה: סָבַר לְאוֹקְמֵי אָמוֹרָא עֲלֵיהּ. תּוּרְגְּמָן: וּשְׁלִישִׁי בִּכְלָל. מוּתָּר לְהָנִיחַ תְּפִילִּין. דְּעִיקַּר אֲבֵילוּת אֵינוֹ אֶלָּא ב' יָמִים: וְאִם בָּאוּ פָּנִים חֲדָשׁוֹת. בְּיוֹם ג', אַף"ה אֵינוֹ חוֹלֵץ תְּפִילִּין. אע"ג דְּאִיכָּא לְמֵיחַשׁ דִּלְמָא אָמְרִי [בִּשְׁנֵי] יָמִים הָרִאשׁוֹנִים נַמִּי הֵנִיחַ תְּפִילִּין: רַבִּי יְהוֹשֻׁעַ אוֹמֵר וכו'. דְּעִיקַּר אֲבֵילוּת אֵינוֹ אֶלָּא יוֹם אֶחָד: וְאִם בָּאוּ פָּנִים חֲדָשׁוֹת. בְּיוֹם שֵׁנִי — חוֹלֵץ תְּפִילִּין: מ"ט דר"א. דְּסָבַר עִיקַּר אֲבֵילוּת שְׁנֵי יָמִים: דִּכְתִיב וַיִּתְּמוּ יְמֵי. דְּמַשְׁמַע ב' יָמִים: עִיקַּר מְרִירָא יוֹם אֶחָד. אֲבָל אֲבֵילוּת ב' יָמִים: הֲלָכָה כר"א בַּחֲלִיצָה. שֶׁאִם בָּאוּ פָּנִים חֲדָשׁוֹת בְּג' — אֵינוֹ חוֹלֵץ, וַהֲלָכָה כְּרַבִּי יְהוֹשֻׁעַ בַּהֲנָחָה — דִּבְשֵׁנִי מוּתָּר לְהָנִיחַ תְּפִילִּין: בְּשֵׁנִי לְעוּלָּא חוֹלֵץ. בִּשְׁלִישִׁי קָאָמַר הֲלָכָה כר"א דְּאָמַר אֵינוֹ חוֹלֵץ, אֲבָל בְּשֵׁנִי — לָא יָדַעְנָא אִי חוֹלֵץ אִי לָא: חוֹלֵץ וּמֵנִיחַ. בְּשֵׁנִי. אֲפִי' מֵאָה פְּעָמִים בַּיּוֹם. וְכִי בָּאוּ פָּנִים חֲדָשׁוֹת — חוֹלֵץ, וְכִי לֵיכָּא פָּנִים חֲדָשׁוֹת — מֵנִיחַ: רָבָא אָמַר כֵּיוָן שֶׁמֵּנִיחַ. בְּשֵׁנִי, שׁוּב אֵינוֹ חוֹלֵץ לְפָנִים חֲדָשׁוֹת: וְהָאָמַר רָבָא. לְעֵיל (דף כ.) בִּכְפִיַּית הַמִּטָּה, הֲלָכָה כְּתַנָּא דִּידַן דְּאָמַר ג' יָמִים עִיקַּר אֲבֵילוּת. ה"נ — נִבְעֵי ג' יָמִים (א) לְהָנִיחַ תְּפִילִּין:

מִצְוָה

תורה אור

אלא מעתה ועמד ואמר ה"נ. משמע: ועמד ואמר — היינו אפי' מיושב. והא דאמרינן פרק "מצות חליצה" (יבמות דף קו.) בתי עמודי — לכתחילה שמא צריך עמידה מדרבנן. מיהו קשה: ד"ועמדו שני האנשים" (דברים יט) דבעינן עומד! וי"ל: ד"ועמד ואמר" ודאי משמע אפי' מיושב, כמו "ועמדו וקדשו" (לעיל דף יח:) אבל "ועמד" לחוד לא משמע הכי*: **דאי** לא תימא הכי וישכב ארצה וכו'. אע"ג ד"ושכב ארלה" כתיב נמי אצל הילד דבת שבע, אע"ג דלא גבי מת כתיב אלא על בנו? ושמא: הואיל והנביא אמר לו "מות ימות" — הרי הוא כמת, ואע"פ שהתפלל עליו שיחיה. וכענין זה אמר בירושלמי: הקב"ה שהיה יודע שעתיד להיות מבול — היה מתאבל על עולמו קודם המבול. ובתוס' הרב הקשה, כי הסוגיא משונה: בתחילה אומר מלתא יתירתא עבד, דאי לא תימא הכי, והדר מקשה דלא יצא ידי חובתו! וצ"ל דהכי פי': מלתא יתירתא, וה"נ כפה מטתו ושכב ע"ג קרקע, וא"כ עבד מלתא יתירתא. דליכא למימר ושכב — היינו כפיית המטה — דהא לא יצא ידי חובתו מכפיית המטה. א"ל: כעין, וליכא שום יתור. וניחא ליה לשנויי הכי מלומר שהיה מלתא יתירתא, ולהוכיח קריעה מכפיית המטה:

אלו דברים שאבל אסור בהן. הכא לא חשיב דברים שמצווה עליהן כגון כפיית המטה ועטיפת הראש, דלא חשיב אלא מילי דאסור בהן. תפילין ושאילת שלום לא חשיב, דאין זה כל ימי האבל, כדאמר לקמן. תכבוסת לא חשיב — דהויא בכלל רחילה. אע"ג דלעיל (דף טו.) מייתי תרי קראי לרחילה ולתכבוסת. אבל הני דלא נוהגים כל השבוע — לא. לאפוקי מפי' הר"א שפירש שרבינו שמואל היה מתיר לאבל לעשות מלאכה אחר ג' ימים. ומה שאין נוהגין עתה לעשות עטיפת הראש וכפיית המטה — סמכינן אהא דאמרינן בירושלמי: אכסנאי אינו חייב בכפיית המטה, דלא לימרון חרש הוא. פי': מכשף. וכמו כן, אנו בין הנכרים, ויש בינינו עבדים ושפחות. ועוד יש ליתן טעם בכפיית המטה: לפי שמטות שלנו כך יכולין לשכב בנחת מלד זה כמו מלד זה, ואין ניכרת הכפייה, דיש להן ד' קונדיסים מלמעלה כעין רגלים. וכדאמרינן לקמן: דרגש אין צריך לכפותו. ועוד יש ליתן טעם בעטיפת הראש — שלא היה מביא כי אם לידי שחוק •ענין עטיפת ישמעאלים:

ואסור לקרות בתורה. בתשובת רבינו יצחק זקני כתב כי רבינו יעקב היה אוסר בימי אבלו באיוב ובקינות ובדברים הרעים שבירמיה, מדלא תני ליה בשמעתין, כמו ט' באב שילהי תענית (דף ל.). ובימי זקנותו חזר והתיר. ובירושלמי אמר: אבל שונה במקום שאינו רגיל. משמע ששונה כמו בט' באב, שאומר בפרק בתרא דתענית (שם): אבל קורא במקום שאינו רגיל. וה"ק התם: כל מצות הנוהגות באבל — נוהגות בט' באב, ואסור לקרות בתורה כו' אבל קורא במקום שאינו רגיל, וקורא באיוב וקינות וכו'. משמע לכאורה דאבל וט' באב שוין, כדקאמר בירושלמי. ומיהו, אבל שונה במקום שאינו רגיל, משמע דהא דוקא שרי, ולא באיוב ובקינות ובירמיה. ומה שהביא רבי יצחק ראיה לאסור מדקאמר לעיל (ד' טו.) אסור בדברי תורה, שנאמר "האנק דום" ומשמע הכל — אין נ"ל ראייה, דלא קאמר אלא מדבר המשמחו. כדאמר בתענית (ד' ל.) משום שנאמר "פקודי ה' ישרים משמחי לב". תדע דכולהו לאו דוקא, דהא קאמר אסור בתפילין, שנאמר "פארך חבוש עליך" ואינו אסור כל ימי אבלו:

משלישי ואילך. ושלישי חשבינן [מקצתו] ככולו. ומדרבנן, דהא לא מייתי קרא אלא לשני ימים, דכתיב "ויתמו ימי בכי אבל משה" הר"א. והאי "ויתמו" — בתפילין. וכן "ואחריתה כיום מר" — טפי מכל שאר מילי, דכל שעה שהוא מר נפש מתעולל בעפר ואין זה פאר, כדפירש בקונטרס בכתובות (ד' ו:) ריב"א. ובט' באב היה אומר ר' יצחק זקני דשרי, כמו בשלישי דשרי:

חולץ ומניח אפילו מאה פעמים. פי': חולץ בפנים חדשות, ומניח כשילכו. וכן כל שעה שילכו, אפה פעמים ביום. וטעמיה משום בין לר"א בין לרבי יהושע בפנים חדשות — אסור, לר"א — להניח אסור, ולרבי יהושע — אפי' חולץ:

מכאן

עין משפט נר מצוה

קיט א מיי' פ"ד מהל' יבום וחליצה הל' ו סמג עשין נב טוש"ע אה"ע סי' קסט סעי' סד:

קכ ב מיי' פ"ה שם הלכה יח:

[וע"ע תוס' יבמות קג. ד"ה בין ותוס' שבועות ל. ד"ה מצוה ותוספות זבחים טז. ד"ה מיושב]

קכא ג מיי' שם הל' א סמג עשין דרבנן ג טוש"ע י"ד סימן שפ סעיף א:

קכב ד ה ו ז מיי' שם הלכה טז סמג שם טוש"ע שם וסימן שפד סעיף א:

[גירסת הרי"ף (דף רלה:) גדולה מכולן אמרו אפילו על גבי קרקע לא יצא כו']

קכג ח מיי' שם פ"ד הלכה ט טוש"ע שם סימן שפח סעיף א:

רבינו חננאל

מטתה ונוהגת עמו אבלות. אמימר שכיב ליה בר ברא קרע עליה *) א"ל קרעתי מעומד קם קרע מעומד א"ל רב אשי ומנ"ל דבעינן קריעה מעומד א"ל דכתיב ויקם איוב ויקרע אי הכי בענין חליצה דכתיב ועמד ואמר לא חפצתי הכי נמי דמעומד. והתניא בין עומד בין יושב בין מוטה חליצתה כשרה אלא מהכא ויקם המלך ויקרע את בגדיו ודלמא קריעה מעומד מלתא יתירתא הוא דעבד כמה דעבד בשכיבתו ארצה דלא הוה צריך דתניא ישן על גבי מטה על גבי כסא ע"ג אודייני גדולה מכולן אפילו על גבי קרקע לא יצא וא"ר יוחנן שלא (יצא) קיים כפיית המטה א"ל מאי וישכב ארצה לאו ארצה ממש הוא אלא כעין ארצה כדמפרש בירוש' ר' יוחנן אמר וישבו אתו לארץ אינו כתוב על הארץ אלא לארץ בדבר הסמוך לארץ מיכן שהיו ישינין על מטות כפויות וכיון שישן על מטה כפויה ניעור בלילה ונזכר שהוא אבל: אלו דברים שאבל אסור בהן במלאכה ברחיצה וסיכה ובנעילת הסנדל ובתשמיש המטה ואסור לקרות בתורה בנביאים ובכתובים ולשנות במשנה ובמדרש ובתלמוד בהלכות ובאגדות ואם היו רבים צריכין לו אינו נמנע. ומעשה ומת בנו של ר' יוסי בצפורי ובתו של ר' בבית שערים ויצאו ודרשו כל היום ואסיקנא ובלבד שלא יעמיד המתורגמן אלא יושב לו אחר בצידו של אבל ולוחש לו והוא משמיע לתורגמן והתורגמן משמיע לרבים. גרסינן בפרק יש בכור לנחלה מת הבן ביום שלשים כיום שלפניו פי' כיום ל"א וחייב לתת ה' סלעים לכהן. ר' עקיבא אומר אם נתן לא יטול ואם לא נתן לא יתן. אמר רב אשי הכל מודים לענין אבלות דיום שלשים כיום שלפניו דמי וחשוב כיום שלפניו ובשלשים ואחד שמע והנה **) היא שמועה רחוקה ואינו נוהג אלא יום אחד בלבד כשמואל דאמר הלכה כדברי המיקל באבל: ת"ר אבל שלשה ימים הראשונים אסור להניח תפילין משלישי ושלישי בכלל מניח ואם באו פנים חדשות אינו חולץ דברי רבי אליעזר ורבי יהושע אומר משני ושני בכלל מניח ואם באו פנים חדשות חולץ. אמר עולא הלכתא כרבי אליעזר בחליצה שאם באו פנים חדשות משלישי ואילך אינו חולץ ***) והלכתא כרבא דאמר כיון שהניח אינו חולץ כר' יהושע בהנחה שמיום שני מניח מ"ט דר' אלעזר דכתיב ויתמו

*) אולי צ"ל אמר לא קרעתי מעומד קם וכו'. **) דברי רבינו בכאן הובא ברי"ף כאן בשם איכא מ"ד ועי' היטב מש"כ על דברי רבינו בזה. ***) נראה דצ"ל משלישי ואילך אינו חולץ וכר"י בהנחה שמיום שני מניח והלכתא כרבא דאמר כיון שהניח שוב אינו חולץ.

מסורת הש"ס

יבמות קג.

לקמן כז. ע"ש

[עי' תוס' ב"ב קמד. ד"ה אודייני]

[נ"ל אלו]

[מס' שמחות פ"ו]

[עי' בה"ג דסוכה (דף רמב.) ד"ה אבל חייב וכו' ותבין למה נקט בכך לישנא]

הגהות הב"ח

(א) רש"י ד"ה והאמר רבא כו' נבעי ג' ימים שלא להניח תפילין:

גליון הש"ס

גמ' ודלמא מילתא יתירתא. עיין לקמן דף כו ע"א תד"ה משכם: תוס' ד"ה אלו דברים וכו' ענין עטיפת ישמעאלים. עי' לקמן דף כד ע"א תוס' ד"ה ושמואל לטעמיה:

קכד א מיי' פ"ה מהל' אבל הלכה ח סמג עשין דרבנן ב טוש"ע י"ד סימן שפ סעיף ב:
קכה ב מיי' שם פ"ז הלכה ה טוש"ע שם סימן שצג סעיף א:
קכו ג מיי' שם פ"ה הלכה כ טוש"ע שם סימן שפה סעיף א:
קכז ד טוש"ע שם בהג"ה:
קכח ה ו טוש"ע שם סעיף ב:
קכט ז ח ט י מיי' שם הלכה כ וטוש"ע שם סעיף א:
קל כ מיי' שם טוש"ע שם סעיף ב:
קלא ל טוש"ע שם:
קלב מ נ מיי' שם פ"ז הלכה ד סמג עשין דרבנן ב טוש"ע שם סימן שעה סעיף א:

מכאן ואילך עושה בצינעא בתוך ביתו. פי' בתוספת הרב: במתפרנס מן הצדקה קאי והכי משמע לעיל. דקאמר לעיל (ד' יט:): הקובר מתו ג' ימים קודם הרגל מונה ה' ימים אחר הרגל ומלאכתו נעשית ע"י אחרים. משמע דהאבל אסור כל ז' והתם נמי לא שרינן לעצמו שיהא עושה מלאכה. וה"נ תניא במסכת שמחות (פ"ה): אבל כל ז' ימים, אסור בעשיית מלאכה הוא ובניו ובנותיו ועבדיו ושפחותיו ובהמתו, כשם שהוא אסור לעשות לו – כך אחרים אסורים לעשות לו. פי': חוץ מזיתיו הפוכים ומלאכת האבד. מיום ג' ואילך עושה מלאכה, דוקא במי שמתפרנס מן הצדקה ובצינעא, אבל אמרו חכמים תבא מארה לשכיניו כו'. בר קפרא אומר: אף בשלישי לא יעשה כך. הביא בתוס' הרב. ולכאורה נראה דכיון דילפינן (לעיל דף כ.) מ"והפכתי חגיכם לאבל" מה חג ז', לענין מלאכה איירי. וגם הר"א מסופק דלמא אעני דוקא קאי. אבל בשם רבינו שמואל אמר: בכל אבלים קאי, מדלא קתני מכאן ואילך עושה עני בצינעא ולא כדפרישית:

מכאן ואילך הולך. פי' בתוספת הרב: ועל זה סומכים שבאים בבהכ"נ בט' באב, ואיני יודע אם הוא מנהג טוב. ומדבריו מאינו למדין שחושב ט' באב כמו לאחר שלשה, ונפקא מינה לענין תפילין, כדפי' לעיל:

מדבר עמו תנחומין ואינו שואל. וקשיא למ"ד מכאן ואילך שואל ומשיב:

מתה אשתו ונשא אשה אחרת. משמע בתוך ל' יום דאי לאחר ל' יום היכי קאמר אינו רשאי ליכנס לביתו לדבר עמו תנחומין הא בשאר מתים נמי אמרו אינו מדבר עמו תנחומין וצריך לאוקמי באין לו בנים לפי' ר"ת שמתיר לישא אשה אחר שבעה א"נ בהניחה לו בנים קטנים שמותר לישא מיד ולבעול אחר ל' יום לפירוש רבינו יצחק והאריך בתוספות פרק קמא דכתובות (דף ד. ושם בד"ה אבל איפכא) ובליקוטין רחוב נתבונח:

מקום קרוב. פירשו בהלכות גדולות דהיינו י' פרסאות:

אפילו בא ביום שביעי ממקום קרוב. וא"ת: והא מקצת היום ככולו! וי"ל: א] כגון שלא עמדו עדיין מנחמין מאצלן. ויש נמי בפ"ק דכתובות (דף ח:): ברכת אבלים בעשרה כל ז', ומסתמא היינו ביום. א"נ י"ל: מקצת היום ככולו לא הוי בלילה לענין שום דבר, כדאמרינן במגילה בפ"ב (דף כ.) דשימור לילה לאו שימור הוא, לענין שבעה נקיים:
הלך

מִצְוָה שָׁאנֵי. ת"ר: [א]אָבֵל, ג' יָמִים הָרִאשׁוֹנִים – אָסוּר בִּמְלָאכָה. וַאֲפִילּוּ עָנִי הַמִּתְפַּרְנֵס מִן הַצְּדָקָה. מִכָּאן וְאֵילָךְ – עוֹשֶׂה בְּצִינְעָא בְּתוֹךְ בֵּיתוֹ, וְהָאִשָּׁה טוֹוָה בְּפֶלֶךְ בְּתוֹךְ בֵּיתָהּ. [ב]ת"ר: אָבֵל, ג' יָמִים הָרִאשׁוֹנִים – אֵינוֹ הוֹלֵךְ לְבֵית הָאָבֵל, מִכָּאן וְאֵילָךְ – הוֹלֵךְ, וְאֵינוֹ יוֹשֵׁב בִּמְקוֹם הַמְנַחֲמִין אֶלָּא בִּמְקוֹם הַמִּתְנַחֲמִין. [ג]תָּנוּ רַבָּנַן: אָבֵל, ג' יָמִים הָרִאשׁוֹנִים – אָסוּר בִּשְׁאִילַת שָׁלוֹם, מִשְּׁלֹשָׁה וְעַד שִׁבְעָה – מֵשִׁיב וְאֵינוֹ שׁוֹאֵל, מִכָּאן וְאֵילָךְ – שׁוֹאֵל וּמֵשִׁיב כְּדַרְכּוֹ. שְׁלֹשָׁה יָמִים הָרִאשׁוֹנִים אָסוּר בִּשְׁאִילַת שָׁלוֹם? וְהָתַנְיָא: *מַעֲשֶׂה וּמֵתוּ בָּנָיו שֶׁל ר"ע, נִכְנְסוּ כָּל יִשְׂרָאֵל וְהִסְפִּידוּם הֶסְפֵּד גָּדוֹל. בִּשְׁעַת פְּטִירָתָן עָמַד ר"ע עַל סַפְסָל גָּדוֹל וְאָמַר: אַחֵינוּ בֵּית יִשְׂרָאֵל שִׁמְעוּ! אפי' שְׁנֵי בָּנִים חֲתָנִים – מְנוּחָם הוּא בִּשְׁבִיל כָּבוֹד שֶׁעֲשִׂיתֶם. וְאִם בִּשְׁבִיל עֲקִיבָא בָּאתֶם – הֲרֵי כַּמָּה עֲקִיבָא בַּשּׁוּק. אֶלָּא כָּךְ אֲמַרְתֶּם: °"תּוֹרַת אֱלֹהָיו בְּלִבּוֹ" וְכ"ש שֶׁשְּׂכַרְכֶם כָּפוּל, לְכוּ לְבָתֵּיכֶם לְשָׁלוֹם. [ד]כְּבוֹד רַבִּים שָׁאנֵי. מִג' וְעַד ז' – מֵשִׁיב וְאֵינוֹ שׁוֹאֵל, מִכָּאן וְאֵילָךְ – שׁוֹאֵל וּמֵשִׁיב כְּדַרְכּוֹ. וּרְמִינְהוּ: *[ה]הַמּוֹצֵא אֶת חֲבֵירוֹ אָבֵל, בְּתוֹךְ ל' יוֹם – מְדַבֵּר עִמּוֹ תַּנְחוּמִין וְאֵינוֹ שׁוֹאֵל בִּשְׁלוֹמוֹ, לְאַחַר ל' יוֹם – שׁוֹאֵל בִּשְׁלוֹמוֹ וְאֵינוֹ מְדַבֵּר עִמּוֹ תַּנְחוּמִין. [ו]מֵתָה אִשְׁתּוֹ וְנָשָׂא אִשָּׁה אַחֶרֶת – אֵינוֹ רַשַּׁאי לִיכָּנֵס לְבֵיתוֹ לְדַבֵּר עִמּוֹ תַּנְחוּמִין. מְצָאוֹ בַּשּׁוּק – אוֹמֵר לוֹ בְּשָׂפָה רָפָה וּבְכוֹבֶד רֹאשׁ! אָמַר רַב אִידִי בַּר אָבִין: [ז]הוּא שׁוֹאֵל בִּשְׁלוֹם אֲחֵרִים – שֶׁאֲחֵרִים שְׁרוּיִין בְּשָׁלוֹם, אֲחֵרִים אֵין שׁוֹאֲלִין בִּשְׁלוֹמוֹ – שֶׁהוּא אֵינוֹ שָׁרוּי בְּשָׁלוֹם. וְהָא מִדְּקָתָנֵי מֵשִׁיב – מִכְּלָל דְּשָׁיְילִינַן לֵיהּ! [ח]דְּלָא יָדְעִי. אִי הָכִי, הָתָם נַמִּי! הָתָם [ט]מוֹדַע לְהוּ, וְלָא מְהַדַּר לְהוּ. [י]הָכָא – לָא צָרִיךְ לְאוֹדוּעִינְהוּ. וּרְמִינְהוּ: *[כ]הַמּוֹצֵא אֶת חֲבֵרוֹ אָבֵל, בְּתוֹךְ י"ב חֹדֶשׁ – מְדַבֵּר עִמּוֹ תַּנְחוּמִין וְאֵינוֹ שׁוֹאֵל בִּשְׁלוֹמוֹ, לְאַחַר י"ב חֹדֶשׁ – שׁוֹאֵל בִּשְׁלוֹמוֹ וְאֵינוֹ מְדַבֵּר עִמּוֹ תַּנְחוּמִין, אֲבָל מְדַבֵּר עִמּוֹ מִן הַצַּד. א"ר מֵאִיר: הַמּוֹצֵא אֶת חֲבֵרוֹ אָבֵל לְאַחַר י"ב חֹדֶשׁ, וּמְדַבֵּר עִמּוֹ תַּנְחוּמִין, לְמָה הוּא דּוֹמֶה – לְאָדָם שֶׁנִּשְׁבְּרָה רַגְלוֹ וְחָיְתָה, מְצָאוֹ רוֹפֵא וְאָמַר לוֹ: כַּלֵּךְ אֶצְלִי, שֶׁאֲנִי שׁוֹבְרָהּ וַאֲרַפְּאֶנָּה, כְּדֵי שֶׁתֵּדַע שֶׁסַּמְמָנִין שֶׁלִּי יָפִין. לָא קַשְׁיָא: [כ]הָא – בְּאָבִיו וְאִמּוֹ, הָא – בִּשְׁאָר קְרוֹבִים. הָתָם נַמִּי יְדַבֵּר עִמּוֹ תַּנְחוּמִין מִן הַצַּד! אִין, ה"נ. וּמַאי אֵינוֹ מְדַבֵּר עִמּוֹ תַּנְחוּמִין – כְּדַרְכּוֹ, [ל]אֲבָל מְדַבֵּר עִמּוֹ מִן הַצַּד. *ת"ר: אָבֵל, ג' יָמִים הָרִאשׁוֹנִים בָּא מִמָּקוֹם קָרוֹב – מוֹנֶה עִמָּהֶן, בָּא מִמָּקוֹם רָחוֹק – מוֹנֶה לְעַצְמוֹ. מִכָּאן וְאֵילָךְ, אפי' בָּא מִמָּקוֹם קָרוֹב – מוֹנֶה לְעַצְמוֹ. ר"ש אוֹמֵר: [מ]אפי' בָּא בַּיּוֹם הַשְּׁבִיעִי מִמָּקוֹם קָרוֹב – מוֹנֶה עִמָּהֶן. אָמַר מָר: ג' יָמִים הָרִאשׁוֹנִים, בָּא מִמָּקוֹם קָרוֹב – מוֹנֶה עִמָּהֶן. א"ר חִיָּיא בַּר אַבָּא א"ר יוֹחָנָן: [נ]וְהוּא שֶׁיֵּשׁ גְּדוֹל הַבַּיִת בַּבַּיִת. אִיבַּעְיָא לְהוּ:
הָלַךְ

תהלים לז

חולין נ:

מִצְוָה שָׁאנֵי. כְּלוֹמַר: הוֹאִיל וּמִצְוָה לְהָנִיחַ תְּפִילִּין – מַאי לְהָנִיחַ לְאַלְתַּר בַּשֵּׁנִי: אִשָּׁה. חֲבִילָה, טוֹוָה בְּפֶלֶךְ: אֶלָּא בִּמְקוֹם הַמִּתְנַחֲמִין. סָמוּךְ לָאֲבֵלִים: אֲפִי' ב' בָּנִים חֲתָנִים. קָבַרְתִּי, מְנוּחָם אֲנִי מֵרוֹב כָּבוֹד שֶׁעֲשִׂיתֶם לִי: וְאִם בִּשְׁבִיל עֲקִיבָא בָּאתֶם הֲרֵי כַּמָּה עֲקִיבָא בַּשּׁוּק. שֶׁלֹּא הֲלַכְתֶּם לְנַחֲמָן: כ"ש שֶׁשְּׂכַרְכֶם כָּפוּל. שֶׁלִּכְבוֹד הַתּוֹרָה בָּאתֶם: לְכוּ לְבָתֵּיכֶם לְשָׁלוֹם. הֲרֵי שָׁאַל בִּשְׁלוֹמָן: וּרְמִינְהוּ. דִּבְתוֹךְ ל' יוֹם אֵינוֹ שׁוֹאֵל: וְנָשָׂא אִשָּׁה. בְּתוֹךְ שְׁלֹשִׁים יוֹם, כְּגוֹן שֶׁאֵין לוֹ בָּנִים, כִּדְלְקַמָּן: אֵינוֹ רַשַּׁאי לִיכָּנֵס לְבֵיתוֹ. לְנַחֲמוֹ, מִשּׁוּם חֲלִישַׁת דַּעַת דְּאִשָּׁה אַחֲרוֹנָה. קָתָנֵי מִיהַת: בְּתוֹךְ ל' יוֹם אֵינוֹ שׁוֹאֵל בִּשְׁלוֹמוֹ. כ"ש שֶׁהָאָבֵל עַצְמוֹ אֵינוֹ שׁוֹאֵל בִּשְׁלוֹמוֹ שֶׁל זֶה. וּלְעֵיל קָתָנֵי: מִשִּׁבְעָה וְאֵילָךְ מֵשִׁיב וְשׁוֹאֵל כְּדַרְכּוֹ: אָמַר רַב אִידִי הוּא שׁוֹאֵל בִּשְׁלוֹם אֲחֵרִים. כְּלוֹמַר: תָּרִיץ הָא דְּתָנֵי מִכָּאן וְאֵילָךְ שׁוֹאֵל כְּדַרְכּוֹ – בְּתוֹךְ שְׁלֹשִׁים יוֹם דְּהוּא שׁוֹאֵל בִּשְׁלוֹם אֲחֵרִים, שֶׁהֵן שְׁרוּיִין בְּשָׁלוֹם וְהָא דְּקָתָנֵי בְּתוֹךְ ל' יוֹם אֵינוֹ שׁוֹאֵל בִּשְׁלוֹמוֹ – אֵין אֲחֵרִים שׁוֹאֲלִין בִּשְׁלוֹמוֹ: מִכְּלָל דְּשָׁיְילֵי. בְּתוֹךְ ל' יוֹם, וְקַשְׁיָא לְמַאן דְּתָנֵי בְּתוֹךְ ל' יוֹם אֵינוֹ שׁוֹאֵל: דְּלָא יָדְעִי. כְּלוֹמַר, הָא דְּתָנֵי דְּמֵשִׁיב – לְהָנֵי דְּשָׁאֲלֵי לֵיהּ וְלָא יָדְעִי דְּאָבֵל הוּא, אֲבָל מַאן דְּיָדַע דְּאָבֵל הוּא – לָא שָׁאֵיל לֵיהּ בְּתוֹךְ ל' יוֹם: אִי הָכִי. דְּאוֹקְמַתְּ לָהּ בְּלָא יָדְעִי, אֲפִי' ג' יָמִים נַמִּי מֵשִׁיב (לְמַאן דְּשָׁאֵיל לֵיהּ (א) וְאָמַר דְּאָבֵל הוּא) לְמַאן דְּלָא יָדַע וְשָׁאֵיל לֵיהּ בְּתוֹךְ ג' יָמִים: הָתָם מוֹדַע לְהוּ. הָא דְּקָתָנֵי כָּל ג' יָמִים אָסוּר בִּשְׁאִילַת שָׁלוֹם – אֲבָל מוֹדַע לְהוּ דְּאָבֵל הוּא, וְלָא מְהַדַּר לְהוּ: הָכָא. לְאַחַר ג' לָא צָרִיךְ לְאוֹדוּעִינְהוּ לְמַאן דְּלָא יָדְעִי דְּאָבֵל הוּא, אֶלָּא מֵשִׁיב: וּרְמִינְהוּ בְּתוֹךְ י"ב חֹדֶשׁ אֵינוֹ שׁוֹאֵל בִּשְׁלוֹמוֹ. וְקָשֶׁה לְהָךְ דְּתָנֵי לְאַחַר שְׁלֹשִׁים יוֹם שׁוֹאֵל בִּשְׁלוֹמוֹ: מִן הַצַּד. שֶׁאוֹמֵר לוֹ "תִּתְנַחֵם", וְאֵינוֹ מַזְכִּיר שֵׁם הַמֵּת: הָא בְּאָבֵל עַל אָבִיו וְעַל אִמּוֹ. אֵינוֹ שׁוֹאֵל בִּשְׁלוֹמוֹ עַד י"ב חֹדֶשׁ: הָא בִּשְׁאָר קְרוֹבִים. שׁוֹאֵל בִּשְׁלוֹמוֹ לְאַחַר ל' יוֹם: הָתָם נַמִּי. שְׁלֹשִׁים, דְּמוֹקְמַתְּ לֵיהּ בִּשְׁאָר קְרוֹבִים: יְדַבֵּר עִמּוֹ תַּנְחוּמִין מִן הַצַּד. לְאַחַר ל', כִּי הֵיכִי דִּבְאָבִיו וְאִמּוֹ מְדַבֵּר עִמּוֹ תַּנְחוּמִין מִן הַצַּד לְאַחַר י"ב חֹדֶשׁ. וְאַמַּאי קָתָנֵי לְאַחַר ל' אֵינוֹ מְדַבֵּר עִמּוֹ תַּנְחוּמִים כְּלָל? ה"נ. וּמַאי לְאַחַר ל' אֵינוֹ מְדַבֵּר עִמּוֹ תַּנְחוּמִים – כְּדַרְכּוֹ: מוֹנֶה עִמָּהֶן. עִם הָאֲבֵלִים שֶׁבְּאוֹתוֹ מָקוֹם. הוֹאִיל דְּבְמָקוֹם קָרוֹב הֲוָה, וְיָכוֹל לָבֹא בִּתְחִלַּת הָאֲבֵילוּת – חָשְׁבִינַן לֵיהּ כְּמוֹ דַּאֲתָא, דְּאֵינוֹ מוֹנֶה אֶלָּא ה' יָמִים עִם שְׁאָר אֲבֵלִים: מוֹנֶה לְעַצְמוֹ. שִׁבְעָה שְׁלֵימִין: שֶׁיֵּשׁ גְּדוֹל הַבַּיִת בַּבַּיִת. שֶׁבָּא וּמָצָא גְּדוֹל הַבַּיִת בַּבַּיִת – מוֹנֶה עִמָּהֶן עִם אֲבֵילֵי הַבַּיִת. וְזֶה שֶׁבָּא הוּא הַצָּעִיר מִמֶּנּוּ. אֲבָל אִם הָיָה גָּדוֹל בַּדֶּרֶךְ, וּבָא בְּתוֹךְ שְׁלֹשָׁה יָמִים, אֲפִי' מִמָּקוֹם קָרוֹב – מוֹנֶה לְעַצְמוֹ, דְּלָא חָשִׁיב אֲבֵילוּת דְּצָעִיר לְאִצְטְרוּפֵי גָּדוֹל בַּהֲדֵיהּ:
הָלַךְ

עיין שמחות פ"ח

[שמחות פי"ד]

רבינו חננאל

ויתמו ימי בכי אבל משה מיעוט ימי אבל שנים ור' יהושע אמר ואחריתה כיום מר יומא קמא בלבד: ת"ר אבל שלשה ימים הראשונים אסור בעשיית מלאכה ואפילו עני המתפרנס מן הצדקה מיכן ואילך עושה בצנעא בתוך ביתו ואשה טווה בפלך בתוך ביתה: **ירושלמי** תבא מאירה לשכיניו שהצריכוהו לאבל לעשות ולאכול: ת"ר ג' ימים הראשונים אסור לילך לבית האבל מיכן ואילך הולך כדרכו ואינו יושב במקום המנחמין אלא במקום המתנחמין. ג' ימים הראשונים אסור בשאילת שלום. והא כשמתו בני ר"ע באו כל ישראל והספידום הספד גדול ובשעת פטירתן עמד ר' עקיבא על ספסל גדול ואמר אחינו בית ישראל שמעו אפילו בנים חתנים קבר מנוחם הוא בשביל כבוד שעשיתם וכמה עקיבא בשוק אלא כך אמרתם תורת אלהיו בקרבו לא תמעד אשוריו וכ"ש ששכרכם כפול לכו לבתיכם לשלום. ופרקינן כבוד רבים שאני. ומקשינן מיכן ואילך שואל ומשיב כדרכו והתניא המוצא חבירו אבל בתוך שלשים יום מדבר עמו תנחומין ואינו שואל בשלומו לאחר שלשים יום שואל בשלומו ואינו מדבר עמו תנחומין מתה אשתו ונשא אשה אחרת כו' הנה אין בשלומו אפילו לאחר ז' בשלומו ופריק רב אידי בר אבין אחרים אין שואלין בשלומו שהוא אינו שרוי בשלום אבל

הגהות הב"ח

(א) רש"י ד"ה הכי כו' מ משיב למאן דשאיל ל הס"ד ואח"כ מה"ד הת מודע להו. הא דקתני שלשה אסור בשאלת של ולמאן דלא ידע ושאיל ל בתוך שלשה ימים מוד להו דאבל הוא ולא מה להו כצ"ל:

הגהות מהר"ב רנשבורג

א] תוס' ד"ה אפי' וכ וי"ל כגון וכו'. נמחק תיב כגון וכ"ב כיון כצ"ל לענ" ור"ל כיון דלקמן דף כ ע"א מוקמינן לדר"ש והו שבא ומצא מנחמין אצל א"כ לא הוי מקצת היו ככולו כל זמן שהמנחמי אצלו ודוק:

הלך גדול הבית לבית הקברות מהו. פי': מי מונה לעצמו או לא? דשמא כיון שהוא טרוד בעניני מת, וכששמעו הם שמע גם הוא – ימנה עמהן. או שמא מונה לעצמו. ולא ידענא מאי הוי דינא בגדול הבית שבא ממקום קרוב, אי מונה עמהן הואיל והוא עיקר. ויש ליתן טעם לומר שהוא מונה לבדו, הואיל ואינו יודע האבילות. או טעם להיפך, דהואיל משום המת הלך – ימנה עמהם:

דאתא בגו תלתא יומין. כשאתא גדול הבית בתוך ג' ימים – מונה הוא עמהן. וכדאמרינן לעיל: ג' ימים הראשונים מונה עמהם. וקשיא לי: דהא קיי"ל כר"ש, דאפי' ביום ז' מונה עמהן, כדאמרינן לקמן, וא"כ, מה לי תוך ג' מה לי לאחר ג'? ונראה מתוך ה"ג דאפי' לר"ש (בר יוסי) הוי חילוק, דתוך ג' ואחר ג' מקום רחוק. שפי' הא דאתא בגו תלתא יומי מונה עמהן – אפי' בא ממקום רחוק. אתא לבתר תלתא יומי ממקום קרוב – אפי' תוך ז' מונה עמהן, ונסמוך פירש: אפי' לר"ש אתיא הך מילתא. ועוד יש לפרש, דה"פ: הלך גדול הבית לבית הקברות מהו? דמיבעיא ליה אם אותו שבא מונה עם הנשארים. וכך פי' ר' יצחק ז"ל. והוא כשיש גדול הבית בבית – אז מונה עמהן הבא אצלם ממקום קרוב ומצאם אבלים, שאע"פ שאבלותם חל מקודם לשלו, ומצאם יום או יומים – יסיים עמהן *לרבנן כשבא גדול הבית תוך ג' ימים, שפירש גדול הבית ג' ימים, ולר"ש אפי' ביום השביעי. ודוקא כשיש גדול הבית בבית, כי אז בטל אצלם. והכי פי': איבעיא להו הלך גדול הבית לבית הקברות, פי': הלך ללות מת עד עיר אחרת, וקברו שם, מהו שיהא מונה עמהן אותו שבא אצל אבלים שבעיר, שמת בה מונה עמהן, אע"פ שאין גדול הבית עמהן שם. [או לא?] דהא דבעינן גדול הבית בבית – למעוטי האי נמי קאתי, אע"ג דידע בהאי אבילות ושייך בה. או דלמא לא אתא למעוטי אלא היכא דליתא גדול הבית בדוכתא אחריתי, דלא ידע בהאי אבילות כלל. אבל הלך לבית הקברות, כיון דידע בהאי אבילות – חשיב אבילות דידהו עיקר, ובטל האורח גבייהו. א"ל: מונה עמהן. והתניא מונה לעצמו! לא קשיא: הא – דאתא גדול הבית בגו תלתא יומי מבית הקברות, דאז הוא מונה עמהן, וגם האורח מונה עמהן, אם בא בתוך שלשה לרבנן או בתוך שבעה לרבי שמעון. הא דלא אתא גדול הבית בגו תלתא יומי – דלא חשיב אבילות דידהו עיקר, דלימני הא דאתא מעלמא בהדייהו, מאחר שאין גדול הבית מונה עמהן. ולא מיבעיא לרבנן שאין גדול הבית מונה עמהן כי לא אתא בגו תלתא, אלא אפי' לר"ש דאמר אפי' ביום ז' מונה עמהן – ה"מ אחר דלא הוה ידע ביה בתחילה, ובטל לגבייהו, כיון דגדול הבית נמי מני בהדייהו, והם תחילת האבילות ועיקרו יותר ממנו, שלא ידע בתחילת האבילות. אבל החוזר מבית הקברות, שהיה בתחילת האבילות – אינו מונה עמהן היכא דלא אתא בגו תלתא יומי, בין אם יש גדול הבית בין אם אין גדול הבית. כי הא דא"ל רב לבני הצלפוני דאתי בגו תלתא, החוזר מבית הקברות בגו תלתא – לימנו בהדייכו, דלא אתו בגו תלתא יומי – מימני לנפשיה, עכ"ל. ז"ל הירושלמי: הרי שבא ומצא אבל בתוך ביתו, בשני ובשלישי – משלים עמהן, ברביעי – מונה לעצמו. ר"ש אומר: אפי' בז' משלים עמהם. ריב"ל אומר: הלכה כר"ש כשיש גדול המשפחה בבית, אבל כשאין גדול המשפחה – מונה לעצמו. ולפי הירושלמי היה נ"ל דאינו פוסק כר"ש אלא כשיש גדול המשפחה בבית, אבל אם אין גדול המשפחה – הלכה כרבנן, דבתוך ג' ימים – מונה עמהם, לאחר ג' – מונה לעצמו. ולפ"ז אתי שפיר אפי' אליבא דהלכתא דאתי בגו תלתא – לימנו *בהדייכו בגדול הבית בבית, דכמו שאין גדול הבית הלכתא כרבנן – כמו כן בגדול הבית עצמו, והוי דינא כרבנן:

מהדריתו אפייכו אתחילו מנו. אבל אותם ההולכים עם המת, משיסתם הגולל בין גדול הבית בבית בין הולך לבית הקברות, וכן המנהג. ובירושלמי אינו כן, דהכי תנן מת שהוליכו אותו ממקום למקום, כגון אלו דקברין במקום אחר, אית תניא תני: אלו שכאן מונין משיצא המת, ואלו ששם מונין משנסתם הגולל. ואית תני: הני והני משנסתם הגולל. ורב סימון בשם ריב"ל: הכל הולך אחר גדול המשפחה. ר' יעקב בשם ר' יוסי: לחומרין. מהו לחומרין? שאם היה גדול המשפחה כאן – *אלו שכאן מונין משיצא המת, ואלו ששם מונין משנסתם הגולל. וגדול המשפחה שם – אלו ואלו מונין משיסתם הגולל. וקשיא: מהו לחומרא? הא זימנין אזלינן לקולא בתר גדול הבית, כגון שגדול המשפחה כאן – שכולם מונין משיצא המת מן הבית, דהוה קולא! לכן נראה לפרש: שאם גדול המשפחה כאן – מונין מיד, ומתחילין להתאבל עמו לכבודו מיד כשישמעו, אפי' שלא בפניו. אבל עיקר אבילות יתחילו למנות משיסתום הגולל. וכן איתא בהדיא: ר"ג זוגה, דמכת *אחתיה, סליק אחיה עמה. אמר ליה רבי מנא: כיון שיש גדול הבית – מסלקת גבי אחוך, שלוף סנדלא. ובתוספות הרב פירש שהש"ס אינו מחלק כך:

מעשה

הָלַךְ גְּדוֹל הַבַּיִת לְבֵית הַקְּבָרוֹת מַהוּ? תָּא שְׁמַע, דְּאָמַר רַבִּי חִיָּיא בַּר אַבָּא אָמַר רַבִּי יוֹחָנָן: אֲפִילּוּ הָלַךְ גְּדוֹל הַבַּיִת לְבֵית הַקְּבָרוֹת [א]מוֹנֶה עִמָּהֶן. מוֹנֶה עִמָּהֶן? וְהָתַנְיָא מוֹנֶה לְעַצְמוֹ! לָא קַשְׁיָא: הָא – [ב]דַּאֲתָא בְּגוֹ תְּלָתָא, וְהָא – דְּלָא אֲתָא בְּגוֹ תְּלָתָא. כִּי הָא דַּאֲמַר לְהוּ רַב לִבְנֵי הַצְלֶפּוֹנִי: דְּאָתוּ בְּגוֹ תְּלָתָא – לִימְנוּ בַּהֲדַיְיכוּ, דְּלָא אָתוּ בְּגוֹ תְּלָתָא – לִימְנוּ לְנַפְשַׁיְהוּ. אֲמַר לְהוּ רָבָא לִבְנֵי מְחוֹזָא: אַתּוּן דְּלָא אָזְלִיתוּ בָּתַר עַרְסָא, [ג]מִכִּי מְהַדְּרִיתוּ אַפַּיְיכוּ מִבָּבָא דְּאַבּוּלָא – אַתְחִילוּ מְנוּ.§ "ר"ש אוֹמֵר אֲפִילּוּ בָּא בַּיּוֹם הַשְּׁבִיעִי מִמָּקוֹם קָרוֹב מוֹנֶה עִמָּהֶן".§ א"ר חִיָּיא בַּר גַּמְדָּא א"ר יוֹסֵי בֶּן שָׁאוּל אָמַר רַבִּי: [ד]וְהוּא שֶׁבָּא וּמָצָא מְנַחֲמִין אֶצְלוֹ. [ה]בָּעֵי רַב עָנָן: נִנְעֲרוּ לַעֲמוֹד וְלֹא עָמְדוּ, מַהוּ? תֵּיקוּ. *גְּמִירִי חַבְרֵיהּ דְּר' אַבָּא בַּר חִיָּיא מַר' אַבָּא, וּמַנּוּ – ר' זֵירָא, וְאָמְרִי לָהּ: חַבְרֵיהּ דְּר' זֵירָא מֵרַבִּי זֵירָא, וּמַנּוּ – ר' אַבָּא בְּרֵיהּ דְּר' חִיָּיא בַּר אַבָּא, א"ר יוֹחָנָן: *הֲלָכָה כְּרַבִּי שִׁמְעוֹן בֶּן גַּמְלִיאֵל בִּטְרֵיפוֹת, וַהֲלָכָה כְּרַבִּי שִׁמְעוֹן בְּאֵבֶל. כְּרַבִּי שִׁמְעוֹן בְּאֵבֶל – הָא דַּאֲמָרַן. כְּרשב"ג בִּטְרֵיפוֹת – דִּתְנַן: בְּנֵי מֵעַיִם שֶׁנִּיקְּבוּ וְלֵיחָה סוֹתַמְתָּן – כְּשֵׁרָה, דִּבְרֵי רשב"ג. מַאי לֵיחָה? אֲמַר רַב כַּהֲנָא: שִׁירְקָא דְּמֵעַיָּא דְּנָפֵיק אַגַּב דּוּחְקָא. *אֲמַר מַאן דְּהוּא: *אִיזְכֵּי וְאַסֵּיק וְאַגְמְרָא לִשְׁמַעְתָּא מִפּוּמֵּיהּ דְּמָרֵיהּ. כִּי סְלֵיק אַשְׁכְּחֵיהּ לְר' אַבָּא בְּרֵיהּ דְּרַבִּי חִיָּיא בַּר אַבָּא, א"ל: אֲמַר מָר הֲלָכָה כְּרשב"ג בִּטְרֵיפוֹת? א"ל: אֲנָא "אֵין הֲלָכָה" אֲמָרִי. כְּר"ש בְּאֵבֶל מַאי? א"ל: פְּלוּגְתָּא נִינְהוּ. דְּאִיתְּמַר, רַב חִסְדָּא אָמַר: הֲלָכָה, וְכֵן א"ר יוֹחָנָן: הֲלָכָה, ר"נ אָמַר: אֵין הֲלָכָה, [ו]וְאֵין הֲלָכָה כְּרשב"ג בִּטְרֵיפוֹת. וַהֲלָכָה כְּר"ש בְּאֵבֶל. *דְּאָמַר שְׁמוּאֵל: הֲלָכָה כְּדִבְרֵי הַמֵּיקֵל בְּאֵבֶל. *)עַל כָּל הַמֵּתִים כּוּלָּן, [ז]מַדְחֶה מִטָּתוֹ – הֲרֵי זֶה מְשׁוּבָּח, עַל אָבִיו וְעַל אִמּוֹ – הֲרֵי זֶה מְגוּנֶּה. הָיָה עֶרֶב שַׁבָּת, אוֹ עֶרֶב יוֹם טוֹב (א) – הֲרֵי זֶה מְשׁוּבָּח, שֶׁאֵינוֹ עוֹשֶׂה אֶלָּא לִכְבוֹד אָבִיו וְאִמּוֹ. [ח]עַל כָּל הַמֵּתִים כּוּלָּן, [ט]רָצָה מְמַעֵט בְּעִסְקוֹ, רָצָה אֵינוֹ

מְמַעֵט

*) שמחות פ"ט

הָלַךְ גְּדוֹל הַבַּיִת לְבֵית הַקְּבָרוֹת. אַחַר מִטָּתוֹ לְקוֹבְרוֹ, וְשָׁהָה שָׁם ג' יָמִים: מַהוּ. מִי חָשְׁבִינַן לֵיהּ כְּמַאן דַּהֲוֵי בְּבֵיתֵיהּ, הוֹאִיל וּלְצוֹרֶךְ הַמֵּת הָלַךְ אִתּוֹ: מוֹנֶה עִמָּהֶן. דַּאֲבֵילוּת שֶׁלָּהֶם הִתְחִילָה מִשֶּׁחָזְרוּ פְּנֵיהֶם מִן הַמֵּת וַאֲבֵילוּת שֶׁל גָּדוֹל (ב) עַד שֶׁיִּסְתּוֹם הַגּוֹלֵל: לִבְנֵי הַצְלֶפּוֹנִי. מָקוֹם: דְּלָא אָזְלִיתוּ בָּתַר עַרְסָא. דְּמַאן דְּהָוֵי בָּתַר עַרְסָא לָא חָיְילָא עֲלֵיהּ אֲבֵילוּת עַד שֶׁנִּסְתַּם הַגּוֹלֵל. כְּשֶׁמּוֹלִיכִין הַמִּטָּה מִבָּבֶל לְא"י לִקְבּוֹר, וְאֵין כָּל הַקְּרוֹבִים כּוּלָּם יְכוֹלִין לַעֲלוֹת עַד א"י, וּמְלַוִּין הַמֵּת פַּרְסָה אוֹ מִיל וְחוֹזְרִים: מִכִּי אַהַדְרִיתוּ אַפַּיְיכוּ מִבָּבָא דַּאֲבוּלָא. מִשַּׁעַר הַחִיצוֹן שֶׁל הָעִיר וּמִגְרָשֶׁיהָ, דְּאָתֵיתוּ לְבֵיתָא: אַתְחִילוּ מְנוּ. יְמֵי אֲבֵילוּת, אע"ג דְּלֹא נִקְבַּר הַמֵּת עַד יָמִים רַבִּים. וְאע"ג דַּאֲבֵילוּת אֵינוֹ חָל עַד שֶׁיִּסְתּוֹם הַגּוֹלֵל – לְדִידְכוּ, דְּלָא מֶחֱזֵי – חֲזָרַתְכֶם כִּנְסִתַּם הַגּוֹלֵל: ה"ג: וְהוּא שֶׁלֹּא עָמְדוּ מְנַחֲמִין מֵאֶצְלוֹ. שֶׁבָּא בַּשְּׁבִיעִי שַׁחֲרִית, עַד שֶׁלֹּא עָמְדוּ מְנַחֲמִין אֵצֶל זֶה שֶׁבַּבַּיִת: נִנְעֲרוּ לַעֲמוֹד. מְנַעְנְעִים וְרוֹצִים לַעֲמוֹד: אָמַר מַאן דְּהוּא. אָדָם אֶחָד, מַאן דַּהֲוָה: מִפּוּמֵּיהּ דְּמָרֵיהּ. מַר' אַבָּא בְּרֵיהּ דְּרַבִּי חִיָּיא אוֹ רַבִּי זֵירָא: אֵין הֲלָכָה אֲמָרִי. כְּלוֹמַר: אֵין הֲלָכָה כְּרַבִּי שִׁמְעוֹן: מַדְחֶה מִטָּתוֹ. מְמַהֵר לְהוֹצִיאוֹ: מְמַעֵט בְּעִסְקוֹ. כְּגוֹן סְחוֹרָה:

רָצָה

עין משפט נר מצוה

קלג א ב טוש"ע י"ד סימן שעה סעיף ח בהג"ה:

קלד ג מיי' פ"א מהל' אבל הל' ה טוש"ע שם סעיף ב:

קלה ד ה מיי' שם פ"ז הלכה ד טוש"ע שם סעיף ח:

קלו ו מיי' פ"ו מהל' שחיטה הלכה יד סמג עשין סג טוש"ע י"ד סימן מו סעיף א:

קלז ז מיי' פ"ד מהל' אבל הלכה ז סמג עשין דרבנן ג טוש"ע שם סימן שנז סעיף ב:

קלח ח מיי' שם פ"ו הלכה ט טוש"ע שם סימן שפ סעיף כד:

בחילופי גרסאות מוחק מן תיבת לרבנן עד ביום השביעי. וגורס לעיל מינה עם הנשארים לרבנן כשבא גדול הבית תוך ג' ימים ולר"ש אפילו ביום ז' וכן פי' ר"י וכו'

רבינו חננאל

הוא שואל בשלום אחיו שהן שרויין בשלום: ת"ר אבל ג' ימים הראשונים בא ממקום קרוב מונה עמהן. ואמר ר' חייא בר אבא אמר ר' יוחנן והוא שיש גדול הבית ואפילו הלך גדול הבית לבית הקברות ובא בתוך ג' מונה עמהן. בא לאחר ג' ומצא שהלך גדול הבית לפני הקברות מונה לעצמו כדאמר להו רב לבני הצלבוני דאתו בגו תלתא לימנן בהדייכו דאתו לבתר תלתא לימני לנפשיה. בא ממקום רחוק בתוך ג' מונה לעצמו מיכן ואילך אפילו בא ממקום קרוב מונה לעצמו ר' שמעון אומר אפילו בא ביום ז' ממקום קרוב מונה עמהם ואוקמה ר' יוסי בן שאול והוא שבא ומצא מנחמין אצל אבלים כלומר עדיין לא נסתלקו מן האבלות כדאמרינן מקצת היום ככולו. ואיבעיא להו נגערו האבלים לעמוד ובא ממקום קרוב ומצאן שעדיין לא עמדו מהו ועמדה בתיקו. אמר משמיה דר' יוחנן הלכה כר' שמעון באבל הא דאמרן דאמר שמואל הלכה כדברי המיקל. הא דאמרינן בגררה בהדין אתרא הלכתא כרשב"ג בטריפות כבר פירשנוה בשחיטת חולין ופשוטה היא. אמר להו רבא לבני מחוזא אתון דלא אזליתו בתר ערסא מכי הדריתו אפייכו מבבא דאבולא אתחילו למימני: **ירושלמי** הרי שבא ומצא בתוך ביתו בשני ובשלישי מונה עמהן ברביעי מונה לעצמו ר"ש אומר אפילו *) בששי משלים עמהן אריב"ל הלכה כר' שמעון בשאין גדול משפחה אבל אם הוא גדול משפחה מונה לעצמו. כר' מנא שהורה לר' יעקב ארמניא מכיון שאתה גדול מנה לעצמך: על כל המתים המדחה מטתו משובח על אביו ועל אמו מגונה. אלא אם היה ע"ש או עיו"ט או שהיו גשמים מזלפין על מטתו ועושה לכבוד אביו הרי גם זה משובח על כל המתים אם רצה שלא למעט בעסקו אלא אם רצה לישא וליתן בסחורתו כל היום הרשות בידו. אבל על אביו ועל אמו חייב למעט פי' בשאר מתים אינו ממעט

מסורת הש"ס

חולין נ. ע"ש

[שם]

[ביצה כז.]

חולין נ. [נדה מח.]

[לעיל יח. וש"נ] עירובין מו. לקמן כו:

הגהות הב"ח

(א) גמ' היה ע"ש או עיו"ט או שהיו גשמים מזלפין על מטתו ה"ז משובח: (ב) רש"י ד"ה מונה כו' ואבילות של גדול לא התחיל עד שיסתום הגולל:

גליון הש"ס

גמ' רצה ממעט בעסקו. עיין לקמן דף כז ע"א תוספות ד"ה אם יכול:

בהדייכו כמו בגדול הבית בבית דבשאין גדול הבית כו' עצמו הוי דינא כרבנן כנ"ל

[עי' נוסחת הירושלמי שהביא הרא"ש בסימן לט]

[פי' מתה אחותו]

תורה אור

מְמַעֵט. עַל אָבִיו וְעַל אִמּוֹ – מְמַעֵט. ^אעַל כָּל הַמֵּתִים כּוּלָּן, רָצָה – חוֹלֵץ, רָצָה – אֵינוֹ חוֹלֵץ. עַל אָבִיו וְעַל אִמּוֹ חוֹלֵץ. וּמַעֲשֶׂה בִּגְדוֹל הַדּוֹר אֶחָד שֶׁמֵּת אָבִיו וּבִיקֵּשׁ לַחֲלוֹץ, וּבִיקֵּשׁ גְּדוֹל הַדּוֹר אַחֵר שֶׁעִמּוֹ לַחֲלוֹץ – וְנִמְנַע וְלֹא חָלַץ. אָמַר אַבַּיֵי: גְּדוֹל הַדּוֹר – רַבִּי, גְּדוֹל הַדּוֹר שֶׁעִמּוֹ – ר' יַעֲקֹב בַּר אַחָא. וְאִיכָּא דְּאָמְרִי: גְּדוֹל הַדּוֹר – ר' יַעֲקֹב בַּר אַחָא, גְּדוֹל הַדּוֹר שֶׁעִמּוֹ – רַבִּי, בִּשְׁלָמָא לְמ"ד גְּדוֹל הַדּוֹר שֶׁעִמּוֹ רַבִּי – הַיְינוּ דְּנִמְנַע וְלֹא חָלַץ. אֶלָּא לְמ"ד רַבִּי יַעֲקֹב בַּר אַחָא – אַמַּאי נִמְנַע וְלֹא חָלַץ? רשב"ג נָשִׂיא הֲוָה, ^בוְכוּלֵּי עָלְמָא מִיחַיְּיבִי לְמִיחְלַץ! קַשְׁיָא. *^געַל כָּל הַמֵּתִים כּוּלָּן מִסְתַּפֵּר לְאַחַר ל' יוֹם, עַל אָבִיו וְעַל אִמּוֹ – עַד שֶׁיִּגְעֲרוּ בּוֹ חֲבֵרָיו. ^דעַל כָּל הַמֵּתִים כּוּלָּן – נִכְנָס לְבֵית הַשִּׂמְחָה לְאַחַר ל' יוֹם, עַל אָבִיו וְעַל אִמּוֹ – לְאַחַר י"ב חֹדֶשׁ. אָמַר רַבָּה בַּר בַּר חָנָה: וּלְשִׂמְחַת מְרֵיעוּת. מֵיתִיבִי: וּלְשִׂמְחָה וְלִמְרֵיעוּת ל' יוֹם! קַשְׁיָא. אֲמֵימָר מַתְנֵי הָכִי: אָמַר רַבָּה בַּר בַּר חָנָה, ^הוּלְשִׂמְחַת מְרֵיעוּת – מוּתָּר לִיכָּנֵס לְאַלְתַּר. וְהָא תַּנְיָא: לְשִׂמְחָה שְׁלֹשִׁים, וְלִמְרֵיעוּת שְׁלֹשִׁים! ל"ק; ^והָא – בַּאֲרִיסוּתָא, הָא – בְּפוּרְעָנוּתָא. ^זעַל כָּל הַמֵּתִים כּוּלָּן – קוֹרֵעַ טֶפַח, עַל אָבִיו וְעַל אִמּוֹ – עַד שֶׁיְּגַלֶּה אֶת לִבּוֹ. א"ר אַבָּהוּ: מַאי קְרָא – "וַיַּחֲזֵק דָּוִד בִּבְגָדָיו וַיִּקְרָעֵם" (שמואל ב א) וְאֵין אֲחִיזָה פָּחוֹת מִטֶּפַח. ^חעַל כָּל הַמֵּתִים כּוּלָּן, אֲפִילּוּ לָבוּשׁ עֲשָׂרָה חֲלוּקִין – אֵינוֹ קוֹרֵעַ אֶלָּא עֶלְיוֹן. עַל אָבִיו וְעַל אִמּוֹ – קוֹרֵעַ אֶת כּוּלָּן, ^טוְאַפִּיקַרְסוּתוֹ אֵינָהּ מְעַכֶּבֶת, אֶחָד הָאִישׁ וְאֶחָד אִשָּׁה. ר"ש בֶּן אֶלְעָזָר אוֹמֵר: ^יהָאִשָּׁה קוֹרַעַת אֶת הַתַּחְתּוֹן, וּמַחֲזַרְתּוֹ לַאֲחוֹרֶיהָ, וְחוֹזֶרֶת וְקוֹרַעַת אֶת הָעֶלְיוֹן. *^כעַל כָּל הַמֵּתִים כּוּלָּן רָצָה – מַבְדִּיל קַמֵּי שָׂפָה שֶׁלּוֹ, רָצָה – אֵינוֹ מַבְדִּיל. עַל אָבִיו וְעַל אִמּוֹ – מַבְדִּיל. רַבִּי יְהוּדָה אוֹמֵר: ^לכָּל קְרִיעָה שֶׁאֵינוֹ מַבְדִּיל קַמֵּי שָׂפָה שֶׁלּוֹ – אֵינוֹ אֶלָּא קֶרַע שֶׁל תִּיפְלוּת. אָמַר רַבִּי אַבָּהוּ: מ"ט דְּר' יְהוּדָה – דִּכְתִיב: "וַיַּחֲזֵק בִּבְגָדָיו וַיִּקְרָעֵם לִשְׁנַיִם קְרָעִים" (מלכים ב ב), *מִמַּשְׁמַע שֶׁנֶּאֱמַר "וַיִּקְרָעֵם" אֵינִי יוֹדֵעַ שֶׁהֵן לִשְׁנַיִם? אֶלָּא: שֶׁנִּרְאִין קְרוּעִים כִּשְׁנַיִם. ^מעַל כָּל הַמֵּתִים כּוּלָּן – שׁוֹלֵל לְאַחַר שִׁבְעָה, וּמְאַחֶה לְאַחַר שְׁלֹשִׁים. עַל אָבִיו וְעַל אִמּוֹ – שׁוֹלֵל לְאַחַר ל' וְאֵינוֹ מְאַחֶה לְעוֹלָם. *^נוְהָאִשָּׁה שׁוֹלַלְתּוֹ לְאַלְתַּר, מִפְּנֵי כְּבוֹדָהּ. כִּי אֲתָא רָבִין א"ר יוֹחָנָן: ^סעַל כָּל הַמֵּתִים, רָצָה – קוֹרֵעַ בַּיָּד, רָצָה – קוֹרֵעַ בִּכְלִי. עַל אָבִיו וְעַל אִמּוֹ – בַּיָּד. וְא"ר חִיָּיא בַּר אַבָּא א"ר יוֹחָנָן: ^עעַל כָּל הַמֵּתִים כּוּלָּן – מִבִּפְנִים, עַל אָבִיו וְעַל אִמּוֹ – קוֹרֵעַ מִבַּחוּץ. אָמַר רַב חִסְדָּא: ^פוְכֵן לְנָשִׂיא. מֵיתִיבִי: לֹא הוּשְׁווּ לְאָבִיו וּלְאִמּוֹ אֶלָּא לְאִיחוּי בִּלְבַד. מַאי לָאו – אֲפִילּוּ לְנָשִׂיא? לֹא, לְבַר מִנָּשִׂיא. נְשִׂיאָה שְׁכִיב. א"ל רַב חִסְדָּא (*לְרַב חָנָן בַּר רָבָא:) כְּפֵי אָסִיתָא וְקוּם עֲלַהּ, וְאַחְוֵי קְרִיעָה לְעָלְמָא. ^צעַל חָכָם חוֹלֵץ מִיָּמִין, עַל אַב ב"ד מִשְּׂמֹאל, עַל נָשִׂיא – מִכָּאן וּמִכָּאן. ת"ר: ^קחָכָם שֶׁמֵּת – בֵּית מִדְרָשׁוֹ בָּטֵל, ^ראַב ב"ד שֶׁמֵּת – כָּל בָּתֵּי מִדְרָשׁוֹת שֶׁבְּעִירוֹ בְּטֵלִין, וְנִכְנָסִין לְבֵיהכ"נ, וּמְשַׁנִּין אֶת מְקוֹמָן; הַיּוֹשְׁבִין בַּצָּפוֹן – יוֹשְׁבִין בַּדָּרוֹם, הַיּוֹשְׁבִין בַּדָּרוֹם – יוֹשְׁבִין בַּצָּפוֹן. ^שנָשִׂיא שֶׁמֵּת – בָּתֵּי מִדְרָשׁוֹת כּוּלָּן בְּטֵלִין, וּבְנֵי הַכְּנֶסֶת נִכְנָסִין לְבֵית הַכְּנֶסֶת, וְקוֹרִין

[וגי' הערוך לרב נחמן בר אמי]

רש"י

רָצָה חוֹלֵץ. כְּתֵיפוֹ: וְנִמְנַע. הָאָבֵל וְלֹא חָלַץ, מִשּׁוּם כְּבוֹד גְּדוֹל הַדּוֹר שֶׁעִמּוֹ, שֶׁבִּקֵּשׁ לַחֲלוֹץ גַּם הוּא: אֶלָּא לְמ"ד גְּדוֹל הַדּוֹר שֶׁעִמּוֹ ר' יַעֲקֹב. וְרַבִּי הֲוָה אָבֵל: עַד שֶׁיִּגְעֲרוּ בּוֹ חֲבֵרָיו. שֶׁכְּבָר גִּידֵּל פֶּרַע יוֹתֵר מִדַּאי: אָמַר רַבָּה. הָא דְּתַנְיָא: נִכְנָס לְבֵית הַמִּשְׁתֶּה לְאַחַר ל' יוֹם: לְשִׂמְחַת מְרֵיעוּת. סְעוּדָה שֶׁעוֹשִׂין רֵיעִים וַאֲהוּבִים זֶה עִם זֶה, וְלָא הָוֵי שִׂמְחָה כָּל כָּךְ. אֲבָל סְעוּדָה דְּשִׂמְחָה, כְּגוֹן דְּנִישּׂוּאִין – לָא: הָא בַּאֲרִיסוּתָא הָא בְּפוּרְעָנוּתָא. אֲרִיסָא הַיְינוּ שֶׁמַּתְחִיל אֶחָד מֵהֶן לַעֲשׂוֹת סְעוּדָה, וּמַלְוֶה לְכוּלָּם כְּדֵי שֶׁיַּעֲשׂוּ גַּם הֵם נַמִּי כָּךְ – לְאוֹתָהּ סְעוּדָה אֵינוֹ נִכְנָס עַד לְאַחַר שְׁלֹשִׁים יוֹם. אֲבָל בְּפוּרְעָנוּתָא, שֶׁמְּשַׁלֵּם לָהֶם סְעוּדוֹת שֶׁנַּעֲשׂוּ לוֹ – יִכָּנֵס לְאַלְתַּר, שֶׁאִי אֶפְשָׁר לוֹ שֶׁלֹּא לְשַׁלֵּם: וְאַפִּיקַרְסוּתוֹ. שֶׁעַל רֹאשׁוֹ, אֵינָהּ מְעַכֶּבֶת. כְּלוֹמַר, אֵינוֹ צָרִיךְ לְקוֹרְעָהּ: אֶחָד אִישׁ וְאֶחָד אִשָּׁה. חַיָּיבִין לִקְרוֹעַ: הָאִשָּׁה. שֶׁמֵּת אָבִיהָ אוֹ אִמָּהּ – קוֹרַעַת חָלוּק הַתַּחְתּוֹן מִשּׁוּם צְנִיעוּת: וּמַחֲזֶרֶת. הַקֶּרַע לַאֲחוֹרֶיהָ: וְחוֹזֶרֶת וְקוֹרַעַת הָעֶלְיוֹן. וְהַתַּחְתּוֹן מְכַסֶּה לִבָּהּ: רָצָה מַבְדִּיל קַמֵּי שָׂפָה. שֶׁאֵינוֹ בַּשָּׂפָה שֶׁלִּפְנֵי הַצַּוָּאר, אֶלָּא קַמֵּי שָׂפָה – שֶׁלִּפְנֵי הַשָּׂפָה, שֶׁלִּפְנֵי הַצַּוָּאר, שֶׁאֵינָהּ קְרוּעָה, וְקוֹרֵעַ תַּחְתֶּיהָ כְּדֵי שֶׁיִּהְיֶה נִרְאֶה הַקֶּרַע: רָצָה אֵינוֹ מַבְדִּיל. אֶלָּא קוֹרֵעַ שֶׁל בֵּית הַצַּוָּאר, אע"ג דְּאֵינוֹ נִרְאֶה הַקֶּרַע, דְּהַכֹּל בֵּית הַצַּוָּאר הוּא: עַל אָבִיו וְעַל אִמּוֹ מַבְדִּיל. קַמֵּי שָׂפָה, כְּדֵי שֶׁיְּהֵא נִרְאֶה הַקֶּרַע: קֶרַע שֶׁל תִּיפְלָה. כְּלוֹמַר: לֹא יָצָא יְדֵי קְרִיעָה, לְפִי דְּנִרְאֶה דְּבֵית צַוָּאר הוּא הַכֹּל: וַיִּקְרָעֵם לִשְׁנַיִם. אֵין קוֹרְעִין, אֶלָּא שֶׁנִּרְאֶה כִּשְׁנַיִם, מַבְדִּיל קַמֵּי שָׂפָה, וְנִרְאֶה בֵּית הַצַּוָּאר קֶרַע אַחֵר: שׁוֹלֵל. בלשטיר"י: מְאַחֶה. קוסט"ר, תּוֹפֵר כְּדַרְכּוֹ: קוֹרֵעַ בִּכְלִי. סַכִּין, כְּדֵי שֶׁלֹּא יַפְסִיד הַבֶּגֶד: קוֹרֵעַ מִבִּפְנִים. תַּחַת הַמִּקְטוֹרֶן שֶׁלּוֹ, שֶׁאֵינוֹ קוֹרֵעַ מִחוּץ לְעֵינֵי הַכֹּל: וְכֵן לְנָשִׂיא. קוֹרֵעַ מִבַּחוּץ: לֹא הוּשְׁווּ. רַבּוֹ וְאַב ב"ד וְנָשִׂיא, וְכָל הָנָךְ דְּתָנֵי בְּמַתְנִיתָא לְאָבִיו וּלְאִמּוֹ: אֶלָּא לְאִיחוּי. שֶׁאֵין מִתְאַחִים לְעוֹלָם. אֲבָל לֹא הוּשְׁווּ לְאָבִיו וּלְאִמּוֹ לִקְרוֹעַ מִבַּחוּץ. לְהַאי לֹא הוּשְׁווּ, דְּעַל אָבִיו קוֹרֵעַ מִבַּחוּץ, וְעַל כּוּלָּן אֵינוֹ קוֹרֵעַ מִבַּחוּץ: כְּפֵי אָסִיתָא. הֲפוֹךְ הַמַּכְתֶּשֶׁת, וַעֲמוֹד עָלֶיהָ וּקְרַע, כְּדֵי שֶׁיִּרְאוּךָ כָּל הָעָם כְּשֶׁתִּקְרַע: חָכָם. מְמוּנֶּה עַל הָעִיר, שֶׁמְּבַקְּשִׁים מִמֶּנּוּ הוֹרָאָה: חוֹלֵץ. כָּתֵף מִיָּמִין: בֵּית מִדְרָשׁוֹ בְּטֵלִין. אוֹתָן שֶׁרְגִילִין לִלְמוֹד תּוֹרָה מִפִּיו:

וְקוֹרִין

שמחות פ"ט | הוריות יב: | [לקמן כו. ע"ש סנהדרין ס. ע"ש ול"ע] | [לקמן כו:]

תוספות

מעשה בגדול הדור. אין זה מעשה לסתור דהא דנמנע ולא חלץ – זהו מפני גדול *הדור שעמו. ובמס' שמחות (פ"ט) קתני עלה: ואין ראוי לחלק כבוד לו. והאחרים הראויין לחלוץ, אף על אביו ועל אמו. ואם אינן ראויין – אינו חולץ, כדי שלא יחללו אחרים ומעשה בר' יעקב כו':

עד שיגערו בו חביריו. נראה דרגל אינו מבטל דבר זה, מדאמרינן בירושלמי: רבי שמואל בר אבדימי דמנה תלתין יומין קמי מועדא, שאיל לרבי מנא. א"ל: כל דבר שהוא תלוי בז' ול' – הרגל מפסיק, ברם הכא – עד שישלח פרע ויגערו בו חביריו, ויאמרו לו לך עמנו. ובשמחה נמי אשכחנא הכא י"ב חדש, ואין רגל מבטל. ויש ספרים שכתוב בהן: או יגערו בו חביריו, בירושלמי. ונראה שהוא טעות סופרים, כי אם כמו שכתבתי: עד שישלח פרע ויגערו בו:

ולשמחת מריעות. פירש בקונטרס: סעודות שעושים ריעים ואהובים זה לזה. וכ"נ, דדוקא לשמחת מריעות מותר לאחר ל' יום, אבל שמחת חתן – אסור אפילו לאחר ל' יום. והא תניא לשמחה ל' ולמריעות ל'! וה"נ פריך בריש פ"ק דבבא מציעא (דף ב.): והא זה וזה קתני! וכן בפ"ק דסנהדרין (דף ח.) גבי זימון בג', וברכת המזון בג', וטובא איכא. ויש מקומות שאינו שואל, כגון בפ"ק דנדרים (דף ז:) *גבי אסור אסור, ובפרק "גיד הנשה" (חולין דף צח. ושם) גבי אסורות אסורות, ובפרק "בית כור" (ב"ב דף קד.) גבי "בית כור" אני מוכר לך כבית כור. וי"מ: ולשמחת מריעות מותר ליכנס לאלתר. ואגן בסעודת חתן איירינן. הא דאמרינן בירושלמי ובמסכת שמחות (פ"ט): אם היה סעודה של מצוה – מותר, לא ידענא מהו קורא סעודת מצוה להתיר באבל. אם דוקא סעודת קידוש ר"ח. פירש הר"א בשם רבינו שמשון: דלסעודת ברית מילה מותר ליכנס, דלא חשיבא שמחה, כדאמרינן בפ"ק דכתובות (דף ח.) דלא מברכינן בה "שהשמחה במעונו" משום דטרידי, וליכא שמחה. ולהר"א לא היה פשוטו לג"ע משמחת מריעות. וגם פירש דאסור לאכול אפי' עם המשמשין ואין לחלק בין סעודת המשמשין לסעודה עצמה. ופסק דכניסה בלא אכילה – שרי, דאין שמחה בלא אכילה ושתיה. ובתוספות הרב פוסק כלישנא דאמימר דמיקל טפי:

אחד האיש ואחד האשה. ובתוס' הרב פוסק כר"ש בן אלעזר, דהלכה כדברי המיקל. ולא ידענא מאי קאמר, דלקמן (דף כו:) אמרינן: אבילות לחוד וקריעה לחוד:

רבי

עין משפט נר מצוה

עי' מהרש"א ולפי הנראה יש כאן ערבובי דברים וכצ"ל הדור שעמו ואין ראוי לחלק כבוד לו כדי שלא יחללו אחרים ובמס' שמחות קתני עלה ואם אין ראוי לחלוץ אף על אביו ואמו לא יחלוץ ומעשה כו' כצ"ל והבוחר יבחר. העתק מחילופי גרסאות

קלט א מיי' פ"ח מהל' אבל הלכה ג סמג עשין דרבנן ב טוש"ע י"ד סימן שמ סעיף טז:

קמ ב מיי' שם פ"ט הלכה טו סמג שם טוש"ע שם סעיף יז:

קמא ג מיי' שם פ"ו הלכה ג סמג שם טוש"ע שם סימן שצ סעיף יז:

קמב ד ה ו מיי' שם הלכה ו ז סמג שם טוש"ע שם סימן שצא סעיף ב:

קמג ז ח ט מיי' שם פ"ח הלכה ב ג סמג שם טוש"ע שם סי' שמ סעיף ט י:

קמד י טוש"ע שם סעיף יא:

קמה כ מיי' שם טוש"ע שם סעיף יב:

קמו ל טוש"ע שם בהג"ה:

קמז מ נ מיי' פ"ט שם הלכה א טוש"ע שם סעיף טו:

[שם בנדרים פריך הש"ס אסור אסור ל"ל וכ"כ תוספות בכורות לא: ד"ה א"כ וכו' דבנדרים פריך כן ולכך צריכים אנו לומר דהכא בדברי תוס' נפל טעות ומ"ש כגון בפ"ק דנדרים גבי אסור אסור שייך לעיל קודם וטובא איכא וכו' ודע עוד דגם במ"ש תוספות הכא ובפ' בית כור וכו' צריך תיקון בזה כי בב"ב קד. שואל הש"ס ע"ש וכך איתא בתוספות בכורות הנ"ל וע"ש]

קמח ס מיי' שם פ"ח הלכה ב ג טוש"ע שם סעיף יד:

קמט ע מיי' שם טוש"ע שם סעיף יג:

קנ פ צ מיי' שם פ"ט הלכה ב יד טו טוש"ע שם סעיף יז:

קנא ק ר ש מיי' שם טוש"ע שם סי' שמ סעיף יח:

רבינו חננאל

ממעט על אביו ועל אמו ממעט בעסקו. ואפילו שהוא על ידי אחרים: ירושל' מרבה בעסקי אביו ואמו משמע בתכריכין והספדו. על כל המתים רצה חולץ פי' חליצת כתף. מוציא ידו מתחת הקרע ונמצאת כתיפו חלוצה מן החלוק. רצה אינו חולץ. על אביו ועל אמו חולץ. ומעשה בגדול הדור שמת אביו ובא לחלוץ. ובקש גדול הדור (עצמו) [שעמו] לחלוץ ולא חלץ. ואסיקנא גדול הדור (שמת) הוא ר' יעקב בר אחא ובקש רבינו הקדוש הוא גדול הדור שעמו לחלוץ עמו מפני כבודו. ונמנע ר' יעקב ולא חלץ. אבל במיתת רשב"ג אבי רבינו הקדוש כ"ע חייבין לחלוץ דנשיא הוא. קיי"ל היכא דחל יום שמיני של אביו ושל אמו להיות בשבת ערב הרגל מגלח ואפילו ביום ששי בע"ש. דלענין כבוד יו"ט ל"ש אב ואם ול"ש שאר קרובים. הלכה כאבא שאול בזה ובזה. על כל המתים מותר להסתפר לאחר שלשים. על אביו ועל אמו מגדל שער עד שיגערו בו חביריו. על כל המתים נכנס לבית המשתה לאחר שלשים יום. ואוקמה אמימר במשתה שמחת מריעות בפורענותא נכנס לאלתר. אבל באריסותא. כלומר הוא אינו פורע אלא מתחיל הוא אחר שלשים יום. אבל על אביו ועל אמו אינו נכנס עד י"ב חדש על כל המתים קורע טפח שנאמר ויחזק בבגדיו ויקרעם לשנים. ואין אחיזה פחותה מטפח. אבל על אביו ועל אמו קורע עד שמגלה את לבו. ואפילו לבוש מאה חלוקים קורע את כולן ומבדיל קמי שפה דבעינן קרע הנראה לשנים קרעים כדכתיב ויקרעם לשנים קרעים ואפיקרסותו אינה מעכבת והאשה על אביה ועל אמה קורעת חלוקה התחתון ומחזרת הקרע לאחוריה וחוזרת וקורעת את העליון. ואינו קורע על אביו ועל אמו בכלי כגון סכין וכיוצא בו אלא בידו קורע ואינו קורע אלא מבחוץ ואינו מאחה הקרע לעולם: **ירושלמי** זהו איחוי העשוי כאריג. אבל על שאר מתים אינו קורע אלא העליון. ואם אינו רוצה להבדיל קמי שפה אינו מבדיל ושולל לאחר שבעה ומאחה לאחר שלשים. והאשה קורעת ושוללתו לאלתר מפני כבודה. ואם רוצה לקרוע בכלי קורע. על אביו ועל אמו קורע מבחוץ. אמר רב חסדא וכן לנשיא. נשיאה שכיב א"ל רב חסדא לרב חנן כפי אסיתא וקום עליה ואחוי קריעה לעלמא. על חכם חולץ מימין על אב ב"ד משמאל. על נשיא מיכן ומיכן. פירוש חליצת כתף. ת"ר חכם שמת מדרשו בטל. אב ב"ד שמת כל מדרשות שבעירו בטילין. ובני הכנסת נכנסין ומשנין את מקומן. היושבין בצפון יושבין בדרום. בדרום יושבין בצפון. נשיא שמת כל בתי מדרשות בטילין ונכנסין לכנסת וקורין

וקורין שבעה ויוצאין. רבי יהושע בן קרחה אומר: לא שילכו ויטיילו בשוק, אלא יושבין ודומין. [א]ואין אומרים שמועה ואגדה בבית האבל. אמרו עליו על ר' חנניה בן גמליאל שהיה אומר שמועה ואגדה בבית האבל. *ת"ר: [ב]אבל, שבת ראשונה — אינו יוצא מפתח ביתו, שניה — יוצא ואינו יושב במקומו, (א) שלישית — יושב במקומו ואינו מדבר, רביעית — הרי הוא ככל אדם. רבי יהודה אומר: לא הוצרכו לומר שבת ראשונה לא יצא מפתח ביתו — שהרי הכל נכנסין לביתו לנחמו. אלא: שניה — אינו יוצא מפתח ביתו, שלישית — יוצא ואינו יושב במקומו, (ב) רביעית — יושב במקומו ואינו מדבר, חמישית — הרי הוא ככל אדם. *ת"ר: [ג]כל שלשים יום לנישואין, מתה אשתו — אסור לישא אשה אחרת, עד שיעברו עליו שלשה רגלים. רבי יהודה אומר: רגל ראשון ושני — אסור, שלישי — מותר. [ד]ואם אין לו בנים — מותר לישא לאלתר, משום ביטול פריה ורביה. [ה]הניחה לו בנים קטנים — מותר לישא לאלתר, מפני פרנסתן. *מעשה שמתה אשתו של יוסף הכהן, ואמר לאחותה בבית הקברות: לכי ופרנסי את בני אחותך. ואעפ"כ לא בא עליה אלא לזמן מרובה. מאי לזמן מרובה? אמר רב פפא: [ו]לאחר שלשים יום. *ת"ר: כל שלשים יום לגיהוץ, אחד כלים חדשים ואחד כלים ישנים יוצאין (ג) מתוך המכבש. רבי אומר: לא אסרו אלא כלים חדשים בלבד. רבי אלעזר בר' שמעון אומר: [ז]לא אסרו אלא כלים חדשים לבנים בלבד. אביי נפיק [*]בגרדא דסרבלא, כרבי. רבא נפיק בחימוצתא רומיתא סומקתא חדתי, כרבי אלעזר בר' שמעון. § "מפני שאמרו שבת עולה ואינה מפסקת". § בני יהודה ובני גלילא, הני אמרי:

יש

[שמחות פ"י ע"ש] [שמחות פ"ז] [שם וע"ש] [שם וע"ש]

וקורין שבעה. בספר תורה. דאין מתפללין יחד בבית הכנסת, אלא כל אחד ואחד מתפלל בביתו: לא הוצרכו לומר שבת ראשונה. שודאי לא יצא מפתח ביתו: כל שלשים יום לנישואין. עד שלשים יום לאחר אבלו אינו יכול לישא אשה: ואחד כלים ישנים יוצאין מתוך המכבש. פירוש: שהן כחדשים: בגרדא דסרבלא. מלבוש לבן מגוהץ ישן: כרבי. דאמר: לא אסרו לבן אלא חדש: בחימוצתא. חלוק: רומיתא. שבא מרומי: כרבי אלעזר. דאמר: לא אסרו אלא לבנים, וזו אדומה היתה:

אפסוקי

רבי יהודה אומר לא הוצרכו. בירושלמי פוסק הלכה כדברי המוסיף בימים (שבעה). וראיתי כשהייתי קטן רבינו יצחק זקני שלא היה יושב במקומו עד שבוע רביעי. ולא ידעתי טעמו, שאם היה סובר כר' יהודה — א"כ יסבור כמותו בשניה, שאינו יוצא מפתח ביתו. מיהו, י"ל בהא אשכחנא טובא לעיל דאבילות שבעה, וקי"ל הכי. ושמא טעמו כרבנן, ומשום דצריך לישב במקומו ואינו מדבר — וטוב יותר שישב חוץ למקומו, דשמא אין אסור לדבר כי אם במקומו: **עד** שיעברו שלשה רגלים. עד שיהיה שלשה רגלים בלא שמחה, ולא ישכח אהבת אשתו. אי נמי: כדי שישא אשה אחרת ולא יהא זכור מן הראשונה, [שלא] יהא ב' דעות במטה. ועוד: פן יזכירנה אהבת אשתו, לקנטרה. ודומיא דהכא אמרי' לעיל (ד' כא:): מתה אשתו ונשא אשה אחרת — אינו רשאי ליכנס לביתו כו'. פירש ה"ר יונה: דאין שייך לפסוק כרבי יהודה דאמר שני רגלים משום דקי"ל לעיל (ד' כב.) כדברי המיקל באבל — דהא מילתא דפליגי בה הכא אין זו באבל, דימי אבלו כלו להן: **ואמר** לאחותה בבית הקברות. לאו דוקא, שהאבל כל שבעה אסור. וריב"א מפרש: דזו היא האשה שאומר בזבחים פ' "טבול יום" (ד' ק.) שמתה בערב הפסח, ואמרי' לעיל: אפי' יום אחד אפילו שעה אחת — בטלה ממנו גזרת שבעה. ומיהו, משמע שסובר כאותו הפירוש שפי' למעלה בשם ה"ר יונה: שאסור ברחילה עד הערב — זהו מבעוד יום. ודין הניחה לו בנים קטנים מיד [*]מותר לישא ולבעול, וכן אין לו בנים — פירשתי בתוספות יבמות (ד' מג: ושם*), וכן [וכד"ה שלא] בכתובות פ"ק (ד' ד.*), ובתשובות. [וכד"ה אבל] ומה שאמר במס' שמחות (פ"ז) בהאי מילתא דנסיב לאלתר ולא בא עליה עד זמן מרובה. והאי דאמרינן אין לו מי שישמשנו מותר, ואין צריך להמתין שלשה רגלים — כתבתי במקום אחר:

כל שלשים יום לגיהוץ. דוקא גיהוץ אסור, אבל בלא גיהוץ, כגון כיבוס — מותר. דאמרינן לקמן (ד' כז:) "אל תבכו למת" הא כיצד? שלשים יום — לגיהוץ ולתספורת. ובמסכת שמחות (פ"ז): שלשים יום לגיהוץ כילד כו'. ובירושלמי: גזרת שלשים — גיהוץ ותספורת. אבל כיבוס משמע דשרי, מדאמרינן פ' "החולץ" (יבמות מג:) גבי אלמנה מפני האיבול, וקאמר: באיבול שלה שלשים יום. ופריך: קל וחומר, מה במקום שאסור לכבס — מותר לארס, במקום שמותר לכבס — אינו דין שמותר לארס. והדתניא במסכת שמחות (פ"ז) שמונה ימים קודם הרגל, אם רצה לכבס ולספר — הרשות בידו, לא ספר לא כיבס ערב הרגל — אסור לספר ולכבס עד שישלימו שלשים יום. משמע דכיבוס נמי אסור! נראה ההוא כיבוס היינו גיהוץ, ומאחר דכיבוס שרי — גיהוץ נמי שרי לדידן, כדאמרי' פ"ק דכתובות (ד' י:) ופ"ד דתענית (ד' כט:): דגיהוץ שלנו ככיבוס שלהן. והקשה ה"ר שמואל מוורדו"ס: דהא בשמעתין באביי נפיק כו', והא בבבל הוו קיימי, דגיהוץ דאינהו אינו אלא כיבוס ומ"מ אסרי! ותירץ רבינו יצחק: דפעמים שהיו מביאים מא"י כלים מגוהצין, או שמא פעמים שמביאין אומנין יודעין לגהץ כבארץ ישראל. והא דתניא בתוספתא (פ"ב): כל אלו שאמרו מותר לספר במועד — מותר לספר בתוך שלשים יום, אבל כל אלו שאמרו מותר לכבס במועד — אסור בתוך שלשים יום של אבל! צריך לומר דכיבוס נמי היינו גיהוץ. ומורי ריב"א זצ"ל היה אוסר לכבס בתוך שלשים יום, ואין נראה לו לדחות כל אלו. והא דקאמר בפרק "החולץ" (יבמות ד' מג. ושם) מקום שמותר לכבס — היינו בהני דהתירו לגלח ולכבס, בריש פירקין (ד' יג:): בא ממדינת הים, ויוצא מבית האסורין. ומה שאסור שם בתשעה באב לכבס — היינו דוקא טעמא שיכול להמתין אחר תשעה באב, הואיל ואיסורו אינו מושך כל כך. וגרסינן שפיר במקום שמותר לספר, כדפרישית. וא"צ למוחקו, וא"צ ליישבו באשה, או בגילוח כל הראש, כדברי המפרשים שרוצים ליישב גירסת הספרים. והארכתי בתוספות יבמות (ג"ז שם). וגרסינן לקמן (ד' כז:): אל תבכו כו', הא כילד? שלשים יום לתכבוסת ולתספורת. והא דאמר לעיל (ד' טו.) אבל אסור בתכבוסת, משמע לאחר שבעה — שרי! התם במים איירי ולא בנתר וחול, וזה יוכל להיות מותר לאחר שבעה. בתוספות הרב כך פירש לאסור, ובשם רבו פירש היתר. ולפי מה שפירש דכיבוס אסור כמו גיהוץ — ניחא קושיית ה"ר שמואל מוורדו"ס. מיהו, מורי לא היה מפרש ממש לאסור כל כיבוס, אלא היה מפרש: דהאי ברייתא דאסרה כיבוס — היינו בא"י, דכיבוס שלהן כגיהוץ שלנו. והיא דקתני גיהוץ ולא כיבוס — היינו בבבל. מיהו, לפי זה לא היה אסור לדידן כי אם גיהוץ. אכן היה ר"י מפרש בלא ראייה כמו שפירש רבינו יצחק הזקן, דבבבל היו פעמים אומנים מא"י יודעין לגהץ, וכלי פשתן אין בהן משום גיהוץ. וחולק על התלמוד ירושלמי, דקתני התם: כל שלשים יום לגיהוץ אסור ללבוש כלי צמר מגוהצין חדשים, וכלי פשתן מגוהצים לבנים. פירש בתוספות הרב, דהא דאסרי גיהוץ — דוקא ללבוש, אבל לגהץ — מותר. והא דקתני כל שלשים יום לגיהוץ — היינו אסור ללבוש כלים מגוהצין כו'. עד מותר להוליך כלים לגיהוץ בתוך שלשים. ואיני יודע אם היה אומר הרב היתר בכיבוס תוך שבעה, ומחלק נמי בין לכבס או ללבוש. מיהו, רבינו יצחק זקני מפרש בתשובתו דאפי' לכבס ולהניח אסור, מדאסרינן בפרק בתרא דתענית (ד' כט.) לכבס ולהניח. ועוד פירש בתשובתו דכיבוס שלנו מותר בט' באב, כדאמרינן דגיהוץ שלנו ככיבוס שלהן, משמע דכיבוס שלנו אינו ככיבוס שלהם. והכי איתא בהדיא בפ"ק דכתובות (ד' י:). מיהו, לענין ימי אבילות — אסור בכיבוס שלנו. אפי' בתשעה באב מחמירין העולם בכיבוס שלנו מתוך המנהג, כמו שהחמירו לענין אבילות דבשר מליח, דשרי כהלכה ורגילין לנהוג בו איסור. ומיהו, איני מבין מנין לו להקל בתשעה באב יותר מימי אבלו? דאדרבה, בפרק בתרא דתענית (שם) נראה לי שמחמיר יותר לענין גיהוץ כלי פשתן בימי אבלו מבמועד. ובמטפחות ידים הסיב רבינו שאף על פי שהתירו במועד — אסורין בימי אבלו, כדאמרינן לעיל (דף יז:): כל שאמרו מותר לגלח במועד כו' והתניא אסורים — ומוקי לה בתכפוהו אבליו: **רבא** נפיק כו'. ופי' בתוספות: דאביי ורבא הלכה כרבא. וא"כ מותר ללבוש כלים מגוהצין לבועין אפילו חדשים, או ישנים אפילו לבנים, וכן פסק ר"ת:

יש

רבינו חננאל

וקורין שבעה ויוצאין ודוין א) ולא יטיילו בשוק ואין אומרים שמועה והגדה בבית האבל. אמרו על ר' חנינא בן גמליאל שהיה אומר שמועה והגדה בבית האבל: ת"ר אבל שבת ראשונה אינו יוצא מפתח ביתו. שניה יוצא ואינו יושב במקומו. שלישית יושב ואינו מדבר. רביעית שוה לכל אדם. ר' יהודה אומר לא הצריכו לומר שבת ראשונה שהכל נכנסין אצלו לנחמו אלא שניה אינו יוצא מביתו. שלישית יוצא ואינו יושב במקומו. רביעית יושב ואינו מדבר. חמישית שוה לכל אדם. ב) והיכן דרגילין אבלים לצלויי כנסת קדמי ואתו ויתבי במקום אבלים מצלו. ואיכא נמי בבבל דעבדי הכי: ת"ר כל שלשים אסור לישא. מתה אשתו אסור לישא אחרת עד שיעברו עליו שלש רגלים. ר' יהודה אומר רגל ראשון ושני אסור שלישי מותר ואם אין לו בנים מותר לישא לאלתר משום ביטול פריה ורביה. הניחה לו בנים קטנים מותר לישא אשה לאלתר מפני פרנסתן. ומעשה שמתה אשתו של יוסף הכהן ואמר לאחותה ועדיין הן בבית הקברות לכי ופרנסי בני אחותך ואעפ"כ לא בא עליה אלא לאחר שלשים וכן עשה ר' טרפון ומפורש בתלמוד א"י: ת"ר כל שלשים יום לגיהוץ אחד כלים חדשים ואחד כלים ישנים יוצאין מתחת מכבש רבי אומר לא אמרו אלא כלים חדשים בלבד אביי נפק בגרדא דסרבלא כר'. רבא נפק ג) בהמיצתא רומניתא סומקתא חדתי כר' [אלעזר בר'] שמעון וקיי"ל כרבא ואליבא דר' אלעזר בר' שמעון: ירושלמי ב' אחין. ב' שותפין, ב' טבחין ב' חנוונין שאירע לאחד מהן דבר הרי אלו נועלין חנותן ופועלים עושין בצינעא במקום אחד: מתני' מפני שאמרו שבת עולה ואינה מפסקת בני יהודה ובני גלילא דהני אמרי יש אבלות

א) כ"ה גרסת הרי"ף ויושבין ודוין כו'. ב) וכן הביא הרמב"ן ז"ל בס' תה"א בשער האבלות בשם רב האי גאון ז"ל ועי' ברא"ש כאן. ג) כ"ה גי' הערוך בערך המלתא וע"ע בערך חמלתא והרי"ף ז"ל גרס בהימייטתא רומייתא.

קנב א מיי' פי"ג מהל' אבל הל' ט טוש"ע י"ד סי' שפח סעיף ז:

קנג ב מיי' שם פ"ז הלכה ה סמג עשין ב טוש"ע שם סי' שלג סעיף ב:

קנד ג ד ה ו מיי' שם פ"ו הל' ה טוש"ע שם סי' שלב סעיף א ב:

קנה ז מיי' שם פ"ה הל' ג ופ"ו שם הלכה ד סמג עשין דרבנן ב טוש"ע שם סי' שפט סעיף ה:

הגהות הב"ח

(א) גמ' שניה יוצא ואינו יושב במקומו ואינו מדבר שלישית יושב במקומו: (ב) שם ואינו יושב במקומו ואינו מדבר רביעית יושב כו': (ג) שם ואחד כלים ישנים יוצאין מתחת המכבש רבי אומר:

גליון הש"ס

גמ' שבת ראשונה אינו יוצא. עיין לקמן דף כז ע"א תוס' ד"ה אם יכול: **שם** בגרדא דסרבלא כרבי. עיין לקמן דף כד ע"ב תוס' ד"ה ברכת אבילים: **תוס'** ד"ה ואמר לאחותה וכו' מותר לישא ולבעול. נ"ל שתיבת ולבעול ט"ס הוא:

קנו א מיי' פ"ד מהל' אבל הל"ז סמג עשין מד"ס ב טוש"ע י"ד סי' שמא סעיף א וטוש"ע א"ח סי' קלט סעיף ה:
קנז ב מיי' פ"י שם הלכה א סמג עשין ב טוש"ע י"ד סי' ת סעיף א:

רבינו חננאל

אבלות בשבת מדקתני במתני' ושבת עולה: והני אמרי אין אבלות בשבת מדקתני אינה מפסקת דאי ס"ד יש אבלות בשבת [השתא אבלות] נהיג אפסוקי דלא מפסקא מיבעיא כו'. לימא כתנאי מי שמתו מוטל לפניו אוכל בבית אחר וכו'. עד ובשבת מיסב ואוכל בשר ושותה יין ומברך ומזמן ומברכין עליו ומזמנין עליו וחייב בתפלה ובק"ש ובתפילין ובכל מצות האמורות בתורה. ר"ג אומר מתוך שנתחייב באלו כך נתחייב בכולן א"ר יוחנן תשמיש המטה איכא בינייהו. מאי לאו בהא קא מיפלגי ת"ק סבר יש אבלות בשבת ור"ג סבר אין אבלות בשבת אפילו תשמיש המטה שרי ודחינן ממאי דלמא עד כאן לא קאמר ת"ק הכא דאסור בתשמיש המטה אלא משום דמתו מוטל לפניו כו':

גליון הש"ס

גמ' וחייב בק"ש ובתפלה ובתפילין ובכל מצות. בברכות בברייתא זו איתא וחייב בכל מצות האמורות בתורה והרי"ף גם חייב בק"ש ותפלה ובכל מצות האמורות בתורה.

יֵשׁ אֲבֵילוּת בְּשַׁבָּת, וְהָנֵי אָמְרִי: אֵין אֲבֵילוּת בְּשַׁבָּת. מַאן דְּאָמַר יֵשׁ אֲבֵילוּת בְּשַׁבָּת – דְּקָתָנֵי: עוֹלָה. מַאן דְּאָמַר אֵין אֲבֵילוּת בְּשַׁבָּת – דְּקָתָנֵי: אֵינָהּ מַפְסֶקֶת. אִי סָלְקָא דַּעְתָּךְ יֵשׁ אֲבֵילוּת בְּשַׁבָּת – הַשְׁתָּא אֲבֵילוּת נָהֲגָא, אִפְסוּקֵי מִיבַּעְיָא? וְאֶלָּא הָא קָתָנֵי עוֹלָה! אַיְידֵי דְּקָבָעֵי לְמִיתְנָא סֵיפָא אֵינָן עוֹלִים, תָּנָא רֵישָׁא עוֹלָה. וּלְמַאן דְּאָמַר יֵשׁ אֲבֵילוּת בְּשַׁבָּת, הָא קָתָנֵי אֵינָהּ מַפְסֶקֶת! מִשּׁוּם דְּקָבָעֵי לְמִיתְנָא סֵיפָא מַפְסִיקִין – תָּנָא רֵישָׁא אֵינָהּ מַפְסֶקֶת. לֵימָא כְּתַנָּאֵי: *אמִי שֶׁמֵּתוֹ מוּטָל לְפָנָיו – אוֹכֵל בְּבַיִת אַחֵר, אֵין לוֹ בַּיִת אַחֵר – אוֹכֵל בְּבֵית חֲבֵרוֹ, אֵין לוֹ בֵּית חֲבֵרוֹ – עוֹשֶׂה לוֹ מְחִיצָה עֲשָׂרָה טְפָחִים, אֵין לוֹ דָּבָר לַעֲשׂוֹת מְחִיצָה – מַחֲזִיר פָּנָיו וְאוֹכֵל. וְאֵינוֹ מֵיסֵב וְאוֹכֵל, וְאֵינוֹ אוֹכֵל בָּשָׂר, וְאֵינוֹ שׁוֹתֶה יַיִן וְאֵין מְבָרֵךְ, וְאֵין מְזַמֵּן, וְאֵין מְבָרְכִין עָלָיו, וְאֵין מְזַמְּנִין עָלָיו, וּפָטוּר מִקְּרִיאַת שְׁמַע, וּמִן הַתְּפִלָּה, וּמִן הַתְּפִילִּין, וּמִכָּל מִצְוֹת הָאֲמוּרוֹת בַּתּוֹרָה. וּבְשַׁבָּת – מֵיסֵב וְאוֹכֵל, וְאוֹכֵל בָּשָׂר, וְשׁוֹתֶה יַיִן, וּמְבָרֵךְ, וּמְזַמֵּן, וּמְבָרְכִין וּמְזַמְּנִין עָלָיו, °וְחַיָּיב בִּקְרִיאַת שְׁמַע וּבִתְפִלָּה וּבִתְפִילִּין וּבְכָל מִצְוֹת הָאֲמוּרוֹת בַּתּוֹרָה. *רַבָּן גַּמְלִיאֵל אוֹמֵר: מִתּוֹךְ שֶׁנִּתְחַיֵּיב בְּאֵלּוּ – נִתְחַיֵּיב בְּכוּלָּן. וְאָמַר ר' יוֹחָנָן: בתַּשְׁמִישׁ הַמִּטָּה אִיכָּא בֵּינַיְיהוּ. מַאי לָאו בְּהָא קָא מִיפַּלְגִי; דְּמָר סָבַר: יֵשׁ אֲבֵילוּת בְּשַׁבָּת, וּמָר סָבַר: אֵין אֲבֵילוּת בְּשַׁבָּת. מִמַּאי? דִּלְמָא עַד כָּאן לָא קָאָמַר תַּנָּא קַמָּא הָתָם – אֶלָּא מִשּׁוּם דְּמֵתוֹ מוּטָל לְפָנָיו, אֲבָל הָכָא דְּאֵין מֵתוֹ מוּטָל לְפָנָיו – לָא. וְעַ"כ לָא קָאָמַר ר"ג הָתָם – דְּאַכַּתִּי לָא חָל אֲבֵילוּת עֲלֵיהּ, אֲבָל הָכָא דְּחָל אֲבֵילוּת עֲלֵיהּ – הָכִי נַמִּי.

בְּעָא

אִפְסוּקֵי מִבָּעֲיָא. כְּלוֹמַר: מִי צְרִיכָא לְמֵימַר דְּאֵינָהּ מַפְסֶקֶת: **אֵין מְבָרֵךְ.** לְהוֹצִיא אֲחֵרִים יְדֵי חוֹבָתָן: **מִתּוֹךְ** שֶׁנִּתְחַיֵּיב בְּאֵלּוּ. קְרִיאַת שְׁמַע כו' נִתְחַיֵּיב בְּכוּלָּן: **תַּשְׁמִישׁ הַמִּטָּה אִיכָּא בֵּינַיְיהוּ.** הָא דְּקָאָמַר נִתְחַיֵּיב בְּכוּלָּן – סָבַר: מוּתָּר בְּתַשְׁמִישׁ הַמִּטָּה, וְתַנָּא קַמָּא סָבַר: אָסוּר בְּתַשְׁמִישׁ הַמִּטָּה: **מָר.** דְּאָסַר בְּתַשְׁמִישׁ, סָבַר: יֵשׁ אֲבֵילוּת בְּשַׁבָּת: **וּמָר.** דְּשָׁרֵי, סָבַר כִּשְׁמוּאֵל דְּאָמַר: אֵין אֲבֵילוּת בְּשַׁבָּת: **עֲדַיִין לֹא חָלָה אֲבֵילוּת עָלֶיהָ.** דְּלֹא נִקְבַּר: אָבֵל

יש אבילות בשבת. בדברים שבצנעא מיירי, כדפירש בקונט'. ובסמוך נמי: לימא כתנאי, מייתי פלוגתא דרשב"ג ורבנן – דהוי דברים שבצנעא. והכי משמע קצת בירושל' דלעיל אמתניתין דהשבת עולה, פליגי רבי יוחנן וריב"ל אם אסור בשבת בתשמיש המטה – משמע דפליגי כעין פלוגתא דהכא, ואליבא דרבי יוחנן יש שאומרים שם מותר, ואותו חולק על התלמוד שלנו, דא"ר יוחנן בפ"ק דכתובות (דף ד. ושם): אע"פ שאמרו אין אבילות בשבת – אבל דברים שבצנעא נוהג. וקצת קשה לי תימה בשמעתין: אביי אשכחיה לרב יוסף דפריס סודרא ארישיה, אמר ליה לא סבר לה מר אין אבילות בשבת? אמר ליה: הכי אמר ר' יוחנן: דברים שבצנעא נוהג! שמא היה סבור דפריס סודרא ארישיה הוה דברים שבפרהסיא, וכמאן דאמר פריעת הראש חובה, ולא היה מחלק בין בביתו בין חוץ לביתו. והוא השיב לו: בביתו חשיב צנעא: **מאן** דאמר יש אבילות בשבת מדקתני עולה. פירש הר"א ז"ל: מדקתני ולא פירש "ואין בה אבילות" – אלמא: אבילות נוהג בה, דאם לא כן – היה לו לפרש הכי בהדיא, אע"ג דעולה לא נהג בה אבילות. דכיון דעולה – משמע דנוהג בה אבילות. ומשני: איידי דקתני סיפא אין עולין סתם, תנא ברישא עולה סתם. ולא נהירא. ופירש ר' שמעון זצ"ל מרבו: מאן דאמר יש אבילות דקתני עולה – משמע דעולה לכל מנין שבעה, ולאבילות – שינהג בשבת מה שנהג אתמול. ומתוך כך תעלה שבת לחשבונו, כשם שעי"ש עולה לחשבונו. מ"ד אין אבילות בשבת, דקתני אינה מפסקת, אע"ג דחשיבא כולי האי לבטל אבילות בגוה – מ"מ אינו מפסיק. דאל"כ פשיטא. וקפריך: ואלא הא דקתני עולה, דמשמע דנוהג אבילות כשאר ימים! ומשני: איידי דקתני גבי י"ט אין עולין לגמרי, לא למנין ולא לאבילות, משום שמחה דכתיב בהן כדפרישית, תנא רישא נמי עולה, באותו לשון עצמו דתנא בי"ט תנא בשבת, דלא להפליג בלשון המשנה. ומיהו, עולה דשבת *אינו למנין דלאבילות לא סלקא, אלא אי נהגא אבילות בגויה. וא"כ, לפי פירוש זה ואלא הא דקתני עולה, ומשני לעולם לא נהגא, ואיידי דתנא כו'. וא"כ המשנה – אין שטת התלמוד לומר "איידי דתנא הא תנא נמי הא" – אלא במילתא דאמת, אלא דלא צריכי. אבל דברים נראים שקר – אין לו לשנות! ועוד יש להקשות: לפי מה שמפרש אי הכי ליתני שבת אינו עולה, והוי דומיא דסיפא יותר. עד כאן לשון הר"א. ובתו' הרב מקשה: דמשמע אפילו למאן דאמר דלא נהגא עולה למנין שבעה, וא"כ ברגל נמי, אע"ג דלא נהגא – יהא עולה. ולעיל אמרי' לענין שבעה לא קמבעיא ליה דלא נהגא מצות שבעה ברגל! ומתרץ: אע"ג דשבת עולה – רגל אינו עולה, הואיל ואין אבילות כלל, משום דכתיב בהן שמחה. שבת מיהא לא כתיב שמחה, אפילו אינה נוהגת – עולה. בירושלמי מפרש טעמא דשבת דאין אבילות נוהג בו – משום דכתיב (משלי י) "ברכת ה' היא תעשיר ולא יוסיף עצב עמה" ושבת כתיב ביה ברכה*: **ואינו** אוכל בשר ואינו שותה יין. נראה דכי היכי דשרי בפרק בתרא דתענית (דף ל.) גבי ערב תשעה באב בשר כל זמן שאינו כשלמים, ויין מגתו – הכי נמי שרי באונן. מיהו, אין רגילין לנהוג בהן היתר לא בכאן ולא בתשעה באב. תימה: משמע דאונן חמור מאבל, דלא מצינו אבל שיהא בו איסור בבשר וביין. ולענין קדשים אשכחן דאבל אוכל וקדשים, ואונן אסור. ובשאר דברים החמירו באבילות: בכפיית המטה, ונעילת הסנדל, ועטיפת הראש, וטובא איכא, ובאונן שרי! וי"ל: דדברים שהן משום אבל – מותר גבי אונן, ובאבילות אחורין. אבל דבר"ש שאינם אסורין משום אבילות, אלא משום שיש לו להיות טרוד בקבורת מתו, ולא ימשך אחר דברים אחרים – כגון אכילת בשר ושתיית יין – אסירי באונן דוקא. ותשמיש המטה, דמשמע בסמוך דאסור באונן – בהא נמי שמא ימשך, או שמא שמחה יתירתא ותולפה, כך מלאתי, ובתגלחת ובתכבוסת לא ידעינן אי שרי באונן. ואין ללמוד איסור לגלח, מדתני' במס' שמחות*: היה מגלח ואמרו לו מת אחד מקרוביו – הרי זה יגמור. משמע: הא לא התחיל – אסור. דלמא בשמועה איירי, ולאחר שנקבר. ובשם ריב"א כתבתי: דתגלחת אסור, דנפקא לן מ"ראשיכם אל תפרעו" (ויקרא י) הא כולי עלמא – אסירי. ואינהו אוננים הוו. ובתשמיש המטה דאסרינן בסמוך, ורצו להתיר באנינות כדאמרינן פ"ק דכתובות (דף ד. ושם), ובאבילות אסרו. דקאמרינן התם: מכניסין את המת לחדר ובועל בעילת מצוה ופורש. והא דקאמרינן התם אבילות דהכא קילא ואתי לזלזולי בה, ומקשה: מאי קולא? אילימא דקתני בועל בעילת מצוה, משום דלא חיילא אבילות עליה. אינו רוצה לומר שאין קולא בדבר, אלא הכי קאמר: אין קולא באבילות, כי אם באנינות ולא אתי לזלזולי באבילות: **ואין** מברכין עליו. פירש בקונטרס בברכות פרק "מי שמתו" (דף יח. ושם): ברכת המוציא, ואין מזמנין – ברכת המזון. ותימה: גבי המוציא מה שייך לומר אין מברכין עליו? בשלמא גבי ברכת המזון – שייך זירוף, אלא גבי המוציא מאי שייך זירוף? ויש לפרש: דבגמרא קאמרינן דאין מברכין עליו, אלא מצוה לחלק, דהוו כשנים שאכלו שמצוה ליחלק, ואין זה האונן מצטרף עמהן, ואין מזמנין עליהן = עמהן, לומר: נברך שאכלנו משלו. ואי לא הוה תני אלא חדא הוה אמינא: לענין נברך שאכלנו משלו דאין מצטרף אבל מצטרף, להיות להם דין שלשה, לברך אחד מהן בעבור חברו, להכי תני תרתי. וריב"א מפרש: דאין מברכין ומזמנין, חדא לומר "נברך שאכלנו משלו", וחדא לברך בשם, כמו שמזכירין שם בעשרה. פירש בקונטרס בפרק "מי שמתו" (ג"ז שם): ואינו מברך – אין צריך לברך ברכת המזון. משמע מפירושו דאין אסור לברך. ובשמעתין נמי פירש כענין זה. ומיהו, מדקאמר בריש פרק "מי שמתו" התם למאן דאמר [תוך] ארבע אמות הוא דאסור – פירש רבינו יצחק בברכות: דאיכא איסור לברך. וגם בתוספות הרב פירש דאסור לברך. ותימה לרבי יצחק: דהשתא נהגו לברך ולזמן! והיה אומר דלא איירי הכא רק כשהוא עוסק בצרכי המת, שאין לו להתבטל מן המצוה. אבל בשעה שאינו עוסק – שרי. אי נמי: בשעה שאחרים עוסקים, והוא אינו עושה כלום. ומיהו, בירושל' אינו משמע כן, והכי איתא התם*: אינו אוכל כל צורכו, ואינו שותה כל צורכו כו', ואינו מברך. ואם בירך – אין עונין אחריו אמן. ואם ברכו אחרים – אינו עונה אחריהם אמן. ואם משום ביטול מצות עסק במתו – מה ביטול יש בעניית אמן? מיהו, נראה לי משום שמיעת הברכה, שלא תהיה אמן יתומה. ועוד: דאמרינן לקמן הן עומדין ומתפללין והוא יושב ומצדיק עליו את הדין, ומשמע שאינו עוסק בו כלל, אלא יושב ודומם. ונראה דאסור לברך. ושוב מצאתי בירושל' דריש פרק "מי שמתו" תני: אם רצה להחמיר על עצמו – אין שומעין לו, למה – מפני כבודו של מת או משום שאין לו מי שישא משאוי. ופריך: והא תניא פטור מנטילת לולב? וקא סלקא דעתיה דמיירי ביום טוב, ובו אינו טרוד לישא במשאוי! ומשני: תפתר בחול. פירוש: בחולו של מועד. ופריך: והתניא פטור מתקיעת שופר, אית לך למימר בחול ולא ביום טוב? אמר ר' חנינא: מכיון שהיו זקוקים להביא לו ארון ותכריכין, דתנינן תמן: מחשיכין על התחום לפקח על עסקי כלה ועל עסקי המת, להביא ארון ותכריכין – נמי כמו שהוא נושא משאוי דמי. *משמע דפליגי בשבת וביום טוב דאינו מברך במאי דאמרינן. מיהו, הא קשיא לן: דאמרינן בסיפא: בשבת מברך ומזמן, וצריך עיון:

בעא

ברכות יז: שמחות פ"י

[במס' שמחות א' כדהכא אבל בברכו' יח. איתא ר"ש בן גמליאל]

אינו אלא למנין דאבילות ולא נהגא אבילות כצ"ל

[ויברך אלהים את יוס השביעי כ"ה במ"ר ויחי פ"ק]

פ"ה ה"ח

רש"א

שמחות פ"ו

משמע דפליגי בשבת כצ"ל

בעא מיניה ר' יוחנן משמואל: יש אבילות בשבת או אין אבילות בשבת? אמר ליה: אין אבילות בשבת. יתבי רבנן קמיה דרב פפא וקאמרי משמיה דשמואל: אבל ששימש מטתו בימי אבלו – חייב מיתה. א"ל רב פפא: [א]אסור אתמר, ומשמיה דר' יוחנן אתמר. ואי שמיעא לכו משמיה דשמואל – הכי שמיע לכו: אמר רב תחליפא בר אבימי אמר שמואל: [א]אבל שלא פרע ושלא פירם – חייב מיתה, שנאמר: "ראשיכם אל תפרעו ובגדיכם לא תפרומו ולא תמותו" וגו', הא אחר שלא פרע ושלא פירם – חייב מיתה. אמר רפרם בר פפא, תנא באבל רבתי: אבל אסור לשמש מטתו בימי אבלו. ומעשה באחד ששימש מטתו בימי אבלו, ושמטו חזירים את גוייתו. אמר שמואל: [ב]פח"ז – חובה, נת"ר – רשות. פריעת הראש, חזרת קרע לאחוריו, זקיפת המטה – חובה. נעילת הסנדל, תשמיש המטה, רחיצת ידים ורגלים בחמין ערבית – רשות. ורב אמר: [ג]אף פריעת הראש רשות. ושמואל, מאי שנא נעילת הסנדל דרשות – דלאו כולי עלמא עבידי דסיימי מסאנייהו, פריעת הראש נמי לאו כולי עלמא עבידי דמגלו רישייהו! שמואל לטעמיה, דאמר שמואל: [ד]כל קרע שאינו בשעת חימום – אינו קרע, [ה]וכל עטיפה שאינה כעטיפת ישמעאלים – אינה עטיפה. מחוי ר"נ [ו]עד גובי דדיקנא. א"ר יעקב א"ר יוחנן: לא שנו אלא שאין לו מנעלים ברגליו, אבל יש לו מנעלים ברגליו – מנעליו מוכיחין עליו. כל קרע שאינו בשעת חימום אינו קרע? והא אמרו ליה לשמואל: נח נפשיה דרב. קרע עליה תריסר מני, אמר: אזל גברא דהוה מסתפינא מיניה. א"ל לרבי יוחנן: נח נפשיה דר' חנינא. *קרע עליה תליסר אצטלי מלתא, אמר: אזל גברא דהוה מסתפינא מיניה. שאני רבנן, דכיון דכל שעתא מדכרי שמעתייהו – כשעת חימום דמי. א"ל רבין בר אדא לרבא: אמר תלמידך רב עמרם, תניא: אבל, כל שבעה – קורעו לפניו, ואם בא להחליף – מחליף, וקורע. [ז]בשבת – קורעו לאחוריו, ואם בא להחליף – מחליף, ואינו קורע! כי תניא ההיא – בכבוד אביו ואמו. אותן קרעין מתאחין או אין מתאחין? פליגי בה אבוה דרב אושעיא ובר קפרא. [ח]חד אמר: אין מתאחין, וחד אמר: מתאחין. תסתיים דאבוה דרב אושעיא דאמר אין מתאחין, דאמר רב אושעיא, אין מתאחין. ממאן שמיע ליה – לאו מאבוה? לא, מבר קפרא רביה שמיע ליה. אמר רבא: אבל מטייל באונקלי בתוך ביתו. אביי אשכחיה לרב יוסף דפרים ליה סודרא ארישיה, ואזיל ואתי בביתיה. א"ל: לאו סבר לה מר אין אבילות בשבת? א"ל: הכי א"ר יוחנן: *דברים שבצינעא נוהג. § "ר"א אומר משחרב בית המקדש עצרת כשבת" וכו'. § אמר רב גידל בר מנשיא אמר שמואל: הלכה כר"ג. ואיכא דמתני להא דרב גידל בר מנשיא אהא: [ט]כל ל' יום *תינוק יוצא בחיק, ונקבר באשה אחת ושני אנשים, אבל לא באיש אחד ושתי נשים.

אבא

רש"י

אבל רבתי. מסכת שמחות: גוייתו. כל גופו, ואיכא דאמרי: אבר שלו. פריעת הראש. שמגלה האבל ראשו בשבת, ואינו מתעטף. וחזרת קרע לאחוריו, וזקיפת המטה – חובה בשבת: נעילת הסנדל. דלאו כולי עלמא סיימי מסאנייהו בשבת, ולא מוכח דאבל הוא: לא כולי עלמא מגלו רישייהו. בשבת, ואע"פ שמתעטף – לא מיחזי כאבל: בשעת חימום. בשעת התחלת הצער, בשעת מיתה: וכל עטיפה שאינה כעטיפת ישמעאלים. הלכך, כיון דכל ימי שבוע שהוא אבל מתעטף כישמעאל, אם אינו עוטה בשבת – נראה כנוהג אבילות, דכ"ע לא נהיגי בעטיפה זו, אלא אבלים בלבד: מחוי ר"נ. עטיפת ישמעאלים: גובי דיקנא. גומות שבלחי, למטה מפיו: לא שנו. פריעת הראש בשבת, דצריך לגלות חוטמו ושפמו וזקנו שהיה מכוסה בימי אבלו, להודיע כי אין אבילות בשבת: אלא שאין מנעלים ברגליו אבל יש מנעלים ברגליו מנעליו מוכיחין עליו. דאינו אבל. אבל לגלות ראשו – אינו צריך. ואם בא להתעטף בצינעא, אפי' כעטיפת הישמעאלים – אין בכך כלום: דמסתפינא מיניה. בקושיות: מחליף וקורע. אע"פ שאינו שעת חימום: כבוד אביו. שנו. אבל לכולי עלמא – אין קורע אלא בשעת חימום: ממאן שמיעא. לרב אושעיא הא דאמר אין מתאחין – שמע מינה האי דאמר אין מתאחין – אבוה דרב אושעיא: אונקלי. שייפינ"ש, חלוק שקורעו: בתוך ביתו. שבצינעא מותר לנהוג אבילות בשבת: דפרים סודריה ארישיה. בשבת, משום עטיפה, דנהיג אבילות: כל ל' יום יוצא בחיק. בן ל' יום מוציאו בחיק לבית הקברות, ולא בארון: אבל לא באיש אחד. שאין מתייחדין עם האשה:

דלוסקמא

תוספות

בעא מיניה ר' יוחנן משמואל. מיהו ר' יוחנן לא קיבל משמואל, דאיהו סבירא ליה: דברים שבצינעא נוהג, כדפרישית לעיל:

הא אחר שלא פרע כו'. אע"ג דפשטי' דקרא הא אחר פורע ופורם, ואם הם יעשו ימותו – נראה דאסמכתא בעלמא הוא, דהא לא מייתי להו סוף פרק "הנשרפין" (סנהדרין דף פג.) גבי אלו שבמיתה:

ושמואל לטעמיה. פי' בתוספ' הרב: דרב סבר דעטיפת הראש שאינה כעטיפת ישמעאלים הויא עטיפה, ומסתמא רב ושמואל הלכה כרב. יש מפרשין דרחיצת ידים דקאמר הכא רשות – היינו כמ"ד פרק "במה מדליקין" (שבת דף כה:) דבלא אבילות הוא רשות. אבל לר"נ בר יצחק דאמר התם: ואני אומר מצוה – באבל נמי הוי מצוה, ולא רשות. ונראה דלא צריך למימר הכי, אלא הכי פירושו: הכא דמשום אבילות – אינו חובה להראות אבילות בשבת:

לא שנו שאין לו מנעלים ברגליו. תימה: דכי היכי דמנעליו מוכיחין עליו, אמאי לא אמרי' אחד מהני מוכיחין? ונמצא דאינו חובה כי אם האחד! ושמא במנעלים יש הוכחה יותר:

וכל קרע שאינו בשעת חימום אינו קרע. נראה דהא דאמר לעיל (דף כ:) מי שנזדמן לו חלוק בתוך ז', אע"פ שאינו שעת חימום – שמא דוקא כגון שקרע כבר. והכא מיירי בשלא קרע עדיין. א"נ: כגון שאין לו חלוק בשעה ראשונה – חייב לקרוע כשיהיה לו, אפי' שלא בשעת חימום. ולי נראה, דבכל שעה שיוכל להתחמם על מתו, אפי' לזמן מרובה אחר מיתתו – קרוי שפיר בשעת חימום, כמו שאמרו ברבנן: משום דמדכרי שמעתייהו, הוא הדין נמי בכל מת שיוכל להתחמם עליו. והא דפריך בסמוך ולא משני הכי – משום דבלאו הכי משני שפיר:

כי תניא ההיא בכבוד אביו ואמו. ומכאן קשה לי על מה שפי' למעלה (דף כ:) *)דגרסי': רבי חנינא מי שאין לו אלא חלוק אחד, דמיירי בכה"ג דמחליף וקורע. דהא גבי אביו ואמו אמר הכא: מחליף וקורע כל שבעה, ולעיל (שם) אמרי': על אביו ואמו קורע לעולם! וצ"ע:

הכי א"ר יוחנן דברים שבצינעא נוהג. פסק בהלכות גדולות כר' יוחנן, לאפוקי מרב ושמואל דאמרי לעיל: תשמיש המטה רשות, ודברים שבצינעא הוא. ובפ"ק דכתובות (דף ד.) נמי קאמר עלה: מסייע ליה לר' יוחנן, דאביי ורבא סברי כוותיה. ואע"ג דקיימא לן (לעיל דף יח. כב.) הלכה כדברי המיקל – ה"מ במחלוקת של תנאים, אבל במילתא דאמוראי – לא אמרן. מספקא לי, כי היכי דשרי בתוך ביתו הני דברים דקריעה, אי הוה אסור נעילת הסנדל בצנעא, וכל שאר דברים:

עצרת בשבת. וכ"ש ר"ה ויוה"כ, ר"ג אומר ר"ה ויוה"כ כרגלים וכ"ש עצרת לאחר חורבן. ולישנא לא אתי שפיר, דהוה ליה למתני: ר"ג אומר אף ר"ה ויוה"כ כו':

וחכמים אומרים לא כדברי זה כו'. ולא שייך למימר: היינו תנא קמא! דנימא כולהו אתו לפרש מילתא דתנא קמא, כי ההיא דלא ירבה לו נשים בפרק ב' דסנהדרין (דף כא.), וההיא (דהמקדש*):

הלכה כר"ג. תימה: כיון דאמר שמואל (לעיל דף יח. כב.) הלכה כדברי המיקל באבל, אמאי איצטריך למיפסק הלכה כר"ג? וי"ל: דחומרא נמי היא, דאם קברו סמוך לחשיכה ולא היה לו שעה אחת לנהוג בו אבילות, או קברוהו נכרים ביום טוב, או שמע שמועה קרובה ביום טוב, אם הם כרגלים – אינם עולים למנין שבעה, ואם הם כשבת – עולים:

אבא

*) אבל הגי' שם מי שאין לו חלוק לקרוע כו' ואולי גיר' אחרת היתה לפניהם ועיין במהרש"א

רבינו חננאל

בעא מיניה ר' יוחנן משמואל יש אבילות בשבת אי לא. א"ל אין אבילות בשבת. אמרי רבנן משמיה דשמואל אבל ששימש מטתו חייב מיתה. א"ל רב פפא אסור אתמר ומשמיה דר' יוחנן אתמר אמר רב תחליפא אמר שמואל אבל שלא פרע ראשו ולא פירם בגדיו חייב מיתה שנאמר ראשיכם אל תפרעו ובגדיכם לא תפרומו ולא תמותו מכלל שאחר שלא פירע ושלא פירם חייב מיתה. אמר רפרם תנא באבל רבתי אבל אסור לשמש מטתו ומעשה באחד ששימש מטתו בימי אבלו ושמטו חזירים את גויתו. אמרו משמיה דשמואל פח"ז חובה. פריעת הראש. חזרת קרע לאחוריו. זקיפת המטה לעשותן בשבת [חובה] להודיע שאינו נוהג אבל בשבת. אבל נ'ת'ר'. נעילת סנדל. תשמיש המטה. רחיצת ידים ורגלים בחמין רשות. ורב אמר אף פריעת הראש בשבת רשות. מקשינן לשמואל מ"ש נעילת הסנדל דאמר רשות דלאו כ"ע מסגי במסני. פריעת הראש נמי לאו כ"ע עבידי דמגלי רישייהו. ופרקינן שמואל לטעמיה דאמר כל קרע שאינו בשעת חימום אינו קרע. וכל עטיפה שאינה כעטיפת ישמעאלים אינה עטיפה. פי' עטיפת ישמעאלים דאמר שמואל מכסה שפמו וזקנו וחוטמו במצנפתו או בטליתו. והוא אלמתה בלשון ערב. ובשבת צריך לגלות חוטמו ושפמו וזקנו שהיה מכסה בימי אבלו כי אין אבל בשבת אבל לגלות ראשו אין צריך. ועוד כמה מכסי מחוי רב נחמן עד גובי דדיקנא. א"ר יוחנן לא שנו אלא שאין מנעלין ברגליו אבל יש מנעלין ברגליו מנעליו מוכיחין עליו. וקיי"ל כרב דאמר פריעת הראש נמי בשבת רשות. ואם בא להתעטף בצנעא כעטיפת ישמעאלים אין בכך כלום *) ולא בעי עטיפה כולי האי. דהא רב יוסף דהוא בתרא עבד כרב. אמר רבא אבל מטייל באונקלי בתוך ביתו. ואונקלי היא מצנפת כגון מצנפת של כה"ג כדגרסינן בסוף מנחות. מעשה בחוני ושמעי בני שמעון הצדיק הלבישו באונקלי וחגרו בצלצול. אביי אשכחיה [לרב יוסף] דפרים סודרא ארישיה כעטיפת ישמעאלים וקאזיל ואתי בביתיה. א"ל לא סבר לה מר אין אבילות בשבת א"ל דברים שבצנעא נוהג. ומקשינן תוב לשמואל וכל קרע שאינו בשעת חימום אינו קרע. והא אמרו ליה לשמואל נח נפשיה דרב וקרע עליה תליסר כברי מאניה. ור' יוחנן קרע על ר' חנינא י"ג אצטלי דמלתא. א"ל אזל ליה גברא דהוה מסתפינא. הנה קרעו בשעת שמועה שלא בשעת חימום. ופרקינן שאני רבנן דכיון דכל שעתא מדכרי שמועתיה שעת שמועה כשעת חימום דמי. רבא אמר מהכא דתניא אבל כל שבעה קורעו לפניו ואם בא להחליף חלוקו מחליף וקורע החלוק שלובש הנה קריעתה שלא בשעת חימום. ופרקינן כי תניא ההיא שקורע כל חלוק שלובש אפילו כל שבעה בכבוד אביו ואמו: (ירושלמי הרי שהיה מחליף בגדיו) תשלום הברייתא ובשבת קורעו לאחוריו כדאמרן חזרת [קרע לאחוריו בשבת חובה] ואם בא בשבת להחליף חלוקו מחליף ואינו קורע. הרי שהיה מחליף בגדיו [כל] שבעה חייב לקרוע כולן. אותן קרעין מתאחין או אינן מתאחין. אסיקנא חלוקת אבוה דר' אושעיא ובר קפרא: ירושלמי אבל שבא מן הדרך והיה רגליו קיהות מותר לרחוץ שאין רחיצת צונן רחיצה. תני אבל ומנודה שהיו מהלכין בדרך מותרין בנעילת הסנדל. ולכשיבואו לעיר יחלוצו וכן בט' באב. וכן בתענית צבור. תני מקום שנהגו לשאול בשלום אבלים בשבת שואלין. ר' אושעיא חמא אבלין בשבת ואמר להו שלום עליכם כמנהג מקומנו. ר' יוסי בן חלפתא הוה משתבח בר"מ קומי ציפוראי. אדם גדול קדוש צנוע הוא. חד (יומא) זמן חמון ליה שאיל בשלום אבילא בשבת. ותו אמרו ליה ר' אהן הוא דאת משני שבחיה אמר להן [מה עביד] א"ל שאיל בשלום אביליא בשבתא. אמר לון בעין אתון מידע חייליה. אתא להודעאן דאין אבלות בשבת דכתיב ברכת ה' היא תעשיר. זו ברכת שבת. ולא יוסיף עצב עמה. זו אבלות כמו דאמר נעצב המלך אל בנו. תני ארוסתו לא מתאבל ולא אונן עליה. תני כל שמתאבלין עליו מתאבלין עמו. רב מתה אחותו פקיד לחייא בריה כד תיסליק לגביי של נעליך מעל רגליך. ר' יונה סליק לגביה ר' גוריון בשבת בגו ז' ימי אבלו. נפיק לגביה לביש סנדלי. א"ל אנת דכר דילפון עובדא מינך דבשבת [מותר] בנעילת הסנדל לא ילפון עובדא מבר נש זעיר. ואין דובר עליו דבר. אפילו דבר תורה א"ר יוחנן שלא היו יודעין במה לפתוח אם ביסורין שבגופו אם בחסרון ממונו אם בנפש בניו ובנותיו: מתני' משחרב בית המקדש ר' אלעזר אומר עצרת בשבת. ר"ג אומר ר"ה ויוה"כ כרגלים. דייקינן מינה וכ"ש עצרת שהיא כרגלים. אמר גידל בן מנשי אמר שמואל הלכה כר"ג

*) נראה דצ"ל דלרב גם בחול א"צ להתעטף כעטיפת ישמעאלים ועי' בתוס' ד"ה ושמואל.

עין משפט נר מצוה

קנח א מיי' פ"ח מהל' אבל הל' א סמג עשין מד"ס ב:

קנט ב ג מיי' פ"י שם הל' א סמג שם טוש"ע י"ד סי' ת סעי' א:

קס ד מיי' פ"ח שם הל' ג סמג שם טור י"ד סי' שמ:

קסא ה ו מיי' פ"ה שם הל' יט טוש"ע י"ד סי' שפו:

קסב ז מיי' פ"י שם הל' א טוש"ע י"ד סי' ת סעי' א:

קסג ח מיי' שם פ"ט הל' א טוש"ע י"ד סי' שמ סעי' יד:

קסד ט מיי' שם פי"ב הל' י סמג שם טוש"ע י"ד סי' שנג סעי' ד:

תורה אור

ויקרא י

מסורת הש"ס

[עי' תוס' ב"ק לג: ד"ה שוכר]

[כתובות ז.]

קדושין פ: שמחות פ"ג

[שייך במשנה דלעיל יט.]

[ג"ז שייך למשנ' דלעיל יט.]

[נ"ל דהמזבח מקדש (ד' פג.) וע"ע תוספות פסחים פג. ד"ה ר' שמעון אומר ודף קטז: ד"ה וחותם ותוס' עירובין מח. ד"ה ר' יהודה]

גליון הש"ס

גמ' אסור אתמר ומשמיה דר' יוחנן אתמר. לא ידעתי מה חידש בזה הא איתא בבריית' גמ' לעיל דף כא ע"א ואלו דברים שאבל אסור בהם וכו' ובתשמיש:

אַבָּא שָׁאוּל אוֹמֵר: אַף בְּאִישׁ אֶחָד וּשְׁתֵּי נָשִׁים. וְאֵין עוֹמְדִין עָלָיו בְּשׁוּרָה, וְאֵין אוֹמְרִים עָלָיו בִּרְכַּת אֲבֵלִים וְתַנְחוּמֵי אֲבֵלִים. בֶּן שְׁלֹשִׁים יוֹצֵא בִּדְלוּסְקְמָא. רַבִּי יְהוּדָה אוֹמֵר: [א]לֹא דְּלוּסְקְמָא הַנִּיטֶּלֶת בְּכָתֵף, אֶלָּא הַנִּיטֶּלֶת בָּאֲגַפַּיִם. וְעוֹמְדִין עָלָיו בְּשׁוּרָה, וְאוֹמְרִים עָלָיו בִּרְכַּת אֲבֵלִים וְתַנְחוּמֵי אֲבֵלִים. *[ב]בֶּן י"ב חֹדֶשׁ — יוֹצֵא בְּמִטָּה, ר"ע אוֹמֵר: הוּא בֶּן שָׁנָה וְאֵבָרָיו כְּבֶן שְׁתַּיִם, הוּא בֶּן שְׁתַּיִם וְאֵבָרָיו כְּבֶן שָׁנָה — יוֹצֵא בְּמִטָּה. ר' שִׁמְעוֹן בֶּן אֶלְעָזָר אוֹמֵר: [ג]הַיּוֹצֵא בְּמִטָּה — רַבִּים מַצְהִיבִין עָלָיו, אֵינוֹ יוֹצֵא בְּמִטָּה — אֵין רַבִּים מַצְהִיבִין עָלָיו. ר"א בֶּן עֲזַרְיָה אוֹמֵר: [ד]נִיכָּר לָרַבִּים — רַבִּים מִתְעַסְּקִים עִמּוֹ, אֵינוֹ נִיכָּר לָרַבִּים — אֵין רַבִּים מִתְעַסְּקִים עִמּוֹ. וּמָה הֵן בְּהֶסְפֵּד? רַבִּי מֵאִיר בְּשֵׁם רַבִּי יִשְׁמָעֵאל אוֹמֵר: עֲנִיִּים — בְּנֵי שָׁלֹשׁ, עֲשִׁירִים — בְּנֵי חָמֵשׁ. רַבִּי יְהוּדָה אוֹמֵר מִשְּׁמוֹ: [ה]עֲנִיִּים — בְּנֵי חָמֵשׁ, עֲשִׁירִים — בְּנֵי שֵׁשׁ. וּבְנֵי זְקֵנִים כִּבְנֵי עֲנִיִּים. אָמַר רַב גִּידֵּל בַּר מְנַשְּׁיָא אָמַר רַב: הֲלָכָה כְּרַבִּי יְהוּדָה שֶׁאָמַר מִשּׁוּם רַבִּי יִשְׁמָעֵאל. דָּרַשׁ ר' עֲנָנִי בַּר שָׂשׂוֹן אַפִּיתְחָא דְּבֵי נְשִׂיאָה: [ו]יוֹם אֶחָד לִפְנֵי עֲצֶרֶת וַעֲצֶרֶת — הֲרֵי כָּאן אַרְבָּעָה עָשָׂר. שְׁמַע רַבִּי אַמֵּי וְאִיקְפַּד. אֲמַר: אַטּוּ דִּידֵיהּ הִיא? דְּרַבִּי אֶלְעָזָר א"ר אוֹשַׁעְיָא הִיא! דָּרַשׁ רַבִּי יִצְחָק נַפָּחָא אַקִּילְעָא דְּרֵישׁ גָּלוּתָא: יוֹם אֶחָד לִפְנֵי עֲצֶרֶת, וַעֲצֶרֶת — הֲרֵי כָּאן אַרְבָּעָה עָשָׂר. שְׁמַע רַב שֵׁשֶׁת אִיקְפַּד, אֲמַר: אַטּוּ דִּידֵיהּ הִיא? דְּר"א אָמַר ר' אוֹשַׁעְיָא הִיא. דְּא"ר אֶלְעָזָר א"ר אוֹשַׁעְיָא: [ז]מִנַּיִן *לַעֲצֶרֶת שֶׁיֵּשׁ לָהּ תַּשְׁלוּמִין כָּל שִׁבְעָה — שֶׁנֶּאֱמַר: °"בְּחַג הַמַּצּוֹת וּבְחַג הַשָּׁבוּעוֹת" (א) מָה חַג הַמַּצּוֹת יֵשׁ לָהּ תַּשְׁלוּמִין כָּל שִׁבְעָה — אַף חַג הַשָּׁבוּעוֹת יֵשׁ לָהּ תַּשְׁלוּמִין כָּל שִׁבְעָה. *אַדְבְּרֵיהּ רַב פַּפָּא לְרַב אָוְיָא סָבָא, וְדָרַשׁ: [ח]יוֹם אֶחָד לִפְנֵי רֹאשׁ הַשָּׁנָה, וְרֹאשׁ הַשָּׁנָה — הֲרֵי כָּאן אַרְבָּעָה עָשָׂר. אָמַר רָבִינָא: הִלְכָּךְ, [ט]יוֹם אֶחָד לִפְנֵי הֶחָג, וְחַג, וּשְׁמִינִי שֶׁלּוֹ — הֲרֵי כָּאן עֶשְׂרִים וְאֶחָד יוֹם. רָבִינָא אִיקְּלַע לְסוּרָא דִּפְרָת, א"ל *רַב חֲבִיבָא מְסוּרָא דִּפְרָת לְרָבִינָא: אָמַר מָר יוֹם אֶחָד לִפְנֵי רֹאשׁ הַשָּׁנָה וְרֹאשׁ הַשָּׁנָה הֲרֵי כָּאן אַרְבָּעָה עָשָׂר? אֲמַר לֵיהּ: אֲנָא מִסְתַּבְּרָא כְּרַבָּן גַּמְלִיאֵל הוּא דְּאָמֵינָא.§

מתני' [י]אֵין קוֹרְעִין, [כ]וְלֹא חוֹלְצִין, [ל]וְאֵין מַבְרִין, אֶלָּא קְרוֹבָיו שֶׁל מֵת. [מ]וְאֵין מַבְרִין אֶלָּא עַל מִטָּה זְקוּפָה.§

גמ'

רש"י

דְּלוּסְקְמָא. אָרוֹן: וְאֵין עוֹמְדִין עָלָיו בְּשׁוּרָה. אֵין צָרִיךְ לַעֲמוֹד עָלָיו בְּשׁוּרָה. כְּשֶׁחוֹזְרִין מִבֵּית הַקְּבָרוֹת עוֹבְרִין לִפְנֵי הָאָבֵל בְּשׁוּרָה, וְכָל אֶחָד אוֹמֵר לוֹ: "תִּתְנַחֵם": בִּרְכַּת אֲבֵלִים. בְּרָכָה שֶׁאוֹמֵר בָּרְחָבָה, כִּדְאָמַר בִּכְתוּבּוֹת (ד' ח:): תַּנְחוּמֵי אֲבֵלִים. כָּל שִׁבְעָה הוֹלְכִין לְנַחֲמוֹ בְּבֵיתוֹ: הַנִּיטֶּלֶת בְּכָתֵף. כְּאָדָם אֶחָד: בָּאֲגַפַּיִם. בִּשְׁנֵי בְּנֵי אָדָם, דֶּרֶךְ כָּבוֹד: וְאֵבָרָיו כְּבֶן שְׁתַּיִם. שֶׁאֵבָרָיו גְּדוֹלִים: מַצְהִיבִין. מַרְגִּישִׁין וּמִצְטַעֲרִין: נִיכָּר לָרַבִּים. שֶׁהָיוּ מַכִּירִין כְּבָר, שֶׁהָיָה רָגִיל לָצֵאת מִן הַבַּיִת: מַה הֵן בְּהֶסְפֵּד. כַּמָּה יְהֵא גָּדוֹל שֶׁמִּצְוָה לְהַסְפִּידוֹ: עֲנִיִּים בְּנֵי שָׁלֹשׁ. לְפִי שֶׁהֶעָנִי מִצְטַעֵר עַל בָּנָיו יוֹתֵר מִן הֶעָשִׁיר, לְפִי שֶׁאֵין לוֹ שִׂמְחָה אַחֶרֶת: יוֹם אֶחָד לִפְנֵי עֲצֶרֶת. הָיָה אָבֵל: הֲרֵי כָּאן אַרְבָּעָה עָשָׂר. דַּעֲצֶרֶת חָשׁוּב כְּשִׁבְעָה, וְזֶהוּ יוֹם שֶׁלִּפְנֵי עֲצֶרֶת — חָשׁוּב ז', דְּסָבַר כִּי הַאי תַּנָּא דִּלְעֵיל (ד' כ.), דְּאָמַר: אֲפִילּוּ יוֹם אֶחָד, אֲפִילּוּ שָׁעָה אַחַת. וּכְמַאן דְּאָמַר עֲצֶרֶת כִּרְגָלִים: **מתני'** עַל מִטָּה זְקוּפָה. יוֹשְׁבִין הַמְנַחֲמִין: חוֹלְצִין. כְּתֵפֵיהֶן:

תוספות

אבא שאול אומר אף באיש אחד ושתי נשים. מפורש במסכת קדושין (דף פ: ושם): אע"ג דאין איש אחד מתייחד עם שתי נשים, בשעת אבילות דטרידא — שרי:

ואין אומרים עליו ברכת אבלים. פירש בקונטרס: דמיירי בלא כלו לו חדשיו. ומיהו, אפי' מיירי בכלו לו חדשיו, נהי דמתאבלים עליו, כדאיתא בפרק "ר"א" (שבת ד' קלו. ושם) ובפרק "יש בכור לנחלה" (בכורות דף מט.) — מ"מ אין מחמירין עליו כל כך לצערו. כדאשכחן בהני דסמוך, דלפי מה שהוא גדול מחמירין לכבודו:

ברכת אבלים ותנחומי אבלים. שמנחמים אותו בדברים: לעיל (ע"א) פירש בקונטרס דאסור להחליף בגדים שכבסו קודם הרגל, ללבוש בגדים שהן מכובסין כי חלוק הוא מַלְבּוּשׁ. ומכאן *משמע שר' שמעון היה מתיר בגדים שכבסו קודם הרגל. ובתוס' פי': אסור להחליף ללבוש בגדים שאינם מכובסים, כי חלוק הוא מלבוש, ורגילים ללובשו ולהחליף בלא כיבוס. ור' יצחק זקיני סובר כך. ועל פירש"י הקשה: דאי שרי בגדים שכבסו קודם אבלו, ומסתמא הכי נמי שרי בגדים המגוהצים קודם אבילות, וא"כ מנין לו למעלה דאביי כרבי *מנא ב"ר אלעזר בן שמעון? שמא מקודם אבלו היו מגוהצין! וי"ל: דמדשרו הני דוקא ולא חדשים לגמרי — ש"מ דסבירא להו הכי. ומיהו, זהו המנהג עתה שמלבישין אותו לאדם אחר יום או חצי יום, ואין זה קרוי בגד מכובס לדידיה: **רבי** עקיבא אומר בן שנה כו'. ולא סגי בי"ב חדשים. ובמסכת שמחות *נראה לי ר"ע כו'. פירוש: דלא בעי ג' שנים, ואם מת ביום שלשים — פוסק בפ' "יש בכור" (בכורות ד' מט.) שלשים יום באדם אינו נפל, ויום שלשים לענין אבילות כיום שלפניו, ואינו מתאבל. וה"ה מסתמא לענין בכור:

דרבי אלעזר א"ר אושעיא היא. והא דלא מייתי ברייתא דר"א בן יעקב, דמפיק תשלומין מ"וקראתם ובקצרכם" איזהו חג שאתה קורא וקוצר — הוי אומר זה חג השבועות. וריש לקיש אמר: חג הקציר, איזהו חג שאתה חוגג וקוצר בו — הוי אומר זה עצרת? ויש לומר: דלא ידעינן כמה ימים, אי לאו מדרבי אושעיא. כדאיתא פרק "אין דורשין" (חגיגה דף יז: ושם). אלא קשיא: מנא ליה דעצרת ררגלים בזמן הזה נמי ליכא תשלומין! ונהי דמתני' הכי משמע, מדקאמרי עצרת כרגלים — משמע לגמרי, נהיו היא גופא מנא ליה? י"ל: כיון דעצרת חד יומא, ונחשב כמו פסח וסוכות בזמן שבית המקדש קיים לענין תשלומין — חשיב נמי לדידן כרגל דפסח וסוכות. מיהו, בר"ה ויום הכפורים משמע דלא סבירא להו הכי דליהוו חשיבי כשבעה ימים, מדלא נקט אלא עצרת. ולית ליה דרבן גמליאל ורב פפא דבסמוך, דאמרי: אפילו ר"ה ויוה"כ ישנן כרגלים, דלעולם הוא במקום פסח וסוכות. הקשה בתוספות הרב: מה אנו צריכים שיהא ראש השנה כשבעה ימים? בלאו הכי נמי מותר לגלח ערב יום כפורים, דהוי קובר את מתו שמונה ימים קודם יום כפורים — דבטלה הימנו גזרת שלשים! ותירץ: דנפקא מינה אם לא גילח ערב יום כפורים, דאינו מגלח אחר יום כפורים. אבל עתה, דחשבינן ראש השנה כשבעה ויום הכפורים כשבעה, וערב ראש השנה כשבעה ימים קודם, ובין ראש השנה ליום כפורים שבעה, ונקיט ליה בתר יום כפורים שני ימים, ומגלח. ואין נראה לי תירוץ זה, דהא קיימא לן כאבא שאול, דאמר לעיל (ד' יט:): מגלח אחר הרגל. אלא יש לפרש: דנפקא לן מינה לענין שמועה רחוקה, דחשבינן לה שמועה רחוקה בהני שני ימים אחר יום כפורים. וזהו דוחק גדול, כי זה אינו מפורש בשום מקום שתחשב שמועה רחוקה פחות משלשים יום. ויותר היה יכול לומר לענין דחשבינן אחר ראש השנה שבת שלישית, דאמר לעיל: יושב במקומו. מיהו, אין זה נראה שום קושיא כלל, דהא דאמר שמונה ימים קודם הרגל בטלה ממנו גזרת שלשים יום — היינו דוקא היכא דנהג אבילות שבעה ימים, אבל זה שלא נהג אבילות כי אם יום אחד — לא אמרינן יום כפורים תבטל שלשים. ותמהתי למה לא פירש הרב כך, כי דבר זה פשוט! ובסמוך פירש כענין זה הרב, יום אחד לפני החג וחג ושמיני שלו — הרי כאן כ"א יום, דדוקא בהני אומרים דשמיני עצרת הרי כ"א יום. אבל מת ברגל, שלא נהג אבילות קודם הרגל — לא הוי שמיני עצרת כי אם יום אחד למנין שלשים. כך נראה לי, ואיני יודע הבירור. כך פירש הרב. ופירש בהלכות גדולות: השתא דאית לן תרי יומי, אי שכיב ליה שיכבא ביום טוב ראשון — לא ינהוג אבילות עד מוצאי יום טוב שני (ימים), ואותו יום טוב שני עולה למנין שבעה. ואי שכיב ביום שני — ההוא יומא נוהג אבילות, דכיון דיום טוב שני דרבנן — אתי אבילות דאורייתא דיום ראשון, דהוי מן התורה, כדאמרינן בזבחים (ד' ק:), ומבטל יום שני דרבנן. ואין נראה לר"י, וגם אין נוהגין כלל. ובמקום אחר פירשתי*:

אלא קרוביו. ירושלמי: ובלבד קרובים הראוין להתאבל. כהדא דרבי אבין דמך במועדא, לא גמל ר' מנא הספדא. אמר: בתר מועדא ניעבדא ליה יקרא, ואסיק: חכם שמת הכל כקרוביו: מברין עליו אלו ואלו. נראה לי: מכאן משמע שיש הבראה בלא אבילות, [נ]כגון ברגל. ולקמן (ד' כה:) אמר: אפי' רבו שלמדו חכמה אינו יושב עליו אלא יום אחד. ותמיהני, אם כן נצטרך הבראה לשמועה רחוקה, ולא מצינו ברבי חייא שעשו לו הבראה, אלא קאמר לעיל (דף כ:): והולך כלי אחרי לבית המרחץ! ושמא לענין הבראה החמירו משום כבוד החכם:

וכף

עין משפט נר מצוה

קסה א ב ג ד מיי' פי"ב הל' אבל הל' י והל' יא טוש"ע יו"ד סי' שנג סעי' ה:

קסו ה מיי' שם הל' ט סמג עשין מד"ס ב טוש"ע י"ד סי' שמד סעיף ד:

קסז ו מיי' פ"י שם הל' ג סמג שם טוש"ע י"ד סי' שלט סעי' ח:

קסח ז מיי' פ"א מהל' חגיגה הלכה ז:

קסט ח מיי' פ"י מהל' אבל הל' ג סמג שם טוש"ע י"ד סי' שלט סעי' ט:

קע ט מיי' שם הל' ד טוש"ע שם סעי' יא:

משמע שרש"י היה מתיר בגדים שכבסו קודם האבל ובתוס' פי' כנ"ל

קעא י מיי' פ"ז מהל' י"ט הל' כג ופ"א מהל' אבל הל' ב סמג שם ולאוין עה טוש"ע א"ח סי' תקמז סעי' ו וטוש"ע י"ד סי' תא סעי' ב:

דאביי כרבי ורבא כראב"ש עי' רש"ש

קעב כ מיי' שם טוש"ע א"ח שם סעי' ז וי"ד שם סעי' ד:

קעג ל מ מיי' שם הל' ג טוש"ע א"ח שם סעי' ח וי"ד שם:

חגיגה יז. ר"ה ד:

פ"ג גרסי' בן ג' שנים יוצא במטה ר' עקיבא כו' פי' דלא בעי ג' כו' כנ"ל

רבינו חננאל

כר"ג. איכא דאמרי להא דרב גידל אהא דתניא תינוק כל ל' יום יוצא בחיק ונקבר באשה אחת ובשני אנשים אבל לא באיש אחד ושתי נשים. אבא שאול אומר אף באיש אחד ובשתי נשים. ואין עומדין עליו בשורה ואין אומרין עליו ברכת אבלים ותנחומי אבלים. בן ל' יום יוצא בדלוסקמא. ר' יהודה אומר לא דלוסקמא הניטלת על הכתף אלא הניטלת על אגפיים. ועומדין עליו בשורה ואומרין עליו ברכת אבלים ותנחומי אבלי'. בן י"ב חודש יוצא במטה. ר' עקיבא אומר בן שנה ואבריו כבן שנתיים בן שנתיים ואבריו כבן שנה יוצא במטה. רבי שמעון בן אלעזר אומר היוצא במטה רבים מצהיבין עליו. ר' אלעזר בן עזריה אומר ניכר לרבים רבים מתעסקין בו. אין ניכר לרבים אין רבים מתעסקין בו מה הן בהספד. ר' מאיר אומר משום ר' ישמעאל עניים בני שלש. עשירים בני חמש. ר' יהודה אומר משום ר' ישמעאל עניים בני חמש. עשירים בני שש. ובני זקנים כבני עניים. אמר גידל בר מנשיא אמר שמואל הלכה כר' יהודה שאמר משום ר' ישמעאל: **ירושלמי** תני אין מראין פנים לא בר"ה ולא ביוה"כ. ר' חזקיה הוה ליה עובדא. סלקין רבנן למחמי ליה אפין בצומא רבא א) אמר לון כלום אמרו אין מראין פנים לא בר"ה ולא ביוה"כ לא מפני התפלה שנייה הוא יוה"כ שחל להיות בשבת. ב) דריש ר' ענני מי שקבר את מתו יום אחד לפני עצרת חשוב כשבעת ימי האבל ופסקו ז' ימי אבלו ועצרת חשוב כשבעת ימי הרגל. דאמר ר' אלעזר מניין לעצרת שיש לה תשלומין שבעה שנאמר בחג המצות ובחג השבועות ובחג הסוכות. מה חג המצות יש לה תשלומין כל שבעה. שאם לא הקריב ביום הראשון יש לו להקריב כל ימי החג. כך עצרת יש לה תשלומין שבעה כחג המצות. הרי ז' לפני עצרת ועצרת ז' הרי י"ד משלים ט"ז יום והרי גמרו לו ל' ומותר בתספורת. אדבריה רב פפא לרב אויא סבא ודרש יום אחד לפני ר"ה ור"ה הרי י"ד אמר רבינא הלכך הקובר את מתו יום אחד לפני החג שבעה והחג שבעה. ושמיני שלו שהוא רגל בפ"ע הרי כאן כ"א יום וזהו שאמר רגל בפ"ע לענין פו"ר קש"ב. פירוש ג) רגל בפ"ע זהו כדי לחשב יום שמיני של חג הסוכות ז' ימים לאבל למנין שלשים: **מתני'** אין קורעין ואין חולצין כתף ולא מברין אלא קרובין של מת

א) פי' ויוה"כ חל אז בשבת. ב) בירושלמי שם איתא שנייה הוא יוה"כ שחל להיות בחול ופי' דאין חילוק לבין שחל בשבת ובין שחל בחול לעולם אין מראין פנים. ג) דברי רבינו אלו הובא בתוס' ר"ה דף ד' ע"ב ד"ה פו"ר קש"ב בשמו של רבינו ז"ל.

הגהות הב"ח

(א) גמ' בחג המצות ובחג השבועות ובחג הסוכות מה חג המצות:

גליון הש"ס

תוס' ד"ה אלא כו' כגון ברגל. עיין לעיל דף כ ע"א תד"ה שכבר:

מסורת הש"ס

[שמחות פ"ג ע"ש]

דברים יז

[ע' פרש"י ביצה כט.]

בכ"מ סא: הגי' רב חנינא

[עיין תוס' ברכות מז: ד"ה מצוה דרבים שאני]

גמ׳ ואפי׳ חכם? וְהָתַנְיָא: *חָכָם שֶׁמֵּת – הַכֹּל קְרוֹבָיו. הַכֹּל קְרוֹבָיו סָלְקָא דַעְתָּךְ?! אֶלָּא: הַכֹּל כִּקְרוֹבָיו; הַכֹּל קוֹרְעִין עָלָיו, וְהַכֹּל חוֹלְצִין עָלָיו, וְהַכֹּל מַבְרִין עָלָיו בָּרְחָבָה! לָא צְרִיכָא דְּלָאו חָכָם הוּא. וְאִי אָדָם כָּשֵׁר הוּא – חִיּוּבֵי מִיחַיֵּיב לְמִיקְרַע, דְּתַנְיָא: מִפְּנֵי מָה בָּנָיו וּבְנוֹתָיו שֶׁל אָדָם מֵתִים כְּשֶׁהֵן קְטַנִּים – כְּדֵי שֶׁיִּבְכֶּה וְיִתְאַבֵּל עַל אָדָם כָּשֵׁר. יִבְכֶּה וְיִתְאַבֵּל? עֶרְבוֹנָא קָא שָׁקֵיל מִינֵּיהּ?! אֶלָּא: מִפְּנֵי שֶׁלֹּא בָּכָה וְהִתְאַבֵּל עַל אָדָם כָּשֵׁר. שֶׁכָּל הַבּוֹכֶה וּמִתְאַבֵּל עַל אָדָם כָּשֵׁר – מוֹחֲלִין לוֹ עַל כָּל עֲוֹנוֹתָיו בִּשְׁבִיל כָּבוֹד שֶׁעָשָׂה לוֹ! דְּלָאו אָדָם כָּשֵׁר הוּא. אִי דְּקָאֵי הָתָם בִּשְׁעַת יְצִיאַת נְשָׁמָה – חִיּוּבֵי מִיחַיֵּיב, דְּתַנְיָא, רַבִּי שִׁמְעוֹן בֶּן אֶלְעָזָר אוֹמֵר: *הָעוֹמֵד עַל הַמֵּת בִּשְׁעַת יְצִיאַת נְשָׁמָה – חַיָּיב לִקְרוֹעַ. לְמָה זֶה דּוֹמֶה – לְסֵפֶר תּוֹרָה שֶׁנִּשְׂרָף, שֶׁחַיָּיב לִקְרוֹעַ! דְּלָא קָאֵי הָתָם בִּשְׁעַת יְצִיאַת נְשָׁמָה. כִּי נָח נַפְשֵׁיהּ דְּרַב סָפְרָא לָא קְרָעוּ רַבָּנַן עֲלֵיהּ. אָמְרִי: לָא גָּמְרִינַן מִינֵּיהּ. אֲמַר לְהוּ אַבָּיֵי: מִי תַּנְיָא הָרַב שֶׁמֵּת? חָכָם שֶׁמֵּת תַּנְיָא. וְעוֹד: כָּל יוֹמָא שְׁמַעְתָּתֵיהּ בְּפוּמִין בְּבֵי מִדְרְשָׁא. סְבוּר: מַה דַּהֲוָה – הֲוָה. אֲמַר לְהוּ אַבָּיֵי, תְּנֵינָא: חָכָם, כָּל זְמַן שֶׁעוֹסְקִין בְּהֶסְפֵּד – חַיָּיבִין לִקְרוֹעַ. סְבוּר לְמִיקְרַע לְאַלְתַּר. אֲמַר לְהוּ אַבָּיֵי, תַּנְיָא: חָכָם כְּבוֹדוֹ בְּהֶסְפֵּידוֹ. כִּי נָח נַפְשֵׁיהּ דְּרַב הוּנָא, סְבוּר לְאוֹתוּבֵי סֵפֶר תּוֹרָה אַפּוּרְיֵיהּ. אֲמַר לְהוּ רַב חִסְדָּא: מִילְּתָא דִּבְחַיֵּיהּ לָא סְבִירָא לֵיהּ, הַשְׁתָּא לֵיקוּם (לֵיהּ) לֵיעֲבַד לֵיהּ? דְּאָמַר רַב תַּחְלִיפָא: *אֲנָא חֲזִיתֵיהּ לְרַב הוּנָא דְּבָעֵי לְמֵיתַב אפוריי׳, וַהֲוָה מַנַּח סֵפֶר תּוֹרָה עֲלֵיהּ, וְכָף כַּדָּא אַאַרְעָא וְאוֹתִיב סֵפֶר תּוֹרָה עִילָּוֵיהּ. אַלְמָא קָסָבַר: אָסוּר לֵישֵׁב עַל גַּבֵּי מִטָּה שֶׁסֵּפֶר תּוֹרָה מוּנָּח עָלֶיהָ. לָא הֲוָה נָפֵיק פּוּרְיָא מִבָּבָא, סְבוּר לְשַׁלְשׁוּלֵי דֶּרֶךְ גַּגִּין, אֲמַר לְהוּ רַב חִסְדָּא: הָא גְּמִירְנָא מִינֵּיהּ: חָכָם כְּבוֹדוֹ דֶּרֶךְ פֶּתַח. סְבוּר לְאַשְׁנוּיֵי מִפּוּרְיָא לְפוּרְיָא. אֲמַר לְהוּ רַב חִסְדָּא, הָכִי גְּמִירְנָא מִינֵּיהּ: חָכָם, כְּבוֹדוֹ בְּמִטָּה רִאשׁוֹנָה. דַּאֲמַר רַב יְהוּדָה אָמַר רַב: מִנַּיִן לְחָכָם שֶׁכְּבוֹדוֹ בְּמִטָּה רִאשׁוֹנָה – שֶׁנֶּאֱמַר: (ש"ב ו) "וַיַּרְכִּיבוּ אֶת אֲרוֹן הָאֱלֹהִים אֶל עֲגָלָה חֲדָשָׁה". פְּרוּם בָּבָא, וְאַפְּקוּהָ. פְּתַח עֲלֵיהּ רַבִּי אַבָּא: רָאוּי הָיָה רַבֵּינוּ שֶׁתִּשְׁרֶה עָלָיו שְׁכִינָה, אֶלָּא שֶׁבָּבֶל גָּרְמָה לֵיהּ. מְתִיב רַב נַחְמָן בַּר *חִסְדָּא, וְאָמְרִי לַהּ רַב חָנָן בַּר חִסְדָּא: (יחזקאל א) "הָיֹה הָיָה דְבַר ה׳ אֶל יְחֶזְקֵאל בֶּן בּוּזִי הַכֹּהֵן בְּאֶרֶץ כַּשְׂדִּים"! *טְפַח לֵיהּ אֲבוּהּ בְּסַנְדְּלֵיהּ. א"ל: לָאו אֲמִינָא לָךְ לָא תִּיטְרוֹד עָלְמָא? מַאי "הָיָה" – שֶׁהָיָה כְּבָר. כִּי אַסְקוּהּ לְהָתָם אֲמָרוּ לֵיהּ לר׳ אַמִי ולר׳ אַסִי: רַב הוּנָא אָתֵי. אֲמָרוּ: כִּי הֲוֵינַן הָתָם לָא הֲוָה לָן לְדַלּוּיֵי רֵישִׁין מִינֵּיהּ, הַשְׁתָּא אָתֵינַן הָכָא אָתָא בָּתְרִין? אֲמָרוּ (*לֵיהּ:) אֲרוֹנוֹ בָּא. ר׳ אַמִי וְר׳ אַסִי נְפוּק, ר׳ אִילָא וְר׳ חֲנִינָא לָא נְפוּק. אִיכָּא דְאָמְרִי: רַבִּי אִילָא נְפַק, ר׳ חֲנִינָא לָא נְפַק. דִּנְפַק מַאי טַעְמֵיהּ – דְּתַנְיָא: אֲרוֹן הָעוֹבֵר מִמָּקוֹם לְמָקוֹם – עוֹמְדִים עָלָיו בְּשׁוּרָה, וְאוֹמְרִים עָלָיו בִּרְכַּת אֲבֵלִים וְתַנְחוּמֵי אֲבֵלִים. דְּלָא נְפַק מַאי טַעְמָא – דְּתַנְיָא: אֲרוֹן הָעוֹבֵר מִמָּקוֹם לְמָקוֹם – אֵין עוֹמְדִין עָלָיו בְּשׁוּרָה, וְאֵין אוֹמְרִים עָלָיו בִּרְכַּת אֲבֵלִים וְתַנְחוּמֵי אֲבֵלִים. קַשְׁיָין אַהֲדָדֵי! לָא קַשְׁיָא, כָּאן – שֶׁשִּׁלְדּוֹ קַיֶּימֶת, כָּאן – בְּשֶׁאֵין שִׁלְדּוֹ קַיֶּימֶת, וְרַב הוּנָא שִׁלְדּוֹ קַיֶּימֶת הֲוָה. דְּלָא נְפַק – לָא סַיְּימוּהָ קַמֵּיהּ. אָמְרִי: הֵיכָא נֵינְחֵיהּ? רַב הוּנָא רִיבֵּץ תּוֹרָה בְּיִשְׂרָאֵל וְר׳ חִיָּיא רִיבֵּץ תּוֹרָה בְּיִשְׂרָאֵל הֲוָה. מַאן מְעַיֵּיל לֵיהּ? אֲמַר לְהוּ רַב חַגָּא: אֲנָא מְעַיֵּילְנָא לֵיהּ, דְּאוֹקְמֵתֵיהּ לְתַלְמוּדַאי כִּי הֲוֵינָא בַּר תְּמָנֵי סְרֵי שְׁנִין וְלָא חֲזִי לִי קֶרִי, (א) וּמְשַׁמַּשׁ לֵיהּ קַמֵּיהּ וְיָדַעְנָא בְּעוֹבָדֵיהּ. דְּיוֹמָא חַד אִתְהַפִּיכָא לֵיהּ רְצוּעָה דִּתְפִילִּין, וִיתִיב עֲלָהּ אַרְבָּעִין תַּעֲנִיתָא. עַיְּילֵיהּ, הֲוָה גְּנֵי יְהוּדָה מִימִינֵיהּ דַּאֲבוּהּ, וְחִזְקִיָּה מִשְּׂמָאלֵיהּ. אֲמַר לֵיהּ יְהוּדָה לְחִזְקִיָּה: קוּם מִדּוּכְתִּיךְ, דְּלָאו אוֹרַח אַרְעָא דְּקָאֵים רַב הוּנָא. בַּהֲדֵי דְּקָאֵים – קָם בַּהֲדֵיהּ עַמּוּדָא דְּנוּרָא, חַזְיֵיהּ רַב חַגָּא, אִיבְעִית, זַקְפֵיהּ לַאֲרוֹנֵיהּ וּנְפַק, אֲתָא. וְהַאי דְּלָא אִיעֲנַשׁ עֲנַשׁ – מִשּׁוּם דְּזַקְפֵיהּ לַאֲרוֹנֵיהּ דְּרַב הוּנָא. כִּי נָח נַפְשֵׁיהּ דְּרַב חִסְדָּא סְבוּר לְאוֹתוּבֵי סֵפֶר תּוֹרָה אַפּוּרְיֵיהּ, אֲמַר לְהוּ ר׳ יִצְחָק: מִילְּתָא דִּלְרַבֵּיהּ לָא סְבִירָא לֵיהּ, אֲנַן נֵיקוּם נַעֲבֵיד לֵיהּ? סְבוּר דְּלָא לְמִישְׁלַף קְרָעַיְיהוּ. אֲמַר לְהוּ ר׳ יִצְחָק בַּר אַמִי: חָכָם, כֵּיוָן שֶׁהֶחְזִירוּ פְּנֵיהֶם מֵאֲחוֹרֵי הַמִּטָּה – שׁוֹלְלִין. כִּי נָח נַפְשׁ׳ דְּרַבָּה בַּר הוּנָא וְרַב הַמְנוּנָא אַסְקִינְהוּ לְהָתָם, כִּי

רש"י

גמ׳ לְסֵפֶר תּוֹרָה. דְּתוֹרָה קְרוּיָה נֵר, שֶׁנֶּאֱמַר (משלי ו): "כִּי נֵר מִצְוָה וְתוֹרָה אוֹר", וּנְשָׁמָה נִקְרֵאת נֵר דִּכְתִיב (שם כ): "נֵר *(אֱלֹהִים) נִשְׁמַת אָדָם": שְׁמַעְתָּתֵיהּ בְּפוּמִין. וְהָוֵי כְּמַאן דִּגְמָרִינַן מִינֵּיהּ: מַאי דַּהֲוָה הֲוָה. הוֹאִיל דְּלָא קָרְעוּ בִּשְׁעַת מִיתָה – תּוּ לָא קָרְעֵי: לְמִקְרַע לְאַלְתַּר. בְּלֹא הֶסְפֵּד: לְאוֹתוּבֵי ס"ת אַפּוּרְיֵיהּ. וְלוֹמַר: קִיֵּים זֶה מַה שֶּׁכָּתוּב בָּזֶה: לָא הֲוָה נָפֵיק פּוּרְיָא מִבָּבָא. דְּזוּטָר הֲוָה בָּבָא: מִפּוּרְיָא לְפוּרְיָא. לְתֵתוֹ בְּמִטָּה אַחֲרִיתָא, קְטַנָּה, שֶׁתֵּצֵא דֶּרֶךְ הַפֶּתַח: אֶל עֲגָלָה חֲדָשָׁה. אוֹתָהּ עֲגָלָה שֶׁשִּׁיגְּרוּהוּ פְּלִשְׁתִּים בָּהּ, וּבְאוֹתָהּ עֲגָלָה הֱבִיאוֹ דָּוִד מִבֵּית אֲבִינָדָב לְעִיר דָּוִד: פְּרוּם בָּבָא. שָׁבְרוּ הַפֶּתַח וְהִרְחִיבוּהוּ: בָּבֶל גָּרְמָה לוֹ. שֶׁאֵין שְׁכִינָה שׁוֹרָה בְּחוּץ לָאָרֶץ: טְפַח לֵיהּ אֲבוּהּ. רַב חִסְדָּא בְּסַנְדָּלָא, שֶׁטָּפַח לוֹ לְרַב נַחְמָן עַל סַנְדָּלוֹ, כְּאָדָם שֶׁנּוֹגֵעַ עַל רֶגֶל חֲבֵירוֹ בַּחֲשַׁאי כְּדֵי שֶׁלֹּא יִשְׁמְעוּ הָעוֹמְדִים סָבִיב מִטָּתוֹ דְּרַב הוּנָא. ע"א: הִכָּהוּ בְּסַנְדָּלוֹ: לָא תִּטְרוֹד עָלְמָא. לֹא תַּטְרִיחַ בְּקוּשְׁיוֹת: שֶׁהָיָה כְּבָר. כְּלוֹמַר: הַהִיא שַׁעְתָּא הֲוָה, וְלֹא יוֹתֵר. וְיֵשׁ אוֹמְרִים: שֶׁהָיָה כְּבָר – בְּאֶרֶץ יִשְׂרָאֵל, שֶׁשָּׁרְתָה עָלָיו רוּחַ הַקּוֹדֶשׁ: כִּי אַסְקוּהּ לְהָתָם. לְאֶרֶץ יִשְׂרָאֵל לְקוֹבְרוֹ, שֶׁכָּל הַנִּקְבָּר שָׁם נִקְבָּר בְּלֹא חֵטְא, *שֶׁנֶּאֱמַר: "הָעָם הַיּוֹשֵׁב בָּהּ נְשׂוּא עָוֹן", כִּדְאִיתָא בִּכְתוּבּוֹת (דף קיא*): לְדַלּוּיֵי רֵישִׁין. דְּאָדָם חָשׁוּב הָיָה, וַהֲוָה לָן בּוֹשֶׁת לְדַלּוּיֵי רֵישִׁין: וְאָתֵי לְהָכָא. דִּסְבוּרִין שֶׁהוּא חַי: שִׁלְדּוֹ. גּוּפוֹ קַיֶּימֶת – יוֹלְאִין: לָא סַיְּימוּהָ קַמֵּיהּ. דְּשִׁלְדּוֹ הֲוָה קַיֶּימֶת: רַב הוּנָא רִיבֵּץ תּוֹרָה. כִּדְאָמְרִי׳ פֶּרֶק "שְׁנֵי דַּיָּינֵי גְּזֵירוֹת" (כתובות דף קו.): כִּי קָיְימִי רַבָּנַן מִקַּמֵּיהּ וּמְנַפְּצֵי גְּלִימַיְיהוּ – מְכַסֵּי לֵיהּ לְיוֹמָא בְּאַבְקָא: רַבִּי חִיָּיא רִיבֵּץ תּוֹרָה. כִּדְאָמְרִינַן בְּבָבָא מְצִיעָא (דף פה:): אֲנָא עָבְדִי לֵיהּ לַתּוֹרָה דְּלָא תִּשְׁתַּכַּח מִיִּשְׂרָאֵל: מַאן מְעַיֵּיל לֵיהּ. מִי יֵלֵךְ לְהַכְנִיסוֹ לִקְבוּרָה אֵצֶל רַבִּי חִיָּיא: אִיתְהַפִּיכָא לֵיהּ רְצוּעָה דִּתְפִילִּין. הַשָּׁחוֹר בִּפְנִים. דִּרְצוּעָה שְׁחוֹרָה נִרְאֶה בַּחוּץ הֲלָכָה לְמֹשֶׁה מִסִּינַי: אִיבְעִית. נִבְעַת וְנִפְחַד: זַקְפֵיהּ לָאֲרוֹנָא. דְּרַב הוּנָא לְקַמֵּיהּ עַמּוּדָא דְּנוּרָא, דְּלָא לִיזְּקֵיהּ: כִּי

תוספות

וכף כדא אארעא ואנח עליה ספר תורה. ונראה דאפילו הספר תורה מונח נגבוה ממנו לא שרי, מדלא אותבוה לספר תורה נגבוה ממנו. וכן פירשתי במנחות בפרק "הקומץ רבה" (דף לג:) *ושם הארכתי:

ורבי חייא ריבץ תורה וכו׳. והקשה בתוספות הרב: דמשמע בירושלמי *שרב הונא מת קודם רבי חייא. דאמר ליה לרבי חייא: ארונו בא. והכא משמע שרבי חייא מת קודם רב הונא! ונראה לי: דרב הונא אחר היה, ואותו שבימי רבי חייא – אין זה רב הונא תלמידו דרב, ע"כ. ומיהו, קשה: בירושלמי קאמר בעובדא דהכא רב הונא ריש גלותא, ולפי הענין של הירושלמי היה משמע דזקפיה ר׳ חגא לארוניה דרב הונא כדי שלא יהא יושב אצל הצדיקים. והכי איתא בפי׳ רבינו חננאל דרב הונא ריש גלותא:

חכם כיון שהחזיר פניו. פירוש: חכם שמת, כיון שהחזיר פניו אותו שקרע. וגרסינן: אפילו חכם שקרע על החכם, כיון שהחזיר פניו – שולל לאלתר. דמשום כבודו של חכם הקורע התירו, דגנאי הוא לצאת בבגד קרוע. ולא נהיר׳:

ספעו

עין משפט נר מצוה

קעד א ב מיי׳ פ"ט מהל׳ אבל הל׳ יא סמג עשין ב טוש"ע י"ד סי׳ שמ סעי׳ ז:

[עיין שם בתוס׳ ד"ה אסור ליסב]

[סוף כלאים וכתובות פי"ב]

קעה ג מיי׳ שם טוש"ע שם סעיף יז:

קעו ד מיי׳ פי"א שם הלכה ב טוש"ע י"ד סי׳ תא סעיף ד:

קעז ה ו מיי׳ שם פ"ט הל׳ יא ופי"ב הל׳ ב טוש"ע י"ד סי׳ שמ סעיף ו:

קעח ז מיי׳ שם פ"ט הלכה יא טוש"ע שם סעי׳ ה:

קעט ח מיי׳ שם הל׳ ב טוש"ע שם סעי׳ לז:

קפ ט מיי׳ שם הל׳ יג טוש"ע שם סעי׳ ז:

קפא י מיי׳ פי"ב שם הלכה ג טוש"ע שם סי׳ שנג סעי׳ ב:

קפב כ מיי׳ פ"י מהל׳ תפילין הלכה ו טוש"ע שם סי׳ רפב סעיף ז:

קפג ל מ מיי׳ פי"ב מהל׳ אבל הל׳ ג טוש"ע שם סי׳ שנג סעי׳ ג:

קפד נ מיי׳ שם הלכה ז סמג עשין מד"ס ב טוש"ע שם סי׳ שמה סעיף ח:

[בע"י ליתא]

[מנחות לב: ע"ש]

קפה ס מיי׳ שם פ"ט הלכה יב טוש"ע שם סי׳ שמ סעיף יז:

מסורת הש"ס

[נ"ל ה׳]

שבת קה: [תוספתא פ"ב]

[משמע ליה להש"ס דמיירי אפי׳ בחינו כשר כ"כ תוס׳ בשבת שם ד"ה דתניא]

דכל הדר בא"י שרוי בלא עון

ומנין אף המתים ת"ל וכפר אדמתו עמו עיין בילקוט חלק ב סוף רמז תתלג. ובע"י בפרש"י לא גרס כדאיתא בכתובות והוסיף ואין ישיבה בארץ אלא לקבורה ע"ש

[נ"ל רב חסדא]

[ב"ק לב: ב"ב כב.]

[נ"ל להו]

רבינו חננאל

מת וא"ר ירמיה ובלבד הראויין להתאבל. אוקימנא למתני׳ באדם שאינו חכם ולא כשר ולא היה עומד שם בשעת יציאת נשמה. אבל בחכם ובכשר חייב לעולם אע"פ שלא היה שם. דתניא חכם שמת הכל חייבין עליו בקרוביו הכל קורעין הכל חולצין והכל מברין והכל עומדין ברחבה. ואי אדם כשר הוא אע"פ שאינו חכם חייב. דתניא מפני מה בניו ובנותיו של בני אדם מתים כשהן קטנים מפני שלא בכה והתאבל על אדם כשר. שכל הבוכה ומתאבל על אדם כשר מוחלין לו על כל עונותיו. ואי עומד על המת בשעת יציאת נשמה חייב. דתניא ר׳ שמעון בן אלעזר אומר העומד על אדם בשעת יציאת נשמה חייב לקרוע למה זה דומה לס"ת שנשרף שחייב לקרוע. כי נח נפשיה דרב ספרא לא קרעו רבנן עליה. אמרו לא גמרינן מיניה.

אמר להו אביי מי תניא הרב שמת חכם שמת תניא. ועוד שמעתתיה בפומין כל יומא בבי מדרשא. סבור מאי דהוה הוה. אמר להו אביי תניא חכם כבודו בהספדו. כי נח נפשיה דרב הונא סבור לאחותי ס"ת אפורייה אמר להו מלתא דבחייה לא סבירא ליה כו׳. לא הוה נפיק פורייה לבבא סבור לשלשולי כו׳. ואסיקנא חכם כבודו להוציאו דרך פתחים ולא דרך גגות. וכבודו במטה ראשונה ולא ממטה למטה שנאמר וירכיבו את ארון האלהים אל עגלה חדשה. סתרו להו לבבי ואפקוה. פתח עליה ההוא ספדנא ראוי היה רבינו שתשרה עליו שכינה אלא שבבל גרמה לו. וההיא דכתיב היה היה דבר ה׳ אל יחזקאל בן בוזי הכהן בארץ כשדים על נהר כבר מאי היה היה שכבר הוה. תניא ארון העובר ממקום למקום עומדין עליו בשורה ואומרין עליו ברכת אבלים ותנחומי אבלים. אוקימנא בשלדו קיימת. אבל אין שלדו קיימת לא: ירושל׳ בתחלת משקין (הלכה ה) תני ליקוטי עצמות אין אומרים עליהן קינים ונהי ולא ברכת אבלים ולא תנחומי אבלים. ואלו הן ברכת אבלים *) (מה שאומרים בשורה. אבל אומרים עליהן דברי קילוסין. אמרו מנחייה גבמה בבית הכנסת. אלו הן תנחומי אבלים מה שאומרים בשורה. אבל אומרין עליהן דברי קילוסין): אמרי מנחייה גבי ר׳ חייא שריבץ תורה כמותו. אמרי מאן ניעייליה. א"ר חנא אנא מעיילנא דאוקימתיה לתלמודא כד הוינא בר תמני סרי ולא חזו לי קרי ומשמע לי קמיה וידענא עובדיה. יומא חד אתהפיכא ליה רצועא דתפילי ויתיב בתעניתא עייליה הוי גני יהודה בריה מימיניה וחזקיה משמאליה. א"ל יהודה לחזקיה קום מדוכתיך דלאו אורח ארעא דקאי רב הונא אבראי. בהדיה דקם. קם בהדיה עמודא דנורא חזייה רב חגא איבעית זקף לארוניה דרב הונא ונפק. והא דלאו מיענשו דבי ריש גלותא משום

*) דברי רבינו כאן בשבוש וכצ"ל ברכת אבלים מה שאומרים בבהכנ"ס אלו הן תנחומי אבלים מה שאומרים בשורה אבל אומרים עליהן דברי קילוסין [וכ"ה בירושלמי פסחים פ"ח ה"ח ובירושלמי דמכילתין נדפס בשבוש וגם חסר שם פירוש לתנחומי אבלים].

הגהות הב"ח

(א) גמ׳ ומשמע ליה קמיה. נ"ב פירוש הייתי משמש לפניו:

גליון הש"ס

גמ׳ מילתא דלרביה לא ס"ל אנן ניקום נעביד. עיין בבא קמא דף יז ע"א תד"ה אלא שהניחו:

קפו א מיי' פ"ט מהל' אבל הלכה יב טוש"ע י"ד סי' רמב סעיף כה:

[שייך לדף כו.]

שפעו מרזבי דציפורי דמא. מפרש בירושלמי: דיהב נפשיה על גזרתא. פירוש: נשפך דמו על יחוד השם. תוספתא פ"א: שנתן נפשו על המילה:

ועל רבו שלמדו חכמה. בפרק "אלו מציאות" (ב"מ דף לג. ושם) פליגי רבי יהודה ורבי יוסי, שרבי יהודה אומר: כל שרוב חכמתו הימנו, ורבי יוסי אומר: אפילו לא האיר עיניו אלא במשנה אחת – זהו רבו, ומסיק שם, עולא אמר: תלמידי חכמים שבבבל קורעין זה על זה, כרבי יוסי ס"ל. ופוסק רב ששת כרבי יוסי. ופי' רבינו חננאל דהכי הלכתא. ובשאלתות דרב אחאי) פוסק כרבי יהודה, דאמר: כל שרוב חכמתו הימנו. ומפרש בפר' "אלו מציאות" בתוספתא דהיו קורעין קריעה [דאין] מתאחה. וכן פירש רבי יצחק בר יהודה, ויותר היה נראה לי דמעשה רב, דשמואל עבד כרבי יוסי כדאי' התם. ורבא נמי מפרש מילתא דרבי יוסי, ורבי אלעזר בירושלמי נמי עבד כוותיה. ושמא היו מחמירין על עצמן:

*) [פרשת קרח סי' קלא]

ברכת

רבינו חננאל

משום דזקיף ארוניה דרב הונא. כלומר זכותו מגינה עליהם דהוא מדבי ריש גלותא. א"ל רב אשי לרב קיפוק בהא יומא דנח נפשיה דרבינא מאי אמרת עליה. פירוש בר קיפוק הוה ספדנא וכן בר אבין ושאלינהו מהו ההספד שתספדו עליו. וכיון שאמר לו בר קיפוד בארזים נפלה שלהבת מה יעשו אזובי קיר. כלומר כ"ע לגביה כאזוב גבי ארז נינהו כולהו. ובר אבין אמר בכו לאובדין ולא לאבידה כו' חלש דעתיה דרב אשי אמר שויתון לגביה כאזוב של קיר והוא כארז מכלל שהוא גדול ממני. נעשה להן חולי ונהפכו רגליהן שאינן יכולין להלך ולא יצאו בהספד. וזהו שאמר רב אשי כיון שרגליהן של אלו הפוכות אינן ראוין לחליצה. כי נח נפשיה דר' יוחנן יתיב עליה ר' אמי שבעה ושלשים. ואסיקנא אפילו רבו שלמדו תורה אינו יושב עליו אלא יום אחד. וא"ר יצחק בר אמי *)תניא חכם כיון שהחזיר פניו מאחורי המטה שולל. פתח עליה ההוא ספדנא. ארץ שנער הרה וילדה. פי' שנער בבל. ארץ צבי א"י. רקת זו טבריא שמת בה.

תורה אור

כִּי מָטוּ אַגִּישְׁרָא קָמוּ גְּמָלֵי. אֲמַר לְהוּ הַהוּא טַיָּיעָא: מַאי הַאי? אֲמָרוּ לֵיהּ: רַבָּנַן דְּקָא עָבְדִי יְקָרָא אַהֲדָדֵי. מָר אֲמַר: מָר נֵיעוּל בְּרֵישָׁא, וּמָר אֲמַר: מָר נֵיעוּל בְּרֵישָׁא. אֲמַר: דִּינָא הוּא דְּרַבָּה בַּר הוּנָא לֵיעוּל בְּרֵישָׁא. חֲלִיף גְּמָלֵיהּ דְּרַבָּה בַּר הוּנָא, נְתוּר כָּכֵיהּ וְשִׁנֵּיהּ דְּהַהוּא טַיָּיעָא. פְּתַח עֲלֵיהּ הַהוּא יָנוּקָא: "גֶּזַע יְשִׁישִׁים עָלָה מִבָּבֶל וְעִמּוֹ סֵפֶר מִלְחָמוֹת. *קָאַת וְקִפּוֹד הוּכְפָּלוּ, לִרְאוֹת בְּשׁוֹד וְשֶׁבֶר הַבָּא מִשִּׁנְעָר. קָצַף עַל עוֹלָמוֹ וְחָמַס מִמֶּנּוּ נְפָשׁוֹת, וְשָׂמַח בָּהֶם כְּכַלָּה חֲדָשָׁה. רוֹכֵב עֲרָבוֹת שָׂשׂ וְשָׂמַח בְּבֹא אֵלָיו נֶפֶשׁ נָקִי וְצַדִּיק". כִּי נָח נַפְשֵׁיהּ דְּרָבִינָא פְּתַח עֲלֵיהּ הַהוּא סַפְדָּנָא: "תְּמָרִים הָנִיעוּ רֹאשׁ עַל צַדִּיק כַּתָּמָר נָשִׁים לֵילוֹת כְּיָמִים [עַל מֵשִׂים לֵילוֹת כְּיָמִים".] א"ל רַב אַשִׁי לְבַר קִיפּוֹק: הַהוּא יוֹמָא מַאי אָמְרַתְּ? אֲמַר לֵיהּ, אָמִינָא: אִם בָּאֲרָזִים נָפְלָה שַׁלְהֶבֶת – מַה יַּעֲשׂוּ אֵיזוֹבֵי קִיר, לִוְיָתָן בְּחַכָּה הוּעֲלָה – מַה יַּעֲשׂוּ דְּגֵי רְקָק, בְּנַחַל שׁוֹטֵף נָפְלָה חַכָּה – מַה יַּעֲשׂוּ מֵי גֵבִים. א"ל בַּר אָבִין: ח"ו דְּחַכָּה וְשַׁלְהֶבֶת בְּצַדִּיקֵי אָמִינָא. וּמַאי אָמְרַתְּ? אָמִינָא: בְּכוּ לָאֲבֵלִים וְלֹא לָאֲבֵדָה, שֶׁהִיא לִמְנוּחָה וְאָנוּ לַאֲנָחָה. חֲלַשׁ דַּעְתֵּיהּ עֲלַיְיהוּ, וְאִתְהַפּוּךְ כַּרְעַיְיהוּ. הַהוּא יוֹמָא לָא אָתוּ לְאַסְפּוֹדֵיהּ. וְהַיְינוּ דְּאָמַר רַב אַשִׁי: *לָא בַּר קִיפּוֹק חָלֵיץ, וְלָא בַּר אָבִין חָלֵיץ. רָבָא, כִּי הֲוָה אָתֵא לְדִגְלַת א"ל לְבַר אָבִין: קוּם אֵימָא מִילְּתָא. קָאֵי וְאָמַר: בָּאוּ רוֹב שְׁלִישִׁית בַּמַּיִם, זְכוֹר וְרַחֵם. תָּעִינוּ מֵאַחֲרֶיךָ כְּאִשָּׁה מִבַּעְלָהּ, אַל תַּזְנִיחֵנוּ כְּאוֹת מֵי מָרָה. (חָנִין יוֹחָנָן זֵירָא אַבָּא יַעֲקֹב יוֹסֵי שְׁמוּאֵל חִיָּיא מְנַחֵם – סִימָן.) רַבִּי חָנִין חֲתָנֵיהּ דְּבֵי נְשִׂיאָה הֲוָה, לָא קָא הֲווּ לֵיהּ בָּנֵי, בְּעָא רַחֲמֵי וְהָווּ לֵיהּ. הַהוּא יוֹמָא דַּהֲוָה לֵיהּ – נָח נַפְשֵׁיהּ. פְּתַח עֲלֵיהּ הַהוּא סַפְדָּנָא: "שִׂמְחָה לְתוּגָה נֶהְפְּכָה, שָׂשׂוֹן וְיָגוֹן נִדְבָּקוּ, בְּעֵת שִׂמְחָתוֹ נֶאֱנַח, בְּעֵת חֲנִינָתוֹ אָבַד חֲנִינוֹ". אַסִּיקוּ לֵיהּ חָנָן עַל שְׁמֵיהּ. כִּי נָח נַפְשֵׁיהּ דְּר' יוֹחָנָן פְּתַח עֲלֵיהּ ר' יִצְחָק בֶּן אֶלְעָזָר: קָשֶׁה הַיּוֹם לְיִשְׂרָאֵל כְּיוֹם בֹּא הַשֶּׁמֶשׁ בַּצָּהֳרַיִם, דִּכְתִיב: °"וְהָיָה בַּיּוֹם הַהוּא וְהֵבֵאתִי הַשֶּׁמֶשׁ בַּצָּהֳרָיִם". וְאָמַר ר' יוֹחָנָן: זֶה יוֹמוֹ שֶׁל יֹאשִׁיָּהוּ. כִּי נָח נַפְשֵׁיהּ דְּר' יוֹחָנָן יְתֵיב רַבִּי אַמִּי שִׁבְעָה וּשְׁלֹשִׁים. אָמַר רַבִּי אַבָּא בְּרֵיהּ דְּרַבִּי חִיָּיא בַּר אַבָּא: רַבִּי אַמִּי *דַּעֲבַד – לְגַרְמֵיהּ הוּא דַּעֲבַד. דְּהָכִי אָמַר ר' חִיָּיא בַּר אַבָּא אָמַר ר' יוֹחָנָן: אאֲפִילּוּ רַבּוֹ שֶׁלִּימְּדוֹ חָכְמָה – אֵינוֹ יוֹשֵׁב עָלָיו אֶלָּא יוֹם אֶחָד. *כִּי נָח נַפְשֵׁיהּ דְּרַבִּי זֵירָא, פְּתַח עֲלֵיהּ הַהוּא סַפְדָּנָא: "אֶרֶץ שִׁנְעָר הָרָה וְיָלְדָה אֶרֶץ צְבִי גִּידְּלָה שַׁעֲשׁוּעֶיהָ. אוֹי נָא לָהּ אָמְרָה רַקַּת, כִּי אִבְּדָה כְּלִי חֶמְדָּתָהּ". כִּי נָח נַפְשֵׁיהּ דְּרַבִּי אַבָּהוּ אַחִיתוּ עַמּוּדֵי דְּקִסְרִי מַיָּא. דְּרַבִּי יוֹסֵי – *שָׁפְעוּ מַרְזְבֵי דְּצִיפּוֹרִי דְּמָא, דְּרַבִּי יַעֲקֹב – אִתְחַמִּיאוּ כּוֹכְבֵי בִּימָמָא. דְּר' אַסִּי – אִיעַקְרוּ כָּל אִילָנַיָּא, דְּר' חִיָּיא – נְחִיתוּ כֵּיפֵי דְּנוּרָא מֵרְקִיעָא, דְּר' מְנַחֵם *(בְּר' יוֹסֵי) – אִישְׁתָּעוּ צַלְמָנַיָּיא וְהָווּ לִמְחֻלְצַיָּיא, דְּר' תַּנְחוּם בַּר חִיָּיא – אִיתְקַצְּצוּ כָּל אַנְדַּרְטַיָא, דְּר' אֶלְיָשִׁיב – אִיחַתְּרוּ שִׁבְעִין מַחְתַּרְתָּא בִּנְהַרְדְּעָא, דְּרַב הַמְנוּנָא – נְחִיתוּ כֵּיפֵי דְּבַרְדָּא מֵרְקִיעָא, דְּרַבָּה וְרַב יוֹסֵף – נְשׁוּק כֵּיפֵי דִּפְרָת אַהֲדָדֵי, דְּאַבַּיֵּי וְרָבָא – נְשׁוּק כֵּיפֵי דְּדִגְלַת אַהֲדָדֵי, כִּי נָח נַפְשֵׁיהּ דְּר' מְשַׁרְשְׁיָא טְעוּן דִּיקְלֵי שִׁיצֵי. ת"ר:

וְאֵלּוּ

ס"א

עמוס ח

כִּי מָטוּ אַגִּישְׁרָא. כְּשֶׁהִגִּיעוּ לַעֲבוֹר דַּף שֶׁל גֶּשֶׁר קָצָר, שֶׁעַכְשָׁיו לֹא הָיוּ יְכוֹלִין לַעֲבוֹר זֶה בְּצַד זֶה, אֶלָּא זֶה אַחַר זֶה: קָמוּ גְּמָלֵי. עָמְדוּ הַגְּמַלִּים נוֹשְׂאֵי הַמִּטּוֹת בִּמְקוֹמָן: טַיָּיעָא. סוֹחֵר יִשְׁמְעֵאלִים: רַבָּנַן. דְּשָׁכְבֵי, רַבָּה בַּר רַב הוּנָא וְרַב הַמְנוּנָא: עָבְדִי יְקָרָא. דְּהָא לָא בָּעֵי הַאי לְמֵיעַל מִקַּמֵּי הַאי: נְתוּר כָּכֵי. לְחָיָיו, מִשּׁוּם דְּבָזֵי לְרַב הַמְנוּנָא: סֵפֶר מִלְחָמוֹת. סֵפֶר תּוֹרָה. לִישָּׁנָא אַחֲרִינָא: שֶׁנִּלְחַם רַבָּה וְרַב הַמְנוּנָא, וּנְתוּר כָּכֵי דְּהַהוּא טַיָּיעָא. לִישָּׁנָא אַחֲרִינָא: גֶּזַע יְשִׁישִׁים – זֶה רַבָּה בַּר רַב הוּנָא, דְּהוּא בֶּן גְּדוֹלִים, בֶּן רַב הוּנָא דְּהוּא רֹאשׁ גּוֹלָה, וְעָדִיף מִנְּשִׂיא דְּאֶרֶץ יִשְׂרָאֵל. וְעִמּוֹ סֵפֶר מִלְחָמוֹת – עִמּוֹ רַב הַמְנוּנָא: קָאַת וְקִיפּוֹד הוּכְפְּלוּ. קְלָלָה, כְּמוֹ: "וִירֵשׁוּהָ קָאַת וְקִיפּוֹד" (ישעיה לד) כְּלוֹמַר: קְלָלָה בָּאָה וְהוּכְפְּלָה בָּעוֹלָם: לִרְאוֹת שׁוֹד וָשֶׁבֶר. זֶה שֶׁקִּיצֵּץ הקב"ה עַל עוֹלָמוֹ: נָשִׂים לֵילוֹת כְּיָמִים. בְּהֶסְפֵּד, עַל שֶׁשָּׂם לֵילוֹת כְּיָמִים בַּתּוֹרָה: בַּר קִיפּוֹק וּבַר אָבִין. הָווּ סַפְדָּנֵי: (הַהוּא יוֹמָא. דְּנָח נַפְשֵׁיהּ): חָלַשׁ דַּעְתֵּיהּ. דְּהַאי מְדַמֵּי לֵיהּ לְשַׁלְהֶבֶת, וְהַאי לַאֲבֵידָה: וְהַהוּא יוֹמָא. דְּנָח נַפְשֵׁיהּ לָא סַפְדוּהוּ, מִשּׁוּם דְּאֵירַע לְהוּ תַּקָּלָה עַל יָדוֹ: לָא בַּר קִיפּוֹק וְלָא בַּר אָבִין חָלֵיץ. מִשּׁוּם דְּאִיתְהַפְּכוּ כַּרְעַיְיהוּ. וּתְנִינָא (יבמות דף קג.): הַאי מַאן דְּמִסְגֵּי אַלּוּחְתָּא דְּרִיגְלָא – לָא חָלֵיץ, דְּהַתּוֹרָה אָמְרָה "וְחָלְצָה נַעֲלוֹ מֵעַל רַגְלוֹ" וְלֹא מִתַּחַת לְרַגְלוֹ: אָתֵי לְדִגְלַת. חִדֶּקֶל: רוֹב שְׁלִישִׁית. יִשְׂרָאֵל נִקְרְאוּ שְׁלִישִׁית. וְרָבָא שָׁקוּל כְּרוֹב יִשְׂרָאֵל, וַאֲמַר לֵיהּ: קוּם וֶאֱמוֹר מִילְּתָא, כְּלוֹמַר: בַּקֵּשׁ רַחֲמִים: כְּאוֹת בְּמֵי מָרָה. שֶׁאִשָּׁה סוֹטָה נִבְדֶּקֶת בָּהֶן: בְּעֵת חֲנִינָתוֹ. דְּוָלָד: אָבַד חֲנִינוֹ. אָבִיו הַמְחָנְנוֹ: וְהֵבֵאתִי הַשֶּׁמֶשׁ בַּצָּהֳרַיִם. אַשְׁקִיעַ הַשֶּׁמֶשׁ בַּצָּהֳרַיִם: יוֹמוֹ שֶׁל יֹאשִׁיָּה. שֶׁנֶּהֱרַג יֹאשִׁיָּה, קָרֵי יוֹמוֹ אֶחָד: לְגַרְמֵיהּ. לְדַעְתֵּיהּ: רַבִּי זֵירָא הָיָה מִבָּבֶל, וְשָׁם נוֹלַד, וְגָדַל בְּאֶרֶץ יִשְׂרָאֵל, וְהַיְינוּ דְּקָאָמַר: אֶרֶץ שִׁנְעָר הָרָה וְיָלְדָה אֶרֶץ צְבִי גִּדְּלָה שַׁעֲשׁוּעֶיהָ. וְאַהָכִי קָרֵי לֵיהּ רַבִּי זֵירָא וְרַב זֵירָא*: אוֹי נָא לָהּ אָמְרָה רַקַּת. יְכוֹלָה לוֹמַר כֵּן, רַקַּת הִיא טִבֶּרְיָא: אַחִיתוּ. הוֹרִידוּ דְּמָעוֹת: אִיתְחַמִיאוּ כּוֹכְבֵי. נִרְאוּ הַכּוֹכָבִים, שֶׁנִּשְׁתַּנָּה הָעוֹלָם מֵרוֹב צַעַר: כֵּיפֵי דְּנוּרָא. אֲבָנִים שֶׁל אוּר: אִשְׁתָּעוּ צַלְמָנַיָּיא. נִימּוֹחוּ פַּרְצוּף שֶׁלָּהֶן: וַהֲווּ לִמְחֻלְצַיָּיא. כְּלוֹמַר, נֶחֶלְקָה וְנִתְמַעֲכָה כָּל צוּרַת פַּרְצוּף שֶׁל צְלָמִים וְצוּרַ' הַמַּטְבְּעוֹת, מִפְּנֵי צוּרַת הֶחָסִיד שֶׁנִּשְׁתַּנֵּית: דְּרַבִּי מְנַחֵם. בְּנָן שֶׁל קְדוֹשִׁים, שֶׁלֹּא נִסְתַּכֵּל אַף בְּצוּרָה שֶׁל זוּזָא, כִּדְאָמְרִינַן בְּ"עַרְבֵי פְּסָחִים" (דף קד.): וַהֲווּ לִמְחֻלְצַיָּיא. כְּמוֹ שֶׁהוּחְלְקָה בְּמַעְגָּל וּבְמַחֲלָצִים, שֶׁבָּהּ מַטִּיחִין טִיט הַכּוֹתֶל: אַנְדַּרְטָא. צוּרַת הַצְּלָמִים שֶׁעוֹשִׂין עַל שֵׁם הַמֶּלֶךְ שֶׁמֵּת: שִׁבְעִין מַחְתַּרְתָּא. דְּגַנָּבִים דְּבִזְכוּתֵיהּ לָא הֲווּ אָתוּ גַּנָּבִים: כֵּיפֵי דְּבַרְדָּא. אֲבָנִים: נְשׁוּק כֵּיפֵי. כִּיפּוֹת שֶׁל גְּשָׁרִים נִשְׁתַּבְּרוּ, וְנָשְׁקוּ זוֹ אֶת זוֹ: שִׁיצֵי. קוֹצִים:

וְאֵלּוּ

[פי' אפי' עופות רעות באות לראות כשמתו ערוך]

יבמות קג. [ע"ש]

[דרדות מח. וש"נ]

מגילה ו.

[וע"ע רש"י כתובות מג ד"ה אמר ר"ז ועי' תוס' מנחות מ: ד"ה ר"ז אמר]

[סנהדרין קט.]

[נ"ל ברבי סימאי ועי' תוס' שבת קמט. ד"ה ודיוקני ותוס' פסחים קד. ד"ה דלא ותוס' ע"ז נ. ד"ה ה"ג]

ואלו קְרָעִין כו'. בְּאֵבֶל רַבָּתִי בְּמַסֶּכֶת שְׂמָחוֹת (פ"ט): בְּרוֹב צִיבּוּר. רוֹב יִשְׂרָאֵל: וּכְמַעֲשֶׂה שֶׁהָיָה. בְּשָׁאוּל וִיהוֹנָתָן: גָּרְמוּ לְנַפְשַׁיְיהוּ. דְּמָרְדוּ בֵּיהּ. וְהָא דְּקָאָמַר לָא קָטְלֵי יְהוּדִי – רוֹצֶה לוֹמַר: בְּחִנָּם: לְקוֹל יְתֵירֵי. לְקוֹל כִּנּוֹרוֹת, שֶׁמָּרְדוּ: בְּאָתְיָא קְרַע קְרַע (*מִדָּוִד): שָׁלֹשׁ דְּלָתוֹת וְאַרְבָּעָה. כְּלוֹמַר: אַרְבָּעָה פְּסוּקִים: אֲנָא מַלְכָּא. וְאַמַּלְכָּא לָא כְּתִיב כְּלוּם: הָיוּ צָרֶיהָ לְרֹאשׁ. שֶׁהִכָּרִי רֹאשׁ וְלֹא אַתָּה: מִשּׁוּם שְׁמוּעוֹת רָעוֹת. עַל הַגָּלוּת, אִיבָּעֵי לְמִיקְרַע: אֶת הַמְּגִילָּה. זֶה הַגְּוִיל: וְאֶת הַדְּבָרִים. זֶה הַכְּתָב: הַשְׁתָּא. אִי שָׁקֵיל לְהוּ נַעֲמִיתָא – אִיבָּעֵי לִי לְמִיקְרַע עַל הַגְּוִיל וְעַל הַכְּתָב, דְּהָוֵי כְּנִשְׂרָף: בִּזְרוֹעַ. שֶׁאֵין יָכוֹל לְהַצִּילוֹ: וּכְמַעֲשֶׂה שֶׁהָיָה. דִּיהוֹיָקִים. אֲבָל דְּנַעֲמִיתָא דְּמָצֵי לְהַצִּיל – לָא מִיקְרַע: הָא דְּפָגַע בְּמִקְדָּשׁ בְּרֵישָׁא. כְּגוֹן שֶׁנִּכְנַס לִירוּשָׁלַיִם בִּשְׁדֵה תֵּיבָה וּמִגְדָּל, דְּלָא רָאָה יְרוּשָׁלַיִם עַד שֶׁרָאָה בֵּית הַמִּקְדָּשׁ – קוֹרֵעַ עַל הַמִּקְדָּשׁ, וּמוֹסִיף עַל יְרוּשָׁלַיִם. אֲבָל כְּשֶׁלֹּא נִכְנַס בְּתֵיבָה וּפָגַע בִּירוּשָׁלַיִם בְּרֵישָׁא – קוֹרֵעַ עַל יְרוּשָׁלַיִם בִּפְנֵי עַצְמָהּ וְעַל הַמִּקְדָּשׁ בִּפְנֵי עַצְמוֹ: כָּל הַקְּרָעִים רַשָּׁאִין לְמוֹלְלָן. לְקַפֵּל בֶּגֶד בִּתְפִירָה: כְּעֵין סוּלָּמוֹת. שֶׁאֵין מְלַקְּטִין זֶה סָמוּךְ לָזֶה, אֲבָל זֶה רָחוֹק מִזֶּה, שֶׁמְּלַקֵּט בָּרוֹחַב כְּעֵין מַעֲלוֹת סוּלָּמוֹת:

מִתּוֹךְ

(שמחות פ"ט) (מ"ב ב) (שם) (שם) (ש"ב א) (לעיל כב: ע"ש סנהדרין ס.)

תורה אור

*וְאֵלּוּ קְרָעִין שֶׁאֵין מִתְאַחִין: [א]הַקּוֹרֵעַ עַל אָבִיו, וְעַל אִמּוֹ, [ב]וְעַל רַבּוֹ שֶׁלִּימְּדוֹ תּוֹרָה, וְעַל נָשִׂיא, וְעַל אַב ב"ד, [ג]וְעַל שְׁמוּעוֹת הָרָעוֹת, וְעַל בִּרְכַּת הַשֵּׁם, וְעַל סֵפֶר תּוֹרָה שֶׁנִּשְׂרַף, [ד]וְעַל עָרֵי יְהוּדָה, וְעַל הַמִּקְדָּשׁ, וְעַל יְרוּשָׁלַיִם. [ה]וְקוֹרֵעַ עַל מִקְדָּשׁ וּמוֹסִיף עַל יְרוּשָׁלַיִם. [ו]אָבִיו וְאִמּוֹ [ז]וְרַבּוֹ שֶׁלִּימְּדוֹ תּוֹרָה מְנָלַן? דִּכְתִיב: °"וֶאֱלִישָׁע רֹאֶה וְהוּא מְצַעֵק אָבִי אָבִי רֶכֶב יִשְׂרָאֵל וּפָרָשָׁיו". "אָבִי אָבִי" — זֶה אָבִיו וְאִמּוֹ, "רֶכֶב יִשְׂרָאֵל וּפָרָשָׁיו" — זֶה רַבּוֹ שֶׁלִּימְּדוֹ תּוֹרָה. מַאי מַשְׁמַע? כִּדְמְתַרְגֵּם רַב יוֹסֵף: רַבִּי רַבִּי, דְּטַב לְהוֹן לְיִשְׂרָאֵל בִּצְלוֹתֵיהּ מֵרְתִיכִין וּפָרָשִׁין. וְלָא מִתְאַחִין מְנָלַן? דִּכְתִיב: °"וַיַּחֲזֵק בִּבְגָדָיו וַיִּקְרָעֵם לִשְׁנַיִם קְרָעִים", מִמַּשְׁמַע שֶׁנֶּאֱמַר *"וַיִּקְרָעֵם" אֵינִי יוֹדֵעַ שֶׁלִּשְׁנַיִם?! אֶלָּא, מְלַמֵּד שֶׁקְּרוּעִים וְעוֹמְדִים לִשְׁנַיִם לְעוֹלָם. אֲמַר לֵיהּ רֵישׁ לָקִישׁ לְרַבִּי יוֹחָנָן: אֵלִיָּהוּ חַי הוּא! אֲמַר לֵיהּ: כֵּיוָן דִּכְתִיב: °"וְלֹא רָאָהוּ עוֹד" — לְגַבֵּי דִּידֵיהּ כְּמֵת דָּמֵי. [ח]נָשִׂיא וְאַב בֵּית דִּין [ט]וּשְׁמוּעוֹת הָרָעוֹת מְנָלַן? דִּכְתִיב: °"וַיַּחֲזֵק דָּוִד בִּבְגָדָיו וַיִּקְרָעֵם וְגַם כָּל הָאֲנָשִׁים אֲשֶׁר אִתּוֹ וַיִּסְפְּדוּ וַיִּבְכּוּ וַיָּצֻמוּ עַד הָעָרֶב עַל שָׁאוּל וְעַל יְהוֹנָתָן בְּנוֹ וְעַל עַם ה' וְעַל בֵּית יִשְׂרָאֵל כִּי נָפְלוּ בֶּחָרֶב". "שָׁאוּל" — זֶה נָשִׂיא, "יְהוֹנָתָן" — זֶה אַב ב"ד, "עַל עַם ה' וְעַל בֵּית יִשְׂרָאֵל" — אֵלּוּ שְׁמוּעוֹת הָרָעוֹת. א"ל רַב בַּר שַׁבָּא לְרַב כַּהֲנָא: וְאֵימָא עַד דְּהָווּ כּוּלְּהוּ! א"ל: 'עַל' 'עַל' הִפְסִיק הָעִנְיָן. וּמִי קָרְעִינַן אַשְּׁמוּעוֹת הָרָעוֹת? וְהָא אָמְרוּ לֵיהּ לִשְׁמוּאֵל: קְטַל שָׁבוֹר מַלְכָּא תְּרֵיסַר אַלְפֵי יְהוּדָאֵי בְּמָזִיגַת קֵסָרִי, וְלָא קְרַע. לֹא אָמְרוּ אֶלָּא בְּרוֹב צִבּוּר, וּכְמַעֲשֶׂה שֶׁהָיָה. וּמִי קְטַל שָׁבוֹר מַלְכָּא יְהוּדָאֵי? וְהָא א"ל שָׁבוֹר מַלְכָּא לִשְׁמוּאֵל; תֵּיתֵי לִי, דְּלָא קְטָלֵי יְהוּדִי מֵעוֹלָם! הָתָם אִינְהוּ גָּרְמִי לְנַפְשַׁיְיהוּ. דְּא"ר אַמֵּי: לְקָל יְתֵירֵי דְּמָזִיגַת קֵסָרִי פָּקַע שׁוּרָא דְּלוּדְקִיָא. [כ]עַל בִּרְכַּת הַשֵּׁם מְנָלַן — דִּכְתִיב: °"וַיָּבֹא אֶלְיָקִים בֶּן חִלְקִיָּה אֲשֶׁר עַל הַבַּיִת וְשֶׁבְנָא הַסּוֹפֵר וְיוֹאָח בֶּן אָסָף הַמַּזְכִּיר אֶל חִזְקִיָּהוּ קְרוּעֵי בְגָדִים". *ת"ר: [ל]אֶחָד הַשּׁוֹמֵעַ וְאֶחָד הַשּׁוֹמֵעַ מִפִּי הַשּׁוֹמֵעַ חַיָּיב לִקְרוֹעַ, וְהָעֵדִים אֵינָן חַיָּיבִין לִקְרוֹעַ, שֶׁכְּבָר קָרְעוּ בְּשָׁעָה שֶׁשָּׁמְעוּ. בְּשָׁעָה שֶׁשָּׁמְעוּ מַאי הָוֵי, הָא קָא שָׁמְעֵי הַשְׁתָּא! לָא ס"ד דִּכְתִיב: °"וַיְהִי כִּשְׁמֹעַ הַמֶּלֶךְ חִזְקִיָּהוּ וַיִּקְרַע אֶת בְּגָדָיו" — הַמֶּלֶךְ קָרַע, וְהֵם לֹא קָרְעוּ. וְלָא מִתְאַחִין מְנָלַן? *אָתְיָא קְרִיעָה קְרִיעָה. [מ]סֵפֶר תּוֹרָה שֶׁנִּשְׂרַף מְנָלַן? דִּכְתִיב: °"וַיְהִי כִּקְרוֹא יְהוּדִי שָׁלֹשׁ דְּלָתוֹת וְאַרְבָּעָה (א) יִקְרָעֶהָ בְּתַעַר הַסֹּפֵר וְהַשְׁלֵךְ אֶל הָאֵשׁ אֲשֶׁר אֶל הָאָח" וגו'. מַאי "שָׁלֹשׁ דְּלָתוֹת וְאַרְבָּעָה"? אָמְרוּ לֵיהּ לִיהוֹיָקִים: כָּתַב יִרְמְיָה סֵפֶר קִינוֹת. אֲמַר לְהוּ: מַה כְּתִיב בֵּיהּ? °"אֵיכָה יָשְׁבָה בָדָד". אֲמַר לְהוּ: אֲנָא מַלְכָּא. א"ל: °"בָּכוֹ תִבְכֶּה בַּלַּיְלָה". אֲנָא מַלְכָּא. °"גָּלְתָה יְהוּדָה מֵעֹנִי" — אֲנָא מַלְכָּא. °"דַּרְכֵי צִיּוֹן אֲבֵלוֹת" — אֲנָא מַלְכָּא. °"הָיוּ צָרֶיהָ לְרֹאשׁ" — אֲמַר לְהוּ: מַאן אֲמָרָהּ? °"כִּי ה' הוֹגָהּ עַל רֹב פְּשָׁעֶיהָ", מִיָּד קָדַר כָּל אַזְכָּרוֹת שֶׁבָּהּ וּשְׂרָפָן בָּאֵשׁ. וְהַיְינוּ דִּכְתִיב: °"וְלֹא פָחֲדוּ וְלֹא קָרְעוּ אֶת בִּגְדֵיהֶם", מִכְּלָל דְּבָעוּ לְמִיקְרַע. אֲמַר לֵיהּ רַב פָּפָּא לְאַבָּיֵי: אֵימַר מִשּׁוּם שְׁמוּעוֹת הָרָעוֹת! א"ל: שְׁמוּעוֹת רָעוֹת בְּהַהִיא שַׁעְתָּא מִי הָווּ? א"ר חֶלְבּוֹ אָמַר רַב הוּנָא: הָרוֹאֶה סֵפֶר תּוֹרָה שֶׁנִּקְרַע חַיָּיב לִקְרוֹעַ [נ]שְׁתֵּי קְרִיעוֹת: אֶחָד עַל הַגְּוִיל וְאֶחָד עַל הַכְּתָב. שֶׁנֶּאֱמַר: °"אַחֲרֵי שְׂרֹף הַמֶּלֶךְ אֶת הַמְּגִלָּה וְאֶת הַדְּבָרִים". רַבִּי אַבָּא וְרַב הוּנָא בַּר חִיָּיא הֲווּ יָתְבִי* [א]קַמֵּיהּ דְּרַבִּי אַבָּא, בְּעָא לְאַפְנוּיֵי, שְׁקָלֵיהּ לְטוֹטַפְתֵּיהּ אַחְתֵּיהּ אַבֵּי סַדְיָא. אֲתַאי בַּת נַעֲמִיתָא בְּעָא לְמִיבְלְעֵיהּ, אֲמַר: הַשְׁתָּא אִיחַיְּיבִין לִי שְׁתֵּי קְרִיעוֹת, א"ל: מְנָא לָךְ הָא? וְהָא בְּדִידִי הֲוָה עוּבְדָא, וַאֲתַאי לְקַמֵּיהּ דְּרַב מַתָּנָה וְלָא הֲוָה בִּידֵיהּ, אֲתַאי לְקַמֵּיהּ דְּרַב יְהוּדָה, וַאֲמַר לִי: הָכִי אֲמַר שְׁמוּאֵל, לֹא אָמְרוּ [ס]אֶלָּא בִּזְרוֹעַ, וּכְמַעֲשֶׂה שֶׁהָיָה. עָרֵי יְהוּדָה מְנָלַן? דִּכְתִיב: °"וַיָּבֹאוּ אֲנָשִׁים מִשְּׁכֶם מִשִּׁילוֹ וּמִשֹּׁמְרוֹן שְׁמֹנִים אִישׁ מְגֻלְּחֵי זָקָן וּקְרֻעֵי בְגָדִים וּמִתְגֹּדְדִים וּמִנְחָה וּלְבוֹנָה בְּיָדָם לְהָבִיא בֵּית ה'" וגו'. א"ר (א) חֶלְבּוֹ אָמַר עוּלָּא בִּירָאָה [ע]אָמַר ר' אֶלְעָזָר, הָרוֹאֶה עָרֵי יְהוּדָה בְּחוּרְבָּנָן — אוֹמֵר: °"עָרֵי קָדְשְׁךָ הָיוּ מִדְבָּר", וְקוֹרֵעַ. יְרוּשָׁלַיִם בְּחוּרְבָּנָהּ — אוֹמֵר: °"צִיּוֹן מִדְבָּר הָיָתָה יְרוּשָׁלַיִם שְׁמָמָה", וְקוֹרֵעַ. בֵּית הַמִּקְדָּשׁ בְּחוּרְבָּנוֹ — אוֹמֵר °"בֵּית קָדְשֵׁנוּ וְתִפְאַרְתֵּנוּ אֲשֶׁר הִלְלוּךָ אֲבֹתֵינוּ הָיָה לִשְׂרֵפַת אֵשׁ וְכָל מַחֲמַדֵּינוּ הָיָה לְחָרְבָּה", וְקוֹרֵעַ. § "קוֹרֵעַ עַל מִקְדָּשׁ וּמוֹסִיף עַל יְרוּשָׁלַיִם". § וּרְמִינְהוּ: [פ]אֶחָד הַשּׁוֹמֵעַ וְאֶחָד הָרוֹאֶה, כֵּיוָן שֶׁהִגִּיעַ לַצּוֹפִים — קוֹרֵעַ, וְקוֹרֵעַ עַל מִקְדָּשׁ בִּפְנֵי עַצְמוֹ וְעַל יְרוּשָׁלַיִם בִּפְנֵי עַצְמָהּ! לָא קַשְׁיָא: [צ]הָא — דְּפָגַע בְּמִקְדָּשׁ בְּרֵישָׁא, הָא — דְּפָגַע בִּירוּשָׁלַיִם בְּרֵישָׁא. תָּנוּ רַבָּנַן: [ק]וְכוּלָּן רַשָּׁאִין לְשׁוֹלְלָן, וּלְמוֹלְלָן, וּלְלוֹקְטָן וְלַעֲשׂוֹתָן כְּמִין סוּלָּמוֹת, אֲבָל לֹא לְאַחוֹתָן. אָמַר רַב חִסְדָּא:

וּבְאִיחוּי

(מ"ב ב) (שם) (שם) (ש"ב א) (מלכים ב יח) (סנהדרין ס.) (מלכים ב יט) (סנהדרין סס) (ירמיה לו) (איכה א) (שם) (שם) (שם) (ירמיה לו) (שם) [ג"ל קמ רבי אבא] (ירמיה מא) (ישעיה סד) (שם) (שם)

א) [בשאלתות איתא אמר ר' יהודה הרואה כו']

ברכת השם מנלן. ועל ברכת השם דנכרים פליגי הכא בירושלמי, אית דאמרי: רבשקה ישראל מומר הוה, אבל דנכרי – לא, ואית דאמרי: נכרי הוה. ובפרק "ארבע מיתות" (סנהדרין דף ס.) נמי פליגי בה בש"ס שלנו, ובירושלמי: הוה ריש לקיש קורע על ברכת השם:

ואחד השומע מפי השומעים. פירש בתוס': כגון מן העדים שאומרים זה, ואם הוא אומר יכה יוסי את יוסי – אין קורעין על זה, וכן משמע בפ"ד מיתות (שם דף נו.):

אתיא קריעה. תימה: אם כן, נילף כל קריעות שלא יתאחו מ"קריעה" "קריעה"! ושמא לא מיסתבר ליה: **קדר** כל האזכרות. תימה: והא (ב)דקרעה בתער הסופר – משמע כל המגילה! ובירושלמי לא גרסינן האזכרות: **לא** אמרו אלא בזרוע. ובירושלמי גרס: ששרפה מלך ישראל בזרוע:

משכם משילו. לא שייך הכא למיפרך: ואימא עד דאיכא תלתא. אבל קצת קשה: דאימר מילתא יתירתא הוה, דמגלחי זקן(ג) ומתגודדים כתיב בהאי קרא! ויש לומר: דלא שייך למימר דלא נילף כלל אלא קריעה, ולעיל (ד' כא.) הכי קאמר נמי: נהי דגמרת שפיר קריעה – מ"מ לא תילף מינה מעומד:

ובאיחוי

קפז א מיי' פ"ט מהל' אבל הלכה ב ג סמג עשין ב טוש"ע י"ד סי' שמ סעיף טו:

קפח ב מיי' שם הלכה ה טוש"ע שם סעיף יז:

קפט ג מיי' שם הלכה ו טוש"ע שם סעיף לו:

קצ ד מיי' שם הלכה י ופ"ה מהלכות תענית הלכה יו יז טוש"ע שם סעיף לח טוש"ע א"ח סי' תקסא סעיף א:

קצא ה מיי' פ"ה מהל' תענית הלכה טז טוש"ע א"ח סעיף ב:

קצב ו מיי' פ"ח מהל' אבל הלכה ג ופ"ט הלכה ב טור ש"ע י"ד סי' שמ סעיף א:

קצג ז מיי' שם פ"ט הלכה ה ופ"ה מהלכות ת"ת הלכה ט סמג עשין ב טוש"ע שם סעיף ח וסי' רמב סעיף כה:

קצד ח מיי' פ"ט מהל' אבל הלכה ב ו טוש"ע י"ד סי' שמ סעיף יז:

קצה ט י מיי' שם טור ש"ע שם סעיף לו:

קצו כ ל מ נ ס מיי' שם הלכה ב ט טוש"ע שם סעיף לז:

קצז ע פ צ מיי' פ"ה מהלכות תענית הלכה טז טוש"ע א"ח סי' תקסא סעיף א ב:

קצח ק מיי' שם הלכה יז ופ"ט מהלכות אבל הלכה ג טוש"ע א"ח סי' תקסא סעיף ד וטוש"ע י"ד סי' שמ סעיף לט:

הגהות הב"ח

(א) גמ' שלש דלתות וארבעה יקרעה בתער הסופר: (ב) תוס' ד"ה קדר כו' והא דיקרעה בתער: (ג) ד"ה משכם כו' דמגלחי זקן וקרועי בגדים ומתגודדים כו' דלא נילף כלל אפילו קריעה:

רבינו חננאל

ת"ר אלו קרעין שאסורין באיחוי פי' עשרה קרעים הללו הקורע על אביו ועל אמו ועל רבו שלמדו חכמה. ועל נשיא ועל אב ב"ד. ועל שמועות הרעות. ועל ברכת השם. ועל ס"ת שנשרף ועל חורבן ערי יהודה ועל חורבן המקדש [ועל ירושלים] וקורע על חורבן בהמ"ק ומוסיף על חורבן ירושלים: אביו ואמו ורבו שלמדו חכמה מהכא ואלישע ראה והוא מצעק אבי אבי רכב ישראל ופרשיו. אבי אבי זה אביו ואמו. רכב ישראל ופרשיו זה רבו שלמדו חכמה. כדמתרגם רבי רבי דטב להון לישראל בצלותך מן רתיכין ופרשין. ואע"ג דאליהו חי הוא כיון דכתיב ביה ולא ראהו עוד כמת הוא לגביה: **ירושלמי** כשם שקורעין על החכמים כך קורעין על תלמידיהן איזהו ת"ח חזקיה אמר כל השונה הלכות *)ועד תורה. א"ר יוסי הדא דאת אמרו בראשונה אבל עכשיו אפילו הלכות. ר' אבוה בשם ר' יוחנן כל שמבטל עסקיו מפני משנתו. תני כל ששואלין אותו ומשיב. א"ר אושעיא כגון אנא דרבבינן משגיחין עלינו וכן מתיבין ליה. א"ר אבא בר ממל כל שיודע לבאר משנתו ואנן אפילו רבבינן לא יכלי לבאר משנתנו איזהו רבו כל שפתח לו תחלה דברי ר' מאיר. ר' יהודה אומר כל שרוב תלמודו ממנו. שמואל חלץ בההוא שהאיר במשנתו. פי' ביאר לו משנתו זו ששנינו בתמיד. ושתי מפתחות היו לו אחד יורד לאמת השחי ואחד פותח כיון. פי' היה מכניס ידו ומורדה עד שיחין שהוא אמה ואח"כ היה מגיע למנעול ופותחו. והאחד היה נכון לפניו מכניס ידו כנגדו ופותח: ולא מתאחין שנאמר ויקרעם לשנים קרעים. ממשמע שנאמר ויקרעם איני יודע שהקריעה לשנים היא אלא מה ת"ל לשנים מלמד שקורעין לעולם לשנים. נשיא ואב ב"ד ושמועת הרעות שנאמר ויחזק דוד בבגדיו ויקרעם וגם כל האנשים אשר אתו ויספדו ויבכו על שאול ועל יהונתן ועל עם ה' ועל בית ישראל כי נפלו בחרב. שאול זה נשיא יהונתן זה אב ב"ד. על עם ה' על בית ישראל אלו שמועות רעות. ומקשינן ואימא לא קרעינן עד דאיכא כולהו. ופרקינן על על הפסיק הענין למימרא דקרעינן על כל אחד ואחד בפ"ע. ואסיקנא לא אמרו דקרעינן על שמועות הרעות אלא ברוב צבור. וכמעשה דשאול דהא שמואל שמע דקטל שבור מלכא י"ב אלפי יהודאי ולא קרע. ועל ברכת השם אחד השומע. ואחד השומע מפי השומע חייבין לקרוע. והעדים אין חייבין לקרוע שכבר קרעו בעת ששמעו. שנאמר ויהי כשמוע המלך את דבריהם ויקרע את בגדיו המלך קרע והם לא קרעו עכשיו שכבר קרעו שנאמר ויבא אליקים בן חלקיהו אשר על הבית ושבנא הספר ויואח בן אסף המזכיר אל חזקיהו קרועי בגדים ויגידו את דברי רבשקה. ולא מתאחין מנ"ל אתיא קריעה קריעה מהתם: **ירושלמי** מהו לקרוע בזמן הזה משום ר' יוחנן אמרו משרבו הגדפנין בטל מלקרוע. מהו לקרוע על הכנויים נשמעיניה מהדא. ר"ל הוה מהלך בדרך נזדמן לו כותי הוה מגדף והוא קורע מגדף והוא קורע נחת מן חמרא ויהב ליה מרתיקא גו ליביה [באבן או באגרוף על לבו] פי' הכהו באגרוף תרגם מרתוק. אמר ליה רשע אית מאנין לאמך מספקא לי אילין שקרעתי הדא אמרת שקורעין על כנויין בזמן הזה: על שריפת התורה. שנאמר ויהי בקרא יהודי שלש דלתות וארבעה יקרעה בתער הספר והשלך על האש. מהו שלש דלתות וארבע. תלת וארבע פסוקין. ובכולהו אמר אנא מלכא כיון דשמע לפסוקי חמישי היו צריה לראש אמר להו מי אמר אמרו ליה כי ה' הוגה על רוב פשעיה מיד קרעה בתער הסופר. קדר כל האזכרות שבו ושרפן באש. וכתיב ולא פחדו ולא קרעו בגדיהם מכלל דהוה להו למקרע: **ירושלמי** א"ר יוסי בשם רב אין קורעין אלא על ס"ת ששרפו מלך בזרוע. כגון יהויקים בן יאשיהו וחביריו. הרואה ת"ח שמת כרואה ס"ת שנשרף א"ר אבהו יבא עלי אם טעמתי כלום כל אותו היום. ר' יונה הוה בצור שמע [דדמך] בריה דר' אבהו. ואע"ג דאכל גובנא ושתה מיא אסקוה צום כל ההוא יומא. א"ר חלבו אמר רב הונא הרואה ס"ת שנשרף חייב לקרוע שתים. אחת על המגלה ואחת על הדברים. שנאמר ויהי דבר ה' אל ירמיהו אחרי שרוף המלך את המגלה ואת הדברים באש ואסיקנא אמר שמואל אין חייבין לקרוע אלא בשרפת התורה בזרוע כמעשה שהיה. אבל אי בלעה נעמיתה תפילי כדאמר רב הונא בר חייא לא. ערי יהודה שנאמר ויבא אנשים משכם משילו ומשומרון שמונים איש מגולחי זקן וקרועי בגדים. א"ר אלעזר הרואה ערי יהודה בחורבנן אומר ערי קדשך היו מדבר וקורע. הרואה ירושלים בחורבנה אומר ציון מדבר היתה וקורע. בהמ"ק חרב אומר בית קדשנו ותפארתנו אשר הללוך אבותינו היה לשרפת אש וכל מחמדנו היה לחרבה וקורע. ואחד השומע ואחד הרואה כיון שהגיע לצופים קורע. ואי פגע בירושלים בפ"ע ועל מקדש בפ"ע. ואי פגע במקדש תחלה קורע על המקדש ומוסיף

*) בירושלמי הגי' ועוד תורה וע"ש בפ"מ ובק"ע.

הגהות מהר"ב רנשבורג א] גמ' רבי אבא ורב הונא בר חייא הוו יתבי קמיה דרבי אבא. נמחק תיבות קמיה דר' אבא וג"כ קמ ר' אבא. כך שמעתי ולאותי יש מגיהים ולענ"ד אין צורך לזה דכבר בירר בס' באר שבע בהוריות דף ב' ע"א דהלכתא כתב ר' אבא הוו ישוב"ה: ב] רש"י ד"ה אתיא קרע קרע מדוד עכ"ל. עיין שו"ת שער אפרים סי' נו דטעות הדפוס הוא ועיין עוד ספר יד דוד:

[א]וּבְאִיחוּי אֲלֶכְּסַנְדְּרִי. ת"ר: [ב]הַקּוֹרֵעַ מִתּוֹךְ הַשָּׁלָל, מִתּוֹךְ הַמָּלָל, מִתּוֹךְ הַלֶּקֶט, מִתּוֹךְ הַסּוּלָּמוֹת — לֹא יָצָא. מִתּוֹךְ הָאִיחוּי — יָצָא. אָמַר רַב חִסְדָּא: [ג]וּבְאִיחוּי אֲלֶכְּסַנְדְּרִי. ת"ר: רַשַּׁאי לְהוֹפְכוֹ לְמַטָּה וּלְאַחוּתוֹ. ר' שִׁמְעוֹן בֶּן אֶלְעָזָר [ד]אוֹסֵר לְאַחוּתוֹ. [ה]וּכְשֵׁם שֶׁהַמּוֹכֵר אָסוּר לְאַחוּתוֹ — כָּךְ הַלּוֹקֵחַ אָסוּר לְאַחוּתוֹ. וּלְפִיכָךְ מוֹכֵר צָרִיךְ לְהוֹדִיעוֹ לַלּוֹקֵחַ. ת"ר: תְּחִילַּת קְרִיעָה טֶפַח, וְתוֹסֶפֶת שָׁלֹשׁ אֶצְבָּעוֹת, דִּבְרֵי רַבִּי מֵאִיר. רַבִּי יְהוּדָה אוֹמֵר: תְּחִילַּת קְרִיעָה שָׁלֹשׁ אֶצְבָּעוֹת, וְתוֹסֶפֶת כָּל שֶׁהוּ. אָמַר עוּלָּא: הֲלָכָה כְּרַבִּי מֵאִיר בִּקְרִיעָה, וַהֲלָכָה כְּרַבִּי יְהוּדָה בְּתוֹסֶפֶת. תַּנְיָא נַמִּי הָכִי, רַבִּי יוֹסֵי אוֹמֵר: [ו]תְּחִילַּת קְרִיעָה טֶפַח וְתוֹסֶפֶת כָּל שֶׁהוּ. ת"ר: [ז]אָמְרוּ לוֹ מֵת אָבִיו, וְקָרַע, מֵת בְּנוֹ, וְהוֹסִיף, תַּחְתּוֹן מִתְאַחֶה, עֶלְיוֹן אֵינוֹ מִתְאַחֶה. מֵת בְּנוֹ וְקָרַע, מֵת אָבִיו וְהוֹסִיף, עֶלְיוֹן מִתְאַחֶה, תַּחְתּוֹן אֵינוֹ מִתְאַחֶה. מֵת אָבִיו, מֵת אִמּוֹ, מֵת אָחִיו, מֵתָה אֲחוֹתוֹ, קוֹרֵעַ קֶרַע אֶחָד לְכוּלָּן. רַבִּי יְהוּדָה בֶּן בְּתֵירָה אוֹמֵר: עַל כּוּלָּן קֶרַע אֶחָד, עַל אָבִיו וְאִמּוֹ קֶרַע אֶחָד, לְפִי שֶׁאֵין מוֹסִיפִין עַל קֶרַע אָבִיו וְאִמּוֹ. מַאי טַעְמָא? אָמַר רַב נַחְמָן בַּר יִצְחָק: לְפִי שֶׁאֵינָן בְּתוֹסֶפֶת. אָמַר שְׁמוּאֵל: [ח]הֲלָכָה כְּרַבִּי יְהוּדָה בֶּן בְּתֵירָה. וּמִי אָמַר שְׁמוּאֵל הָכִי? וְהָאָמַר שְׁמוּאֵל: *הֲלָכָה כְּדִבְרֵי הַמֵּיקֵל בְּאֵבֶל! אֲבֵילוּת לְחוּד, קְרִיעָה לְחוּד. עַד הֵיכָן קוֹרֵעַ? [ט]עַד טִיבּוּרוֹ, וְיֵשׁ אוֹמְרִים: עַד לִבּוֹ. אע"פ שֶׁאֵין רְאָיָה לַדָּבָר — זֵכֶר לַדָּבָר, שֶׁנֶּאֱמַר: °"וְקִרְעוּ לְבַבְכֶם וְאַל בִּגְדֵיכֶם". הִגִּיעַ לְטִיבּוּרוֹ, מַרְחִיק שָׁלֹשׁ אֶצְבָּעוֹת וְקוֹרֵעַ. נִתְמַלֵּא מִלְּפָנָיו — מַחֲזִירוֹ לַאֲחוֹרָיו. נִתְמַלֵּא מִלְּמַעְלָה — הוֹפְכוֹ מִלְּמַטָּה. [י]וְהַקּוֹרֵעַ מִלְּמַטָּה וּמִן הַצְּדָדִין לֹא יָצָא. [כ]אֶלָּא שֶׁכֹּהֵן גָּדוֹל פּוֹרֵם מִלְּמַטָּה. פְּלִיגוּ בָּהּ רַב מַתָּנָה וּמָר עוּקְבָא, וְתַרְוַיְיהוּ מִשְּׁמֵיהּ דַּאֲבוּהּ דִּשְׁמוּאֵל וְלֵוִי; חַד אָמַר: [ל]כָּל שִׁבְעָה קוֹרֵעַ, לְאַחַר שִׁבְעָה מוֹסִיף. וְחַד אָמַר: כָּל שְׁלֹשִׁים קוֹרֵעַ, לְאַחַר שְׁלֹשִׁים מוֹסִיף. מַתְקִיף לַהּ רַבִּי זֵירָא: מַאן דְּאָמַר כָּל שִׁבְעָה קוֹרֵעַ, אַמַּאי, דְּלָא נִיתַּן לְשׁוֹלְלוֹ, אֶלָּא הָא דְּאָמַר מָר: *הָאִשָּׁה שׁוֹלַלְתּוֹ לְאַלְתַּר, ה"נ הָתָם מִשּׁוּם כְּבוֹד אִשָּׁה הוּא. מַאן דְּאָמַר כָּל שְׁלֹשִׁים קוֹרֵעַ, אַמַּאי, דְּלָא נִיתַּן לְאַחוּתוֹ. אֶלָּא לְאָבִיו וּלְאִמּוֹ, דְּלָא נִיתַּן לְאַחוּתוֹ לְעוֹלָם, ה"נ הָתָם מִשּׁוּם כְּבוֹד אָבִיו וְאִמּוֹ הוּא. ת"ר: *[מ]הַיּוֹצֵא בְּבֶגֶד קָרוּעַ לִפְנֵי הַמֵּת הֲרֵי זֶה גּוֹזֵל אֶת הַמֵּתִים וְאֶת הַחַיִּים. *רשב"ג אוֹמֵר, [נ]הָאוֹמֵר לַחֲבֵירוֹ: "הַשְׁאִילֵנִי חֲלוּקְךָ וְאֵלֵךְ וַאֲבַקֵּר אֶת אַבָּא שֶׁהוּא חוֹלֶה", וְהָלַךְ וּמְצָאוֹ שֶׁמֵּת — קוֹרֵעַ, וּמְאַחוֹ. וּכְשֶׁיָּבֹא לְבֵיתוֹ מַחֲזִיר לוֹ חֲלוּקוֹ וְנוֹתֵן לוֹ דְּמֵי קִרְעוֹ. וְאִם לֹא הוֹדִיעוֹ — הֲרֵי זֶה לֹא יִגַּע בּוֹ. ת"ר: [ס]חוֹלֶה שֶׁמֵּת לוֹ מֵת — אֵין מוֹדִיעִין אוֹתוֹ שֶׁמֵּת, שֶׁמָּא תִּטָּרֵף דַּעְתּוֹ עָלָיו. וְאֵין מְקָרְעִין בְּפָנָיו, וּמַשְׁתִּקִין אֶת הַנָּשִׁים מִפָּנָיו. *וּמְקָרְעִין לְקָטָן מִפְּנֵי עָגְמַת נֶפֶשׁ. [ע]וְקוֹרְעִין עַל חָמִיו וְעַל חֲמוֹתוֹ מִפְּנֵי כְּבוֹד אִשְׁתּוֹ. וְאָמַר רַב פַּפָּא, תָּנָא בְּאֵבֶל רַבָּתִי: [פ]אָבֵל לֹא יָנִיחַ תִּינוֹק בְּתוֹךְ חֵיקוֹ מִפְּנֵי שֶׁמְּבִיאוֹ לִידֵי שְׂחוֹק, וְנִמְצָא מִתְגַּנֶּה עַל הַבְּרִיּוֹת.§ "וְאֵין מַבְרִין *עַל מִטּוֹת זְקוּפוֹת".§ ת"ר: הַהוֹלֵךְ לְבֵית הָאָבֵל, אִם הָיָה לִבּוֹ גַּס בּוֹ — יַבְרוּהוּ עַל מִטּוֹת כְּפוּיוֹת, וְאִם לָאו — יַבְרוּהוּ עַל מִטּוֹת זְקוּפוֹת. רָבָא אִיתְרַע בֵּיהּ מִילְּתָא. עָל לְגַבֵּיהּ אַבָּא בַּר מַרְתָּא, דְּהוּא אַבָּא בַּר מַנְיוּמֵי. רָבָא — זְקִיף, אַבָּא בַּר מַרְתָּא — כָּפֵי. אֲמַר: כַּמָּה לֵית בֵּיהּ דַּעְתָּא לְהַאי צוּרְבָא מֵרַבָּנָן. תָּנוּ רַבָּנָן: הַהוֹלֵךְ מִמָּקוֹם לְמָקוֹם, אם

מִתּוֹךְ הַשָּׁלָל. שֶׁלֹּא קָרַע אֶלָּא בַּשָּׁלָל: מִתּוֹךְ הָאִיחוּי. מְקָרַע הָאִיחוּי: וּבְאִיחוּי אֲלֶכְּסַנְדְּרִי. דַּהֲוֵה כְּשָׁלֵם: רַשַּׁאי לְהָפְכוֹ לְמַטָּה. שֶׁהוֹפֵךְ הַקֶּרַע לְמַטָּה, וְהוֹפֵךְ שֶׁלְּמַטָּה לְמַעְלָה, וּמְאַחֵהוּ, וְעוֹשֶׂה בֵּית הַצַּוָּאר וְלוֹבְשׁוֹ: וְתוֹסֶפֶת שָׁלֹשׁ. כְּגוֹן שֶׁמּוֹסִיף קֶרַע אַחֵר עַל אוֹתוֹ קֶרַע, כְּגוֹן שֶׁאֵירְעוֹ אֵבֶל אַחֵר: עֶלְיוֹן אֵין מִתְאַחֶה. שֶׁקְּרָעוֹ עַל אָבִיו וְעַל אִמּוֹ: שֶׁאֵינָן בְּתוֹסֶפֶת. כְּלוֹמַר, אֵין בַּדִּין שֶׁמּוֹסִיף עֲלֵיהֶן: הִגִּיעַ לְטִיבּוּרוֹ. וּמֵת לוֹ מֵת אַחֵר: מַרְחִיק שָׁלֹשׁ אֶצְבָּעוֹת. בְּצַד אוֹתוֹ קֶרַע, וְקוֹרֵעַ: נִתְמַלֵּא. קְרָעִים מִלְּפָנָיו, מַחֲזִירוֹ לַאֲחוֹרָיו וְחוֹזֵר וְקוֹרֵעַ לְפָנָיו: כָּל שִׁבְעָה. אִם מֵת לוֹ מֵת — קוֹרֵעַ קְרִיעָה אַחֶרֶת: לְאַחַר שִׁבְעָה מוֹסִיף. עַל קֶרַע רִאשׁוֹן: דְּלָא נִיתַּן לְשׁוֹלְלוֹ. תּוֹךְ שִׁבְעָה כְּלָל. וְאִי מוֹסִיף בֵּיהּ — מִיחְזֵי כְּקֶרַע אֶחָד. אֲבָל לְאַחַר שִׁבְעָה, דִּכְבָר שְׁלָלוֹ — קוֹרֵעַ כָּל הַשְּׁלִילוֹת וּמוֹסִיף כָּל שֶׁהוּ, דְּמִינְכַּר דְּעַל מֵת אַחֵר קָרַע: אִשָּׁה שׁוֹלַלְתּוֹ לְאַלְתַּר. אֲפִילּוּ תּוֹךְ שִׁבְעָה: הָכִי נַמִּי. דְּמוֹסִיף דְּקוֹרֵעַ הַשְּׁלִילָה, וּמוֹסִיף בָּהּ פּוּרְתָּא דְּקָא מִינְכַּר. וְקָא פָּסֵיק: כָּל שִׁבְעָה קוֹרֵעַ, וַאֲפִילּוּ אִשָּׁה: מִשּׁוּם כְּבוֹד הָאִשָּׁה הוּא. וְלָא מִן הַדִּין: מִשּׁוּם כְּבוֹד אָבִיו. וְלָא מִן הַדִּין וְהָוֵי כְּאִיחוּי, לְפִיכָךְ מוֹסִיף בּוֹ לְאַחַר שְׁלֹשִׁים: בְּבֶגֶד קָרוּעַ. קוֹדֶם לָכֵן, גּוֹזֵל הַכֹּל. שֶׁמְּרַמֶּה הַכֹּל, שֶׁמַּרְאֶה לָהֶן שֶׁקָּרַע עַל הַמֵּת: וְאִם לֹא הוֹדִיעוֹ. שֶׁהוֹלֵךְ לְבַקֵּר אֶת אָבִיו: יַבְרוּהוּ. לְאוֹתוֹ שֶׁבָּא עַל מִטּוֹת כְּפוּיוֹת: אָבֵל — הַהוֹלֵךְ מִמָּקוֹם לְמָקוֹם: יְגַלְגֵּל

וּבְאִיחוּי אלכסנדרי. בירושלמי: איזהו איחוי — כל שאין מקומו ניכר. ובמסכת שמחות (פ"ט) מפרש: כל שאחוהו כל צורכו: **כך** הלוקח אסור לאחותו. לא שמעתי אם מותר למוכרו לנכרי. נהי דלוקח אסור לאחותו — אם הוא נכרי מותר. ואע"פ דמוכר צריך להודיע ללוקח — היינו כדי שלא יעשה לוקח איסור, אבל אין אנו חוששין אם יתפרנו הנכרי, ולכאורה היה מותר.* ועוד צ"ע. והאי וכשם שהמוכר כו' — הוי פי' לתנא קמא בלא הפיכה, ולר"ש בן אלעזר אפילו על ידי הפיכה. ובמאי דפליגי נראה דהלכה כתנא קמא, וכן פירש הר"א:

תחילת קריעה שלש אצבעות. לא ידענא *ממאי מפיק טעמא, דלעיל (ד' כג:) מפקינן טפח מ"ויחזק": אין אחיזה פחות מטפח:

תניא נמי הכי. רבי יוסי סובר כן, ורבי יוסי הלכה כמותו גבי דרבי מאיר ורבי יהודה, בפרק "מי שהוציאוהו" (עירובין ד' מו:). ועוד, דה"ל מכריע: **קורע** קרע אחד על כולן. במסכת שמחות (פ"ט): א"ל מת אביו וקרע, והוא אינו אלא אמו — יצא. מתה אמו, והוא אינו אלא אביו — יצא. מת אביו, מתה אמו, וקרע, והוא אינו אלא אחד מן הקרובין — יצא, אחד מן הקרובין וקרע, והוא אינו אלא אביו או אמו — לא יצא. ובירושלמי: אמרו לו מת ראובן וקרע, ואמרו שמעון היה — יצא. אמרו לו מת ראובן וקרע, ואח"כ אמרו לו קיים היה ומת, אית תנא: לא יצא. וכן קרע על אביו ונמצא בנו. אם מת על אתר — אין צריך לקרוע. כמה הוא על אתר — כדי דבור. ובסוף פרק בתרא דנדרים (דף פז.) כמו כן היא שנויה: **אמר** רב נחמן בר יצחק לפי שאינן בתוספת. תימה: מאי מוסיף לפרש הטעם מן הברייתא? ופירש הר"א בשם רבינו שמואל: דלא גרסינן "לפי שאין מוסיפין" בברייתא. והר"י הקשה בתוספות: מאי שייך בתוספת? נראה לי דמצי למימר דסבירא כמאן דאמר עד טיבורו. אי נמי: עד שיגלה את לבו — אין זה כל כך כמו עד לבו. מיהו, יותר נראה לי: דקאמר רב נחמן בר יצחק לפי שאינן בתוספת — שצריך לקרוע עד לבו, ואם אירע כך שלא קרע עד לבו — מ"מ, כיון דלא עשה כמו שהיה צריך — אומר אין שייך תוספת. מיהו, לפירושו קסבר רב נחמן בר יצחק כיש אומרים עד לבו. ואפילו למאן דאמר בסמוך עד טיבורו — יש ליישב כמו שפי', שאין צריך לקרוע על אביו ועל אמו רק עד שיגלה את לבו, מכל מקום אם קרע טפי — שפיר, משום כבוד אביו, ואין כאן "בל תשחית": **פורם** מלמטה. בפ' בתרא דהוריות (ד' יב:) מפרש מה קורע למטה, אם בצואר: **לפי** שאין מוסיפין על אביו ואמו. פי' בקונטרס: דאכולהו קאי, דבין אם קרע על אביו קודם, בין קרע על אחד מקרוביו קודם. ולא ידענא מנא ליה, דלישנא משמע דוקא על קרע אביו ואמו שהיה קודם: אם

רבינו חננאל

על ירושלים: ת"ר רשאי להופכו למטה ולעשות לו איחוי. פי' להפך החלוק לחתכו ולתת בית הצואר שלו שולים והשולים יעשה בית שפה. ר' שמעון בן אלעזר אומר באיחוי בין מלמעלן בין מלמטה. וכשם שהבעלים אסורין לאחותו כן הלוקח אסור לאחותו. לפיכך צריך המוכר להודיע ללוקח שזה קרע אסור באיחוי הוא. ת"ר וכולן אלו הקרעין רשאין לשוללן למוללן ללוקטן ולעשותן בתפירה אחת כעין סולמות שיהא ניכר הקרע. אבל אין רשאין לאחותן באיחוי אלכסנדרית שהוא כמין אריגה. ת"ר הקורע מתוך השלל או מתוך המלל או מתוך הליקוט או מתוך הסולמות לא יצא. אבל אם היה איחוי אלכסנדרית שהוא כארינה יצא ידי קריעה: **ירושלמי** כד דמך ר' יוחנן אורי ר' חייא בר אבא לשלול הקרע בו ביום ולנעול הסנדל בו ביום. א"ל ר' תנחום בר חייא לר' חוננא בר פפא ר' צלי עלן. א"ל יסוג תודעתך שכל אותה שנה הדין מתוח כנגד המשפחה דא"ר יוחנן כל שבעה החרב שלופה עד שלשים יום. ומשלשים ועד י"ב חדש אינה רופפת ואינה חוזרת לתערה עד י"ב חודש. למה"ד לכיפת אבנים שנתרועעה אחת מהן נתרועעו כולן. א"ר אלעזר אם נולד להן בן באותה משפחה נתרפאת כל המשפחה כולה: **ת"ר** תחלת הקריעה טפח ואם קרע על המת ועוד מת לו מת אחר ובא לקרוע ולהוסיף על הקרע מוסיף ג' אצבעות דברי ר' מאיר *) ותחלת קריעה ג' אצבעות ותוספת כל שהו. אמר עולא הלכה כר' מאיר בקריעה שתחלת קריעה טפח. והלכתא כר' יהודה בתוספת דדי לו אפילו כל שהו. תניא נמי הכי ר' יוסי אומר תחלת הקריעה טפח ותוספת כל שהו: **ת"ר** מת אביו וקרע. מת בנו והוסיף תחתיו מתאחה. עליון אין מתאחה. מת בנו וקרע מת אביו והוסיף מה... בן בתירה אומר על כולן כגון בנו ובתו אחיו ואחותו ואשתו קורעין להן קרע אחד על אביו ועל אמו קורע קרע אחר. לפי שאין מוסיפין על קרע אביו ואמו פי' לפי שאינו בתוספת מ... אביו ועל אמו מבדיל קמי שפה שלו וקורע והולך עד שמגיע הקרע אל לבו ומגלה. ובשאר מתים קורע טפח ומוסיף כל שהו עד שמגיע אל לבו. ואע"פ שאין ראייה ברורה אשכחן זכ... וקרעו לבבכם ואל בגדיכם. אמר שמואל הלכה כר' יהודה בן בתירה. איני והאמר שמואל הלכה כדברי המיקל באבל. ור' יהודה לגבי ת"ק מחמיר הוא. ופרקינן כי קאמר שמואל בע... ענין קריעה הוא. הלכך הלכתא כר' יהודה בן בתירה. עד היכן קורע עד טיבורו הגיע לטיבורו מרחיק ג' אצבעות וקורע. נתמלא מלפניו מחזירו מלאחוריו נתמלא מלמעלה הופכו למט... מהפך ועושה שולי חלוקו בית הצואר וקורע למעלה. והקורע מלמטה מן השוליים ומן הצדדין לא יצא. אלא שכ"ג פורם מלמטה. פליגי **) עליה משמיה דאבוה דשמואל ולוי. חד אמר ... לאחר שבעה אם מת לו מת אחר מוסיף על הקרע הראשון כל שהו. וחד אמר כל שלשים יום אם ימות לו מת אחר קורע [קרע] אחר לאחר ל' יום מוסיף. מתקיף ליה ר' זירא מאן דאמר ... אמאי אינו מוסיף דלא ניתן לשוללו בתוך ז'. אלא קרע של אשה ששוללתו לאלתר הכי נמי שמוספת לאלתר. ופרקינן התם משום כבוד אשה. מ"ד כל ל' יום אם קורע אמאי כו': ת"ר ה... לפני המת הרי זה גוזל את החיים ואת המתים רשבג"א האומר לחבירו השאליני חלוקך כדי שאלך ואבקר את אבי שהוא חולה. ומצאו שמת קורעו. וכשיבא לביתו מאחו. ומחזירו ... דמי קרעו. ואם לא הודיעו כי הולך לבקר את אביו לא יגע בו. ת"ר חולה שמת לו מת אין מודיעין אותו שמא תטרף דעתו של חולה ואין מקרעין לו ומשתקין הנשים מפניו ומקרעי... אביו שמת או על אמו. וכיוצא בהן מפני עגמת נפש. וקורע על חמיו ועל חמותו מפני כבוד אשתו: תנא באבל רבתי אבל לא יניח תינוק בחיקו מפני הרבים מפני שמביאו לידי שחוק ו... הבריות. ואין מברין אלא על מטות זקופות. ת"ר ההולך לבית האבל אם היה לבו גס בו יברוהו על מטות כפויות. ואם לאו יברוהו על מטות זקופות. רבא איתרע ליה מלתא דאבלות על לגביה רבה וזקי... על אבא בר מרתא וכפה. אמר לית ביה דעתא [להאי צורבא] מרבנן דכפה דהא אין לבי גס בו. ת"ר אבל ההולך ממקום למקום אם יכול למעט בעסקו כלומר שלא יקנה ולא ימכור [ימעט]. ואם לאו י...

*) חסר כאן וצ"ל ר"י אומר תחלת קריעה ג' אצבעות וכו'. **) נ"ל פליגו בה רב מתנה וכו' משמיה דאבוה דשמואל וכו'.

עין משפט נר מצוה:
קצט א מיי' פ"ט מהל' אבל הלכה ג:
ר ב ג מיי' שם סמג עשין ב טוש"ע י"ד סי' שמ סעיף כ:
רא ד ה מיי' שם והלכה ד סמג שם טוש"ע שם סעיף יט:
וכמס' שמחות ספ"ט איתא לאסור
רב ו מיי' שם פ"ח הלכה ב ג סמג שם טוש"ע שם סעיף ג:
[עי' כלים פכ"ז מ"ב ומ"ו] אולי צ"ל פכ"ז
רג ז ח מיי' שם הלכה ט טוש"ע שם סעיף כב:
רד ט מיי' שם הלכה י טוש"ע שם סעיף כג:
רה י מיי' שם הלכה א טוש"ע שם סעיף ג:
רו כ מיי' שם ופ"ז הלכה ו סמג שם וסמג לאוין קא ומיי' פ"ה מהל' כלי המקדש הלכה ז:
רז ל מיי' פ"ח מהלכות אבל הלכה י סמג עשין ב טוש"ע י"ד סי' שמ סעיף כח:
רח מ מיי' שם הלכה ו סמג שם טוש"ע שם סעיף לג:
רט נ מיי' שם הלכה ז טוש"ע שם סעיף לד:
רי ס מיי' שם הלכה ד טוש"ע שם סי' שלה:
ריא ע מיי' שם הלכה ה טוש"ע שם סי' שמ סעיף ז:
ריב פ מיי' פ"ה הלכה כ טוש"ע שם סי' שלה סעיף ג: וסי' שנח סעיף ח:

מסורת הש"ס:
תורה אור
לעיל יח. וש"נ עירובין מו.
יואל ב
לעיל כב:
שמחות פ"ט
שם [תוספתא כ"מ פ"ח]
לעיל יז:
אלא

רש"י

יגלגל עמהן. ואינו עושה סחורה בפני עצמו, אלא עם חבורה: אף על גב שאין לו. לאבל אחר השבת אלא יום אחד: קרביטיו. רצועותיו, שהוא כעין תרניפני"א: ערסא דגדא. מטה שמייחדים אותה למזל טוב, ואין משתמשין בה כלום, אלא מייחדין אותה לשרות מזל טוב עליה: דצלא. עור: סירוגו מתוכו. מכניס רצועות מן חורי עצי המטה: על גבה. והעור כפול על העץ: נקליטי. עצים זוקפין מתוקנין למראשותיו ולמרגלותיו, ונותנין עץ ארוך עליהן, ונותן הסדינין עליהם לשמור מהזבובים: אין מברכין. על הריח בבית האבל: המנחמין. קרוביו, מביאין עניינים של אוכלין: מתני' אסקוטלא. תמחוי: פוטרין את הרבים. שאומרים למנחמין: לכו לבתיכם: אין מניחין מטה במועד ברחוב. להספידו: ולא של נשים לעולם. ששופעות זיבה: גמ' בכליכה

גמרא

אם יכול למעט בעסקו — ימעט, ואם לאו — יגלגל עמהן. תנו רבנן: *מאימתי כופין את המטות? משיצא מפתח ביתו, דברי ר' אליעזר. רבי יהושע אומר: *משיסתם הגולל. מעשה שמת רבן גמליאל הזקן, כיון שיצא מפתח ביתו אמר להם רבי אליעזר: כפו מטותיכם. וכיון שנסתם הגולל, [אמר להם רבי יהושע: כפו מטותיכם.] אמרו לו: כבר כפינו על פי זקן. ת"ר: מאימתי זוקפין את המטות בערב שבת — מן המנחה ולמעלה. אמר רבה בר הונא: אף על פי כן, אינו יושב עליה עד שתחשך. ולמוצאי שבת, אע"פ שאין לו לישב אלא יום אחד — חוזר וכופה. תנו רבנן: הכופה מטתו, לא מטתו בלבד הוא כופה, אלא כל מטות שיש לו בתוך ביתו הוא כופה. ואפילו יש לו עשר מטות בעשרה מקומות כופה את כולן, ואפילו חמשה אחין ומת אחד — כולן כופין. ואם היתה מטה המיוחדת לכלים — אין צריך לכפותה. דרגש — אין צריך לכפותו, אלא זוקפו. רבן שמעון בן גמליאל אומר: דרגש, מתיר את קרביטיו והוא נופל מאיליו. *מאי דרגש? אמר עולא: ערסא דגדא. אמר ליה רבה: אלא מעתה גבי מלך, *דתנן: כל העם מסובים על הארץ והוא מיסב על הדרגש, מי איכא מידי דעד האידנא לא אותביניה — והשתא מותבינן ליה? מתקיף לה רב אשי: מאי קושיא? מידי דהוה אאכילה ושתיה, דעד האידנא — לא אוכליניה ולא אשקיניה, השתא — אוכליניה ואשקיניה! אלא, אי קשיא — הא קשיא: (*דתנן,) דרגש אינו צריך לכפותו אלא זוקפו, ואי ערסא דגדא — אמאי אינו צריך לכפותו? הא (*תנן:) *)הכופה מטתו — לא מטתו בלבד הוא כופה, אלא כל מטות שיש לו בתוך ביתו כופה! ומאי קשיא? מידי דהוה אמטה המיוחדת לכלים, דתניא: אם היתה מטה המיוחדת לכלים — אינו צריך לכפותה! אלא, אי קשיא הא קשיא: רבן שמעון בן גמליאל אומר: דרגש, מתיר קרביטיו והוא נופל מאיליו. ואי סלקא דעתך ערסא דגדא — מאי קרביטין אית ליה? *כי אתא רבין אמר ליה ההוא מרבנן, ורב תחליפא בר מערבא שמיה, דהוה שכיח בשוקא דגילדאי: מאי דרגש — ערסא דצלא. [א]איתמר נמי, אמר ר' ירמיה: דרגש — סירוגו מתוכו, מטה — סירוגה על גבה. אמר רבי יעקב בר אחא אמר רבי יהושע בן לוי: *הלכה כרבן שמעון בן גמליאל. (*איתמר נמי,) אמר רבי יעקב בר אחא אמר רבי אסי: מטה שנקליטיה יוצאין — זוקפה, ודיו. *תנו רבנן: ישן על גבי כסא, על גבי *אודייני גדולה,[ב] על גבי קרקע — לא יצא ידי חובתו. אמר רבי יוחנן: שלא קיים כפיית המטה. תנו רבנן: מכבדין ומרביצין בבית האבל, ומדיחין קערות וכוסות וצלוחיות וקיתוניות בבית האבל, ואין מביאין את המוגמר ואת הבשמים לבית האבל. איני: והא תני בר קפרא: אין מברכין לא על המוגמר ולא על הבשמים בבית האבל. ברוכי הוא דלא מברכין, הא אתויי — מייתי! לא קשיא; הא — בבית האבל, הא — בבית המנחמין.§

מתני' אין מוליכין לבית האבל לא בטבלא ולא באסקוטלא ולא בקנון, אלא בסלים. ואין אומרים ברכת אבלים במועד, אבל עומדין בשורה, ומנחמין, ופוטרין את הרבים. אין מניחין את המטה ברחוב שלא להרגיל את ההספד. ולא של נשים לעולם, מפני הכבוד.§

גמ' תנו רבנן: בראשונה היו מוליכין בבית האבל, עשירים — בקלתות של כסף ושל זהב, ועניים — בסלי נצרים של ערבה קלופה. והיו עניים מתביישים, התקינו שיהו הכל מביאין בסלי נצרים של ערבה קלופה, מפני כבודן של עניים. תנו רבנן: בראשונה היו משקין בבית האבל, עשירים — בזכוכית לבנה, ועניים — בזכוכית צבועה, והיו עניים מתביישין. התקינו שיהו הכל משקין בזכוכית צבועה, מפני כבודן של עניים. בראשונה היו מגלין פני עשירים ומכסין פני עניים, מפני שהיו מושחרין פניהן מפני בצורת, והיו עניים מתביישין. התקינו שיהו מכסין פני הכל, מפני כבודן של עניים. *בראשונה היו מוציאין עשירים בדרגש, ועניים בכליכה

תוספות

אם יכול למעט בעסקו ימעט. פירש בקונטרס: בסחורתו. ונראה דבדבר האבד קאמר, וכן פי' לעיל (ד' כב.) גבי "על כל המתים כולן רצה ממעט בעסקו רצה אינו ממעט". וגם הרב פירש לעיל בדבר האבד עושה בצנעא בתוך ביתו. נראה לפירושו דהכא איירי באביו ואמו, ומשום דהולך בדרך – התירו לו שיגלגל עמהם אם אינו יכול למעט. דבשאר מתים אינו ממעט כלל אם אינו רוצה. ואי איירי הכא בשאר מתים – צריך לומר להפך: הולך בדרך ואינו נוהג אבילות כל כך, ומתנחם יותר – אסור להרבות בעסקו יותר מאותו שיושב בביתו ואינו מתנחם. וה"ר יוסף פירש: דהכא ימעט בעסקו – לקנות צורכי סעודה, ולפי שהולך בדרך רגיל לקנות צורכי סעודה יותר מבביתו, שיש לו קונים עבורו, וגם מוצא בביתו הרבה. משום הכי נקט הולך בדרך. ומה שפירש בקונטרס דאיירי כשאמרו לו על מיתת קרוביו כשהיה בדרך – לא ידענא אי בעי למימר דאיירי במוליך סחורתו ממקום למקום כדפי' בקונטרס, ור"ל דשמא שרי ליה לדידיה למכור סחורתו, דכיון דהוליך אותה כבר וטרח בה ולא פשע בהליכתו, שלא היה יודע לישב בביתו שיכול לשומרה, או שמא הקונטרס ר"ל משום דאמרינן לעיל (דף כג.) שבת ראשונה אינו יוצא מפתח ביתו. וזה אינו קושיא, דאע"פ שאינו יוצא מפתח ביתו בעיר – הא אמרינן (לעיל דף טו:): יצא לדרך (*חולך ונכנס לעיר). אלמא: מותר לצאת (בו). ושמא דוקא בדבר האבד מותר לצאת לדרך: מן המנחה ולמעלה. פי' בתוספות הרב: דמספקא ליה אי מנחה גדולה אי מנחה קטנה, דמקודם לכן אינו יושב עליה. נראה לי, דמכאן סמכו שלא לישב ע"ג כסא וספסל, אע"פ שאין ראיה גמורה, דשאני מטה הואיל וצריך כפייה, ולא מצינו כפייה בכסא וספסל: ואין מוליכין לבית האבל. זאת המשנה כל כרחין נסדרה בהיפך, ושמא כל זה מן הברייתא דלמעלה, כמו שפירש בתוספות בההיא דלעיל. ותמיהני: מדוע לא פירשו גם כאן כמו שפירש למעלה! ושמא בספר הרב היתה כתובה מגוף הברייתא, ולא הוצרך לפרשו. או לא היה כתוב בספרו כלל: ואין מוליכין כו'. וכן מוכיח מתוך פירוש התוספות שפי': לא ידענא אי קאי האי בראשונה היו מוליכים אמוגמר ובשמים, דאמר אין מברכין. הא אתויי – מייתינן. אי אמתניתין קאי, דקתני: מברין, ואותה הברייתא היא בראשונה מוליכין כו' דאמתניתין קאי. ועוד: כיון שפירש התקינו שיהו הכל מוליכין כו', ומתניתין לאחר תקנה:

עין משפט נר מצוה

ריג א מיי' פ"ו מהלכות אבל הלכה י טוש"ע י"ד סי' שפ סעיף כג:
ריד ב מיי' פ"א שם הלכה ב סמג עשין דרבנן ב טוש"ע שם סי' שעה סעיף א:
רטו ג ד ה מיי' שם פ"י הלכה ב טור י"ד סי' ת:
רטז ו ז ח מיי' שם פ"ה הלכה יח טור י"ד סי' שפז:
ריז ט מיי' שם פ"ז הלכה א ופ"ב מהלכות מלכים הלכה ד:
ריח י מיי' פ"ה מהל' אבל הלכה יח טור י"ד שם:
ריט כ ל מיי' פי"ג שם הלכה ו סמג עשין שם טוש"ע שם סי' שעח סעיף ז:
רכ מ טוש"ע שם:
רכא נ מיי' שם הלכה ז טי"ד סי' תא:
רכב ס מיי' שם פי"א הלכה ג טי"ד שם:
רכג ע מיי' שם ופ"ו מהלכות י"ט הלכה כג טוש"ע י"ד סי' תא סעיף א וטוש"ע א"ח סי' תקמז סעיף א:
רכד פ מיי' שם פי"ב הלכה ה טוש"ע שם סי' שנה:
רכה צ ק מיי' שם פי"ג הלכה ז טי"ד סי' שעח:
רכו ר מיי' שם פ"ד הלכה א טוש"ע שם סי' שנג סעיף א:

[נ"ל נועל נכנס לעיר חולך]

רש"א מ"ז וגורס ואמר

מסורת הש"ס

שמחות פי"א
כתובות ד: סנהדרין מז: שבת קנב:
רש"א
סנהדרין כ. ע"ש
נדרים נו. ע"ש סנהדרין שם
[נ"ל דתניא]
[נ"ל תניא]
*) ג"ז שם תענית לג: נדרים שם
נדרים נו. סנהדרין כ. ע"ש
נדרים נו: סנהדרין כ: ע"ש
עי' תוס' כ"ב קמב. ד"ה אודייני
[תוספתא נדה פ"ט]

הגהות הגר"א

א] גמ' ערסא דצלא. אמר ר' כו' כצ"ל. ומלות אתמר נמי ליתא בסנהד' ועי' הגירסא נדרים: [ב] שם גדולה מזו ע"ג כו' כצ"ל:

רבינו חננאל

יקנה צרכי הדרך ודברי' שיש בהן חיי נפש: ת"ר מאימתי כופין המטות משיוציאו המת מן הבית. דברי ר' אליעזר ר' יהושע אומר משיסתם הגולל. וקיי"ל כר' יהושע דאין אבילות נוהגת אלא משיקבר המת ויסתום הגולל: ת"ר הכופה מטתו לא מטתו בלבד הוא כופה אלא כל מטות שיש בבית. ואפילו יש לו עשר מטות בעשר מקומות כופה את כולן. ואפילו ה' אחין ומת אחד מהן כולן כופין. ואם היתה מיוחדת לכלים ואינה עשויה לישן אין צריך לכפותה. דרגש א"צ לכפותו אלא זוקפו ודיו ואמר עולא האי דרגש ערסא דגדא הוא פירוש מטה העשויה לכבוד מזל הבית ואין אדם ישן עליה. ונדחו
בריו. ואסיקנא דרגש הוא ערסא דצלא. פירוש מטה של עור. כי פי' צלא עור הוא עור נטוי וקשור בחבלים על המלבנות ומסורגות מלבנות המטה בחבלים הללו והעור בתוכן. וכיון שמעמידין אותה ישנין ג העור. ואמר רשב"ג דרגש מתיר קרביטין והוא נופל. אתמר נמי א"ר ירמיה דרגש סירוגו מתוכו. מטה שנקליטיה יוצאין זוקפה ודיו. כלומר אינו צריך לכפותה: ת"ר מאימתי זוקפין את המטות בע"ש ן המנחה ולמעלה. ואעפ"כ אסור לו לישן עליה עד שתחשך. ובמו"ש אע"פ שלא נשאר לו משבעת ימי אבלו אלא יום אחד בלבד חוזר וכופה מטותיו: ת"ר ישן ע"ג מטה. וע"ג אודיני. וע"ג ספסל ע"ג קרקע א יצא י"ח. וא"ר יוחנן מפני שלא קיים כפיית המטה: ת"ר מכבדין ומרביצין ומדיחין את הקערות כוסות וקיתוניות וצלוחיות בבית האבל. ואין מביאין מוגמר בבית האבל. ואוקימנא הא דתני בר קפרא ין מברכין על המוגמר ועל הבשמים של בית האבל בהני דמייתי בבית המנחמין: מתני' אין אומרים ברכת אבלים במועד. אבל עומדין בשורה ומנחמין ופוטרין את הרבים: ת"ר בראשונה היו מוליכין בית האבל עשירים בקלתות של כסף ושל זהב ועניים בסלי נצרים כו' וכן היו משקין בבית האבל את העשירים בזכוכית לבנה. ואת העניים בזכוכית צבועה וכו'. וכן היו מגלין את מתין העשירים. והיו מכסין את פני העניים שהיו שחורין מן הרעב וכו' וכן היו מוציאין מתי עשירים ברדגש ועניים בכליכה כו'. ובכל אלו היו העניים מתביישין. התקינו חכמים לעשות לעשירים כדרך שהן עושין לעניים שלא יהא

בְּכְלִיכָה, וְהָיוּ עֲנִיִּים מִתְבַּיְּישִׁין, הִתְקִינוּ שֶׁיְּהוּ הַכֹּל מוֹצִיאִין בִּכְלִיכָה, מִפְּנֵי כְּבוֹדָן שֶׁל עֲנִיִּים. בָּרִאשׁוֹנָה הָיוּ מַנִּיחִין אֶת הַמּוּגְמָר תַּחַת חוֹלֵי מֵעַיִם מֵתִים, וְהָיוּ חוֹלֵי מֵעַיִם חַיִּים מִתְבַּיְּישִׁין, הִתְקִינוּ שֶׁיְּהוּ מַנִּיחִין תַּחַת הַכֹּל, מִפְּנֵי כְּבוֹדָן שֶׁל חוֹלֵי מֵעַיִם חַיִּים. *בָּרִאשׁוֹנָה הָיוּ מַטְבִּילִין אֶת הַכֵּלִים עַל גַּבֵּי נִדּוֹת מֵתוֹת, וְהָיוּ נִדּוֹת חַיּוֹת מִתְבַּיְּישׁוֹת, הִתְקִינוּ שֶׁיְּהוּ מַטְבִּילִין עַל גַּבֵּי כָּל הַנָּשִׁים, מִפְּנֵי כְּבוֹדָן שֶׁל נִדּוֹת חַיּוֹת. בָּרִאשׁוֹנָה מַטְבִּילִין עַל גַּבֵּי זָבִין מֵתִים, וְהָיוּ זָבִין חַיִּים מִתְבַּיְּישִׁין. הִתְקִינוּ שֶׁיְּהוּ מַטְבִּילִין עַל גַּב הַכֹּל, מִפְּנֵי כְּבוֹדָן שֶׁל זָבִין חַיִּים. *בָּרִאשׁוֹנָה הָיְתָה הוֹצָאַת הַמֵּת קָשָׁה לִקְרוֹבָיו יוֹתֵר מִמִּיתָתוֹ, עַד שֶׁהָיוּ קְרוֹבָיו מַנִּיחִין אוֹתוֹ וּבוֹרְחִין. עַד שֶׁבָּא רַבָּן גַּמְלִיאֵל וְנָהַג קַלּוּת רֹאשׁ בְּעַצְמוֹ וְיָצָא בִּכְלֵי פִשְׁתָּן, [א]וְנָהֲגוּ הָעָם אַחֲרָיו לָצֵאת בִּכְלֵי פִשְׁתָּן. אָמַר רַב פָּפָּא: וְהָאִידָּנָא נְהוּג עָלְמָא אֲפִילּוּ *בְּצַרְדָּא בַּר זוּזָא.§ "אֵין מַנִּיחִין אֶת הַמִּטָּה בָּרְחוֹב".§ אָמַר רַב פָּפָּא: *[ב]אֵין מוֹעֵד בִּפְנֵי תַלְמִיד חָכָם, וְכָל שֶׁכֵּן חֲנוּכָּה וּפוּרִים. [ג]וְהָנֵי מִילֵּי — בְּפָנָיו, אֲבָל שֶׁלֹּא בְּפָנָיו — לֹא. אִינִי? וְהָא רַב כָּהֲנָא סַפְדֵיהּ לְרַב זְבִיד מִנְּהַרְדְּעָא בְּפוּם נַהֲרָא! אָמַר רַב פַּפִּי: [ד]יוֹם שְׁמוּעָה הֲוָה, וְכִבְפָנָיו דָּמֵי. אָמַר עוּלָּא: *הֶסְפֵּד עַל לֵב, דִּכְתִיב: °"עַל שָׁדַיִם סוֹפְדִים", טִיפּוּחַ — בַּיָּד, קִילּוּס — בָּרֶגֶל. תָּנוּ רַבָּנַן: הַמְקַלֵּס — לֹא יְקַלֵּס בְּסַנְדָּל, אֶלָּא בְּמִנְעָל, מִפְּנֵי הַסַּכָּנָה. אָמַר רַבִּי יוֹחָנָן: [ה]אָבֵל, כֵּיוָן שֶׁנִּיעֲנַע רֹאשׁוֹ — שׁוּב אֵין מְנַחֲמִין רַשָּׁאִין לֵישֵׁב אֶצְלוֹ. וְאָמַר רַבִּי יוֹחָנָן: [ו]הַכֹּל חַיָּיבִין לַעֲמוֹד מִפְּנֵי נָשִׂיא, חוּץ מֵאָבֵל וְחוֹלֶה. וְאָמַר ר' יוֹחָנָן: [ז]לַכֹּל אוֹמְרִים לָהֶם "שְׁבוּ" חוּץ מֵאָבֵל וְחוֹלֶה. אָמַר רַב יְהוּדָה אָמַר רַב: [ח]אָבֵל, יוֹם רִאשׁוֹן — אָסוּר לֶאֱכוֹל לֶחֶם מִשֶּׁלּוֹ, מִדְּאָמַר לֵיהּ רַחֲמָנָא לִיחֶזְקֵאל: °"וְלֶחֶם אֲנָשִׁים לֹא תֹאכֵל". רַבָּה וְרַב יוֹסֵף [ט]מְחַלְּפֵי סְעוּדָּתַיְיהוּ לַהֲדָדֵי. וְאָמַר רַב יְהוּדָה אָמַר רַב: [י]מֵת בָּעִיר — כָּל בְּנֵי הָעִיר אֲסוּרִין בַּעֲשִׂיַּית מְלָאכָה. רַב הַמְנוּנָא אִיקְלַע לְדָרוֹמְתָא, שְׁמַע קוֹל שִׁיפּוּרָא דְּשִׁכְבָא. חֲזָא הָנָךְ אֱינָשֵׁי דְּקָא עָבְדִי עֲבִידְתָּא, אֲמַר לְהוּ: לֶיהֱווּ הָנָךְ אֱינָשֵׁי בְּשַׁמְתָּא! לָא שִׁכְבָא אִיכָּא בְּמָתָא? אָמְרוּ לֵיהּ: חֲבוּרָתָא אִיכָּא בְּמָתָא. אֲמַר לְהוּ: [כ]אִי הָכִי — שַׁרְיָא (א)לְכוּ. וְאָמַר רַב יְהוּדָה אָמַר רַב: [ל]כָּל *הַמִּתְקַשֶּׁה עַל מֵתוֹ יוֹתֵר מִדַּאי — עַל מֵת אַחֵר הוּא בּוֹכֶה. הַהִיא אִיתְּתָא דַּהֲוַת בְּשִׁיבָבוּתֵיהּ דְּרַב הוּנָא, הֲווּ לָהּ שִׁבְעָה בְּנֵי. מֵת חַד מִינַּיְיהוּ, הֲוַות קָא בָּכְיָא בִּיתֵירָתָא עֲלֵיהּ. שְׁלַח לָהּ רַב הוּנָא: לָא תַּעַבְדִי הָכִי! לָא אַשְׁגְּחָה בֵּיהּ. שְׁלַח לָהּ: אִי צַיְיתַּת — מוּטָב, וְאִי לָא — צְבִית *זְוָודְתָא לְאִידָךְ מִית. וּמִיתוּ כּוּלְּהוּ. לְסוֹף אֲמַר לָהּ: תִּימוֹשׁ זְוָודְתָא לְנַפְשִׁיךְ, וּמִיתָא. °"אַל תִּבְכּוּ לְמֵת וְאַל תָּנֻדוּ לוֹ", "אַל תִּבְכּוּ לְמֵת" — יוֹתֵר מִדַּאי, "וְאַל תָּנֻדוּ לוֹ" — יוֹתֵר מִכְּשִׁיעוּר. הָא כֵּיצַד? [מ]שְׁלֹשָׁה יָמִים — לִבְכִי, וְשִׁבְעָה — לְהֶסְפֵּד, וּשְׁלֹשִׁים — לְגִיהוּץ וּלְתִסְפּוֹרֶת. מִכָּאן וְאֵילָךְ — אָמַר הַקָּדוֹשׁ בָּרוּךְ הוּא: אִי אַתֶּם רַחֲמָנִים בּוֹ יוֹתֵר מִמֶּנִּי. °"בְּכוּ בָכוֹ לַהוֹלֵךְ", *אָמַר רַב יְהוּדָה: בְּלֹא בָּנִים. רַבִּי יְהוֹשֻׁעַ בֶּן לֵוִי לָא אָזֵל לְבֵי *אֲבִילָא אֶלָּא לְמַאן דְּאָזֵיל בְּלָא בְּנֵי, דִּכְתִיב: "בְּכוּ בָכוֹ לַהוֹלֵךְ כִּי לֹא יָשׁוּב עוֹד וְרָאָה אֶת אֶרֶץ מוֹלַדְתּוֹ". רַב הוּנָא אָמַר: זֶה שֶׁעָבַר עֲבֵירָה וְשָׁנָה בָּהּ. רַב הוּנָא לְטַעְמֵיהּ, *דְּאָמַר רַב הוּנָא: כֵּיוָן שֶׁעָבַר אָדָם עֲבֵירָה וְשָׁנָה בָּהּ — הוּתְּרָה לוֹ. הוּתְּרָה לוֹ סָלְקָא דַּעְתָּךְ?! אֶלָּא אֵימָא: נַעֲשֵׂית לוֹ כְּהֶיתֵּר. אָמַר רַבִּי לֵוִי: [נ]אָבֵל שְׁלֹשָׁה יָמִים הָרִאשׁוֹנִים — יִרְאֶה אֶת עַצְמוֹ כְּאִילּוּ חֶרֶב מוּנַּחַת לוֹ בֵּין שְׁתֵּי (*יְרֵיכוֹתָיו,) מִשְּׁלֹשָׁה עַד שִׁבְעָה — כְּנֶגְדּוֹ בְּקֶרֶן זָוִית, מִכָּאן וְאֵילָךְ — כְּאִילּוּ עוֹבֶרֶת כְּנֶגְדּוֹ בַּשּׁוּק.§ "וְלֹא שֶׁל נָשִׁים לְעוֹלָם מִפְּנֵי הַכָּבוֹד".§ אָמְרִי נְהַרְדְּעֵי: לֹא שָׁנוּ אֶלָּא

רש"י

בְּלִיכָה. מִטָּה שֶׁל מֵתִים: עַל גַּבֵּי נִדּוֹת מֵתוֹת. הַכֵּלִים שֶׁנִּשְׁתַּמְּשׁוּ בָּהֶן בְּעוֹדָן בַּחַיִּים, שֶׁנִּטְמְאוּ בִּנְגִיעָתָן. שֶׁהַנִּדָּה מְטַמְּאָה בִּנְגִיעָתָהּ אָדָם וְכֵלִים: וְהָיוּ נִדּוֹת חַיּוֹת מִתְבַּיְּישׁוֹת. שֶׁעוֹשִׂין בָּהֶן מַה שֶּׁאֵין עוֹשִׂין לִשְׁאָר מֵתוֹת: קָשָׁה לִקְרוֹבָיו. בְּתַכְרִיכִין טוֹבִים: צַרְדָּא. קַנְבּוֹס: בַּר זוּזָא. הַנִּקְנֶה בְּזוּז: אֵין מוֹעֵד לִפְנֵי חֲכָמִים. שֶׁיְּכוֹלִין לְהַסְפִּידוֹ: עַל לֵב. מְטַפֵּחַ כְּנֶגֶד הַלֵּב: בְּיָד. קוֹפֵץ יָד זוֹ לְזוֹ: בְּרֶגֶל. מַכֶּה רַגְלוֹ בַּקַּרְקַע: מִפְּנֵי הַסַּכָּנָה. שֶׁהוֹפֵךְ הַסַּנְדָּל וְשׁוֹבֵר רַגְלוֹ: נִיעֲנַע רֹאשׁוֹ. שֶׁנִּרְאֶה שֶׁנִּיחַם מֵעַצְמוֹ: לַכֹּל אוֹמְרִים שְׁבוּ. כְּשֶׁעוֹמְדִין לִפְנֵי הַנָּשִׂיא: חֲבוּרְתָא אִיכָּא. חֲבוּרוֹת הֵן, שֶׁאֵלּוּ קוֹבְרִין מֵתִים שֶׁלָּהֶם לְבַדָּם וְאֵלּוּ קוֹבְרִין מֵתִים שֶׁלָּהֶם לְבַדָּם: וְלֹא יָשׁוּב עוֹד וגו'. מַשְׁמַע: מִכָּאן וְאֵילָךְ לֹא יַעֲשֶׂה לְעוֹלָם תְּשׁוּבָה: אֶלָּא

תורה אור

תוספות

בכליכה . גרס בערוך, בשני כפי"ן, ואית דגרסי כליכה בבי"ת השניה, כמו: הללו חוזרין לכלובן (ביצה דף כה.), וכמו "ככלוב מלא עוף" (ירמיה ה), אי נמי כמו "מכליב" (לעיל דף י.). ופירש הקונטרס: כעין סולם, והיינו כעין תפירות רחוקות זו מזו, ומביא הא דאמרינן במדרש: נטלו את הכרובים ונתנום בכליכה. ואם כן צריך לגרוס בפיוט של חרבן בית המקדש בתשעה באב: עמון ומואב הוציאו את הכרובים, וכליכה היו בם מסובבים. וגרס בב' כפי"ן לגירסת הערוך. וכל זה — שלא לבייש מי שאין לו. וכן איתא במסכת בכורים (פ"ג מ"ז): בראשונה מי שהיה יודע לקרו' כו'. ומאותה ההלכ' ◦מביאין ראיה להא דאמר: שמנה פסוקים שבתורה יחיד קורא אותם, דלא בעי למימר שלא יקרא שליח צבור עמו. כי בימיהם לא היה קורא שליח צבור עם הקורא. ומה שרגילים עתה לקרות — זהו מפני כבודו של קורא, שלא לבייש מי שאינו יודע. וכדאמר גבי בכורים: בראשונה מי שהיה יודע לקרות — קורא, ומי שאינו יודע לקרות (אינו קורא) — מקרין אותו. נמנעו מלהביא בכורים, התקינו שיהו מקרין את הכל (בכורים פ"ג מ"ז): **ונהג** קלות ראש בעצמו. שלוה כן בשעת פטירתו. וי"מ: לאחד מבני ביתו בחייו. ולשון "בעלמו" משמע כפירוש ראשון:

*__אבל__ לא מטפחות. פירוש: סופק כפיו זו בזו. וא"ת: הא תנן פרק "משילין" (ביצה דף לו:) אין מטפחין ביו"ט, ופי' בקונטרס בפרק "המביא כדי יין" (שם דף ל. בד"ה מרקדין): משום שיר או משום אבל. ומאי איריא בי"ט ומשום שמא יתקן כלי שיר — אפילו בחולו של מועד אסור, משום צער? וצ"ל: דמשום שיר קתני, ולא משום אבל: **טפוח** ביד. כדפרישית: סופק כפיו זו על זו. והכי משמע בהוריות בירושלמי: כשתפס רבי יהודה את ריש לקיש שרי רבי יוחנן טפח בחדא ידיה. [א"ל]: ובחדא ידיה טפחין? כו'. ומספקין, פירש בקונטרס בביצה (דף לו:): כף על ירך. ואם כן "ויספק את כפיו" (במדבר כד) על ירך הן, שתי כפים על שתי ירכים. וצ"ע:

ה"ג ר"ח **לא** יקלס במנעל ולא בסנדל מפני הסכנה. פירוש: דיתף שרי טפי, דנזהר היטב פן ינזק:

ה"ג ר"ח **לכל** אומרים להן שבו חוץ מאבל וחולה. פירוש: תלמידי חכמים שעומדין — צריך לומר שְׁבוּ. אבל וחולה, אפילו עמדו — אין צריך לומר "שבו". דלא די שעמדו, שאין צריכין לעמוד, ואם כן — פשיטא שישבו בלא רשות: **יום** ראשון אסור לאכול משלו. פירשתי למעלה: אפילו אוכל כמה פעמים באותו יום, דלא קתני סעודה ראשונה: **אסורין** בעשיית מלאכה. משמע דבתלמוד תורה שרי, ולא אסור אלא חכם שמת, דבית מדרשו בטל. *מיהו, בשעת הוצאת מת — אז מבטלין ת"ת, כדאמרינן פ' שני דכתובות (דף יז: ושם) ובפ"ק דמגילה (דף ג:): מבטלין ת"ת להוצאת המת ולהכנסת כלה. ומיהו, היכא דאיכא חבורתא — מספקא ליה. ועוד האריך רבי יצחק בתשובה, והביא ראיה מן הירושלמי: **לגיהוץ** ולתספורת. למעלה* פי' ריב"א היה אומר [שגרסינן] לכבוס ולתספורת, ופירש למעלה *) דאשה מותרת בנטילת שער לאחר ז'. ובתוספות פירש דלא ידע מנא ליה: **מכאן** ואילך כאילו עוברת כנגדו בשוק. עד י"ב חדש. והכי איתא בירושלמי: כל שבעה — החרב היא שלופה, עד שלשים — היא רופפת, לאחר י"ב חודש — היא חוזרת לתערה. ולמה הדבר דומה — לכפה של אבנים, כיון שנזדעזעה אחת מהן — נזדעזעו כולם. ובתלמוד דידן נמי אמרינן (שבת דף קה:): אחד מן האחין שמת — ידאגו כל האחין כו':
מה

עין משפט נר מצוה

רכז א מיי' פ"ד מהל' אבל הלכה א טור ש"ע י"ד סי' שנב סעיף א:
רכח ב ג ד מיי' פי"א שם הלכה ה ופ"ו מהלכות ת"ת הלכה כב סמג עשין ב ולאוין עה טוש"ע שם סי' תא סעיף ה:
רכט ה מיי' פי"ג מהל' אבל הלכה ג סמג עשין ב טוש"ע י"ד סי' שעו סעיף א:
רל ו ז מיי' שם הלכה ה סמג שם טוש"ע שם סעיף א בהג"ה וסעיף ב:
רלא ח ט מיי' שם פ"ד הלכה ט סמג שם טוש"ע שם סי' שעח סעיף א:
רלב י כ מיי' שם פי"ד הלכה י סמג שם טוש"ע שם סי' שמג סעי' א וסי' שסא סעיף ב:
רלג ל מ מיי' שם פי"ג הלכה יא סמג שם טוש"ע שם סי' שלד סעיף א:
רלד נ מיי' שם הלכה יב טוש"ע שם סעי' ז:

[מגילה ג: ע"ש]
[תוספתא פ"ב]
שייך למתני' דף כח ע"ב

מסורת הש"ס

נדה עא. [תוספ' נדה פ"ט עי' תוס' שם ד"ה אלא טעמי']
כתובות ח: [תוספתא שם]
[גי' הערוך צדרא ועי' ב"מ נא. דאיתא התם צדרייתא פרש"י בגדי קנבוס]
ישעיה לב
יחזקאל כד
[נ"ל המקשיר הכי איתא בע"י ופרש"י לשון וקשרו מספד]
[פי' תכריכין עי' רש"י עירובין מא; ובנו"ז יז ד"ה בזוודתא]
ירמיה כב
שם
ב"ב קטז. ע"ש
[שם]
יומא פו: פז. ע"ש קדושין כ. מ. סוטה כב. ערכין ל:
[בשאלתות אי' כתיפיו]
[לעיל כב:]
[דף כג. ד"ה כל]
*) [דף יח. בד"ה ובגונסטרי ועי' ברא"ש סי' ק]

הגהות הב"ח

(א) גמ' אי הכי שריא (לכו). תז"מ ונ"ב ס"א להו:

גליון הש"ס

תוס' ד"ה בכליכה וכו' מביאין ראיה להא דאמר ב"ב ד' טו ע"א:

רבינו חננאל

יהא הפרש בין עשירים לעניים: ת"ר בראשונה היו מניחין מוגמר תחת מתים בחולי מעיים כו' וכך היו מטבילין את הכלים ע"ג הנשים שהיו מתות נדות וכו' וכך היו מטבילין הכלים ע"ג המתים כשהן זבין והיו בכל אלו החיים מתביישין התקינו שיהו עושין כן לכל. בראשונה היתה הוצאת המת קשה לקרוביו שהיו מוציאין בתכריכין ממון רב והיתה קשה עליהן הוצאתם יותר ממיתתם עד שהיו מניחין ובורחין עד שבא ר"ג וניהג קלות בעצמו וצוה להוציאו בכלי פשתן ונהגו כל העם לצאת בכלי פשתן כמותו. והאידנא נהוג עלמא אפילו בצררא בר זוזא. פי' בחלוק בר זוזא: **מתני'** אין מניחין במועד את המטה ברחוב שלא להרגיל ההספד. אמר רבה בר רב הונא אין מועד בפני ת"ח וכ"ש חנוכה ופורים אלא מספידין בהן. וה"מ בפניו אבל שלא בפניו לא. ויום שמועה כבפניו דמי ומותר אפילו במועד. אמר עולא הספד על לב. שנאמר על שדים סופדים *) טיפוח ביד. קילוס ברגל שנאמר (יחזקאל ו) הכה בכפך ורקע ברגלך: ת"ר [המקלס] לא יקלס לא במנעל ולא בסנדל מפני הסכנה. א"ר יוחנן אבל כיון שנענע בראשו שוב אין המנחמין רשאין לישב אצלו. ואמר ר"י הכל חייבין לעמוד לפני נשיא חוץ מאבל וחולה. ואמר ר' יוחנן לכל אומר' להן שבו חוץ מאבל וחולה. אמר רב יהודה אמר רב אבל אסור לאכול ביום ראשון משלו שנאמר ולחם אנשים לא תאכל. רבה ורב יוסף בימי אבלם היו מחלפין סעודתן בהדדי. אמר רב יהודה אמר רב מת בעיר כל בני העיר אסורין בעשיית מלאכה עד שינתן לקבורתו. וכל המתקשה על מתו יותר מדאי על מת אחר הוא בוכה. דההוא אתתא דהוו לה ז' בני ומת חד מינייהו והוות מתקשת יותר מדאי. ושלח לה רב הונא ולא אשגחה ביה ומיתו לה כולהו ומתה היא נמי: ת"ר אל תבכו למת יותר מדאי. ואל תנודו לו יותר מכשיעור. הא כיצד ג' לבכי וז' להספד. ל' לגיהוץ ולתספורת מיכן ואילך הרי הוא קישוי. בכו בכה להולך. אמר רב להולך בלא בנים. ר' יהושע בן לוי לא הוה אזיל לבי אבילא אלא אמאן דשכיב בלא בני. כי לא ישוב עוד וראה את ארץ מולדתו. זה שעבר עבירה ושנה בה. מיכן ואילך שאינו מהרהר בתשובה מפני שנעשית לו כהיתר: א"ר לוי אבל ג' ימים הראשונים יראה עצמו כאילו חרב מונחת לו בין כתיפיו. מג' ועד ז' כאילו חרב כנגדו בשוק. מיכן ואילך כאילו חרב מונחת בקרן זוית. ואין מניחין מטה של נשים ברחוב לעולם מפני

*) עי' בערוך ערך טפח ד'.

אלא חיה, אבל שאר נשים – מניחין. ר' אלעזר אמר: אפילו שאר הנשים, דכתיב: "ותמת שם מרים ותקבר שם" – סמוך למיתה קבורה. ואמר ר' אלעזר: אף מרים בנשיקה מתה, אתיא "שם" "שם" ממשה. ומפני מה לא נאמר בה "על פי ה'" – מפני שגנאי הדבר לאומרו. א"ר אמי: למה נסמכה מיתת מרים לפרשת פרה אדומה – לומר לך: מה פרה אדומה מכפרת – אף מיתתן של צדיקים מכפרת. א"ר אלעזר: למה נסמכה מיתת אהרן לבגדי כהונה – מה בגדי כהונה מכפרין – אף מיתתן של צדיקים מכפרת. ת"ר: מת פתאום – זו היא מיתה חטופה, חלה יום אחד ומת – זו היא מיתה דחופה. ר' חנניא בן גמליאל אומר: זו היא מיתת מגפה, שנאמר: "בן אדם הנני לוקח ממך את מחמד עיניך במגפה" וכתיב: "ואדבר אל העם בבקר ותמת אשתי בערב". שני ימים ומת – זו היא מיתה דחויה, ג' – גערה, ארבעה – נזיפה, חמשה – זו היא מיתת כל אדם. א"ר חנין: מאי קרא? "הן קרבו ימיך למות", "הן" – חד, "קרבו" – תרי, "ימיך" – תרי, הא חמשה. "הן" חד – שכן בלשון יווני קורין לאחת "הן". מת בחמשים שנה – זו היא מיתת כרת. חמשים ושתים שנה – זו היא מיתתו של שמואל הרמתי. ששים – זו היא מיתה בידי שמים. אמר מר זוטרא: מאי קרא – דכתיב: "תבא בכלח אלי קבר", "בכלח" בגימטריא שיתין הוו. שבעים – שיבה, שמונים – גבורות, דכתיב: "ימי שנותינו בהם שבעים שנה ואם בגבורות שמונים שנה". אמר רבה: מחמשים ועד ששים שנה – זו היא מיתת כרת. והאי דלא חשיב להו – משום כבודו של שמואל הרמתי. רב יוסף, כי הוה בר שיתין עבד להו יומא טבא לרבנן. אמר: נפקי לי מכרת. א"ל אביי: נהי דנפק ליה מר מכרת דשני, מכרת דיומי מי נפיק מר? א"ל: נקוט לך מיהא פלגא בידך. רב הונא נח נפשיה פתאום, הוו קא דייגי רבנן. תנא להו זוגא דמהדייב: לא שנו אלא שלא הגיע לגבורות, אבל הגיע לגבורות – זו היא מיתת נשיקה. אמר רבא: חיי, בני ומזוני, לא בזכותא תליא מילתא, אלא במזלא תליא מילתא. דהא רבה ורב חסדא תרוייהו רבנן צדיקי הוו, מר מצלי ואתי מיטרא, ומר מצלי ואתי מיטרא. רב חסדא חיה תשעין ותרתין שנין – רבה חיה ארבעין, בי רב חסדא – שיתין הלולי, בי רבה – שיתין תיכלי. בי רב חסדא – סמידא לכלבי ולא מתבעי, בי רבה – נהמא דשערי לאינשי, ולא משתכח. ואמר רבא: הני תלת מילי בעאי קמי שמיא, תרתי יהבו לי, חדא לא יהבו לי; חוכמתיה דרב הונא ועותריה דרב חסדא – ויהבו לי, ענוותנותיה דרבה בר רב הונא – לא יהבו לי. רב שעורים אחוה דרבא הוה יתיב קמיה דרבא, חזייה דהוה קא מנמנם. א"ל: לימא ליה מר דלא לצערן! א"ל: מר לאו שושביניה הוא? א"ל: כיון דאימסר מזלא – לא אשגח בי. א"ל: ליתחזי לי מר. איתחזי ליה. א"ל: הוה ליה למר צערא? א"ל: כי ריבדא דכוסילתא. רבא הוה יתיב קמיה דר"נ, חזייה דקא מנמנם. א"ל: לימא ליה מר דלא לצערן. א"ל: מר לאו אדם חשוב הוא? [א] א"ל: מאן חשיב, מאן ספין, מאן רקיע? א"ל: ליתחזי לי מר. אתחזי ליה. א"ל: ה"ל למר צערא? א"ל: כמישחל בניתא מחלבא. ואי אמר לי הקב"ה זיל בההוא עלמא כד הוית – לא בעינא, דנפיש ביעתותיה. רבי אלעזר הוה קאכיל תרומה, איתחזי ליה.[ב] א"ל: תרומה קא אכילנא, ולאו קודש איקרי? חלפא ליה שעתא. רב ששת איתחזי ליה בשוקא, אמר ליה: בשוקא כבהמה? איתא לגבי ביתא. רב אשי איתחזי ליה בשוקא, א"ל: [ה]איתרח לי תלתין יומין, ואהדרי לתלמודאי. דאמריתו: *) אשרי מי שבא לכאן ותלמודו בידו. ביום תלתין אתא, אמר ליה: מאי כולי האי? קא דחקא רגליה דבר נתן,[ג] ואין מלכות נוגעת בחברתה אפילו כמלא נימא. רב חסדא לא הוה יכיל ליה, דלא הוה שתיק פומיה מגירסא. סליק יתיב בארזא דבי רב, פקע ארזא ושתק ויכיל ליה. ר' חייא לא הוה מצי למיקרבא ליה. יומא חד אידמי ליה כעניא, אתא טריף אבבא, א"ל: אפיק לי ריפתא. אפיקו ליה. א"ל: ולאו קא מרחם מר אעניא? אההוא גברא אמאי לא קא מרחם מר? גלי ליה, אחוי ליה שוטא דנורא, אמצי ליה נפשיה.§ מתני'

ה) [גירסת הערוך איתרח.] ג) [ברכות מח: וש"נ]

*) [פסחים נ. ב"ב י: כתובות עז:]

אלא חיה. שמתה מחמת וולד, שהיא שופעת: מת פתאום. שלא חלה: מחמשים שנה. ולמעלה: והאי דלא חשיב ליה. בהדי כרת: כרת דיומי. שמא ימות מיתה חטופה: פלגא. דמכרת דשני מיהא פלטי לי: מנמנם. גוסס: א"ל. רבא לרב שעורים: לימא מר. למלאך המות דלא לצעורי: שושביניה. דמלאך המות: דאימסר מזליה. איתרע מזליה: ליתחזי לי מר. בתר מיתה: מר לאו אדם חשוב. לימא ליה מר: ספין רקיע. מתוקן למיבעי מיניה: ביעתותיה. דמלאך המות: רגליה דבר נתן. למיהוי נשיא: אמאי לא מרחם. דמתפקדנא למייתי ליה למר בההוא עלמא: אחוי ליה שוטא דנורא. וידע דהוא מלאך המות: מתני'

מה פרה אדומה מכפרת. פירוש: על מעשה העגל. וכדאמרינן במדרש: משל לבן השפחה שטינף פלטירין של מלך, אומר המלך: תבא אמו וכו': **מיתת** אהרן לבגדי כהונה. דכתיב (במדבר כ) "והפשט את אהרן את בגדיו ואהרן יאסף ומת שם", וכן פי' בקונטרס. ואין לפרש מיתת בני אהרן ל"בגדי קדש ילבש" – לפי שאינו סמוך כ"כ: **מה** בגדי כהונה מכפרין. בזבחים כו' (דף פח:): **חטופה** ודחופה. לא ידענא מאי שנא הוא, ומנא ליה: **ואדבר** אל העם בבקר. פי': וחלתה ומתה: **הן** קרבו וכו'. לאו דוקא, דלא אשכחנא למשה היה חולה. וביום מותו כתב הרבה (סוטה יג:), ופסע כמה פסיעות בבת אחת, כדפירש בפירוש חומש: **מת** בחמשים זו היא מיתת כרת. בירושלמי (פ"ב דביכורים) דייק מ"אל תכריתו שבט הקהתי" (במדבר ד), ועבודתם עד חמשים דכתיב (שם ח) "מבן חמשים שנה ישוב מצבא העבודה". ועוד: מימי שנותיו ע' שנה, דל עשרין דלא איענש עליהן – נשתיירו חמשים (כדאי' שבת פט:). ותימה לפי', דהא משמע בשמעתין דבחמשים משנולד קאמר. ועוד: יהא חמשים לאחר שנתחייב כרת, והוא מיתת כל אדם: **ומיתה** בידי שמים בששים. בירושלמי מפיק ממתי מדבר, דאמרינן*: לא מת אחד מהן פחות מבן ששים. וממיתה דהכא משמע זו היא מיתה בידי שמים, וכרת – בחמשים עד ששים, ולא ששים בכלל, וזהו שזרעו נכרת. וי"מ: דחמשים היא מיתה שבידי שמים, וכי איתא בהדי זרעו – הוי כרת, וששים מיתת כל אדם. ובשבת פרק שני (כה. בד"ה כרת) וברים יבמות (ב. בד"ה אשת אחיו) הארכתי: **אלא** במזלא תליא מילתא. והקשו בתוספות, הא דאמרן בסוף שבת (דף קנו. ושם): אין מזל לישראל! וי"ל: דלפעמים משתנה ע"י מזל, כי הנהו דהתם, ופעמים שאין משתנה, כדאמרינן בתענית (דף כה.) גבי רבי אלעזר בן פדת, דא"ל: ניחא לך דאחריב עלמא דאולי אברי' בעידנא דמזוני: **שתין** הלולי. יש מפרשים: לאו דוקא: **ספין**. חשוב, למחר (הוא ו) היא מתה. ואין כל בריה *ספונה (כתובות עב.) פירוש*): חשובה. ובמדרש ילמדנו: אין העובדי כוכבים ספונים כלום, שנא' (ישעיה מ) "כל הגוים כאין נגדו" וכן פירש בערוך*, והביא עדיין ראיות אחרות: **מאן** רקיע. פי': מתוקן ותפור. "ונעלות בלות ומטולאות" (יהושע ט) תרגום: בלן ומרוקעים. "למתפרות כסתות" (יחזקאל יג) תרגומו: דמתטטים רקיעי. חשוך, והוא לשון ישמעאל, חתיכת בגד תפורה על הקרע, בערוך. ועוד הביא, דאמרינן בפ' "לא יחפור" (ב"ב דף כ.): חזי למרקע לבוש. מיהו, יש ספרים כתוב שם "לקרעא":

*) [ועי' בערוך ערך ספן ב]

בלע

רלה א מיי' פי"ב מהל' אבל הלכה ה סמג עשין ב טוש"ע י"ד סי' שנה:

רבינו חננאל

מפני הכבוד. אמרי נהרדעי לא שנו אלא חיה דשכיח טינוף אבל של שאר נשים מניחין ר' אלעזר אומר אפילו של שאר נשים אין מניחין שנאמר ותמת שם מרים ותקבר שם תיכף למיתה קבורה א"ר אלעזר אף מרים בנשיקה מתה. אתיא שם שם כתיב הכא ותמת שם מרים וכתיב וימת שם משה עבד ה' מה משה בנשיקה אף מרים בנשיקה. ומפני מה לא נאמר במיתת מרים על פי ה' מפני שגנאי הדבר לאומרו באשה. א"ר אמי למה נסמכה מיתת מרים לפרשת פרה אדומה מה פרה זו מטהרת חטאים ונקראת חטאת וכל חטאת מכפרת עון כך מיתתן של נשים צדקניות מטהרת ומכפרת עונותיהן של ישראל. וכ"ש מיתתן של צדיקים שמכפרת: **ירושלמי** בתחלת יוה"כ א"ר יודן בר שלום למה נסמכה מיתת אהרן לשבירת הלוחות ללמדך שמיתתן של צדיקים קשה לפני הקב"ה כשבירת הלוחו' כתיב ובני ישראל נסעו מבארת בני יעקן מוסרה שם מת אהרן. וכי אהרן במוסרה מת והלא בהור ההר מת. אלא כיון שמת אהרן נסתלקו ענני הכבוד וכו' ובקשו ישראל לחזור למצרים וחזרו ח' מסעות ורץ שבט לוי והרג מהן ח' משפחות וגם הם הרגו מן הלוים ד' משפחות לעמרמי ליצהרי לחברוני לעוזיאלי כו'. אמרו על מה אירע לנו זה על שלא נתעסקנו בהספדו של צדיק כראוי. מיד ישבו במוסרה והספידו וגמלו לו חסד בהספד כראוי והעלה להן הכתוב כאילו במוסרה מת כו'. א"ר אלעזר למה נסמכה מיתת אהרן לבגדי כהונה לומר לך מה בגדי כהונה מכפרין כדגרסינן (בזבחים דף פ"ח:) אף מיתת אהרן מכפרת: ת"ר מת פתאום זו מיתה חטופה. חלה יום אחד ומת זו מיתה דחופה. ר' חנינא בן גמליאל אומר זו מיתת מגפה שנאמר בן אדם הנני לוקח את מחמד עיניך במגפה וכתיב ואדבר אל העם בבקר ותמת אשתי בערב. חלה יומים ומת זו מיתה דחויה חלה ג' ומת זו מיתת גערה. חלה ד' ומת זו היא מיתת נזיפה. חלה ה' ימים ומת זו היא מיתת כל אדם. שמעינן לה מהאי קרא ויאמר ה' אל משה הן קרבו ימיך למות. קרבו תרי. ימיך תרי הן חד הרי ה' ימים. ואח"כ כתיב למות. מי שמת בן חמשים זו היא מיתת כרת. בן נ"ב זו היא מיתתו של שמואל הרמתי. בן ששים זו היא מיתת כל אדם. א"ר זירא מהאי קרא תבא בכלח אלי קבר. בכל"ח בגימטריא שיתין הוו. בן שבעים שיבה. בן שמונים בגבורות שנא' ימי שנותינו בהם שבעים שנה ואם בגבורות שמונים שנה. אמר רבא מי שמת מחמשים ועד ששים מיתת כרת היא. והא דלא חשיב לה משום כבודו של שמואל הרמתי. רב יוסף כי הוה בר שיתין אמר כבר נפקית מכרת דשני. רב הונא נח נפשיה פתאום. הוו רבנן דייגי טובא. תנא להו זווא דמהדייב פי' שם חכם. לא שנו דמיתת פתאום היא מיתה חטופה אלא במי שלא הגיע לגבורות אבל מי שהגיע לגבורות זו היא מיתת נשיקה. אמר רבא חיי בני ומזוני לאו בזכותא תליא מלתא אלא במזלא. דהא רבה ורב חסדא תרוייהו צדיקי גמורי נינהו מר מצלי ואתי מיטרא ומר מצלי ואתי מיטרא. רב חסדא חי' צ"ב שנה. ורבה חיה מ' שנה. בי רב חסדא שיתין הילולי. בי רבה שיתין תכלי. בי רב חסדא נהמא דסמידא לכלבי. בי רבה [נהמא] דשערי לאינשי לא משתכח אמר רבא תלתא בעאי מקמי שמיא. תרי הבו לי וחד לא הבו לי חכמתיה דרב הונא ועותריה דרב חסדא הבו לי ענוותנותיה דרבה בר רב הונא לא הבו לי. רבה חוה יתיב קמיה דרב נחמן והוה רב נחמן גוסס בעי למינח נפשיה. א"ל בעי רחמי דלא ליצערן מלאכא דמיתותא. א"ל ואנת לאו גברא חשיבא גבי שמיא אנת בעי רחמי עלך א"ל מאן חשוב מן ספון מן רקיע פי' כלומר כיון שנמסר אדם ביד מלאך המות אין שם חשיבותו. א"ל אחרי מיתתו אולי תתראה לי בחלום. ביקש מן הקב"ה כדי שיתראה לו בחלום ונתראה לו. אמר לו היה לך צער בשעת מיתה. א"ל לאו ומשל לו משל כהרמת נימא של שיער מתוך החלב. א"ל אילו היה הקב"ה אומר לי לך חזור וחיי כאשר היית בחייך ואח"כ תמות לא הייתי רוצה שאע"פ שלא היה [לי] צער. אימתו של מה"מ גדולה היא מאד. רבא אתחזי ליה בחלמיה לרב שעורים אחוה. וא"ל הוה לך צערא ואמר לי כי ריבדא דכוסילתא. פי' כמו שריטה ששורטין האומנין בצואר למצוץ דמו. כגון אותו הצער היה לי בעת יציאת הנשמה מן הגוף. רב ששת אתחזי ליה מלאך המות בשוק. א"ל כבהמה איתא לגבי ביתא. רב אסי אתחזי ליה מלאך המות. א"ל אתרח לי ל' יומין דאהדריה לתלמודי. דאמריתו אשרי מי שבא לכאן ותלמודו בידו. ביום שלשים אתא. א"ל מאי כולי האי. א"ל דקא דחקא רגליה דבר נתן:

מתני'

הגהות מהר"ב רנשבורג

א] גמ' א"ל מאן חשיב מאן ספון מאן רקיע. פי' מי הוא חשוב בעיניו ומאן ספון מי הוא אדם ראוי לליסתפו מיניה וחייש לדיבוריה ומאן רקיע מי מתוקן אלנו. מפי' ע"י קטן: ב] שם א"ל תרומה קא אכילנא ולאו קדש איקרי. פי' לאו תרומה אכילנא דאיקרי קודש ואי קטלית לי קא מטמיא וכתיב את משמרת תרומתי שצריך לשומרה בטהרה חלפא ליה שעתא ולא מת באותו פרק. מפי' הנ"ל:

רלו א מיי׳ פ״ו מהלכות י״ט הלכה כ ופי״א מהל׳ אבל הלכה ד סמג עשין ב טוש״ע א״ח סי׳ תקמז סעיף ב וטוש״ע י״ד סי׳ תא סעיף ה:

[כדאיתא ב״ב יז:]

רלז ב ג מיי׳ פי״ג מהלכות אבל הלכה ג סמג עשין ב טוש״ע י״ד סי׳ שעו סעיף א:

[בד״ה אמר ר״נ]

רלח ד מיי׳ פ״ד מהל׳ כלי המקדש הלכה ב טוש״ע א״ח סי׳ קכח סעיף יד בהג״ה וסי׳ רא סעיף ב:

בלע המות. כדי לסיים בדבר הטוב. משום דמועד קטן הוא סוף סדר מועד. ומהר״ט מתרץ הרב רבי יעקב מאורליינ״ש הא דאתחיל סדר נשים בט״ו נשים, אע״ג דאתחיל בפורענותא לא מתחיל, כדאמרינן ב״ש נוחלין" (ב״ב דף קח.)! ותירץ, דסומכין פורענות דמועד קטן אלא פרענות דיבמות, דסמכינן פורענותא לפורענותא ונחמתא לנחמתא*:

צדקיהו מלך יהודה. לדיק גמור היה. *אבל במקרא לא מלינו יותר כי אם שלוה להעלות ירמיהו מן הטיט:

ינחם כתיב. בכתובות (דף סט:*) פירשנו בענין אחר, שלא כפירוש הקונטרס דהכא:

וליטול מנה יפה ראשון. פי׳: יש לישראל ליתן לו. אבל הוא אין לו ליטול, כדאמרינן פ׳ "מקום שנהגו" (פסחים דף נ:): הנותן עיניו בחלק יפה כו׳. מיהו, נראה לי דכהן, כיון שזהו דינו – יכול לראות סימן ברכה. ואע״פ שאומרים בפ׳ "הזרוע" (חולין קלג.): "ונתן". ולא שיטול מעצמו, אין זה לוקח מתנות. כי אם רואה שפיר מה שהוא רוצה ואומר ליתן לו:
[וע׳ תוס׳ גיטין נט: בד״ה וליטול מנה]

הדרן עלך ואלו מגלחין וסליקא לה מסכת מועד קטן

מתני׳ *א נָשִׁים בַּמּוֹעֵד מְעַנּוֹת, אֲבָל לֹא מְטַפְּחוֹת. ר׳ יִשְׁמָעֵאל אוֹמֵר: הַסְּמוּכוֹת לַמִּטָּה מְטַפְּחוֹת. בְּרָאשֵׁי חֳדָשִׁים, בַּחֲנוּכָּה וּבַפּוּרִים – מְעַנּוֹת וּמְטַפְּחוֹת, בָּזֶה וָזֶה – לֹא מְקוֹנְנוֹת. נִקְבַּר הַמֵּת – לֹא מְעַנּוֹת וְלֹא מְטַפְּחוֹת. אֵיזֶהוּ עִינּוּי – שֶׁכּוּלָּן עוֹנוֹת כְּאַחַת, קִינָה – שֶׁאַחַת מְדַבֶּרֶת וְכוּלָּן עוֹנוֹת אַחֲרֶיהָ, שֶׁנֶּא׳ °"וְלַמֵּדְנָה בְנוֹתֵיכֶם נֶהִי וְאִשָּׁה רְעוּתָהּ קִינָה". אֲבָל לֶעָתִיד לָבֹא הוּא אוֹמֵר: °"בִּלַּע הַמָּוֶת לָנֶצַח וּמָחָה ה׳ אֱלֹהִים דִּמְעָה מֵעַל כָּל פָּנִים" וגו׳.§ **גמ׳** מַאי אָמְרָן?

ירמיה ט; ישעיה כה

א]אֲמַר רַב: וַיי לְאָזְלָא, וַיי לַחֲבִילָא. אָמַר רָבָא, נְשֵׁי דְּשַׁכַּנְצִיב אָמְרָן הָכִי: וַיי לְאָזְלָא, וַיי לַחֲבִילָא. וַאֲמַר רָבָא, נְשֵׁי דְּשַׁכַּנְצִיב אָמְרָן: *גּוּד גַּרְמָא מִכַּבָּא, וְנִמְטֵי מַיָּא לְאַנְטִיכֵי. וְאָמַר רָבָא, נְשֵׁי דְּשַׁכַּנְצִיב אָמְרָן: ב]*עֲטוּף וְכַסּוּ טוּרֵי, דְּבַר רָמֵי וּבַר רַבְרְבֵי הוּא. וַאֲמַר רָבָא, נְשֵׁי דְּשַׁכַּנְצִיב אָמְרָן: שַׁיּוּל אִצְטְלָא דְּמֵילְתָא לְבַר חוֹרִין דִּשְׁלִימוּ זְוָודֵיהּ. וַאֲמַר רָבָא, נְשֵׁי דְּשַׁכַּנְצִיב אָמְרָן: ג]רָהֵיט וְנָפֵיל אַמַּעְבְּרָא, וִיזוֹפְתָא יָזֵיף. וַאֲמַר רָבָא, נְשֵׁי דְּשַׁכַּנְצִיב אָמְרָן: ד]אַחָנָא תַּגָּרֵי אַזְבִּזְגֵי מִיבַּדְקוּ. וַאֲמַר רָבָא, נְשֵׁי דְּשַׁכַּנְצִיב אָמְרָן: ה]מוֹתָא כִּי מוֹתָא, וּמַרְעִין – חִיבּוּלַיָּא. *תַּנְיָא, הָיָה ר״מ אוֹמֵר: °"טוֹב לָלֶכֶת אֶל בֵּית אֵבֶל" וגו׳ "עַד וְהַחַי יִתֵּן אֶל לִבּוֹ" דְּבָרִים שֶׁל מִיתָה, דְּיִסְפַּד – יִסְפְּדוּנֵיהּ, דְּיִקְבַּר – יִקְבְּרוּנֵיהּ, דְּיִטְעַן – יִטְעֲנוּנֵיהּ. דְּיִדַל – יִדְלוּנֵיהּ. וְאִיכָּא דְּאָמְרִי: דְּלָא יִדַל – יִדְלוּנֵיהּ, דִּכְתִיב: °"כִּי טוֹב אֲמָר לְךָ עֲלֵה הֵנָּה" וגו׳. ת״ר: כְּשֶׁמֵּתוּ בָּנָיו שֶׁל רַבִּי יִשְׁמָעֵאל נִכְנְסוּ ד׳ זְקֵנִים לְנַחֲמוֹ: ר׳ טַרְפוֹן, וְר׳ יוֹסֵי הַגְּלִילִי, וְר׳ אֶלְעָזָר בֶּן עֲזַרְיָה, וְר״ע אָמַר לָהֶם ר׳ טַרְפוֹן: דְּעוּ שֶׁחָכָם גָּדוֹל הוּא, וּבָקִי בָּאַגָּדוֹת, אַל יִכָּנֵס אֶחָד מִכֶּם לְתוֹךְ דִּבְרֵי חֲבֵירוֹ. אָמַר ר״ע וַאֲנִי אַחֲרוֹן. פָּתַח רַבִּי יִשְׁמָעֵאל וְאָמַר: רַבּוּ עֲוֹנוֹתָיו, תְּכָפוּהוּ אֲבֵלָיו, הִטְרִיחַ רַבּוֹתָיו פַּעַם רִאשׁוֹנָה וּשְׁנִיָּה. נַעֲנָה ר״ט וְאָמַר: °"וַאֲחֵיכֶם כָּל בֵּית יִשְׂרָאֵל יִבְכּוּ אֶת הַשְּׂרֵפָה", וַהֲלֹא דְּבָרִים ק״ו: וּמָה נָדָב וַאֲבִיהוּא שֶׁלֹּא עָשׂוּ אֶלָּא מִצְוָה אַחַת, דִּכְתִיב: °"וַיַּקְרִיבוּ בְּנֵי אַהֲרֹן אֶת הַדָּם אֵלָיו" – כָּךְ, בָּנָיו שֶׁל ר׳ יִשְׁמָעֵאל – עַל אַחַת כַּמָּה וְכַמָּה. נַעֲנָה ר׳ יוֹסֵי הַגְּלִילִי וְאָמַר: °"וְסָפְדוּ לוֹ כָל יִשְׂרָאֵל וְקָבְרוּ אוֹתוֹ", וַהֲלֹא דְּבָרִים ק״ו: וּמָה אֲבִיָּה בֶּן יָרָבְעָם שֶׁלֹּא עָשָׂה אֶלָּא דָּבָר אֶחָד טוֹב, דִּכְתִיב בֵּיהּ: °"יַעַן נִמְצָא בוֹ דָּבָר טוֹב" – כָּךְ, בָּנָיו שֶׁל ר׳ יִשְׁמָעֵאל – עַל אַחַת כַּמָּה וְכַמָּה. מַאי דָּבָר טוֹב? ר׳ זֵירָא וְר׳ חִינָּנָא בַּר פַּפָּא; חַד אָמַר: שֶׁבִּיטֵּל *מִשְׁמַרְתּוֹ וְעָלָה לָרֶגֶל, וְחַד אָמַר: שֶׁבִּיטֵּל פַּרְדְּסָאוֹת שֶׁהוֹשִׁיב יָרָבְעָם אָבִיו עַל הַדְּרָכִים שֶׁלֹּא יַעֲלוּ יִשְׂרָאֵל לָרֶגֶל. נַעֲנָה ר׳ אֶלְעָזָר בֶּן עֲזַרְיָה וְאָמַר: °"בְּשָׁלוֹם תָּמוּת וּבְמִשְׂרְפוֹת אֲבוֹתֶיךָ הָרִאשֹׁנִים [אֲשֶׁר הָיוּ לְפָנֶיךָ כֵּן] יִשְׂרְפוּ לָךְ", וַהֲלֹא דְּבָרִים ק״ו: וּמָה צִדְקִיָּהוּ מֶלֶךְ יְהוּדָה, שֶׁלֹּא עָשָׂה אֶלָּא מִצְוָה אַחַת, שֶׁהֶעֱלָה יִרְמְיָה מִן הַטִּיט – כָּךְ, בָּנָיו שֶׁל רַבִּי יִשְׁמָעֵאל – עַל אַחַת כַּמָּה וְכַמָּה. נַעֲנָה ר״ע וְאָמַר: °"בַּיּוֹם הַהוּא יִגְדַּל הַמִּסְפֵּד בִּירוּשָׁלַםִ כְּמִסְפַּד הֲדַדְרִימּוֹן [בְּבִקְעַת מְגִדּוֹ".] *וְאָמַר רַב יוֹסֵף: אִלְמָלֵא *תַּרְגּוּמֵיהּ דְּהַאי קְרָא לָא הֲוָה יָדְעֵנָא מַאי קָאָמַר: בְּעִידָּנָא הַהוּא יִסְגֵּי מִסְפְּדָא בִּירוּשְׁלֵם כְּמִסְפְּדָא דְּאַחְאָב בַּר עָמְרִי דִּקְטַל יָתֵיהּ הֲדַדְרִימּוֹן בַּר טַבְרִימּוֹן, וּכְמִסְפַּד דְּיֹאשִׁיָּה בַּר אָמוֹן דִּקְטַל יָתֵיהּ פַּרְעֹה חֲגִירָא בְּבִקְעַת מְגִדּוֹ. וַהֲלֹא דְּבָרִים ק״ו: וּמָה אַחְאָב מֶלֶךְ יִשְׂרָאֵל, שֶׁלֹּא עָשָׂה אֶלָּא דָּבָר אֶחָד טוֹב, דִּכְתִיב: °"וְהַמֶּלֶךְ הָיָה מָעֳמָד בַּמֶּרְכָּבָה נֹכַח אֲרָם" – כָּךְ, בָּנָיו שֶׁל ר׳ יִשְׁמָעֵאל – עַל אַחַת כַּמָּה וְכַמָּה. א״ל רָבָא לְרַבָּה בַּר מָרִי, כְּתִיב בֵּיהּ בְּצִדְקִיָּהוּ "בְּשָׁלוֹם תָּמוּת" וּכְתִיב °"וְאֶת עֵינֵי צִדְקִיָּהוּ עִוֵּר"! א״ל: הָכִי א״ר יוֹחָנָן: שֶׁמֵּת נְבוּכַדְנֶאצַּר בְּיָמָיו. וַאֲמַר רָבָא לְרַבָּה בַּר מָרִי: כְּתִיב בֵּיהּ בְּיֹאשִׁיָּהוּ: °"לָכֵן הִנְנִי אוֹסִפְךָ עַל אֲבוֹתֶיךָ וְנֶאֱסַפְתָּ אֶל קִבְרֹתֶיךָ בְּשָׁלוֹם" וּכְתִיב: °"וַיֹּרוּ הַיֹּרִים לַמֶּלֶךְ יֹאשִׁיָּהוּ"! *וְאָמַר רַב יְהוּדָה אָמַר רַב: שֶׁעֲשָׂאוּהוּ כִּכְבָרָה! א״ל, הָכִי א״ר יוֹחָנָן: שֶׁלֹּא חָרַב בֵּית הַמִּקְדָּשׁ בְּיָמָיו. א״ר יוֹחָנָן: ב]אֵין מְנַחֲמִין רַשָּׁאִין לוֹמַר דָּבָר עַד שֶׁיִּפְתַּח אָבֵל, שֶׁנֶּאֱמַר: *°"אַחֲרֵי כֵן פָּתַח אִיּוֹב אֶת פִּיהוּ" וַהֲדַר "וַיַּעַן אֱלִיפַז הַתֵּימָנִי". *א״ר אֲבָהוּ: ג]מִנַּיִן לְאָבֵל שֶׁמֵּיסֵב בָּרֹאשׁ – שֶׁנֶּאֱמַר: °"אֶבְחַר דַּרְכָּם וְאֵשֵׁב רֹאשׁ וְאֶשְׁכּוֹן כְּמֶלֶךְ בַּגְּדוּד כַּאֲשֶׁר אֲבֵלִים יְנַחֵם". "יְנַחֵם" אַחֲרִינֵי מַשְׁמַע! אָמַר רַב נַחְמָן בַּר יִצְחָק: יְנָּחֵם כְּתִיב. מָר זוּטְרָא אָמַר מֵהָכָא: °"וְסָר מִרְזַח סְרוּחִים", מִרְזַח – נַעֲשָׂה שַׂר לִסְרוּחִים. אָמַר ר׳ חָמָא בַּר חֲנִינָא: מִנַּיִן לְחָתָן שֶׁמֵּיסֵב בָּרֹאשׁ – שֶׁנֶּאֱמַר: °"כֶּחָתָן יְכַהֵן פְּאֵר", מַה כֹּהֵן בָּרֹאשׁ – אַף חָתָן בָּרֹאשׁ. וְכֹהֵן גּוּפֵיהּ מְנָלַן? *דְּתָנָא דְּבֵי ר׳ יִשְׁמָעֵאל: °"וְקִדַּשְׁתּוֹ" – ד]לְכָל דָּבָר שֶׁבִּקְדוּשָּׁה, *לִפְתּוֹחַ רִאשׁוֹן, וּלְבָרֵךְ רִאשׁוֹן, וְלִיטּוֹל מָנָה יָפָה רִאשׁוֹן. א״ר חֲנִינָא: קָשָׁה יְצִיאַת נְשָׁמָה מִן הַגּוּף כְּצִיפּוֹרִי

מתני׳ *בְּלָא פֵּירוּשׁ: **גמ׳** לַחֲבִילָא. חֲבָלָה: גּוּד גַּרְמָא מִכַּבָּא. נָפְלוּ הַלְּחָיַיִם: נִמְטוּ מַיָּא לְאַנְטִיכֵי. כְּלוֹמַר: הָדְרֵי מַיָּא לְמִפְרַע כְּלַפֵּי לְמַעְלָה: שַׁיּוּל אִיצְטְלָא דְּמֵלְתָא. כְּלוֹמַר: יָפָה מִיתָה כְּמַלְבּוּשׁ שֶׁל מֵילַת: דִּשְׁלִימוּ זְוָודֵיהּ. שֶׁכָּלוּ לוֹ מְזוֹנוֹתָיו, שֶׁהוּא עָנִי: עֲטוּף. תורה אור חוּשֶׁךְ: אַזְבְּזְגֵי. קוֹנִים: מוֹתָא. כָּל אָדָם מֵת: (מַרְעָא חֲבִילָא). מַרְעִין חִיבּוּלַיָּא. הַאִיסּוּרִין הֵן בַּבַּיִת: דְּיִדַל יִדְלוּנֵיהּ. כְּלוֹמַר: מַגְבִּיהִין בְּהֶסְפֵּד לְמִי שֶׁמַּגְבִּיהַּ קוֹלוֹ לְהַסְפִּיד אֲחֵרִים: הִטְרִיחַ רַבּוֹתָיו. שֶׁבָּאִין לְנַחֲמוֹ: מִשְׁמַרְתּוֹ. שֶׁהוֹשִׁיב יָרָבְעָם שֶׁלֹּא לַעֲלוֹת לָרֶגֶל: מָעֳמָד בַּמֶּרְכָּבָה. שֶׁלֹּא יִבָּהֲלוּ: יְנַחֵם אֲחֵרִים מַשְׁמַע. שֶׁמְּנַחֲמִין יוֹשְׁבִין בָּרֹאשׁ: סְרוּחִים. לְשׁוֹן רַבִּים: לִפְתּוֹחַ בָּרֹאשׁ. לִקְרוֹת בַּס״ת: וּלְבָרֵךְ. בִּרְכַּת הַמָּזוֹן: כְּלִיפּוֹרִי

פרש״י על כל עמוד זה תמצא בעין יעקב ע״ש

מגילה ג.

[בערוך ערך גד שני נמצא פירוש ע״ש]

נדרים פג: כתובות עב.

קהלת ז

משלי כה

ויקרא י

שם ט

מלכים א יד

שם

[שהשיבו אביו שומר שלא יעלה איש לרגל ובטל משמרתו ועלה. ז״ל רש״י במלכים]

ירמיה לד

זכריה יב

מגילה ג.

[ועי׳ תוס׳ ב״ק ג: ד״ה כדמתרגם]

מלכים א כב

ירמיה לט

מלכים ב כב

דה״ב לה

תענית כב: [סנהדרין מח:]

[ואין דובר וגו׳ וכתיב אחרי כן פתח איוב את פיהו וענו חביריו כך מצאתי הגי׳ בתורת האדם להרמב״ן ז״ל]

איוב ג

כתובות סט.

איוב כט

עמוס ו

ישעיה סא

ויקרא כא

הוריות יב: נדרים סב. גיטין נט:

[עי׳ תוס׳ חולין פז. ד״ה ותיתן]

[כלאס האומר להרים התעטפו והתכסו במלבושכם נאים כי זה האיש הבא להקבר אצלכם בן גדולים הוא. ערוך]

רבינו חננאל

מתני׳ נשים במועד מענות אבל לא מטפחות מאי אמרן. אמר רבא ויי לאזלא ויי לחבלא. פירוש נשי דשכנציב היו חכמות והיו מענות ואומרות אוי להולך כדכתיב כי הולך האדם אל בית עולמו וסבבו וגו׳ ואוי למי שהוא ממושכן ונתבע לשלם הפקדון שאצלו. כלומר האדם מתמשכן להשלים רוחו שהוא אצלו פקדון לבעליה. פי׳ חבלא משכון. פירוש גוד גרמא מכבא ונמטי מיא לאנטוכיא חתוך המאכל מן השיניים ויגיע חמות המים באנטיכי. כלומר כיון שנחתך המאכל מפי החולה בוערת בו חמות ומחממת מי רגליו כחמות אנטיכי. דתנן אנטיכי אע״פ שגרופה אין שותין הימנה מפני שמחממת הרבה. פי׳ שייול אצטלא דמלתא לבר חורי דשלימו זוודיה. כלומר דומה כאצטלא של מילת לבנה לבן טובים שירד מנכסיו. ושלמה הצידה שלו הקבורה טובה לו מחיים. ויש שאומרים מי שאין לו בגדים ללבוש ישאל וילך ללות בן טובים של מת ושלמו ימי חייו. עטוף וכסוי טורי דבר רברבי ובר רמי הוה. פי׳ כמו אדם האומר להרים התעטפו והתכסו במלבושיכם הנאים כי זה האיש הבא להקבר אצלכם בן גדולים הוא. וי״א לבני אדם אומרים התעטפו והתכסו במלבושיכן ועמדו על ההרים וכסו אותן בשעת קבורתו כי בן גדולים ורמים הוא. אחאנא תגרי דעל זבוגי מיבדקי. פי׳ אחינו התגרים שעל קניינם מיבדקי. כלומר במקום סחורתן נבדקין הנאמנים הם אם לאו. כמו שאומרים (בעירובין סה) בג׳ דברים אדם ניכר בכוסו בכיסו ובכעסו. רהיט ונפיל *) בר אודי ואמבדי יוזפתא יזיף. פי׳ רץ בכל כחו ונופל בין האובדים ועל המעברות מלוה לוה. פי׳ כמו משל הוא. כלומר אע״פ שאדם רץ בכל כחו כל ימיו כשנופל בין האובדים בין אובדי הדרכים. או כשיגיע לעבור בנהר מתחנן למי שמעבירו ואם אין לו נוטל בהלואה ואינו מוצא. מותא כי מותא. ומרעא חבוליא. פי׳ המות של זה כמיתת כל אדם. ואריכות חוליו תוספת כמו הרבית על המלוה. שיש מי שפורע חובו היא המלוה שנתנה לו ודיו. ויש מי שפורע **) המלוה היא נשמתו ותוספת על נשמתו צער חליו. תניא היה ר״מ אומר מ״ד טוב ללכת את בית אבל וגו׳ והחי יתן אל לבו דברים של מיתה. דיספד יספדוניה דטעון יטעוניה דידל ידלוניה. איכא דאמרי לא ידל דאדלוניה כדכתיב כי טוב אמר לך עלה הנה מהשפילך לפני נדיב אשר ראו עיניך. כשמתו בניו של ר׳ ישמעאל נכנסו ד׳ זקנים לנחמו. ר׳ יוסי הגלילי. ור׳ אלעזר בן עזריה ור׳ עקיבא ור׳ טרפון. אמר להן ר׳ טרפון ראו כי חכם גדול ובקי בהגדות הוא אל יכנס אחד לתוך דברי חבירו אמר להן ר׳ עקיבא ואני אחרון. פתח ר׳ ישמעאל ואמר רבו עונותיו תכפוהו אבליו הטריח רבותיו פעמים רבות. נענה ר״ט ואמר ואחיכם כל בית ישראל יבכו את השרפה וגו׳ ומה בני אהרן שלא עשו אלא מצוה אחת שנאמר ויקריבו בני אהרן את הדם אליו. בניו של רבי [ישמעאל] עאכו״כ שחייבין כל ישראל לבכותם. ראב״ע אומר שחייבין כל ישראל לבכות מהכא שנאמר בשלום תמות ובמשרפות אבותיך המלכים הראשונים אשר היו לפניך כן ישרפו לך הוי אדון יספדו לך וגו׳ והלא דברים ק״ו ומה צדקיה שלא עשה אלא מצוה אחת שהעלה ירמיה מן הטיט זכה לכך. בניו של ר׳ עאכו״כ. ריה״ג אומר מהכא וספדו לו כל ישראל וקברו אותו כי זה לבדו יבא לירבעם אל קבר יען נמצא בו דבר טוב. והלא דברים ק״ו ומה אביה בן ירבעם שלא עשה אלא דבר אחד שביטל משמרתו ועלה לרגל. וי״א שביטל פרדסאות שהושיב ירבעם שלא יעלו ישראל לרגל כך. בניו של ר׳ שעשו כמה מצות עאכו״כ. ר״ע אומר מהכא ביום ההוא יגדל המספד בירושלם כמספד הדרימון בבקעת מגידו. ואמר רב יוסף אלמלא תרגומא דהאי קרא לא הוינן ידעי מאי קאמר בעידנא ההיא יסגא מספדא בירושלים כמספד אחאב דקטל יתיה הדרימון בן טברימון. וכמספד יאשיהו בן אמון דקטל יתיה פרעה חגירא בבקעת מגידו. ומה זה שלא עשה אלא דבר אחד דכתיב והמלך היה מעמד במרכבה נוכח ארם עד הערב החזיק בעצמו שלא יאמרו גוסס הוא ויברחו ישראל ותחלת נפילה ניסה בניו של ר׳ עאכו״כ שכל ישראל חייב לספוד ולבכות עליהם. א״ל רבא לרבה בר מרי כתיב ביה בצדקיהו בשלום

הגהות מהר״ב רנשבורג

א] גמ׳ אמר רב ויי לאזלא ויי לחבילא. פי׳ אוי לה להליכה כזו שאינה חוזרת ואוי לה למשאוי כזה שנושאים את המת. פ״א אוי להולך לממושכנים עליו: ב] שם עטוף וכסו טורא. פי׳ התעטפו והתכסו ההרים בחשך שבן גדולים ובן גבוהים היה המת הזה: ג] שם רהיט ונפיל אמעברא ויזופתא יזיף. פי׳ רהיט תגר וטרחן היה כל ימיו ועכשיו נפל ריקם בלי ממון אמעברא כשביקש לעבור מן העולם וצריך ללות ממון לתכריכין: ד] שם אחנא תגרי אזבזגי מיבדקו. פי׳ אחינו הסוחרים דאזבזגי מיבדקו באחריתם נראה עשרם כגון זה שאין לו עכשיו במה לקבור ועל מת עני אומרים אותו כדי שירחמו עליו. מע״י קטן: ה] שם מותא כי מותא ומרעין חיבולא. פי׳ דמיתתו היה כמיתת כל אדם שהכל מתים. אמנם מרעין חיבולא שיסורים קשים הו״ל יותר משאר ב״א ג״ז מצאתי בע״י קטן. ונלע״ד לפ״ז דברש״י בד״ה מרעא חבילא וכו׳ צ״ל היסורין הן בבית עכ״ל וכצ״ל ופי׳ דבריו דהיסורים הם בפנים ואינן ניכרין אף דמיתתו היתה שלימה כמיתת אחרים ודו״ק:

בְּצִיפּוֹרֵי בְּפִי הַוּוֹשֶׁט. רַבִּי יוֹחָנָן אָמַר: כְּפִטּוֹרֵי בְּפִי וֶושֶׁט. *וְאָמַר *רַבִּי לֵוִי בַּר חַיְּתָא: הַנִּפְטָר מִן הַמֵּת לֹא יֹאמַר לוֹ "לֵךְ לְשָׁלוֹם" אֶלָּא "לֵךְ [א] בְּשָׁלוֹם" הַנִּפְטָר מִן הַחַי לֹא יֹאמַר לוֹ "לֵךְ בְּשָׁלוֹם", אֶלָּא "לֵךְ [ב] לְשָׁלוֹם", הַנִּפְטָר מִן הַמֵּת לֹא יֹאמַר לוֹ "לֵךְ לְשָׁלוֹם" אֶלָּא "לֵךְ בְּשָׁלוֹם" — שֶׁנֶּאֱמַר: °"וְאַתָּה תָּבֹא אֶל אֲבוֹתֶיךָ בְּשָׁלוֹם". הַנִּפְטָר מִן הַחַי לֹא יֹאמַר לוֹ "לֵךְ בְּשָׁלוֹם" אֶלָּא "לֵךְ לְשָׁלוֹם", שֶׁהֲרֵי דָּוִד שֶׁאָמַר לְאַבְשָׁלוֹם °"לֵךְ בְּשָׁלוֹם" — הָלַךְ וְנִתְלָה, יִתְרוֹ שֶׁאָמַר לְמֹשֶׁה °"לֵךְ לְשָׁלוֹם" — הָלַךְ וְהִצְלִיחַ. *וְאָמַר רַבִּי לֵוִי: כָּל הַיּוֹצֵא מִבֵּית הַכְּנֶסֶת לְבֵית הַמִּדְרָשׁ, וּמִבֵּית הַמִּדְרָשׁ לְבֵית הַכְּנֶסֶת — זוֹכֶה וּמְקַבֵּל פְּנֵי שְׁכִינָה, שֶׁנֶּאֱמַר: °"יֵלְכוּ מֵחַיִל אֶל חָיִל יֵרָאֶה אֶל אֱלֹהִים בְּצִיּוֹן". אָמַר רַב חִיָּיא בַּר אַשִׁי אָמַר רַב: *תַּלְמִידֵי חֲכָמִים אֵין לָהֶם מְנוּחָה אֲפִילּוּ לָעוֹלָם הַבָּא, שֶׁנֶּאֱמַר: "יֵלְכוּ מֵחַיִל אֶל חַיִל יֵרָאֶה אֶל אֱלֹהִים בְּצִיּוֹן".§

הדרן עלך ואלו מגלחין וסליקא לה מסכת מועד קטן

תורה אור: בְּצִיפּוֹרֵי בְּפִי הַוּוֹשֶׁט. כְּחֶבֶל שֶׁיֵּשׁ בּוֹ קֶשֶׁר, וְיוֹצֵא בְּקוֹשִׁי מִן הַגָּרוֹן: פִּיטּוּרֵי. [נ"ל אמר] שֶׁקּוֹשְׁרִין שְׁתֵּי סְפִינוֹת בְּיַחַד: יֵלְכוּ מֵחַיִל אֶל חָיִל. שֶׁיֵּלְכוּ מִבֵּית הַמִּדְרָשׁ לְבֵית הַכְּנֶסֶת, וּמִבֵּית הַכְּנֶסֶת לְבֵית הַמִּדְרָשׁ — אַחַר יֵרָאֶה אֶל אֱלֹהִים בְּצִיּוֹן, יִזְכּוּ אֶל עֶלְיוֹן:

הדרן עלך ואלו מגלחין
וסליקא לה מסכת מועד קטן

רבינו חננאל

בשלום תמות. וכתיב ואת עיני צדקיהו עור. א"ל הכי א"ר יוחנן שמת נבוכדנצר בחייו. א"ל ביאשיהו כתיב לכן הנני אוסיפך (אל) [על] אבותיך [וגו'] בשלום וכתיב ויורו המורים למלך יאשיהו. ואמר רב יהודה א"ר שעשאוהו ככברה. א"ל הכי א"ר יוחנן שלא חרב ביהמ"ק בימיו. אמר רב יהודה אמר רב א) המנחמין רשאין לומר לישב אלא על הקרקע שנאמר וישבו אתו לארץ וכתיב אחרי כן פתח איוב את פיהו וגו'. ואחרי כן ויען אליפז התימני. א"ר אבהו מניין לאבל שיושב בראש שנאמר אבחר דרכם ואשב ראש ב). מר זוטרא אמר מהכא וסר מרזח סרוחים. מרזח נעשה סר לסרוחים. המרזח הוא האבל כלומר הניזח במרירות ומפורש בכתובות (דף סט). הנפטר מן המת לא יאמר לו לך לשלום אלא לך בשלום שנא' ואתה תבא אל אבותיך בשלום והנפטר מן החי לא יאמר לו לך בשלום אלא לך לשלום. שהרי דוד אמר לאבשלום לך בשלום הלך ונתלה באילן ונהרג. יתרו שאמר למשה לך לשלום הלך והצליח. א"ר חמא בר חנינא מניין לחתן שיושב בראש שנאמר כחתן יכהן פאר וגו'. מה כהן בראש דתני דבי ר' ישמעאל וקדשתו לכל דבר שבקדושה לפתוח ראשון ולברך ראשון וכו' כך חתן בראש. א"ר לוי כל היוצא מן הכנסת למדרש ומבית המדרש לבית הכנסת זוכה ומקבל פני שכינה שנאמר ילכו מחיל אל חיל יראה אל אלהים בציון:

א) ע"ס נפל בכאן בדברי רבינו וכנ"ל אין המנחמין רשאין לישב אלא ע"ג קרקע שנאמר וישבו אתו לארץ ואמר רב יהודה אמר רב אין המנחמין רשאין לומר דבר עד שיפתח האבל שנאמר ואין דובר אליו דבר וכתיב אחרי כן פתח איוב וכו' וכ"ה גי' הרי"ף והרא"ש בכאן ובגי' הש"ס שלפנינו חסר מימרא קמייתא דרב יהודה א"ר. ב) נ"ל ואשב ראש וגו' כאשר אבלים ינחם מר זוטרא אמר מהכא.

הדרן עלך ואלו מגלחין במועד. וסליקא לה מסכת מועד קטן בס"ד

מסורת הש"ס: ברכות סד. [ע"ש] | בראשית טו | ש"ב טו | שמות ד | [ברכות סד. ע"ש] | תהלים פד | ברכות סס

עין משפט נר מצוה: [א] [רמב"ם פ"ד מהל' אבל ה"ד]: [ב] [מג"א סי' קי סק"ט]:

The following paragraph is recited three times:

הַדְרָן עֲלָךְ מַסֶּכֶת מוֹעֵד קָטָן וְהַדְרָךְ עֲלָן, דַּעְתָּן עֲלָךְ מַסֶּכֶת מוֹעֵד קָטָן וְדַעְתָּךְ עֲלָן, לָא נִתְנְשֵׁי מִנָּךְ מַסֶּכֶת מוֹעֵד קָטָן וְלָא תִתְנְשֵׁי מִנָּן, לָא בְּעָלְמָא הָדֵין וְלָא בְּעָלְמָא דְאָתֵי.

יְהִי רָצוֹן מִלְּפָנֶיךָ יהוה אֱלֹהֵינוּ וֵאלֹהֵי אֲבוֹתֵינוּ, שֶׁתְּהֵא תּוֹרָתְךָ אֻמָּנוּתֵנוּ בָּעוֹלָם הַזֶּה, וּתְהֵא עִמָּנוּ לָעוֹלָם הַבָּא. חֲנִינָא בַּר פַּפָּא, רָמֵי בַּר פַּפָּא, נַחְמָן בַּר פַּפָּא, אַחַאי בַּר פַּפָּא, אַבָּא מָרִי בַּר פַּפָּא, רָפְרָם בַּר פַּפָּא, רָכִישׁ בַּר פַּפָּא, סוּרְחָב בַּר פַּפָּא, אַדָּא בַּר פַּפָּא, דָּרוּ בַּר פַּפָּא.

הַעֲרֶב נָא יהוה אֱלֹהֵינוּ אֶת דִּבְרֵי תוֹרָתְךָ בְּפִינוּ וּבְפִי עַמְּךָ בֵּית יִשְׂרָאֵל, וְנִהְיֶה אֲנַחְנוּ וְצֶאֱצָאֵינוּ (וְצֶאֱצָאֵי צֶאֱצָאֵינוּ) וְצֶאֱצָאֵי עַמְּךָ בֵּית יִשְׂרָאֵל, כֻּלָּנוּ יוֹדְעֵי
שְׁמֶךָ וְלוֹמְדֵי תוֹרָתְךָ לִשְׁמָהּ. מֵאֹיְבַי תְּחַכְּמֵנִי מִצְוֹתֶךָ תהלים קיט
כִּי לְעוֹלָם הִיא־לִי: יְהִי־לִבִּי תָמִים בְּחֻקֶּיךָ לְמַעַן לֹא אֵבוֹשׁ: לְעוֹלָם לֹא־אֶשְׁכַּח פִּקּוּדֶיךָ כִּי־בָם חִיִּיתָנִי: בָּרוּךְ אַתָּה יהוה לַמְּדֵנִי חֻקֶּיךָ: אָמֵן אָמֵן אָמֵן סֶלָה וָעֶד.

מוֹדִים אֲנַחְנוּ לְפָנֶיךָ יהוה אֱלֹהֵינוּ וֵאלֹהֵי אֲבוֹתֵינוּ שֶׁשַּׂמְתָּ חֶלְקֵנוּ מִיּוֹשְׁבֵי בֵּית הַמִּדְרָשׁ, וְלֹא שַׂמְתָּ חֶלְקֵנוּ מִיּוֹשְׁבֵי קְרָנוֹת. שֶׁאָנוּ מַשְׁכִּימִים וְהֵם מַשְׁכִּימִים, אָנוּ מַשְׁכִּימִים לְדִבְרֵי תוֹרָה, וְהֵם מַשְׁכִּימִים לִדְבָרִים בְּטֵלִים. אָנוּ עֲמֵלִים וְהֵם עֲמֵלִים, אָנוּ עֲמֵלִים וּמְקַבְּלִים שָׂכָר, וְהֵם עֲמֵלִים וְאֵינָם מְקַבְּלִים שָׂכָר. אָנוּ רָצִים וְהֵם רָצִים, אָנוּ רָצִים לְחַיֵּי הָעוֹלָם הַבָּא, וְהֵם רָצִים לִבְאֵר
שַׁחַת, שֶׁנֶּאֱמַר: וְאַתָּה אֱלֹהִים תּוֹרִדֵם לִבְאֵר שַׁחַת תהלים נה
אַנְשֵׁי דָמִים וּמִרְמָה לֹא־יֶחֱצוּ יְמֵיהֶם וַאֲנִי אֶבְטַח־בָּךְ:

יְהִי רָצוֹן מִלְּפָנֶיךָ יהוה אֱלֹהַי, כְּשֵׁם שֶׁעֲזַרְתַּנִי לְסַיֵּם מַסֶּכֶת מוֹעֵד קָטָן כֵּן תְּעַזְרֵנִי לְהַתְחִיל מַסֶּכְתּוֹת וּסְפָרִים אֲחֵרִים וּלְסַיְּמָם, לִלְמֹד וּלְלַמֵּד לִשְׁמֹר וְלַעֲשׂוֹת וּלְקַיֵּם אֶת כָּל דִּבְרֵי תַלְמוּד תּוֹרָתְךָ בְּאַהֲבָה, וּזְכוּת כָּל הַתַּנָּאִים וְאָמוֹרָאִים וְתַלְמִידֵי חֲכָמִים יַעֲמֹד לִי וּלְזַרְעִי שֶׁלֹּא תָמוּשׁ הַתּוֹרָה מִפִּי וּמִפִּי זַרְעִי וְזֶרַע זַרְעִי
עַד עוֹלָם, וְיִתְקַיֵּם בִּי: בְּהִתְהַלֶּכְךָ תַּנְחֶה אֹתָךְ בְּשָׁכְבְּךָ משלי ו
תִּשְׁמֹר עָלֶיךָ וַהֲקִיצוֹתָ הִיא תְשִׂיחֶךָ: כִּי־בִי יִרְבּוּ יָמֶיךָ משלי ט
וְיוֹסִיפוּ לְךָ שְׁנוֹת חַיִּים: אֹרֶךְ יָמִים בִּימִינָהּ בִּשְׂמֹאולָהּ משלי ג
עֹשֶׁר וְכָבוֹד: יהוה עֹז לְעַמּוֹ יִתֵּן יהוה יְבָרֵךְ אֶת־עַמּוֹ תהלים כט
בַשָּׁלוֹם:

The following paragraph is recited three times:

הַדְרָן We shall return to you, tractate *Moed Katan,* and your glory is upon us. Our thoughts are upon you, tractate *Moed Katan,* and your thoughts are upon us. We will not be forgotten from you, tractate *Moed Katan,* and you will not be forgotten from us; neither in this world nor in the World-to-Come.

יְהִי רָצוֹן May it be Your will, Lord our God and God of our ancestors, that Your Torah will be our avocation in this world and will accompany us to the World-to-Come. Ḥanina bar Pappa, Ramei bar Pappa, Naḥman bar Pappa, Aḥai bar Pappa, Abba Mari bar Pappa, Rafram bar Pappa, Rakhish bar Pappa, Surḥav bar Pappa, Adda bar Pappa, Daru bar Pappa.

הַעֲרֶב נָא Please, Lord our God, make the words of Your Torah sweet in our mouths and in the mouths of Your people, the house of Israel, so that we, our descendants (and their descendants), and the descendants of Your people, the house of Israel, may all know Your name and
study Your Torah for its own sake. Your commandments *Psalms 119*
make me wiser than my enemies, for they are ever with me. Let my heart be undivided in Your statutes, in order that I may not be put to shame. I will never forget Your precepts, for with them You have quickened me. Blessed are You, O Lord; teach me Your statutes. Amen, Amen, Amen, Selah, Forever.

מוֹדִים We give thanks before You, Lord Our God and God of our ancestors, that You have placed our lot among those who sit in the study hall and that you have not given us our portion among those who sit idly on street corners. We rise early and they rise early. We rise early to pursue matters of Torah and they rise early to pursue frivolous matters. We toil and they toil. We toil and receive a reward and they toil and do not receive a reward. We run and they run. We run to the life of the World-to-Come and they run to the pit of destruction,
as it is stated: But You, God, will bring them down into *Psalms 55*
the pit of destruction; men of blood and deceit shall not live out half their days; but as for me, I will trust in You.

יְהִי רָצוֹן May it be Your will, Lord my God, just as you have assisted me in completing tractate *Moed Katan* so assist me to begin other tractates and books and conclude them to learn and to teach, to observe and to perform, and to fulfill all the teachings of Your Torah with love. And may the merit of all the *tanna'im* and *amora'im* and Torah scholars stand for me and my descendants so that the Torah will not move from my mouth and from the mouths of my descendants and the descendants of my
descendants forever. And may the verse: When you *Proverbs 6*
walk, it shall lead you, when you lie down, it shall watch over you; and when you awaken, it shall talk with you
be fulfilled in me. For in the Torah your days shall be *Proverbs 9*
multiplied, and the years of your life shall be increased.
Length of days is in her right hand; in her left hand are *Proverbs 3*
riches and honor. May the Lord give strength to His *Psalms 29*
people; the Lord will bless His people with peace.

The following קדיש *requires the presence of a* מנין.

יִתְגַּדַּל וְיִתְקַדַּשׁ שְׁמֵהּ רַבָּא
בְּעָלְמָא דְּהוּא עָתִיד לְאִתְחַדָּתָא
וּלְאַחֲיָאָה מֵתַיָּא, וּלְאַסָּקָא יָתְהוֹן לְחַיֵּי עָלְמָא
וּלְמִבְנֵא קַרְתָּא דִירוּשְׁלֵם, וּלְשַׁכְלָלָא הֵיכְלֵהּ בְּגַוַּהּ
וּלְמֶעְקַר פָּלְחָנָא נֻכְרָאָה מֵאַרְעָא
וְלַאֲתָבָא פָּלְחָנָא דִשְׁמַיָּא לְאַתְרֵהּ
וְיַמְלִיךְ קֻדְשָׁא בְּרִיךְ הוּא בְּמַלְכוּתֵהּ וִיקָרֵהּ
(נוסח ספרד: וְיַצְמַח פּוּרְקָנֵהּ וִיקָרֵב מְשִׁיחֵהּ)
בְּחַיֵּיכוֹן וּבְיוֹמֵיכוֹן וּבְחַיֵּי דְכָל בֵּית יִשְׂרָאֵל
בַּעֲגָלָא וּבִזְמַן קָרִיב, וְאִמְרוּ אָמֵן.

יְהֵא שְׁמֵהּ רַבָּא מְבָרַךְ לְעָלַם וּלְעָלְמֵי עָלְמַיָּא.

יִתְבָּרַךְ וְיִשְׁתַּבַּח וְיִתְפָּאַר וְיִתְרוֹמַם וְיִתְנַשֵּׂא
וְיִתְהַדָּר וְיִתְעַלֶּה וְיִתְהַלָּל
שְׁמֵהּ דְּקֻדְשָׁא בְּרִיךְ הוּא
לְעֵלָּא מִן כָּל בִּרְכָתָא
/ בעשרת ימי תשובה: לְעֵלָּא לְעֵלָּא מִכָּל בִּרְכָתָא/
וְשִׁירָתָא, תֻּשְׁבְּחָתָא וְנֶחֱמָתָא, דַּאֲמִירָן בְּעָלְמָא
וְאִמְרוּ אָמֵן. (קהל: אָמֵן)

עַל יִשְׂרָאֵל וְעַל רַבָּנָן
וְעַל תַּלְמִידֵיהוֹן וְעַל כָּל תַּלְמִידֵי תַלְמִידֵיהוֹן
וְעַל כָּל מָאן דְּעָסְקִין בְּאוֹרַיְתָא
דִּי בְּאַתְרָא (בארץ ישראל: קַדִּישָׁא) הָדֵין, וְדִי בְּכָל אֲתַר וַאֲתַר
יְהֵא לְהוֹן וּלְכוֹן שְׁלָמָא רַבָּא
חִנָּא וְחִסְדָּא, וְרַחֲמֵי, וְחַיֵּי אֲרִיכֵי, וּמְזוֹנֵי רְוִיחֵי
וּפֻרְקָנָא מִן קֳדָם אֲבוּהוֹן דִּי בִשְׁמַיָּא
וְאִמְרוּ אָמֵן.

יְהֵא שְׁלָמָא רַבָּא מִן שְׁמַיָּא
וְחַיִּים (טוֹבִים) עָלֵינוּ וְעַל כָּל יִשְׂרָאֵל
וְאִמְרוּ אָמֵן.

Bow, take three steps back, as if taking leave of the Divine Presence, then bow, first left, then right, then center, while saying:

עֹשֶׂה שָׁלוֹם/ בעשרת ימי תשובה: הַשָּׁלוֹם/ בִּמְרוֹמָיו
הוּא יַעֲשֶׂה בְרַחֲמָיו שָׁלוֹם, עָלֵינוּ וְעַל כָּל יִשְׂרָאֵל
וְאִמְרוּ אָמֵן.

The following Kaddish requires the presence of a minyan.

Magnified and sanctified may His great name be,
in the world that will in future be renewed,
reviving the dead and raising them up to eternal life.
He will rebuild the city of Jerusalem
and in it re-establish His Temple.
He will remove alien worship from the earth
and restore to its place the worship of Heaven.
Then the Holy One, blessed be He,
will reign in His sovereignty and splendor.
May it be in your lifetime and in your days,
(*Nusaḥ Sepharad:* make His salvation flourish,
and hasten His messiah,)
and in the lifetime of all the House of Israel,
swiftly and soon – and say: Amen.

May His great name be blessed for ever and all time.

Blessed and praised,
glorified and exalted,
raised and honored,
uplifted and lauded
be the name of the Holy One,
blessed be He,
beyond any blessing,
song, praise and consolation uttered in the world –
and say: Amen.

To Israel, to the teachers,
their disciples and their disciples' disciples,
and to all who engage in the study of Torah,
in this (*in Israel add:* holy) place or elsewhere,
may there come to them and you great peace,
grace, kindness and compassion,
long life, ample sustenance and deliverance,
from their Father in Heaven –
and say: Amen.

May there be great peace from heaven,
and (good) life for us and all Israel –
and say: Amen.

Bow, take three steps back, as if taking leave of the Divine Presence, then bow, first left, then right, then center, while saying:

May He who makes peace in His high places,
in His compassion make peace for us and all Israel –
and say: Amen.